Robert Peake, the Elder, *Henry, Prince of Wales* (c. 1610).
Reproduced by permission of the National Portrait Gallery, London.

SKULL BENEATH THE SKIN

The Achievement of John Webster

CHARLES R. FORKER

SOUTHERN ILLINOIS UNIVERSITY PRESS
Carbondale and Edwardsville

Edited by Teresa White
Designed by Quentin Fiore
Production supervised by Loretta Vincent

Library of Congress Cataloging-in-Publication Data

Forker, Charles R.
Skull beneath the skin.

Bibliography: p.
Includes index.
1. Webster, John, 1579?–1634?—Criticism and
interpretation. I. Title.
PR3187.F67   1986   822'.3   85-26144
ISBN 0-8093-1279-4

This project has been supported by the National Endowment for the Humanities, a federal agency which supports the study of such fields as history, philosophy, literature, and languages.

Grateful acknowledgment is made to quote from "Whispers of Immortality" in *Collected Poems 1909–1962* by T. S. Eliot, copyright 1936 by Harcourt Brace Jovanovich, Inc.; copyright © 1963, 1964 by T. S. Eliot. Reprinted by permission of the publisher.

TO HARRY LEVIN

CONTENTS

ILLUSTRATIONS

PREFACE

John Webster is now firmly established (with Marlowe, Jonson, and Middleton) as one of the most important Renaissance dramatists next to Shakespeare. This book attempts to fill the need for a critically detailed and comprehensive study of his entire *oeuvre*, setting a fresh interpretation of the three major (and unaided) plays in the context of the playwright's total career and development as an artist. No scholarly treatment of Webster's minor and collaborative works has appeared in English for many years, with the exception of a handful of books that skate lightly over the lesser writings as a pretext for discussing *The White Devil*, *The Duchess of Malfi*, and, occasionally, *The Devil's Law-Case*. E. E. Stoll's *John Webster: The Periods of His Work as Determined by His Relations to the Drama of His Day* (Boston: Alfred Mudge, 1905) is now obsolete, and Fernand Lagarde's doctoral thesis, *John Webster* (Toulouse: Association des Publications de la Faculté des Lettres et Sciences, 1968), is old-fashioned in its critical methods. Both Stoll and Lagarde wrote before the discovery of important biographical data on Webster that affect interpretation significantly. The recent volume on Webster by M. C. Bradbrook, *John Webster, Citizen and Dramatist* (London: Weidenfeld and Nicolson, 1980), takes some account of the new facts but shows only limited interest in the minor plays, two of which she dismisses altogether from consideration.

In addition, modern techniques of authorship ascription (particularly the study of involuntary linguistic habits such as the use of auxiliary verb forms and contractions) now make it possible to deal with the notorious difficulties of canon in Webster scholarship with a marked increase in precision and objectivity. Accordingly, I have been able to present fresh evidence for including two doubtful plays in Webster's canon—*Anything for a Quiet Life* (a collaboration with Middleton) and *The Fair Maid of the Inn* (a collaboration with Fletcher, Massinger, and Ford). Finally, this study seeks to present Webster's entire achievement in the context of seventeenth-century drama as a body, not only considering important influences (dramatic and nondramatic) upon his work but analyzing (in the Appendix) Webster's virtually unnoticed impact upon his contemporaries as well as upon the major Caroline and Restoration dramatists. What emerges from this latter investigation is the somewhat surprising conclu-

sion that, apart from Shakespeare, Webster seems to have made a more formative impress upon Restoration tragedy than any other dramatist of the
Renaissance.

Webster's career is famous for its apparent shapelessness—a shapelessness
that many critics, however sympathetic they may otherwise be to the poet's genius, see as analogous to his dramaturgy, even in plays so widely admired as *The
White Devil* and *The Duchess of Malfi*. The career, like the most characteristic
dramas, was indeed asymmetrical, but I hope to show, by a more detailed study
of all Webster's writings than has been attempted before, that intelligible and
significant patterns in both the life and the plays are not only discernible but revealing. As in the case of Shakespeare, the study of any individual work by Webster gains significantly by a critical awareness of the entire corpus. One of the
prominent and unifying themes that runs from first to last through Webster's art
is the ironic juxtaposition of love with death. It is a motif that profoundly informs Webster's language, his characterization, his dramatic construction, his
special kind of irony, his theatrical texture and tone, and both his tragic and
comic views of life. This pervasive union of opposites therefore has the deepest
kinds of implication for our judgment of Webster's uniqueness—for his ideas
about sexuality, psychology, politics, social relationship, religion, and even cosmology. It lies at the very heart of the ongoing debate in Webster criticism as to
whether or not the playwright in his greatest tragedies affirms or disaffirms a
universal moral order.

The volume is organized into four major sections. The first of these considers the facts of Webster's biography in the context of the religious, intellectual,
social, and professional climate of Jacobean London. Particular stress is laid
upon the association of Webster and his family with the parish of St. Sepulchre
(near Newgate Prison), with the great livery company of the Merchant Taylors,
and with the flourishing trade in coaches, carts, and other vehicles in which his
father and brother were actively engaged. Public funerals were an important
part of Webster's family experience, and, through personal contact with both
the tailoring and wagon-hiring businesses, the dramatist must have taken a professional as well as a literary interest in the mortuary environment that so colors
his imagery and stage effects. Although we cannot be certain that Webster attended either the Merchant Taylors' School or the Middle Temple, I have discussed both these distinguished institutions in some detail for the light they may
cast on the man and his writings. The second long section takes up the events of
Webster's career in chronological sequence, pausing to describe and analyze in
critical detail the numerous individual works that are ordinarily neglected in
studies of the dramatist. Here, especially in the case of the comedies and tragicomedies, a certain amount of plot summary becomes necessary, not only because these plays are relatively unfamiliar (even to specialists in Jacobean
drama) but also because the plotting itself tends to be unusually intricate (even
by the standards of the day). Part III offers critical analyses of the three plays of

which we can be sure Webster was the sole author, studying these in detail against the background of the love-death conjunction as it appears in his theatrical predecessors and coevals. The last section surveys Webster's reputation in the seventeenth, eighteenth, and nineteenth centuries and attempts some generalizations about the shape of his artistic development, the state of modern scholarship, and the significance of his achievement. As mentioned above, the Appendix is devoted to Webster's impact upon contemporary and later seventeenth-century drama.

Although I have claimed to consider the totality of Webster's known writings in this book, I deliberately exclude a few works that have been attributed to the dramatist within memory. R. G. Howarth assigns the late chronicle play, *The Valiant Scot* (printed 1637), to Webster, as well as a sonnet of commendation ("To his belooued, the *Author*") prefixed to William Barkstead's *Mirrha, the Mother of Adonis* (1607). Both works bear initials that could conceivably designate Webster as the author ("*J. W.* Gent." for the play, and "I. W." for the sonnet); but the hard evidence for identifying either of these with the playwright is, in my opinion, negligible. Readers interested in the Webster apocrypha, however, should consult Howarth's "A Requiem by John Webster," in *A Pot of Gilly-flowers: Studies and Notes* (Cape Town: Privately printed, 1964), pp. 24–26; "*The Valiant Scot* as a Play by John Webster," *Bulletin of the English Association, South African Branch*, 9 (1965), 3–8; and "A Commendatory Sonnet by John Webster," *English Studies in Africa*, 9 (1966), 109–116. George F. Byers, the editor of the standard edition of *The Valiant Scot* (New York: Garland Publishing, 1980), pp. 32–54, convincingly rejects Howarth's ascription on both historical and linguistic grounds.

Without publishing his reasons, Howarth also attributed a third work to Webster—*A Speedie Poste* (1625) by "I. W. Gent." This exceedingly rare book is a collection of model letters in close imitation of such volumes as Nicholas Breton's *A Poste with a Packet of Madde Letters* (1602). The case for the dramatist's authorship of the model letters is linguistically complicated, and although I am now inclined to accept Howarth's ascription as valid, I have decided (in a spirit of caution) to defer presentation of the evidence I have so far assembled until I can study the question more searchingly. *A Speedie Poste* may indeed turn out to be a substantive addition to Webster's canon, but if so, it is not likely to alter our estimate of his artistic achievement significantly.

More recently, Carol A. Chillington has identified Hand D in the manuscript play *Sir Thomas More* (the hand traditionally said to be Shakespeare's) with Webster; see Chillington's "Playwrights at Work: Henslowe's, Not Shakespeare's, *Book of Sir Thomas More*," *English Literary Renaissance*, 10 (1980), 439–479. My refutation of Chillington's claim, originally prepared for a seminar on the *More* problem (organized by Trevor Howard-Hill), and based on evidence of style, idiom, vocabulary, and spelling in the works of Webster and Shakespeare, must also be reserved for publication elsewhere.

A few parts of this book in more rudimentary form have already been printed in journals. In Part II, my discussion of the *Ho* plays by Webster and Dekker originally appeared in *Publications of the Arkansas Philological Association* and that of Webster's prose characters in the *Modern Language Quarterly*. A briefer and differently organized version of the introduction to Part III (on the love-death nexus in Renaissance tragedy) was published by *Shakespeare Studies*; a minor portion of the chapter on *The Duchess of Malfi* (now in substantially altered dress) came out in *Anglia*. I must thank the editors of these publications for permission to reprint. This is also the place to acknowledge with gratitude the permission of Harcourt Brace Jovanovich, Inc., to quote from T. S. Eliot's "Whispers of Immortality," from which the title and epigraph of this volume derive. I owe thanks also to His Grace, the Duke of Northumberland, for allowing me to reproduce Lotto's *Putto with a Skull* from his private collection, as well as to the directors of the National Portrait Gallery, London (for the reproduction of Peake's portrait of Prince Henry), to the Courtauld Institute, London (for the drawing by Bloemart), to the Musée de l'Oeuvre Notre-Dame, Strasbourg (for *Les Amants Tréspassés*), to the Cleveland Museum of Art (for *A Bridal Pair*), and to the Art Institute of Chicago (for the Dürer engraving).

Indiana University generously granted me two leaves of absence at different stages in the writing of this book as well as a grant-in-aid to help defray the substantial costs of preparing the manuscript for publication. I am deeply indebted also to the National Endowment for the Humanities and to the Henry E. Huntington Library (where much of the writing was done) for a year-long fellowship that relieved me of teaching and assisted me importantly in both financial and scholarly ways. Anyone who has had the privilege of carrying on sustained work at the Huntington will know at once how immeasurable must be my debt to that Shangri-la of academic endeavor and to its learned and gracious staff. Other great libraries, too, have been unfailingly responsive to my needs, especially the British Library (where I spent part of a sabbatical), the library of U.C.L.A., the Dartmouth College Library (much used during a visiting professorship in Hanover), the Folger Shakespeare Library, and, not least, the splendid library of my home base, Indiana University.

Skull beneath the Skin was not written in a day. Perhaps I have been unduly influenced by my author, who was notorious for a slow rate of composition and who confessed in the defensive preface to his first major tragedy that he did "not write with a goose-quill, winged with two feathers." I have undoubtedly trespassed upon the patience of several people—perhaps more than anyone, upon that of the director of the Southern Illinois University Press, Kenney Withers, who uncomplainingly allowed me to underestimate the time it would take to complete a long project. He has been unusually supportive and understanding throughout the delays.

In most respects this book is a work of synthesis. The knowledge and insights I have absorbed from my numerous predecessors in the study of Jacobean drama will, I hope, be obvious, even when I have been unable to acknowledge them by name. That my indebtedness is great the footnotes show; and there could have been, *horribile dictu*, even more of them. Over the years I have accumulated debts to many scholars and friends, some of whom may be surprised to find their names listed below. Literary scholarship often proceeds in ways of which its primary abettors and pervasive influencers can hardly be aware. My teacher, the late Alfred Harbage of Harvard University, aroused my interest in Webster when I was still a graduate student, and, at a later but almost equally formative stage, the late R. G. Howarth of the University of Cape Town unselfishly shared some of his as yet unpublished findings with me. I owe an incalculable debt of gratitude to R. W. Dent of U.C.L.A. and to George W. Williams of Duke University, who read most of the manuscript in draft, made invaluable substantive suggestions, and saved me from numerous errors. The blunders, of course, are my own, but I am deeply sensible of the learning, encouragement, and assiduous attention to detail that these two splendid scholar-critics offered me.

Innumerable friends at the Huntington, particularly fellow academics and writers whom I came to know better during my fellowship year, were resourceful and stimulating in ways that no mere roster of names can begin to indicate; discussions with R. A. Foakes, Roland Mushat Frye, S. K. Heninger, Martin Ridge, William A. Ringler, Hallett Smith, John Steadman, Joseph H. Summers, James Thorpe, and Catherine Turney were unusually helpful. A whole platoon of distinguished Renaissance and related specialists at places other than my own university have freely offered their assistance, advice, friendship, and support. Among these I must especially mention Michael J. B. Allen and Daniel G. Calder of U.C.L.A., J. Leeds Barroll III of the University of Maryland, David Bevington of the University of Chicago, George F. Byers of Fairmont State College, Joseph Candido of the University of Arkansas, Mary Edmond of London, Russell A. Fraser of the University of Michigan, Barry Gaines of the University of New Mexico, Cyrus Hoy of the University of Rochester, G. K. Hunter of Yale University, J. R. de J. Jackson of the University of Toronto, Michael Jamieson of the University of Sussex, David Kastan of Dartmouth College, Terrance B. Kearns of Arkansas State University, Elizabeth D. Kirk of Brown University, Norman Rabkin of the University of California at Berkeley, Nicholas F. Radel of St. Lawrence University, Eric S. Rump of York University, Toronto, Susan Snyder of Swarthmore College, and Mihoko Suzuki of the University of Miami.

Closer to home, colleagues and friends in Bloomington (some of whom rejoice to see me lightened of my albatross even more heartily than I) not only have endured my obsession with Webster for many years but have done everything a man could wish—and much more—to help me bring my long task to an end. Among the many persons deserving of mention, I must especially include (from the Indiana University Department of English) Judith Anderson, Roy W. Battenhouse, Mary A. Burgan, Philip B. Daghlian, E. Talbot Donaldson, Georges Edelen, Robert Fulk, Barbara A. Johnson, James H. Justus, Terrence J. Martin,

David J. Nordloh, C. Donald Peet, Melvin L. Plotinsky, Anthony W. Shipps, Stuart M. Sperry, Albert Wertheim, and Wallace E. Williams; and (from Indiana University at large) Ross C. Allen, Henry R. Cooper, Christopher W. Dickson, Timothy Long, Mark Musa, Samuel N. Rosenberg, M. Jeanne Peterson, Gerald L. Strauss, and the Reverend James K. Taylor. To these people my obligations are often as emotional as they are intellectual. Nor could I have done with this series of acknowledgments without mentioning my students in Renaissance drama over the years, even though to do so requires an impersonal herding of them together into a hypothetical "class." Some of them, at least, will know that this book is theirs as much as it is mine. Finally, I want to thank Melvin Heath of the *American Historical Review*, without whose expertise and extended labors on the word processor this book could never have come to light, and Cathryn Lombardi, who prepared the map of Webster's neighborhood.

The text of Webster quoted for most of the minor works is *The Complete Works of John Webster*, ed. F. L. Lucas (London: Chatto & Windus, 1927); in order to distinguish interpolations of my own from Lucas's, I have in most instances silently removed his editorial brackets. Lucas, however, omits the collaborations with Dekker (*Sir Thomas Wyatt*, *Westward Ho*, and *Northward Ho*), and for these plays I use the standard edition of *The Dramatic Works of Thomas Dekker*, ed. Fredson Bowers (Cambridge: Cambridge University Press, 1953–61). Modern editions of the three unaided plays have superseded Lucas's. For *The White Devil* and *The Duchess of Malfi* I cite the Revels editions by John Russell Brown (London: Methuen, 1960 and 1964 respectively); for *The Devil's Law-Case* I quote from the edition by Frances A. Shirley (Lincoln: University of Nebraska Press, 1972). The text of Shakespeare cited throughout is *The Complete Works of Shakespeare*, ed. David Bevington (Glenview, Ill.: Scott, Foresman, 1980). All other relevant editions are duly recorded in the footnotes.

Webster was much possessed by death
And saw the skull beneath the skin;
And breastless creatures under ground
Leaned backward with a lipless grin.

Daffodil bulbs instead of balls
Stared from the sockets of the eyes!
He knew that thought clings round dead limbs
Tightening its lusts and luxuries.
    —T. S. Eliot, "Whispers of Immortality"

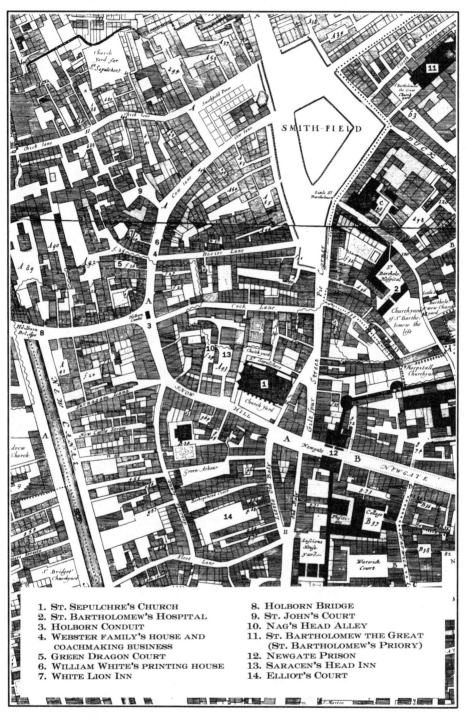

1. Webster's neighborhood, from John Ogilby and
William Morgan's *Large Map of London* (1676).

The key within the image:

1. ST. SEPULCHRE'S CHURCH
2. ST. BARTHOLOMEW'S HOSPITAL
3. HOLBORN CONDUIT
4. WEBSTER FAMILY'S HOUSE AND
   COACHMAKING BUSINESS
5. GREEN DRAGON COURT
6. WILLIAM WHITE'S PRINTING HOUSE
7. WHITE LION INN
8. HOLBORN BRIDGE
9. ST. JOHN'S COURT
10. NAG'S HEAD ALLEY
11. ST. BARTHOLOMEW THE GREAT
    (ST. BARTHOLOMEW'S PRIORY)
12. NEWGATE PRISON
13. SARACEN'S HEAD INN
14. ELLIOT'S COURT

PART I
JOHN WEBSTER,
MERCHANT TAYLOR
AND CITIZEN OF LONDON

No one any longer disputes that the author of *The White Devil* and *The Duchess of Malfi* belongs (with Marlowe, Jonson, and Middleton) among the greatest Renaissance dramatists apart from Shakespeare. Yet until 1976, when Mary Edmond published her all-important researches on Webster, we knew virtually nothing about the playwright's life apart from his early employment by Henslowe, his membership in the Company of Merchant Taylors, and what could be gleaned or inferred from his writings. This was less than our knowledge of any of his famous contemporaries and friends—less, indeed, than that about almost all major figures of English literature except such anonymous and shadowy writers as the *Beowulf* and *Sir Gawain* poets. Ignorance of Webster's life had not been for lack of vigorous and persistent investigation. But the name was so common in the late sixteenth and early seventeenth centuries that the playwright was notoriously difficult to identify among the thicket of John Websters that continued to crop up in contemporary records. The difficulties, as we now know, were compounded by the burning (in the Great Fire of 1666) of the records of the London parish to which Webster belonged—records that undoubtedly contained essential facts about family christenings, marriages, and burials. Edmond's painstaking discoveries about the parish of St. Sepulchre-without-Newgate have done much to fill in the gaps. Webster's birth and death dates still cannot be specified with certainty, but we now possess reliable information about his family, his neighborhood, his church, and even the precise location of his residences. With this foundation to build upon, it is reasonable to hope that additional data may gradually come to light.[1]

The dramatist's father, John Webster senior, may have been a native Londoner, for there is evidence to suggest that various Websters apparently related to him lived in St. Sepulchre's parish, or nearby, as early as the mid-sixteenth century. He was born about 1550 and, in his teenage years, apprenticed to Anne Sylver (widow of Anthony Sylver, Merchant Taylor), who lived in Chick Lane, a street that led westward out of Smithfield Market and crossed the river Fleet. The house that the elder Webster seems to have occupied as a youth was leased by the Sylvers from St. Bartholomew's Hospital, sited on the southeastern edge of Smithfield—originally a monastic foundation whose monks had instituted

3

the annual Bartholomew Fair (held in the adjacent marketplace) of which Ben Jonson gives us such a vivid picture in his famous comedy.

Webster became a wealthy coachmaker and prominent tradesman in the London transport business—a maker and hirer-out of two-wheeled carts, four-wheeled wagons, and the horses and equipment needed for their use. He served his apprenticeship under the auspices of the Merchant Taylors because the coachmaking profession had not yet established its own livery company in Webster's lifetime. There was "a close and obvious connection," as Edmond reminds us, "between tailors, who made trappings for funerals, plays and pageants, and the men who provided hearses for coffins, and vehicles to transport the players' baggage and to serve as platforms for outdoor performances."[2] In 1602, for instance, the Merchant Taylors would pay Webster "for hire of the horses and chariot" used to draw "the scholars" of Merchant Taylors' School "on the triumphing day" when Sir Robert Lee was installed as Lord Mayor and Anthony Munday devised the show.[3] Later, Webster would probably furnish the three "rolling Pageants" or "Triumphs" that Dekker required for the analogous ceremonies of 1612 when Sir John Swinnerton, another Merchant Taylor, was elected mayor.[4]

In 1571 at about twenty-one (the usual age), Webster senior had completed his apprenticeship—a period of at least seven years—and was duly made free of the Merchant Taylors on 10 December of that year. He must have prospered early in the trade, for he soon began taking on apprentices of his own. The records of his livery company show that he presented and made free at least thirteen apprentices, including his younger son Edward, the boys coming up to London from numerous counties throughout the nation. A family friend and neighbor, one Thomas Andrewe, on 8 April 1614 left a legacy of five pounds "vnto all the howsehold men servaunts and apprentices" of the Webster family to be distributed "equallie . . . to and amongest them."[5] Even as early as 1597, Webster the "wagonmaker" was assessed in lay subsidy rolls at a higher rate and was paying a larger tax than almost all others of his parish.[6] Clearly, by the reign of King James, the elder Webster supervised a burgeoning establishment and was approaching the status of a Renaissance Henry Ford or Walter Chrysler. In 1608 he was building coaches for the nobility. On 24 June of that year, for instance, Henry Hastings, Earl of Huntingdon, paid "Webster, the coachmaker" forty-five pounds "for a new coach."[7]

Upon fulfilling his servitude as an apprentice, Webster's father was free to marry, and on 4 November 1577 at St. Giles, Cripplegate (a nearby parish to the east), he did so. His bride, the playwright's mother, was Elizabeth Coates, daughter of Thomas Coates, a blacksmith.[8] It is easy to imagine how the match came about, for Webster's trade obviously necessitated constant dealings with blacksmiths. At least two sons were the issue of this union—John, the dramatist, and Edward, the coachmaker, who succeeded his father as proprietor of the family business. Although the baptismal records have perished, there is good reason to assume that John was the elder (since he bore his father's Christian name) and that Edward was some years his junior. Edward would have been about twenty-one when his father presented him for freedom in the family guild by servitude on 3 February 1611/12.[9] This would place his birth approximately in 1590 or 1591. His older brother John seems to have been born about a decade earlier—probably in 1578 or 1579, a year or so after the marriage of his parents. In all likelihood there were other children as well. The Thomas Andrewe who bequeathed money to the Webster servants and apprentices also left five pounds each to "Iohn Webster the Younger" and his wife Sara, as well as twenty shillings each to "Margery Webster and to hir two sisters"—probably the playwright's siblings.[10]

It is just possible that the young John Webster involved himself with the theatre at a tender age. The evidence, however, is extremely tenuous. One "John Wobster" (an obvious misreading of Webster) is recorded as having been with Robert Browne's troupe of English actors when they performed in Cassel, Germany, in 1596. This John may conceivably be a mistake for the "George Webster" who was also in Germany (in 1598 and later) or, alternatively, the elder brother of George.[11] Lacking the registers of St. Sepulchre's parish, we have no way of checking whether the London coachmaker had a third son named George. But if the actor in Germany was the dramatist-to-be (he would have been about eighteen), Webster may have begun his theatrical career in a traditional way, for his fellow playwrights Munday, Heywood, Rowley, Jonson, and Shakespeare were all apparently players, usually early in life. It is probably safe to disregard the words of the Puritan Thomas Hall, who, in attacking John Webster of Clitheroe (a popular preacher unrelated to the poet), vituperated in 1654 against his enemy by confusing him, perhaps maliciously, with the theatrical Webster and by referring to him on a title page as "the Quondam Player" and in the body of his essay as "a Profane Stage-Player."[12] By this time the dramatist had long been dead—a fact that Hall either did not know or pretended not to know. Hall's title, *Histrio-Mastix, A Whip for Webster*, is undoubtedly borrowed from William Prynne's notorious abuse of the stage, *Histrio-Mastix, the Player's Scourge* (1633); but it is barely possible that Hall was also alluding to the character of Histrio in Jonson's *Poetaster* (1601). This play, which was Ben's principal contribution to the so-called war of the theatres, ridicules both Marston and Dekker, with whom Webster collaborated. Histrio is portrayed as a bumptious, newly prosperous actor of the Lord Chamberlain's Men (Shakespeare's company), who is a companion of Demetrius (Dekker), the writer hired by the same company to answer Jonson's attack. The professional collaboration of Webster and Dekker is certain enough, but there is nothing to suggest that Webster had anything to do with the Lord Chamberlain's Men until 1604 when they had become the King's Men and he was writing the induction for Marston's *Malcontent*. Anyway, there is no need to assume that Jonson intended Histrio to represent a single individual, for the characterization is highly general.

The plausibility of Webster's having become an actor is somewhat increased by his father's transactions with theatre people. The famous actor Edward Alleyn (who played Tamberlaine, Dr. Faustus, and Barabas in Marlowe's plays) and his older brother John (also an actor) acknowledged a debt of fifteen shillings to "John Webster, cytysen and merchauntayler of London" on 25 July 1591, the sum to be repaid by the following 30 September.[13] This debt may well have been connected with a theatrical company (perhaps the Admiral's Men). Moreover, Browne had been associated with Edward Alleyn in 1583 as one of Worcester's servants and in 1589 was still in possession of a supply of costumes, playbooks, and other goods, held in common with the Alleyn brothers and Richard Jones.[14] Philip Henslowe, for whom Webster later began working as a journeyman playwright, was, of course, Edward Alleyn's father-in-law.[15] As an Admiral's man, Alleyn probably acted in the first play that Webster wrote with Munday, Middleton, and Drayton; we know that Dekker, the young playwright's closest early collaborator and a lifelong friend, was on terms of "rich affection" with Alleyn.[16]

Whether the younger John Webster began earning his living as an actor or not, he could scarcely have avoided meeting such people, for his father continued to be associated with civic pageantry and therefore with the actors, poets, and artisans involved in these affairs. The Merchant Taylors assessed Webster senior ten shillings in 1603 toward the cost of shows they were planning for the coronation of the new king.[17] In 1605 they paid eight shillings and sixpence to the elder Webster and his friend John Froome to reimburse them for buying "drincke for the workemen, and for other expences about the pageant" (written by Munday) for Sir Leonard Halliday, the latest member of their fraternity to be elected Lord Mayor.[18] The Taylors gave seven shillings and sixpence "To Mr Webster [for] 3 dayes" in 1607 when the company entertained King James, Queen Anne, and Prince Henry at a banquet at Merchant Taylors' Hall in Threadneedle Street and Ben Jonson was asked for advice about a speech to welcome the visiting royalty.[19] In 1613 Dekker was in debt to John Webster senior for the sum of forty pounds, probably for the rental of wagons or other rolling stock that he had supplied to the poet for his mayoral pageant the year before.[20]

The coachmaker's son would have been naturally cordial with actors, if for no other reason than that his own success as a dramatist depended importantly on theirs. When "his beloved friend" Thomas Heywood came forward in 1612 to defend the profession in his *Apology for Actors*, Webster contributed a sympathetic prefatory poem emphasizing how "well our Actors may approve your paines, / For you give them authority to play, / Even whilst the hottest plague of envy raignes. . . ."[21] He was joined in his enthusiasm by two actor-friends, Richard Perkins (who had played Flamineo in *The White Devil* that very year) and Robert Pallant (whose son was later to take the role of Cariola in *The Duchess of Malfi*). At the end of *The White Devil*, also printed in 1612, Webster took the almost unprecedented step of adding a special encomium of the performers, even mentioning Perkins by name:

> For the action of the play, 'twas generally well, and I dare affirm, with the joint tes-timony of some of their own quality, (for the true imitation of life, without striving to make nature a monster) the best that ever became them: whereof as I make a general ac-knowledgement, so in particular I must remember the well approved industry of my friend Master Perkins, and confess the worth of his action did crown both the beginning and end.[22]

When he came to publish *The Duchess of Malfi* about a decade later, Web-ster again departed from convention by listing opposite their roles the names of players from two separate productions of the play. And, of course, his *Excellent Actor*, one of the most attractive of Webster's Overburian characters, illustrates the poet's admiration for the art of playing more explicitly than any casual praise could do, for this portrait (together with Hamlet's speech to the visiting troupe at Elsinore) defines the highest standard of Elizabethan acting: a good actor (Burbage may have been the model) "fortifies morall precepts with example" and "addes grace to the Poets labours."[23] All this would appear to suggest a close involvement with actors on Webster's part and a concern for the profession re-markable even among the other dramatists of his day. But there is almost no reli-able evidence that the playwright ever trod the boards himself. Indeed, in the praise of Perkins quoted above, he seems to distance himself from active partici-pation in the players' craft by speaking of "their own quality."

Webster probably married on 18 March 1605/06, shortly after he had fin-ished *Northward Ho* (with Dekker), the second of their jointly composed city farces for Paul's boys, and less than two months before a son was born to him. His spouse, who had been baptized at St. Bride's, Fleet Street, on 20 April 1589, was a girl of only seventeen—one Sara Peniall, daughter of Simon Peniall, a prominent member of the Saddlers' Company and in 1605/06 one of its War-dens.[24] Although, as a craft, they tended to be nervous about the new fad of traveling by coach rather than on horseback, saddlers, like blacksmiths, would have obvious business connections with a family, such as the Websters, who needed straps, pillions, harnesses, leather fittings, and other furniture for their horses and drawn vehicles. John Webster III, the first child of John and Sara, was baptized at St. Dunstan-in-the-West on 8 May 1606.[25] Since St. Dunstan's (at the western and more fashionable end of Fleet Street) was now the parish of Sara's parents, the new baby was christened from the house of his grandparents. Like John Webster senior, Simon Peniall was moving up in the world and had trans-ferred his residence from St. Bride's (where his daughter had been baptized) to the more prosperous district along the road from which his wife came. On 15 October 1611, he was granted the lease of a house at Holborn Conduit near the Webster es-tablishment in St. Sepulchre's parish and given a pension 19 February 1617/18.[26]

Under ordinary circumstances the playwright and his young bride would have been married at St. Dunstan's (the Penialls' church) or at St. Sepulchre's (Webster's parish); but since Sara was already seven months pregnant, a certain quiet haste was called for. Accordingly Webster obtained a license to marry outside London—at St. Mary's in the village of Islington north of the city. Mary Edmond has discovered a matrimonial entry in the St. Mary's parish register (dated 18 March 1605/06) for John Webster and Sara "Gimmell" or "Gimnell"—probably a mispelling or misunderstanding of Peniall. As she reminds us, the exceptional fact that the marriage took place during Lent points to the nature of the couple's emergency.[27] Later, when Webster was dramatizing the pressures on the Duchess of Malfi to conceal her pregnancy or focusing on the sexual plight of Angiolella in *The Devil's Law-Case*, perhaps he recalled the embarrassment in which his own fiancée had found herself. Sara Webster was apparently named after her mother Sara Peniall (nee Coxe), who had married Simon Peniall 16 August 1584 at St. Dunstan-in-the-West.[28] We know that additional children were born to the poet and his wife, for the will of a neighbor, Mrs. Margery Pate, left twenty shillings to each of the playwright's daughters Elizabeth and Sara (named obviously for their paternal grandmother and mother), twenty shillings to young John (the dramatist's son), and forty shillings to "the rest of Websters Children."[29]

Although he was proud of his family's connection with the ancient livery of which his father was a member, the playwright appears to have taken little part in the business of coachmaking. When he published his mayoral pageant, *Monuments of Honor*, in 1624, the title page carefully designated the author as "Iohn Webster, Merchant-Taylor"; in his dedication to Lord Mayor Gore, Webster refers to himself as "one borne free of your Company" (l. 14), and in the text proper he speaks of "our Hall" (l. 108) and "our Company" (l. 148).[30] The phrase "borne free" is somewhat misleading. What Webster means is that he was entitled to membership at the age of majority or later (upon payment of the usual fee) "by patrimony"—that is, by virtue of his father's membership—rather than "by servitude," the more common means of gaining admission. As already mentioned, his brother Edward had served a regular apprenticeship in the trade under his father and was admitted to freedom by servitude in 1611/12. John, the older brother, waited until 19 June 1615 to claim membership by right of birth, paying three shillings and fourpence for the privilege. John Webster senior had apparently died between the date on which he made his will (8 April 1614) and the following year when his eldest son formally took up his patrimonial freedom, for he was not present to sponsor him in person. Two unrelated Merchant Taylors, James Williams and William Griffyn, had to testify in his stead to Webster's parentage.[31]

Since the dramatist was now official head of the family, it was appropriate for him to establish his ties to the fraternity in a formal way, for freedom in a City livery company conferred both status and identity upon a man. But he may also have been positioning himself as a candidate to write the Lord Mayor's pageant the next time a brother of the guild should be honored with election. In fact, nine years later, Sir John Gore *was* the next Merchant Taylor to become Lord Mayor, and Webster was the poet duly chosen by his own company to devise the festivities and compose the speeches.[32] In 1615 it would not have been lost upon the playwright that the authorship of such civic pageantry was both honorific and profitable. If Webster was seeking to qualify as the official poet of the Taylors, he would have remembered that his early theatrical colleagues had written similar entertainments for the fraternity in years when a member had been elected mayor—Anthony Munday in 1602, 1605, and 1610, and Thomas Dekker in 1612. Munday and Middleton, both friends of Webster, had between them nearly monopolized the writing of the annual shows for the past ten years. Webster was probably ambitious to share some of this literary prestige.

When Gore was installed as mayor in 1624, the Merchant Taylors must have felt that a member of their own fraternity, an established dramatist who had written plays for the major London theatres, including Shakespeare's, was the logical choice. The financial accounts of the Taylors for that year show a disbursement of 270 pounds "to Iohn Webster yᵉ Poet" and John Terry, William Patten, and George Lovett, who assisted with the building, painting, and gilding of "all the land & water shewes" and "pageantes." The amount also covered the expense of "chariott greene men and theire ffireworkes" (that is, actors gotten up as savages or wild men, who walked in front to clear away crowds by exploding squibs) and "apparell porters" to carry costumes and perhaps equipment and "devices" that could not be readily transported on wheels. The chariot may have been supplied by Webster's brother. Payment had of course been agreed upon in writing between the artists and the officers of the company, but Webster and his fellows were paid an additional ten pounds "over and above the agreemᵗ . . . by way of gratuity."[33] Webster's *Monuments of Honor* was the most lavish and expensive of all the Lord Mayors' pageants in the reign. It cost the Merchant Taylors over a thousand pounds, a gigantic sum for the period.

Webster's laureateship of the Merchant Taylors was, however, to be brief. Six years after Gore's inauguration another member of Webster's guild (Sir Robert Ducy) was elected Lord Mayor, and although the ceremonies were abbreviated that year to a mere triumphal procession, it is clear from the records that Dekker, who had been supplying the Lord Mayors' shows for the immediately preceding years, would have been entrusted with the pageant, had there been one.[34] Probably, except for unusual cause, Webster's professional brethren would not have paid an outsider to do what one of their own number had already proved he could do so well. Webster was apparently not available to produce another pageant in 1630. By then his poetic days must have been over. Or perhaps he was ill.

Webster's younger brother Edward seems, like his father, to have flourished as a citizen, guild member, and businessman. A Star Chamber suit of February

1620/21 identifies him as a coachmaker and constable of Farringdon Ward Without, the precinct of London to the northwest (outside the original city walls) in which the Websters lived.[35] Constables of city wards were officially conservators of the peace, functioned theoretically as police officers, and performed various administrative duties at the local level of municipal government. About a week after gaining his freedom in the Merchant Taylors', Edward probably married Margaret Allen on 10 February 1611/12 at the Church of St. Peter-le-Poor, in Broad Street, just north of Merchant Taylors' Hall;[36] we cannot be sure, however, that this Edward Webster was the poet's brother. If Margaret Allen was Edward's first wife (could she have been a relative of the theatrical Alleyns, whose mother was also named Margaret?), she must have died before 2 October 1621 when Edward married again—like his brother, by license—at New Brentford.[37] This market town several miles to the northwest of London—a part of Brentford or Brainford, as it was often spelled in Jacobean times—had served as the place of assignation for the illicit sexual adventures of *Westward Ho*, and had also been referred to salaciously in *Northward Ho* (V.i.42).

Edward's second wife was Susan Lewellyn, the widow of Walter Lewellyn of Kington, Herefordshire. She was born Susan Walker, whose father John Walker, also of Kington, had married Elizabeth Cage and was living with his wife and daughter, at the time of Susan's marriage, only two minutes' walk from the Webster place of business near Smithfield.[38] In 1632, when Susan Webster's mother Elizabeth died, she left five shillings in her will to every man and maidservant of her son-in-law's substantial household and forty shillings' worth of bread for the poor people of St. Sepulchre's parish to be given out as Edward saw fit. She also left her daughter, Mrs. Edward Webster, a hundred pounds to spend as she chose. Edward initialed this will on each page "EW" and served with his wife as one of the two executors.[39] Susan Webster's paternal uncle Henry Walker, who died in 1616, was a freeman of the Company of Musicians (documents refer to him as a "Minstrell of London") as well as a milliner by trade; it was he who sold Shakespeare the Blackfriars Gatehouse property in 1613.[40]

A large subordinate fraternity of tailors and clothworkers known as the Bachelors' (or Yeomans') Company had come under the direct authority of the Merchant Taylors by Webster's time and were represented in the affairs of the guild by four Wardens Substitute—one for each quarter of London (Watling Street, Candlewick Street, Fleet Street, and Merchant Taylors' Hall) into which, for administrative purposes, the society had been divided. The Bachelors' Company, whose independent records have perished, seems to have consisted largely of the poorer and socially less prominent members of the tailoring craft, and, according to Clode (official historian of the guild), "younger men of the better class held it to be disparagement to serve" as an elected Substitute.[41] An Edward Webster (possibly the dramatist's brother) was assessed four pounds in 1624 toward the cost of the "Triumph" for Lord Mayor Gore, which John Webster planned and wrote. His name appears in the records of the Merchant Taylors as a "Bachelor in Budge" (that is, entitled to wear ceremonial white lamb's wool or fur) with others of the "Fleet Street Quarter," and later as one of the four "Wardens Substitutes of the Batchelors Companie of Merchantailors" in connection with the installation of Sir Robert Ducy as Lord Mayor in 1630.[42] Despite the correct location (the poet's family *did* reside near Fleet Street), this Edward Webster is not easy to identify with the man who took over the management of the Cow Lane coachmaking business, for the "Bachelor in Budge," especially as late as 1624, would seem to be too subsidiary a figure in the Merchant Taylors to fit the circumstances of such a prominent and successful businessman. We have no indication that John Webster senior or his eldest son, the playwright, had ever been members of the inferior Bachelors' Company. But, of course, lacking the Bachelors' account books, we cannot be sure. Perhaps the Warden Substitute was a poorer relative of the Webster clan.

We know the location of the Webster family's house and coachmaking establishment from the apprentice books of the Merchant Taylors (they refer to the playwright's father as being of Smithfield, of St. Sepulchre's parish, and of Cow Lane)[43] and from the manuscript *Journal* of St. Bartholomew's Hospital, which owned the buildings that housed the family quarters and business including a "great y[ar]d and workhowse" for the construction and storage of vehicles.[44] John Webster senior seems to have died before 26 February 1614/15 because Edward, who was then managing the enterprise, negotiated a new twenty-one-year lease of the property in Cow Lane for a hundred pound fee (half the sum to be paid immediately) with an annual rent of ten pounds. Still another lease was granted to Edward Webster on 20 June 1618 for the same premises with the yard behind it, the yearly rent being increased by thirty-three shillings and fourpence.[45] By 1643/44 the payment had risen to twelve pounds. The St. Bartholomew ledgers list Edward Webster as of both Cow Lane and Hosier Lane, because the buildings which the family occupied were located at the junction of the two streets. Cow Lane curved southwards from the northwest side of Smithfield Market where the sheep pens were located. Hosier Lane ran almost due west from the lower part of Smithfield near Pie Corner to its intersection with Cow Lane. In their map of 1676 Ogilby and Morgan show the actual configuration of the buildings at the corner of Cow and Hosier Lanes (the fire of 1666 had spared them) with the yard behind and the alley leading to it from the Cow Lane side (see fig. 1). The site was a natural one because Cow Lane had become the London street in which coachmaking was concentrated. Pepys and his wife shopped there on 5 November 1668, "spen[ding] all the afternoon going up and down among the coachmakers in Cow lane," and finally chose "a little Chariott, whose body was framed but not Covered" with which "we are mightily pleased."[46]

Just south of the Webster business—on the western side of Cow Lane and below its junction with Hosier Lane—lay Green Dragon Court (marked f. 26 by Ogilby and Morgan). It was here that Edward Webster's in-laws, the Walkers, lived. After Elizabeth Cage Walker (Edward's mother-in-law) died in 1632, Edward inherited the quarters his wife had occupied before her marriage, and the couple presumably moved their residence there or at least continued to hold onto the two tenements that the Walkers had been leasing. The St. Bartholomew records show Edward making annual payments of twenty-six shillings and eightpence for one of the buildings, and three pounds, six shillings, and eightpence for the other, while of course retaining the business premises in Cow Lane.[47] Robert Peake (c. 1551–1619), official picturemaker to Henry, Prince of Wales, had also lived in Green Dragon Court from 1585/86 to about 1599, and his son William signed as a witness in 1632 to Elizabeth Walker's will.[48]

Immediately next door to the Websters' Cow Lane establishment and apparently sharing a northern wall with it was the printing house of William White, for several years Master Warden of the Stationers' Company. Much of White's custom consisted of setting Puritan theological works in type; indeed, the coachmaker's neighbor issued a couple of sermons by Thomas Adams, the author of the famous *White Devil, or the Hypocrite Uncased* (1613), who picked up the same title phrase that the dramatist Webster used for his first unaided tragedy. White also printed several editions of a work on equine medicine, telling "how to know the age of a horse" (the horsemarket was just up the street in Smithfield) as well as *A Strange Report of Six Most Notorious Witches* (1601), an anonymous account of the "devilish practices" of certain women in Germany who were said to have murdered more than four hundred children.[49] In addition, he printed plays, including Shakespeare's. The first quarto of *Love's Labor's Lost* (1598) bears his initials, as do the second quarto of *3 Henry VI* (1600), the fourth quarto of *Richard II* (1608), and the fifth quarto of *1 Henry IV* (1613). He also saw part of the first edition of *Pericles* (1609) through the press. White printed five editions of Kyd's *Spanish Tragedy* (quartos 3 through 7— 1599, 1602, 1603, 1611, and 1615), the second edition of Peele's *Edward I* (1599), the second quarto of the anonymous *Wily Beguiled* (1614), and the first of Haughton's *Englishmen for My Money, or A Woman Will Have Her Will* (1616). The printer identified his shop as being "over against the White Lion,"[50] an inn whose courtyard entrance can be located on the Ogilby-Morgan map (marked f. 24) at the western side of Cow Lane directly opposite the Webster and White buildings. A description of the Webster quarters in St. Bartholomew's *Journal* (the record of a lease dated 20 June 1618, a few months after White's death) mentions "p[ar]te of the ground whearon the pryntinge howse nowe standeth."[51] Shakespeare could have visited the White printshop, a possible place (outside the theatre) for Webster the dramatist to have met his more famous coeval. Perhaps, as Mary Edmond suggests, Shakespeare's reference in Mercutio's best-known speech to Queen Mab's "chariot"—"an empty hazel-nut, / Made by the joiner squirrel or old grub, / Time out o' mind the fairies' coachmakers" (*Romeo and Juliet*, I.v.59–61)—may reflect the older playwright's personal knowledge of the Webster coachmaking site even though the fanciful speech antedates the *Love's Labor's Lost* quarto by several years.[52]

White died in March 1618. One of the witnesses to his will (another member of St. Sepulchre's parish) was none other than George Eld, the printer of Webster and Dekker's *Northward Ho* (1607), of the fourth edition of Overbury's *A Wife* (1614), which the dramatist may have edited, and of several works that Webster drew upon for "sentences" and verbal inspiration—Goulart's *Admirable and Memorable Histories* (1607), Matthieu and de Serres's *General Inventorie of the History of France* (1607), and Matthieu's *Heroyk Life and Deplorable Death of Henry the Fourth* (1612). Eld supervised the printing of many plays, including those by Marlowe, Jonson, Chapman, Dekker, Middleton, Marston, and Shakespeare; he printed the second quarto of *The Shoemaker's Holiday* (1610), the first quartos of *The Revenger's Tragedy* (1607) and *Troilus and Cressida* (1609), and the bewildering first edition of Shakespeare's *Sonnets* (1609).

The third printer with whom Webster had dealings was, of course, Nicholas Okes, who, from 1607 to about 1617, kept his shop near Holborn Bridge, just a stone's throw to the southwest from the Webster-White complex in Cow Lane. Nicholas's father, John Okes, was a freeman of the Company of Horners and a fellow parishioner of John Webster senior, with whom he signed a vestry minute at St. Sepulchre's in 1608.[53] It was Okes who printed Webster's most prestigious works—*The White Devil* (1612), *A Monumental Column* (1613), *The Duchess of Malfi* (1623), and *Monuments of Honor* (1624)—as well as Heywood's *Apology for Actors* (for which the dramatist wrote verses) and John Stephens's *Satirical Essays, Characters, and Others* (1615), which prompted Webster's character, *An Excellent Actor*. Of course Okes also set the plays of others, including Shakespeare: the first quartos of *King Lear* (1608) and *Othello* (1622) were produced under his supervision in addition to well-known dramas by Dekker, Marston, Chapman, Heywood, Jonson, and Ford. For a number of years Okes regularly printed the annual mayoral pageants, often by Middleton. He also set Donne's *Ignatius his Conclave* (1611), which Webster undoubtedly read. Okes knew White and Eld personally and on occasion even shared the printing of books with them. Heywood, praising the printer's "honest indeauours," addressed Okes in his *Apology* as "my approued good Friend," so it is not improbable that Webster felt a similar warmth and respect.[54]

By 1641 (after the death of John Webster, dramatist) Edward and Susan Webster were living in St. John's Court, a small street that began at Cow Lane to the north of the old Webster property (midway between the Smithfield sheep pens and Hosier Lane) and wound irregularly in a northwesterly direction to Chick Lane. Their house was closer to the Cow Lane than the Chick Lane end, and they employed two maidservants named Martha and Mary.[55] Edward Webster's will (he died about 16 November 1644) makes no mention of his older brother the playwright, who had predeceased him by some years. Edward's widow

Susan died shortly after her husband in February 1645/46, requesting burial "in the Vault" of St. Sepulchre's church "as neere my Mother & husband as maie convenientlie bee. . . ." (As a rule, burial in the vault or crypt of a church cost more than burial in the nave or churchyard and was therefore a mark of affluence or social prestige.) So far as we know, the Edward Websters had no children. After Susan's death, her relatives inherited the Cow Lane and Green Dragon Court leases.[56] The playwright John Webster lived in Nag's Head Alley (marked f. 29 by Ogilby and Morgan), a court that opened northwards off Snow Hill just west of the parish church and only a few minutes' stroll from the Webster tenements in Cow Lane and Green Dragon Court. Since John and Sara Webster were residing in Nag's Head Alley in 1606 when their first child was baptized, presumably the dramatist had moved there at the time of his marriage six weeks or so earlier.[57]

* * *

The parish church that the author of *The Duchess of Malfi* attended and in which his parents, his brother, and his sister-in-law almost certainly were buried, was the largest in Jacobean London and one of the most prominent architecturally. In the early Middle Ages it had been named "St. Edmund-without-Newgate" and then, in crusading times (because of a connection with the Knights of the Holy Sepulchre) was apparently renamed "St. Edmund and the Holy Sepulchre." After 1137, when the Bishop of Salisbury bestowed it upon the prior and canons of St. Bartholomew in West Smithfield, the official name got abbreviated to St. Sepulchre-without-Newgate and, in popular speech, to "St. Pulcher's." After the dissolution of the monasteries in 1538, the church came under the direct patronage of the crown, but in 1636 the President and Fellows of St. John's College, Oxford, were given administration of the living; indeed, they hold it to this day. The dramatist lived almost within the shadow of a very imposing structure with one of the tallest bell towers in the city. In 1598 Stow wrote that it had been "newly reedified or builded, about the raigne of *Henry* the sixt, or of *Edward* the fourth" by Sir John Popham, Henry VI's Chancellor of Normandy. What Stow terms the "fayre Porch . . . towardes the South," erected in perpendicular style by Popham, is still visible today.[58]

The great tower with its four pinnacles (some 153 feet above street level) was the scene of at least one suicide in Webster's time, for William Dodington, a lawyer, officer in the Exchequer, and brother-in-law of Sir Francis Walsingham, hurled himself from it on 11 April 1600. Francis Bacon referred wittily to the incident in a conversation with Queen Elizabeth about Essex: "If I do break my neck, I shall do it in a manner as Mr. Dorrington [i.e., Dodington] did it, which walked on the battlements of the church many days, and took a view and survey where he should fall."[59] Perhaps Webster recalled this event when, in writing *The Devil's Law-Case*, he had Leonora threaten to "leap these battlements"

(V.v.12) rather than endure imprisonment in her turret. The main body of the church Webster knew was gutted in the Great Fire of 1666 and rebuilt, probably by Sir Christopher Wren, on the ruins (using the walls, porch, and tower, which still stand). Since then the fabric has been several times modified or "restored" and the churchyard largely eliminated, but the outer dimensions of the edifice are essentially the same as in Renaissance times. In Webster's day the church tower boasted a magnificent set of bells (probably the "bells of Old Bailey" in the famous nursery rhyme since St. Sepulchre's dominated the district that Stow calls "the Bayly"), which had originally belonged to the nearby Priory of St. Bartholomew and which tolled almost ceaselessly in time of plague or to announce the impending execution of prisoners, incarcerated in Newgate Prison across the street and sometimes buried, after being hanged at Tyburn, in the churchyard. Jonson refers to the "bells / Of loud Sepvlchres with their hourely knells" (Epigram 133, ll. 173–174).[60]

The parish was one of the most populous in the city, serving some "Twentie thowsand sowles" according to a petition in behalf of Dr. John Spencer, vicar during Webster's most creative years;[61] and it had the reputation of being crowded, noisy, rambunctious, and smelly—partly, of course, because of the horse, swine, sheep, and cattle market in its midst and the bulging prisons nearby. In *The Devil is an Ass*, in a passage that seems to glance at the notorious filth of the area, a jailor at Newgate remarks on the "infernall stincke, and steame" that the escaping Pug leaves behind—a vapor so thick "You cannot see St. *Pulchars Steeple*" (V.viii.132–133). The induction to *Bartholomew Fair* also speaks of Smithfield as "dirty" and "stinking" (ll. 161–162),[62] and Stow uses very similar language about the neighborhood. Indeed, Webster's father was accused by one Ellis Wyn in a Star Chamber suit of 7 November 1592 of "causing noisome airs" by "heaping dung and other filth upon a laystall" in the vicinity.[63]

Pie Corner at the southern entrance to Smithfield (named after an inn placard depicting a magpie) was well known for cookshops and stalls and the indigents who loitered there. Jack Dawe, a writer of 1623, mentions those who "walke snuffing vp and downe in *Winter* Euenings through *Pie-corner*, yet haue not one crowne to replenish their pasternes." Further north near the horse market lay an area called Ruffians' Hall where various kinds of sporting contests had traditionally been held. Thomas Fuller in his *Worthies of England* speaks of men meeting "casually and otherwise" there "to try Masteries with Sword and Buckler."[64] More formal tournaments, jousts, and spectacles for the benefit of royalty or visiting dignitaries from abroad had also taken place at Smithfield in medieval days. The market was not paved until 1615. The parish contained a large number of inns and taverns to accommodate the constant stream of cattle drovers, travelers, and transients into the area from the provinces or from the continent. One of the largest and most prominent, standing next to the church itself, was the Saracen's Head, named (according to John Lydgate) for its having been visited by Richard Coeur de Lion in 1194 on his return from captivity in Austria. Dekker alludes to it as the "Sarsens-head at Newgate" in *Satiromastix* (I.ii.301).[65] St. Sepulchre's had become the hub of London's busy agricultural and manufacturing trade.

A certain amount of crime, sharp practice, and debauchery were inevitable in a parish, like St. Sepulchre's, that drew such huge crowds, particularly in August during Bartholomew Fair, and a special court, known as the Court of Piepowders (a corruption of *pieds pouldreux* or "dusty feet") had been summoned to adjudicate offenses in connection with the annual event.[66] The area appears to have been noted for beggars, cozeners, and knaves, a whole catalogue of whom had been stereotyped in John Awdeley's *A Fraternity of Vagabonds* (1565). Awdeley, a printer who flourished during the youth of John Webster senior and who lived and sold books in nearby Little Britain Street "by great St. Bartholomew's," refers more than once to sites in the neighborhood of Smithfield. Cow Lane itself, which, according to Stow, had recently acquired many new buildings, was notorious for fortune-tellers. We learn, for instance, in Jonson's *Bartholomew Fair*, that Dame Purecraft developed her passion for an insane husband after "the cunning men in Cow-lane" assured her "she shall never have happy hour, unless she marry . . . a madman" (I.ii.44–47).[67]

A number of famous names are associated with Webster's parish. John Rogers (1500?–1555), Calvinistic vicar of St. Sepulchre's, was the first Protestant martyr to be burned at the stake under Queen Mary. His execution, which the dramatist's father may have witnessed as a boy, took place in Smithfield in the presence of his wife and eleven children and is memorialized at length in Foxe's *Acts and Monuments*. The burning of heretics, incidentally, continued into the dramatist's own lifetime. The last person to suffer such a fate at Smithfield was the Arian, Bartholomew Legate, who was executed by fire among a vast "conflux of people" in 1612, the year of *The White Devil*, after being confined at Newgate where his brother Thomas had already died. Since he lived so close to the celebrated place of martyrdom, the playwright could easily have been one of the assembled crowd. William Camden, the historian, antiquary, and teacher of Ben Jonson, was born in the Old Bailey precinct of the parish in 1551 (when Webster senior was an infant) and attended the famous Bluecoat School, Christ's Hospital, just steps away from the church in which both he and the future coachmaker were probably baptized. Queen Elizabeth's tutor, Roger Ascham, the author of *The Schoolmaster*, died in the parish in 1568 and was buried in the church. Captain John Smith, whose adventures in Europe, Asia, and America have become legendary and whom Pocahontas saved from death by stoning in Virginia, was living just outside Newgate at the time of his death (21 June 1631) and also lies in St. Sepulchre's, where a tablet still commemorates him. He may have received Holy Communion at one of the altars there on the eve of his departure for the new world. Webster could have attended his funeral.

Roger Williams, colonist, religious separatist, and founder of Providence, Rhode Island, was born about 1603 when Webster was just beginning his career as a playwright. The Williamses were neighbors of the Websters (they also lived in Cow Lane), and Roger's father James, a Merchant Taylor like his friend down the street, signed as a witness to certify that John Webster, dramatist, was "the sonne of John Webster merchauntaylor" when the playwright was admitted to freedom in the guild by patrimony in 1615.[68] After James Williams's death, Edward Webster performed the same service for Sydrach Williams, Roger's older brother, when Sydrach took up his freedom by patrimony in February 1620/21.[69] Dr. William Harvey (1578–1657), the discoverer of the circulation of the blood, was married in November 1604 at St. Sepulchre's (Harvey's wife Elizabeth was the daughter of Lancelot Brown, physician to both Queen Elizabeth and James I), and regularly attended patients at St. Bartholomew's Hospital, where the court of governors offered him an adjoining house and garden. His lectures first setting forth his new anatomical theories were presented at a college in Knightrider Street just south of nearby St. Paul's. An earlier resident of the hospital had been the unfortunate Roderigo Lopez, the Portugese Jew, who was hanged, drawn, and quartered at Tyburn in 1594 on suspicion of having tried to poison the queen after becoming her chief physician. Lopez had been highly respected as a medical authority at St. Bartholomew's when Webster was a boy.

The great lady of the area was Penelope Devereux, sister of Essex, the "Stella" of Sidney's sonnets, and (before her marriage to Lord Rich) under the guardianship of the same Earl of Huntingdon who later purchased a coach from Webster's father. Lady Rich appears to have lived for a time in Bartholomew Close at the Priory of St. Bartholomew in Smithfield, one of her husband's London properties. The despicable Sir Richard Rich (1496?–1567), Attorney-General, later Lord Chancellor, betrayer of Fisher and More, toady of Cromwell, and grandfather of Penelope's husband, had acquired the estate in 1546 for 1,064 pounds, eleven shillings, and threepence after Henry VIII dissolved the monasteries, and the Prior's mansion became his principal London establishment.[70] Although, after her separation from Lord Rich, Penelope preferred Essex House in the Strand (the home of her brother the Earl), St. Bartholomew's was her official town residence. During Penelope's lifetime, Baron Rich greatly built up or "developed" the whole area around Bartholomew Close. In the adjoining church, St. Bartholomew the Great, Webster could have seen a tablet thematically suggestive of his greatest plays. The inscription, above which are figures of a husband and wife lying nude on a couch, reads:

> Behowlde youreselves by us;
> Sutche once were we as you;
> And you in tyme shal be
> Even duste as we are now.[71]

St. Sepulchre's had a reputation for learned clergy—particularly those of Puritan inclinations. The martyr John Rogers had been greatly influenced by

William Tyndale, with whose translation of the scriptures (the so-called Matthew's Bible) he became connected. Webster's own parish priest, John Spencer (1559–1614), was a distinguished Greek scholar. President of Corpus Christi College, Oxford, prebendary of St. Paul's Cathedral, and chaplain to James I as well as vicar of St. Sepulchre's (from 1599 until his death), Spencer served on the New Testament committee for the authorized version of the Bible (1611) and contributed to the translation of the Epistles. He was also a close friend of Richard Hooker, whose *Laws of Ecclesiastical Polity* he saw through the press. The Cromwellian cleric Hugh Peters (1598–1660) was appointed to a lectureship at St. Sepulchre's in the late 1620s where the dramatist could have heard him. According to Peters's own account, "the resort [to the lectures] grew so great that [his words] contracted envy and anger."[72] Peters, whose religious views quickly became too heterodox for the Anglican establishment, went first to Holland to preach and, thence, in 1635, to Salem, Massachusetts. He returned to England during the Civil War, became an influential chaplain in Fairfax's army, was later given rooms in Whitehall Palace by the Lord Protector, inherited the private library of Archbishop Laud (confiscated by Parliament), and was finally hanged as a regicide at the Restoration.

One final divine, Henry Airay, an evangelical Calvinist preacher and Oxford don, deserves mention in connection with St. Sepulchre's church because of an arresting anecdote concerning his chance visit to the parish. The story cannot be traced further back than the early nineteenth century and may therefore be apocryphal, but, if true, it occurred during Webster's residence nearby (probably when the poet was at Nag's Head Alley) and would undoubtedly have appealed to his taste for the macabre:

Dr. Airy, Provost of Queen's College, Oxon. (1599–1616), passing with his servant accidentally through St. Sepulchre's churchyard, in London, where the sexton was making a grave, observing a skull to move, showed it to his servant, and then to the sexton, who, taking it up, found a great toad in it, but withal observed a tenpenny nail stuck in the temple-bone; whereupon the Doctor presently imagined the party to have been murdered, and asked the sexton if he remembered whose skull it was. He answered it was the skull of a man who died suddenly, and had been buried twenty-two years before. The Doctor told him that certainly the man was murdered, and that it was fitting to be inquired after, and so departed. The sexton, thinking much upon it, remembered some particular stories talked of at the death of the party, as that his wife, then alive, and married to another person, had been seen to go into his chamber with a nail and hammer, etc.; whereupon he went to a justice of the peace, and told him all the story. The wife was sent for, and witnesses were found who testified that and some other particulars; she confessed, and was hanged.[73]

Such graveyard scenes, reminiscent of Hamlet with the skull of Yorick, were not unusual in Webster's day. The dramatist's friend Middleton, in his *Blacke Booke* (1604), speaks of "sheets smudged so dirtily" that they might have "been stolen by night out of Saint Pulcher's churchyard when the sexton had left a grave open, and so laid the dead bodies wool-ward," that is, without linen.[74]

Artists and their ilk were no less familiar to Webster's parish than businessmen, scholars, and clergy. In fact the area seems to have fostered something like a colony of painters and related "artificers." As mentioned earlier, the portrait painter Robert Peake, famous for his numerous canvases of contemporary royalty (see the frontispiece for a striking example), had lived in Green Dragon Court during the playwright's minority. Peake's son William, also a painter resident in the parish, was a personal friend of the Webster clan and witnessed the will of Edward Webster's mother-in-law. Perhaps, as Mary Edmond suggests, the dramatist "sat to the Peakes."[75] By 1619, the year he died, Robert Peake had moved south to the Old Bailey precinct, and William inherited the unexpired lease of the house he rented there. John Mattingley, King James's Master-Joiner, had also lived in Green Dragon Court with Peake and Edward Webster's in-laws when Webster was a boy.[76] John de Critz, another artist of the period (he made, painted, and gilded the elaborate escutcheon and "achievements" of Prince Henry installed in Westminster Abbey after the royal funeral in 1612) also lived for thirty years very near St. Sepulchre's parish (in St. Andrew's, Holborn) and was assessed in 1607 as a parishioner of Webster's parish where his studio may have been located. He and Peake the elder were jointly appointed to the office of Serjeant-Painter to the king in 1607.[77]

The Peakes and de Critz were freemen of the Goldsmiths' Company, a fraternity appropriate to the gilding and making of gold leaf required by their art. Isaac Oliver, miniaturist (d. 1617), the distinguished pupil of Nicholas Hilliard, although born in France, had lived as a child in the Fleet Lane section of St. Sepulchre's (from 1568 to 1571 or later);[78] as an adult he lived in Blackfriars, near the theatre where *The Duchess of Malfi* was performed, and was buried in the local church, St. Anne's. Francis Meres in 1598 grouped Hilliard, Oliver, and de Critz as "very famous for their painting."[79] Robert Peake's exact contemporary William Larkin (d. 1619), who made portraits of the third Earl of Dorset, the Countess of Somerset (murderess of Overbury), and Mrs. Turner (her accomplice)— he was freeman of the Painter-Stainers' Company—was also a parishioner, for about 1605 his father signed an undated request for an increase in the vicar's allowance.[80] Inigo Jones, architect, designer, and collaborator with Jonson on court masques, was born in Smithfield and baptized 29 July 1573 in the Church of St. Bartholomew the Less, the adjoining parish to the east.

Given the number of painters in his immediate neighborhood, it is not difficult to explain Webster's interest in the motif of portraiture that figures so prominently in *The Devil's Law-Case* and, more briefly, in *The White Devil* and *The Duchess of Malfi*. In the first tragedy Isabella meets her death by kissing a poisoned picture (II.ii); in the second Cariola says that her mistress, the Duchess, looks "Like to your picture in the gallery, / A deal of life in show, but none in practice" (IV.ii.31–32). Leonora's words from the tragicomedy seem to reflect immediate experience on the dramatist's part with contemporary painters and their studios:

> With what a compell'd face a woman sits
> While she is drawing! I have noted divers
> Either to feign smiles, or suck in the lips
> To have a little mouth; ruffle the cheeks
> To have the dimple seen; and so disorder
> The face with affectation, at next sitting
> It has not been the same; I have known others
> Have lost the entire fashion of their face
> In half an hour's sitting.
> . . . .
> In hot weather,
> The painting on their face has been so mellow,
> They have left the poor man harder work by half
> To mend the copy he wrought by. . . .
> (*The Devil's Law-Case*, I.i.168–181)

The Cardinal's instruction to Bosola for the purpose of tracing Antonio may also betray Webster's familiarity with portrait painters: "go to th' picture-makers and learn / Who bought [the Duchess's] picture lately—" (*The Duchess of Malfi*, V.ii.141–142).

Obviously the dramatist would have known theatre people residing in his vicinity. He clearly had dealings with Ralph Savage—for a time manager of the Red Bull, his local playhouse situated just north of Smithfield in the parish of St. James, Clerkenwell. (The Queen's Men performed *The White Devil* at the Bull in 1612; later *The Devil's Law-Case* probably opened there as well.) Savage, with Nicholas Okes (Webster's printer), had been involved in 1613 with John Webster senior in a King's Bench litigation against Dekker for the recovery of forty pounds.[81] And in 1624 Savage employed Webster, Dekker, Ford, and Rowley to write *Keep the Widow Waking*, a play (now lost) that took advantage of a sensational local scandal concerning Anne Elsdon, a widow of means, whom an outrageous charlatan, Tobias Audley, had inebriated, debauched, and defrauded of her property. Anne Elsdon, her sister Mrs. Elizabeth Freshwater, and Audley himself all lived or had lived in St. Sepulchre's parish, and Webster could hardly have failed to gain firsthand knowledge of the affair.[82] Elizabeth, Anne Elsdon's daughter, who lived in St. James's parish near the theatre, was married to Benjamin Garfield (the son of another St. Sepulchre's parishioner), who brought a Star Chamber suit against the nefarious Audley as well as some of those connected with the theatrical production. Aaron Holland, who owned the lease of the property on which the Red Bull stood, was a defendant in this suit with Dekker, Rowley, and others. He, too, lived near Webster (in Clerkenwell) and is likely to have known the playwright personally.

John Webster

*   *   *

We know that Webster's father, one of the most prosperous and influential men of the parish, took a significant role in its affairs. Edmond points out that he signed no fewer than three documents as a Common Councilman of the church, one of which is preserved at Hatfield House, the ancestral home of the Cecil family.[83] This is a petition (written about 1605) to Robert Cecil, Earl of Salisbury, for a supplement to the stipend of the vicar "Whose living is very small" and "not sufficient to maintaine his familie" in so "greate and spacious" a parish. Eighteen leading parishioners besides Webster signed the paper including the "Pictormaker" Robert Peake (as a churchwarden), the Master-Joiner John Mattingley, William Larkin the elder (an innkeeper of the Holborn Cross precinct and father of the portrait painter William Larkin), and Ralph Smyth (a Merchant Taylor like Webster). Webster's signature appears seventh in the list. Signing as Alderman's Deputy was none other than Ralph Garfield, the father of Benjamin Garfield, who sued those involved in the production of *Keep The Widow Waking* for defaming his mother-in-law, Anne Elsdon.[84]

The elder Webster's second signature as a leading member of St. Sepulchre's has a curious connection with his son's greatest tragedy, *The Duchess of Malfi*. In 1605 Robert Dowe (or Dove), one of Webster's fellow Merchant Taylors and a notable benefactor of the guild, gave an endowment of fifty pounds to the parish officers for the purpose of ministering to the spiritual needs of condemned criminals in Newgate Prison, diagonally across the street. Webster's father, grouped with three other members of the Common Council of the parish, was also one of twenty-four signatories to this benevolence. A sexton or clerk, appointed by the vicar, churchwardens, and vestry, and paid at the rate of one pound, six shillings, and eightpence, was to visit prisoners appointed for execution by means of an underground passage between the church and the prison, exhorting them to prayer and repentance and ringing a handbell, donated by Dowe himself. The procedure was very well known (there is an account of it in an expanded edition of Stow's *Survey of London*, 1618), and the dramatist alludes specifically to it in the words he gives Bosola as he supervises the strangling of the Duchess:

> I am the common bellman
> That usually is sent to condemn'd persons
> The night before they suffer. . . .
>
> (IV.ii.173–175)

Shakespeare also may have referred to the macabre ceremony in *Macbeth* (written the year after Dowe's benefaction) when he made Lady Macbeth say, "It was the owl that shriek'd, the fatal bellman, / Which gives the stern'st good-night" (II.ii.3–4).

Dowe's directions for this ministry were detailed and specific: "about the hour of tenn of the clock in the quiet of the night next before everie execution daie," the officiant was

to goe unto Newgate there to stand soe neere the window as he can where the condemned prisoners do lye in the Dungeon the night before they shall be executed and wth a hand bell . . . give there twelve solemn tolls with doble strokes and then after a good pawse to deliver with a lowd and audible voice (his face towards the prisoner's window) to the end the poore condemned sowles maie give good care and be the better stirred up to watchfulness and praier certain words of exhortation and prayer . . . and then he shall toule his bell again.[85]

At the cell the bellman was to recite the following syntactically pauseless exhortation:

Yee Prisoners within who for your wickedness and sinns after many former mercies shewed you are nowe appointed to be executed to death to morrow in the forenoon give care and understand that to morrow morning from six of the clock till tenn the greatest Bell of St. Sepulchres parish shal be touled for You in manner and order of the passing Bell used to be touled for those that lye at the point of death to the end that all godly people hearing that bell and knowing that [it] is for You going to your death maie be stirred up to praie hartelie to God to bestow his mercie and his grace upon You while you yet live and therefore seeing the praiers of other Men can doe you noe good unless you turn to the Lord in true sorrow for your own wickedness and praie with them for yourselves also I beseech you all and everie of you for Christ his Sake to continue this night in watching and hartelie praie for the Salvation of your own sowles while there is yet time and place for mercie considering that to morrow You are to appeere before the Judgment of yor Creator and to give an accompt to him of yor lives past and to suffer eternal torment for your sinns comytted against him unlesse upon your hartie and unfeigned repentance in this world by faithful and earnest praier you obtain pardon and forgiveness at the hand of God through the death and passion of your Redeemer Ihesus Christ who came to save Synners and now sitteth at the right hand of his ffather to make intercession for as manie of you as penitentlie turn to God by him (then end saying two severall tymes) our Lord take Mercie on You all our Lord take Mercie on You all.[86]

The next morning when prisoners were to be taken to Tyburn to be hanged, the cart (very likely supplied by the Webster cart-and-wagon business) drew up to the wall of St. Sepulchre's, where the prisoners received nosegays, the bellman again used his handbell, and the "passing bell" in the tower above rang out its mournful knell. The handbellman was to stand "bareheaded . . . having first given twelve solemne toules with double strokes for better stirring up . . . the prisoners' mynde as other good peoples' harts to praie for God his mercie towards them. . . ."[87] Dowe directed that he should address a briefer speech on this occasion:

All good People praie hartelie to God for these poor Synners going to their deaths for whome this great Bell doth toule and all you that are condemned to die repent yourselves with lamentable tears and ask mercy for the Salvation of your Souls by the merritts passion and death of Ihesus Christ our onely Saviour and Redeemer (and then with a lowde voice say two several times) our Lord take mercie upon You all our Lord take mercie upon You all.[88]

On one such occasion in 1607 when a papist named Humphrey Lloyd was condemned for murdering a yeoman of the king's guard in a quarrel over religion, the prisoner refused to listen to the exhortation of a Protestant:

> When he was drawne in the Carte (with others) toward execution, and all the Carts beeing stayed before Saint Sepulchers Church, where the most Christian and charitable deed of Master *Dooue* [i.e., Dowe], at euery such time is worthily performed, to moue prayer and compassion in mens harts, for such so distressed: All the while that the man spake, *Lloyd* stopte his eares, not willing to heare any thing, but if any Romaine Catholicks were neere, he desired such to pray for him. And so at Tyborne he did in like manner. . . .[89]

Apparently the ritual of preparing the condemned for their ordeal was elaborated even further. According to at least one antiquarian, it was the custom to recite rhymed verses to the prisoners on the night before their execution:

> All you that in the condemned hold do lie,
> Prepare you, for to-morrow you shall die;
> Watch all and pray, the hour is drawing near,
> That you before the Almighty must appear;
> Examine well yourselves, in time repent,
> That you may not to eternall flames be sent.
> And when St. Sepulchre's bell to-morrow tolls,
> The Lord above have mercy on your souls.
> Past twelve o'clock![90]

The tolling of St. Sepulchre's "passing bell," theoretically rung for all deaths in the parish, must have been nearly a daily occurrence, especially in plague years. Dowe provided that, for executions, "the greatest bell of Saint Sepulchres shall alwaies begyn to toule from the 25th of March unto the 29th of September at six A.M. and from the 29th of September unto the 25th of March before seaven A.M. in manner as the passing Bell is used and that this Bell shall alwaies continue towling until tenn of the clock or until such tyme as the Sheriffs' Officers shall return home from the execution to the end and purpose that all good people hearing this passing Bell may be moved to pray for these poor Synners going to execution after which the said Bell shall cease towling and be rung out the space of one half hower or thereabouts."[91] In *The Devil's Law-Case*, when Ercole and Contarino are thought to have killed each other in a duel, Leonora exclaims:

> What a dismal noise yon bell makes!
> Sure some great person's dead.
> (II.iii.83–84)

Then, a few lines later, "*Two Bellmen*" enter with the Capuchin friar, who requests prayers for the "two unfortunate nobles"; in dying, they had "No churchman's prayer to comfort their last groans" (II.iii.93–95). We can readily understand how close to home these sentiments and their accompanying ceremonial effects must have been to John Webster, most funereal of Jacobean playwrights. The execution handbell that Dowe provided with his gift still exists and can be seen today in St. Sepulchre's church.[92]

Three years after Dowe gave money for exhorting the condemned of Newgate, a fellow philanthropist and Merchant Taylor, Robert Smith (originally from Leicestershire and unrelated, apparently, to the Ralph Smyth who signed the Salisbury petition),[93] donated fifty pounds to supply four small Bibles each year as Easter gifts to "towardly honest and diligent" poor children of the parish. The Bibles were to be "well bound, buffed and bossed." The money was also to be used (every week in perpetuity) to purchase a penny loaf of wheat bread for each of twelve poor persons of St. Sepulchre's. John Webster senior also signed the vestry minute, dated 1608, pertaining to this charity. Among the other twenty-six signatures (Webster signed fourth) were James Hodgson, who had also signed the petition in behalf of Spencer, and John Okes, the father of the printer Nicholas Okes, mentioned earlier.[94]

* * *

The dramatist's family connection with a thriving transport business was, of course, only too well known. Henry Fitzgeffrey of Lincoln's Inn, a friend of the John Stephens who attacked the author of Webster's anonymously published character, *An Excellent Actor*, published a poem entitled *Notes from Black-Fryers* (1617) that includes a hostile portrait of Webster. Fitzgeffrey alludes to him discourteously as "The *Play-wright, Cart-wright*," glancing doubly at his supposedly clumsy playmaking and at his brother Edward's trade in two-wheeled vehicles—the crudest and least fashionable aspect of his custom.[95] Two of Fitzgeffrey's fellows at the same Inn (John Stephens and John Cocke) seem to have jibed similarly at Webster in the second edition of Stephens's *Satirical Essayes, Characters, and Others* (1615), where they refer to Webster's writing as being "dressed ouer with oyle of sweaty Post-horse" and as employing "hackney similitudes" (see n. 33, pp. 546–547, below).[96] More amusingly, William Hemminge's manuscript *Elegy on Randolph's Finger* (c. 1632)—Hemminge was the son of Shakespeare's partner at the Globe—also adverts to the family enterprise. The poet Thomas Randolph had lost his finger in a tavern skirmish, and Hemminge's couplets burlesque its ceremonious funeral—a cortège to the river Styx, accompanied by the other grieving poets:

> that wch soe ofte has toumbled ore a Verse
> Is toumbled now ytt selfe Into a hearse,
> Borne to yttes graue, by Art Inuention

Thrice blessed Nature, Imitation.
Ytt had byn drawne and wee In state aproche
but websters brother would nott lend a Coach:
hee swore thay all weare hired to Conuey
the Malfy dutches sadly on her way,
And wittye fortune ytt seemes thought ytt more meett
to haue our Poettes quayntly vse thayr feett.

(ll. 33–42)[97]

These lines suggest that Edward Webster regularly hired out coaches and hearses for funeral processions, which could be more or less elaborate in Jacobean times depending on the rank, wealth, and prestige of the deceased. Cymoent's retrieval of the wounded body of Marinell in Spenser's *Faerie Queene* seems to reflect the late Elizabethan use of coaches and other vehicles for the most important burials:

Tho vp him taking in their tender hands,
They easily vnto her charet beare:
Her teme at her commaundement quiet stands,
Whiles they the corse into her wagon reare,
And strow with flowres the lamentable beare:
Then all the rest into their coches clim. . . .

(III.iv.42)[98]

Somewhat unusually, the Marchioness of Winchester was conveyed to her grave "in a charrett" on 4 February 1558/59, but the practice became more common in the seventeenth century with the growing popularity of wheels.[99] The term "hearse" originally designated the wooden frame for supporting the pall with its candles but gradually came to refer also to the vehicle that transported the corpse to church. By 1659 at least, the word had acquired the latter meaning, for a diarist of this date refers to "an herse" being brought from London to Worcester to convey the body of his friend to its grave in Earles Colne, Essex.[100] By the interregnum, John Evelyn was measuring the social significance of various funerals by the number of coaches present. At Lady Browne's burial at Deptford (6 October 1652) the hearse was "accompanied with many Coaches of Friends, & other persons of qualitie"; the widow of Thomas Russell was laid to rest (22 December 1656) at Charleton where "neere 100 *Coaches*" could be seen. On 3 August 1667 the body of the poet Abraham Cowley was "conducted to Westminster Abby in an *Hearse* with 6 horses, & all funebral decency, neere an hundred Coaches of noble men & persons of qualitie following . . ."; and when Evelyn buried his own brother (21 March 1670) at Epsom, "about 20 Coaches of six-horses" attended.[101] Many of these vehicles, as might be expected, were made in London.

Royal funerals, of course, were the most sumptuous of all and traditionally featured lifelike wax effigies of the corpse, richly clothed, placed on top of the coffin, and pulled through the streets on a horse-drawn "chariot" canopied and decorated heraldically in the showiest possible manner. More than one scholar has suggested that the "representation" of Prince Henry, mounted on his funeral car in 1612, drawn through the city by eight black horses, and then set up for display in Westminster Abbey, may well lie behind the conception of the wax corpses in *The Duchess of Malfi*.[102] Since Walter Rippon, the maker of Queen Elizabeth's funeral chariot in 1603, had been a member of St. Sepulchre's parish where coachbuilders naturally clustered,[103] it is not unlikely that the dramatist's father was similarly employed on the later occasion. We know from both *A Monumental Columne* and *Monuments of Honor* that King James's oldest son was one of the playwright's special heroes. Also Prince Henry had been an honorary Merchant Taylor, had been feasted by the company at their hall in 1607, and, only a year before his untimely death, had presented "Two brace of fatt bucks" to the fraternity, hunted in His Highness's deerpark and sent to the hall "in a coach."[104] There may possibly have been an official connection between the royal family and the Webster coachmaking establishment despite the tendency of the dramatist to take a deliberately antisycophantic tone toward the aristocracy.

Webster was certainly reflecting upon the commercial advantages of funerals in a speech he wrote for the cynical Romelio:

> Funerals hide men in civil wearing,
> And are to the drapers a good hearing,
> Make the heralds laugh in their black raiment,
> And all die worthies, die worth payment
> To the altar offerings . . . [i.e., all who
> die worthy of having gifts offered in their name
> are socially acclaimed].
> (*The Devil's Law-Case*, II.iii.121–125)

If the drapers stood to profit from the funerals of the wealthy (because of the quantities of black cloth required), so, too, did the Merchant Taylors (who made pennons, canopies, escutcheons, velvet coverings for hearses and catafalques, and the more grandiose trophies or insignia of mortuary pomp) and the coachmakers (who supplied vehicles when they were used). Henry Machyn, the best-known furnisher of funerals when the dramatist's father was a boy, belonged to Webster's livery company.[105]

But links between Webster's family business and the grim realities of death must, as a rule, have been considerably humbler than those having to do with noble or state funerals. The "carting" of condemned criminals from Newgate to the gallows has already been mentioned, and, in addition, lesser offenders were sometimes tied to such carts and whipped through the streets. Webster alludes to this latter punishment in *The Devil's Law-Case* (IV.ii.524). When an epidemic of plague broke out, there was the necessity of transporting scores of corpses on carts or wagons—often to pest pits some distance from the home parish, to relieve pressure on overcrowded churchyards and to lessen the risk of infection.

F. P. Wilson in his horrifying account of the plague in Renaissance England reveals that in Webster's parish alone 2,223 deaths were recorded during the half year between 14 July and 22 December 1603, of which 1,861 were caused by the dread disease. He quotes some uncommonly gruesome lines by George Wither (a poet, in his way, as "much possessed by death" as Webster), describing the shallow mass graves of a later plague year (1625) in which one might see (and smell) an "arme, or shoulder, or a leg," "a heape of skulls," a "halfe unburied . . . Corpse," a "locke of womans hayre," or a "dead mans face / Uncover'd." The collectors of cadavers bore a red wand (the symbol of contagion) and announced their approach by ringing a bell as their carts went from street to street and by crying "Cast out your dead." Wilson reprints an illustration of the "dead-carts" from the plague of 1665 as well as two others depicting the panicky flights from London by barge and wagon on the part of many people to escape contamination.

The intermittent demands for coaches and other vehicles for escape purposes must have augmented the profits of both Edward Webster and his father. Smithfield, logically enough, became one of the regular locations for their rental. A woodcut of 1630 (also reproduced by Wilson) shows runaways fleeing the city by coach. The infected, too ill to walk or ride horseback, were forced to hire coaches to get about, and in 1625 the situation became so alarming that on 23 April the Court of the East India Company purchased a secondhand coach for twenty pounds to avoid the peril of renting "mercenary coaches which are common to all kind of people whole or sick."[106] For those who could afford them, coaches were a popular means of upper-class travel out to Tyburn to witness notable executions. When the notorious Anne Turner, hanged for complicity in the Overbury murder, met her fate in 1615, many courtiers came in their coaches to see her suffer. One witness wrote to a friend that her body, "being taken down [from the gallows] by her brother . . . was in a coach conveyed to St. Martin's of the Fields, where in the evening of the same day she had an honest and decent burial."[107]

By the first decade of the seventeenth century coaches had already become the rage in London. Stow in the 1603 edition of his *Survey of London* remarks that "Of olde time Coatches were not knowne in this Island . . . but now of late yeares the vse of [them] . . . is taken vp, and made so common, as there is neither distinction of time, nor difference of persons obserued. . . ."[108] Edmond Howes, in an expansion of Stow's *Annals* (1631), amplifies the earlier passage, perhaps from notes, manuscripts, or books left by the original author:

little by little [coaches] grew usuall among the Nobilitis, and others of Sort, and within twentie yeeres became a great trade of Coachmaking.[109] About that time began long Waggons to come in use, such as now come to London from Canterbury, Norwich, Ipswich, Glocester, &c., with passengers and commodities. Lastly, even at this time, 1605, began the ordinary use of Caroaches.[110]

Many (including Fynes Moryson, Samuel Rowlands, Henry Peacham, and the Venetian envoy Orazio Busino)[111] deplored the new fad, bringing, as it did, unprecedented increases in dung, noise, the bumptious behavior of impatient drivers, and general congestion. The streets, still essentially medieval in their irregular and narrow layout, were ill designed for the traffic jams that resulted from the proliferation of two- and four-wheeled vehicles and from the burgeoning use of hackneys, which were tending to threaten the old form of hired travel on the Thames. The water poet John Taylor dashed off a pamphlet, *The World Runnes on Wheeles* (1624), satirizing the new fashion of "*Hackney hell-Carts*" that "*haue vndone my poore Trade*" of waterman, and emblematizing the whole business of coachmaking and coach hiring as a wicked manifestation of degeneracy and pride. In more honorable times, he writes, such national heroes as Sidney, Drake, and Essex, being "deadly foes to all sloth and effeminacy," "did make small vses of Coaches. . . ." Taylor's generalization about the affluence of the manufacturers would undoubtedly fit Webster's brother and, probably, his father as well:

your Coach-makers trade is the most gainefullest about the Towne, they are apparelled in Sattens and Veluets, are Masters of their Parish, Vestry-men, who fare like the Emperors *Heliogabalus* or *Sardanapalus*, seldome without their Mackroones, Parmisants, Iellyes and Kickshawes, with baked Swannes, Pasties hot, or cold red Deere Pyes, which they haue fro[m] their Debtors worships in the Country: neither are these Coaches onely thus cumbersome by their Rumbling and Rutting, as they are by their standing still, and damming vp the streetes and lanes, as the *Blacke Friers*, and diuers other places can witnes, and against Coach-makers doores the streets are so pestered and clogg'd with them, that neither man, horse or cart can passe for them. . . .[112]

As this passage makes plain, the theatre district in the city was especially affected by the nuisance of coach-driven playgoers arriving for, and departing from, performances of dramas such as Webster's own *Duchess of Malfi* or Jonson's *Alchemist*. The personified coach in Peacham's *Coach and Sedan* (1636) boastfully claims that "my imployment is so great, that I am never at quiet, day or night: I am a Benefactor to all Meetings, Play-houses, Mercers shops, Taverns, and some other houses of recreation, for I bring them their best customers, as they all know well enough."[113] Churches, too, were annoyed. Taylor complains of the "hideous rumbling in the streetes by many Church dores" so that "peoples eares are stop'd with the noyse, whereby they are debard of their edifying. . . ."[114] As early as 1606 Dekker had remarked on the disturbance to afternoon nappers—on the "thundring" caused by "carts and Coaches" "in euery street"—implying by his very title (*The Seuen Deadly Sinnes of London: Drawne in Seuen Seuerall Coaches Through the Seuen Seuerall Gates of the Citie. . . .*) the multifarious evils that attached to the habit of being driven in preference to walking or riding a mount.[115]

It would have been surprising indeed if the plays of the period had not shown the marks of such a momentous change in social behavior. Mistress

Quickly in *The Merry Wives of Windsor* refers to "knights, and lords, and gentlemen, with their coaches, I warrant you, coach after coach" (II.ii.61–63), while Vindice in *The Revenger's Tragedy* tries to prostitute his own sister by painting a picture of frenetic court luxuries that include "Nine coaches waiting—hurry, hurry, hurry" (II.i.206).[116] The coach had obviously become an important symbol of status and upward mobility, especially for the merchant classes. In Jonson's *Poetaster* Chloe exclaims, "I doe long to ride in a coach most vehemently" (IV.ii.17–18),[117] and the absurdly romantic Gertrude of *Eastward Ho*, a goldsmith's daughter, regards the chance to experience the new means of travel as one of the chief attractions of marriage to her new-made knight, Sir Petronel Flash. Quicksilver, in the latter comedy, remarks that "there was never child longed more to ride a cock-horse, or wear his new coat, than she longs to ride in her new coach" (II.ii.307–309); moreover, he observes (correctly in Gertrude's case) that a woman who will "marry to ride in a coach . . . cares not if she ride to her ruin" (III.ii.210–211).[118] Chapman, Jonson, and Marston actually write a speaking part for a coachman into *Eastward Ho* and represent the bride as totally obsessed with her new toy when it arrives in town to convey her to her imaginary Eastward Castle. The departure is enough to attract crowds, and a citizen's wife predicts that there "will be double as many people to see her take coach as there were to see [a new ship] take water" (III.ii.19–21).[119] The lady herself shrieks ecstatically, "Now, heaven! methinks I am e'en up to the knees in preferment" (III.ii.42–43).[120]

The unsettling roughness of such rides also occasioned much comment. The father of the Jeweller's Wife in Middleton's *Phoenix* warns his daughter about the dangers of miscarriage when she is about to ride off with her knight: "take heed the coach jopper not too much; have a care to the fruits of your body" (II.iii.17–18).[121] *The Roaring Girl* by Middleton and Dekker, which also includes a speaking part for a coachman, alludes to the "vild swaggering [i.e., the contemptuous demeanor of passengers] in coaches now-a-days"; "the highways are stopt" (III.i.15–16)[122] with such pretentious travelers, a circumstance that promotes competitively fast driving. The same scene (III.i.18–19) also refers to the well-known use of coaches, because of their greater privacy, as a means of transporting women to inns on the outskirts of the city (such as that at Ware, the village that figures so prominently in *Northward Ho*) where extramarital rendezvous often took place. John Taylor, in the pamphlet already cited, points scornfully to the coach as a convenient locus for sexual misconduct: a coach "is neuer vnfurnished of a bedde and curtaines, with shop-windowes of leather to buckle Bawdry vp as close in the midst of the street, as it were in the Stewes. . . ."[123] Not surprisingly, the popular stage exploited this aspect of the new coach-hiring culture as well. Dekker's *Match Me in London* and Middleton's *A Chaste Maid in Cheapside* (both c. 1611–1613) provide examples. The first play refers to a "Caroach" as a "Bawdy house" that "runs on foure wheeles" (II.iv.108–110), and the second mentions that Lady Kix's "coach will serve" for the cure of her childlessness by means of a "physic" whose sexual nature the lady obtusely fails to anticipate (III.iii.140–143).[124] Marston in *The Scourge of Villanie* (1599) had joked obscenely about a wife so bored with her husband's priapic inadequacy that she uses her coach (with the aid of a glass dildo) as a vibrator or sex machine:

> Shal *Lucea* scorne her husbands luke-warme bed?
> (Because her pleasure being hurried
> In ioulting Coach, with glassie instrument,
> Doth farre exceede the *Paphian* blandishment). . . .[125]

Despite his family's involvement in the business of making and lending coaches, Webster (or at least his collaborators) missed few opportunities to indulge in the same kind of allusion—usually with a satiric or moralistic thrust. Typically, *Westward Ho* makes reference to the London traffic problem, especially at a major festival such as the inauguration of a Lord Mayor: the accelerating birthrate in the city reminds Justiniano of the speed with which the multiplying "Coaches" run "into Cheap-side vppon *Symon* and *Iudes* day" (II.i.171–173). The same play refers to the jostling on bumpy roads that coaches guarantee their riders: the very suggestion of such a journey provokes Mistress Tenterhook to object, "O fie vpont: a Coach? I cannot abide to be iolted" (II.iii.69). But preponderantly, Webster's allusions to coaches carry overtones of lust or illicit sexuality. The bawd Birdlime arranges for Mistress Justiniano to be called for in style by the lecherous Earl of *Westward Ho*: "the *Caroche* shall come" (I.i.133). In *The White Devil*, Bracciano pays his initial visit to Vittoria in a "caroche" (I.ii.8), which is then sent on ahead so that he may pursue the object of his infatuation with greater freedom. Later, at her arraignment, we hear of Vittoria's extravagant and courtesanlike style of entertaining, "Her gates [being] chok'd with coaches" (III.ii.73). In *The Devil's Law-Case* Romelio worries lest "a hackney coachman, if he can speak French" (I.ii.192), may abet his sister in a love affair of which he disapproves. A madman in the torture episode of *The Duchess of Malfi* imagines that he has been cuckolded on wheels: "Woe to the caroche, that brought home my wife from the masque, at three o'clock in the morning! it had a large featherbed in it" (IV.ii.104–106). And a similar detail shows up in a Websterian scene of *The Fair Maid of the Inn*, where the Host informs the foolish suitors for Bianca's hand that the mountebank Forobosco will soon attract diverse nyphomaniacal ladies "hurrying hither in Fetherbeds . . . fetherbeds that move upon 4 wheels, in Spanish caroches" (IV.ii.28–31).

* * *

After considerable investigation, the nature and extent of Webster's formal education remain in doubt. Uncertainty on the issue has inevitably fostered speculation and not a little scholarly disagreement. We possess no documentary evidence of the playwright's schooling and are therefore driven to inferences based on his father's economic and professional standing and on such classical knowledge as the works themselves may be thought to evince. Attendance at Merchant Taylors' School, the famous institution founded and operated by the elder Webster's own brotherhood, would seem very likely, but the records, admittedly incomplete, give no indication of the future poet's presence there, and debate continues as to his mastery of Latin.

Unfortunately, the single reference that perhaps connects Webster with the Inns of Court—a very tempting possibility—cannot certainly be accepted as applying to the playwright. The dramatist's editor, F. L. Lucas, discovered an entry in the records of the Middle Temple dated 1 August 1598 admitting a "Master John Webster, lately of the New Inn, gentleman, son and heir apparent of John Webster of London, gentleman" to the society of Middle Templars.[126] This date fits nicely (the coachmaker's son would have been between eighteen and twenty) as does the intellectual environment. Moreover, this John Webster was never called to the bar, which is precisely what we should expect of someone who turned to playwriting as a career. The same inn claimed Thomas Overbury, John Marston, and John Ford as members—the first two, significant influences on Webster (especially in the characters and *The Malcontent*), and the last, his friend and theatrical collaborator. Add to these considerations Webster's obvious interest in the legal world, his quarrel with John Stephens of Lincoln's Inn in *An Excellent Actor*, and his fondness for courtroom scenes and judicial disputes (important in *The White Devil*, *The Devil's Law-Case*, *A Cure for a Cuckold*, and *Appius and Virginia*), and the law school record might seem irresistible. But there were other John Websters in London, satire on litigiousness and legal corruption had become a popular convention in the drama of the period, and the term "gentleman" (applied to both father and son) gives cause for hesitation. As Lucas reminds us, Edmond Howes does list "Iohn Webster, gentleman" among "Our moderne and present excellent Poets" in his continuation of Stow's *Annals* (1615),[127] but one wonders whether Webster senior, though already a thriving merchant in 1598, would be entitled to such a designation. (The rank seems to have been applied more loosely in later decades.) Webster alludes occasionally to university life in his plays, but the only trace of a John Webster at either university in the sixteenth century is a record of one who matriculated as a "sizar" at St. John's College, Cambridge, in the Easter term of 1585 but took no degree.[128] The earliness of this date clearly eliminates the dramatist, who could not have been more than seven years old at the time. Webster, of course, could have moved directly from Merchant Taylors' School to the New Inn. Some Inns-of-Court men entered directly from grammar school, usually via the adjunct Inns of Chancery, of which the New Inn was one.

Doubtless in emulation of poets such as Chapman and Jonson, Webster was eager to give the impression of learning. In his dedication of *Monuments of Honor* (1624) he speaks of doing the new mayor, the Merchant Taylors, and the

City of London "honor" by writing "in the quality of a Scholler" (ll. 7–8); and in the body of the same work he boasts self-consciously that his own "light of Learning" is "as great . . . as any formerly imployed" (ll. 1–2) by poets who have composed such pageants in past years—presumably comparing himself to Munday, Dekker, and especially Middleton (who had been to Queen's College, Oxford). If there had been space, Webster informs us, he would have described "the Original and cause of all Tryumphes . . . in the Time of the *Romans*" (ll. 3–4) in addition to providing a history of such ceremonies in his own metropolis. Then he concludes the book by apologizing for his style, which he could have made "more curious and Elaborate" but for the fear of being "too teadious . . . or too weighty" and so "troubl[ing]" the mayor himself and "pusl[ing] the understanding of the Common People" (ll. 375–378).[129] The year before, when he published *The Devil's Law-Case*, Webster quoted Horace in gratuitous demonstration of "be[ing] free from those vices which proceed from ignorance" ("To the Judicious Reader," ll. 2–3), at the same time observing complacently in his dedication to Sir Thomas Finch that "the greatest of the Caesars have cheerfully entertain'd less poems than this . . ." (ll. 8–9).[130]

Webster's preface to *The White Devil* (1612), going well beyond the patronizing and self-congratulatory, rises to the contemptuous, even the splenetic. His unreceptive audience at the Red Bull, little better than "ignorant asses" who prefer "new books" to "good books" (ll. 8–10), could hardly have appreciated a tragedy in classical style—one properly furnished with "the sententious *Chorus*" and "the passionate and weighty *Nuntius*"; indeed, had the author provided these, such an "uncapable multitude" would be "able to poison" the play "ere it be acted" (ll. 18–22).[131] And, insultingly, he appropriates a couple of Horatian tags to imply that ordinary playgoers are mere yokels with garlic breath—no more discriminating in taste than pigs who feed on the scraps of their keepers.

As has been pointed out by more than one commentator, such aggressive displays of cultural and intellectual superiority sound suspiciously defensive and may reflect a writer who felt profoundly insecure about his own educational attainments. R. G. Howarth, who has conducted the most thorough examination of Webster's classical knowledge and R. W. Dent, who has painstakingly documented the poet's verbal borrowings, have both demonstrated the derivative and often inaccurate nature of Webster's scholarship.[132] His ability in modern languages must certainly have been slight, for he never used a foreign work when he could find an English translation, and we cannot be positive that he ever read a continental book in the original. Though he loved to deck out his prefaces, title pages, and dedications with a show of classical learning and quoted frequently from such ancients as Virgil, Martial, Ovid, Seneca, perhaps Juvenal, and especially Horace, most of his appropriations are either commonplace Latin tags, mottoes, and legal terms, or borrowings at second or third hand from the preliminary matter of contemporaries such as Dekker and Jonson. He seems to have known no Greek, and such Latin as he had he may have picked up gradually, perhaps from better educated friends like Heywood and Ford, toward the latter half of his literary career. A Latin work is the only known book that could have served as Webster's main source for *Appius and Virginia* (c. 1627)—unless we posit a lost version in English—and he was able to translate (perhaps even compose) some brief Latin verses to members of the royal family about 1624. One might well conclude from the internal evidence that Webster could hardly have been an educated man in the full tradition of Elizabethan humanism. Howarth therefore rejects the identification of the Middle Templar with the dramatist and regards Webster's Latin as so insecure as probably to rule out even a sustained grammar school education: "From *The White Diuel* onwards [Webster] merely poses as a scholar."[133]

If we accept Howarth's low estimate of Webster's learning, the picture that emerges is that of a dramatist whose literary talents greatly exceeded his formal training and who, even more than Shakespeare, was largely self-taught. Unlike Shakespeare, however, Webster hankered after scholarly prestige and highbrow eminence. In his self-important address "To the Reader" at the front of *The White Devil*, he compares himself complacently to Euripides in the very act of mistaking Alcestis for the nonexistent "Alcestides, a tragic writer" (l. 28), either through his own or an intermediary's blunder in Latin grammar.[134] Moreover, Webster appears to suggest, although he carefully exculpates himself from the charge of invidious comparisons, that he prefers to be thought of as a peer of Chapman and Jonson, the two most scholarly playwrights of the age, rather than of Shakespeare, Dekker, and Heywood, whom he groups together after Beaumont and Fletcher at the base of his literary hierarchy:

for mine own part I have ever truly cherish'd my good opinion of other men's worthy labours, especially of that full and height'ned style of Master Chapman, the labour'd and understanding works of Master Jonson: the no less worthy composures of the both worthily excellent Master Beaumont, and Master Fletcher: and lastly (without wrong last to be named) the right happy and copious industry of Master Shakespeare, Master Dekker, and Master Heywood, wishing what I write may be read by their light. . . .

(ll. 34–43)[135]

Webster seems to have possessed some of the "industry" that he attributes, with a hint of condescension, to Shakespeare and the other runners-up in his roster of models, but in the work he cared to be judged by he tried harder than they to impress readers by striving for the "full and height'ned style" of Chapman and by emulating the "labour'd and understanding works" (the term "works" is revealing) of Jonson. Webster never mentions Marston; he was probably respectful of the ex-satirist's desire, after his ordination to the priesthood, of severing all ties with his theatrical past. But the fashionable corrosiveness of plays such as *The Malcontent* must have struck him almost as much as more classically oriented scripts by Chapman and Jonson.

The judgment minimizing Webster's schooling may, however, be too severe. Howarth, writing before Mary Edmond had published her data on Webster's family, assumed incorrectly that the tragedian was "the poor son of a London tailor" and "a member of a socially inferior class."[136] In addition, some of Howarth's evidence for the poet's classical incapacity is dubious. Since history records no Greek poet by the name of Alcestis, the misrendering, Alcestides, is far more understandable than if a well-known literary figure had been referred to; anyway, in this case, Webster seems merely to have accepted the mistake of another writer without correcting it. It is true that Webster often seems ignorant of the context when he quotes from a classical author, but we know that he kept a commonplace book and in most cases would have little reason, months or even years after copying an extract, to consult the original source. Such exactitude was hardly required of a writer for the popular stage.

Howarth makes much of Webster's supposedly weak Latin vocabulary. He instances "torvèd" in *Appius and Virginia* (V.ii.67) and "lenitive" in *The Duchess of Malfi* (III.i.75), both of which words, he believes, could not have been misused by a poet familiar with their Latin roots. "Torvèd" in the phrase, "his least torvèd frown," ought logically to appear as "torvid" (from *torvidus* = fierce) rather than as a form that implies the nonverb, *to torve*; while "lenitive" (= soothing; from *lenis* = smooth) in the expression, "lenitive poisons," might seem to be a contradiction in terms. But Jacobean orthography is notoriously erratic (many English spellings of the period, even in the works of learned writers, falsify the Latin roots from which the words derive), and, in any case, the word "torvèd" appears in a scene of *Appius and Virginia* that has often been attributed to Heywood. As for "lenitive poisons," the phrase is not so impossible as Howarth supposed. Brown points out that Webster was later to use the word "lenatively" in its normal sense in *Anything for a Quiet Life* (I.i.91) and plausibly suggests that, in *The Duchess*, Ferdinand simply refers to potions that were sweet or pleasant to the taste but that nevertheless caused insanity—"lenitive poisons, such as are of force / To make the patient mad" (III.i.75–76).[137] F. L. Lucas, himself a distinguished classicist, could annotate Webster's supposed solecisms without concluding that the playwright lacked formal training; indeed, it was Lucas, as mentioned above, who discovered and provisionally accepted Webster's connection with the Inns of Court. Also Howarth somewhat undermines his own argument by conceding that dramatists such as Marlowe, a Cambridge man, and Chapman, who could genuinely claim classical learning, were capable of mistranslating their originals, although he thinks Webster's blunders more akin to the notorious "howler" of Thomas Kyd, a nonuniversity man, who rendered Virgil's "ad lumina" ("until dawn") as "by candlelight" in *The Housholders Philosophie* (1588).[138] What Howarth oddly fails to mention is that Kyd himself was an entrant at Merchant Taylors', the very school that he seems to doubt Webster attended.

Although E. E. Kellett spoke of the dramatist's "ambiguous classical knowledge," believing that "his close association with so good a scholar as Heywood" would sufficiently account for "the scraps of Martial and Horace which adorn his pages," and although Dent has concluded that "Webster's indebtedness to the classics" was "consistently at second hand,"[139] most scholars have assumed that Webster had more formal education than Howarth allows him. Peter Haworth attributed Webster's sluggish rate of composition, his relatively meager output, and his unevenness in dramatic vitality to his being "pre-eminently a scholar with . . . gifts of a purely literary quality," even going so far as to compare him to Milton; while W. A. Edwards, a disciple of Leavis, praised Webster as belonging to a sophisticated elite of "young wits" whose "tradition of elegant writing" derived from such learned authors as "Sidney and Lyly."[140]

Certainly Webster read widely and eclectically in contemporary and Renaissance literature, especially when this could be consulted in his own language; we know that he drew upon such diverse works as Sidney's *Arcadia*, Montaigne's *Essays* (in Florio's version), Erasmus's colloquy "Funus," North's *Plutarch*, William Alexander's *Monarchicke Tragedies*, Matthieu's French history (in translations by Grimestone), Donne's *Ignatius his Conclave* and *Anatomy of the World*, Painter's *Palace of Pleasure*, Guazzo's *Civil Conversation* (retranslated from a French version by Pettie), Nashe's *Unfortunate Traveller*, Montreux's *Honours Academie* (Englished by Tofte), Adams's *The Gallants Burden*, Guevara's *Diall of Princes* (another of North's translations), and Goulart's *Admirable and Memorable Histories* (in an English version by Grimestone). No wonder Fernand Lagarde tends to give Webster the benefit of the doubt as regards formal schooling. Nor is it entirely surprising that M. C. Bradbrook, with her accustomed intrepidity, can state flatly that "it does not . . . seem open to any question that Webster would have attended the school founded by his father's company, the school for which his father provided pageant waggons." And she goes on to assert that "It would have been an act not merely of eccentricity but of ostracism for a member of the company to send his child anywhere else."[141] If skepticism about Webster's enrollment at either Merchant Taylors' School or the Middle Temple constitutes the only safe position, we must grant that these places are the likeliest sources of his literary and linguistic nurture.

If Webster did attend Merchant Taylors' School, he was taught at one of the handful of most distinguished academies in the nation, St. Paul's (established by John Colet), St. Peter's College (or Westminster School, as commonly referred to), Winchester, and Eton being the nearest rivals in intellectual eminence. Founded in 1561 by two philanthropic Merchant Taylors—Sir Thomas White (who also founded St. John's College, Oxford, and who figures in Webster's own *Monuments of Honor*) and Richard Hilles (who donated five hundred pounds for purchase of the Manor of the Rose, the mansion in Suffolk Lane where instruction took place), the school had been dedicated from its inception to "the better educac[i]on and bringing vp of Children in good manners and L[ite]rature."[142] Although enrollment was strictly limited to two hundred and fifty boys, a hundred paying no tuition at all and the rest paying either two shillings and twopence, or five shillings, a quarter, depending on their circumstances, the school was unusually large for its day and attracted pupils from the provinces as well as from London. According to the statutes drawn up by the Merchant Taylors, a headmaster "in body whole, sober, discreete, honest, verteous, & learned, in good & cleane Latine l[ite]rature, & also, in Greeke, yf such may be gotten," was to be appointed. A chief usher and two subordinate ushers were to assist. The boys to be admitted (in addition to qualified children of the Taylors themselves) might be "of all nations & countryes indifferently" but must already know "the catechism in English or Latyn" and be able to "read perfectly & write competently." School began at seven o'clock in the morning and continued until five in the evening with a two-hour recess at eleven. Prayers were recited thrice daily (morning, noon, and evening) "with due tact and pawsing," the boys kneeling. They studied by the light of expensive "wax candles," the cheaper tallow candles, which smoked, being disallowed. Merchant Taylors' was a day school. There were no provisions for boarding, and indeed the statutes specifically forbade the consumption of food and drink during teaching hours, although there might be special banquets on days of celebration. Physical exercise was encouraged, but cockfighting, tennis, "riding about of victoring," and "disputing abroad, which is but foolish babling & losse of tyme" were proscribed. Liturgical holidays excepted, scholars were to have "leave to play . . . only once in the weeke."[143]

Richard Mulcaster (1530?–1611), the first headmaster, established the school's reputation for excellence from the start. Mulcaster, who authored two treatises on education, *Positions* (1581) and *The First Part of the Elementarie* (1582), was a notable scholar of Latin, Greek, and Hebrew. He had studied under Nicholas Udall at Eton and afterwards at both King's College, Cambridge, and Christ Church, Oxford. A product of enlightened humanist ideals and training (Sir John Cheke had been his mentor at Cambridge), Mulcaster believed in cultivating the whole boy, tomorrow's Renaissance man. Consequently he fostered such activities as singing, playing musical instruments, drawing, the putting on of plays, wrestling, archery, dancing, and other social and physical graces in addition to strictly academic disciplines. In the 1570s Merchant Taylors' boys performed regularly before the queen (like the child actors at St. Paul's, for whom John Lyly wrote), and also (before an ordinance of the guild forbade such theatricals on their own premises) to more boisterous audiences at Merchant Taylors' Hall. In Webster's time the boys still took part in municipal pageants and civic ceremonies. In 1603, for instance, the then headmaster William Hayne was reimbursed for "p[re]paring his schollers to make a shew and speech in Cheapsyde" on Lord Mayor's day the previous October. Charges are recorded for banqueting "the children of the pageant at the rehearsal of their parts" before the Master and Wardens of the company and for Hayne's expenses of "preparing a wagon and apparelling 10 scholars who represented the 9 muses and the god Apollo."[144] This was the same show, mentioned above, for which Webster's father had supplied horses and a chariot.

Sir James Whitelocke (1570–1632), one of Mulcaster's more successful pupils (he went on—perhaps like Webster—to the New Inn, then to the Middle Temple, and ultimately became a Justice of the King's Bench), gives us a first-hand account of the regime at Suffolk Lane:

> I was brought up at school under mr. Mulcaster, in the famous school of the Marchantaylors in London, whear I continued untill I was well instructed in the Hebrew, Greek, and Latin tongs. His care was also to encreas my skill in musique, in whiche I was brought up by dayly exercise in it, as in singing and playing upon instruments, and yeerly he presented sum playes to the court, in whiche his scholers wear only actors, and I on[e] among them, and by that meanes taughte them good behaviour and audacitye.[145]

Whitelocke does not mention the corporal punishment in which Mulcaster also believed, but a humorous anecdote, told of the famous schoolmaster after he had left Merchant Taylors' and was teaching at St. Paul's, conveys some notion of his unique combination of harsh discipline, wit, and capacity for leniency:

> He being one day whippinge a boy, his breeches being down, out of his insulting humour he stood pausing a while over his breech; and there a merry conceit taking him he said, "I aske ye bannes of Matrymony between this boy his buttockes of such a parish on ye one side and Lady Birch of ye parish on ye other side, and if any man can shew any lawfull cause why yey should not be joyned together let yim speake, for yis is ye last time of askinge." A good sturdy boy and of a quick conceit stood up and sayd, "Master, I forbid ye bannes." The master takinge this in dudgeon sayd, "Yea, Sirrah, and why so?" The boy answered, "Because all partyes are not agreed." Whereat the master likinge that witty answer spared the one's fault and the other's presumption.[146]

The school in Suffolk Lane quickly became known for its middle-class progressivism. Mulcaster even argued for the education of girls although he accepted none into his school. Irascible, stiff-necked, and difficult (at least from the perspective of his employers), he was nevertheless large-minded. Famous as a teacher of classical learning, he also reverenced his mother tongue and therefore did much to encourage a style of expression indigenous to his own culture. He saw the development of the vernacular as a patriotic duty and knew the value of enriching English with borrowings from other languages. His much-quoted statement in the *Elementarie*, with which Webster, at least privately, could hardly have disagreed, is revealing:

> is it not in dede a meruellous bondage, to becom seruants to one tung for learning sake, the most of our time, with losse of most time, whereas we maie haue the verie same treasur in our own tung, with the gain of most time? our own bearing the ioyfull title of our libertie and fredom, the *Latin* tung remembring vs, of our thraldom & bondage? I loue

Rome, but *London* better, I fauor *Italie*, but England more, I honor the Latin, but I worship the *English*.[147]

Mulcaster's pedagogical principles and the traditions to which his leadership gave rise rapidly bore fruit in a succession of famous alumni—several of these major names in literary history and a few of them dramatists. Edmund Spenser is the best known among the English poets, but Thomas Lodge (from whom Webster may have borrowed), Thomas Kyd (already mentioned), and James Shirley (the last leading playwright to serve the King's Men) were also Merchant Taylors' boys. So too was the minor Latin dramatist, poet, physician, and friend of John Florio, Matthew Gwynne. The school naturally produced a goodly share of prelates and churchly scholars. Launcelot Andrewes, the great bishop of Winchester and part translator of the King James Bible, began his training as a linguist at Merchant Taylors', as did five of his fellows on the committee of translators—Ralph Huchenson (President of St. John's College, Oxford), Giles Thompson (Proctor of Oxford University, chaplain to the queen, Dean of Windsor, and ultimately, Bishop of Gloucester), John Spencer (Webster's vicar at St. Sepulchre's), Ralph Ravens (Doctor of Divinity, of St. John's, Oxford), and John Peryn (Regius Professor of Greek and Canon of Christ Church, Oxford). Thomas Dove, another chaplain to Queen Elizabeth, Dean of Norwich, Church Commissioner at the Hampton Court Conference, and Bishop of Peterborough, studied ancient languages at the school. So did William Juxon, Bishop of London during the Civil War, and Matthew Wren, successively Bishop of Hereford, Norwich, and Ely. Juxon was Charles I's confessor, attended the royal martyr on the scaffold, and at the Restoration was elevated to the see of Canterbury; Wren suffered imprisonment for eighteen years under the Commonwealth and on his release built the chapel at his old college (Pembroke Hall, Cambridge), which his architectural nephew, Christopher Wren, designed. Bishops John Buckeridge (of Rochester, then of Ely) and Rowland Searchfield (of Bristol) were Merchant Taylors' students, as were Peter Heylyn (the biographer of Archbishop Laud), Samuel Foxe (son of John, the Protestant martyrologist), and the third and fourth headmasters of the school, Edmund Smith (who would have taught Webster) and William Hayne. Two close friends of Richard Hooker, students together at Corpus Christi, Oxford, began their educations at Merchant Taylors'—Sir Edwin Sandys (the traveler, treasurer of Virginia, and son of Archbishop Sandys) and George Cranmer (a great nephew of the martyred archbishop who contributed so memorably to *The Book of Common Prayer*). Not surprisingly, the philanthropic Robert Dowe, a Warden of the Merchant Taylors, sent his sons, John and Henry, to the school.

Boys generally entered Merchant Taylors' at age nine or ten (although Kyd was only seven) and—if they could hold their own in the rigorously challenging program of study—remained until their mid-teens. Of course some boys, among whom Webster might have been one, dropped out earlier. The future tragedian would have been enrolled about 1587–1588—the tense period of the Armada and a year or two after Mulcaster, ending a tenure of twenty-five years, had resigned as headmaster. The crotchety pedagogue had apparently quarreled once too often with the Court of Merchant Taylors and in 1586 was replaced as head, first by Henry Wilkinson and then by Edmund Smith—both Cambridge graduates and former chief ushers of the school. Wilkinson lasted only six years in the headmastership, Smith only seven, whereupon the fourth headmaster, William Hayne, entered in 1599 upon another long period of uninterrupted leadership. Wilkinson and Smith, Webster's presumed masters, were less remarkable and colorful men than Mulcaster, but they taught on the same humanist principles and inculcated the same Reformation values that had been the hallmark of Richard Hilles, the chief inspiration behind the school at its founding. If Webster failed to excel in Latin, Greek, and Hebrew to the degree exhibited by some of his more academically inclined schoolfellows, he must at least have refined his natural taste for sententious eloquence and for wit, meter, imagery, and the pleasures of the spoken word—all significant components of dramatic verse. Perhaps, too, the school reinforced or helped to form that bitter, quasi-Calvinist emphasis on human depravity that was later to color his most distinctive plays, although this tone would more likely have been fostered by the Middle Temple. The distance between Cow Lane and Suffolk Lane is close to a mile and a quarter—a twenty-minute walk or so through the heart of the city on a dark winter morning for a lad of nine. One wonders whether he would have been permitted to undertake the daily journey unaccompanied. A servant of the large Webster household may have walked with him to school or perhaps driven him in one of his father's carts.

* * *

If Webster went to the New Inn after his grammar school years at Merchant Taylors', he probably entered about 1596 or 1597, when he was something like sixteen or seventeen. This Society was an Inn of Chancery, professionally affiliated with the Middle Temple and serving mainly as a preparatory institution for younger men on their way to an Inn of Court. Sir Thomas More, for instance, studied there before becoming a member of Lincoln's Inn. Usually residence at an Inn of Chancery lasted only a year or two. Most, though by no means all, New Inn students graduated to the Middle Temple, officially their senior house; and the Parliament of the upper Society regularly appointed Readers to present test cases and expound statutory principles to its subordinate Inn as part of their legal education. In 1608, a decade after Webster would have left the junior Society, the Temple became its landlord by acquiring a freehold of its property.

With rooms arranged in a quadrangle around a courtyard and with gardens and a dining hall attached, the New Inn resembled a university college. Dating apparently from the mid-fifteenth century, it had originally been founded as the result of a migration from St. George's Inn (no longer extant in Webster's lifetime but formerly located near the junction of Seacoal and St. George's Lanes, very close to Newgate and St. Sepulchre's Church). According to Stow, the New Inn buildings before the students took them over had been "a common hostery, called of the signe our Lady Inne"; Sir John Fineux, Lord Chief Justice of the King's Bench, seems to have arranged the new tenancy, for which the prospective lawyers paid the bargain rent of only six pounds a year.[148] The entrance lay on the northern side of Wych Street (near the eastern end of Aldwych in modern London) due west of the Church of St. Clement Danes—the church, incidentally, that served as the chapel for the contiguous Inn of Chancery (St. Clement's), the Inn about which Justice Shallow reminisces in *2 Henry IV*.[149] Along the southern side of the church nave ran the Strand; the street on the northern side (called "Back Side of St. Clement's") forked into Wych Street (the northern tine) and Holywell Street (the southern tine) at the western extremity of the churchyard. Wych Street, in effect, was a western extension of Butcher Row, a street that branched off the Strand near its origin at Temple Bar.

The Middle Temple, to which the "Master John Webster, lately of the New Inn" moved in August 1598, was not far away. It lay immediately south of Temple Bar, the wooden gateway that marked the westernmost limit of the old city and the end of Fleet Street. As in Elizabethan times, one still enters the Inn from this thoroughfare. Middle Temple Lane ran southwards from Fleet Street to the Thames, bisecting the Society's extensive grounds. Its magnificent new hammer-beamed hall (forty-five feet high, a hundred feet long, forty feet wide, pierced by graceful windows bearing stained-glass coats of arms of illustrious alumni, furnished with a large gallery, and adorned by a richly carved screen) had been erected earlier in the reign (it was completed about 1572) and occupied a site on the western side of Middle Temple Lane north of the Temple gardens, which fronted the river. These are the famous gardens, constituting a sort of *rus in urbe*, where Shakespeare in his earliest chronicle play sets his fictional commencement of the Wars of the Roses with the symbolic plucking of the red and white badges of Lancaster and York. The dynastic quarrel (begun, as might be expected, in the offical place for legal debates—the dining hall) moves outdoors:

> Within the Temple hall we were too loud.
> The garden here is more convenient.
> (*1 Henry VI*, II.iv.3–4)

Spenser in his *Prothalamion* (1596) also gives us a sense of the idyllic setting of the Temple when he alludes to

> those bricky towres,
> The which on *Themmes* brode aged backe doe ryde,
> Where now the studious Lawyers haue their bowers

Where whylome wont the Templer Knights to byde,
Till they decayd through pride. . . .

(ll. 132–136)[150]

Visitors, including royalty, often arrived at the Temple by water, mounting the stairs that descended from a pier or "bridge" at the lower end of the Lane. The famous Temple Church, built in the twelfth and thirteenth centuries by the Knights Templars, served as the chapel for both the Middle Temple and the Inner Temple, its sister society immediately to the east. The round part dates from about 1185; the nave or choir was consecrated in 1240.

The Inns of Court, grouped together with their subsidiary Inns of Chancery in the fashionable suburb outside the old city walls and southwest of such bustling, crowded, and intensely commercial areas as Smithfield, formed an enclave of intellectual and social privilege in Renaissance London. Although the city had already encroached upon them to some extent, especially near the river, the geography was symbolically as well as practically significant; for, of course, the Inns occupied the space between the merchant-dominated jurisdiction of the Lord Mayor on the one hand and, on the other, the royal court at Whitehall and the Palace of Westminster, which housed the Lords, the Commons, and the most important court of law in the land. Governmentally speaking, the Inns were considered to occupy a Liberty, even though the Middle Temple, for instance, fell within the boundaries of Farringdon Ward Without. The Reformation had brought with it a rapid expansion of the legal profession in England, so that, by the end of the sixteenth century, some association or at least familiarity with the law (even if admission to the bar were not contemplated) was perceived as the principal means of advancement to the corridors of power. According to one authority, the rate of annual admissions to the Inns "quadrupled between 1500 and 1600," although residence did not increase at the same rate, since nonstudent and occasionally poorer student members sometimes lived away from the premises.[151]

Theoretically, only "gentlemen," young men of pedigree, could be admitted to the Inns, but by Webster's time this rule had become virtually impossible to enforce, and, in practice, the sons of wealthy tradesmen were often accepted, thereby becoming gentlemen de facto. Perhaps the designation of Webster's father as "gentleman" (*generosus*) in the record of entry is to be explained simply as the fiction necessary to the new status of his son. Edward Sharpham, himself a Middle Templar, writes a joke on the gratuitousness of rank into his comedy *The Fleire* (1606):

Florida. . . . draw neere us, hence foorth we accept you as our owne, and so wee bid you welcome: are you a Gentleman?
Gentleman. Yes sure Madam, for I was both borne & begotten in an Innes Court.

Madame Fromaga. Sure Madam then hees a Gentleman, for he thats but admitted to the house is a Gent. much more he thats begotten in the house.

(I, 136–143)[152]

Sir Thomas Smith, as early as 1583, could write that "whosoeuer studieth the
lawes of the realme, who studieth in the uniuersities, who professeth liberall sciences, and to be shorte, who can liue idly and without manuall labour, and will
beare the port, charge and countenaunce of a gentleman . . . shall be taken for a
gentleman. . . ."[153] It was all very well for Sir George Buc, James I's Master of
Revels, to inveigh against the idea that the sons of "merchants, tradesmen or artificers" and others of humble birth "can be made gentlemen" by "admittance" to
an "inne of court, for no man can be made gentleman but by his father";[154] but
Smith's assessment of how matters stood was closer to the social realities.

Although technically independent of each other, the four Inns of Court
(Lincoln's, Gray's, and the Middle and Inner Temples) together with their respective Inns of Chancery constituted "The Third Vniuersitie of England"—a
term coined by Buc in 1615 but derived obviously from Stow's description of the
Inns in 1598, the same year the John Webster of the records became a Middle
Templar: "there is in and about this Citie, a whole Vniuersitie, as it were, of students, practisers or pleaders and Iudges of the lawes of this realme, not liuing of
common stipends, as in other Vniuersities . . . but of their owne priuate mainte-
nance. . . ."[155] As Stow's statement implies, undergraduates at Oxford and
Cambridge were often poor and dependent on scholarships provided by a college, school, or other charitable source, whereas Inns-of-Court men had to have
funds of their own and were expected to maintain themselves with some affluence as befitted gentlemen born. Occasionally there were levies for new buildings, as had been the case when the Middle Templars were financing their
impressive hall. Members paid significant fines of admission, and, in addition to
keeping chambers and not infrequently a servant, were regularly assessed for all
sorts of banquets, entertainments, and other activities associated with the social
and professional life of their Society, which functioned somewhat in the manner
of a great house. They were also expected to dress elegantly, even under their
gowns, despite certain sumptuary regulations against undue ostentation. The
wearing of gaudy colors, of stuffed breeches, of long hair, of fancy cloaks,
boots, and rapiers—especially in hall—was theoretically forbidden, but evidence suggests that by Webster's day such infractions were often winked at. And
Inns-of-Court men were notorious for their constant patronizing of theatres and
other pleasures available to those with ready cash to expend. It cost at least forty
pounds a year to live at an Inn with any dignity; many, of course, spent far more.

Studies were by no means confined to the law. The social environment inevitably spawned a certain amount of dilettantism, but Mulcaster's ideals of
breadth and diversification had significantly influenced higher as much as secondary education. Lessons in fencing, singing, dancing, and other social attain-

ments—indeed, in almost any polite discipline—could be had from private tutors or ancillary academies that proliferated within or around the edges of the Inns. Buc's addendum to the 1615 edition of Stow's *Annals* gives an extensive list of "Arts and Sciences Read and Tavght in This Vniversitie," including theology, grammar, rhetoric, poetry, logic, philosophy, physic (or medicine), astronomy, music, languages, calligraphy, swimming, dancing, painting, and, not least, "Art Memorative" and "Art of Reuels" (p. 963). No wonder Ben Jonson, who claimed *"friendship with diuers . . . great Names in learning"* at the Inns, could dedicate *Every Man Out of His Humour* to the famous Societies—in his words, "the Noblest Novrceries of Hvmanity and Liberty in the Kingdome."[156]

Like all institutions of learning in Webster's age, the Inns were rigidly hierarchical in organization. The Middle Temple, for instance, housed about two hundred Inner Barristers (the equivalent of undergraduates), who studied under the guidance of Utter Barristers. These, in turn, elected the most accomplished of their number as Benchers, who became the governors or Parliament of the Inn. The older men who actually practiced law received clients in their chambers, and the Inns became regular houses of resort, both professional and social, for persons of prominence. Benchers could extend the privileges of affiliation, including residence, to influential visitors, as social clubs do today. Honorary memberships were sometimes conferred upon peers or other dignitaries.

There was no teaching faculty as such. Those who had already been admitted to the bar bore the duty of initiating their younger brethren into the profession, much as masters in a livery company passed on their skills to apprentices. In the learning intervals between terms (particularly in the Lent and August vacations) a Reader, chosen from among the Benchers, customarily lectured the entire house in the Great Hall on some statute, after which the Utter Barristers and Benchers, in order of seniority, argued a point or question of law in detail and were answered at the end of the proceedings by the Reader. But the Inner Barristers learned mainly by participating in "moots" and "boltings"—exercises in legal argumentation. The moot was a mock debate at which a young student pleaded a questionable point of law in law French before three Benchers. Then a pair of Utter Barristers, taking opposite sides of the question, argued the issue further (also in law French), after which the Benchers rendered their opinions in English. Boltings, held regularly after meals, were similar legal disputations, conducted among Inner and Utter Barristers, ranged three against three. In addition, students might read classic cases compiled in standard textbooks and attend public trials at Westminster or the Guildhall, where a special section called "le cribbe" was reserved for them. There were no formal examinations. Admission to the bar depended chiefly on the number of moots in which a student had participated.[157]

The full course of legal studies leading to qualification as a practicing barrister ran at least seven years, but some Inns-of-Court men made their Society a more or less permanent home. When John Marston arrived at the Middle Temple in 1594 or 1595 (a few years ahead of Webster), he moved into chambers built by and shared with his own father, a prosperous lawyer, Bencher, and resident during legal terms since 1570. John Marston senior was buried in the Temple Church in 1599, and the dramatist, his son and heir, was laid to rest beside him in 1634, having returned home, so to speak, after living for years as a clergyman outside London. Many members, like Marston and Webster, had no intention of pursuing the law formally as a career, although the cleverness, mental agility, and verbal command developed by moots and boltings would undoubtedly bear fruit in other ways. Attached as they were to the fringes of the court (Sir Walter Raleigh and Sir Henry Wotton, Essex's secretary, were Middle Templars) and associated with the functions of national government (committees of Parliament sometimes met under their roofs), the Inns became finishing schools in which young men on the rise sought to acquire the skills, fashions, manners, poise, tastes, and ideas—in brief, the sophistication—of the movers and shakers of the realm. These youths often thought of themselves as the cognescenti of the culture—as potential taste makers, writers, courtiers, ambassadors, privy councillors, and members of Parliament, if not specifically as future judges, pleaders, or justices of the peace.

An inevitable competitiveness, social as well as intellectual, defined the ethos of the Inns, and their environment bred a style characterized by wit, *sprezzatura*, studied frivolity, breezy irreverence for the stodgier manifestations of authority, youthful brashness, and cynicism—sometimes in tandem with a strenuous intellectual, artistic, political, religious, or professional seriousness. Inns-of-Court sparks had the reputation, more than half self-promoted, of being wild, rebellious, lazy, licentious, and pleasure-seeking. The poet Sir John Davies, himself one of Webster's contemporaries at the Middle Temple, produced an amusing caricature of the type—the none too bright son of a landed aristocrat who violates the dress regulations and indulges his coarse tastes (brought with him from the country) by deserting his law books for his favorite bears in the pit:

> Publius student at the common law,
> Oft leaves his bookes, and for his recreation:
> To Paris Garden doth himselfe Withdrawe,
> Where he is ravisht with such delectation
> As downe amongst the dogges and beares he goes,
> Where whilst he skipping cries To head, To head,
> His Satten doublet and his velvet hose,
> Are all with spittle from above be-spread.
> Then is he like his Fathers cuntrey hall,
> Stinking with dogges, and muted all with haukes.
> And rightly too on him this filth doth fall,
> Which for such filthie sports his bookes forsakes,

Leaving olde Ployden, Dier and Brooke alone,
To see olde Harry Hunkes and Sacarson.
(*Epigrammes*: "In Publium," 43)[158]

Theological and political disputation must have been just as prevalent at the Inns of Webster's day as the arguing of legal points; at all events, by the late sixteenth century, the law societies had gained a reputation for controversy—even subversiveness—especially in matters of religion. As early as 1571 the Archbishop of Canterbury, Matthew Parker, was deploring the tendency of the Inns to grow "of late . . . very disordered and licentious in over bold speeches and doings touching religion."[159] Elizabeth's church settlement of 1559 had met some initial resistance among lawyers, and several prestigious members of Inns remained papists or were known Catholic sympathizers. According to one calculation, the Catholic population in 1574 (particularly at Gray's Inn and the Inner Temple) ran as high as twenty percent. The distinguished Bencher Edmund Plowden (the "olde Ployden" of Davies's epigram, who, as treasurer, had supervised the building of Middle Temple Hall) exerted considerable Romish influence until his death in 1585; and two peers later suspected of complicity in the Gunpowder Plot (Henry Percy, Earl of Northumberland, and Anthony Browne, Viscount Montague) both became Middle Templars only four years prior to Webster's own admission. With their select clientele and obvious potential for leadership, the Inns became natural targets for infiltration by Jesuit missionaries, who might seek out fresh converts while enjoying the protection of well-placed recusants in the heart of the capital city. In 1580 Plowden and a few of his "dearest and most familiar friends" were said by his Protestant enemies at the Middle Temple to have caused the whole house to be "pestered with papistes."[160] Richard Hopkins (d. 1594), the translator of the Spanish mystic Luis de Granada, had entered the same Inn in 1561; "wear[ying] of the heresy of the place," he removed to Louvain, then to Spain, and finally to France, but he dedicated his translations to the gentlemen of the Inns of Court.[161]

As Hopkins's objection to the religious climate of the Middle Temple may in part suggest, nonconformist opinions of a Puritan cast were probably more characteristic of the house than Roman Catholic loyalties. Sermons and theological lectures constituted a prominent feature of Inn life, for all the societies employed regular preachers, in addition to whom a stream of visiting divines competed for the attention of members on an occasional basis. Gray's and Lincoln's Inns established permanent lectureships in divinity apart from their support of chaplains to celebrate Holy Communion and conduct ordinary services. The master of the Temple Church, chief ecclesiastic for the Middle and Inner Temples, enjoyed a crown appointment, but the other clerical posts—curacies, assistant chaplaincies, lectureships, and the like—lay within the gift of the Inns themselves, so that incumbents inevitably reflected the religious biases of the Benchers at whose semiautonomous pleasure they served. During the latter half of Elizabeth's reign the Inns became noted centers of radical Protestantism, places where Calvinist scholarship, partisan pulpit oratory, and doctrinal politicking were not only tolerated but to some extent encouraged, as they had earlier been (especially while Edmund Grindal was primate), by pragmatic bishops and privy councillors, who seem to have regarded the voices of heterodoxy as an effective antidote to Roman Catholic subversion.

Typical of the spirit of religious antagonism at the Inns was the celebrated disagreement between the fiery Calvinist and convinced presbyterian, Walter Travers, and his more quiescent superior at the Temple Church, Richard Hooker. Appointed by the Benchers in 1585 to serve as preacher, Travers hoped also to secure the mastership when the post became vacant later the same year. The queen in her wisdom, however, bestowed the plum upon Hooker, while Travers temporarily retained his subordinate office; and the two men in their sermons vied for the ideological allegiance not only of the students but of the senior barristers as well. Learned and intensely partisan congregations, who took notes for further discussion, collected around both spokesmen. As Thomas Fuller famously phrased it, "Here the pulpit spake pure Canterbury in the morning, and Geneva in the afternoon."[162] The central issue, of course, was predestination, but questions about such matters as valid ordination, the structure of church government, and ecclesiastical vestments and ceremonies were also in the air. Fuller noted colorfully that "in this Temple not only much knocking was heard, but (which was the worst) the nails and pins which one master-builder drave in, were driven out by the other."[163] Hooker, indeed, found the *noise and oppositions* of his post intolerable, pointing out in a letter to Archbishop Whitgift (who had worried from the beginning about Travers's large and schismatic following) that *God and Nature did not intend* [him] *for Contentions, but for Study and quietness.*"[164] Hooker had left the Temple Church by the time Webster entered the adjoining Inn, but when the playwright came to write *The Devil's Law-Case*, he echoed a famous passage from the *Ecclesiastical Polity* at IV.ii.264–265 ("the law of Nature / Is the stay of the whole world") that his connection with the Middle Temple may somehow have prompted.[165]

Puritan theology with its cocksure and often acrimonious tone had become chic among youthful intellectuals and those who saw themselves as progressives. Influential figures like Leicester had hoped to see the English church go further in the direction of the continental reformers. Lord Burghley had plumped for Travers as the senior cleric at the Temple, and Sir Edward Coke (one of the notetakers at Travers's sermons) saw in the nonconformist emphasis on private conscience a strong argument for the supremacy of common law with its implied corollary—greater limitation of the royal prerogative. It is no accident that as antimonarchical sentiment and Parliamentary recalcitrance grew stronger under James and Charles, the Inns of Court supplied many of the opposition's most articulate leaders; nor is it surprising that the regicides during the Civil War were often men with Inns-of-Court backgrounds. As early as 1584 or thereabouts,

Richard Bancroft, who was to become Archbishop Whitgift's successor in the battle against rampant Puritanism, complained of "Seducers in the Innes of Courte" who were corrupting "the flower of the Gentilitie of England" and training them up "in a disobedient mislikinge of the present estate of the Churche. . . ."[166]

But it would be wrong to assume that the Inns had become homogeneously precisian or left wing in their sympathies. Loyal Anglicans and royalists were still to be found defending the establishment in chapel, hall, and garden. Archbishop Whitgift had silenced Travers only a year after Hooker's installation as master of the Temple Church, and Nicholas Balguy, master at the time of Webster's admission, was a true son of the *via media*. Orthodoxy had a brilliant exponent in John Donne, who, by the time he was made Dean of St. Paul's, had become the most popular of the preachers at Lincoln's Inn. Certainly Webster would have been exposed to other clergymen of Donne's high-church party. And, in addition, there were staunchly anti-Puritan laymen at the Middle Temple such as the minor poet and rhetorician John Hoskyns and the friend (later enemy) of John Davies, Richard Martin, who became Recorder of London. Sir Ralph Clare, admitted in 1602, was a passionate royalist and attended Charles I during the Great Rebellion.

The religiopolitical milieu of the law societies during the nineties seems to have bred a good deal of witty irreverence and youthful iconoclasm, in both behavior and literary style. The rage for pungent satire, a taste for disenchantment, parody, and the flouting of convention, and the desire to shock were symptoms of a mind-set among Inns-of-Court wits, the poetic results of which could be sampled in such diverse writings as Davies's mocking epigrams, Marston's Thersitean *Scourge of Villanie*, and Donne's libertine elegies. The typical epigrammatist, according to Jonson, was "bold, licentious, full of gall, / Wormewood, and sulphure, sharpe, and tooth'd withall . . . a petulant thing, hurle[ing] inke, and wit, / As mad-men stones: not caring whom [he] hit" ("To my Booke," ll. 3–6).[167] Factionalism and ambition made for raillery in commons and quarreling in the streets.

The most notorious incident at the Middle Temple (it occurred on 9 February 1598, less than a year before Webster's admission, and would, in any case, have been unforgettable) was Davies's cudgeling of his former companion Martin while the latter dined peacefully in hall. Martin, a handsome and popular figure, had been elected Lord of Misrule or "Prince d'Amour" (the title analogous to Prince of Purpoole at Gray's Inn) for the Christmas Revels of 1597–1598. The ungainly and pockmarked Davies (nicknamed Stradilax by his fellows) had been one of the organizers of this solemn merriment and had himself aspired to the role of Prince. Instead he had to content himself with playing the buffoon's part and reciting, among other orations, an obscene poem dispraising women, referred to in the account of Benjamin Rudyerd, a co-participant, as a "comparison of pork." The Christmas Prince reigned from the eve of the Nativity (24

December) until Candlemas (2 February), presiding in the interim over a series of banquets, processions, masques, comedies, sporting events, dicing contests, dances, and mock ceremonies, financed in part by a noble sympathizer, the Earl of Shrewsbury. The schedule of entertainments had involved a public satire on Stradilax, but Davies, during the course of the entire season, seems somehow to have been singled out for *ad hominem* ridicule in a way that enraged him—especially, perhaps, since Martin, as Prince, must have appeared to collude in the humiliation of his closest friend. At this distance, we can only guess at the volatile compound of jealousy, derisiveness, resentment, frustrated ambition, and tomfoolery gone off the rails that eventuated in Martin's broken head and Davies's three-year expulsion from the Society; but this tragifarcical denouement was only the most extreme example of disciplinary problems that apparently beset a whole circle of brilliant but unruly Middle Templars in Webster's day, the core of whom had been together at Winchester College. Seven years earlier, for instance, on another occasion of Lord-of-Misrule revelry, Martin, Davies, and their set had been censured for noisiness, rioting, and "forcibly breaking open chambers in the night," Martin being temporarily expelled and Davies forbidden to enter commons.[168] Heavy fines were also imposed upon offenders.

The spirit of rebellion that these quasi-festive eruptions reveal was more than mere adolescent rumpus-rousing, for several of Davies's and Martin's friends at the Middle Temple continued to get themselves into hot water in later life through acts of self-destructiveness and indiscretion. In 1614 John Hoskyns, by then an M.P., alluded insultingly in the House of Commons to the voraciousness of James I's Scottish favorites and was summarily confined to the Tower for a year in a room with shuttered windows. Imprisonment gave him leisure to concoct a clever bit of rhymed advice to his son on the dangers of intemperate wit:

> Sweet Benedict whilst thou art younge,
> And know'st not yet the vse of Toung,
> Keepe it in thral whilst thou art free:
> Imprison it or it will thee.[169]

Sir Henry Wotton, another friend from the same circle, nearly wrecked his distinguished career by defining an ambassador in a moment of flippancy as "an honest man, sent to *lie* abroad for the good of his country."[170] Sir Henry was imprudent enough to put his quip into writing, which, after it had embarrassed King James, cost its author dearly in royal patronage and advancement. His mistake was not unlike the disastrous outburst of Essex about Elizabeth after his fall from favor—namely, that "the Queen's conditions were as crooked as her carcase."[171] Marston, too, may have suffered a brief imprisonment with his collaborators, Jonson and Chapman, for their anti-Scottish dialogue in *Eastward Ho*, although probably he escaped, perhaps because of his father's prominence in legal circles.

The Middle Temple in Webster's period seems to have fostered jibes of all kinds—some of them unanswerable in their obstreperous crudity. The diarist John Manningham (admitted to the Society the same year as Webster) wrote of John Davies, now reinstated after his brutal attack on Martin, that he "goes wadling with his arse out behinde as though he were about to make every one that he meetes a wall to pisse against."[172] And Webster's friend Marston was himself the victim of a similarly excretory jest when, as the satirist "Monsieur Kinsayder," he was caricatured by undergraduates at St. John's College, Cambridge, in *The Return from Parnassus, Part II* for "lifting vp [his] legge and pissing against the world" (I.ii; ll. 267–268).[173] Some of the satirical wit for which the Middle Temple had become notorious seems to have been an extension into language of aggressions for which its inhabitants were occasionally fined. Just one month prior to Webster's arrival at the house, the Benchers felt called upon to restrain members from certain boorish practices:

Divers grievances are daily committed by reason of water, chamberpots, and other annoyances cast out of gentlemen's chambers to the great offence of gentlemen of good worth passing by, as well as of the House and others; in future the owner of a chamber where such an offense is committed shall be fined 40s.[174]

Webster almost seems to be writing out of the traditions of his own Inn when in the *Characters* he describes his "Puny-clarke," who "doth itch towards a Poet," as

most chargeable to the butler of some *Inne of Chancery*, for pissing in their Greene-pots. Hee eates Ginger-bread at a Play-house; and is so saucy, that he venters fairely for a broken pate, at the banketing house, and hath it. He would never come to have any wit, but for a long *vacation*, for that makes him bethinke him how hee shall shift another day. He praies hotely against fasting: and so hee may sup well on Friday nights, he cares not though his master be a Puritan.

(*Works*, IV, 28)

Links between the Inns of Court and the drama have frequently been studied. Finkelpearl has performed this service admirably for Marston, and Bradbrook, following suit, has discussed the same data fruitfully in connection with Webster.[175] In consequence, there is little need to retrace old ground in detail. It is clear that the legal societies were natural breeding grounds for playwrights. In addition to Marston and, perhaps, Webster, Sharpham and Ford were both Middle Templars, while Beaumont was a member of the Inner Temple and Lodge of Lincoln's Inn. That such men could become writers for the stage indicates the growing respectability of drama as a profession, nor were they necessarily driven into the entertainment world for merely economic reasons. Marston, and later, Webster, wrote for the fashionable children's companies, partly, no doubt, for reasons of prestige. A unique tradition of theatricality had been built into the calendar and routines of legal training; as one satirist of the period wrote, "the Innes . . . vse Reuels more then any men."[176] In addition to various kinds of in-house entertainment, written and performed by the lawyers themselves, professional companies were sometimes imported to present plays with wider audience appeal.

Both kinds of work could reach high levels of artistry. When the Inner Templars, Sackville and Norton, diverted their fellows on Twelfth Night 1561/62 with *Gorboduc*, they produced a sententious and politically significant tragedy worthy of presentation before the queen at Whitehall later the same month. Gray's Inn hired Shakespeare's company to play *The Comedy of Errors* in their hall for the Christmas festivities of 1594. Eight years later, analogous Revels at the Middle Temple concluded with a performance of Shakespeare's *Twelfth Night* (2 February 1601/02), an occasion at which Webster could have been present. In the next reign, both Shakespearean plays were performed at court. Attending the public and private theatres was a much celebrated habit of men at the Inns, so that a kind of professional symbiosis seems to have developed between the actors and the lawyers. Finkelpearl cites a passage from William Prynne's *Histrio-Mastix* (1633) that indicates a mutual dependency: according to the censorious Prynne, himself a Lincoln's Inn man addressing the young gentlemen of the four societies, the law students become "afternoons men" or frequenters of "Stage-playes" "as soone as they are admitted" to an Inn, while the players, for their part, are the Inns' "chiefest guests and imployment. . . ." Davies in one of his epigrams refers to "the clamorous frie of Innes of court / Fill-[ing] up the privat roomes" of London theatres.[177]

Life at the Middle Temple involved various kinds of ritual, which lent to its banquets and entertainments a tone similar to that of the royal court. Nobles, courtiers, and high officials were sometimes present to honor the house by their attendance, to add glamor, and even to participate in the lavish spectacles, especially the dancing. The queen's favorite, Leicester, had presided over the Grand Christmas of the neighboring Inner Temple in 1561–1562 as "Palaphilos, Prince of Sophie." Christopher Hatton, then a student, was Master of the Game at the same festival and danced so elegantly that, when the masque was afterwards taken to court, he dazzled Her Majesty into making him another of her darlings. Hatton later wrote an act of *Tancred and Gismund*, acted before the queen in 1566 or 1567. The Prince d'Amour Revels of 1597–1598 at Webster's Inn included a mock coronation and proclamation of the Prince's titles, a formal challenge by a stranger knight and a defense by a champion, the rendering of homage, a "Tufftaffeta Oration" and "Fustian answer," a ceremony entitled "the Sacrifice of Love," the bestowing of knighthoods in the order of "the Quiver," a procession through the streets (with caparisoned horses) of masquers, torchbearers, and dignitaries sumptuously appareled and heralded by trumpet fanfares and "a peal of Ordnance," a "solemn Barriers," a formal embassage from Lincoln's Inn, and the "Arraignment of a discontented and jealous lover."[178] In addition to all this, there were two comedies (undoubtedly acted by hired professionals), four masques, another combat at barriers, and "law sports." Bartholomew Young, the translator of Montemayor's *Diana* (1598), tells us that he performed "in a publike shewe at the Middle Temple" in the presence of Lady Rich (to whom he dedicated his book) and many other "noble Lordes and faire Ladies."[179]

The Grand Christmas celebrated just before Webster became a Middle Templar was unusually elaborate, but he could not have helped noticing, even if his studies at the Inn were short-lived, that piquant admixtures of elevated ceremonial with raucous clowning, of noble idealism with cynical debunking, were endemic to the fashion of the law societies. At the regular Readers' Feasts, for instance, and at similar banquets given for Judges and Serjeants (who attended in their scarlet and purple robes) on All Saints' Day and the Purification of the Virgin, it was obligatory by ancient custom for the Reader to tread the "measures"; formally called forth by the Master of the Revels, he would lead all the other members of his society in their order of precedence in a slow processional dance, at the end of which low bows were made to those being honored and symbolic refreshments (a kind of secular communion) were ritually presented. The younger students of Webster's period apparently hated this old-fashioned rite and had to be forced by their elders to participate on pain of being fined or even disbarred. Perhaps they managed to guy such rituals in sly ways or even openly to travesty them. Certainly many elements of Inns-of-Court revelry required burlesque, and still others must have invited it.

Such an atmosphere of "solemn foolerie," as John Evelyn was later to term it,[180] could hardly have failed to impress a young playwright on the threshold of his career, especially if he himself, like Davies and Martin, had played a creative role in the activities. Webster's plays are replete with effects that owe much to the traditions of the masque; they also contain notable discontinuities—scenes of formal splendor and public solemnity in which order and dignity are presented as unstable, are undercut by destructive commentary, are threatened by the sense of impending chaos, or are even ruptured by the intrusion of some terrible surprise. In *The White Devil* Vittoria's arraignment, Bracciano's nuptial barriers, and Lodovico and Gasparo's administration of extreme unction and later "matachin" involve the same collision of the ceremonial and the disruptive (put now to tragic uses) that the dramatist could have observed or taken part in at the Middle Temple. And so, in other ways, do comparable scenes from *The Duchess of Malfi*—the Cardinal's arming, for example, and the painfully drawn-out but formalized tormenting of the heroine. Somewhat analogous examples, where the comic aspect is more salient, are the tribunals of *The Devil's Law-Case* and *Appius and Virginia*. Here, like his fellow Middle Templar Marston, Webster delights to satirize the corruptions and pomposities of legal argument and procedure while nevertheless upholding the value of justice to which the bogus practitioners and prating windbags are supposedly dedicated. Farcical interjections and the broad caricaturing of lawyers complicate our response to events and issues that are potentially or actually tragic. A degree of mirth undermines the gravity without wholly annihilating it. These effects, also, are not dissimilar to those that must have been evident during the "law sports" of the Inns or even during the more serious moots and boltings of the training exercises per se. Webster also seems to have seized upon the theatrical capital inherent in the way specific testimony may quickly alter the direction of a court case or a clever argument reverse expectation. The intellectual appeal of serpentine reasoning or the rhetorical cunning of a "Quick-silver" tongue (*Appius and Virginia*, IV.i.211) must have been part of the daily experience of a receptive Utter Barrister.

The theatre provided a kind of public forum for young men trained in rhetoric (as the Inns-of-Court students were) and nurtured in the national center of satire, love poetry, and philosophical discourse. What better medium than the stage for the clever wordsmith, eager to comment obliquely on the mores and leadership of his age, bent upon taking up the latest ideological posture, or keen to explore ethical and metaphysical ideas through the disturbing implications of borrowed or invented plots and through the personae of fictional characters? Marston's plays, as Finkelpearl has shown, reflect such concerns, and there is good reason to suspect that Webster's, though perhaps less overtly, do so as well. If Sir John Davies had written for the stage, he might have composed a drama that combined his notion of life as a cosmic dance (eloquently articulated in *Orchestra*) with the music and choreography of galliards and corantos, with salacious speeches such as Stradilax's "comparison of pork," and with witty impertinences like his own epigram on being imprisoned after the quarrel with Martin: "Now Davis for a birde is in, / But yet it is but for a Martin."[181] Ford *did* write plays in which the most exquisite refinements of neo-Platonism and the languors of love melancholy could be mingled with grotesque violence and the coarsest bawdry. Accordingly, Webster's characteristic mixtures of skepticism and received wisdom may owe something to the intellectual climate of the Inns. His greatest plays betray a paradoxical respect for and suspicion of book learning such as may well have found parallels in an atmosphere where "official" study was highly specialized, theoretical, and based largely on musty precedents.

We know that Montaigne was a favorite author of both Marston and Webster, partly, perhaps, because the French essayist unblinkingly acknowledged the naturalness and power of the sex drive and gave cachet to the idea that experience could often teach more reliably than some quasi-infallible authority, who might, in any case, be contradicted by a rival sage. In *What You Will* (1601), Marston created the character of Lampatho, who, with typical Inns-of-Court disillusionment, expatiates on the fruitless quest for certainty:

> I was a scholler: seaven use-full springs
> Did I defloure in quotations
> Of crossd oppinions boute the soule of man;
> The more I learnt the more I learnt to doubt,
> Knowledge and wit, faithes foes, turne fayth about.
>   (II.i)[182]

Webster works the same kind of protest against meaningless scholarship—especially when it is absurdly oriented to the pedantic irrelevancies of the mythic past—into his characterization of Bosola, a figure who "hath studied himself half blear-eyed . . . to gain the name of a speculative man" by inquiring "to know how many knots was in Hercules' club, of what colour Achilles' beard was, or whether Hector were not troubled with the toothache . . ." (*The Duchess of Malfi*, III.iii.42–47).

Marston's classic formulation of Jacobean melancholy, put into the mouth of Malevole, is almost parodically one-sided, but we have no difficulty imagining such attitudes gaining self-conscious expression among the more radical and pretentious students of the Middle Temple:

Think this—this earth is the only grave and Golgotha wherein all things that live must rot; 'tis but the draught wherein the heavenly bodies discharge their corruption; the very muck-hill on which the sublunary orbs cast their excrements. Man is the slime of this dung-pit, and princes are the governors of these men; for, for our souls, they are as free as emperors', all of one piece; there goes but a pair of shears betwixt an emperor and the son of a bagpiper; only the dyeing, dressing, pressing, glossing, makes the difference.

(*The Malcontent*, IV.v.110–119)[183]

In *Antonio's Revenge* (c. 1600) Marston could make the title character, in like mood, refer to human kind as "vermin bred of putrefacted slime" (IV.iv.2).[184]

Webster's dramatic expressions of pessimism, of the hopelessness of the human plight, are imagistically less repulsive than Marston's, but they can sometimes suggest a comparable sensation-mongering and self-referential extremism. Thus the somberness of Flamineo just before feigning death and of Bosola before actually expiring:

> Whether I resolve to fire, earth, water, air,
> Or all the elements by scruples, I know not
> Nor greatly care,—Shoot, shoot,
> Of all deaths the violent death is best,
> For from ourselves it steals ourselves so fast. . . .
> (*The White Devil*, V.vi.113–117)

>   O, I am gone!—
> We are only like dead walls, or vaulted graves,
> That ruin'd, yields no echo. . . .
> . . . .
>   O, this gloomy world!
> In what a shadow, or deep pit of darkness,
> Doth womanish and fearful mankind live!
> (*The Duchess of Malfi*, V.v.96–102)

These speeches, of course, gain tragic force and complexity from their contexts, but, in isolation, they sound like the sort of thing a resourceful but disconsolate

Inns-of-Court intellectual might invent or quote from his copybook in a jaundiced conversation with contemporaries after dinner in commons.

If Webster was, in fact, a Templar, his association with a famous legal society would have opened doors, actual and potential, to the great world of ideas and affairs. All four Inns can boast of illustrious memberships, but the long list of Middle Temple entrants in the sixteenth and seventeenth centuries, even apart from names mentioned earlier in this account, reads like a Renaissance *Who's Who*.[185] Among the great nobles of the house (including those who later inherited or rose to high titles) were Ludovick Stuart, Duke of Richmond, George Villiers, Duke of Buckingham, and James Scott, Duke of Monmouth (the illegitimate son of Charles II). Henry Somerset, afterwards Marquess of Worcester, was admitted the same year as Webster. His grandfather, third Earl of Worcester, was also a member, as were the earls of Banbury, Carlisle, Devonshire, Manchester, Northampton, Northumberland, Portland, and Shrewsbury. Devonshire was Charles Blount, also called Lord Mountjoy, who served under Essex and was Penelope Rich's lover as well as Sir John Davies's patron. Northumberland, nicknamed "the wizard earl" because of his mathematical and scientific studies, languished fifteen years in the Tower for supposed complicity in the Gunpowder Plot; it was he, among others, who helped Davies gain reinstatement after his disgrace in the Martin incident. Prominent Middle Templars during the Cromwellian and Restoration periods were the earls of Sandwich, Clarendon, and Winchilsea. Baron Rich, Henry VIII's unscrupulous servant and the grandfather of Lady Penelope's enormously wealthy husband, had been a Reader at the house in 1529, rising later to the Lord Chancellorship. Lord Hastings, Master of the Horse in Queen Mary's time and one of Queen Elizabeth's escorts to London at her accession, had been a Templar as well.

An important court connection for Webster would have been Sir George Buc, a member since 1585 and James I's Master of the Revels. Another member, Sir Thomas Puckering, son of the Lord Keeper of the Great Seal, was official companion to Prince Henry from 1605 to 1610, the years just before Webster began work on his two major tragedies. Sir Francis Windebank, admitted in 1603, became Secretary of State in the reign of Charles I; a convert to Catholicism, he fled to France in 1640 under suspicion of treason. Sir George Carew, Sir Christopher Hatton's secretary during Elizabeth's reign and later ambassador to Poland and France, had become an influential Middle Templar by the time of Webster's membership. Of course, visits to the banqueting hall from great courtiers like the Earl of Essex could occur from time to time. The young Webster would have had the chance to observe such august figures at firsthand taking dinner with the Benchers at high table.

Important churchmen such as James Montague, Bishop of Winchester, and George Montaigne, Archbishop of York, had been admitted to the Middle Temple in their earlier days. Winchester was chosen to edit the works of James I. Sir Herbert Croft, in later life a devout apologist for the Church of Rome, had become a Middle Templar and was already sitting in Parliament four years before Webster entered the Society. The well-known Puritan preacher, William Crashaw (father of the Roman Catholic poet), became master of the Temple Church in 1605. Webster would hardly have known these men, since, in at least three cases, their connection with his Inn postdated his own, but their names help to illustrate the religious diversity of his house. More glamorous in the traditions of the Middle Temple are the famous Elizabethan soldiers, sailors, and men of action. The seamen Sir Francis Drake, Sir John Hawkins, and Sir Martin Frobisher, were all admitted in the 1590s, apparently as honorary members. The geographer Richard Hakluyt and the explorer of the American east coast, Bartholomew Gosnell (or Gosnold), also belonged to the Inn.[186] Sir Francis Vere, whose campaign in the Netherlands is well known, Sir Edward Norris, who fought with Sidney and was knighted by Leicester, and his younger brother, Sir Thomas Norris, officer in Ireland and patron of Edmund Spenser, also passed through the house.

Not unexpectedly, the Middle Temple garnered a strong reputation for governmental leadership in Webster's era. Six speakers of the House of Commons and a handful of Lord Mayors (including a couple of the dramatist's fellow guild members, Sir Robert Lee and Sir John Swinnerton) belonged to the Society. As mentioned earlier, two old boys from Merchant Taylors' School went on to become prominent representatives of the Inn—Sir James Whitelocke (Reader, M.P., Sergeant-at-Law, Chief Justice of Chester, Judge of the King's Bench) and Sir Edwin Sandys (leading Parliamentarian, statesman in colonial affairs, treasurer of the Virginia colony). Bulstrode Whitelocke, eldest son of Sir James, also became a Templar, who, as Master of the Revels for the house, organized a masque in 1633 to be performed before King Charles and his queen. He became a Bencher and, in the Long Parliament, promoted the impeachment of the Earl of Strafford, rising during the interregnum, first to the speakership of the House, and then to the upper chamber as one of "Cromwell's Lords." Bulstrode's friend, Sir Richard Lane (Reader, treasurer of the Inn, Lord Keeper of the Great Seal) defended Strafford at his trial and supported the royal cause until its ruin at the execution of Charles I. The republican John Pym, great enemy of Strafford and Laud in the Long Parliament, had also been trained at the Middle Temple, as had Edward Bagshaw (another hater of episcopacy and a figure of republican sympathies) and John Lisle (the violent antimonarchist, who drafted King Charles's death sentence). An earlier lawyer of the house, who rose to the top position of treasurer, was Thomas Greene, remembered today as Shakespeare's cousin. For a time, Greene occupied New Place, the dramatist's house at Stratford, and communicated with his kinsman about the enclosure of lands in which they both had a financial interest. Greene seems to have had some literary inclinations, for he wrote a commendatory poem for Michael Drayton's long historical epic, *The Barons' Wars* (1603).

As the careers of Greene, Davies, Hoskyns, and numerous others attest, the Middle Temple drew no rigid line between lawyerly skills and dabbling in the arts. Webster's Inn, in fact, helped educate a long roster of men more noted to-day as poets, writers, and scholars than as barristers. The range is impressive. Several of the most relevant names (Raleigh, Hooker, Overbury, and Ford, for instance) have already appeared above; but to them may be added Thomas Carew (poet, friend of Suckling), Richard Carew (rhetorician and critic), George Sandys (translator of Ovid, brother of Sir Edwin), George Puttenham (author of *The Arte of English Poesie*), Fulke Greville (poet, philosophical dramatist, biographer of Sidney), Sir Norton Knatchbull (biblical scholar), Robert Chester of Roysdon (supposed author of *Love's Martyr*, associated with Shakespeare's "Phoenix and the Turtle"), Sir John Salisbury (versifier and patron of Chester), Sir Benjamin Rudyerd (poet, friend of Jonson, author of *Le Prince d'Amour or the Prince of Love* [published 1660], politician), William Fleetwood (antiquarian, Latin poet, Recorder of London, friend of John Stow, freeman of the Merchant Taylors), Thomas Eliot (dedicatee of Meres's *Palladis Tamia*), George Salterne (legal historian, author of the Latin play *Tomumbeius* [c. 1603]), Daubridgecourt Belchier (author of the comedy *Hans Beer Pot* [published 1618]), and William Fowler (Scottish sonneteer, uncle of William Drummond of Hawthornden). Inigo Jones, the architect and designer of masques, was likewise a Middle Templar. It is noteworthy that the tradition of dramatically talented members continued through the later seventeenth and eighteenth centuries. Shadwell, Southerne, Congreve, and Sheridan were all admitted to the Inn.

Webster's Society even nurtured its share of historically important malefactors. Sir Charles Danvers, admitted shortly after the future dramatist, was one of the rebels who supported Essex in 1601 and went to the block on Tower Hill for treason. Thomas Winter, who entered the Middle Temple in 1590, became a Gunpowder Plot conspirator and was executed (with his brother Robert) in 1606. Sir Gervase Helwys, a member of the Society since 1579, was appointed Lieutenant of the Tower in 1613 when Overbury was imprisoned there. He was accused, perhaps unjustly, of intentionally allowing his charge (a fellow Middle Templar) to be poisoned at the behest of the Earl of Northampton and Robert Carr, Lord Rochester, who had procured him his office; he was condemned and duly hanged. However briefly Webster may have been associated with the Temple, he would have entered there an environment with far-reaching implications for the history, religion, politics, and culture of his era. In more than one respect it would have been the setting for his coming of age.

* * *

The circumstances of Webster's death and the place of his burial unfortunately remain as speculative as the nature of his education. The tragedian may well lie near his brother, sister-in-law, and parents in the vault of St. Sepulchre's. Interment in his home parish would be normal if he continued in later years to live in Nag's Head Alley or near Smithfield, and, as we have seen, such burial appears to have been a family tradition. Since the parish records are lost, however, no one can be certain. Largely for the same reason, the date of death is equally questionable. In 1635 Webster's old friend Thomas Heywood published his *Hierarchie of the Blessed Angels* in which he alluded to the nicknames of his fellow dramatists in a passage that seems by its use of tenses to distinguish between the living and the dead:

> Our moderne Poets to that passe are driuen,
> Those names are curtal'd which they first had giuen;
> And, as we wisht to haue their memories drown'd,
> We scarcely can afford them halfe their sound.
>   *Greene*, who had in both Academies ta'ne
> Degree of Master, yet could neuer gaine
> To be call'd more than *Robin*: who had he
> Profest ought saue the *Muse*, Serv'd, and been Free
> After a seuen yeares Prentiseship; might haue
> (With credit too) gone *Robert* to his graue.
> *Marlo*, renown'd for his rare art and wit,
> Could ne're attaine beyond the name of *Kit*;
> Although his *Hero* and *Leander* did
> Merit addition rather. Famous *Kid*
> Was call'd but *Tom*. *Tom*. *Watson*, though he wrote
> Able to make *Apollo's* selfe to dote
> Vpon his Muse; for all that he could striue,
> Yet neuer could to his full name arriue.
> *Tom*. *Nash* (in his time of no small esteeme)
> Could not a second syllable redeeme.
> Excellent *Bewmont*, in the formost ranke
> Of the rar'st Wits, was neuer more than *Franck*.
> Mellifluous *Shake-speare*, whose inchanting Quill
> Commanded Mirth or Passion, was but *Will*.
> And famous *Iohnson*, though his learned Pen
> Be dipt in *Castaly*, is still but *Ben*.
> *Fletcher* and *Webster*, of that learned packe
> None of the mean'st, yet neither was but *Iacke*.
> *Deckers* but *Tom*, nor *May*, nor *Middleton*.
> And hee's now but *Iacke Foord*, that once were *Iohn*.[187]

Most scholars, reading very literally, have assumed that these couplets settle Webster's death as having occurred before 7 November 1634 when Heywood's book was licensed. But the tenses are not altogether to be trusted, for it is possible that Heywood only meant to imply that Webster was no longer writing. Everyone, after all, has heard living people referred to in the past, especially when their present activities are not known or not the subject of interest. In any case, Dekker and Middleton *were* both dead by 1634, despite Heywood's apparent assertion to the contrary, and the coupling of Webster with Fletcher, who certainly *was* dead as Heywood implies, may have influenced the poet's choice of the preterite.[188] If Heywood was merely suggesting that Webster's active career was over in 1634, we might perhaps be tempted to accept as also applying to him a notation in the parish register of St. James, Clerkenwell, that "John Webster was buried" on 3 March 1637/38.[189] This is the parish, just north of Smithfield, where two of Webster's theatrical partners, Dekker and Rowley, were both buried, and it is near the Red Bull where *The White Devil* and, later, *Keep the Widow Waking* were performed. It is perhaps not an unlikely place for Webster to have lived at the end of his life, although, coming from a prosperous family, he probably did not die in debt as did his old friend Dekker. Webster was almost certainly alive in 1632, for Hemminge's facetious allusion to Edward Webster's refusal to "lend a Coach" for the hearsing of Randolph's finger ("hee swore thay all weare hired to Conuey / the Malfy dutches sadly on her way") would lose much of its point and perhaps even offend if the playwright had recently died. If the burial record at St. James's be taken as referring to the dramatist, Webster would have been fifty-nine or sixty at the time of his death—a few years younger if we rely on Heywood's past tense. He probably lived longer than Shakespeare, who died at fifty-two.

Beyond the dates, titles, and payments by Henslowe for some of his lost plays, his extant works themselves, and a few contemporary or near-contemporary references to him, we know almost nothing more about Webster. No physical likeness survives. Henry Fitzgeffrey's caricature of the dramatist in *Notes from Black-Fryers*, published in 1617 after Webster had already composed his two greatest tragedies, gives us our only description of the playwright. Written by an enemy at Lincoln's Inn long after Webster would have left the Middle Temple—an enemy who was clearly an ally of the John Stephens with whom Webster had quarreled in print—this portrait is intentionally destructive; but it seems to be based on some, though probably not much, firsthand knowledge. Fitzgeffrey mocks the poet as one of the foolish members of a Blackfriars audience arriving for a performance at the fashionable private theatre. The dramatist shows up in the company of "Fantastick," a foppish singer:

> Bvt h'st! with him Crabbed (*Websterio*)
> The *Play-wright*, *Cart-wright*: whether? either! *ho*—
> No further. Looke as yee'd bee look't into:
> Sit as ye woo'd be *Read*: *Lord*! who woo'd know him?
> Was euer man so mangl'd with a *Poem*?
> See how he drawes his mouth awry of late,
> How he scrubs: wrings his wrests: scratches his Pate.
> A *Midwife*! helpe! By his *Braines coitus*,
> Some *Centaure* strange: some huge *Bucephalus*,
> Or *Pallas* (sure) ingendred in his *Braine*,
> Strike *Vulcan* with thy hammer once againe.

> This is the *Crittick* that (of all the rest)
> I'de not haue view mee, yet I feare him least,
> Heer's not a word *cursiuely* I haue *Writ*,
> But hee'l *Industriously* examine it.
> And in some 12. monthes hence (or there *about*)
> Set in a shamefull sheete, my errors *out*.
> But what care I it *will* be so obscure,
> That none shall vnderstand him (I am sure.)[190]

This doggerel unfortunately tells us very little about Webster that we could not infer from his surviving works. The contemptuous reference to the family trade of cart- and wagonmaking has been mentioned above. Fitzgeffrey's attack associates Webster with the most fashionable and highbrow of the London theatres, where his own *Duchess of Malfi* had been performed, and with the King's Men, who were then playing there. Like most Inns-of-Court men, Fitzgeffrey and Stephens probably went there themselves often. The epithet "Crabbed (*Websterio*)" is interesting, for the Lincoln's Inn satirist is probably glancing at the dramatist's attraction to Italian subject matter; and the adjective, if taken literally, might conceivably refer to a physical deformity of some sort, although it is more likely a double hit at Webster's peevish or cantankerous manner and his reputation for a knotty and contorted style. Fitzgeffrey's mythological figures for Webster's characteristic writing—"Some *Centaure* strange: some huge *Bucephalus*"—would seem to ridicule the unnaturally mixed or hybrid quality of plays like *The White Devil*, *The Duchess of Malfi*, and perhaps *The Devil's Law-Case*, plays that combine satire with elements of love and revenge tragedy. In a way, too, the reference to "*Pallas*," the goddess of wit or intelligence (who was conceived in Jove's forehead after Vulcan had split it open), suggests not only the labored nature of Webster's style but also the junction of sexuality and violence so thematically central to his greatest dramas.

Certainly the portrait confirms what Webster himself admits, namely his painful slowness and difficulty of composition, his apparently known habit of fussing, worrying, and straining over a manuscript. In the preface to *The White Devil* he had written defensively, "To those who report I was a long time in finishing this tragedy, I confess I do not write with a goose-quill, winged with two feathers" ("To the Reader," ll. 25–27). And the lampoon implies also that costive, scurrilous, almost atrabiliar strain in Webster's personality that seems to have found dramatic release in malcontent cynics like Flamineo, Bosola, and Romelio, or in acrid personal exchanges such as that between Webster and Fitzgeffrey's legal friend Stephens. Indeed, as Lucas has suggested, the portrait itself, especially the reference to "a shamefull sheete" setting out "my errors," may have been written in retaliation for Webster's thrust at Stephens in *An Excellent Actor*.[191] The shameful sheet also, of course, refers to the garment worn by those doing public penance.

Allowing for the heavy-handed burlesque that defines the limit of Fitzgeffrey's talent as a satirist and that, in any case, is conventional in the amateur style of much Inns-of-Court raillery, we can just make out the public personality of John Webster under the distortions of this cartoon. Webster, at least in the eyes of nonintimates, must have seemed, in Lucas's apt phrase, "something of a porcupine."[192] The tone of self-congratulation, the hypersensitivity to criticism, the finicky delight in pedantic allusion, dense syntax, and sententious opacity, the modish scorn of popularity, the overinsistent disclaiming of flattery to patrons, the laboriousness, the pomposity—all the less irenic and gracious traits or attitudes, in fact, that Webster's prefaces and dedications express—seem to chime remarkably with Fitzgeffrey's cruel but doubtless recognizable caricature.

Of course, the Lincoln's Inn lawyer would purposely exclude all of Webster's literary and dramatic strengths, even if he were intelligent and sensitive enough to perceive them. The artistic taste of a man who (in the same volume that includes the dispraise of Webster) could publish the following epigram, "Of an Egregious Whoore," does not seem notably refined:

> *Thy Belly is thy God*. I well may say!
> All thy care is to *serue* it *Night* and *Day*.
> *Feare* then thy God: least (whil'st thou worship so!)
> *He Rise*, and *Hellish* torments put the[e] to.[193]

But Fitzgeffrey may secretly have admired Webster's work somewhat more than he pretends. One of his longer "Satyricall Epigrams," also printed in the collection that contains *Notes from Black-Fryers*, might have been suggested by a typically Websterian equivocation in the opening scene of *The Devil's Law-Case*, a device used in the play to complicate and trouble the relationship between Contarino and Leonora. Contarino asks the lady "to bestow your picture on me" (I.i.154), explaining later in soliloquy that he had meant by "picture" not a literal portrait but Leonora's daughter—her likeness in another sense. Fitzgeffrey's Epigram 62, entitled "Of 2 Painters contending for Preeminence," is essentially a ribald joke in couplets about a pair of artists who quarrel about which of them excels the other in lifelike portraiture. The first shows a picture of his wife, virtually challenging the other to surpass its excellence. The second painter then borrows his rival's spouse on the pretext of painting her yet more verisimilarly. The wife becomes pregnant by the competing painter, gives birth to an illegitimate daughter who closely resembles her, and finally presents the child to her husband as a better representation of her person than his painting: "Loe heere my Picture: Trie if you can mend it."[194]

The possibility of influence here has to contend with certain difficulties of timing. The date of *The Devil's Law-Case* is difficult to specify precisely; but the play cannot have been performed before 1617, the same year as Fitzgeffrey's bawdy tale, for Webster borrows at I.i.38–41 from William Cecil's *Certaine Precepts for the Well Ordering and Carriage of Mans Life*, published in 1617. Lord

Burghley's book was licensed early (3 May 1615), whereas Fitzgeffrey's was not entered until 9 October 1617, late in the probable year of Webster's tragicomedy. Obviously, in order for Fitzgeffrey to have picked up the suggestion about actual and metaphoric portraits from *The Devil's Law-Case*, he would have had to see the play before October of the year in which he published his epigram. Although not impossible, this timing pushes Webster's tragicomedy rather far forward. Perhaps the similarity between the two works is mere coincidence—the result of two writers drawing independently upon a familiar idea. Or, conceivably, Webster fell upon Fitzgeffrey's epigram in the book that contained the satiric portrait of him and worked an idea from it into his play. The nature of the borrowing, however (if borrowing is involved at all), does not seem like the kind we have come to expect from the author of *The White Devil* and *The Duchess of Malfi*. Like so much else in the life of our dramatist, the exact relationship between him and Fitzgeffrey contains a note of mystery and uncertainty. Finally, the most reliable avenue to understanding the genius of Webster must be through a comprehensive examination of his works.

PART II
THE CANON

THE EARLY CAREER

Webster's literary career has to be pieced together in the most fragmentary way. We meet our subject first in the pages of Henslowe's account book as one of the journeyman dramatists whom that busy entrepreneur was employing to turn out profitable popular successes for the Admiral's and Worcester's Men. It seems probable that Webster began playwriting under the tutelage and encouragement of the more experienced Dekker, who already had such successful plays as *The Shoemaker's Holiday* and *Old Fortunatus* to his credit. The earliest records show a regular collaboration between them, and the association continued throughout their professional lives.

On 22 May 1602 Henslowe "lent" five pounds to be divided among Webster, Munday, Middleton, Drayton, and others "in earnest of a book called *Caesar's Fall*."[1] On the twenty-ninth, only seven days later, Thomas Downton received three pounds from Henslowe on behalf of Dekker, Drayton, Middleton, Webster, and Munday "in full payment for their play called *Two Shapes*."[2] In view of their closeness in time to each other and the common authorship stated, these references undoubtedly represent alternative titles for the same play. The drama is lost, and we know nothing of it except that it was written for Marlowe's old company, the Admiral's Men, but the earlier of the two entries indicates a tragedy on a very popular subject—not improbably in competition with Shakespeare's *Julius Caesar*, which had been performed in 1599 at the Globe and which continued to hold the stage throughout the period. As a beginner working with older and better-known writers, Webster probably had little option in the selection of a subject. Nevertheless, the appointed one must have been congenial to him, for his interest in tragic history, whether classical or modern, never deserted him. Some fifteen years later Webster was to write a speech for a central character of *The Devil's Law-Case* that shows that the irony inherent in the death of the great Roman would not have been lost upon him:

> O great Caesar, he that pas[sed] the shock
> Of so many armed pikes, and poison'd darts,
> Swords, slings, and battleaxes, should at length,
> Sitting at ease on a cushion, come to die
> By such a shoemaker's awl as this, his soul let forth

At a hole no bigger than the incision
Made for a wheal [i.e., a blister]!
(III.ii.100–106)

Six months after *Caesar's Fall* Webster was again working with Dekker and others on a historical play. Henslowe's records show that on 15 October 1602, Chettle, Dekker, Heywood, Wentworth Smith, and Webster received an advance of fifty shillings "in earnest of a play called *Lady Jane*," undoubtedly a tragedy dramatizing the sad fate of Lady Jane Grey and probably referred to elsewhere in the *Diary* as "the play of *The Overthrow of Rebels*." By the twenty-first, the play had apparently been completed, for Henslowe records the sum of five pounds, ten shillings "in full payment" to Heywood and his four collaborators. It must have pleased because we find Henslowe laying out an additional five shillings to Dekker on 27 October in earnest of a *Lady Jane, Part II*.[3] Both plays in their original form have perished, but, as Webster's editors have suggested,[4] a condensed and mutilated version of the two almost certainly survives in *The Famous History of Sir Thomas Wyatt, With the Coronation of Queen Mary and the Coming In of King Philip*.

This is the "bad quarto" of 1607, a pirated text for which no entry in the *Stationers' Register* was made. Its title page attributes the play to Dekker and Webster alone and tells us that it was acted by Queen Anne's Men, the company for which *Lady Jane* had been composed but known before the accession of James I as the Earl of Worcester's Servants. The play, as printed, does not fulfill the promise of its title, for it contains neither Mary's coronation nor Philip's arrival in England. It does, however, present the plight of Lady Jane Grey and her young husband, Lord Guilford Dudley, from the moment of their forced involvement in their parents' ill-conceived dynastic plot until their execution. The sources are clearly Holinshed's *Chronicle* and Stow's *Annals*. Foxe's *Book of Martyrs* and Grafton's *Chronicles* were also used.[5] Just how much of this play is Webster's work the corruption of its text, probably the result of "memorial reconstruction," makes it hazardous to assess. Cyrus Hoy, recognizing the impossibility of attributing entire units of action to any single author in so garbled a play, plausibly sees "signs of Webster"[6] in the first two and final two scenes of the tragedy. The most one can say is that the mention of Dekker and Webster on the title page and the absence of the other names associated with *Lady Jane* encourage us to suppose, however hesitantly, that the two men specified may have had controlling hands in the revised version of the play even if they were not the sole authors. The piece must have been popular, for the publisher brought out a second edition in 1612.

Sir Thomas Wyatt belongs to that immensely favored genre of the 1590s and the years just following—the play on some phase of native, often recent, history, which combines elements of biography, political contention, nationalistic pride, and religiomoral homily. Other examples are *Thomas of Woodstock*, *Sir*

John Oldcastle, Thomas, Lord Cromwell, Rowley's *When You See Me, You Know Me* (on the fall of Wolsey), and Heywood's *If You Know Not Me, You Know Nobody* (on the early hardships of Elizabeth I). Shakespeare's plays on English kings had, of course, done much to create the appetite to which Dekker, Webster, and their collaborators were appealing, and, in fact, *Sir Thomas Wyatt* contains a couple of possible echoes of *Richard II* and a certain borrowing from *1 Henry IV*.[7]

Typically, the play stresses the familiar *de casibus* motifs of earthly instability and *contemptus mundi*. Northumberland and Suffolk, the play's twin examples of dangerous ambition, open the first scene with heavy irony by likening the ebbing life of Edward VI "to quicke light[n]ing . . . no sooner seene, / But . . . extinct" (I.i.3–4). If the overreaching fathers are blind to the doom they so actively court, their innocent children, Guilford and Jane, are only too conscious of the brevity of earthly life and especially of the cosmic links between high place and mortality, between rise and fall:

> Alasse, how small an Vrne contaisnes a King?
> He that ruld all, euen with his princely breath,
> Is forc'd to stoope now to the stroake of death.
> (I.ii.2–4)

When Northumberland and Suffolk enter a moment later to proclaim Jane queen and to lead her and her husband in a "*dead march*" to the Tower to prepare for the coronation, the lady whom Dudley will later call his "faire Queene of sorrowe" (V.i.98) already expresses presentiments of their tragic end:

> We are led with pompe to prison.
> O propheticke soule,
> Lo we ascend into our chaires of State,
> Like funerall Coffins, in some funerall pompe
> Descending to their graues.
> (I.ii.62–66)

This ominous beginning points directly to the final scene that presents the trial and execution of the young lovers, a scene to which Dudley can self-consciously refer as the "blacke conclusion of our Tragedie" (V.ii.56).[8] Again, the brevity and capriciousness of life are insisted upon:

> The time was Lords, when you did flock amaine,
> To see her crownd, but now to kill my *Iane*,
> The world like to a sickell, bends it selfe,
> Men runne their course of liues as in a maze,
> Our office is to die, yours but to gaze.
> (V.ii.61–65)

The earliest surviving work in which Webster had a hand is entirely orthodox, both politically and theologically. Eternity offers man his only assurance, and the figures of the drama, whether guilty or innocent, rush toward it. On his way to the block Lord Guilford pauses to comment (with a metaphysical shudder of which later Websterian characters would be capable) upon the decapitated head of his beloved:

> *Winchester.* My Lord, the time runs on.
> *Guilford.* So does our death.
>   Heeres one has run so fast shee's out of breath,
>   But the time goes on, and my faire *Ianes* white soule,
>   Wil be in heauen before me if I doe stay:
>   Stay gentle wife, thy *Guilford* followes thee. . . .
>   (V.ii.170–175)

What Lagarde seems to disapprove of as a "détail horrible" dictated by the coarseness of "les goûts du public contemporain"[9] is of course a striking example of how medieval ideas continued to imbue Jacobean sensibilities.

Hardly an episode between the death of young Edward and the execution of his ill-starred cousin fails to underscore the folly of putting one's faith in men rather than in God; repeatedly, politics is shown to be a treacherous master, and there is more than a mere suggestion of that seesaw effect that we associate with Shakespeare's plays on Henry VI. Arundel, a critical voice in the Privy Council, at first supports Jane; then, yielding to the persuasions of Wyatt, he deserts Northumberland, denounces his former ally as a traitor, and prompts him to muse on how quickly "fiue hundred friendes" (II.ii.75) can melt away to nothing. The Lord Treasurer of England attempts to defect from Northumberland's faction under color of returning home on private business and has to be brought back by force. Suffolk, Northumberland's co-conspirator, escapes to a remote cabin where his trusted servant, Judas-like, betrays him with a kiss and then strangles himself in remorse. Queen Mary's plan to marry Philip II turns Wyatt, the patriot-hero of the play, from fervent loyalist to misguided rebel. Sir George Harper, one of Wyatt's anti-Spanish adherents, defects to Norfolk, the defender of Mary's policy, but Captain Bret is no sooner appointed by Norfolk to lead the vanguard against Wyatt's insurrection than he, in turn, joins forces with the enemy. Wyatt and his Kentish followers march on London only to discover the gates of the city barred and popular support evaporated:

> O *London, London,* thou perfidious Town,
> Why hast thou broke thy promise to thy friend?
> That for thy sake, and for the generall sake,
> Hath thrust my selfe into the mouth of danger?
>   (IV.iii.44–47)

A stage direction at this juncture, "*Heare they all steale away from* Wyat *and leaue him alone,*" is emblematic of a melancholy truth that the play unwearyingly reiterates.

Few aesthetic virtues must be expected in a text as mutilated as *Sir Thomas Wyatt*; accordingly, the play's ragged style with its limping meter and obtrusive rhymes, its mainly sentimental characterization and conventional moralism, offer few rewards or surprises. Although the drama as we have it is hardly more than the ruins of a play, we can nevertheless glimpse intermittently some features of the more imposing structure from which it derives. It is apparent, for instance, that the collaborating dramatists had an instinct for effective contrasts and parallels—an instinct that should make us pause over M. C. Bradbrook's flat declaration that "Dekker could not achieve formal structure."[10] The title character, like Shakespeare's Talbot or Henry V, is clearly meant to embody the finest qualities of English soldiership—fidelity to his men, courage, kindness, honesty, love of country—and his armed protest against the queen's marriage is portrayed as a fatal error of judgment, a tragic confounding of desirable ends with presumptuous means, rather than as a thrust for personal power. In his misguided idealism, he stands out sharply against such self-interested politicians as the ambitious Northumberland, the weaker Suffolk, and the implacable Winchester. Just before his execution, for instance, Wyatt confronts the cruel bishop, who exults in his fall, with a trenchant pun:

> When that houre comes, wherein my blood is spilt,
> My crosse will looke as bright as yours twice guilt.
>
> (V.ii.23–24)

Such moments recall the antithesis that Shakespeare sets up between good Duke Humphrey and the wicked Cardinal Beaufort in *2 Henry VI*.

The titular hero, incidentally, is the most persistent punster of the drama, so that his penchant for wordplay becomes a device of characterization. This sort of wit usually serves to sharpen or underscore political judgments of a choric kind, to establish him as an intrepid and downright spokesman for the national good. Thus, he can attack Suffolk and Northumberland for treasonably backing Lady Jane by glancing at his own feet, which are "booted and spur'd" (I.i.21):

> It bootes me not to stay,
> When in this land rebellion beares such sway.
>
> (I.i.23–24)

And again, a little later:

> You haue set your handes vnto a will.
> A will you well may call it:
> So wils *Northumberland*: so wils great *Suffolke*,
> Against Gods will. . . .
>
> (I.i.27–30)

And still again:

> And if the Dukes be crosse, weele crosse their powers.
>
> (I.vi.111)

The dramatists set up a further contrast and parallel between the soldier and the young lovers. Wyatt's self-generated martyrdom "to keepe Spaniards from the Land" (V.ii.33) throws the political helplessness of Jane and Guilford into poignant relief. Yet the basic analogy between the two situations is also part of the dramatic design. Wyatt's awareness, for instance, that his fall completes a larger pattern ("Then here's the end of *Wyats* rising vp" [V.ii.32]) echoes Jane's earlier premonition on the interdependence of ascent and descent.

Mary and Jane, the two queens of the play, are alike in their religious dedication, in their longing for wedded love, and also in their domination by older and self-aggrandizing men, but Mary first appears "like a Nun, not like a Princesse borne," frustrated in her exclusion from "pompe and state" (I.iii.1–4), whereas the only "Kingdome" Jane craves is that of a husband's devotion: "What care I though a Sheep-cote be my Pallace . . ." (I.ii.15–17). Shakespeare had already exploited the contrast between the desire for royal power (Richard of York) and the desire for pastoral escape (Henry of Lancaster) in *3 Henry VI*, but the dramatic tension between emotional needs and public affairs is, of course, inherent in the chronicle genre. Mary appears with a Catholic prayer book at the beginning of her reign; Jane prepares for the end of hers by reading its Anglican counterpart. The contrast obviously provides an effective touch of irony, but the parallel has an equally important function: it helps clarify the significant distinction between political and religious partisanship, for the play, though ardently anti-Spanish, scrupulously refrains from fanatical anti-Catholicism. As Jane says when Winchester accuses her of heresy:

> We are Christians, leaue our conscience to our selues:
> We stand not heere about Religious causes
> But are accused of Capitall Treason.
>
> (V.i.112–114)

The priority of royal legitimacy over ecclesiastical allegiance is strongly enforced by another striking contrast. When Northumberland proclaims Queen Jane at Cambridge, the stage direction reads, "*A Trumpet sounds, and no answere*" (II.ii.19); some twenty lines later, recognizing that his supporters have failed him, the duke reluctantly proclaims Mary, and instead of embarrassed silence, the trumpet now elicits "*a shoute and a flourish*" (II.ii.53). Northumberland's essential isolation in this scene balances the later plight of Wyatt, whose rebellion also collapses for lack of popular backing and as a result of broken faith.

Sir Thomas Wyatt contains other suggestive juxtapositions. For instance, the suicide of Holmes, Suffolk's treacherous servant, is immediately preceded by the entrance of a clown who ravenously devours the food that had been meant to preserve the condemned nobleman before his capture; the clown also steals the blood money. In this episode physical need and spiritual crisis are permitted to jostle each other in such a way as to suggest that ironic mix of comic and tragic attitudes that any broad view of experience must entail. As an entertainer the clown may be tedious; in so death-oriented a play, he nevertheless reminds us that life is partly an affair of animal satisfactions and bodily survival. However rudimentarily, the clown is plainly meant to endow the play with the same sort of contrasting perspective with which Falstaff enriches *Henry IV*.

No doubt we should resist the temptation to look too closely for traces of Webster in a play whose tone and spirit seem manifestly so like Dekker. Sporadically *Sir Thomas Wyatt* does sound notes that an admirer of *The White Devil* or *The Duchess of Malfi* might regard as anticipating the Italian tragedies, although most of these are conventional. Wyatt, the blunt man of action, does, for instance, inveigh against the treacheries and corruption of a court that has "chang'd since Noble *Henries* daies" (I.i.26), and the imagery occasionally takes on a Websterian intensity: Guilford, confronting execution, moralizes bitterly on the hopeless plight of political impotence:

> Great men like great Flies, through lawes Cobwebs breake,
> But the thin'st frame, the prison of the weake.
>
> (V.i.99–100)

Even this example, however, contains a strong element of the proverbial, as Tilley's *Dictionary* makes clear.[11] The prominence of the trial scene (V.i) in which the youthful defendants verbally dominate their accusers reminds us of the later Webster, as does the interest in female characters who are resiliently individual or who (as in the case of Jane) achieve their fullest selfhood by confronting death. Jane's self-assertive line, "I was proclaimde Queene, I the Crowne should weare" (V.i.59), may even be thought to anticipate in regality and courage the more famous "I am Duchess of Malfi still" (IV.ii.142). That Jane is presented as psychologically stronger than her husband reminds us of the similar imbalance in the characterization of Antonio and the Duchess. When Jane is led out to the scaffold, for instance, Guilford *falles in a trance* (V.ii.150). It is apparently to gain such an operatic effect that Webster and Dekker deliberately reverse the order of the two executions as they appear in the source material. But, as Cyrus Hoy points out, we may be observing here "a first tentative sketch of the dramatic ground plan that would fashion the elaborately suspended catastrophes" of Webster's later tragedies: "the beheading first of Jane and then of Dudley is to *Sir Thomas Wyatt* what the murder first of Brachiano and then of Vittoria is to *The White Devil*, and the murder first of the Duchess and then of Antonio is to *The Duchess of Malfi*."[12]

Despite the explicitly Christian emphasis of the play and the stress on humility that this necessitates, the authors are also interested in postures of stoic defiance and the more humanistic expressions of personal dignity. Wyatt's words when he is captured give perhaps some foretaste of the mature Webster:

> I am wounded, let me haue a surgion,
> That I may goe sound vnto my graue.
> Tis not the name of Traitor paules me,

Nor pluckes my weapon from my hand.
Vse me how you can,
Though you say Traitor, I am a Gentleman.
Your dreadfull shaking me, which I defie,
Is a poore losse of life, I wish to die,
Death frights my spirit, no more then can my bed,
Nor will I change one haire, loosing this head.
. . . .
I hope for nothing, therefore nothing feare.

(IV.iv.29–41)

Flaccid and pedestrian though the writing is (at least in the mangled state that has come down to us), the dark resolution, particularly of the final line, is not without Websterian overtones.

But more suggestive than these is the Webster-like concern in *Sir Thomas Wyatt* with the ironies of union and separation, with the divisive propensity of politics to scatter friends, to dissolve loyalties, to come between parents and their children, and even to separate lovers. Perhaps this emphasis accounts for the early appearance of a theme that Webster was to explore more deeply later— the paradoxical interrelation of love and death. Like Romeo and Juliet, Jane and Guilford fulfill their romantic passions for each other by dying. "Seuered" in life by their "Fathers pride," the couple are nevertheless united "in one graue, as fits their loues" (V.ii.184–186), and indeed they are painfully eager for the "fatal de-clynation" of the axe that will "make [them] earth" (V.ii.123–124). Jane kisses her beloved but moments before she "must kisse the blocke" (V.ii.97). This blend of the pathetic with the macabre has in fact been prepared for by earlier details. Guilford, for instance, dreams that his father "Was marryed to a stately Bride" (III.ii.17) and poisoned at the nuptial feast just before he learns that he has been beheaded on Tower Hill. Already in Webster's apprentice work, romance seems to imply doom.[13]

* * *

Webster's next play, again a collaborative effort for Worcester's Men (this time with Dekker, Chettle, and Heywood), was commissioned by Henslowe on 2 November; at least Henslowe paid Heywood and Webster an advance of three pounds on that date toward their share in it.[14] The title was *Christmas Comes But Once a Year*, which suggests a comedy hurriedly thrown together against the approaching festival season of 1602–1603. The play is lost, but we know that it was performed, probably at the Rose, where Worcester's Men were then playing, because Henslowe twice paid for costumes in connection with it during successive weeks.

Our only other trace of Webster's activity in 1602 is a short, unmemorable but smoothly competent poem, "*To my kinde friend . . .*" that the poet wrote in commendation of the third part of Anthony Munday's translation of *Palmerin of England* published that year. Dekker also contributed some verses. The prolific Munday, who was nearly a generation older than Webster, eked out a living as a professional hack, producing pageants, lyrics, pamphlets, ballads, and translations of romances in addition to plays. Webster probably met him through Dekker or some of the other writers in Henslowe's clutch of needy dependents. At all events, they were both working on *Caesar's Fall* in 1602. Munday's translation from the Italian (probably through a French intermediary) is a dreary affair of questing knights, imperiled ladies, and (as Webster describes one aspect of the subject) "Strange Pigmey-Singleness in Giant-fights," but, as the dramatist's regular dependence on English versions of foreign material would seem to imply, Webster was writing more than a facile compliment to a full-fledged professional when he came to his final couplet:

> Translation is a traffique of high price:
> It brings all learning in one Paradise.
> (Lucas, ed., *Works*, III, 259)

Henslowe's regular entries stop in 1603, and we hear nothing more about Webster from the account book. It is likely that his professional association with Dekker was interrupted at this point, for the London theatres had to close because of the plague in 1603, and some of the companies were probably on tour in the provinces. The queen died that year, and among the inevitable lamentations that appeared to commemorate her funeral was one called *England's Mourning Garment* by Henry Chettle, with whom Webster had worked on both *Lady Jane* and *Christmas Comes But Once a Year*. R. G. Howarth has suggested that Chettle's poem, in which the author takes various contemporary poets to task for not rising properly to the royal occasion, alludes to the friendship between Dekker and Webster.[15] After referring to Jonson as "our English *Horace*" and Shakespeare as "silver tonged *Melicert*," Chettle speaks of "Quicke *Antihorace* . . . Together with yong *Moelibee* thy friend"; the last named persons are both described as "deere" and as possessing "vertues" that "highly I commend."[16] "Antihorace" must of course be Dekker, for Jonson had portrayed himself as Horace in *The Poetaster*, the play that attacks Dekker, and the latter had immediately riposted by having Horace tossed in a blanket at the end of his own *Satiromastix*. Most scholars have thought that "yong Moelibee" is Marston, a writer also satirized by Jonson in *The Poetaster*,[17] but Howarth may have been correct in supposing that the allusion is to Webster.

In 1604 we find Webster and Marston themselves associated with the production—at the Globe—of the latter's most famous play, *The Malcontent*. Whether Webster had been impressed earlier by Marston's work is uncertain, but the contact with it on this occasion must have had a profound influence, for Webster's greatest plays are shot through with effects of tone, attitude, and style that not only are Marstonian in general but seem, in certain respects, especially imitative of this play. The date of *The Malcontent* has been much disputed, but it was certainly written between 1602 and 1604, the year when no fewer than three separate editions were published.[18] The third edition differs from the other two in containing eleven additional passages as well as an "Induction." The induction itself could not have been written earlier than 12 March 1603, for John Lowin, one of the King's Men who appears in it, was on this date still a member of Worcester's company.[19] From this "addition" we learn that the play had originally been performed at the Blackfriars theatre by the Children of the Chapel Royal (the boy actors or "little eyases" to whom Hamlet refers), that the playbook had been "lost," and that the King's Men, having in effect stolen it, were acting the play and justifying their piracy on grounds that the children had also been known to steal a popular theatre piece. "Jeronimo" is mentioned, which perhaps means that the boys' company had pirated Kyd's *Spanish Tragedy*, a drama that officially belonged to the Admiral's Men.[20]

The original production of *The Malcontent* at the private theatre had involved incidental music, probably a concert before the play as well as entre-act ensembles—music that was not customary at the Globe. For this reason the adult company seems to have hired Webster, probably in collaboration with Marston, to lengthen the play by nearly six hundred lines. As G. K. Hunter has pointed out, the passages added to the play text proper fall into two categories—those that merely expand or enlarge upon existing situations and those that introduce Passarello the clown, an entirely new role perhaps written for Robert Armin, the comic of the King's Men who has been associated with Feste, Lear's Fool, and other such parts.[21] The augmentations of the first type are recognizably by Marston because of their style. The Passarello passages, however, sometimes constitute whole scenes and betray no clear evidence of their authorship. They seem to be based on material from jestbooks. The phraseology on the title page of the altered version of the tragicomedy is ambiguous at best: "*THE MALCONTENT*. Augmented by *Marston*. With the Additions played by the Kings Maiesties servants. Written by *Ihon Webster*." These words are susceptible to various interpretations, but it appears very likely that Webster was responsible for the new material added specifically with the King's Men in mind (the induction and the Passarello passages) and that the other augmentations are by Marston and represent cuts restored from the Blackfriars performances or fresh expansions to enlarge the text for its new production at the Globe or some combination of the two.[22] This likelihood has been further strengthened by D. J. Lake, who corroborates Hunter's apportionment of shares on the basis of linguistic evidence. Lake considers that Webster's responsibility for the induction and the Passarello additions is now "proved beyond reasonable doubt."[23]

Apart from its considerable literary interest, the induction is important historically for the vivid impression of the Globe players that it leaves with us and for the early evidence of Webster's association with the company. It rather looks as though the dramatist were working with Shakespeare's fellows for the first time. At any rate, three of the actors for whom he wrote parts were later to play important roles in *The Duchess of Malfi*. Richard Burbage was, of course, the most distinguished tragedian of his day, the man who became famous not only for his portrayal of Webster's Ferdinand but also for his performances in the title roles of *Richard III*, *Hamlet*, *King Lear*, and *Othello*. Henry Condell, who was to act the Cardinal in *The Duchess*, is remembered today, along with John Hemminge, as a sponsor of the Shakespeare First Folio. John Lowin, who is said to have excelled as Falstaff, Volpone, and Sir Epicure Mammon, was to create the role of Bosola. Webster seems to have had the personalities of these and other players in mind as well as their particular talents and, of course, their roles in the new play.

The author of *The Malcontent*, unlike Dekker, was a prominent figure of the intellectual *avant-garde* in Webster's formative years. After an undergraduate education at Oxford, he had come up to London in the '90s and had entered the Middle Temple, where he dabbled with legal studies and associated with the rebellious, semi-Bohemian society that the new environment afforded. Residence at one of the Inns of Court gave him entree to an elite literary circle composed of such figures as John Donne, Sir John Davies, Richard Barnfield, Everard Guilpin, John Weever, and Ben Jonson—angry young men, many of them, who were smitten by the new satirical way of writing, who cultivated a taste for Juvenal and Persius, and who were fond of epigrams and harsh, elliptical, somewhat pretentious assaults upon pretension. Such men often tended to go in for a style characterized by skepticism, self-conscious parody, libertine explicitness, Senecan *sententiae*, abruptness, discontinuity, disgust, and neostoical gloom. Marston himself quickly became one of the most distinctive voices of the new trend, and his verse satires such as *The Scourge of Villainy* (1598) taken together with his plays, mostly written for private performance by companies of boy actors, illustrate how the fashion could be adapted to dramatic purposes.

In his early dramas such as *Antonio's Revenge* and *The Malcontent*, Marston built upon the foundations of the revenge play laid by Kyd, but he managed not only to shift the emphasis of the older tradition by introducing the snarling satire and stoical moralizing for which he was already notorious but also to increase the shock value by fusing "camp" or absurdist humor, violence, horror, and sex against a background of Italianate decadence. Later masterpieces such as Tourneur's *Revenger's Tragedy* and Webster's *Duchess of Malfi* were to owe much to these innovations, and it is surely more than mere coincidence that Marston and Webster often draw upon the same passages from Montaigne, that Francisco in *The White Devil* quotes the same popular Virgilian tag that Marston had used in his dedication of *Antonio and Mellida*,[24] and that Forobosco (the word suggests sneaking or prying) is the name of a character in both *Antonio and Mellida* and *The Duchess of Malfi*.[25] By writing an induction for *The Malcontent* in 1604, then, not only was Webster introducing the Globe audience to a new genre, what one of his characters refers to as the "bitter play" (Induction, l. 51); he was also schooling himself in a vogue that Marston partly typifies by his dedication of the drama to Ben Jonson, "poetae elegantissimo gravissimo," most elegant and weighty of poets. The induction, in fact, bristles with "sallets" and modish ridicule after the manner of the play it introduces.

The assignment of helping to refit Marston's masterpiece for the Globe required ingenuity, tact, and subtlety of Webster, for the induction had to fulfill a challenging diversity of functions. It must whet interest in a less mimetic technique than would be expected, at the same time endowing an already complex drama with still another dimension. Not only must Webster account for the peculiar circumstances by which a play associated with child actors had come to be produced by the leading troupe of adult competitors; but he also must do so without laborious explicitness or any apparent loss of spontaneity and casualness, without violating the tone of sophisticated mockery essential to the original. Accordingly, Webster incorporates the necessary explanation in a throwaway jest:

> *Condell.* Faith, sir, the book was lost; and because 'twas pity so good a play
> should be lost, we found it, and play it.
> *Sly.* I wonder you would play it, another company having interest in it.
> *Condell.* Why not Malevole in folio with us, as Jeronimo in decimo-sexto
> with them? They taught us a name for our play: we call it *One for an-*
> *other.*
>
> (Induction, ll. 74–80)

Such exchanges produce an improvisatory, even slap-dash effect, but on closer reading it becomes clear that Webster, who was doubtless eager to impress the King's Men with his initial efforts on their behalf, was not content merely to attach a topical and separable prefix to Marston's work. Instead, he built a kind of antechamber to *The Malcontent* cleverly designed to prepare his audience psychologically, aesthetically, and intellectually for the new kind of dramatic experience they would encounter once inside the larger edifice.

Marston's play presents us with a kaleidescope of exaggerated effects, what Arthur Kirsch has called "a gamut of emotional displays,"[26] at the same time dwelling restlessly upon its own artifice. With its curious amalgam of sordid intrigue and satirical moralism, of aborted crime and pretentious folly, of ethical ideas and flippancy, and also with its constant stress on posturing, disguise, and role playing, *The Malcontent* makes the absurdly corrupt court of Genoa an intricate metaphor for the actual world where men as individuals and as a society must wrestle with pain and conflict. The deposed Duke Altofront, who masquerades throughout most of the action as the acerbic Malevole in order to observe and ultimately overturn the usurper's regime, lives a lie (like Hamlet in his antic disposition) that he may express his deeper feelings, attack hypocrisy, and expose truth; yet his very disguise symbolizes the interior divisions, the philosophic and emotional ambivalences, that inevitably beset the man of moral sensitivity. As the substitute duke remarks of Malevole, ironically without recognizing his true identity, "The elements struggle within him; his own soul is at variance within herself . . ." (I.ii.26–27).

The entire drama thus exploits the ironic interplay of conscious with unconscious impostors, of characters who deceive others by intention, whether for good or ill, and themselves by blindness, stupidity, and pride. The villainous Mendoza states the principle in its most reductive terms when he designs that Malevole and Pietro, whom he believes to be his agents, shall neatly eradicate each other:

> One stick burns t' other, steel cuts steel alone.
> 'Tis good trust few; but, O, 'tis best trust none!
>   (IV.iii.143–144)

All the members of this semifarcical triangle present themselves as other than they are: Mendoza believes that he is Duke of Genoa, not realizing that his "confessor" is the supposedly murdered Pietro or that Malevole is the banished Altofront. Pietro occupies a medial position between Mendoza's ignorance and Malevole's omniscience, so that the state of each character's awareness corresponds, as the epilogue confirms, to that character's ethical level on the play's moral scale. It is typical of Marston's reflexiveness that Altofront, the master actor and stage manager of the play, should reprove Pietro's magniloquent response to villainy with a metaphor from the boards: "O do not rand [i.e., rant], do not turn player" (IV.iv.4); nor are we surprised that the climax in which the intrigues are resolved, the identities disclosed, the judgments rendered, and humane values restored should be brought about through the agency of a masque in which Altofront represents himself as one of "four high-famèd Genoan Dukes" (V.vi.58) come as ghosts from the dead.

Marston never lets us forget that illusion may coincide with truth as well as separate us from it. So it is that while the sycophant Bilioso can be portrayed as quintessentially protean, a figure whose satiric point is his adjustibility to all roles, the venial Pietro can assume the cowl of a "holy father" merely to protect himself and then experience a conversion that makes the costume appropriate:

> O, I am changed . . .
> In true contrition I do dedicate
> My breath to solitary holiness,
> My lips to prayer; and my breast's care shall be,
> Restoring Altofront to regency.
>   (IV.v.127–131)

The disguised Altofront prompts Pietro to disguise and then brings him to himself; only at this point can Pietro know Malevole's secret and in turn help his mentor to resume his proper role as Altofront. Both men in some sense win their true identities *through* rather than in spite of their playacting.

Webster devised his induction to anticipate and harmonize with these ideas by focusing attention on the theatrical medium itself, on the processes of an art in which actors live a dual existence—outside as well as inside their own plays. In one way players are symbolic extensions of the audience; in another they are "characters" in a fiction who nevertheless keep us aware of the deception to which we have assented. *One for Another*, Condell's alternate title for *The Malcontent*, describes the profession of acting as truly as the plot of Marston's tragicomedy. As early as Medwall's *Fulgens and Lucres* (c. 1490–1501), an induction had been used to bridge the gulf between actuality and art, and several Elizabethan plays employ the device; few, however, are so elaborately integrated with the substance of the dramas they introduce as this of Webster.

He commences by having one of the King's Men, Will Sly, enter in the role of a foolish playgoer fresh from Blackfriars, a self-appointed connoisseur who customarily sits onstage, has seen *The Malcontent* often, and has copied "most of the jests here in my table-book" (l. 17). In his first speech Sly reminds us of his real-life identity by asking the tireman who reluctantly provides him with a stool, "Dost think I fear hissing? I'll hold my life thou tookest me for one of the players" (ll. 4–5). Webster instantly involves his audience in the doubleness of Sly's role as entertainer and as entertained. Sinklo, another actor of the company, joins Sly, and together they enact a bumptious audience who demand to see some of the Globe's star performers: "Where's Harry Condell, Dick Burbage, and Will Sly? Let me speak with some of them" (ll. 11–13). Burbage, Condell, and Lowin now enter in their own persons and make possible a conversation in which the ironies of role playing and role shifting are multiplied just as they are about to be in the play that will follow. Initially, Sly takes the part of an auditor, but so brazenly does he involve himself with the function of the performers that they have some difficulty persuading him to leave the stage, and he does so only after he has presumed to address the entire theatre in an extemporaneous prologue. Lowin has earlier offered to "help" him "to a private room" (ll. 125–126), and in a fictional sense we must suppose that the intruder rejoins the larger audience out of which he hypothetically emerged. But, of course, Sly would quickly re-enter the Globe stage (after a change of costume) to play one of the characters of *The Malcontent*. That Burbage acted Malevole is the only casting decision of which we can be certain, but, if Bernard Harris is right in guessing that Sly played Bilioso,[27] this timeserver's chameleonic changes of persona might be symbolically prefigured in Sly's overlapping roles (all of them implied by Webster's introductory skit) as actor, spectator, presenter, and dramatic character. The expulsion of Sly from the stage at the end of the induction also parallels the kicking out of Mendoza at the conclusion of *The Malcontent*.

Marston had distanced his play from its Blackfriars audience by incorporating into it an element of self-parody, a spirit of travesty that undercuts the conventions of plot and rhetoric in which the work is grounded. Webster carries this process a step further by facetiously imitating the defensiveness that often characterizes the inductions of Jonson. In *Cynthia's Revels*, for instance, Jonson had endorsed the talents of the child actors by having them defend their own style

78

while mimicking the stupidities of pretentious critics who call them "rascally *Tits* . . . so manie *wrens*, or *pismires*" (Induction, ll. 121–122).[28] Webster also has an effete auditor (Sinklo) who "durst lay four of mine ears, the play is not so well acted [by the men at the Globe] as it hath been" (ll. 88–89) by the boys. Thus he sides with the adult performers as against the children while laughing at the propogandistic fashion of the rival company.

Webster also attacks the malicious or paranoid tendency of the audience to misapply the satire in too personal a way. Again following Jonson's lead, he builds his critical principles into the induction, providing Burbage, for instance, with an opportunity to condemn hypocritical spectators and assert the responsibilities of the playhouse: "Why should not we enjoy the ancient freedom of poesy? Shall we protest to the ladies that their painting makes them angels? or to my young gallant that his expense in the brothel shall gain him reputation? No sir, such vices as stand not accountable to law should be cured as men heal tetters, by casting ink upon them" (ll. 64–70). Such preachments are complex in their effect. Threatening to become the Jacobean equivalent of a Shaw preface, they nevertheless remain dramatically objective; they incorporate the authorial voice while preserving the distinction between writer and performer. Again we are aware of overlapping roles—Burbage as the spokesman for Webster (and also for Marston), Burbage as an actor defending his profession before fools, and Burbage as a scourge of vice in a warming-up exercise for his portrayal of Malevole, who in a few minutes will describe himself to a confidant as a "free-breathed discontent" (I.iv.31), a man whose "affected strain gives me a tongue / As fetterless as is an emperor's" (I.iii.164–165).

In composing the induction Webster even appears to have chosen a few of his jokes with specific reference to details or motifs of the play proper. An allusion to the garlic breath of the groundlings provides a forescent of the evil smells that pervade the Genoan court. Sly's foppish by-play with his hat plume satirizes the dandyism of the stereotypical patron at the Blackfriars while it illustrates in advance Malevole's remark that there is "no fool but has his feather" (V.iii.40).[29] References to cosmetics, tobacco, the habits of marmosets, and the bawdy symbolism of the apricot appear in both induction and play, and Webster's jest about a homosexual relation between Sly and Sinklo sets up the attack of Malevole upon Ferrardo, the minion of Pietro, as "Duke's Ganymede" and "smooth-chinned catamite" (I.ii.6–9).

Webster's deceptively offhand prelude to *The Malcontent*, which Stoll has called "wooden" and Rupert Brooke "valueless,"[30] is thus an impressive and surprisingly calculated performance. Already, though in a minor form, we glimpse that mixture of effects and significances so characteristic of the dramatist at his most memorable—a comic preview of the planned chaos that informs the structure of, say, *The White Devil*. Parody is mingled with seriousness; commentary on the theatre points forward to social and moral criticism; a high degree of aesthetic self-consciousness is embodied in the racy prose of circumstantial particularity and realistic badinage. Much of this is already in Marston and builds upon him. But some of it sounds like authentic Webster. The complementary principles of unity and multiplicity, of connection and disjuntion that Ralph Berry has related so interestingly to the techniques of the baroque,[31] were already beginning to shape Webster's art.

If, as now seems probable, Webster also invented the character of Passarello to take advantage of Armin's special talents, he was at once extending the range of Marston's satire and adding variety and lightness of wit to the play. As the professional jester of the piece, the only fool by definition among a galaxy of fools, Passarello personifies folly in Marston's Genoa, expressing it visually by his distinctive dress and by his style of converting everything to laughter. His verbal currency belongs to the familiar convention of the court fool, consisting largely of puns, bawdy double-entendres, the standing of intended meanings on their heads, choplogic, and startling similes, as, for instance, "I am as common in the court as an hostess's lips in the country" (I.viii.59–60). He functions in some respects as a vignette of the play's doubleness and role playing, for he is both a critic of the society whose absurdities he exists to ridicule and a *reductio ad absurdum* of it. Having no psychological depth, he can be another mouthpiece for raillery against the pretensions and vices of the world that employs him—cuckoldry, sexual debauchery, social ambition, the cosmetic excesses of women, flattery, greed—and, like Lear's fool, he is wiser than his master. Malevole encapsulates this paradox in a cynical couplet delivered aside:

> O world most vild, when thy loose vanities,
> Taught by this fool, do make the fool seem wise!
> (I.viii.55–56)

But Passarello is equally an extension of the world he reproves. He dresses in velvet like his idiotic patron, and, when Bilioso protests that his own velvet "shall be embroidered, because I'll differ from the fool somewhat" (III.i.67–68), it is the parallel rather than the contrast that makes the comic point. When Malevole comments on the fool's "guarded" or richly trimmed clothes, Passarello appeals to custom, "even as footmen and bawds wear velvet . . ." (I.viii.9). The paid wag is, of course, never at a loss for words, but, when Passarello describes his own habits of speech ("Nay, I shall talk when my tongue is a-going once; 'tis like a citizen on horseback, evermore in a false gallop" [I.viii.30–32]), he self-consciously parodies the mindless chatter of the court by promoting more of it. He exposes Bilioso's affected drinking of wine by falling in with the fashion and drinking in public himself:

Malevole. What hast thou there, fool?
Passarello. Wine. I have learned to drink since I went with my lord ambassador; I'll drink to the health of Madam Maquerelle.
Malevole. Why? Thou wast wont to rail upon her.
Passarello. Ay; but since, I borrowed money of her.
(V.ii.13–18)

As licensed fool, he wittily crystallizes the supine "humour" of Bilioso ("He'll lie like to your Switzer or lawyer; he'll be of any side for most money" [I.viii.47–48]), yet is cynically content to "dog" and "fawn upon" him because he "feeds" and maintains him. Yet there is a hint of self-loathing also: "when I snap him . . . he spits in my mouth. If a dog's death were not strangling, I had rather be one than a serving-man" (III.i.145–149).

Passarello, then, stands both for a critical awareness of what is amiss in Genoa and for a shoulder-shrugging compliance with it. He regards himself as a necessity; as he says, "the court cannot possibly be without me" (I.viii.61–62). But neither can he be without the court, and in this sense he parallels Malevole. He functions dramatically as a minor and more frivolous commentator upon a social order whose aberrations sustain him. The scenes pairing him with Bilioso, in which he serves as the release mechanism or "straight man" for his master's ludicrous self-exposure, help to clarify the values of the play by polarizing two extremes of folly—vacuousness and imbecility as against amusing but ultimately complacent intelligence. Whoever composed the Passarello episodes was clearly making additions, like the writer of the induction, that would capitalize upon the brilliant new cast at the Globe and yet reinforce effects of form, idea, and tone that were the hallmark of Marston's original.

* * *

Whether the contact with Marston had anything to do with Webster's next theatrical activities we cannot be sure, but it is interesting to find him writing a pair of plays—apparently in 1604 and 1605 and again in collaboration with his old mentor and friend Thomas Dekker—for a private company of boys, the Children of Paul's. These were the players for whom Marston had regularly written and who had lately succeeded in enlisting the talents of both Chapman and Middleton. Marston's *Antonio and Mellida* and its afterpiece *Antonio's Revenge* had been acted a few years earlier by Paul's boys, but, if we may judge from the rather fragmentary evidence, their repertory at this time ran, with the possible exception of Chapman's *Bussy D'Ambois*, to racy comedies of intrigue and cuckoldry, usually depicting middle-class life and mores in London—plays such as Middleton's *Michaelmas Term*, *A Mad World, My Masters*, *Your Five Gallants*, and *A Trick to Catch the Old One*. The contributions of Webster and Dekker to this fashion were two energetic, slightly cynical, farces called *Westward Ho* and *Northward Ho*.

The title of the first play derives from the familiar cry of London watermen who operated a sort of taxi service up and down the Thames, but in the hands of Dekker and Webster the phrase comes to stand for illicit sexual adventure. The complicated plot, controlled with more than ordinary deftness and economy, concerns three restless citizens' wives who scheme with the aid of Justiniano, a clever manipulator, to escape "westward" to Brentford for an overnight tryst with a trio of young rakes. Their jealous husbands, whose morality is no better than their spouses', pursue them in the expectation of catching the women *in flagrante delicto*, only to be foiled when they discover that their wives have remained technically chaste after all; as a joke the coquettes have decided to tease the gallants by arousing their desires but withholding the expected intimacies. In the subplot a lecherous old peer, abetted by the bawd Birdlime, attempts to seduce Justiniano's wife. Although nearly yielding, she ultimately converts him to virtue by pretending to choose death rather than dishonor. The two dramatists treat this seamy subject matter with frothy vivacity and abandonment, interweaving sexual and financial concerns in a manner that betokens a kind of equivalence between them. The tone of the play, which is gaily cooler, more mannered, and less sentimental than that of Dekker's characteristic productions, was obviously conceived with a wealthier and rather more sophisticated audience in mind than would typically be the case with a play for Worcester's or the Admiral's Men. Some of Dekker's inveterate heartiness and optimism nevertheless undercut the attempt at Middletonian disengagement, so that the comedy makes a broader, or at least more mixed, appeal than we might expect at a fashionable theatre in the vicinity of St. Paul's.

The success of *Westward Ho* at the end of the 1604 season must have been considerable. At any rate, it provoked a brilliant rival comedy about six months later. This was *Eastward Ho*, written by Jonson, Chapman, and Marston (all three of whom Webster admired) and acted by the competing boys' company, the Children of the Queen's Revels, at Blackfriars. This hilarious play, built upon a double contrast between a London tradesman's two daughters (one absurdly romantic, the other sensible) and his two apprentices (one prodigal, the other industrious) is very genial in its response to Dekker and Webster; as such, it shows that the old personal animosity between Jonson and Dekker expressed in earlier plays such as *The Poetaster* and *Satiromastix* had by now evaporated. With some justification, the prologue disclaims envy and imitation of *Westward Ho*, "that which is opposed to ours in title, / For that was good, and better cannot be . . ." (ll. 5–6),[32] but the play obviously capitalizes upon the same themes of cuckoldry and money, and its title, even more than in the earlier play, becomes a kind of symbolic shorthand for various kinds of adventurous folly—licentious, spendthrift, or romantically pretentious. Like *Westward Ho*, the new play contained fashionable allusions to Kyd's *Spanish Tragedy* and to *Hamlet*.

Both Jonson and Chapman got into serious trouble because of some incidental satire on James I's newly created Scottish knights that *Eastward Ho* contained, but the authors' imprisonment and the threat of having their nostrils slit and ears lopped off did not deter Webster and Dekker from nearly exhausting the popular vein in yet a third comedy, *Northward Ho*, which the children of Paul's were acting by the end of 1605. Again the title carried obvious sexual overtones, for the action begins and ends at an inn in Ware, a village on the northern outskirts of London notorious for extramarital assignations. One of the hostels there was famous for a huge bed capacious enough to accommodate four couples at once, and Shakespeare had referred to it in *Twelfth Night* (III.ii.46). The whirligig of trickery and countertrickery is even more dizzying in *Northward Ho* than in the two preceding plays, and both the subject matter and the attitude taken toward it suggest that Webster and Dekker were hoping to cap their earlier success. The central plot elaborates two opposed but interlocking intrigues. Luke Greenshield, who has unsuccessfully attempted to seduce Mistress Mayberry, tries to avenge himself upon the woman and her furiously jealous husband by making Mayberry think she is unfaithful. Meanwhile, Mayberry, with the active assistance of his friend Bellamont, turns the tables on Greenshield by tricking the latter into procuring his own wife for Mayberry (the lady having been disguised) and then exposing him as a self-cuckolder. A number of subsidiary deceptions are woven into the pattern, two of which are typical: Featherstone, an ally of Greenshield at the beginning, betrays his friend by conniving to seduce his wife, and then is himself betrayed and punished by being manipulated unwittingly into marriage with a whore; Bellamont, in addition to plotting against Greenshield and Featherstone, is victimized by a prodigal son, who bilks him of both his silver plate and his reputation, and also by his traveling companion, who arranges to have him locked up in a madhouse on the way to Ware.[33]

Neither *Westward Ho* nor *Northward Ho* matches *Eastward Ho* for vigor of characterization or freshness, but the third play in the sequence was clearly intended as a final variation on the materials of the earlier two. *Northward Ho*, for instance, explicitly alludes to the Brentford of the first play and takes up the theme of the prodigal so effectively managed in the second. One interesting new feature of the final play is the character of Bellamont, who is represented as a "little hoary Poet" (IV.i.258) sometimes "haunted with a Fury" (IV.i.25) of supernatural inspiration. Allusions to certain classical and French subjects known to interest Chapman make it clear that Dekker and Webster were amusing themselves (and doubtless their audience) by gently burlesquing one of their professional rivals—a collaborator on *Eastward Ho* and possibly its guiding genius.[34] The scene in which Bellamont is detained at Bedlam may be a humorous reference to Chapman's recent imprisonment. But, as Allardyce Nicoll has pointed out,[35] the portrait is good-natured and contains little of the vitriol that had embittered the caricatures of the *poetomachia* a few years earlier. Chapman could scarcely have taken umbrage, and it is almost certain that Webster, at least, would have wished to avoid offending his more learned and prestigious contemporary whose "full and height'ned style" he was to admire in his preface to *The White Devil*. The quarto, published in 1607, tells us that *Northward Ho* was "*Sundry times Acted*"; the title page of *Westward Ho* (also 1607) bears the corresponding designation "*divers times Acted*." John Day's *Isle of Gulls*, onstage in February 1606, alludes to all three plays, and Edward Sharpham's *The Fleire* of the same year carries the joke of the sexual journey to its logical conclusion: "goe Southwardes, my Gallants, South-wards hoe" (II.400–401)[36]—that is, to a brothel on the south bank of the Thames.

Although the names of both dramatists appear on the title pages of *West-ward Ho* and *Northward Ho*, it used to be assumed that Dekker rather than Webster must have determined the conception of both and probably have done most of the writing. Recent scholarship forces us to modify such assumptions drastically. Peter B. Murray, through analysis of linguistic forms, has demonstrated that Webster wrote about forty percent of each play. Dekker's custom of using "has" and "does" in preference to Webster's characteristic "hath" and "doth" throws important light on the method of their collaboration, for both plays fall neatly into a pattern of five or six sections in which one set of linguistic habits alternates with the other set, cutting across plot lines. Murray's conclusion is worth quoting:

[Webster and Dekker] probably sat down together and worked out the whole story line, then assigned the first unit of action to Webster and what followed to Dekker. Webster, notoriously the slower of the two writers, was thus given a definite goal to write towards. Dekker, on the other hand, had the freedom to write ahead as far as he could while Webster was toiling over his share. When Webster finished his assignment, they met again, compared what they had done, and divided the next section of the play in the same way.[37]

The only exception to the clear demarcation of sections, which incidentally coincide with the ends of scenes, is at the end of *Northward Ho* where the various strands of the preceding action are unraveled. Here, presumably, the problems of composition were sufficiently complex to necessitate working together.

The superior richness and vitality of *Eastward Ho* have cast the twin comedies by Webster and Dekker into virtual eclipse. The few recent critics who have bothered to mention *Westward Ho* and *Northward Ho* have generally been dismissive or condescending, or else have addressed themselves chiefly to historical, biographical, or bibliographic questions. G. R. Price, for instance, speaks of their "Silly intrigues" lacking in "pungency" and Brian Gibbons of the "*exclusion* of moral and didactic considerations which are the primary impetus of satiric drama."[38] Though more favorably disposed, Alexander Leggatt is content to pass both plays off with only brief discussion as "relaxed and easygoing."[39] L. C. Knights, who pronounces the dramas of Dekker with "few exceptions . . . uniformly dull," grudgingly praises "some interesting thumbnail sketches" in *Westward Ho*, but accounts for these by attributing the best satire to Webster alone.[40] Rupert Brooke (with the same play in mind) responded to the "tang of delightful, coarse gaiety, like a country smell in March,"[41] but his laudations are too aggressively aimed at Victorian prudery to be trusted for balance or judgment. Cyrus Hoy convicts *Westward Ho* of "ultimate incoherence,"[42] although he finds more to admire in its companion piece. The most sympathetic criticism of the two comedies to date has been supplied by Fernand La-garde,[43] although even his more serious treatment rests too heavily on the relative depth or shallowness of individual characterizations. E. E. Stoll seems to have summed up modern opinion with fair accuracy long ago when he remarked on the looseness of the plays, on their lack of "edge and fitness, discrimination and taste . . . [and] meaning";[44] so it is hardly surprising to find a recent editor of *Eastward Ho*, eager to elevate his text on the shoulders of its competitors, referring to "the 'claptrap appeal' and shoddy realism" of Dekker and Webster's work.[45]

Although *Eastward Ho* is unarguably a funnier and richer play than its rivals in the sequence, the two Dekker-Webster comedies are overdue for fresh scrutiny and deserve more detailed analysis than they have customarily received. Theatrically successful in their own day (as the quarto title pages attest), these frothy entertainments written for Paul's Boys serve as revealing examples of efficient and skillful collaboration between dramatists of widely differing bents. Taken together, they testify impressively to the ability of both authors to adjust their respective styles to each other as well as to new professional exigencies, and, working under pressure, to produce comedies that, while catering to fashionable taste and exploiting familiar conventions, are technically deft, possess unity of theme and structure, and sparkle with a unique blend of bourgeois heartiness and sophisticated disengagement. Even for a seasoned playwright like Dekker, such achievements are scarcely to be despised. For Webster, who was still apparently in his apprentice years, they are remarkable.

The low valuation of *Westward Ho* and *Northward Ho* has stemmed in most cases from a lack of sympathy with the frankly farcical techniques that Webster and his senior collaborator were trying to exploit. City comedy, still a relatively new genre in 1604, tended by the nature of its audience and its material to encourage brittle and two-dimensional writing. Even Shakespeare in his nearest approach to the form did not hesitate to shrink Falstaff from the comic giant of *Henry IV* to the more pitiable bungler of *The Merry Wives of Windsor*. Jonson's sardonic tone and "humours" characterization increasingly gave place to Middleton's more studiedly detached articulations of folly. Interest in the twists and turns of intrigue took precedence over richly elaborated portraiture or careful motivation; the values of escapist entertainment tended to dilute the old moral intensities, to underscore traditional ethics sporadically and more as a pretext for the fun than for their own sake. Probably the stylized acting of the childrens' companies promoted a certain flatness of characterization and an emphasis on clever surface effects of language and situation. Practical men of the theatre such as Webster and Dekker were in no position to ignore these fashions. Consequently, in their two plays for Paul's Boys, they sketched their characters lightly in order to concentrate in each case on an amusing collection of tricks and rogueries that derive from the popular tradition of jestbooks, fabliaux, and cony-catching literature. The didactic element, though visible, they intentionally subordinated to verbal merriment and liveliness of event.

Playfulness is the *raison d'être* of the two comedies, and the influence of Chaucerian imitations such as *The Cobler of Caunterburie* (1590) and *Westward for Smelts* (c. 1603) is anything but accidental.[46] The tone and purpose of both plays are well illustrated by Mayberry's excited remark to Bellamont in *Northward Ho* when the jealous husband informs the poet of his plan to surprise Kate Greenshield and Featherstone during their clandestine lovemaking: "A Commedy, a Canterbury tale smells not halfe so sweete as the Commedy I haue for thee old Poet: thou shalt write vpon't Poet" (IV.i.208–210). A little later Bellamont follows through on Mayberry's suggestion by borrowing from Chaucer's Harry Bailly; as Mayberry and his party ride toward Ware, the poet proposes that for "mirth on the high way" the travelers "practise iests one against another, and hee that has the best iest throwne vpon him, and is most gald . . . shall beare the charge of the whole iourney" (IV.iii.14–18). The contest of jest and counterjest, the insistence on a world of congenial victimization, determines in fact the structure and style of both plays. As their parallel titles suggest, the journey motif with its picaresque associations and its implications of escape from London reinforces the idea (as in Chaucer's original) of a holiday for characters and audience alike. The vacation from workaday affairs that both comedies offer verges constantly upon sexual holiday as well, but the plays draw back from total amorality because the adulterous alliances (at least for the wives) stop short of consummation, and because Webster and Dekker inject enough self-recognition, forgiveness, and bonhomie into the resolutions to rob the injuries, whether contemplated or actually committed, of their sting. At the end of *Westward Ho*, Justiniano speaks chorically for both comedies when he laughingly teaches the frustrated philanderers that "all is but merriment, all but a May-game" (V.iv.278).

The collaborating dramatists betray their gamelike attitude toward seduction and cuckoldry through a proliferation of images from cardplaying, dicing, and popular pastimes, and especially from sports such as hunting, fishing, fencing, riding, tilting, bowling, falconry, archery, and shooting. When Justiniano, for instance, volunteers to disguise himself and facilitate the wives' escape to Brentford with a false report to Wafer that the latter's child is ill, the master intriguer of *Westward Ho* says of himself that he is "borne still to draw Dun out ath mire" (II.iii.92); the sport alluded to is a Christmas game in which members of a company, pretending that a heavy log is a mired horse, contrive to let it drop on each others' toes as they gradually enlist enough strength to pull it across a room. The image not only suits Justiniano as the chief controller of the play's direction and resolution but also suggests the surprises and difficulties that lie in store for the other characters. Here, in fact, we have something approaching the "figure in action and figure in language" of which Hereward T. Price speaks so admiringly in his influential essay on Webster's major tragedies but which he specifically denies to the poet's collaborative plays.[47]

Closely allied to the sporting motif in both comedies is the athletic energy conveyed by a pervasive sense of motion. The characters (two of them are named Leapfrog and Whirlpool) are forever dispatching, trotting, galloping, running, driving, spurring, racing, outstripping, flying, sallying forth, leaping into the saddle, calling for oars, kicking up heels, bestirring their stumps, or striking while the iron is hot. Collectively, such actions portray an unsettled, hurried, upwardly mobile society, tireless in its pursuit of pleasure, profit, or persons suspected of some ruse. A stage direction in *Northward Ho*, "*Enter* Bellamont, Mayberry, Greensheild, Phillip, Leuarpoole, Chartley: *all booted*" (IV.iii.1), fairly suggests the propulsiveness of both plays. Webster and Dekker produce this effect not merely through the action proper but through incidental details—old Honeysuckle in *Westward Ho* boasting as he dresses of a morning that he is "as Lymber as an Antiant that has flourisht in the raine, and as Active as a *Norfolk* tumbler" (II.i.7–8); Captain Whirlpool joking about the unseemly haste with which food is devoured at court banquets "eare I could say grace" and the need to wear gauntlets "for feare I lose my fingers in the dishes" (III.ii.31–35); Squirrel in *Northward Ho* affirming that Featherstone's lust is as hard to restrain as "a Bull noynted with Sope, and baited with a shoale of Fidlers in *Staffordshire*" (III.ii.33–34); a bawd in the same play commenting on how "your country Gentlemen . . . as soone as they come to their lands get vp to *London*, and like squibs that run vpon lynes . . . keepe a Spitting of fire, and cracking till they ha spent all" (IV.iii.86–91).

An ironic corollary of this ceaseless activity is the feeling both plays occasionally provoke of the treadmill futility of mere cleverness. In lives so furiously accelerated, broader perspectives and deeper emotions contract; forgetful of larger contexts, obsessed by immediate goals, men begin to resemble mechanical dolls. Some such significance seems implicit in Justiniano's stress on the transitoriness of life in the sex and money capital of England:

men and women are borne, and come running into the world faster than Coaches doe in Cheap-side vppon *Symon* and *Iudes* day: and are eaten vp by Death faster, then Mutton and porridge in a terme time. Who would pin their hearts to any Sleeue: this world is like a Mynt, we are no sooner cast into the fire, taken out agen, hamerd, stampt, and made Currant, but presently wee are changde. . . .

(II.i.171–177)

Behind the willfulness, agility, and need for individual control that farce traditionally portrays, there lurks a disturbing hint of determinism; and the comparison of men to coins with its implication of hardness, sameness, and random exchange sounds a dehumanizing note. The playfulness of these comedies is double-edged. Like all good games, they offer us a certain relief from our deeper concerns by a process of systematic simplification and reduction, by a recasting of the conflicts of life into fictive and symbolic forms that admit of neat resolutions. Pain is not negated in these plays so much as it is acknowledged and purged through laughter. If the rules of play are conventionalized and predictable in comedies of cuckoldry, that is essential to their function of combining fun with psychological reassurance.

One of the most amusing games that Webster and Dekker play in the *Ho* plays is chiefly verbal and consists of sustaining a sexual conversation for as long as possible in the vocabulary of an unrelated or distantly related subject. A particularly inventive example occurs in *Westward Ho* when Justiniano, masquerading as Parenthesis, a teacher of writing, discusses his pupil's progress with her husband, Citizen Honeysuckle. That the wives of London burghers should take up penmanship in their spare time comments satirically of course on bourgeois pretensions to culture, on the beginnings of a more feminist social ethic, and on the problems of communication that faced married women who wished to toy secretly with an affair. Justiniano in his role as tutor to the ladies thus functions as their mentor in adultery, although he intends ultimately to expose his "sweete Scholler[s]" (II.i.192) by betraying them to their husbands. The following dialogue is notable not only for its extraordinary resourcefulness within an artificially narrow frame of reference but also for the ironic complacency of Honeysuckle, who enjoys the game of bawdy double-entendre as much as Justiniano or the theatre audience:

> *Honeysuckle.* And how does my wife profit vnder you sir? hope you to do any good vpon her.
> *Justiniano.* Maister *Honisuckle* I am in great hope shee shall fructify: I will do my best for my part: I can do no more then another man can.
> *Honeysuckle.* Pray sir ply her, for she is capable of any thing.
> *Justiniano.* So far as my poore tallent can stretch, It shall not be hidden from her.
> *Honeysuckle.* Does she hold her pen well yet?
> *Justiniano.* She leanes somewhat too hard vppon her pen yet sir, but practise and animaduersion will breake her from that.
> *Honeysuckle.* Then she grubs her pen.
> *Justiniano.* Its but my paines to mend the neb agen.
> *Honeysuckle.* And where abouts is shee now maister *Parenthesis*? Shee was talking of you this morning, and commending you in her bed, and told me she was past her letters.
> *Justiniano.* Truely sir she tooke her letters very suddenly: and is now in her Minoms.
> *Honeysuckle.* I would she were in her Crotchets too maister *Parenthesis*: ha-ha, I must talke merily sir.
> *Justiniano.* Sir so long as your mirth bee voyde of all Squirrility, tis not vnfit for your calling: I trust ere few daies bee at an end to haue her fal to her ioyning: for she has her letters *ad vnguem*: her A. her great B. and her great C. very right: D. and E. dilicate: hir double F. of a good length, but that it straddels a little to wyde: at the G. very cunning.

Honeysuckle. Her H. is full like mine: a goodly big H.

Justiniano. But her double LL. is wel: her O. of a reasonable Size: at her p. and q. neither Marchantes Daughter, Aldermans Wife, young countrey Gentlewoman, nor Courtiers Mistris can match her.

Honeysuckle. And how her v.

Justiniano. You sir, She fetches vp you best of al: her single you she can fashion two or three waies: but her double you, is as I would wish it.

Honeysuckle. And faith who takes it faster; my wife, or mistris *Tenterhook?*

Justiniano. Oh! Your wife by ods: sheele take more in one hower, then I can fasten either vpon mistris *Tenterhooke*, or mistris *Wafer*, or Mistris *Flapdragon* (the Brewers wife) in three.

(II.i.69–107)

After Judith Honeysuckle's entrance, the punning game is pursued still further:

Mistress Honeysuckle. . . . how does my master? troth I am a very trewant: haue you your *Ruler* about you maister? for look you, I go cleane awry.

Justiniano. A small fault: most of my schollers do so: looke you sir, do not you thinke your wife will mend: marke her dashes, and her strokes, and her breakings, and her bendings?

Honeysuckle. She knowes what I haue promist her if shee doe mende: nay by my fay *Iude*, this is well, if you would not flie out thus, but keepe your line.

Mistress Honeysuckle. I shal in time when my hand is in: haue you a new pen for mee Maister, for by my truly, my old one is stark naught, and wil cast no inck. . . .

(II.i.113–123)

Such a virtuoso exchange illustrates the historical connections between the conceited and "metaphysical" style of the late Elizabethans and the calculated prurience of Wycherley's "china scene" in *The Country Wife*. The writing-fornicating analogy reappears later in the episode where Justiniano, after arranging for Mrs. Honeysuckle to meet her gallant at a wine-drinking party, goes to "set" her fellow "Wenches the selfe same Coppy" (II.i.225–226). Webster and Dekker then vary the motif ironically in Act IV by applying it to one of the husbands: Tenterhook visits a brothel where he tries to pass himself off as a scrivener in order to avoid detection.

Eating, hunting, and fishing, though in less concentrated form, replace writing as the prevailing sex analogies of *Northward Ho*, but both plays make bawdy capital out of music. In *Westward Ho*, for instance, the drunken Sir Gosling Glow-worm baits Birdlime by forcing her to perform upon a stringed instrument before she bursts in upon the amorous couples:

Birdlime. Alas Sir, I'me an olde woman, and knowe not how to clutch an instrument.

Sir Gosling Glow-worm. Looke marke too and fro as I rub it: make a noyse: its no matter: any hunts vp, to waken vice.

89

Birdlime. I shall neuer rub it in tune.
Sir Gosling Glow-worm. Will you scrape?
Birdlime. So you will let me go into the parties, I will sawe, and make a
    noyse.
Sir Gosling Glow-worm. Doe then . . . and part 'hem. . . .
Birdlime. If I must needes play the Foole in my olde dayes, let mee haue the
    biggest instrument, because I can hold that best. . . .

                        (V.iii.58–69)

A similar passage appears in the Bedlam scene of *Northward Ho* where Bellamont observes a demented bawd and musician:

Bawd. Me thought this other night, I saw a pretty sight,
    Which pleased me much.
    A comely country mayd, not squeamish nor afraid,
    To let Gentlemen touch.
    I sold her maiden-head once, and I sold her maiden-head twice,
    And I sould it last to an Alderman of *Yorke*.
    And then I had sold it thrice.
Musician. You sing scuruily.
Bawd. Mary muffe, sing thou better, for Ile goe sleepe my old sleepes. *Exit.*
Bellamont. What are you doing my friend.
Musician. Pricking, pricking.
Bellamont. What doe you mean by pricking?
Musician. A Gentleman like quallity.

                        (IV.iii.93–106)

Both plays follow up this conjunction of dissimilars by ending with the raucous
"noyse of Musitians" (*Northward Ho*, V.i.514)—a mixed sound that seems to
echo the social and moral cacophonies of past action as much as it celebrates the
joys of harmony restored. Justiniano, however, chooses to demonstrate that
music may also signify legitimate sexuality as he leads the other husbands of
Westward Ho in their kisses of reconciliation: "put all instruments in tune, and
euery husband play musicke vpon the lips of his Wife whilst I begin first"
(V.iv.282–284). Indeed, in Act V of *Westward Ho*, Dekker and Webster offer a
comic variant of the symbolism of the broken lute that Heywood had employed
for pathetic effect in *A Woman Killed with Kindness* (1603). As the wives arrive
at Brentford with their gallants, they call for music, only to hear harsh noises
that the musicians are making in a neighboring room, as they gather to rub their
instruments with rosin and repair a broken fiddle; music is restored to the play at
the beginning of the following scene, but only after the wives have decided to
double-cross their would-be lovers and remain true to their husbands.

    In addition to the witty exuberance that the games of linguistic indecency
disclose, their simple recurrence helps portray a society that has come, somewhat wearily perhaps, to accept lust as the universal determinant of behavior.

Birdlime, with appropriate cynicism, expresses this libertine outlook in her homily to Mrs. Justiniano:

you must thinke that the commodity of beauty was not made to lye dead vpon any young womans hands: if your husband haue giuen vp his Cloake, let another take measure of you in his Ierkin: for as the Cobler, in the night time walks with his Lanthorne, the Merchant, and the Lawyer with his Link, and the Courtier with his Torch: So euery lip has his Lettice to himselfe: the Lob has his Lasse, the Collier his Dowdy, the Westerne-man his Pug, the Seruing-man his Punke, the student his Nun in white Fryers, the Puritan his Sister, and the Lord his Lady: which worshipfull vocation may fall vppon you, if youle but strike whilest the Iron is hot.

(II.ii.186–196)

Sex becomes (as often in Middleton) a kind of lowest common denominator of the *Ho* plays. Nearly all the characters are involved in the game of bedding new partners, exposing rival alliances, or assisting these schemes for profit or revenge. The constant reference to promiscuity in terms of civilized pursuits such as writing, music, dining, hunting, and the like, establishes a denigratory link between human and animal norms already evident in the proliferation of beast images—in forms of address such as "lamb" and "good mouse," in names such as Birdlime, Sir Gosling Glow-worm, Dogbolt, Sir Fabian Scarecrow, Leapfrog, Hornet, and Squirrel, and in taverns called The Greyhound, The Lion, and The Dolphin. *Westward Ho* mentions no fewer than forty animals, *Northward Ho* even more. As is conventional in satiric drama, most are bestial metaphors intended to imply stupidity, grossness, or vulnerability, but it is interesting in the light of Webster's mature practice to note how prominently birds figure in the verbal pattern.[48]

The stress on animality is not wholly negative in effect, for it can suggest health, vitality, and frolicsome spirits. "Ranke excesse," as the randy Earl of *Westward Ho* admits, may "Turne . . . man into a beast" (IV.ii.21–22), but Dekker and Webster agglomerate this conventional moralism with obvious relish for the natural appetites and earthier instincts of the human body. An aging merchant, returned from abroad, finds the "change of pasture" restorative (*Westward Ho*, II.i.9), while the typical lusty female will "break ouer any hedge to change" (V.i.88) her grazing place; secret intriguers "hatch an egge of iniquity" (II.i.194); jealous husbands are "Weasell[s] . . . going to catch Quailes" (V.iv.162–163) or "colts . . . kicking" (V.iv.108) at a door; an unfaithful wife is a blackbird for whom "her husband whissels" (II.iii.129)[49] or a "wild-ducke" lying at night "ith segges" (*Northward Ho*, V.i.249–250) with her paramour. When Bellamont outrages Kate Greenshield by comparing ladies to horses, the poet can reply (with the apparent approval of the dramatists): "And no disparagment; for a woman to haue a high forhead, a quick eare, a full eye, a wide nostrell, a sleeke skin, a straight back, a round hip, and so forth is most comely" (V.i.321–323).

Nowhere is the gamelike approach of Webster and Dekker to their material more evident than in the deliberate self-consciousness of their dramaturgy. Both *Westward Ho* and *Northward Ho* constantly italicize their own artifice as plays, and the awareness of medium becomes at once a condition of audience response and a feature of the characterization. As the dramatists play upon the increasingly familiar conventions of city comedy, they invite us to participate vicariously in their manipulative skills; but they also project the games of manipulation into the fiction proper, thus creating, as it were, internal "stage managers" or "playwrights" who involve themselves knowingly in a kind of make-believe. However moralistic or licentious their stated motives, the deceivers and deceived alike take part in a sequence of practical jokes, for which the ultimate justification is the laughter of all. The collaborating dramatists have in a sense expressed their own function as entertainers by making it the subject of their work.

In *Westward Ho* the obvious focus of this self-reference is the character of Justiniano, a rich merchant of, significantly, Italian extraction. A more frivolous cousin to Marston's Altofront, he pretends to go on a journey but remains behind in disguise to trigger the mechanisms of the plot and observe its effects.[50] As the most omniscient figure of the cast and the one most given to managing and commenting upon the action, he derives from the medieval Vice; as a constitutionally jealous husband obsessed with proving that his imagined cuckoldom extends to his fellow tradesmen, he is a descendant of "humours" comedy and recalls such men as Shakespeare's Ford and Jonson's Kitely. Thus, he combines almost antithetical functions: he is at once an embodiment of folly and, as his name implies, the play's chief agent of exposing folly in others. Moreover, he seems aware of the distinction. While he plots and spies with a blend of gusto and Machiavellian ingenuity, he pauses periodically to reflect upon the foolishness of his own position:

O the villany of this age, how ful of secresie and silence (contrary to the opinion of the world) haue I euer found most women. I haue sat a whol afternoone many times by my wife, and lookt vpon her eies, and felt if her pulses haue beat, when I haue nam'd a suspected loue, yet all this while haue not drawne from her the least scruple of confession. I haue laine awake a thousand nights, thinking she wold haue reuealed somewhat in her dreames, and when she has begunne to speake any thing in her sleepe, I haue iog'd her, and cried I sweete heart. But when wil your loue come, or what did hee say to thee ouer the stall? Or what did he do to thee in the Garden-chamber? Or when wil he send to thee any letters, or when wilt thou send to him any mony, what an idle coxcombe iealousie wil make a man.

(III.iii.40–53)

Justiniano plays a circular game; he operates as a force for disorder that he may preside over the comic solution of difficulties that, for the most part, have been manufactured.

Having delightedly encouraged his female "pupils" in their sexual escapade, he can step back to moralize upon his role before initiating the preventive countermovement:

wel, it rests now that I discouer my selfe in my true shape to these Gentlewomens husbands: for though I haue plaid the foole a little to beguile the memory of mine owne misfortune, I woulde not play the knaue, though I be taken for a Banquerout, but indeed as in other things, so in that, the worlde is much deceiued in me, for I haue yet three thousand pounds in the hands of a sufficient friend, and all my debts discharged. I haue receiued here a letter from my wife . . . with protestation to gyue me assured tryall of her honesty. I cannot tell what to thinke of it, but I will put it to the test, there is great strife betweene beautie, and Chastity, and that which pleaseth many is neuer free from temptation: as for Iealousie, it makes many Cuckoldes, many fooles, and many banquerouts: It may haue abused me and not my wifes honesty: Ile try it: but first to my secure and doting Companions.

(III.iii.96–110)

Serving as the play's presenter, he stands between the other characters and us, so that he functions in one sense as a surrogate for the authors. In his first soliloquy, he refers to his "Citty dames" as "indeede the fittest, and most proper persons for a Comedy," then leaves the stage to set his "comicall businesse" (I.i.225–229) in motion. But in terms of the fiction, his scenario amounts to self-administered therapy. Justiniano is actuated by the need to project his own shame as a putative cuckold upon three others—to multiply images of himself in a comedy of his own devising and to assume false identities toward this end. As in *The Malcontent*, to which Webster had contributed his sophisticated induction, so in *Westward Ho* the techniques and layering of illusion become part of the comic point. The boy actor portraying Justiniano challenges the audience to smile at his parody of a familiar type, the neurotically suspicious husband; but the character in the play proper is at once detached from and engaged with the action. Webster and Dekker ask us to appreciate the complexities of a child simultaneously playing a chorus and a London merchant, and of a London merchant playing a schoolmaster, who in turn masquerades as a collier. "Master Parenthesis" exults in his role as stage manager and producer of surprises. At the Stillyard drinking party he jokingly tests the bravado of the wives by pretending that their husbands are just outside the door—an ironic anticipation of his bringing them actually onstage at Brentford. And he clearly enjoys the game of disguises. Before he decides to impersonate the coal vendor, we see him speculating about his costume: "Let me see: Ile breake out in some filthy shape like a Thrasher, or a Thatcher, or a Sowgelder, or something: and speak dreamingly. . . . Ile go make ready my rusticall properties" (II.iii.95–110). In the end, of course, Justiniano renounces the role of "a Foxe in a Lambes skin" (II.iii.64), and, removing his schoolmaster's wig, reveals himself with maximal theatricality: "I will now play the Merchant with you" (V.iv.289–290).

Although Justiniano symbolizes the principle of inventiveness in *Westward Ho*, the comic initiative passes at several points to other hands; the play-producing game is shown to be contagious. Mrs. Honeysuckle, one of Parenthesis's "scholars," conceives the ruse of the sick child in which Mrs. Wafer and Justiniano, as cooperative performers, play their parts. Clare Tenterhook, another pupil, stages the whole episode of Monopoly's arrest, then feigns sickness in order to avoid the sexual experience she has taken such pains to arrange. Perhaps we may discern here, as in *Sir Thomas Wyatt*, another early pointer towards Webster's developing interest in strong and self-sufficient women, but the matter to be emphasized is the sense of spontaneity and improvisation that the comedy conveys as more characters begin intriguing on their own. Justiniano regains supremacy over events in Act V when he redirects the husbands in their plan to expose the wives.

The underplot of the comedy, with its melodramatic story of the voluptuous Earl and his conversion to rectitude, is handled with the same elaborate awareness of theatre that marks the central intrigue. Birdlime, the old panderess who arranges the meeting between Justiniano's wife and the peer, gains entrance to the merchant's house by masking as a dealer in cosmetics, and the rich gown that she delivers as a bribe from the nobleman prompts Mrs. Justiniano to compare herself to a player (II.ii.109). A little later Birdlime invokes a more startlingly theatrical simile: "A woman when there be roses in her cheekes, Cherries on her lippes, Ciuet in her breath, Iuory in her teeth, Lyllyes in her hand, and Lickorish in her heart, why shees like a play. If new, very good company, very good company, but if stale, like old *Ieronimo*: goe by, go by" (II.ii.181–185). Like Justiniano, she takes pleasure in stage-managing. When Honeysuckle, Tenterhook, and Wafer arrive in rapid succession to be serviced at her brothel, and when she is faced with the problem of keeping the men unrecognized and apart from each other, she exploits the full resources of the Jacobean stage. Honeysuckle, with whom she plays cards on the lower platform, must twice be hidden in a "closet" to avoid encountering the other two. She ushers Tenterhook "*aboue*" for a fling with the prostitute Luce while the card game continues below. When the entrance of Wafer threatens to precipitate a meeting between him and Tenterhook, Birdlime concocts separate charades for the two husbands to play, casting one as a scrivener and the other as Luce's outraged brother. The use of the two stage levels to reinforce the analogy between sex play and card play emblematizes the relation between a major theme of the comedy and the fascination with technique; also, of course, it looks forward to those refinements of irony that Middleton was to actualize so brilliantly in the chess scene of *Women Beware Women*. The shelving of one character, so that the next may be accommodated without interference, recalls a strategy that Jonson polished to high gloss in *The Alchemist*. When Birdlime's whole structure of deception collapses in mutual recognition, the outrageous manipulator passes the whole thing off as a diversion: "If I did it not to make your good worships merry, neuer beleeue me, I wil drinke to your worship a glasse of Sack" (IV.i.158–159).

The two plots of *Westward Ho* come nicely together in the purposely stagy episode of the Earl's regeneration, for here Justiniano is as actively the dramatist and role player as elsewhere. It is ironic and typical of the play's procedure that a seducer who tempts his intended victim by means of music and a banquet presented in dumbshow should himself be awakened to virtue by a grotesque theatrical trick. Justiniano, now disguised as a woman, takes the place of his own wife and shows to the Earl the face of moral ugliness by confronting him in an ambiguous shape that the peer interprets for a witch.[51] As in *Hamlet*, to which Justiniano later alludes (V.iv.51), drama becomes the way to prick a conscience. But even after he has revealed his true identity to the shaken Earl, Justiniano continues to make artifice the vehicle of truth. Drawing a curtain to disclose Mrs. Justiniano's "corpse," he tells the "fleshly Lord" (IV.ii.143) that he has poisoned the lady in a desperate attempt to preserve her chastity; after allowing the shock to register, he then raises "sweete *Moll*" from the dead with a compliment that applies equally to the skill of the boy actor and the wife's resistance to temptation: "Awake . . . th'ast played / The woman rarely, counterfetted well" (IV.ii.151–152). What Justiniano punningly calls "My Act" (IV.ii.149) finally produces the intended moral spasm in the Earl:

> Mirror of dames, I looke vpon thee now,
> As men long blind, (hauing recouered sight)
> Amazd: scarce able are to endure the light:
> Mine owne shame strikes me dumb: henceforth the booke
> Ile read shall be thy mind, and not thy looke.
>
> (IV.ii.162–166)

The simulated death and resurrection of a lady become the emblems of an old man's sin and rebirth. Honeysuckle, whom Justiniano has peripherally involved with the other husbands in his stratagem, remarks that he wishes their "wiues [were] heere to see this Pageant" (IV.ii.168). Thus, a scene crammed with tragicomic effects, so seemingly at odds with the realism of city comedy, consists surprisingly well with the play as a totality. Although its operatic tone, jingling rhymes, and sentimental emotion may jar, it nevertheless carries out, albeit in different colors, the pattern of self-conscious theatricality that defines the structure of the whole. Moreover, there are a few hints—the absurd Petrarchanism of the Earl's love rhetoric, for instance—that, even in the subplot, the dramatists may have written with their tongues at least half in their cheeks.

The influence of Jonson, Marston, and Middleton—all of them highly self-conscious dramatists—is already apparent in *Westward Ho*. One wonders therefore whether the audience at Paul's would catch reminiscences of the even more popular Shakespeare. In addition to Hamlet (who is mentioned directly),

Sir Andrew Aguecheek, Mistress Quickly, and Juliet's Nurse are all present in shadowy form. The silly carpet knight Sir Gosling Glow-worm, with his "lank thighes" (III.iv.77), his passion for dancing and drinking, and his tendency to be drawn into brawls, appears to have been suggested by Sir Toby's mindless companion in *Twelfth Night*; and Sir Fabian Scarecrow, Gosling's nonappearing likeness, probably derives from the same source.[52] Mrs. Tenterhook departs briefly (V.i.94–100) from her usual astuteness to assume the malapropistic speech of the Hostess in *Henry IV*; and Birdlime, whose bones ache "with iaunting" (II.ii.7), who tipples *aqua vitae*, and who provokes the epithet "stale damnation" (II.ii.153),[53] teases the Earl by holding back news of her visit to Mrs. Justiniano in a patent imitation of the Nurse's delayed report to Juliet (*Romeo and Juliet*, II.v). Since they expected their audiences to be familiar with *The Spanish Tragedy* and *Hamlet*, it is at least possible that Webster and Dekker intended their other borrowings to be obvious as well, thus adding further stimulus to audience awareness of the theatre.

Northward Ho delights in its own artifice almost more insistently than its predecessor, but now the two dramatists embody the spirit of comic invention literally in a member of their own craft. If Bellamont was conceived as a kindly burlesque of Chapman, this hardly prevented his also serving as a symbolic extension of the authors themselves, for Philip's "old poeticall dad" (III.i.2) gives as good as he gets in the matter of trickery and can, moreover, laugh at himself. Despite the jests at his expense and, in another sense, because of them, the character focuses the principle of dramatic creativity in the play, a principle that spreads out to embrace the other major figures of the cast. When Allardyce Nicoll complains that Bellamont's traits "have no integral association with the comedy's plot,"[54] surely he overlooks the thematic significance of the character; for the contest of practical jokes that Bellamont initiates on the road to Ware merely formalizes a game that Greenshield and Featherstone are already playing at the opening of the comedy and that Mayberry, Philip, Kate, and Doll (with her seedy accomplices) take up in due course.

Bellamont's association with drama, and especially comedy, is rarely permitted to escape our notice. When we first meet the poet, he is telling his friend Mayberry how the fair at Sturbridge "afforded me mirth beyond the length of fiue lattin Comedies" (I.i.40–41), remarking that he himself "could make an excellent discription" of the sights "in a Comedy" (I.i.54–55). Two scenes later, after Bellamont chides his companion for jealous exaggeration ("Sfoot you talke like a Player"), Mayberry replies by challenging the dramatist "to bring my wife vpon the Stage" where her supposed flirtations could indeed "please Gentlemen" (I.iii.28–33). When the muse attends him, the little author will speak with no one, not even "a Sharer . . . Of the big company," let alone a mere "plaier" (IV.i.2–5); but Captain Jenkins is in fact granted audience only to be told about "the Tragedy of young *Astianax*" (IV.i.36–37), baffled by details of its forthcoming production at the French court, and read some lines that sound like a parody of the execution scene in Chapman's *Tragedy of Charles, Duke of Byron.*[55] At the entrance of Doll, Bellamont thrusts the captain "behind the hangings" to "heare the peece of a Commedy" (IV.i.116–117) that exposes her for a common trollop and the listener for a gull; he later jests about the episode as "a most villanous female Tragedie" (IV.i.212). By the final act, Bellamont is rewriting Mayberry's script, spontaneously altering his friend's strategy to have Greenshield surprise Kate in Featherstone's arms, for, as he explains, his cleverer drama "will haue a more neate and unexpected conueyance" (V.i.6–7). Accordingly, he assigns Mayberry a new role as lecher ("this is your part of the Comedy" [V.i.19–20]), encourages Greenshield in his scheme to play falconer equipped with wig and beard from "a company of country plaiers" (V.i.82–83), masks Kate as "a *Yorkeshire* Gentlewoman" (V.i.75), and coaches Mayberry's wife to dissemble shock and "come out vpon her qu" (V.i.117)—all this to trick a would-be seducer into pandering his wife to the man he would have cheated. When Philip, in a later "shuffling" of the deck, "turne[s] vp" Doll "for the bottom carde at *Ware*" (V.i.369–370), Bellamont continues to maneuver his characters about the stage: he traps the improvident Featherstone and the prostitute into hasty wedlock by passing them off respectively to each other as heir and heiress.

Thus does the poet and playwright of the piece outreach his competitors in gamesmanship, and thus, too, does he exemplify poetic justice, for he punishes the sexual intriguers by casting them in roles that call upon their talents as amorists. But such moral judgment as he makes is free of self-righteousness or arrogance. The Welsh captain notes Bellamont's habit of talking to himself when alone "as if hee were in Bed-lam" (IV.i.20), a detail that suggests the man's interior life and that prepares us for the actual trapping of the playwright in the famous madhouse. Although Bellamont protests his sanity as he is bound, kicked, and humiliated, he preserves a kind of dignity by taking the joke in good part and by observing darkly to his laughing companions that "your best Poets indeed are madde for the most part" (IV.iii.192–193). Of course, he intends, like the others, to exact comic revenge upon his tormentors, but, in another sense, he represents the man apart, and his comment may be read as a suggestion that, compared to Mayberry's irrational jealousy, his son's prodigality, and the endless deceptiveness of Featherstone and the Greenshields, his "madness" is the only sanity. Better than most, he can distinguish between appearance and reality, as he proves when he warns Mayberry that Greenshield's story about the ring may be a hoax. In the characterization of Bellamont, Webster and Dekker appear to be making Dryden's point that "Great wits are sure to madness near allied"; and their transformation of raw sexual energies into self-effacing unions, if only by authorial fiat at the end of the play, may distantly reflect Duke Theseus's vision that "The lunatic, the lover, and the poet / Are of imagination all compact."[56] The moral imaginativeness of *Northward Ho* may appear rudimentary—a mere affair of tit for tat; but Bellamont does become the symbolic spring from which cleverness combined with humor and common sense wells out. Witty in himself, he also stands for the cause that wit is in other men; and just as Justiniano's theatricality in *Westward Ho* infected the entire comedy, so Bellamont's profession as dramatist spills over into nearly every episode of the more complexly plotted *Northward Ho*.

Leverpool and Chartley consent to "playe [their] partes" in Doll's tavern-bawdy house, for, as their mistress announces, "The world's a stage, from which strange shapes we borrow" (I.ii.99–101). When the trull sets up a scene between herself and Bellamont with Philip as unseen audience, the pranksters rejoice in "any scaffold to execute knauery vpon" (II.i.277), and we infer that in the gulling of her foolish suitors, Doll has learned a trick or two from the many actors with whom she has had traffic (III.i.130). Once convinced of his wife's fidelity, Mayberry forces her to play the gracious hostess; she is to welcome her would-be seducers as though they were women newly come up to London "to see the Pageant" (II.ii.5) on Lord Mayor's Day, and Bellamont is at hand to instruct her in the specifics of her part. Later Mayberry calls his plan for vengeance "A Comedy" (IV.i.208). Kate Greenshield poses as her husband's sister, pretending to sleepwalk as a means of getting into Featherstone's room and feigning illness as a means of getting out. Her final role, suggested, of course, by Bellamont, is that of a woman traveler from Yorkshire. In shedding this mask, she sums up the entire game of role playing on which the comedy is based, at the same time defining its moral tone: "I protest . . . I haue playd this knauish part only to be witty" (V.i.231–232). Entertainment is the true motive behind almost everyone's trickery.

The sheer joy in contrivance that Webster and Dekker display in the *Ho* plays precludes any thoroughgoing realism, and it would be naive to regard either as a literal transcript of Jacobean city life or, in Dyce's words, "a picture of the manners and customs of the time."[57] Both comedies, nonetheless, reflect the sociology and economics of their era, and the surfaces of both are studded with a rich particularity that stems, like the studied self-consciousness, from the satiric styles of Jonson and Marston. A texture of contemporaneity is guaranteed by repeated allusions to people, places, and events—the voyages of Cavendish and Drake, the siege of Ostend, Bankes and his famous horse, Kempe's dance to Norwich, Gunpowder Alley, Long-Lane, Blackwall, Limehouse, the Rhenish winehouse in the Stillyard, and so forth. Startling, even grotesque, pictures crowd the dialogue—"Iack-dawes dung[ing] the top of *Paules* Steeple" (*Westward Ho*, II.i.31–32); "forty maim'd souldiors" in a cart "looking as pittifully as Dutchmen first made drunke, then carried to bee-heading" (III.iii.25–27); "the leg of a dead horse hang[ing] in the But of Sacke to keepe it quicke" (IV.i.53–54); university Freshmen at a goose market "stuck here and there, with a graduate: like cloues with great heads in a gammon of bacon" (*Northward Ho*, I.i.44–46). We get Brobdingnagian close-ups—a wrinkled forehead with "more cromples, then the back part of a counsellors gowne, when another rides vppon his necke at the barre" (*Westward Ho*, II.i.12–13); a face "witherd and pale like the tree in Cuckolds Hauen in a great snow" (*Northward Ho*, III.ii.13–14); "a *Darby-shere* woman discouer[ing] her great teeth, in laughter" (III.ii.3–4). Such details impart a cartoonlike emphasis to the prose and point ahead to the mannered discordancies of the Overburian character, a genre in which both Dekker and Webster were to excel.

Vivid touches of local color enliven the canvas. *Parvenus* at court buy their knighthoods for 200 pounds; merchants spend their substance, "consorting . . . with Noble men" or "building a summer house" (*Westward Ho*, I.i.189–190); Inns-of-Court sparks swagger about in "Cloakes and Rapiers, Boots and Spurs," instead of "in their Caps and Gownes, ciuilly, and modestly" (IV.i.14–16). "Respectable" wives, like Jacobean versions of Emma Bovary, farm their children out to wet nurses and meet their lovers secretly in church; the prostitutes, continually harried out of town by officialdom, "come . . . dropping into the freedome by Owle-light sneakingly" (*Northward Ho*, I.ii.75–76). Apprentices smash brothel windows in a Shrove Tuesday riot. When gallants spend a night out of town, they retire to smoke and spit before bedding their women; "When your cittizen comes into his Inne, wet and cold, dropping, either the hostis or one of her maids, warmes his bed, puls on his night-cap, cuts his cornes, puts out the candle, [and] bids him command ought, if he wants ought" (V.i.66–69). Such is the social backdrop against which Webster and his friend manufacture their artificialities of plot and character.

The didactic element in these comedies is anything but solemn, yet their moral point of view is oddly blurred, halting as it does between sympathy for bourgeois values on the one hand and laughter at them on the other. The mockery of middle-class husbands ("they which are most violent dotards before their marryage are most voluntary Coucouldes after" [*Westward Ho*, I.i.88–89]) collapses into something like approval when the aristocrats with whom their spouses flirt are inevitably worsted by the winning combination of citizenly resourcefulness and wifely self-discipline in the crisis. But the husbands themselves seem to waver between attacks of conventional righteousness and the amoral excitements of intrigue for its own sake. Justiniano can worry about the propriety of his deceiving Wafer ("Heauen pardon me, and pray God the infant be not punisht fort" [II.iii.94–95]), yet positively relish his plans to spirit the ladies off to Brentford. Once he has got them there, moreover, he shows more interest in preserving their husbands' reputations than in actually preventing adultery. The double standard in sexual mores goes blithely unchallenged: husbands coming fresh from the brothel can speak of each other as "three innocent Cittizens so horribly, so abhominably wrung" (V.iv.16–17), and they are ready to summon the police to punish their rivals for "their wickednesse" (V.iv.25). With the wives, this hypocrisy is more a matter for jesting than reproof.

Undisguised exhilaration in success and competition mingle with old-fashioned doubts about means. Mrs. Tenterhook, for example, betrays the uncertain ethic of *Westward Ho* by trying to square aggressiveness toward lovers with traditional fidelity to husbands:

They shall know that Cittizens wiues haue wit enough to out strip twenty such guls; tho we are merry, lets not be mad: be as wanton as new married wiues, as fantasticke and light headed to the eye, as fether-makers, but as pure about the heart, as if we dwelt amongst em in Black Fryers. . . . Oh yes: eate with em as hungerly as souldiers: drinke as if we were Froes: talke as freely as Iestors, but doe as little as misers, who (like dry Nurses) haue great breastes but giue no milke. . . . the Iest shal be a stock to maintain vs and our pewfellowes in laughing at christnings, cryings out, and vpsittings this twelue month: how say you wenches, haue I set the Sadle on the right horse.

(V.i.159–174)

If strenuous individualism was the hallmark of the rising capitalist, erotic adventure might provide his wife with the psychological equivalent of her husband's enterprise. In both comedies the implied parallel between wealth and sex is ambiguously treated. The passing of jewelry from hand to hand is repeatedly associated with amorous intrigue, and the name of one of the gallants, Monopoly, also suggests the proximity of sexual and financial appetites.[58] Yet the jewels not only cloud reputations; they also clear them and, in the end, revert to their original owners. When Mrs. Justiniano calls her chastity a great "sum," "a debt thats due / But to one Man" (*Westward Ho*, II.ii.112–114), her husband, we are meant apparently to take her words without irony; but then she is paid for her virtue by being allowed to keep the Earl's jewels, a somewhat too worldly reward for her moral absolutism. At the end of *Northward Ho*, Featherstone gamely accepts that his "fate" (union with a whore) spells poverty, and wearily assents to Mayberry's crass jibe, "Now a man may haue a course in your Parke?"; yet a moment later Doll is protesting that she will forever be "true," and he announces cheerfully that "all the Dogs in *France* shall not part vs" (V.i.501–509). Idealism and cynicism, sentiment and hardness, optimism and pessimism nudge each other curiously. It is as though the Dekker of *The Shoemaker's Holiday* and the Middleton of *Michaelmas Term* or *A Chaste Maid in Cheapside* had uncomfortably joined hands on the same stage.

The oddly mixed outlook of *Westward Ho* and *Northward Ho* is probably due less to differences in the sensibility of Webster and Dekker than to their common circumstances as partners. Both had chiefly been associated with the public theatre, although neither was a stranger to the ways of the boys' companies;[59] now they were attempting to please the affluent of the City, who thought of themselves as more sophisticated than the penny regulars at the Fortune or the Rose. The fashion of jeering the bourgeoisie doubtless flattered those patrons of Paul's who attached themselves to the court or who were nurturing social ambitions; but the audience must also have included rich citizens like Justiniano and Mayberry, whose clever handling of the gentry would strike sympathetic chords and reinforce mercantile pride. The remarkable evenness of the prose in both comedies suggests that both playwrights aimed at writing in a way that would straddle such tensions, dissolving conflicts of class and value in general hilarity.

Distant as they are from Webster's masterpieces in tone, complexity, and depth, the two *Ho* plays do contain some faint adumbrations of the later plays. The most suggestive links are to *The Devil's Law-Case*, a drama whose intricacies of plot and artifice reflect the experience of Webster's apprentice efforts for the boy actors. The tragicomedy makes much of role playing and deliberately refers to its own "comical events" (V.vi.63) in terms of theatrical performance. The lawyer Crispiano, who disguises himself to spy on his son and "to curb the insolencies / Of . . . women" (III.i.29–20), recalls Justiniano in his function as an interventionist; his patient treatment of Julio is, of course, a variant of the prodigal son motif, less moralistically presented in the Bellamont-Philip relationship of *Northward Ho*. Despite its Italian setting, *The Devil's Law-Case* explores in greater depth those social oppositions of city and court that the London comedies skate over so merrily. Also the little "pageant" of Mrs. Justiniano's "death" and revival in a context of illicit romance encapsulates a major theme of the tragicomedy, in which no fewer than three characters, believed dead, return to life, and in which Romelio, symbolically prompted by coffin and shroud, pretends to undergo a spiritual regeneration. Romelio even refers to his "right excellent form / Of penitence" as "this dumb pageant" (V.iv.146–147). A variation on the Lucrece situation, Justiniano's reported killing of his wife to preserve her honor, was, of course, to figure more prominently in *Appius and Virginia*. The use of mad folk to torment Bellamont, combined with the satirical treatment of the insane, makes the imprisonment scene of *Northward Ho* a comic precursor of its tragic counterpart in *The Duchess of Malfi*; even Greenshield's invasion of the bedchamber where Featherstone is seducing the intruder's wife represents the farcical handling of a situation that Webster was to use again with terrifying effect in the scene of *The Duchess* where Ferdinand interrupts his sister preparing to go to bed with Antonio. Cyrus Hoy has detected in Justiniano "a typically Websterian creation" who is

strenuously ironic and hysterically bent on mastering a world in which, as he never tires of telling himself and others, nothing is what it appears to be. Raised to a tragic power, this satiric sense of life's discrepancies was to issue in the characters of Flamineo and Bosola, mysteriously shaping and exploiting and recoiling from and finally destroyed by the violent and devious forces that sweep through [the great Italian tragedies].[60]

The *Ho* plays, like the dramas to come, have no want of tough-nerved women, but Mrs. Mayberry's robust self-defense in the later of the two comedies suggests a continuity with such episodes as Vittoria's arraignment in *The White Devil*.

Occasionally in the city comedies we find those violent or macabre details that foreshadow the tragic Webster—the image of drunken Dutchmen being carried to decapitation (*Westward Ho*, III.iii.26–27), jokes about hanging, drawing, quartering, and the dismemberment of cadavers in the midst of an absurd wooing scene (*Northward Ho*, IV.i.139–142), the association of unsheathed blades, "naked weapons" (*Northward Ho*, I.ii.6, V.i.356), with the male sexual organ (compare *The Duchess of Malfi*, I.i.331–337, III.ii.71–72), the comparison of women to defective cannon that fly to pieces when fired (*Northward Ho*, II.ii.136–140).[61] A sexual pun on the sport of "running at the ring" (*Northward Ho*, I.iii.91–92) seems to anticipate the series of ironic double-entendres in *The Duchess of Malfi* that begins with the news, on Ferdinand's initial entrance, that Antonio "took the ring offenest" (I.i.88).[62] Birdlime's ludicrous description of her wares (*Westward Ho*, I.i.116–122) hints at the more grotesque and disgusting account of cosmetics that Bosola gives in response to the Old Lady in *The Duchess* (I.i.35–40), and the curious mention of a mathematical instrument or "Ingin" in connection with artificial alterations of the face (*Westward Ho*, I.i.78) also reappears in the later play (I.i.136–137). The habit of introducing strained or conceited anecdotes into dramatic dialogue, a characteristically Websterian trait, already shows up in Justiniano's account of how colliers acquired a reputation for venereal disease (*Westward Ho*, III.iii.9–31).

It would be overhasty to assign all these pre-echoes to Webster, and, indeed, Murray's apportionment of shares, if we accept it, would yield more than half to Dekker. But the authorship itself is less important than the developing evidence of Webster's accretive and imitative approach to style. Whoever may have invented individual scenes or passages, Webster, whether consciously or not, was already storing up themes, turns of plot, and effects of rhetoric that would prove useful to him later on.

* * *

With the two *Ho* plays, written in 1604 and 1605 respectively, the first phase of Webster's literary career seems to close. His collaboration with Dekker had been almost continuous from 1602 to the end of 1605. Not only had the two poets worked on plays together, they had also associated themselves with at least two nondramatic projects during this period. Their assistance to Munday in launching the publication of his *Palmerin of England, Part III* has already been mentioned. Both also seem to have been involved in one of the most magnificent examples of Jacobean spectacle, prepared by the City of London to welcome Elizabeth's successor, James I, to his new capital in 1603. The architect Stephen Harrison was commissioned to design seven triumphal arches, elaborately decorated and allegorically conceived, through which the sovereign and his train would pass in procession from the Tower of London to Temple Bar. Two of the arches were contributed by the committees of Italian and Dutch merchants then resident in London—affluent men such as Webster and Dekker were representing on the stage in the Justiniano of *Westward Ho* and the Hans Van Belch of *Northward Ho*. Over three hundred craftsmen worked for five months erecting the arches in the year of His Majesty's accession, but the plague, which was raging in the City by August, necessitated a postponement of the state entry, and the construction had to be interrupted until the following February. When the procession finally did occur on 15 March 1604, the king was greeted with appropriate speeches by Jonson, Dekker, and Middleton.

One of the splendid memorials of this grand occasion is a handsome folio volume, published the same year, containing William Kip's beautiful engravings of the seven triumphal arches and a detailed description of each. Both Dekker and Webster wrote commendatory "Odes" for this volume, entitled *Arches of Triumph*. The latter's poem is a graceful lyric that contrasts the triumphs of war with the peaceful celebration of the king's accession and comments conventionally on the power of the volume to redeem Harrison's art from oblivion. It is not unlikely that Webster was employed along with Dekker to write speeches for the ceremony itself, or to assist with the published description. If so, however, Dekker failed to acknowledge his junior friend in his published *Magnificent Entertainment Given to King James* (1604).[63] No doubt, the young playwright was already gaining experience in the traditions of municipal pageantry that would serve him well when he came to plan his Lord Mayor's show twenty years later.

2

MATURITY

Although the dates of Webster's more important and mature plays are in some cases problematic, we seem to be confronted at this point with a gap of some five years in the dramatist's career. Possibly the plague, which continually forced the public playhouses to shut down for months at a time between 1605 and 1610, was responsible. Anyway, after 1607, when all three of his surviving plays with Dekker appeared in print, the next certain event is the publication of *The White Devil* in 1612. It is interesting to note that his first unaided play (unless *Appius and Virginia* is an exception) turned out to be one of the two acknowledged masterpieces for which Webster is famous. The playwright is defensive in his preface about being "a long time in finishing this tragedy," which not only helps explain the period of apparent unproductivity but also the achievement, for the first time, of a fully distinctive and individual style. Since the play contains borrowings from Robert Tofte's translation of Montreux's *Honours Academie* (1610), some of the actual writing of *The White Devil* must have been done after this date, but from what we know of Webster's working habits, we can imagine him beginning to assemble his materials well before this. Most of Webster's other borrowings in the play are from works published in 1608 or earlier.[1] The first performance probably occurred in the early months of 1612, the same year as publication. The company was Queen Anne's Men, with whom Webster had previously been associated in *Sir Thomas Wyatt*. The theatre was the Red Bull in Clerkenwell, which was tending to supersede the same company's older and inferior Curtain.

The principal writer for the Queen's Men at this time was Thomas Heywood, who was providing them with plays such as *The Rape of Lucrece* and a series of dramas on the *Golden, Silver, Brazen,* and *Iron Ages*. The traditions of the Red Bull were popular, not to say lowbrow, and the company sought to compete with the King's Men at the Globe and the Prince's at the Fortune by offering plays that contained clowning, battles, noise, spectacle, and tireless bustle. Webster's densely written and thought-provoking tragedy was a signal departure from the normal fare.

The play that appears to have immediately preceded Webster's on the boards of the Red Bull was Dekker's *If This Be Not a Good Play, the Devil Is in*

It, published a few months before *The White Devil*. The two titles suggest a relationship, but, whereas Webster's use of the word *devil* is metaphoric and symbolic, Dekker's is literal. His play, in the old tradition of *Doctor Faustus*, is constructed around a three-pronged diabolic mission to earth in which individual fiends, each in disguise, assail the different worlds of court, church, and marketplace. Since Dekker presents his demons as more jocularly human than supernatural, they come off as "white devils" of a kind, but the play is much more corrosive than was usual with that genial poet; and the overall effect amounts to a cruel indictment of contemporary society at three distinct levels. The emphasis on sex in a context of guilt and torture may be crudely proleptic of Webster's tragedy: the King of Naples, for instance, suddenly rejects a fiancée, his "earthly blisse" (I.ii.246), with the opinion that "A woman is an insatiate graue / Wherein hee's dambd that lyes buried" (III.i.28–29), and a cloistered monk, furnished with candle, death's head, and crucifix, is later tempted with a procession of courtesans who dance erotically before him.[2] Dekker's preface, which complains that in these hard days "*Merit goes a Begging*, and *Learning starues*,"[3] sounds a note of disillusionment that was to become all too familiar in the writings of his younger friend and colleague Webster. Probably both were having a lean time of it economically at this period. Dekker must have known that Webster was struggling to finish *The White Devil* and have thought highly of the work, for he seems to herald its appearance in the dedication of his own play. Speaking to members of the company, he writes, "I wish a *Faire* and *Fortunate Day*, to your *Next New-Play* (for the *Makers-sake* and your *Owne*,) because such *Braue Triumphes* of *Poesie*, and *Elaborate Industry*, which my *Worthy Friends Muse* hath there set forth, deserue a *Theater* full of very *Muses* themselues to be *Spectators*. To that *Faire Day* I wish a *Full*, *Free*, and *Knowing Auditor*."[4]

But Dekker's good wishes for the reception of *The White Devil* were not fulfilled in the event. Webster was pleased by the acting and praised the performers—especially his friend Richard Perkins—but from what he says in his published preface "To the Reader," we gather that in other respects conditions were unfavorable and the audience indifferent, if not downright hostile. We catch in his words those characteristically Websterian accents of frustration, disappointment, and contempt. The play "was acted in so dull a time of winter, presented in so open and black a theatre, that it wanted . . . a full and understanding auditory." Moreover, "most of the people that come to that playhouse"—that is, the Red Bull—"resemble those ignorant asses (who visiting stationers' shops their use is not to inquire for good books, but new books) . . ." (ll. 4–10). Webster goes on to abuse "the uncapable multitude" and dazzle the intelligentsia, who he hopes will be his readers, with a fusillade of allusions to Martial, Horace, and Euripides. He insists that in modifying the strict Senecan conventions in the direction of popular taste he has "willingly, and not ignorantly . . . faulted," for if a dramatist for the Red Bull were to "present . . . the most sententious tragedy that ever was written, observing all the critical laws, as height of style, and gravity of person, enrich it with the sententious *Chorus*, and as it were lifen death, in the passionate and weighty *Nuntius*: yet after all this divine rapture" the breath of the illiterate unwashed, reeking with garlic, would be "able to poison it, and ere it be acted . . ." (ll. 15–22).[5]

Ironically, it is precisely the artistic compromise about which Webster was fretting in this absurdly overwritten preface that resulted in one of the greatest tragedies in English. For the play does possess a high degree of literary self-consciousness—the "height of style," "gravity of person," and sententiousness that its author so obviously admired—without sacrificing either dramatic tension and subtle characterization or the movement, color, and excitement that are essential for popular success in the theatre. There is plenty of action in *The White Devil*, and the play is, in fact, full of thrills, shocks, and surprises, but its poetic texture is richly concentrated and "difficult" (in the fashion of Chapman), its plot occasionally elliptical, and the view of life presented relentlessly terrible and dark. Webster's tragedy requires unflagging attention and makes intellectual as well as emotional demands. It was perhaps to be expected that audiences used to the comparative simplicity and unreflectiveness of Heywood's typical pieces would be put off by a deliberately "hard" writer such as Webster, one who emulated Jonson and Marston in his unconcealed scorn of mere crowd pleasers and who was bent on what Dekker described as "*Braue Triumphes* of *Poesie*, and *Elaborate Industry*."

The White Devil, despite its showy artifice and its utilization of conventions from revenge tragedy and Renaissance satire, represents in an important sense a return to history, for the dreadful events on which Webster based his plot had actually occurred, and in the very recent past. The subtitle summarizes these as "The Tragedy of *Paulo Giordano Ursini*, Duke of Brachiano, With the Life and Death of Vittoria Corombona the famous Venetian Curtizan."[6] The death mentioned was in fact a sensational murder in Padua that had taken place only twenty-seven years before *The White Devil* was first performed and that marked the climax in a whole series of violent and mysterious deaths. The bare facts of the case were ready-made for drama.

Vittoria Accoramboni, born in 1557 at Gubbio, a small town in the Tuscan hills, came from a poor but locally aristocratic family. Because of her extraordinary charm and beauty and in spite of a modest dowry, she was able to marry Francesco Peretti, a nephew of the powerful Cardinal Montalto, at Rome. She was only sixteen at the time. Peretti seems to have adored his attractive young wife, but about seven years after their marriage she met Paulo Giordano Orsini, the obese but highly influential Duke of Bracciano. Although twenty years her senior and physically gross, he pressed his attentions upon her and soon became Vittoria's lover, assisted in part by the encouragements of the girl's ambitious mother and the sinister machinations of her brother Marcello. But the duke, too, was already married—to the sister of the Grand Duke of Tuscany, Isabella de' Medici, upon whom he had fathered three children including Virginio (his son and heir), and who had herself entered into an adulterous love affair with one Troilo Orsini, a blood relation of her husband. This embarrassing situation eventuated in at least three premeditated murders. Isabella's brother, the Duke of Florence, arranged to have Troilo Orsini killed in Paris. Isabella "accidentally" met death—at the hands of her fat husband, it was rumored, or of her reigning brother eager to keep the honor of the House of Medici unspotted, or perhaps of both men in complicity with each other. Then, having engineered the assassination of Vittoria's husband Peretti (he was lured to a late rendezvous by Marcello, then in Bracciano's service, and shot in a deserted passageway), the recent widower secretly married the irresistible widow.

Pope Gregory XIII immediately ordered Bracciano and Vittoria to separate, and while an inquiry into the death of Peretti was being conducted, she was temporarily imprisoned at Rome in the Castello San Angelo. But nothing came of the investigations, and, upon her release, she rejoined her new husband, married him a second time, and held court with him as his duchess at the duke's ancestral estate in Bracciano. When Pope Gregory, who had harried the couple more or less continuously for four years, died in 1585, they immediately celebrated what they thought was their freedom by a third wedding, this time in public. Less than an hour after the nuptial blessing had been pronounced, however, the cardinals in conclave (with irony portentous for the lovers) decided to bestow the triple tiara of St. Peter upon Peretti's aggrieved uncle, Cardinal Montalto, who now took the title of Sixtus V. From this pontiff, of course, it was bootless to expect indulgence, and Bracciano with his duchess soon fled the papal states, first to Venice and then to Padua. The journey north had severely taxed the duke's health, and, plagued with an abcess on his leg in addition to his excessive corpulence, he moved to Salò on Lake Garda, where he died 13 November 1585, after ignoring his doctor's caution to eat nothing.

Vittoria tried to kill herself, failed, and then returned to Padua to live on the extravagant inheritance her late husband had provided for her in his will. But Isabella's relatives, the Medici, were furious at Vittoria's status, which they interpreted as menacing the welfare of Virginio, Bracciano's legitimate heir. A compromise was attempted, but when Vittoria refused to come to terms, the Duke of Florence allowed (if he did not specifically command) her to be ruthlessly murdered (along with Flaminio, her younger and innocent brother) by a band of ruffians under the direction of Lodovico Orsini. The assassin was a kinsman of Bracciano who had returned from banishment after a life of banditry and who detested Vittoria. She was twenty-eight at the time of her death. Lodovico was ultimately seized by the Venetian authorities and strangled in private with a red silk cord; the thugs under his command were severally tortured and executed in public. The Duke of Florence died a couple of years later, probably by poison, while Vittoria's intriguing brother Marcello, who had by chance escaped Lodovico's henchmen in Padua, was extradited from Venice to Ancona and beheaded there. A Greek sorceress whom Marcello had used to inflame Bracciano's passion for Vittoria was burned alive at the same time.

The White Devil deviates radically from these historical facts, some of which Webster could hardly have known except through gossip or rumor so soon after their occurrence. Gunnar Boklund, who has made an elaborate study of the possible sources for the play, numbers 109 different manuscript accounts and six published versions of the story, all theoretically available to Webster, but none of these can account for the particular combination of details that make up the play. The version that agrees best with the plot of Webster's tragedy (one of the least accurate historically) survives in the form of a brief newsletter written in German from Venice for the Fugger banking house. It seems likely, as Boklund has concluded, that Webster read some lost English translation or amplification of this document, probably in conjunction with other materials including an anonymous *Letter Lately Written from Rome* Englished from the Italian by John Florio (1585) and *A Treatise of the Election of Popes*, translated from the French of Hierome Bignon (1605). The Latin incantations over the dying Bracciano were based on *Funus*, one of the *Colloquies* of Erasmus. A possible influence that has not been suggested before is Chapman's *Bussy D'Ambois* (1604), a play that, like Webster's, involves in its denouement the conjuring up of spirits, the appearance of a ghost, a revenger disguised as a friar, pistol shots, and the sudden invasion of a gang of murderers. Webster praises Chapman in his preface and could well have imitated certain features of the earlier tragedy.

Many of Webster's departures from fact or shifts in emphasis were doubtless the result of poetic invention and dramatic license. The Vittoria of *The White Devil*, for instance, is directly implicated in the murders of her first husband and of Bracciano's wife. The corrupt brother (Flamineo in Webster, Marcello in history) plays a more important role in the drama than he did in life. Webster complicated Lodovico's motive for the murder of Vittoria by giving him an unrequited passion for Isabella. Also Prince Giovanni (the historical Virginio) becomes at the end of the play a titular force for the dispensation of justice and the restoration of civil order. Other incongruities were probably due to omissions, distortions, or misinformation in Webster's sources. The dramatist probably knew nothing of Isabella's adulterous affair with Troilo Orsini, of Bracciano's two private marriages to Vittoria and his morbid obesity, or of the Greek witch who was said to have given him love philtres. Webster may also have believed incorrectly that the real Bracciano was murdered, as he is in the play, and that Pope Sixtus had discouraged Lodovico from taking vengeance on Vittoria. But however incomplete his background knowledge or however freely he may have used it, Webster obviously regarded *The White Devil* as a major artistic effort, not just an ordinary potboiler. No wonder he was piqued by the cold response it provoked at the Red Bull. The evidence suggests that he revised and corrected a holographic or scribal copy before giving it to the printer.[7]

Webster's title, *The White Devil*, is pregnant with subtlety, for although its most obvious application is to Vittoria (Bracciano, referring to her beauty, describes her at one point as "the devil in crystal" who has led him "with fatal yokes of flowers" to his "eternal ruin" [IV.ii.88–91]), it also fits other leading characters—such as Flamineo and Bracciano—who commit and suffer the blackest evils while managing, some of the time at least, to preserve a luminous courage and stoical independence. Thus, the term comes to stand for the mysterious way in which good and evil interpenetrate, for it evokes the idea of hypocrisy (evil masking itself as good) as well as the paradoxical truth that certain "good" traits may only be embodied or expressed through evil. As Shakespeare's Henry V had observed, "There is some soul of goodness in things evil, / Would men observingly distill it out" so that men may "make a moral of the devil himself" (*Henry V*, IV.i.4–12). The title phrase was current in Webster's day, but the dramatist may well have been prompted by Cyril Tourneur's earlier use of it in *The Revenger's Tragedy*, a play that also exploits revenge, illicit passion, and horror in an Italian setting and that is probably based in part on another phase in the sensational history of the Medici.[8]

The same year *The White Devil* came out, Heywood published his *Apology for Actors*. Webster had mentioned him favorably with Dekker and Shakespeare in his preface to the tragedy, and now he showed his personal affection by writing a forceful poem to adorn his colleague's defense of the stage against Puritan attack. Heywood's argument is based chiefly on the antiquity of the theatre as a civilized institution and the tonic moral effect that plays can have on audiences. The second point had, in effect, been dramatized already by Webster and Dekker in *Westward Ho*, in which the lustful Earl is brought to repentance by theatrical means. Webster's endorsement is warm, and, exhilarated by the battle, he delights to level his satirical wit at the enemy:

> Such men who can in tune both raile and sing,
>   Shall, viewing this, either confess 'tis good,
> Or let their ignorance condemn the spring,
>   Because 'tis merry and renewes our blood.

But even in so slight a poem as "To his beloved friend, Master Thomas Heywood," we get Webster's characteristic view that a good piece of work is its own commendation:

> Be, therefore, your owne judgement your defence,
>   Which shall approve you better than my praise.[9]

* * *

On 6 November 1612 Henry, Prince of Wales, died suddenly of typhoid fever at the age of eighteen. Handsome, athletic, chivalrous, candid, and a hater of flattery, he was the precise opposite, in most respects, of his father, King James. Moreover, the prince, an honorary Merchant Taylor like Webster, had been the patron of a troupe of actors (including, at one point, Edward Alleyn) for whom the dramatist's colleagues, Middleton and Dekker, had both written plays.[10] Death had cruelly robbed the country of her national idol and future hope. The display of grief, which was elaborate, included such features as a waxen effigy of the prince fastened to the top of his coffin (the spectacular wax likenesses in *The Duchess of Malfi* may owe something to the event) and over thirty funeral laments composed by eminent poets such as Donne, Chapman, Giles Fletcher, Henry King, and Drummond of Hawthornden. Webster's contribution, written within six weeks of the burial, was an elegy entitled *A Monumental Column*, which the author dedicated, with his usual ostentation, to the king's favorite Sir Robert Carr, Viscount Rochester, and published in a volume, funereally decorated with black pages, as a companion to the elegies by two fellow dramatists, Tourneur and Heywood.[11] It seems oddly inconsistent to find Webster, whose plays regularly attack ambitious hypocrisy and the immorality of courts, addressing his "night-peece" to Carr—a name that has become synonomous with Jacobean sycophancy and corruption at their worst. But Webster was a friend of Carr's friend, Sir Thomas Overbury, and, in any case, may have been ignorant of the favorite's infatuation with the detestable Countess of Essex—an affair that was to lead in rapid succession to a scandalous annulment of her first marriage, a second marriage to Carr, and the horrible poisoning of Overbury in the Tower, which she instigated and for which they were both tried and convicted. Webster's use of the term "night-peece" in both the dedication (l. 11) and the poem proper (l. 295), literally a painting that depicts a nocturnal scene, was thus replete with unintended irony, for the playwright had used it earlier to describe the mass murders that conclude *The White Devil* so sensationally (V.vi.297). Moreover, since Pierre Matthieu's tribute to the assassinated Henry IV of France (translated by Grimestone in 1612) was Webster's chief source for the language of *A Monumental Column*, the violent death of royalty could scarcely have been excluded from the poet's mental context.

Webster crammed his elegy, an ambitious poem of some 330 lines in decasyllabic couplets, with sententiae, classical allusions, and metaphysical conceits, and, in the curious magpie fashion that was now becoming his hallmark, with echoes and appropriations from a number of poets, some of them personal friends, including Jonson, Chapman,[12] Sidney, Donne, Daniel, and perhaps Shakespeare. His conception of the poem as a "monumental column" erected to the prince's memory may even owe something to the ceremony of *Prince Henry's Barriers*, presented at court on Twelfth Night, 1610. This elaborate entertainment, for which Inigo Jones designed the decor and Jonson wrote speeches, presented a fallen house of chivalry complete with "*Obelisks* and *Columnes* broke, and downe" (l. 37) to symbolize the decay of those heroic and manly values that the valiant prince (on the threshold of his installation as Prince of Wales) was about to revivify.[13] To modern taste Webster's performance seems labored and structureless, but if it is less controlled than Tourneur's, it is also less pedestrian than Heywood's. The content is, of course, traditional. Webster develops the conventional Christian paradox that death has conferred immortal life upon the prince, "Whose happinesse is growne our punishment" (l. 145), and that his virtue and stoic preparedness for "larger titles, more triumphant wreathes" (l. 227), should serve those left behind as a *memento mori*:

> Now view his death-bed; and from thence let's meet
> In his example our owne winding-sheete.
> There his humility, setting apart
> All titles, did retire into his heart.
> O blessed solitarinesse that brings,
> The best content, to meane men and to Kings!—
>
> (ll. 201–206)

Webster struggles to balance contempt for the world, confidence in eternity, and the assertion that Providence is justified against the more immediate pain, and even horror, inflicted by "the al-controuling power of Fate" (l. 114). He opposes "the tempestious weather" (l. 295) of the season in which Henry died to "that glorious day" (l. 303) a few months in prospect when Princess Elizabeth will marry the Elector Palatine. But the harsh realities of the present rather than hopes for the future dominate the tone and much of the most vivid imagery. The emphasis on transience, the sense that "all our Scepters and our Chaires of State / Are but glasse-metal" (ll. 115–116) recalls, of course, the theme of *Sir Thomas Wyatt*.

Readers of Webster's tragedies will recognize in *A Monumental Column* some familiar techniques and preoccupations. A long apologue allegorizes the idea that Pleasure is but Sorrow disguised; Prince Henry, alive and dead, is like a "Christall glasse" (l. 234) broken in the blowing and then refashioned more perfectly to be sent as a present to "some great Prince" (l. 240).[14] Edward, the Black Prince, cut off before he could inherit his father's throne, becomes the heroic type of his descendant in an extended parallel that dwells with macabre wit upon the gruesome aspects of death and battle; Edward, like Henry, exemplified valor, humility, and steadfastness, and his

> resolution was so fiery still,
> It seem'd he knew better to die then kill:
> And yet drew Fortune, as the Adamant, Steele,
> Seeming t'have fixt a stay upon Her wheele:
> Who jestingly, would say it was his trade
> To fashion death-beds, and hath often made
> Horror looke lovely, when i' th' fields there lay
> Armes and legges, so distracted, one would say
> That the dead bodies had no bodies left.
>
> (ll. 80–88)

The startling grostesquerie of this passage, obviously designed to jolt the sensibility of the reader, would probably have offended Lucas less (he pronounced the lines "Surely the most detestable . . . in all Webster")[15] had he grasped the aesthetic principle behind it. In much of his most powerful work, Webster strove consciously to wrest some modicum of order from the most violent, threatening, and chaotic of experiences; to make "Horror looke lovely" and the ugly beautiful by means of artifice was, in fact, a major object of his poem, and it is equally an object of his most characteristic plays. The rhetorical distortions of *A Monumental Column*, "a broken *Columne*" (l. 143) like the youth it honors, are meant to express stylistically that sense of radical dislocation that is one of Webster's specialties. Here, as elsewhere, Sidney had supplied a precedent. The account of Amphialus's battle against Basilius in the *Arcadia* employs similar rhetoric for a similar purpose:

In one place lay disinherited heads, dispossessed of their natural seignories; in another whole bodies to see to, but that their hearts, wont to be bound all over so close, were now with deadly violence opened: in others, fouler deaths had uglily displayed their trailing guts. There lay arms, whose fingers yet moved as if they would feel for him that made them feel; and legs, which contrary to common reason, by being discharged of their burden, were grown heavier.

(III, 7)[16]

Employing a favorite association of ideas, Webster images death as the tyrant who lies in wait for "glorious *Youth*," then changes "his love into fell ravishment" (ll. 194–196); and he stresses earthly fame, which it is the poet's function to keep fresh, as a consolation for death.

The author's two references to the forthcoming marriage of the Prince of Wales's sister in the dark context of the poem's occasion seem more than merely consolatory, for they serve to exemplify the idea, abstractly expressed in the extended parable, that pleasure and sorrow are linked. Again, as so often in Webster, we have a disquieting juxtaposition of opposites in which dramatic possibilities are inherent. No more than a year after her brother's death had forced the princess Elizabeth to postpone her wedding, Shakespeare and Fletcher produced *The Two Noble Kinsmen* for the Blackfriars, a play that begins with the interruption of Duke Theseus's nuptial procession by a trio of mourning queens veiled in black and that ends with the summoning of Palamon from the executioner's block, "the stage of death" (V.iv.123),[17] to a happy reunion with Emilia. Webster himself was much attracted to the theme of death intruding upon marriage. It had figured importantly in *Sir Thomas Wyatt* and was to become a principle of dramatic construction in the three great plays of his middle period—the plays for which everyone remembers him. That the dramatist was aware of the theatrical implications of his material appears readily enough from the succession of images that evoke the stage: "till death made hope erre," the Prince's admirers "stood as in some spacious theater / Musing what would become of him" (ll. 47–49); the Black Prince, Henry's prototype, knew that heroic action, "not the gaudy show / Of ceremonies, do on Kings bestow / Best Theaters" (ll. 90–92); the royal figure lying on his deathbed confronted the press of "weeping visitants . . . As Kings at Revels sit," wishing "the crowd away . . . and himselfe asleepe" (ll. 215–217).

Not surprisingly, since it was Webster's habit to borrow from himself as well as others, we meet the same line applied to Henry that the dramatist also used for Antonio's description of the Duchess of Malfi: the beams from the prince's "hollow Tombe, / Staine the time past, and light the time to come" (l. 278).[18] Even the Old Lady of *The Duchess*, whose face is so full of "deep ruts and foul sloughs" that "to behold [her] not painted inclines somewhat near a miracle" (*The Duchess of Malfi*, II.i.23–25) makes a preliminary appearance in the poem: the allegorical Sorrow, who dons Pleasure's garments, meets an "old Court Lady" who "paints" herself "to adde a grace, / To the deformity of her wrinkled face." Although there is no phrasal similarity, Webster continued to be much concerned with the cosmetic excesses of courtly women and the "impost[ure]" and "haggish false-hood" of which they were symbolic (ll. 172–179).

Hampered by his slow rate of composition, Webster was obviously pressed by the need to produce his elegy quickly. "I hasted, till I had this tribute paid / Unto his grave, so let the speede excuse / The zealous error of my passionate *Muse*" (ll. 310–312), he writes, not scrupling to hit at competitors who have already been before him with their "waste Elegies" and "scraps of commendation more base / Then are the ragges they are writ on" (ll. 260–262).

*   *   *

Slow composition notwithstanding, Webster seems to have completed his greatest play within a year after writing *A Monumental Column*. Actually, as careful study of the sources shows, *The Duchess of Malfi* was probably begun as early as 1612, when *The White Devil* made its unsuccessful bow at the Red Bull; Webster then interrupted work on Act III in order to compose the elegy on Prince Henry (*The Duchess* at this point levied upon many of the same works as the poem), but he continued apparently to work on the later acts of the tragedy well into 1613. Although not published until a decade later, *The Duchess of Malfi* could be seen in London at least by 1614, for William Ostler, who took the part of Antonio in the first production, died on 16 December of that year. The new tragedy must have made its first appearance on the stage during the winter season of 1613–1614 or perhaps during the following spring or autumn.

The company was the King's Men, the most popular and talented group of actors in the kingdom, for whom Webster had ten years earlier written his Induction to *The Malcontent*. The change in auspices from the Queen's to the King's Men meant an obvious rise in prestige, for Shakespeare's company performed at court oftener than the others and, besides, regularly occupied the two best playhouses in London—the Globe on the bankside, which was partially open and depended on daylight, and the Blackfriars in the city proper, which was enclosed and artificially illuminated by torch or candlelight. The title page of the 1623 quarto says that *The Duchess* was performed at both theatres, but mention of the Blackfriars first and in larger type may indicate that the tragedy was thought of more as a play for "private" than for "public" performance. Indeed, John Russell Brown has suggested that the play calls for certain effects of lighting and dramatic silence that would be especially appropriate to the conditions of the smaller and more intimate private house.[19] If this was the case, Webster must have been highly gratified; his new audience would have been several cuts above "the uncapable multitude" that had received *The White Devil* so indifferently. When the play was published in 1623, it included a list of the cast, giving two names each for the parts of Ferdinand, the Cardinal, and Antonio. This is good evidence that the play had been revived with a different cast around 1619, the date of Burbage's death, after which Joseph Taylor, Burbage's replacement in the role of Ferdinand, joined the King's Men. An earlier revival is also likely, for the Venetian envoy Orazio Busino, writing from London on 7 February 1618, described a performance that he had presumably seen not long before:

they showed a cardinal in all his grandeur, in the formal robes appropriate to his station, splendid and rich, with his train in attendance, having an altar erected on the stage, where he pretended to make a prayer, organizing a procession; and then they produced him in public with a harlot on his knee. They showed him giving poison to one of his sisters, in a question of honour. Moreover he goes to war, first laying down his cardinal's habit on the altar, with the help of his chaplains, with great ceremoniousness; finally he has his sword bound on and dons the soldier's sash with so much panache you could not imagine it better done. And all this was acted in condemnation of the grandeur of the Church, which they despise and which in this kingdom they hate to the death.[20]

After publication there was a third revival on 26 December 1630, when *The Duchess* was played before King Charles I in the new Cockpit Theatre at Whitehall,[21] and the play continued to hold the stage at the Restoration.

Some of the most prominent members of Shakespeare's company performed in the tragedy. In addition to Burbage and Taylor (the successive Ferdinands), John Lowin, Henry Condell, William Ostler, Richard Sharpe, John Thompson, and Robert Pallant all took parts. Lowin, who appeared as Bosola, later (according to T. W. Baldwin) played the title role in Fletcher's *Valentinian* and Alberto in *The Fair Maid of the Inn* by Fletcher, Massinger, Webster, and Ford.[22] Condell, who acted the Cardinal, was of course one of the supervisors of the First Folio. Ostler, who, as already mentioned, played Antonio, also took roles in Jonson's *Poetaster*, *Alchemist*, and *Catiline*. Sharpe, Thompson, and Pallant were boys who acted the Duchess, Julia, and Cariola respectively. Sharpe was apparently the "leading lady" of the troupe for some years prior to 1623.[23] Obviously, the acceptance of this tragedy by the King's Men demonstrates that

Webster had achieved—and in his own lifetime—a substantial measure of professional recognition.

For *The Duchess of Malfi* as for *The White Devil*, Webster again went to sixteenth-century Italian history. But this time he got his facts only after they had been fictionalized by Matteo Bandello in his twenty-sixth novella, greatly expanded and moralized in a French adaptation by François de Belleforest (the second volume of his *Histoires Tragiques*, 1565), and finally translated from French into English, with minor shifts of emphasis, by William Painter in his *Palace of Pleasure* (1567). Whether or not Webster could read Italian (there is some reason to suspect that he could not), Painter was obviously his main source, and the dramatist may not have realized that the historical Delio, who in Bandello's account tries to warn Antonio of his impending assassination, was very likely the Italian author himself.[24] The ultimate source behind Webster's tragedy seems, then, to have been written by a man who had some firsthand knowledge of the people and events he describes under the guise of an entertaining tale. The case of the Duchess of Amalfi, who mysteriously disappeared with two of her children a few months before her husband's murder in October 1513, occasioned much less scandal than the death of Vittoria Accoramboni seventy-two years later, but in this instance the principals, although noble, were less prominent and the revengers more discreet and efficient.

In life the duchess was the daughter of Enrico d'Aragona, a half brother of King Federico, the last Aragonian to occupy the throne of Naples. Her brother, Lodovico d'Aragona, was born in 1474, created Marquis of Gerace in 1489, married to the granddaughter of a pope in 1493, almost immediately made a widower, and then installed as Cardinal of Aragon in 1494. He fought in various military campaigns despite his ecclesiastical calling, enjoyed considerable influence, political, cultural, and military, especially under Pope Julius II, and died quietly at Rome in 1519. His younger and more obscure brother assumed the secular title of Marquis of Gerace upon Lodovico's acceptance of the red hat. Their sister Giovanna, a few years younger than Lodovico, was married in 1490 as a child of twelve to Alfonso Piccolomini, who three years later inherited the dukedom of Amalfi but who did not live to see the birth of a son, Alfonso, in 1499. For some ten years Giovanna presided over the duchy as regent for her young son. Then she suddenly fled Amalfi in November 1510 with a great retinue, ostensibly to visit the religious shrine at Loretto, but actually to join Antonio Bologna at Ancona. The man she met was her former household steward, whom she had secretly married. The couple had tried to conceal their relationship for several years, but the birth of three children, the last not until after the duchess reached Ancona, made matters increasingly difficult, and she and her lower-born husband (like Vittoria and Bracciano) seem never to have had a moment's peace once their marriage became public knowledge. They soon moved from Ancona to Siena and then again from Siena toward Venice, but were intercepted at Forli. Antonio with his eldest son escaped to Milan, where he was murdered in October 1513, but the duchess with their two other children was conducted back to Amalfi and never seen again. She was probably murdered. Alfonso, the duchess's son by her first marriage, became Duke of Amalfi.

Amalfi was only a minor duchy, and the few contemporary documents independent of Bandello that survive contain little to suggest that the brothers of the duchess were responsible for her death or her second husband's. Nevertheless, Bandello's remarkably objective, slightly cynical account is probably true in essentials. Here we learn, for instance, that the relationship between Antonio and the lady was a genuine love match, that their secret marriage was witnessed by a chambermaid who, despite Antonio's suspicions to the contrary, remained loyal to her mistress and died with her, that the Aragonian brothers (their motives are not probed) had their sister and two of her children strangled in Amalfi, that Antonio, living in Milan, was kept ignorant of his wife's death even while he hoped naively for a reconciliation with the cardinal, and that Delio, who had tried to warn him, witnessed his murder there at the hands of Daniele da Bozolo (a Lombard captain employed by the avenging brothers) and three assistants.

Belleforest, inflating Bandello's version to four times the original size, not only casts much of the story into long dialogues and soliloquies but, with his penchant for sermonizing, entirely alters the point of view. He stresses the incredible savagery of the cardinal and his brother, bringing out particularly at one point the latter's violent anger. Although he still treats their victims with a certain amount of sympathy, he strongly disapproves of the secret marriage between a person of royal blood and a commoner as a breach of degree, regarding it, despite the technical religious validity, as a cover for folly and wantonness; and he makes Antonio more prudential, ambitious, and sentimental in motive than Bandello had done. But heavy-handed as Belleforest's treatment is in many respects, it nevertheless provided Webster, through Painter's translation, with a basis for characterizations of impressive subtlety and complexity.

We know that Webster was influenced, incidentally, by a few other works besides Painter's for certain aspects of the narrative line, and indebtedness to still other writers for different purposes is probable as well. He drew upon Edward Grimestone's translation of Simon Goulart's *Admirable and Memorable Histories* (1607) for Ferdinand's lycanthropy in Act V, and may therefore have read that author's version of the fatal romance between Antonio and the duchess in the same volume—a romance that Goulart without hesitation condemns as unchaste. An equally unsympathetic version had appeared in Thomas Beard's *Theatre of God's Judgements* (1597), but Webster had also read George Whetstone's somewhat more indulgent *Heptameron of Civil Discourses* (1582) in which it is said of the duchess's "base choice" that "a woman looseth none of her general titles of dignitie by matching w' her inferior."[25] Webster may have gone to Geoffrey Fenton's English version of Guicciardini's *History of Italy* (1579) and a passage in Dekker, Haughton, and Day's drama *Lust's Dominion* (II.i.39–53) for suggestions about the martial side of the cardinal's character.[26] He may also have got Ferdinand's trick with the severed hand in Act IV out of Herodotus— either through Bandello (in the novella immediately preceding the story of the duchess) or through Barnabe Riche's English translation of *The Famous History of Herodotus* (1584). If Webster could understand Italian or Spanish, possibily he derived some of his ideas from Cinthio's novella about the love of Oronte for Orbecche or from Lope de Vega's play *El Mayordomo de la Duquesa de Amalfi*,[27] both of which offer some striking parallels to the English tragedy. That he used Sidney's *Arcadia* is certain, for the play abounds in verbal borrowings from that source besides adapting details for the Duchess's sufferings in Act IV from Sidney's episode in which Queen Cecropia imprisons and torments the princesses Pamela and Philoclea, exposes them to darkness and noise, and makes one of them witness the apparent execution of the other. Probably, the echo scene is also indebted to Sidney's romance. Certain ritualistic aspects of the torture episodes Webster very likely took from the tradition of the antimasque, a grotesque parody (sometimes involving madmen) that in the early seventeenth century often preceded the main or regular elements of a court masque. Two of the three lavish entertainments presented at the festivities for Princess Elizabeth's wedding (by Campion and by Beaumont) included "frantics" who appeared "in sundry habits and humours."[28]

Webster made some meaningful changes in the story as he found it in Painter. Most of these enrich the play's characterization, intensify its irony, and enlarge its scope, thereby complicating the moral impression and deepening the tragic effect. For instance, he amalgamated the various instruments of the Aragonian brothers into the single character of Bosola, a minor figure in the source who appears only at the very end. Webster's Bosola thus becomes essential to the action from the start; he is given an internal life that changes and develops; and he kills Antonio, not deliberately as in Painter, but ironically in an attempt to save him. Not only does he die himself in the play after having presided over the torture and execution of the Duchess, but also, by stabbing both the Cardinal and Ferdinand, he becomes, with still further irony, a justicer. In fact, the entire fifth act, devoted as it is to the aftermath of the Duchess's murder, is Webster's invention. The finale includes Antonio's mysterious vision of his wife from the grave, the Cardinal's relationship with his mistress Julia (a wholly new character in Webster), Ferdinand's madness, the violent deaths of all the remaining characters, and the establishment of Antonio's son as Duke of Amalfi. In Painter, the wicked brothers and Bosola survive, and the Duchess's eldest son by her first marriage inherits the title.

A few other alterations are worth mentioning. Webster made Painter's Delio a friend and confidant of Antonio. He changed the character of Castruchio from a cardinal to a superannuated husband for Julia and made the shadowy midwife of the source into a repulsive "Old Lady," in both cases for satiric purposes. He increased sympathy for Antonio by playing down the ambitious and prudential side of his nature; he altered the figure of Cariola, making her less sophisticated and more conventionally pious (in Painter she invents the escape strategy of feigning a religious pilgrimage whereas in Webster she opposes it); and he gave Bosola the function of commentator by re-creating him as an odd compound of cynicism and conscience, a frustrated railer of the type Webster already knew from Marston's *Malcontent*. He balanced the lovers against the two brothers by giving the latter a continuous prominence that they did not have in Painter; he cleverly differentiated their temperaments so as to make them embody different kinds of evil; and he completely altered their relationship to the Duchess by having them warn her about remarriage and spy upon her before she weds for the second time. Webster invented the terrifying scene in which Ferdinand breaks into the Duchess's bedchamber; he delayed the escapes of both the lovers, and greatly increased the effect of pity and fear by prolonging the heroine's suffering and death. Most subtly of all, he managed to assimilate and reconcile contradictory or ambivalent attitudes to both the Duchess and her steward that could be found in various parts of the source material.

One other source for *The Duchess*, as yet unmentioned, was the dramatist's earlier *White Devil*. To quote Brown's perceptive words,

Webster had a persistent and brooding mind, and for him creation often involved repetition; he worked in series, like a painter who re-aligns the elements of one composition in his next to suggest less obvious inter-relations, new astringencies, or sudden simplifications of form. Within Webster's plays, scenes echo each other, and his two great tragedies, both set at court and with a central heroine, are in important ways two versions of a single subject.[29]

Bosola, for instance, is in some respects a reworking of Flamineo in the sister tragedy. Webster's fascination with such malcontent figures, impoverished intellectuals forced to degrade their talents and corrupt their integrity in the service of naked power or courtly values they despise, may have had its foundation to some extent in Webster's own life. Much of this, no doubt, derives from the fashion of Renaissance satire that pervades the dramatic and nondramatic literature of Jacobean England. Nevertheless, the intense bitterness and disillusionment that the characters often express coupled with Webster's own repeated lashings out at toadyism and flattery tempt the biographer, lacking facts, to posit some abiding resentment in the dramatist's personal experience that finds expression in the plays.

The Duchess of Malfi proved to be one of the most respected tragedies of the period, and when Webster published it in 1623 almost a decade after its composition, he did so with some of the ponderous self-importance that had marked his publication of *The White Devil*. Bibliographical evidence suggests that Webster took pains to see that the printed edition would be fully authoritative. Probably he had helped correct his earlier tragedy in press, and now he followed the same procedure in the case of its successor.[30] His characteristic indifference to clear or complete stage directions, which the quarto of 1623 betrays, is merely an indication that he thought of the volume more as a reading than an acting version, but his interest in the printed text, likely set from a transcript prepared by the well-known scrivener Ralph Crane and approved by the author, may be inferred from certain details. The title page advertises the "perfect and exact Coppy, with diuerse *things Printed, that the length of the Play would* not beare in the Presentment" (in other words, the restoration of acting cuts); and the lyrics sung in Act III for the ceremony of the Cardinal's arming are printed with the marginal notation, "The author disclaims this ditty to be his." Everything about the quarto, in fact, suggests a studied formality. Not only are the names of the performers given—a most unusual feature at the time—but also the play, unlike the first quarto of *The White Devil*, is carefully divided into acts and scenes, and (as is standard in manuscripts prepared by Crane) the names of characters are grouped together at the start of a scene instead of being located where the entrances actually occur in the action. This latter arrangement recalls the "classical" practice of learned dramatists such as Jonson, the first Elizabethan to regard his plays as "works" and to superintend their publication personally.

Webster, of course, was eager to attract patronage, and he dedicated *The Duchess* to George Harding, Baron Berkeley, a young Oxford man who, as a direct descendant of the first and second Lords Hunsdon, had obvious connections with the King's Men. Harding was already the dedicatee of Burton's *Anatomy of Melancholy*, and in the future received dedications of plays from both Massinger and Shirley. Webster's attitude is complacent, even bumptious, but in this too he may have been affecting the posture of "learned" men like Jonson and Chapman: "I do not altogether look up at your *title*, the ancientest *nobility* being but a *relic* of time past, and the truest *honour* indeed being for a man to confer *honour* on himself. . . . I am confident this work is not unworthy your *Honour*'s perusal; for by such *poems* as this, *poets* have kissed the hands of *great princes*" (ll. 12–19). It is surely significant that Webster nowhere uses the word "play" in the dedication but refers to *The Duchess* as a "work," a "poem" that, if favorably received, will enhance his Lordship's reputation not merely as a patron but as an "example" of learning.[31] An approving response, Webster writes, "shall make you live in your grave and *laurel* spring out of it, when the ignorant scorners of the *Muses* (that like worms in *libraries* seem to live only to destroy *learning*) shall wither, neglected and forgotten" (ll. 22–25). An obscurely abbreviated Latin motto on the title page (a tag from Horace) sounds even more blatant: "If you know wiser precepts than these of mine, kindly tell me; if you do not, practice these with me." Such is the sense of Horace's original, and by quoting from it, Webster seems to dare readers to name a better or at least more thoughtful play than his own. The quotation, however, was not uncommon, and our suspicions as to how Webster may have come by it are instantly aroused by the discovery that Dekker had appropriated the same words for his *Lanthorne and Candle-light* (1609). The application to *The Duchess* is strained, and one wonders whether Webster did not include the cryptic Latin more for scholarly effect than for sense.

Middleton, Rowley, and Ford, all at one time or another collaborators with Webster, composed verses of commendation for the volume. Middleton, signing himself "Poet and Chronologer of London," wrote with more professional detachment than the others and in terms that could hardly fail to please "that well-deserver, Mr. John Webster," since he pays court to the author's artistic integrity and much-cultivated forthrightness. After calling *The Duchess* "this masterpiece of tragedy," "this work of fame," Middleton manages through his choice of images to associate the author's literary achievement with the tragic dignity of the play's heroine:

> Thy monument is rais'd in thy life-time;
> And 'tis most just; for every worthy man
> Is his own marble, and his merit can
> Cut him to any figure and express
> More art than Death's cathedral palaces,
> Where royal ashes keep their court. Thy note
> Be ever plainness, 'tis the richest coat:
> Thy epitaph only the title be—
> Write, 'Duchess,' that will fetch a tear for thee.

Rowley's brief verses "To his friend . . ." are more routine and emphasize the verisimilitude of the title character, how she is "lively body'd in thy play." But Ford's are the most generous of all, for they claim that the drama challenges comparison with the great tragedies of antiquity:

> Crown him a poet, whom nor Rome, nor Greece,
> Transcend in all theirs, for a masterpiece.

Although this praise is partly conventional, it nevertheless gives some indication of the high regard in which *The Duchess of Malfi* was held by Webster's fellows. The play continued to be popular throughout the remainder of the century, and reprints were issued in 1640, 1678, and 1708. A certain emotional coloring creeps into the eighteenth-century titles: the fourth edition was called *The Unfortunate Duchess of Malfi, or the Unnatural Brothers*, and Theobald's adaptation of 1735 was presented as *The Fatal Secret*.

*   *   *

Early in 1614, after Webster finished *The Duchess of Malfi* (or perhaps slightly before), Sir Thomas Overbury's didactic poem *A Wife* appeared in print. The prominent author, secretary to the king's favorite Sir Robert Carr and a friend of Jonson widely admired for his cultivation and wit, had died appallingly by poison only months earlier on 15 September 1613. Thus it is not surprising that these pedestrian stanzas, written in the form made popular by Shakespeare's *Venus and Adonis*, should have enjoyed such posthumous success, particularly after the scandal became public. The poem characterizes the ideal Jacobean wife as a woman of modesty, circumspection, domestic efficiency, discretion, intellectual unpretentiousness, and devotion to her husband, and generalizes sententiously about the theological, natural, social, and sexual purposes of matrimony. It is possible, as some have speculated, that one of Overbury's motives in composing what amounts to a versified character was to warn his master Carr against the disastrous marriage to the Countess of Essex. If so, Overbury would unwittingly have been exacerbating the grotesque hatreds that culminated in his own murder. That Webster admired the poem is clear from the fact that he twice lifted a phrase out of it for his own use—once in *The Devil's Law-Case* and again in his dedication of *The Duchess* to Baron Berkeley.[32] But his association with *A Wife* must have been somewhat closer than mere verbal borrowing would imply.

A few months after the first edition of *A Wife* was published, a second edition appeared bearing a title page that announced the addition of "many witty Characters . . . *written by* [Overbury] *himselfe and other* learned Gentlemen his friends." This volume, which contains twenty-two of the famous sketches or portraits in the genre forever linked with Overbury's name, became the core of a rapidly expanding collection that by 1622 had reached an eleventh edition enlarged to a total of eighty-three characters by various contributors, mostly anonymous. Since the characters added to later editions imitate the original twenty-two in style and method, and since not even these first are wholly by Overbury, the problems of attribution are complex. Nevertheless, certain conclusions are possible.

Webster's enemy John Cocke claimed that three characters in the sixth edition were his own, but had been tampered with by "the ridiculous and bold dealing of an vnknowne botcher" whom he identifies as the author of *An Excellent Actor*—that is, Webster.[33] Dekker probably contributed six characters on the theme of debt and prison life to the ninth edition of 1616.[34] Donne seems to have written the final sketch, *A True Character of a Dunce*, anonymously added to the eleventh edition of 1622, but reprinted as Donne's thirty years later in his son's edition of his father's works.[35] Webster had become connected with the anthology at least by 1615, and perhaps earlier. Verbal parallels with the playwright's other works of the same period, the use of several of his favorite sources, his habit of adapting the same borrowing to more than one context, the chronology (as closely as it can be reconstructed), and the dramatist's known attraction to the form of the character in his plays,[36] together provide strong evidence that Webster is the author of a group of thirty-two characters added to the sixth edition of 1615.[37] Webster was probably the editor of this sixth edition, for apart from contributing a major section of the book, no doubt composed expressly to feed the public appetite for more new characters "drawne to the life," he appears to have been responsible for the general title page, which carries one of his favorite Latin mottoes, *non norunt haec monumenta mori* ("These are the monuments that know not how to die"). Webster had already used this quotation (from Martial) in his preface to *The White Devil* (1612), and would use it again to adorn the title page of his mayoral pageant, *Monuments of Honor* (1624).

Although the evidence is admittedly tenuous, Webster may have supervised the four editions of the characters that immediately preceded the sixth and perhaps even have contributed to them as one of Overbury's "learned" friends. An unsigned preface in the second edition headed "*The Printer to the Reader*" and dated 16 May 1614 adopts the characteristic Websterian tone of arrogant condescension. After sneering at his audience's probable "*ignorance*" of "*the deepe Arte of Poetry*," their "*usuall contempt or aspersion*" of both "*frivolous, and fantasticke labours*," and their predictable failure to distinguish between "*a quaffing fellowes barbarisme*" and "*a worthy-written stile in Tragedies*," the writer goes on to speak of the characters *not* by Overbury ("*the first author*") as "*little inferior to the residue . . . and first transcrib'd by Gentlemen of the same qualitie. . . .*" All twenty-two of the characters that constitute the "*surplusage*" over the original edition of *A Wife* the writer now claims to publish "*upon good inducements*" from Overbury and the other contributors "*with warrantie of their and my owne credit.*"[38] The publisher of all the earliest editions was Lawrence Lisle, but the tone of this preface, several times reprinted after its initial appearance, could hardly be that of a professional bookseller; it was almost certainly written by an editor commissioned for the task, and its deliberately crabbed, obscurely contorted style fits Webster exactly. The whole preface, in fact, sounds like the product of an actual member of Overbury's fashionable circle of wits and intellectuals, or at least of someone who was straining very hard to give that impression. Indeed, the preface and Webster's virtually established role in the sixth edition of the characters a year later tempt one to conclude that the dramatist, in effect, became Overbury's literary executor, and further that he was personally responsible for collecting the original group of characters that had doubtless been circulating in manuscript and seeing them through the press. The trial of Carr and Frances Howard in 1615 for the murder of Overbury undoubtedly added to the notoriety (and hence to the salability) of the volume.

The prose character, which erupted into fashion with Joseph Hall's *Characters of Vertues and Vices* (1608) and the Overbury collection (directly influenced by Hall's book), had a complex literary ancestry. In the distant background, of course, lay the work of Theophrastus (c. 373–284 B.C.), the Greek delineator of specific vices, whose brief essays were translated into Latin by Casaubon in 1592 and whom Hall acknowledged as a model. In the middle distance, Chaucer's sharply observed portraits of the Canterbury pilgrims must have influenced the taste for colorful figures in whom the universal qualities of humanity were given a local habitation. But more important than either of these precedents was a combination of elements from recent or contemporary literature. Familiar or local types satirically struck off by means of a few traits or mannerisms dextrously chosen for their social particularity and vividness, as well as for the moral animus they might excite, could already be found in the satire, pamphlets, and drama of the age. A parade of would-be courtiers and fops, blustering cowards, hypocritical Puritans, and foolish travelers already strutted upon the stage in Jonson's comedy of humours. The rogue literature and "cony-catching" pamphlets of Greene, Nashe, and Dekker had already set the style for descriptions of vagabonds, gulls, petty criminals, and other lower-class types. The satires of Hall and Marston and the epigrams of Jonson seem to have influenced the scurrilous tone and pithy style of many of the characters and to have suggested the recurrent emphasis on certain social affectations and absurdities in the professional and wealthier classes.

In the hands of Overbury, Webster, and their fellows, the character often became more an exercise in witty exposure and malicious mockery than the serious examination of an isolable evil. For the author of characters, unlike the strict allegorist, accidents of environment could assume an importance semi-independent of the human failings therein illustrated. Even when they turned to the portraiture of virtues rather than vices, the Overburian writers tended to conceive their ideal figures in terms of a social milieu and to use their subjects as vehicles for elaborately "conceited" writing. The rhetorical technique, calculated to dazzle, jar, or surprise the reader with verbal acrobatics, paradoxes, puns, "metaphysical" analogies, sententiae, and abrupt shifts of direction, was fundamentally unsuited to sustained or searching analysis. The method encouraged a monadic paragraph structure in which a series of discrete sentences, each with its own witty kernel or distillation of meaning, required the reader to move by jerks from one emphatic point to the next until he reached a concluding aphorism that put the stamp of finality upon all that had gone before.

The characters sometimes have a racy, journalistic interest. Their quaint appeal includes historical impressions of dress, social behavior, and setting, such as a Jacobean diarist might offer; but the realism, particularly in its visual aspect, is nearly always introduced in the service of generalization, analogy, a pun, *discordia concors*, or some other device of wit. The idea seems to have been to build up a generic portrait, whether idealized or satiric, by presenting a random but more or less typical collection of details—mental habits, beliefs, opinions, social mannerisms, moral attitudes, clothes, pastimes, occupational activities—that in combination would reveal the essence behind the facade. The purpose, of course, was didactic; the athletic brevity and ingenuity of style were, theoretically at least, a means of combining moral weight with lightness of touch. One of the late additions to the Overbury collection, a sort of character of a character, conveys the self-consciously "wrought" quality of the style by its recourse to metaphors from carpentry, drawing, and music:

To square out a Character by our English levell, it is a picture (reall or personall) quaintlie drawne in various collours, all of them heightened by one shadowing.
It is a quicke and softe touch of many strings, all shutting up in one musicall close: It is wits descant on any plaine song.

(Paylor, ed., p. 92)

This description applies so accurately to the best of Webster's thirty-two characters, which are generally more controlled and unified than the others in the collection, that it might well serve as the epigraph for the dramatist's particular contribution to the anthology.

The Webster group is impressive in variety and range. Country types, tradesmen, servants, upstarts of various sorts, and even criminals are intermingled with gentle folk and people from the military, ecclesiastical, legal, and medical professions. Twice, in calculated contrasts of the idealizing mode with the satiric, Webster pairs characters, balancing *A Worthy Commander in the Wars* against *A Vainglorious Coward in Command* and *A Virtuous Widow* against *An Ordinary Widow*. These latter two illustrate the incidental interest that the characters may sometimes hold for readers of Websterian drama. Both express a decidedly negative attitude toward remarriage and therefore serve to modify overly simple responses to the Duchess of Malfi's secret alliance with Antonio in the tragedy. Webster's magpie method of composition in the characters could be predicted by any student of the plays, for here, as there, the dramatist lifts ideas freely both from himself and from others. *A Worthy Commander*, for instance, contains obvious debts to Hall's *Of a Valiant Man*, and numerous details of style and content show that Webster regularly levied upon earlier characters in the Overbury collection, as well as upon his own characters among the thirty-two. His sketch of the carping academic, the intellectually fraudulent *Fellow of a House*, merely embroiders ideas set forth earlier in the anonymous *Mere Fellow of an House* that immediately precedes the Webster group in the sixth edition. His *Devilish Usurer* is ridiculed, in the terms he also applies to his *Mere Pettifogger* (an unscrupulous attorney), as avaricious enough to hide money with the intention of recovering it after his own death, and inhumane enough to take *The Penal Statutes* for his favorite reading.

Much of the local color in the characters, heightened as it frequently is by mild or outrageous hyperbole, undoubtedly reflects personal experience. As a publishing dramatist, Webster must have known young scribes such as *A Puny Clerk*—a country bumpkin apprenticed to an Inns-of-Court man who "doth itch towards a Poet," "greases his breches extreamely with feeding without a napkin," "eates Gingerbread at a Play-house," and tries to disguise his laziness by making the words in his copy "spread" and by affecting the "swooping *Dash*" (Lucas, ed., *Works*, IV, 28). Since the poet's family was connected with the livery trade, Webster clearly had firsthand knowledge of such Smithfield swindlers as *An Arrant Horse-courser*. This rascal furnishes hackneys that break down ten miles out of London, and practices endless deceptions upon buyers of horses—powdering the animals' "eares with Quicksilver" and giving them "suppositories of live Eeles" to make them appear spirited, disguising "all manner of Diseases" in a beast fit only for the slaughterhouse, and regretting that he cannot make the wretched animal "goe on a wodden legge and two crutches" (*Works*, IV, 31). The fop whom Webster characterizes in *An Improvident Young Gallant* was certainly familiar to him, as we know already from his satirical induction to Marston's *Malcontent*. Webster's contempt is almost Swiftian. The impudent "phantastique" is frizzled "like a Baboone," squanders his money on wagers and whores, and sits upon the stage of a private theatre—Webster may well have had one or both of the two Blackfriars auditoriums in mind, where *The Malcontent* and *The Duchess of Malfi* were performed—to show off his newest clothes: "and when the Play is done, if you but mark his rising, 'tis a kind of walking Epilogue betweene the two Candles, to know if his Suite may passe for currant" (*Works*, IV, 33).

Colorful bits of Jacobean social history abound. We are introduced to the noisy London *Waterman* whose familiar cries had supplied the titles for *Westward Ho*, *Eastward Ho*, and, by extension, *Northward Ho* a decade earlier when Webster was regularly collaborating with Dekker, and who is especially busy in the afternoons ferrying playgoers to and from the bankside. Webster sees him as a surly opportunist (we recognize at once the ancestor of a certain species of modern cab driver) for whom London Bridge is "the most terriblest eye-sore" (*Works*, IV, 38) because it offers an alternative means of crossing the river. Two of the characters convey some sense of the sizable Dutch population then resident in England. *A Drunken Dutchman* and *A Button-maker of Amsterdam* recall Jonson's self-indulgent Puritans. The first, obese from drinking beer, "stinks of Butter, as if he were noynted all over for the Itch"; he and his ilk "swarme in great Tenements like Flyes: six House-holds will live in a Garret" (*Works*, IV, 32). The second, having fled Holland for his conscience's sake and "left his wife and children upon the Parish," hates Latin, the sign of the cross, and feasts as Popish abominations, yet can nevertheless "out-eat six of the fattest *Burgers*; "his zeale consists much in hanging his Bible in a Dutch button" (*Works*, IV, 33). *A Canting Rogue* gives a glimpse of a whole class of vagrant ne'er-do-wells, constantly on the move throughout the countryside, unemployed, indigent, babbling their strange argot, and sleeping in groups as large as forty wherever a barn offers shelter.

The scornful portraits greatly outnumber the sympathetic ones, and if we read the whole group at a sitting, it is easy to tire of the insistent debunking.

Therefore we welcome the grateful radiance of the idealized characters, which often project a genuine poetic charm and suggest the world of a George Herbert or an Izaak Walton. Webster's *Noble and Retired Housekeeper* and his *Franklin* remind us that hospitality, sweet reasonableness, sincerity, cheerfulness, humility, and piety without ostentation could still persist quietly among the rural gentry in an era that we often think of as almost irremediably cynical and worldly. Webster's *Franklin*, more highly idealized than Chaucer's, evokes nostalgia for a merrier and less sophisticated age:

His outside is an ancient Yeoman of England. . . . He is taught by nature to be contented with a little. . . . He allowes of honest pastime, and thinkes not the bones of the dead any thing brused, or the worse for it, though the Countrey Lasses daunce in the Churchyard after Evensong.

(*Works*, IV, 43–44)

The *Noble Housekeeper* can face death tranquilly with resignation and dignity in the same spirit as the Duchess of Malfi. Not surprisingly, in this character Webster even echoes words that he had already assigned to his tragic heroine:

He hath this hand over *Fortune*, that her injuries, how violent or sodaine soever, they doe not daunt him; for whether his time call him to live, or die, he can do both nobly: if to fall, his descent is breast to breast with vertue; and even then, like the *Sunne* neare his Set, hee shewes unto the world his *clearest countenance*.

(*Works*, IV, 29)[39]

Despite such eloquence the style is uneven. Too many of the characters are more memorable for a few of their ingredients than for wholeness of impression, and Webster's wit can be so forced, garish, or disproportionate to its subject that the overall effect is like that of a new costume wearing its owner. The incessant punning is partly responsible, for one of Webster's favorite devices is the sentence that reads like the solution to a conundrum. The *Usurer* loves no "Good Deedes" unless they be "Seal'd and Delivered; nor doth he wish any thing to thrive in the Countrey, but Bee-hives; for they make him waxe rich" (*Works*, IV, 36). *A French Cook* is "a very saucy companion" (*Works*, IV, 41); the bibulous *Sexton*, who prepares corpses for burial, is "a grave drunkard" and, though "a sloven, yet . . . loves cleane linnen extreamely, and for that reason takes an order that fine holland sheets be not made wormes meate" (*Works*, IV, 41–42). *An Ordinary Fencer* shows his good nature by being "open-breasted to his friends; for his foile, and his doublet, weare not above two buttons: and resolute he is, for he so much scornes to take blowes, that he never weares *Cuffes*" (*Works*, IV, 27). This sort of thing, in which the context is created for the sake of the joke, reads like the feebler scenes of low comedy familiar to every student of minor Renaissance drama. Indeed, the connection in Webster's case is probably more than fortuitous.

Traits of the "baroque" manner are obvious: the syntax replete with doublets and triplets, the personifications and learned allusions, the juxtaposition of the concrete with the abstract and of Latinate with earthy diction, the occasional ornate sentence interspersed among the epigrammatic "hard lines," the alliteration used to bind the elements of an antithesis, the farfetched comparison, the love of paradox. The following passage from *A Mere Pettifogger* illustrates some of these features:

[He is] *one of Sampsons Foxes*: He sets men together by the eares, more shamefully then *Pillories*. . . . *Cowardise* holds him a good Common-wealths-man; his Pen is the Plough, & Parchment the Soyle, whence he reapes both Coyne and Curses. He is an *Earthquake*, that willingly will let no ground lye in quiet. Broken titles make him whole; to have halfe in the County breake their Bonds, were the onely liberty of conscience.

(*Works*, IV, 35)

Webster can use chiasmus effectively, as when he writes of *An Ordinary Widow*, "The end of her husband beginnes in teares; and the end of her teares beginnes in a husband" (*Works*, IV, 39). And he has the metaphysical poet's gift for arresting, often bizarre, images. His poetaster, *A Rimer*, is "a Dung-hill not well laide together" (*Works*, IV, 44); his *French Cook*, "an enemy to Beefe and Mutton," concocts gourmet dishes that "wee may rather call a drinking, then a meale" (*Works*, IV, 41). The *Intruder into Favour*, who in some respects suggests Robert Carr, is so practiced at "shrowding dishonestie under a faire pretext" that "hee seemes to preserve mud in Chrystall";[40] his "whole body goes all upon *screwes*, and his face is the *vice* that mooves them" (*Works*, IV, 29). The *Worthy Commander*

doth not thinke his body yeeldes a more spreading shadow after a victory then before;[41] and when he lookes upon his enemies dead bodie, tis with a kinde of noble heavinesse, not insultation. . . . Lastly, when peace folds him up, his silver head should leane neere the golden Scepter, and die in his *Princes* bosome.

(*Works*, IV, 25–26)

Webster's description of *An Excellent Actor*, perhaps based upon Richard Burbage, the most famous tragedian of the age,[42] is surely one of history's noblest and most eloquent defenses of the thespian's art. No less feelingly than Shakespeare, Webster knew that all the world's a stage:

an excellent Plaier . . . addes grace to the Poets labours: for what in the Poet is but ditty, in him is both ditty and musicke. . . . All men have beene of his occupation: and indeed, what hee doth fainedly that doe others essentially: this day one plaies a Monarch, the next a private person. Heere one Acts a Tyrant, on the morrow an Exile: A Parasite this man to-night, to-morrow a Precisian, and so of divers others. I observe, of all men living, a worthy Actor in one kind is the strongest motive of affection that can be: for when he dies, we cannot be perswaded any man can doe his parts like him. . . . I valew a worthy Actor by the corruption of some few of the quality, as I would doe gold in the oare; I should not minde the drosse, but the purity of the metall.

(*Works*, IV, 43)

Such passages, in which rhythmic modulation and sonorous cadence are artfully adjusted to the sentiment, in which a feeling of weight or substance is achieved without heaviness, entitle Webster to a place with Sir Thomas Browne among the great prose writers of the period.

Despite the rich surface variety of Webster's thirty-two characters, the themes and attitudes that underlie them are few and predictable. A reader of the Italian tragedies will already have met most of them. The assault on hypocrisy and pretension, now broadened to embrace a wider cross section of humanity, is carried beyond the world of the courtier and politician into that of the trades-man, the professional man, the artist. Although Webster's form naturally accommodates the satirical emotions more readily than the tragic, the character-ist, like the tragedian, delights to stress the gap between words and actions, to strip moral corruption and absurdity of their meretricious vesture, to exemplify repeatedly the struggle of the ego against social norms and facts of nature. Meanness of motive, "self-opinion," and petty greed may replace the more gran-diose evils of Webster's Italy, and the contumelious tone may rob them of their power to frighten, but the prose characters nevertheless present us with the same grotesque energies exhausting themselves in death that give such ironic power to the dramas of a year or so earlier. After all, as a perceptive critic of Marston re-minds us,[43] the difference between English folly and Italian vice could be for Jac-obean audiences more a distinction of mode than of substance.

Webster's religious attitude appears to emerge fairly clearly in the charac-ters, and though it is always hazardous to extrapolate major views from minor works or to assume that such views never alter with time or context, we must take the evidence where we find it. The repeated slurs upon papistry and Puri-tanism and the obvious respect for the seemly pieties of a settled faith would im-ply that Webster, like his father, was a loyal Anglican. For a man with theatrical and courtly connections, however, a formal allegiance to the established church would be taken for granted. Consequently, we need not rule out a vein of deep pessimism in his spiritual makeup or even the despair some critics have seen em-bodied in the tragedies. As in his plays, nobility of character, stoic resolution, and the preservation of a good name remain the stoutest defenses against the worst that Fortune and Death can inflict.

Nor are we surprised to find in the characters Webster's taste for the maca-bre. His sketch of a gravedigger who rejoices in sickbed and gallows and regards "a great plague" as "his yeere of Jubile" (*Works*, IV, 42) sounds the expected note, and so does that of the cowardly captain who longs for the death of his sol-diers so that he may continue dishonestly to draw their wages in "dead paies"

(*Works*, IV, 26). *A Virtuous Widow* ends characteristically with the Websterian association of death with love:

No calamity can now come neere her, for in suffering the losse of her husband, shee accounts all the rest trifles: she hath laid his dead body in the worthyest monument that can be: Shee hath buried it in her owne heart. To conclude, shee is a Relique, that without any superstition in the world, though she will not be kist, yet may be revernc't.

(*Works*, IV, 39).

Had nothing of Webster's survived except the characters, T. S. Eliot's observation that the poet "was much possessed by death" would still be apt, for roughly half of the thirty-two end, like the example above, with a reminder of mortality.

A Fair and Happy Milkmaid, the most famous and best-loved of all the Overburian characters, illustrates Webster's absolute mastery of the form. Almost universally admired, as its reappearance in innumerable anthologies and its mention by most literary historians attest, it has curiously escaped the serious analysis it deserves. Walton, who quoted from it in the fourth chapter of his *Compleat Angler*, seems to have been the most eminent, if not the first, to recognize in this charming idyl a classic expression of the pastoral ideal. He must have sensed (since his allusion occurs in a context that also offers full texts of Marlowe's "Come Live With Me" and Raleigh's answer) that the prose character at its best could approach the finest lyrics of the period in precision of detail, subtlety of rhythm and tone, complexity of organization, and simple unity of effect:

A fayre and happy Milke-mayd,
Is a Countrey Wench, that is so farre from making her selfe beautifull by Art, that one looke of hers is able to put *all face-Physicke* out of countenance. She knowes a fayre looke is but *a dumbe Orator* to commend vertue, therefore mindes it not. All her excellencies stand in her so silently, as if they had stolne upon her without her knowledge. The lining of her apparell (which is her selfe) is farre better then outsides *of Tissew*: for though shee bee not arrayed in the spoyle of the *Silkeworme*, shee is deckt in *innocence*, a farre better wearing. She doth not, with lying long a-bed, spoyle both her *Complexion & Conditions*; nature hath taught her *too Immoderate sleepe is rust to the soule*: she rises therefore with *Chaunticleare*, her Dames Cocke; & at night makes the *Lambe* her *Courfew*. In milking a Cow, and strayning the Teates through her fingers, it seemes that so sweet a Milke-presse makes the Milke the whiter, or sweeter; for never came *Almond Glove or Aromatique Oyntment* on her Palme to taynt it. The golden eares of Corne fall and kisse her feete when shee reapes them, as if they wisht to bee bound and led prisoners by the same hand fell'd them. Her breath is her owne, which sents all the yeere long of *June*, like a new-made Hay-cocke. She makes her hand hard with labour, and her heart soft with pittie: and when winter evenings fall early (sitting at her merry wheele) she sings a defiance to the giddy *Wheele of Fortune*. Shee doth all things with so sweet a grace, it seemes *ignorance* will not suffer her to doe ill, being her minde is to do well. She bestowes her yeeres wages at next Faire; and in choosing her Garments, counts no brav-

ery i' th' worlde like decency. The *Garden* and *Bee-hive* are all her *Physicke & Chyrurgery*, & she lives the longer for't. She dare goe alone, and unfold sheepe i' th' night, and feares no manner of ill, because she means none: yet to say truth, she is never alone, for she is still accompanied with *old songs, honest thoughts*, and *prayers*, but short ones; yet they have their efficacy, in that they are not pauled with insuing idle cogitations. Lastly, her dreames are so chaste, that she dare tell them: only a Frydayes dreame is all her *superstition*: that shee conceales for feare of anger. Thus lives she, and all her care is, She may dye in the *Spring-time*, to have store of flowers stuck upon her winding-sheete.

(*Works*, IV, 30)

Webster's method here is to build up a structure that unites generality with concreteness. The figure of the milkmaid serves as an emblem for a particularly attractive combination of virtues—humility, unself-consciousness, freedom from fear, industry, chastity, religious devotion, in a word, innocence—but he renders these universals almost wholly in terms of sense experience. By calling attention to the girl's natural beauty, her songs, her "strayning the Teates through her fingers," her breath like the scent of new-mown hay, and the products of her husbandry (corn, milk, honey), he draws all five senses into harmonious relation and creates an impression of healthful stability that becomes morally normative for the reader as well as fresh and satisfying aesthetically. The milkmaid's world is one in which everything is related to everything else, in which a pleasing variety of activities and objects combines to reflect the spiritual richness of inner simplicity. Dressing, milking, spinning, singing, praying, dreaming—all are seen as variant manifestations of a soul at peace with God and the world. Since the milkmaid's life symbolizes the triumph of virtue over corruption, ordinary oppositions—between work and play, waking and sleeping, action and thought, life and death, time and eternity—are caught up in a unity that implies the doctrine of plenitude and the synthesis of the Many in the One. Vital yet Platonically remote, she appears simultaneously both separate from and at one with her surroundings. Her aloneness is not lonely.

Webster adopts the most conventional images only to employ them with delicate originality. The golden ears of corn that the maid harvests are wittily anthropomorphized into worshipers who "fall and kisse her feete" and so suggest the reciprocal mode of her involvement with nature. And the color of the grain seems to characterize a world that somehow harmonizes the mythical golden age, an autumn landscape, and the golden rule of Christianity. We are already halfway to Traherne's "Orient and Immortal Wheat." The garden and the beehive—those traditional emblems of social order so familiar to students of Shakespeare's histories—are linked rhetorically so as to convey the idea that leisure and effort, pleasure and utility are ideally one. Her milk and honey are natural, not man-made products—as much the gifts of Grace as rewards for human labor, and their traditional associations invite the reader to connect the local

English setting with the biblical Promised Land and the pastoral landscapes of classical literature.[44]

The recurrent contrast between nature and art helps unify the character thematically. The girl forgoes the sophistications of cosmetics, "the spoyle of the *Silkeworme*" or the palm tainted with "*Almond Glove or Aromatique Oyntment*," in order that she may be "deckt in *innocence*" and so deserve the "store of flowers" that one day will adorn her shroud. Webster establishes an architectonic unity by superimposing several kinds of progression upon the paragraph structure. The generalized movement of the character is from work to rest and from the active to the contemplative—from an emphasis upon the dangers of "*Immoderate sleepe*" that is "*rust to the soule*" to the relaxation of "*old songs, honest thoughts*, and *prayers*." The temporal span of the milkmaid's day, bounded by the crowing cock at morning and the bleating lamb at night, is reinforced by a rhetorical organization that focuses upon her dressing in the early sentences and her dreams in the penultimate one.

But the progression from morning to evening is made to serve also as a microcosm of the life cycle itself. The final sentence, by idealizing the milkmaid's death and imagining its occurrence "in the *Spring-time*," evokes the appropriate religious connotations. In addition, it brings the earlier references to autumn harvests, summer haying, and long winter evenings into fresh relationship and endows them with a more profound significance. The maid defies "the giddy *Wheele of Fortune*" by plying her "merry wheele," and when her life is spent, she completes the larger cycle of which her spinning is the symbol by returning to earth in "her winding-sheete." Thus does Webster subtly imply that the movements from day to night, from winter to spring, from labor to rest, from outer to inner reality, from life to death are but variations of a cosmic rhythm, earthly adumbrations of the circle of divine perfection.[45] Although its theological implications are not precisely Wordsworthian, *A Fair and Happy Milkmaid* may be read as a Renaissance anticipation of lyrics like "The Solitary Reaper" or "A Slumber Did My Spirit Seal" in which the heroines seem to participate mysteriously in the harmony of nature or are ultimately "rolled round in earth's diurnal course."

"The Hand of Providence," said Sir Thomas Browne, "writes often by Abbreviatures, Hieroglyphicks or short Characters, which . . . are not to be made out but by a Hint or Key from that Spirit which indited them."[46] Webster's character of the milkmaid, though actually of earlier composition, might well be an application of Browne's metaphysic to literary form, a calculated illustration of the doctor's precept that "a contented Mind enlargeth the dimension of little things."[47] The Christian virtues that the medical philosopher recommends to the lowly of station—"Submission, Humility, Content of mind, and Industry"—are exactly those of the milkmaid, and Webster so arranges the *visibilia* of her life as to compose an emblem or symbolic representation of the difference between human and divine standards of measurement. Again Browne's words are pertinent:

To be low, but above contempt, may be high enough to be Happy. But many of low Degree may be higher than computed, and some Cubits above the common Commensuration; for in all States Virtue gives Qualifications and Allowances, which make out defects. Rough Diamonds are sometimes mistaken for Pebbles, and Meanness may be Rich in Accomplishments, which Riches in vain desire. If our merits be above our Stations, if our intrinsecal Value be greater than what we go for, or our Value than our Valuation, and if we stand higher in God's, than in the Censor's Book; it may make some equitable balance in the inequalities of this World, and there may be no such vast Chasm or Gulph between disparities as common Measures determine. The Divine Eye looks upon high and low differently from that of Man.

(Christian Morals, pp. 113–114)

The Arcadian nostalgia of the piece, although Webster in fact draws upon Sidney's romance for one of his sentences,[48] was, of course, a conventional literary attitude of the period; we have only to recall other queens of curds and cream—Greene's fair Margaret of Fressingfield or Shakespeare's Perdita, for instance—of whom this character with its subtle blend of idealism and earthiness seems a cameo reproduction. But in an age whose darkest cruelties and despairs Webster chose to mirror so terrifyingly in the Italian tragedies, it is not hard to imagine the peculiar appeal of this happy, almost prelapsarian vision. Indeed, he had already dramatized the contrast that pastoral inevitably implies by having Bosola taunt the Duchess of Malfi just before her execution with a merciless reminder of its charms: "Thou art some great woman, sure, for riot begins to sit on thy forehead, clad in gray hairs, twenty years sooner than on a merry milkmaid's" (IV.ii.135–137). The flower-strewn winding-sheet of the milkmaid, emblem of natural fulfillment, is worlds away from its grotesque counterparts in the tragedy—the metaphorical "winding-sheet" in which the Duchess secretly marries Antonio (I.i.389) and its paradoxical equivalent, the "*shroud*" that Bosola bids her "*quickly don*" as he brings her "By degrees of mortification" (IV.ii.177–181). Webster was particularly fond of the winding-sheet as a symbol; consequently, we are not astonished to find him elaborating its possibilities dramatically a few years later in *The Devil's Law-Case* (c. 1617–1619). At the end of this tragicomedy, a Capuchin friar tries to reclaim Romelio and Julio from their pride and worldliness by staging a little pageant intended to enforce the lesson of *contemptus mundi*. According to Webster's stage direction, Leonora enters "*with two coffins borne by her servants, and two winding-sheets stuck with flowers . . .*"; she presents "*one to her son, and the other to* Julio." Romelio's response to these gifts is one of the poet's famous dirges that, although it deserves to be appreciated for its own delicate artistry, may serve also as an uncommonly beautiful gloss on an attitude that profoundly informs *A Fair and Happy Milkmaid*:

> 'Tis very welcome; this is a decent garment
> Will never be out of fashion. I will kiss it.
> All the flowers of the spring

Meet to perfume our burying:
These have but their growing prime,
And man does flourish but his time.
Survey our progress from our birth:
We are set, we grow, we turn to earth.
Courts adieu, and all delights, *Soft music.*
All bewitching appetites;
Sweetest breath, and clearest eye,
Like perfumes, go out and die;
And consequently this is done,
As shadows wait upon the sun.
Vain the ambition of kings,
Who seek by trophies and dead things
To leave a living name behind,
And weave but nets to catch the wind.

                                          (V.iv.126–143)

All Webster's portraits, whether idealized or satiric, are founded on the principle of organized distortion, on a harmony of disproportions manifested in the wit of clashing imagery, syntactic restlessness, and rhythmic instability. In most, the distortion is deliberately downward and so approaches, by verbal means, those "Pictures and Draughts in *Caricatura*," of which Sir Thomas Browne speaks, "wherein, among others, the Painter hath singularly hit the signatures of a Lion and a Fox in the face of Pope Leo the Tenth."[49] Like Browne's caricaturist, Webster consistently employs animal imagery as an instrument of degradation. His *Pirate* "is a *cruell Hawke* that flies at all but his owne kind" (*Works*, IV, 27), his *Intruder into Favour* a "*Mountaines Monkie*" (Webster borrows the image from Montaigne)[50] "that climbing a tree, and skipping from bough to bough, gives you backe his face; but comne once to the top, hee holdes his nose up into the winde, and shewes you his taile" (*Works*, IV, 30). The *Drunken Dutchman* is "Like a Horse . . . onely guided by the mouth" (*Works*, IV, 32); the *Quacksalver* (a medical charlatan) "hath more . . . doubles then a Hare" (*Works*, IV, 40). The *Jesuit* is not only "a gray Woolfe" but a prose version of the portrait of Pope Leo: "in his Seminary, hee's a Foxe; but in the Inquisition, a Lyon Rampant" (*Works*, IV, 42). Recognizing, like the authors of *Volpone* and *King Lear* before and of *Christian Morals* after him, that humanity is "a composition of Man and Beast,"[51] Webster repeatedly illustrates in his characters one of the pious doctor's dicta: "Un-man not therefore thy self by a Beastial transformation, nor realize old Fables. Expose not thy self by four-footed manners unto monstrous draughts, and Caricatura representations."[52] Indeed, Webster had already applied this idea dramatically, most consistently perhaps in the early city comedies.[53]

But distortion upwards is no less evident than its contrary in Webster's art. *A Worthy Commander, A Noble and Retired Housekeeper, A Fair and Happy*

Milkmaid, *A Franklin*, *A Virtuous Widow*, and *A Reverend Judge* are all portraits whose outlines and colors are antinaturalistically—I had almost said romantically—softened by the transforming pressure of the idealisms that inspired
them. They are kinetic rather than static in moral effect, characters less of what
man is than of what he might be. Yet, for all their ameliorative motivation, they
do not falsify human nature so much as they regulate, stylize, shape, and emphasize one side of it. The representation of *la belle nature* necessitates purposeful
omission. And here again Webster is curiously at one with the gentle wisdom of
Browne:

Affection should not be too sharp-Eyed, and Love is not to be made by magnifying
Glasses. If things were seen as they truly are, the beauty of bodies would be much
abridged; and therefore the wise Contriver hath drawn the pictures and outsides of
things softly and amiably unto the natural Edge of our Eyes, not leaving them able to
discover those uncomely asperities, which make Oyster-shells in good Faces, and
Hedghoggs even in Venus's moles.

(*Christian Morals*, p. 127)

The prose characters of John Webster lay a claim upon our attention that
goes beyond the attractions that have usually been granted them—the appeal of
the merely grotesque on the one hand or of the merely quaint and pretty on the
other. In a style that is frequently mordant, sometimes sonorous, and always
witty, they limn the externals of humankind against a backdrop that impels us to
reconsider individual values in broadest perspective. They show us man caught
in the great Renaissance tension between angel and beast—a tension potentially
tragic despite the comic emphasis upon which Webster's genre insists. A hasty
reading of the characters may impress us more with the bestial than with the an-
gelic possibilities of the subject matter, and here again the seeming dominance of
evil over good in the tragedies may be relevant. But Webster was not unaware in
his characters of the obverse position. To quote once more from Sir Thomas
Browne, with whom, surprisingly, Webster shares more than a few traits of style
and thought: "There is no excuse to forget what every thing prompts unto us. To
thoughtful Observators the whole World is a Phylactery, and every thing we see
an Item of the Wisdom, Power, or Goodness of God."[54] The largely secular
"plaine songs," upon which Webster in the characters elaborates his rhetorical
descants, keep a resonance from plain song and (by metaphorical extension)
echo the more awesome modalities of canticle and psalter.

*   *   *

In 1615 Webster was at the height of his powers. If his next play was *The Guise*,
as there is some reason to suspect, its loss may well be the most regrettable of all
the lost plays in his canon. We know of its existence because the poet himself refers to it in his dedication of *The Devil's Law-Case* to Sir Thomas Finch: "Some

of my other works, as *The White Devil, The Duchess of Malfi, Guise,* and others, you have formerly seen" (ll. 4–6). The play was probably in print by 1623, when this dedication appeared, for in the same volume Webster invites "the Judicious Reader," having already "approved my other works" (l. 18), to "read" *The Devil's Law-Case* with them specifically in mind. The year of *The Guise* is impossible to establish with any certainty, but the position of the play in Webster's own list and the painful slowness with which he usually composed would seem to imply a date later than *The Duchess* but earlier than *The Devil's Law-Case* (1617–1619?). Howarth has plausibly suggested 1615,[55] although Webster could conceivably have written the play any time before 1623.

The nature of the lost drama is also doubtful, for the various catalogues of printed plays compiled just before and after the Restoration do not agree on the point. The earliest list, that of Rogers and Ley (1656), assigns a play called "Guise" to Marston, perhaps a slip for Marlowe. Edward Archer's catalogue of the same year lists "Guise" as a comedy by John Webster. "Guise" appears again in two separate editions of a similar list by Francis Kirkman—in 1661 without designation of authorship or genre and in 1671 anonymously as a tragedy. Henry Marsh's list of 1663 mentions a "Guise" that was supposedly a comedy. Howarth, relying on the testimony of Archer and Marsh and discounting that of Kirkman, argues that Webster's play was indeed a comedy. And he goes on to speculate that it might have had something to do with the fourth Duke of Guise's official visit to London in the spring of 1607 or that the title, instead of referring to a French nobleman, merely meant "custom, habit, or fashion" as in the usage of Shakespeare and others. Howarth's conclusion might be right, but since the early play lists are notoriously unreliable and contradictory, and since we have no assurance in any case that all the references are to Webster's play, there is good reason for skepticism. It seems more natural, in fact, to think of Webster's lost *Guise* as another drama of scandal and corruption, based, like the two Italian tragedies, on fairly recent continental history. This supposition is the more warranted because Webster quarried so much in his other works from the French history of Pierre Matthieu. In one of the two volumes by Matthieu that he used extensively Webster could have read a detailed account of the rise and fall of the third Duc de Guise, a larger-than-life figure of "inuincible valour and courage," a man about whom the writer moralizes in terms that might well excite the imagination of a tragedian: "Thou seekest oh Duke! to touch the heauens with thy forehead, and hell with thy foote: but learne, that our histories are full of the violent deaths of those proud spirits, who seeke their glory and profit with the ruine of their Country, the preiudice of States, and the subuersion of common peace."[56]

The shocking assassination of this arrogant noble on Christmas Day, 1588, at the instigation of Catherine de Medici's weakling son Henry III, attracted international attention, and the events that led up to it as well as its immediate aftermath would have provided Webster with a heady mixture of political intrigue, sex, treachery, and revenge exactly suited to his tastes and talents. The subject was a popular one with Renaissance playwrights. Marlowe had dramatized it in his *Massacre at Paris*, also referred to as *The Guise* (variously spelled *Gvyes*, *Gwies*, and *Gwisse*) in Henslowe's *Diary*; Chapman, whom Webster especially admired, had dealt with it in his two semihistorical *Bussy D'Ambois* plays, even punning on the name Guise in a way that shows how Howarth's reading of Webster's title might be reconciled with the tragic genre;[57] and even the obscure Henry Shirley, murdered in 1627 like his own title character, composed a play (now lost) called *The Duke of Guise*, which undoubtedly offered a third version of the same or related incidents. Marlowe's character is a typically Machiavellian "overreacher" who commits atrocity after atrocity in his campaign to possess the French crown. He poisons a queen with perfumed gloves, has a Lord Admiral stabbed to death in bed (the victim is taunted with the cross of his assassin's dagger as he tries to pray), sends the victim's severed head and hands to the Pope, and schemes against the king with his wicked brother, a cardinal, who is later strangled onstage. When King Henry in a counterplot lures the Guise to his doom in "his royal cabinet," the duke faces death with stoic defiance and a heroic assertion of his identity:

> Let mean conceits and baser men fear death:
> Tut, they are peasants; I am Duke of Guise;
> And princes with their looks engender fear.
> . . . .
> O that I have not power to stay my life,
> Nor immortality to be reveng'd!
> To die by peasants, what a grief is this!
> (xxi.68–81)[58]

The play, which is highly episodic, ends only after the king himself has been assassinated by a friar who plunges a poisoned knife into him while delivering a letter.

Marlowe's tragedy is crude work, at least in the mutilated state that has survived, but its possibilities are splendid. It is therefore tantalizing to imagine what Webster could have done with the same material. A line here and there even seems to prefigure the later dramatist's manner: "I go as whirlwinds rage before a storm" (xi.29) recalls imagery of tempestuous motion that Webster also applied to Isabella in *The White Devil* (II.i.149) and to Ferdinand in *The Duchess of Malfi* (III.ii.161). "Is Guise's glory but a cloudy mist . . . ?" (xv.29) reminds us of the deaths of Flamineo and Antonio "in a mist," and "Tut, they are peasants; I am Duke of Guise" reads like a coarser rendering of the feeling expressed by "I am Duchess of Malfi still" (IV.ii.142). It is even possible to project thematic linkages between Marlowe's tragedy and Webster's. Judith Weil in a stimulating reassessment of *The Massacre at Paris* notes the pervasive "associations of love and blood" that inform the play, beginning with the marriage of Navarre, which the Queen Mother intends to "dissolve with blood and cruelty" (i.25), and "run-[ning] throughout the violent ceremonies" of the drama: "The word 'sweet' is invariably yoked with blood and death."[59]

The possibilities of a literary connection between the two dramatists were not lost on F. P. Wilson, who also recognized the drama inherent in the historical subject matter. Marlowe apparently made no use of Henry III's enigmatic words while "spurn[ing] with his foot" the corpse of the Guise: "Il paraît encore plus grand que vivant." But, as Wilson points out, the king's remark "is one of those instinctive reflections which while they may come from the top layer of the mind yet illuminate at deeper levels the speaker and the situation. One might say that it was only waiting for a great context in order to become art: then, it might have been signed by Middleton or Webster."[60] Samuel Sheppard, writing in his *Fairy King* sometime between 1648 and 1654, spoke of Webster's "three noble Tragedies."[61] We can only wonder whether he meant to include *The Guise* in his trilogy. If he did, he would seem to have been following the author's own grouping of the play with the two other acknowledged masterworks.

*   *   *

Whether Marlowe actually influenced *The Guise* or not, he obviously exerted some posthumous force upon the next of Webster's plays, *The Devil's Law-Case*. Romelio, the most interesting character of that drama, is a Neapolitan merchant who, disguising himself as a Jew, advertises his Machiavellianism in such a way as to remind the audience unmistakably of Barabas in *The Jew of Malta*:

> Excellently well habited! Why, methinks
> That I could play with mine own shadow now,
> And be a rare Italianated Jew;
> To have as many several change of faces
> As I have seen carv'd upon one cherry stone;
> To wind about a man like rotten ivy,
> Eat into him like quicksilver, poison a friend
> With pulling but a loose hair from's beard, or give a drench,
> He should linger of't nine years, and ne'er complain
> But in the spring and fall, and so the cause
> Imputed to the disease natural; for slight villainies,
> As to coin money, corrupt ladies' honors,
> Betray a town to th' Turk, or make a bonfire
> O' th' Christian navy, I could settle to't,
> As if I had eat a politician
> And digested him to nothing but pure blood.
>
> (III.ii.1–16)[62]

We know that Webster's friend Richard Perkins, the original Flamineo of *The White Devil*, played the part of Barabas in a revival of Marlowe's play around

1632, for Thomas Heywood in a special prologue composed for the purpose, praised his characterization by comparing it favorably to Edward Alleyn's a generation earlier. It is by no means impossible, as Bentley suggests,[63] that Perkins also played the role of Romelio and was adverting in the lines quoted—especially the mention of "play[ing] with mine own shadow"—to similarities between this new part and one he was already known to have played successfully before, for there is good evidence to show that Marlowe's *Jew* remained popular from the time of its original production about 1590. If this was the case, Webster may well have written Romelio's lines with Perkins's special talents in mind. At any rate, the character would give Perkins ample scope to display the same witty cynicism that the role of Flamineo had called for—a role, it will be remembered, for which Webster thought Perkins especially well qualified.

The argument for Marlowe's influence, however, rests on broader grounds than an isolated allusion to *The Jew of Malta*, for *The Devil's Law-Case* shares several elements of plot with the earlier play. Both dramas portray avaricious merchants who boast of great wealth and cynically manipulate others, including female relatives—a daughter in one case, a sister in the other—in order to augment it; both contain outrages against nuns and ridicule of friars; both have innocent heroines for whose hand rival suitors contend in a duel that is mortal (or apparently mortal) to both men. It is perhaps worth noting in addition that during the period in which Webster's play was performed, the same troupe revived Marlowe's *Edward II*. It may be that *The Guise* (the death of the historical Duke of Guise is actually mentioned in the prologue to *The Jew of Malta*) and *The Devil's Law-Case* together represent a phase of Webster's career during which Marlowe's plays, perhaps because of recent productions involving friends and associates, stimulated the younger dramatist's imagination.

The Devil's Law-Case is difficult to date precisely, but the title page of the 1623 quarto tells us that this "*new Tragecomoedy, the true and perfect Copie from the Originall . . . was approouedly well Acted by her Maiesties Seruants.*" Since Queen Anne's Company dissolved after Her Majesty's death on 2 March 1619, and since the play clearly borrows from Jonson's *The Devil Is an Ass* (acted 1616) and from Lord Burghley's *Certaine Precepts . . . for the well ordering . . . of a man's Life* (1617), it is possible to narrow the limits significantly.[64] The play was probably first performed either at the Red Bull or at the newer Cockpit Theatre in 1617 or 1618. The modish tone of the drama certainly suggests the latter playhouse, for the Cockpit (or Phoenix, as it was also called) was essentially a "private" theatre that catered, like the rival Blackfriars, to an elite clientele.[65] After having written *The Duchess of Malfi* and perhaps other plays for the King's Men, Webster was again associated with the players for whom he had labored on *The White Devil*.

Although *The Devil's Law-Case* is recognizably Websterian in poetic style, its plot, which is full of rapid shifts, surprises, and improbabilities, and its characters, whose motivation frequently seems insufficient or cloudy, show that

Webster was trying, at least superficially, to adapt his more somber tastes to the tragicomic mode that Beaumont and Fletcher had recently made so fashionable. The result is a curiously hybrid play in which moments of genuine feeling and sardonic scorn are somewhat uncomfortably contained by action that is incredible, highly contrived, and fundamentally theatrical. Glossy artifice of the Fletcherian sort had not been Webster's strength. Yet even in an uncongenial form he managed now to write with much of his former energy and brilliance, to sustain whole scenes of vigorous dialogue and dramatic excitement. There is an intellectual sinuousness—and even at times a moral earnestness—about the play that sets it apart from such performances as *Philaster* or *A King and No King*. Gabriele Baldini in his sympathetic study has called attention to the strain that this play sets up between interest in the mechanisms of plot and interest in the deeper aspects of personality; more recently Ralph Berry has seen the apparently facile ending as "a cross between Jonson and Fletcher."[66] Tragicomedy is by definition a mixed genre, but Webster seems in *The Devil's Law-Case* to have produced a play that is (even for him) peculiarly Janus-faced—a work that carries over themes, attitudes, techniques of characterization, and stage effects from the major tragedies, yet nevertheless points forward to the thinner and more relaxed dramaturgy of his final phase.

The play is plotted around two major situations, the first of which directly causes the second. Two noblemen, Contarino and Ercole, although long-time friends, are rivals for the hand of Jolenta. The girl loves Contarino, but her brother Romelio furthers the match with Ercole for selfish and materialistic reasons, while her widowed mother Leonora assists him in his schemes because she is herself secretly in love with Contarino. This state of affairs leads to a duel between Ercole and Contarino in which both men wound each other seriously. Romelio, in order to prevent Contarino from changing a will in which he has bequeathed everything to Jolenta, disguises himself as a Jewish doctor and stabs the stricken Contarino, as he believes, fatally. But the intended murder ironically cures Contarino, for Romelio's dagger has only "made free passage for the congealed blood" (III.ii.161) in the original wound. When Romelio, unaware of the recovery he has just effected, triumphantly informs his mother that he has killed Contarino, she can barely hide the cause of her distress; then, in soliloquy, she confesses her passion for the supposedly murdered man and decides to stop at nothing in a campaign to take revenge upon her own son. The revenge action (not surprisingly for the author of *The White Devil* and *The Duchess of Malfi*) occupies most of the second half of the play. Leonora tries to disinherit Romelio by trumping up the charge that he is the bastard son of her own adulterous union some forty years earlier with an old friend of her husband, one Crispiano, and by having the whole question brought to open trial. Here, as in the famous courtroom scene of *The White Devil* where Vittoria is arraigned, Webster is at his dramatic best, and the episode culminates effectively in a sensational reversal by which the judge suddenly steps down from the bench, reveals himself as that very Crispiano with whom Leonora had claimed to have sexual relations, and exposes the whole tale as a malicious fraud.

The concluding action of the play is convoluted and somewhat cryptic. Ercole, who, by concealing his recovery from the duel, has been supposed dead and who has observed the legal proceedings "muffled" and undetected, publicly accuses Romelio of having murdered Contarino in his bed. Since supporting testimony is lacking, the issue must be settled by a second duel in which Contarino, also unrecognized (in a Danish disguise), serves as Ercole's second against Romelio. According to Webster's stage direction, the combat is "*continued to a good length*" (V.vi.16), perhaps providing the sort of spectacle that audiences at the Red Bull are known to have delighted in. The inconclusive battle stops only after Leonora and a friar enter to inform the astonished antagonists that Contarino is not only alive but Ercole's second. The two friends embrace, ironically concluding their rivalry in mutual affection. Ercole claims Jolenta, who has earlier sworn to love him in the false belief that Contarino originally preferred her mother; Contarino converts the former lie into present truth by announcing, most improbably, that he has indeed "entirely vowed [his] life" (V.vi.26) to Leonora. Webster then triples the pairing off of partners by having Romelio, at last repentant, marry a nun whom he has got with child. Comic byplay, as well as further complexity, is provided by secondary characters such as Crispiano, who disguises himself as a merchant in order to spy on a spendthrift son; by Ariosto, who moralizes satirically on various evils and who serves, somewhat to the embarrassment of the defendant, as Romelio's advocate at trial; by Sanitonella and Contilupo, two ludicrous representatives of the legal profession; by Winifrid, Leonora's mendacious maid, who perjures herself in court; and by two venal surgeons who are accessories to Romelio in the supposed murder but then double-cross him. The Capuchin friar introduces an otherworldly dimension, thereby deepening and expanding the play's moral and spiritual contexts.

No one has discovered a comprehensive source for this complicated story, and it seems likely that Webster invented the plot himself, no doubt prompted by earlier works for certain elements and motifs. Indeed, it would almost appear that in planning the sequence of episodes, he adopted a method analogous to his tesselation of commonplace-book material for individual scenes and speeches. The result is a curiously spasmodic effect upon the narrative line. Apart from the obvious influence of Marlowe, especially on the character of Romelio, Webster probably consulted Goulart's *Histoires Admirables*, available in Grimestone's English translation (1607), for the tale of the stab wound that effects an unexpected cure. This is the same book from which Webster had borrowed the symptoms of Ferdinand's lycanthropy in *The Duchess of Malfi*. There are numerous analogues to the story of the mother who falsely proclaims her own son a bastard.[67] One likely source is the anonymous play *Lust's Dominion* (c. 1600), now pretty certainly attributed to Dekker, Haughton, and Day. This drama, which contains a military cardinal, may have influenced Webster's conception of the

Duchess of Malfi's ecclesiastical brother,[68] and, in any case, might well be familiar to the playwright, since it was written for the Admiral's Men and dates from the period of Webster's first association with them and with Dekker. But the motif of the mother disowning her son also appears in Middleton and Rowley's *A Fair Quarrel* (probably acted about 1616–1617) and in Warner's *Continuance of Albion's England* (1606) and Holland's translation of Camden's *Britain* (1610); Webster seems to have known both nondramatic works.

Boklund has suggested most interestingly that Webster may have drawn upon *The Malcontent* for the supposed death and sudden reappearance of a wounded man (Marston's Ferneze, like Contarino, is believed dead by both his friends and enemies).[69] Boklund also thinks it probable that the names of Crispiano and Winifrid derive from William Rowley's play *A Shoemaker a Gentleman* (c. 1608). The latter suggestion is attractive for several reasons: Rowley was a friend of Webster, as we know from his commendatory poem for *The Duchess* and from his later collaboration with the playwright in *Keep the Widow Waking* and *A Cure for a Cuckold*; Rowley's play, like Webster's, was probably written for Queen Anne's Company; and Crispianus, like the Crispiano of Webster's tragicomedy, conceals his true identity, only to reveal it at a crucial point late in the action. Moreover, as Boklund points out, *A Shoemaker a Gentleman* contains a scene in which a queen woos and wins a man of apparently low rank that "comes astonishingly close"[70] to the similar matter in *The Duchess of Malfi*. We might add that when the Duchess proposes to Antonio in the tragedy, she swears ironically by St. Winifred (I.i.390), the very saint whose wedding and martyrdom (both with St. Hugh) form the sanguinary climax of *A Shoemaker a Gentleman*.

Since Jonson's *Sejanus* provided Webster with a few phrases for *The Devil's Law-Case* (as also had been true for both *The White Devil* and *The Duchess of Malfi*), it is possible that Eudemus, the poisoning doctor of the Roman tragedy, influenced the conception of Romelio as a would-be murderer masquerading as a physician; but Webster's most unquestionable appropriation from *Sejanus*, Contarino's threat to "make" Ercole's "bravery fitter for a grave / Than for a wedding" (I.ii.251–252),[71] only suggests Webster's return to themes and motifs treated already in the two Italian tragedies. The trial of Romelio with its combination of willful courage in the defendant, malice in the accuser, and bureaucratic pomposity in the court is an obvious reworking of attitudes from *The White Devil*, and the Capuchin who tries to "startle" proud men into learning "how to die" (V.vi.121–122) functions, like Bosola, as *agent provocateur* of the condemned."[72] Even the name of Webster's tragicomedy evokes the earlier masterpieces, for devil imagery is a prominent feature of all three plays and is clearly used to intensify the psychic and moral hell that Webster delighted to portray. The rather pleonastic second title, *When Women Go to Law, the Devil Is Full of Business*, may glance backward to Dekker's *If This Be Not a Good Play, the Devil Is in It*; indeed, Jonson's *The Devil Is an Ass*, from which Webster borrows some satirical words against lawyers and ostentatious dress, alludes in its prologue to the Dekker comedy. If *The White Devil* and *The Duchess of Malfi* may be considered "in important ways two versions of a single subject,"[73] *The Devil's Law-Case* in an equally qualified sense must represent a third. The departures may appear more significant than the continuities, but these have to do with a new genre and a homelier social sphere more than with theme, moral climate, poetic texture, and tone. *The Devil's Law-Case*, despite its technical hesitations and awkward joins, is authenticallly Websterian in its persistent exploration of a grotesque, yet vital, world—a world deformed by the crosscurrents of love and vengeance where intelligence, pride, malevolence, and irrationality syncretize or intertwine disturbingly.

Even in the unlikely context of tragicomedy, Webster managed to reveal once more his abiding interest in the drama of recent history. According to a legend current at the time, Queen Elizabeth would have spared her favorite, Essex, from the headsman's axe, had he but humbled himself by returning to her a ring given him as a love token long before. He did send the ring from his prison, so the story goes, but, falling into the hands of the Countess of Nottingham, it miscarried, and the queen spent her final years in bitterness and remorse for his death.[74] In *The Devil's Law-Case* Leonora draws a parallel between her passion for Contarino and the old queen's love for the young earl:

> Let me die
> In the distraction of that worthy princess
> Who loathed food, and sleep, and ceremony,
> For thought of losing that brave gentleman
> She would fain have saved, had not a false conveyance
> Express'd him stubborn-hearted.
>
> (III.iii.295–300)

It is possible also, as Lucas points out,[75] that Webster based the actions of Winifrid in the courtroom scene on the behavior of an actual servant. In 1618–1619 during the scandalous Star Chamber trial in which Sir Thomas Lake, his wife, and children were convicted of libeling the Countess of Exeter with letters forged to show incest and attempted murder, Lady Lake's maid, one Sarah Swarton, perjured herself on behalf of her mistress. Certainly, this law case had its devilish ingredients, and women seem to have been the worst offenders.

Webster oversaw the publication of *The Devil's Law-Case* carefully, which is not surprising, since the play appeared in print the same year as *The Duchess of Malfi* with which he took equal care. The 1623 quarto, which contains features that suggest nontheatrical copy as well as one or two authorial press corrections, makes it evident that the publisher had the dramatist's full backing. The dedicatee was Sir Thomas Finch, Bart., later Earl of Winchilsea, an ancestor of the eighteenth-century poetess. In his bid for patronage Webster again tried hard to avoid the possible imputation of cringing humilty. Not content with the usual disclaimer of flattery, a vice "which I hate," he comes close to impudence: "Nor do I much doubt [Sir Thomas's acceptance of the play], knowing the greatest of the Caesars have cheerfully entertain'd less poems than this; and had I thought it unworthy, I had not enquired after so worthy a patronage" (Dedication, ll. 3–11).

Although Finch lived in Drury Lane, the same street where the new Phoenix had opened, patron and poet had apparently not met, for Webster says, "Your self I *understand* to be all courtesy" (l. 11; italics added), but the baronet had "formerly seen" (probably in manuscript or printed form but perhaps in the theatre) "Some of my other works, as *The White Devil*, *The Duchess of Malfi*, *Guise*, and others" (ll. 4–6). The title page carries part of a motto from Seneca, *Non quam diu, sed quam bene* ("With life, as with a play, it matters, not how long, but how good the performance is"), and a preface "To the Judicious Reader" manages to work a trio of quotations from Horace into the first three sentences. Webster is so confident that the "play will ingeniously acquit itself" to those readers whose approval is worth the having and so disdainful of "the rest," the ignorant and windy commonalty, "that I have not given way to divers of my friends, whose unbegg'd commendatory verses offered themselves to do me service in the front of this poem" (ll. 4–13). However immodest Webster's show of modesty may seem to us and however much we may regret the loss of the complimentary poems, this address to the reader does throw important light upon the dramatist's aesthetics. Again we find Webster paying tribute to the actors who had performed the play: "A great part of the grace of this (I confess) lay in action" (that is, the acting); and indeed it would require subtlety and skill in performance to make Contarino's final coupling to Leonora acceptable to audiences or Romelio's last-minute repentance consistent with his earlier cynicism. But the playwright goes on to state the cardinal principle by which he would be judged in this as well as "my other works": "no action [can] ever be gracious, where the decency of the language, and ingenious structure of the scene, arrive not to make up a perfect harmony" (ll. 13–17). Webster was underlining the obvious but frequently ignored point that in poetic drama the word must be cousin to the deed, that the poetry and the performance must depend for their success on each other. Moreover, his mention of language in collocation with structure should alert us to one of the specialties of tragicomedy and of Websterian technique in general—namely, the effect of equivocal or ambiguous language upon plot and upon the promotion of deliberate uncertainty in responses to character and motive. In addition, the reference to "ingenious structure" seems to imply that Webster tended to conceive of dramatic form in terms of semiautonomous scenes, each with its independent coherence, rather than in terms of larger units. This might partly account for the elliptical or rough connections that sometimes mar even the greatest of Webster's plays despite their tonal and thematic integrity.

With the publication of *The Duchess of Malfi* and *The Devil's Law-Case* in 1623, the same year that Hemminge and Condell brought out their famous collected edition of Shakespeare, Webster had reached the zenith of his career as a professional dramatist. By then his most distinctive and original works could be widely read, and it is impossible not to feel that the eclectic achievements of his final years—such of them, at any rate, as survive or can be hesitantly identified—represent a sharp and disappointing decline in quality. One symptom of this is the apparent reversion to the collaborative practice of his earlier years, for again we find him writing plays with others—William Rowley, John Ford, his old friend Dekker, and probably Middleton.

THE FINAL PHASE [I]

About 1621 Middleton wrote *Anything for a Quiet Life*, one of his numerous city comedies for the King's Men at the Blackfriars. The play was not published until the Restoration, long after the author's death, with a title page attributing it solely to him. There is no external evidence whatever to indicate that Webster shared in the writing, but since H. Dugdale Sykes attributed more than half of the drama to him in 1921, his name has nevertheless been connected with the play by most scholars who have dealt with the comedy.[1] The text of 1662 does contain several striking verbal parallels to Webster's undoubted work and also borrows at a few places from sources (including Sidney's *Arcadia*) that were among Webster's favorite quarries. Obviously, no certainty as to his participation can be supported on this basis alone, but since Middleton is not known to have shared Webster's unusual borrowing habits (especially the borrowing from Sidney), and since the two playwrights had not only worked together before (on *Caesar's Fall*) but were still friends two decades later, when Middleton praised *The Duchess*, it is hard to dismiss this internal evidence as mere coincidence.

Of course, the Restoration publisher Francis Kirkman would have no reason to falsify the attribution deliberately (as he might have done if the claim had been for Shakespeare or even Fletcher), but, if he was uncritical enough to ascribe *The Thracian Wonder* to Rowley and Webster,[2] he would certainly be capable of omitting a name from a title page, whether ignorantly or carelessly. William Power, who stops short of urging Webster's entitlement, has argued that certain features of the text, especially the doubling of the name George (George, the apprentice, and George Cressingham) in scenes where the two characters appear together, as well as inconsistencies of characterization, support the likelihood of dual authorship.[3] Certainly, this is a more plausible way of accounting for some of the text's anomalies than the mere haste suggested by Ward and endorsed by Holmes.[4] Moreover, no other play by Middleton has been shown to contain so many suggestive and varied links with Webster as *Anything for a Quiet Life*—links that too many careful readers of both dramatists have perceived for the theory of shared responsibility to be rejected without hesitation. It is true that Middleton might have been imitating Webster; two of the Sidneyan phrases, "O you sweet-breath'd Monkey" (II.i.55) and "creatures of the field that only live / On the wilde benefits of *Nature*" (IV.i.81–82), are much closer both in wording and context to *The Devil's Law-Case* and *The Duchess of Malfi* respectively than to the *Arcadia*.[5] We know on the one hand that Middleton admired *The Duchess* and borrowed from it several times in later plays.[6] On the other, Webster often echoes himself and appears to do so again in *Anything for a Quiet Life*. Several critics have judged the play to be metrically uncharacteristic of Middleton and in places closer to Webster's prosody.[7]

Analysis of the play's linguistic usage in the matter of favorite contractions, affirmatives, and other expressions largely confirms the division between Middleton and Webster made originally by Sykes and endorsed by F. L. Lucas and R. H. Barker. David J. Lake has shown that *Anything for a Quiet Life* includes the exclamation "Pue wawe" (II.i.64) and the unusual contraction *of't* (V.i.223, 225), forms that Middleton never employs but that are duplicated or closely paralleled in Webster's acknowledged plays.[8] In addition, Webster's clear preferences, particularly in his later work, for *I am* (over *I'm*), for *them* (over *'em*), for *yes* (over *ay*), his fondness for *i'th*, *o'th*, and *'s* (= *his*), and his total avoidance of *betwixt* all coincide with the very scenes (excepting III.i) that Sykes and Lucas ascribe to Webster on other grounds. Lake's linguistic arguments are too technical and complex to be summarized adequately here, and, as G. B. Shand has pointed out, Lake neglects the influence that problems of spacing might have had upon a compositor's use of contractions.[9] But it is surely significant that MacD. P. Jackson, working independently of Lake and using similar, but slightly different, data, also concludes that the play is partly Webster's, although he would assign a bit more of the text to Middleton:

For the main plot concerning the Cressinghams Webster seems to have been largely responsible, and the verse speeches of the Cressinghams in Act V may well be his work. Indeed, very little of the play's verse sounds to me like that of Middleton: it is especially remote from the Middleton of 1621, the year to which *Anything for a Quiet Life* is generally assigned and a likely composition date for *Women Beware Women*. . . . That both authors are in the extant play can be regarded as highly probable, at the very least.[10]

The date of the play's printing (some forty years after its composition) may cast a degree of doubt on the validity of the kind of orthographical evidence assembled by Lake and Jackson, for we cannot know what vicissitudes the manuscript may have undergone during the interim. But taken together with the internal evidence of other kinds, the linguistic data confirm beyond reasonable doubt that *Anything for a Quiet Life* is a collaborative play and that the author of roughly forty-five percent of it (I, II.i, IV.i, the beginning of IV.ii, the end of V.i) is indeed Webster. Certainly until strong evidence to the contrary can be produced, we are justified in placing the play within the Webster canon.

In substance, *Anything for a Quiet Life* is a collection of intrigues and tricks, evidently derived in part from jestbooks[11] and held together in a tenuous unity under the umbrella of its title, a proverbial saying that applies in different ways to every aspect of the crowded plot. As the prologue puts it,

> *How ere th'intents and appetites of men*
> *Are different as their faces, how and when*
> *T'employ their actions, yet all without strife*
> *Meet in this point*, Any thing for a Quiet Life.
>
> (ll. 1–4)[12]

In typical Middletonian fashion the familiar themes of sex and money are worked hard so as to satirize the mores of contemporary London, a city in which the quest for cash has almost obliterated traditional distinctions of class. As Lagarde has noticed, we are dealing with a society in which the son of a country gentleman can pass himself off as a knight and yet call a barber cousin, in which a genuine knight can marry a lady of the court but board his children with a mercer and plan to apprentice them.[13] We learn that Knavesbee, the most contemptibly avaricious bourgeois of the piece, has been a student at Cambridge with a peer who calls him "worthy friend" (I.i.286), and that Sir Francis Cressingham's daughter-in-law, disguised as a boy, has gone into service as a page, presumably for reasons of poverty. More absurdly, a French whore supports the claim of the youthful rake Franklin that he belongs to her nation's ambassadorial service by reporting that she knows his father, a fishmonger.

Strained marital relationships are the chief obstacles to quiet life, but these are counterpointed by difficulties between two pairs of fathers and sons. In the main plot, Sir Francis Cressingham, a *senex amans* obsessed with alchemy and gambling, is persecuted by his second wife, a shrewish girl of fifteen "bred up i' th Court" (I.i.12) who has married him for his money and now dominates him completely. She withholds jewels from the three children of the first marriage bequeathed to them by their mother, tries to disinherit them by getting her husband to sell his land, and farms out the two youngest to live in the household of Water-Chamlet, a rich mercer. Meanwhile, she spends her doting husband's money extravagantly and by taking absolute control over his financial affairs reduces him to the status of a pensioner in his own family. Only at the end of the play do we discover that her outrageous behavior has been part of a calculated program of therapy to save her husband from the economic ill effects of his two hobbies—gaming and the "Consuming Chymistry" (V.i.532) of his laboratory.

A number of subsidiary actions buttress this preposterous situation. Water-Chamlet, the cloth merchant, is married to an even fiercer virago than Lady Cressingham, a stentorian woman who nags him on every subject from business ethics to sexual infidelity. But Water-Chamlet loves her despite her curst ways, and when she deserts his house for her cousin's, threatening divorce, he finds his life as unquiet without her as he had with her. He finally tames his shrew with the help of his apprentice by pretending to cast her off and (so as to arouse her jealousy) by staging a wedding at which the French prostitute poses as the new bride. A second by-plot varies the motif of the aggressive wife and beleaguered husband by reversing the relationship. The depraved lawyer Knavesbee, in an action that reminds us of the Greenshields' situation at the end of *Northward Ho*, undertakes to pander his own wife to Lord Beaufort on the promise of "Threescore pounds a year" (III.i.97). She extricates herself from this degrading plight by making shameless advances to Lord Beaufort's page (really George Cressingham's wife in disguise) and so offending the peer by her preference for a mere servant that he rejects her in disgust as "a base strumpet" (III.i.146). Mistress Knavesbee nevertheless reports to her husband that in carrying out her erotic assignment she has come to prefer Lord Beaufort to him, and Knavesbee is therefore astonished to receive only scorn and abuse when he claims his expected reward.

A third strand of plot concerns two indigent sons thrown upon the resources of their own wit. Franklin, disappointed by Lord Beaufort's broken promise to finance his captaincy of a ship, and George Cressingham, deprived of support by his stepmother's newfangled financial policies, combine their talents to defraud Water-Chamlet of his goods. Disguising themselves, they visit Water-Chamlet's shop, where they dupe two apprentices into letting them have fifty pounds worth of valuable cloth on the promise of payment at a neighboring barber shop. The climax of this episode is a hilariously bawdy confrontation between Sweetball, the barber-surgeon, and one of the apprentices. Misunderstanding each other's intent, they talk entirely at cross-purposes. While Ralph, the apprentice, angrily insists on being paid, Sweetball thinks the lad has come to be treated for venereal disease and is not only too bashful to be candid about his ailment but also mentally affected by it. The brandishing of "Dis-membring Knife" and "Cauterizing-Iron" (II.iii.68–70) make for excellent farce, but Middleton exploits the situation verbally for a superb parody of medical jargon and a whole series of salacious double-entendres. Sexual jokes that utilize terms from the cloth trade ("ware," "tissue," and "yard") recall the punning games of the *Ho* plays.

The final act of the comedy contains more diversions such as an absurd suicide pact between Sweetball and Knavesbee (ultimately frustrated, of course) and a scheme by which Franklin's father settles his son's debts at half-rate by pretending that the boy is dead. Although its various deceptions are linked together somewhat mechanically, *Anything for a Quiet Life* is a lively performance. Middleton and Webster's method is to keep their audience ignorant of much of the trickery until it is actually in train or even over. Not only are three critical surprises—the revelation of Lady Cressingham's reforming motive, the existence and disguise of George Cressingham's wife, and the feigning of young Franklin's death—reserved for the final hundred lines of the play, but the withholding of crucial information amounts to a continuing game with the spectators by means of which the playwrights engage their attention.

The inventor of the elaborate confidence trick upon the mercer, his apprentice, and the barber deliberately declines to explain his strategy in advance:

> *Franklin.*   I have a Project
>   Reflects upon yon Mercer, Master *Chamlet,*
>   Shall put us into money.
> *George Cressingham.* What is't?
> *Franklin.* Nay,
>   I will not stale it afore-hand, 'tis a new one. . . .
>   (I.i.267–272)

Middleton thus places his audience disquietingly in a position midway between the sophistication of the cozener and the naiveté of the gulls. Much is left to inference; we see only the *effects* of the collusion between the French bawd and Franklin when she helps him evade the police (III.ii) and between her and the apprentice when she pretends to be Chamlet's new bride (IV.iii). When the apprentice George enters to read a list of guests supposedly invited to his master's feast and to detail the hecatomb of animals to be slaughtered for the occasion (IV.ii.44), he pointedly neglects for some thirty lines to inform his auditors both on stage and off that a wedding is in prospect. It is only after Mrs. Chamlet's return to heel at the end of the following scene that we discover no celebration was ever planned. Intention is purposely concealed. We watch Mistress Knavesbee attempt to seduce Selenger, then bargain to sleep with Lord Beaufort if he in turn will force the page into her bed, before she explains in soliloquy that the whole procedure has been an oblique strategy to arouse disgust in the peer and so preserve "honesty" (III.i.170).

Middleton and Webster spice the game of mystification and surprise by tucking vague clues and veiled hints into the dialogue. The resistance of Sir Francis to Lord Beaufort's criticism of his "rash" marriage (I.i.35), for instance, establishes the initial impression of a doting fool, yet, in retrospect, serves as preparation for the wife's *volte-face* at the denouement; and just as George's resentment of his stepmother is reaching its apogee, we hear her promising oracularly that she "will not be / The woman to you hereafter you expected" (V.i.234–235). Although Mistress Knavesbee's device to repulse the lecherous nobleman remains unclear until it has been executed, the author at this point does warn us to expect trickery by giving the lady an ominously sententious couplet:

> Women though puzzel'd with these subtile deeds,
> May, as i'th Spring, pick Physick out of weeds.
>   (II.i.182–183)

Even Franklin's father undercuts the "sad appearance" of his mourning dress by punning on the word with a hint that his son may still be alive: " 'tis no more then as your Honor says, indeed—appearance; it has more form then feeling sorrow Sir, I must confess . . ." (V.i.309–311). The comedy is designed to clarify itself progressively and, like a jigsaw puzzle, to satisfy its beholders only when the final piece is correctly in place. Such dramaturgy serves to keep up suspense and challenge perceptivity while discouraging emotional involvement. By driving a wedge between our immediate responses to behavior and subsequent interpretations and judgments of it, the playwrights stimulate skepticism and disturb predictable reactions. However coarse-grained the farcical materials of the play may appear, the systematic detachment of its technique lends it a certain intellectual appeal.

Controversy over attribution has so distracted scholars that they have woefully neglected *Anything for a Quiet Life* as a work of art. Swinburne discerned "very good stuff in the plot" but pronounced "the workmanship . . . hardly worthy of the material."[14] Lagarde and Holmes, two fairly recent commentators, both treat the play routinely—more out of duty, one guesses, than respect. Criticism on the whole has been content to ignore the play entirely as drama or to apologize for it as inferior work, "maledroite," failing in "vraisemblence," or lacking "structural integrity and coherence."[15] Lucas goes so far as to label the main plot "imbecile" and the comedy as a whole "trash" except for its interest as "social history."[16] Intemperate as this opinion undoubtedly is, very little energy has been enlisted to modify it or to re-examine the play for possible strengths.

We might begin the reassessment by noting the "uneasiness of tone" that R. B. Parker in a provocative essay identifies as a general feature of Middletonian comedy.[17] Parker points to the characteristic strain we often feel in Middleton's work between the dramatist's impulse to scarify vice on the one hand and to regard it with sardonic amusement on the other. Moralistic intensity and farcical aloofness elbow each other in a way that sometimes threatens a play's equilibrium or unfocuses its point of view. In *Anything for a Quiet Life* Middleton experiments with a new solution to an old problem. In the earliest comedies his difficulty had been the bringing of "immoral comic characters" too abruptly "to severe condemnation."[18] Influenced now by the romantic conventions of tragicomedy, he avoids retributive harshness altogether by suggesting that reprehensible behavior is more often apparent than real—that actions that look sordid, ugly, or selfish may in fact be the means to reform, forgiveness, reconciliation, and harmony. Enlargement of context is supposed to make all the difference. Lady Cressingham has been cruel, we are told, only to be kind; Mistress Knavesbee has been disingenuous only to be true to her own ideals. In a less serious but nevertheless indicative vein, Water-Chamlet describes the deception of his wife as "knavery with a good purpose in't" (IV.iii.69), and the entire cast in chorus heartily endorses Old Franklin's trick with his son: "You have beguil'd us honestly sir" (V.i.620). Middleton and Webster would almost appear to be invoking a stage doctrine of *felix culpa* in order to justify sudden or unexpected reversals.

The theatrical surprises of the fifth act do smack suspiciously of Fletcherian sentimentality, for they suggest an attempt through sheer sensationalism to divert attention from the ethical issues presented earlier.[19] But the tremulous imbalance between ends and means is not a feature of the fifth act only. The collaborating authors expose us throughout the play to a blurred ethos replete with ambiguous or self-contradictory moral attitudes. The long-suffering patience of the mercer or the ebullient mateyness of his apprentice may evoke a wholesome world of Dekkerian affirmation, but this is more than counterweighted by technically "good" characters whose words and actions project the darker vision that young Cressingham sums up when he speaks of "a world so dull as this, / Where faith is almost grown to be a miracle" (V.i.29–30). If it is true that "an honest man may look like a knave, and be ne're the worse for't" (III.ii.103–104), as Chamlet says optimistically in the scene where his cozener evades him, the very irony of the situation forcibly recommends the obverse of the speaker's postulate to our consideration. If the play as a whole betrays any harmony of conception, it is clearly, like Chamlet's marriage, a "harmony in Discords" (II.ii.233). The most interesting characters of *Anything for a Quiet Life* are in fact presented with a kind of doubleness that forbids much security of judgment about them.

Before we actually meet Lady Cressingham, her spouse describes her to us in curious terms. Conventionally, we might expect January to dwell upon the sexual allurements of May; instead, we get a very moral portrait indeed, one that emphasizes how "Discretion . . . beyond her years . . . does more improve / Her goodness." Preferring church to revelry, she has "A Matrons sober staidness in her eye, / And all the other grave demeanor fitting / The Governess of a House . . ." (I.i.37–52). Although Lord Beaufort discounts this praise as special pleading ("Come, come, you read / What you would have her to be, not what she is" [I.i.54–55]), the actual resolution of the conflict, if we accept it at face value, proves the husband's opinion truer in a sense than his critic's. Yet this prim beginning and end merely demarcate the dubiously antiperjorative margins between which Lady Cressingham overwhelms us with repeated demonstrations of her pride, rapacity, willfulness, irresponsibility, paranoia, malice, and all that is unnatural in a wife and stepmother. No doubt her parade of ungracious deeds speaks louder than her husband's loyalty at the opening or her self-defense in the finale, but Middleton and Webster include just enough on the plus side to preclude a simple negative response.

Moreover, the dramatists raise without quite answering the question of whether the character is to be taken as a psychologically rounded figure or as a mere pawn. Looked at in one way, she is an inexperienced girl bent on testing the limits of her newly acquired power and blind to her own faults until her stepson has "Ripen'd [her] pity with his dews of duty" (V.i.518); viewed from a greater distance, she may be seen as a static figure whose "harsh-seeming usage" (V.i.525) of her family has been nothing more than an overelaborate disguise contrived for commendable, if hidden, purposes. The dual perspective produces something akin to a comic version of *The Changeling*, that masterful tragedy that was to provoke an analogous question: does Beatrice-Joanna degenerate from naif to murderess or does she merely reveal her innate corruption under the stimulus of a particular catalyst, De Flores? Inherent in both characterizations is the mysterious problem of the degree to which persons control or direct their own natures, and it may be more than fortuitous that the phrase, to "play the Changeling" (II.i.71–72) with its full freight of irony, crops up twice in the Knavesbee subplot of *Anything for a Quiet Life*.

A complementary ambiguity attends the portrayal of Sir Francis, the lady's apparently brainwashed husband. In Lord Beaufort's estimation, he has simply forfeited his common sense and exposed himself to shame, exploitation, and even cuckoldom, since the old man is as cold sexually as "some bleak Banquetting-house / I'th dead of Winter" (I.i.32–33). Saunder, the impertinent steward, thinks his master as malleable as wax (IV.i.142), and the dutiful son who reluctantly consents to be disinherited shows up his father for a very caricature of uxoriousness. In the main Sir Francis comes off as a human character, a simpleton defined almost exclusively by his infatuation with a beautiful monster. Yet, as his fortune dwindles and his pain increases, his sense of reality expands so that by the final act he has won some sort of self-recognition. At the nadir of his humiliation, he sighs out, "man is never truly awake / Till he be dead" (V.i.195–196), and later, when his immediate wants have been relieved by his son, the kindness jolts him into an *éclaircissement*:

> I am amazement to my self;
> I slept in poverty, and am awake
> Into this wonder. . . .
> . . . .
> But I am my sons childe, sir, he knows of me
> More then I do my selfe.
>
> (V.i.478–486)

The emergence of Sir Francis from darkness into light under the pressures of suffering and love accords imperfectly with the cardboard dotard of the early acts, and both impressions are hard to reconcile with the wise fool who divines from the start his wife's quintessential rectitude. To blur the picture further, Middleton and Webster refrain from dramatizing the gaming and alchemical propensities that supposedly activate Lady Cressingham in her campaign of reform. Indeed, we learn from Chamlet early in the first scene that, although Sir Francis has "been a Gamester" in the past, he has now "given it o're" (I.i.88), and by the end of the scene that his laboratory is about to be smashed (I.i.332–333). Having nearly forgotten these matters by the time the new wife gets around to explaining her conduct, we are tempted to accuse her, in Coleridgean phrase, of the "motive-hunting of a motiveless malignity."

Mistress Knavesbee, although technically on the side of virtue, is nearly as repellent as her mate. Again, the two playwrights confront us with an almost total divorce between acceptable means and ends. Like Mrs. Justiniano of *West-ward Ho*, Sib Knavesbee finds herself in the squalid situation of being prostituted to a nobleman, but since her mode of self-protection requires her to be a sexual tease, a liar, and the cause of an innocent page's dismissal, it calls the sincerity of her outrage gravely into question. Young Cressingham can refer to her as "a modest Gentlewoman" (V.i.584), but almost everything about her up to this point has suggested the Machiavel and the canting hypocrite. Young Franklin calls her a "witty rogue" (I.i.239) before she makes her first entrance, and a little later she deliberately plays upon her husband's jealousy by confessing to a secret flirtation with "a handsom Scholar" (II.i.53) on her last visit to Sturbridge Fair. After accepting the lawyer's shocking proposal with minimal protest, she tells her would-be seducer that she married for money, "not fashion," on the teaching of "Goldsmiths Wives" (II.i.145–146); later she vents her loathing of both husband and page by wishing them on the gallows: "One Mourning-Gown shall serve for both of them" (III.i.169). The scene in which she entraps Selenger with a skein of golden yarn perfectly symbolizes the blend of materialism and sexual aggressiveness in her nature. Yet the authors ordain that this complacent wearer of the fox's skin—the metaphor is her own (III.i.173)—should be the play's chief railer against corruption and lust.

Even the subsidiary characters can provoke a mixed response. In the opening dialogue Lord Beaufort would appear to be the voice of reason, and it is he again who in the final speech crowns the reconciliations with a feast and reconfirms the social and moral ideals of the play. But in his actions he has shown himself to be a lecher, a snob, and a "most un-lordly" promise breaker (IV.iii.12), nor does he anywhere betray the slightest consciousness of fault. Kicking and reviling Knavesbee as the "basest of knaves" (V.i.295), he wholly ignores his own complicity in the attempt to bed Sib, and it is notable that even the rebarbative pander feels more guilt than his customer. For Beaufort—Middleton and Webster would seem to hold—the failure to satisfy an appetite is punishment enough.

As for Old Franklin, the deus ex machina who makes his first appearance in the final act, everyone in the play seems pleased to regard him as the soul of charity. Young Cressingham, whose inheritance he saves, says that his purchase of the family property is sufficient to "style you our Preserver" in the memory of "all posterity," and the gentleman himself claims, not insincerely, that his action looks only "to the end of the good deed it self" (V.i.36–40). But the repolishing of his own "good name" (V.i.328) by settling the debts of his son who has besmirched it through "dissolute course[s]" (V.i.7) will not bear much ethical scrutiny. Not only does he get by with paying half the money owed, he cheerfully accepts the praise and respect of creditors who, assuming the debtor deceased, believe that legally they "could have nothing claim'd" (V.i.327). Half a loaf is better than none, of course, but no one, least of all any of the tradesmen, bothers to point out that the gentleman has come off better than they and, strictly speaking, has not at all "fully satisfied" (V.i.605) the obligation. Old Franklin has in fact been guilty of sharp practice while reaping the guerdon of the idealist—apparently without any awareness of the contradiction. Moreover, his justification of the trick is rooted in sophistry—the contention that spiritual "death" (by which he means his son's errant conduct) can be equated with physical (or legal) death. The whole argument is semantic sleight of hand. Examined carefully, the father's morality comes off as worse than the son's.

The pranks of the two scapegrace youths and of Chamlet's agent George must be taken like the Gadshill robbery in *1 Henry IV*, an incident to which young Cressingham appeals in self-defense. The losses of the barber and the mercer are made good, and the spirit of playful aimiability that envelops their cozenage forbids solemnity.[20] But even these relatively innocent high jinks in the context of the play as a whole intensify rather than dissipate our sense of being caught in the cross fire of two irreconcilable attitudes. On the one side, cleverness, guile, and wit need no justification but their efficacy as entertainment; on the other, conventional standards of morality must be upheld and compel a didactic emphasis. By presenting the trickery first and explaining or moralizing it later, the two playwrights would seem to be having their ethical cake and eating it too. The inescapable problem that such an incongruous mix of values poses is, of course, the degree to which it is deliberate. Perhaps we may explain a measure of the play's fuzziness by ascribing haste or carelessness to its collaborating authors. The most startling shifts of perspective could conceivably have resulted from flawed coordination with Webster, from the attempt to dress the satiric staples of city comedy in the more romantic fashions of the new genre, or from some combination of the two. But the play's duality of outlook is too consistently sustained to be wholly inadvertent.

The discordancies of characterization are supported fairly evenly by a careful junction of gay hilarity with queasy disrelish. The text contains so many casual allusions to death that a kind of thematic undertow is established that pulls against the comic flow. The metaphor of death and resurrection suggested by Chamlet's remarriage (IV.i.110–112, IV.iii.70–77), by Cressingham's restoration (V.i.195–200), and by young Franklin's reappearance (V.i.607–708) is considerably weakened by the frequent expressions of hostility and sadism that pervade the text. Many of these are as macabre as they are funny. Sweetball, for instance, is a particularly effective grotesque because his attitude to violence is so absurdly clinical, even when he himself is to be a victim. For the barber-surgeon, technical jargon has a value horribly independent of human pain, whether the project at hand involves cutting off the "Member" (II.iii.57) of a boy who already "has but one stone" (II.ii.65), wishing Franklin executed so he can "vex every vein about him" (III.ii.26) at the next anatomy lecture, or confederating with Knavesbee to "make incission . . . by his *Jugulars*" (V.i.433–434) in exchange for being strangled himself. Here the hiatus between means and ends, between causes and results, contributes an effect of black comedy, traces of which appear throughout the play.

When Knavesbee fails of his reward, he threatens to "go home and cut my Wife's Nose off," to "turn over a new Leaf, and hang up the Page," and "lastly" to "drown my self" so as to "sink at *Queen-hive*, and rise agen at *Charing-cross*" (V.i.302–305). Rachel Water-Chamlet is eager to attack her supposed rival with "one of my knives" freshly whetted or a "Bird-spit" (IV.ii.120–123), and to make her husband's "Bastards . . . as blinde as Puppies" (IV.iii.30–31); she also wants to "cut off [George's] ears" (IV.iii.66). No wonder her husband sometimes calls her "*Rac*" (V.i.572), a discourteous pun on "rack" or perhaps "wrack" (= vengeance, persecution, injury).[21] Lord Beaufort wants the "branded head" of Knavesbee to know only darkness until the villain's "execution day" (V.i.282–283). Selenger can imagine the hangman's rope as a possible release from Sib Knavesbee's embarrassing addresses (III.i.74), and the mercer at his gloomiest "would be prest to death" (III.ii.142). The exaggeration that such details involve precludes any real fear from intruding upon the laughter, but the details themselves remind us continually of actual punishments and sufferings that prevail beyond the theatre walls and of the bitterness that familiarly invades domestic relationships. A certain amount of repulsive imagery also undermines the play's levity—references to caterpillars, worms in the belly, poison, gangrene, feeding kites with carrion, the sexual exertions of monkeys, fleas in the rushes, stinking sweet-balls (with the genital pun intended), genetically malformed children, diarrhea, pustular rheum, and so forth. Middleton and Webster consistently modify the romanticism of the comedy with touches of gallows humor and physical disgust.

It would appear, then, that *Anything for a Quiet Life* has been self-consciously designed to evoke a bifocal response to which ambiguities of character, motivation, action, morality, and tone all contribute a share. But the collaborators contrive to keep the antitheses unstable, evolving and shifting their alignments, rather than fixed. The sense of doubleness arises mostly from a posteriori considerations, from comparison of present effects with earlier and apparently contradictory ones. The very tentativeness inherent in this method conduces to a weakening of commitment and tends to shrink judgment to mere opinion. If standards of virtue and vice, of wisdom and folly, must be perpetually revised, what of absolutes? Do they not dissolve and perhaps abandon us to a limbo of existential absurdity? The conventions of tragicomedy, which often seem to impose a factitious order too neatly upon the disturbing confusions that have gone before, can, of course, be made to heighten this feeling, and the authors seem to use the very abruptness at the end of the play as a vehicle for contrasting the facile solutions of the stage with the untidy actualities of life. The cleavage forces us to become aware of characters (and their actions) both as functions of a mechanism and as mimetic representations. George Cressingham dramatizes the point by challenging his stepmother to assume a virtue if she has it not and to answer his moralistic criticisms "not . . . In your own person." Her indignant response, "A fine Puppet-play!" (V.i.238–240), reminds us that in one sense the whole performance has been an affair of marionettes, that the entertainment value of the comedy depends to a great extent on our acceptance of characters who dance on strings to a conclusion foreordained by the two dramatists.

The technique of the comedy as well as its content suggests a concern not only with traditional problems of self-knowledge but also with the ambiguities of moral and aesthetic identity—with the endless search for the mind's construction in the face and with the pursuit of authenticity though dramatic artifice. The multiple disguises of the play bear on these issues, and it is obvious that the prominent motif of cloth and clothing carries more than literal significance. Young Franklin must take on three distinct personae before he can be revealed and reaccepted in his true nature; his friend must pretend to be a French tailor, a professional dealer in fashionable surfaces, in order to get by in a world where fathers are blind to the legitimate status of their sons. The male disguise of George Cressingham's wife, impenetrable to everyone except her husband on and off the stage, is primarily a fillip of the plot but secondarily a reminder of the difference between stage and real gender as well as a lesson in the folly of trusting appearance. All the marriages of the play entail role playing and so help reinforce the connections between moral and physical disguise. Water-Chamlet's name and trade point to a milieu in which clothes may hide as much as they reveal. Watered camlet (or chamlet), a sumptuous fabric variegated lustrously by wavy lines and, in the seventeenth century, woven usually of silk and Angora goat hair, would suggest not only ostentation and exotic theatricality but perhaps also (because of the subtle lights in its texture) a certain changeableness, inconstancy, or deceptiveness. While posing as an unnatural wife, Lady Cressingham tries to bankrupt her husband by extravagances of dress; then she signalizes her allegiance by entering "*in civil habit*" (V.i.508). But which of the two modes agrees best with her character? And when her husband whom she has "confin'd . . . t' one sute" (V.i.141–142) appears "bravely" attired in the final scene (V.i.476), can the bright new finery really be taken as the sign of a changed man? Do the "*gallant*" clothes (V.i.508) of the previously neglected children and the new suits with which Mrs. Chamlet finally rewards the apprentices herald a brave new world from which malice, egotism, and the manipulation of others have miraculously vanished?

The cheerfulness at the conclusion seems somehow to turn back upon itself, as if the startling revelations and reverses were more a retreat into illusion than a withdrawal from it. The frequent mention of sleeping and dreaming makes this possibility the likelier. One can take the pat theatricalities of the ending as a Swiftian joke or as a desperate attempt to show the mischievous world of city life as better than it looks. Perhaps Middleton and Webster themselves were ambivalent on the point and embodied their doubts in a comedy that stirs rather than settles our queries. In any case, they ended the play on an interrogative note:

> *I am sent t'enquire your Censure, and to know*
> *How you stand affected?*
>
> (Epilogue, 1–2)

The words of the epilogue may perhaps be taken to involve the audience in the problem of meaning as well as in a judgment upon the skill of the performers.

It has been usual to depreciate *Anything for a Quiet Life*, but closer inspection shows that the collaborating playwrights took some pains to deploy their materials in a patterned way. Contrast plays an obvious part here. Chamlet's pretended wedding banquet finds its counterpart in the actual feast of unity at the end. The intensity of Mistress Knavesbee's hatred for her husband ("I loathe the memory of every touch / My lips hath tasted from thee" [IV.ii.21–22]) balances Chamlet's affection for his wife ("The tongues bitterness must not separate / United souls" [III.ii.167–168]). Satirical acridness is opposed by appeals to sentiment, the least subtle of which (as in Dryden's *All for Love*) is the bringing on of Sir Francis's children to "beget more compassion" (IV.i.104) and shame in the father. Unhealthy materialism is set against legitimate pleasure in goods: Knavesbee's willingness to barter his wife and Lady Cressingham's conspicuous consumption do not negate the lyric delight we are intended to feel when George cries his "Stuffs," his "Silk-Grograns, Sattins, Velvet fine, / The Rosie-colour'd Carnadine" (II.ii.2–4). Clearly the cloth of gold so often mentioned in the dialogue is both positively and negatively charged. "Fresh wedding robes, and *Georges* fresh new sute" (IV.iii.77) gain our approval, but there is equal emphasis on what lies beneath. Sweetball's longing to dissect Franklin's heart to see if it be English or French (III.ii.86–88) merely burlesques the concern with exposure implicit in satire, and later George Cressingham preaches to his father that his stepmother's "Beauty" must not be allowed to obscure "her ugly heart" (IV.i.95–100).

Middleton and Webster often lace distinct parts of the comedy together with repetitions of a purely verbal or nominal sort. Sometimes lacking thematic force, these links might almost pass unnoticed; yet the number of them is striking, and, occasionally, when they occur back to back, they seem to function, almost subliminally, as ligatures between contiguous scenes or between sections of a larger scene. Franklin, describing the villainies of Knavesbee, exclaims, "Hang him, hang him" (I.i.233) only to be echoed in the following episode by Mistress Knavesbee's retort to her husband, "Go hang" (II.i.56). Water-Chamlet speaks of his unquiet home life as "a grief" (II.ii.221), an "affliction" (II.ii.231), and a few minutes later the barber-surgeon with much talk of "exulceration" and a "*Penis . . .* endanger'd" is soliciting Ralph to "open your griefs freely to me" (II.iii.38–47). Sweetball plays obscenely on his own name in the final line of II.iii

157

to be followed instantly by Selenger and Mistress Knavesbee, who use the words "sweeter" and "sweetest" in the first four verses of their amorous encounter. A plea for the hanging of Knavesbee and the page (III.i.168) almost immediately precedes a plan to deliver Franklin over "to the Hangman" (III.ii.24). Lady Cressingham pacifies her stepchildren with "Sweet-meats" (IV.i.146) just before the lawyer welcomes his wife from Lord Beaufort's: " 'tis as sweet as e'er 'twas . . . buss me, Sugar-candy" (IV.ii.13). Pretending to have cuckolded her spouse, Sib Knavesbee calls him "a horned beast, an Ox" (IV.ii.36); then eighteen lines later Chamlet's apprentice has entered and is regaling the couple with the list of meats including "One Ox" (IV.ii.54) that are to be served to his master's wedding guests. When the repetitions are spaced further apart, their effect is less comical or ironic; nevertheless, they testify to the dramatists' unifying instincts. The dialogue mentions silkworms, glass, ships, organs, the court chapel, cheese, storms, and poison all more than once and in widely divergent contexts.

A searcher intent enough upon finding the more familiar Webster in this play could perhaps discover a few recognizable elements, but only a few. The parallel between Lord Beaufort and the Earl in *Westward Ho* with their unsuccessful attempts to seduce a citizen's wife has already been mentioned. Water-Chamlet's shrew keeps her husband under her thumb by recording all his misdemeanors in a "*Black-book*" (I.i.148) of the same kind that Cardinal Monticelso uses in *The White Devil* to list the "names of all notorious offenders" (IV.i.31), but Middleton himself had already used the phrase for the title of a pamphlet in 1604. *Anything for a Quiet Life* contains three aggressive, strongwilled females, a type in which Webster was obviously interested, and Selenger calls one of them (Mistress Knavesbee) "filthy Beauty" and "a white witch" (III.i.88–89) in expressions that recall Webster's title epithet for Vittoria. When Knavesbee proposes that his wife lie with Beaufort, he approaches the matter circuitously by means of a supposed dream (II.i) in a fashion like that in which Vittoria suggests murder to Bracciano. Several speeches by Sir Francis, Lady Cressingham, and Old Franklin are Webster-like in their dependence on equivocation.

Apart from these similarities of plot and style, there are a few other places where the text distantly suggests the tragic Webster—the mention of a soap-boiler in a context of madness (V.i.64),[22] a brief echo scene (V.i.375–411), an Aesopian apologue (V.i.161–164), and a satiric "character" of Lady Cressingham spoken to her face but in the third person:

> *Envy* and *Pride* flow in her painted breasts,
> She gives no other suck; all her attendants
> Do not belong to her husband, his money is hers—
> Marry his debts are his own—she bears such sway,
> She will not suffer his *Religion* be his own,
> But what she please to turn it to.
>
> (V.i.249–254)

One of Lord Beaufort's speeches (I.i.7–11) alludes to Overbury's poem, *A Wife*, which Webster probably edited. Mistress Knavesbee's move to "winde" Selenger "into [her] service" (III.i.30) could be read as a literalization of Julia's metaphor about her relation to the Cardinal: "You shall see me wind my tongue about his heart, / Like a skein of silk (*The Duchess of Malfi*, V.iii.222–223). Such details are suggestive, but the fact that nearly half of them occur in passages probably written by Middleton (according to Lake's linguistic evidence) only shows, as in the case of the *Ho* plays, how thoroughly the collaborators were able to conform their ideas and the larger features of their style to each other and, in so doing, at least partly to subdue their individual natures, like the dyer's hand, to what they were working in.

More obvious than typical Websterisms are a number of Shakespearean overtones, especially in the last act. Young Cressingham explicitly compares his cheating of the merchant to Prince Hal's purse stealing. Water-Chamlet in a probable allusion to *The Tempest* thinks of retiring to a peaceful Bermuda island, once full of thunder, lightning, and "amazing Noises" (V.i.356) but now disenchanted. His wife's submission to obedience seems to imitate Kate's famous speeches at the end of *The Taming of the Shrew*. The elder Cressingham's unnatural relinquishing of all authority to his harpylike wife and his irrational disinheriting of a loyal son are presented almost as domestic parodies of the tragic mistake in *King Lear*. Sir Francis, like Shakespeare's great hero,

> could not
> Come to see order, until foul disorder
> Pointed the way to't—
> So inconsiderate, yet so fruitful stil
> Is dotage to beget its own destruction.
> (V.i.148–152)[23]

And Sweetball's frustrated wish to anatomize the disguised Franklin in order to know his "heart" may be taken as a travesty of Lear's crazed behavior in the imaginary trial scene: "Then let them anatomize Regan; see what breeds about her heart. Is there any cause in nature that make these hard hearts?" (*King Lear*, III.vi.75–77).

* * *

In 1623 Webster contributed eight lines of negligible verse in commendation of Henry Cockeram's *English Dictionarie*, one of the earliest lexicons to be published in the language. This pocket-sized volume, which went through eleven editions by 1658, was elaborately subtitled *An Interpreter of hard English Words, Enabling as well Ladies and Gentlewomen, young Schollers, Clarkes, Merchants, as also Strangers of any Nation, to the understanding of the more difficult authors already printed in our Language, and the more speedy attaining of an elegant perfection of the English tongue, both in reading, speaking and writing*. As the title indicates, the book limits itself in the main to difficult words, devoting a section wholly to fancy or pompous synonyms, *"fustian termes,"* for the use of those "who study rather to be hearde speake, than to understande themselves."[24] Webster's couplets "To his industrious friend," understandably omitted from all but the first edition, pay Cockeram the backhanded compliment of satirizing an important segment of the volume's potential readership:

> while Words for paiment passe at Court,
> And whilst loud talke and wrangling make resort
> I'th Terme to Westminster, I doe not dread
> Thy leaves shall scape the Scombri, and be read.[25]

The poem is undistinguished, but it is typical of Webster in its downright tone, its hit at court life, and its repetition of the hackneyed classical joke, used by Horace, Martial, and others, about bad poetry used as a wrapping for fish ("Scombri").

The next theatrical enterprise in which Webster is known to have engaged was a play quickly written to exploit a pair of sordid local scandals. The first of these, pathetic enough in actuality, was rich in comic potential for the stage. Late in July 1624, Anne Elsdon, a respectable sixty-year-old widow of substantial wealth and too convivial for her own good, fell in with one Tobias Audley, a disreputable tobacconist, vendor of strong drink, and, as his enemies later charged, "a most notorious Lewd person and of noe worth of Creditt."[26] He was in his twenties. Audley conducted the woman to a tavern in Blackfriars, where four of his cronies—two prostitutes and a couple of down-at-heels clergymen— had already gathered for a drinking party. This gang of sharpers, who sound from the documents like characters out of Jonson's *Alchemist*, immediately proceeded not merely to get Mrs. Elsdon drunk but to keep her so for a period of five days. During this interval Audley, assisted by the others (who, of course, expected to profit by the scheme), prevented her from returning to her own house, forced her into a contract of marriage before witnesses, and purchased the necessary license with her money. One of the two priests married the couple at the Nag's Head, a tavern in Cheapside, and, before the poor woman was sober enough to realize what was happening, Audley had bedded his "bride," ransacked the house for money, jewelry, plate, and property deeds, and got her, as he thought, legally within his power. The conspirators then scoffed at her as an "old hag" and "old jade." By this time, however, Anne Elsdon's son-in-law Benjamin Garfield had discovered her disappearance and took the first of a series of legal actions against Audley. Garfield's mounting frustration with the ineffectual processes of common law prompted him at length to lay his case before the Court of the Star Chamber. But before any settlement could be reached, both the widow and her conniving suitor died—he, still unconvicted, in Newgate Prison, she in her devastated house, partly, perhaps, from the physical effects of her recent ordeal. Mrs. Elsdon's heirs seem never to have recovered the stolen property, and Garfield himself died a few years after his mother-in-law, to be buried in St. James's, Clerkenwell, the parish church where Webster himself may lie.[27]

As noted already in Part I, the principals in this affair were probably people of whom Webster had personal knowledge. The widow Elsdon lived in his parish, St. Sepulchre's, as did Audley for a time. Garfield lived in the adjoining parish north of Smithfield, where Webster's local theatre, the Red Bull, was located. Moreover, Garfield's father, Ralph Garfield, had been a friend of Webster's father. Both men, as leading members of St. Sepulchre's, had joined in petitioning Lord Salisbury to supplement the insufficient stipend of their vicar.[28]

The second crime was more shocking still and certainly as dramatic, for it was based on a matricide in Whitechapel. Only a few months prior to Anne Elsdon's comitragic adventure, on 9 April 1624, Nathaniel Tindall, a youth, brutally stabbed his mother to death. History does not record the boy's motive, but he pleaded guilty at his trial in the Old Bailey and was duly hanged (lest the grisly warning be lost upon his neighbors) near the house in which the violence had been committed.

Webster collaborated with Dekker, Rowley, and Ford, three of the most prominent dramatists of the day, in turning these two sensational episodes into a popular play whose double plot is proclaimed by its title, *A Late Murther of the Son upon the Mother, or Keep the Widow Waking*. Hardly more than a month after Mrs. Elsdon was kidnapped and despite Garfield's attempt to prevent him, the Master of the Revels licensed the play for performance at the Red Bull.[29] As a result of the production, which added public ridicule to the widow's other tribulations, Garfield's case against Audley got entangled with charges of libel against various theatrical persons thought to be responsible for putting the play on at the expense of the old lady's reputation. Among these were the part authors Rowley and Dekker, Aaron Holland (who had built the Red Bull and had been for some years an important sharer in its profits), Rafe Savage (who, acting as business manager, commissioned the play and paid the dramatists), and Ellis Worth, an actor well known for his performances at the playhouse. Although the drama is lost, we know a good deal about it from statements made at the official investigation and since uncovered by C. J. Sisson.[30] Dekker was the only dramatist who testified, but from his deposition and related documents the probable process by which the play got written can be reconstructed with unusual completeness.

Dekker and Rowley seem to have worked out a scenario in which episodes from the tragic murder plot were to be interlaced with mirthful scenes from the story of the widow Elsdon's misadventure. Dekker apparently controlled the shape of the play, for we know that he wrote the entire first act, in which the major characters of both plots would be introduced, and a set speech in the final scene for Tindall, undoubtedly the protagonist's penitent oration on the scaffold. Webster and Ford, doubtless having studied Dekker's initial work, must then have been summoned to join Rowley in writing the intermediate sections. Probably they each composed a single act separately and then came together with Dekker to work on Act V and adjust their respective portions to the whole. Webster, like the others, would then have a hand in both plots. This in fact is what we should expect from our knowledge of his collaborative method with Dekker in *Westward Ho* and *Northward Ho* and with Middleton in *Anything for a Quiet Life*.

Three of the men had already collaborated in rushing a topical sensation onto the boards. Rowley, Dekker, and Ford produced a script together in the summer of 1621 based on the recent trial and execution of the pathetic Elizabeth Sawyer and entitled *The Witch of Edmonton*. It is even possible that Webster assisted them in this earlier play as well as in *A Late Murder*, for the title page (1658), which atttributes the work to "divers well-esteemed Poets: *William Rowley, Thomas Dekker, John Ford*, &c.," implies that not all the authors receive mention. The four obviously had to work rapidly on *Keep the Widow Waking*, for only about five weeks elapsed between the Elsdon affair and Sir Henry Herbert's license. Haste, of course, would be essential if the theatre were to capitalize fully on the topical subject matter, and, besides, the players at the Red Bull were competing with a rival troupe whom Herbert allowed to present their own version of the Tindall murder one day after the play by Webster and his colleagues opened.[31] Dekker and Rowley were both accustomed to such pressures, but one wonders what inconvenience they occasioned Webster, by his own confession a notoriously slow writer. Perhaps he was assigned a somewhat smaller share than the others.

Contemporary evidence gives us some knowledge of both the content and tenor of *A Late Murder*. No fewer than two broadside ballads on the subject of the Tindall killing appeared shortly after the lad's trial, and must have encouraged the writing of the play. These stressed the "*most bloudy, vnnatural, and vnmatchable*" nature of the crime and the "penitent . . . Teares" of the murderer.[32] The matter obviously cried out for homiletic treatment in the tradition of such "domestic" tragedies as *Arden of Faversham*, *A Warning for Fair Women*, and *A Yorkshire Tragedy*, nor would Dekker and his partners have shrunk from squeezing every drop of horror and pathos from the uncommonly lurid events.

A third ballad enlightens us on how the subplot was handled. This is revealingly called "keeping the widow wakeing or lett him that is poore and to wealth would aspire gett some old rich widdowe and grow wealthye by her, to the tune of the blazing torch."[33] Here we are given the crude success story of a resourceful young hero who competes with three suitors (a pawnbroker, a horse courser, and a comfit maker) for the widow's hand and who cheats them of their prize by superior wit. This, of course, is Audley, who cleverly makes his fortune by plying his victim with drink and thereby tricking her into matrimony. No sympathy is wasted on the foolish woman, who, the writer implies, ought to know better

than to consort with a man less than half her age. On the contrary, all the approbation is reserved for Audley:

> Thus sometimes that haps in an houre,
>   that comes not in seaven yeare,
> Therefore lett yong men that are poore,
>   come take example here,
> And you whoe faine would heare the full
>   discourse of this match makeing,
> The play will teach you at the Bull,
>   to keepe the widdow wakeing.[34]

It is quite clear that the ballad, which gives the play's underplot in outline
and takes its title for a refrain, was written afterwards as a means of drumming
up business for the theatre. Benjamin Garfield even charged that Aaron Holland, one of the men with financial interests in the Red Bull, deliberately sent a
balladmonger to sing it beneath Anne Elsdon's window. The testimony from the
records of the Star Chamber case contains additional detail about how Mrs. Elsdon was derided on the stage. There was a scene in which Audley gleefully describes to his shop assistant how, in applying for the wedding license, he told
those in charge "that it was for the marrieing of an old bedd ridden woman and a
young fellow together."[35] If the audience had already seen the widow prostrated
from tippling, such a scene would of course add insult to injury and heighten the
farcical irony of her plight. The play naturally contained tavern scenes. In one of
them Audley and his gang of conspirators humiliated the widow by making her
think she was about to receive a basket of apricots from an acquaintance and
then rudely letting her down. A drawer is put up to disguising himself as a girl
and pretending to deliver the fruit. Someone then cries out for a drink and the
drawer, reverting to habit, responds with "Anon, anon, Sir," thus revealing his
true identity. The subtitle of the play was a proverbial expression and would
have served as bawdy shorthand for the familiar situation in which a clever
rogue takes possession of a rich widow both sexually and financially at the same
time. Fletcher had already used the phrase with this implication in *Wit Without
Money* (1614–1620), and Etherege was to do so again in *The Comical Revenge*
(1664).[36]

The artistic level of *Keep the Widow Waking* does not sound particularly
high. The two plots have little in common except their middle-class origin and
their appeal as a sort of Jacobean yellow journalism. It would be difficult to fuse
them into an organic whole, although something might be done with the striking
parallels and contrasts inherent in the combination. The principals of both stories are an older woman and a younger man. One of the female victims would be
presented tragically to evoke moral outrage—and perhaps tears—while the other
would be exploited as the butt of farcical tricks and jokes. Doubtless, too, there
would be a certain dramatic effectiveness in watching Tindall sink to his doom

in an agony of conscience while Audley blithely rose to riches on the strength of his ruthless ingenuity. The counterpointing of murder and sex would perhaps appeal to Webster. Nevertheless, it is hard to imagine his taking great pride in a play so hurriedly thrown together and so obviously tailored to the vulgar tastes of the Red Bull. This was the theatre whose audience and physical conditions he had held in contempt when *The White Devil* was first produced. But Webster must have been glad of the money he got for his part in the project. The intense outrage of Mrs. Elsdon's son-in-law and especially his haling such a variety of stage people into court imply that the play was a huge success at the box office.

* * *

Webster undoubtedly took his other major assignment of 1624, the pageant for Sir John Gore's inauguration as mayor on October 29, rather more seriously than the potboiler at the Red Bull. Planning and preparation for the show had begun as early as the preceding June, and Webster was probably at work on his contribution to the festivities well before *A Late Murder* was acted. His guild, the Right Worthy and Worshipful Fraternity of Merchant Taylors, had been licensed by Edward I and numbered among its honorary brothers most of the English monarchs since that time. It was one of the largest, richest, and most influential of the great London livery companies, with three lord mayors already to its credit since James I's accession. Ten years, however, had elapsed since the last Merchant Taylor was chosen, and there was now special cause for fraternal pride and a budget lavish enough to express it ostentatiously. Although the high inflation of the period must be taken into account, the Taylors spent over a thousand pounds on the pageant—a greater sum than they had ever spent for such a purpose in three centuries.

The ritual for Lord Mayor's day was "Deriued from remarkable Antiquity," as Webster's title puts it. It consisted basically of a "riding" or triumphal procession "the morrowe after Simon and Jude's Day" to and from Westminster, where the Lord Mayor elect took the oath of allegiance at the Exchequer.[37] The "bachelors" of the guild of which the new mayor was free always served as ceremonial attendants and were splendidly garbed to set them apart from the freemen of other companies. The Merchant Taylors traditionally wore blue gowns with crimson hoods. The mayor himself, dressed in a long gown of scarlet with a black velvet hood and his gold chain of office, was accompanied in procession by his immediate predecessor as mayor and by the other most important municipal officers—aldermen, sheriffs, and the recorder. A series of elaborately decorated barges took the entire party up river for the oath. On their return, the mayor landed at St. Paul's Wharf, "where he and the reste of the Aldermen take their horses, and in great pompe passe throwgh the greate streete of the citie called Cheapsyde,"[38] there to be greeted by the assembled representatives of all the other livery companies. Antic figures "apparelled lyke devells" and "wylde men" with firecrackers cleared the crowded streets for a colorful parade in which the mayor was preceded by the regalia of his new position—the sword of the City of London, a scabbard set with pearls, and the great mace. The procession stopped at the Guildhall for a banquet at which the new mayor feasted a huge assemblage of citizens; then it continued to St. Paul's Cathedral for solemn evensong and was afterwards lighted through the streets with special torches for the mayor's journey home.

Much of the expense was laid out for cloth—taffeta, silk, lace, satin, sarcenet, velvet—to make coats, gowns, hoods, caps, ribbons, streamers, pennons, and heraldic banners. The City Carpenter was employed to erect and dismantle special signposts as were a whole crew of decorators, painters, and gilders to prepare the arms and escutcheons of the prominent institutions and officers of state. The music of hautboys, flutes, trumpets, and drums accompanied the progress at various points; at others it was greeted by the booming of cannons. The account books of the Merchant Taylors contain a carefully itemized bill of expenses showing disbursements for both services and material—thirty-three pounds, six shillings, and eight pence, for instance, "paid for double discharging one hundred and fforty chambers and ffireworks in the little ship upon ye triumph day." Not even the five shillings "given to a little boy that went in ye Company's barge wth his drum" is omitted.[39] It is highly probable that Webster's brother Edward supplied the pageant wagons as the playwright's father had done a dozen years earlier when Dekker wrote the Lord Mayor's show for the previous Merchant Taylor to hold the office.

Webster's part in these ceremonies was to design and supervise the execution of several spectacles or "devices" that would pay honor to Sir John Gore, the Merchant Taylors, and the whole municipality by combining the arts of carpentry and painting with that of verse. As was customary, the dramatist immediately published a description of his *Monuments of Honor*, including, naturally, the poetic speeches he had written to be delivered on the occasion. When Sir John and his retinue took water "at the *Three Cranes*" (l. 37), they were presented with a symbolic glorification of London as the navigational center of the world. Mounted on a barge that approached the mayor's "in maner of a Sea-Triumph" were "two Eminent Spectacles" (l. 23). In the first, allegorical figures representing Oceanus and Thetis received the watery tribute of their subordinates, the Thames and the Medway. The companion device, "a faire Terrestiall Globe, Circled about, in convenient Seates, with seaven of our most famous Navigators" (ll. 27–29) signified that "*Oceanus* in gratefull recompence" returned "the memory" (ll. 33–34) of such distinguished mariners as Drake, Hawkins, Frobisher, and Gilbert. An exchange in couplets between Thetis and Oceanus, heralded by "a peale of Sea-Thunder" (l. 38), compared London to Venice in beauty and importance and concluded with a salutation to the mayor and aldermen, wishing them a prosperous year.

A variety of "land shews" or floats awaited His Lordship in the cathedral churchyard after he debarked at St. Paul's Wharf. The first, called the *Temple of Honor*, had a person representing "*Troynovant*" (London) at its apex. Supported upon pillars encircled with roses and enthroned "in rich Habilaments," she presided over the five "eminent" (ll. 96–97) but lesser cities of Antwerp, Paris, Rome, Venice, and Constantinople, under each of which, in turn, sat a renowned English scholar and poet. Webster's choice of Chaucer, Gower, Lydgate, Sir Thomas More, and Sidney was calculated to celebrate London's reputation for learning, its hospitality to literature, and the traditional association of letters with the court. Riding "afore this *Temple*" (l. 105) were figures associated with the origin of the Merchant Taylors themselves—Henry de Royall, the first master of the guild elected in 1300, and John of Yeacksley, who in 1331 purchased the land in Threadneedle Street where their hall was later built. After a speech by Troynovant explaining the visual symbolism, the actor playing Sidney briefly underlined the conventional function of poets as perpetuators of men's fame. Webster's special attraction to Sidney, whose turns of phrase he liked to copy and work into his own compositions, appears plainly from the fact that he alone of the five authors impersonated on the pageant was given a speaking part. Webster, of course, was touching on a favorite theme in mentioning the avoidance of flattery:

> To Honor by our *Wrightings Worthy Men*
> *Flowes as a duty from a judging pen,*
> *And when we are emploid in such sweet praise,*
> *Bees swarme and leave their honey on our bayes:*
> *Ever more Musically Verses runne,*
> *When the loth'd veine of flattery they shun.*
> (ll. 132–137)[40]

The omission of Shakespeare and other dramatic poets was, of course, to be expected, for their profession would have been thought too "popular" and undignified for such an occasion.

After the *Temple of Honor* came a figure personating Sir John Hawkwood, one of the Merchant Taylors' most important heroes. Originally a humble apprentice of the trade, he had risen to distinguish himself in battle under the Black Prince, and after fighting in the Holy Land and serving "divers Princes of *Italy*" (l. 145) as a general, had died at Florence and been honored by a magnificent tomb in the Duomo. Mounted on horseback "in compleate Armour" (l. 141) and resplendent in plumes of pale blue and white, the colors of the Company, he symbolized the glorious possibilities open to a brother, even if his birth were mean. Hawkwood rode in front of a horse-drawn chariot, emblazoned with the arms of the Fraternity, that under a crimson canopy contained eight English kings "that have bin free of this Worshipfull Company" (ll. 67–68). These were the monarchs of Shakespeare's great history cycle, including even "the bad man, but the good King, *Richard* the third, for so the Lawes he made in his short Government doe Illustrate him" (ll. 178–180). The appropriate roses, red for Lancaster and white for York, garnished the various chairs of state and were significantly combined for the chair of Henry VII. Edward III spoke for all the royalty in praise of the Taylors, concluding his verses with their motto, "*By unity the smallest things grow great*" (l. 202), which was then echoed in chorus by the other kings. Behind the chariot in order of rank rode various celebrities—peers, churchmen, and knights—who throughout the years had been granted honorary freedom of the company. These numbered almost two hundred and ranged from Richard II's queen to Sir John Harrington, Queen Elizabeth's godson and the translator of Ariosto's great epic *Orlando Furioso*. Two foreigners were represented by reason of the ancient association of the Knights of St. John in Jerusalem with the Merchant Taylors, for the livery company and the knightly order shared the same patron saint, John the Baptist. A special subgroup commemorated the great feast, held in 1607, when the company had conferred membership upon Prince Henry and a large body of his counselors and attendants.

The "Sea-Tryumphs" (l. 235), which had meanwhile been removed to land, made their appearance for the second time that day and were now followed in parade by two emblems dear to the Merchant Taylors: first, a little ship called the Holy Lamb that ordinarily hung from the rafters in Merchant Taylor's Hall but that now bore the golden fleece in its rigging to signify that the tailoring trade fell under the special protection and providence of God; second, a camel and a lion, "the two beasts . . . proper to the Armes of the Company" (ll. 239–240), ridden respectively by a Turk and a Moor, to suggest the commerce of the Taylors with faraway and exotic regions of the world.

Webster concluded his pageantry with two more elaborately wrought spectacles. The first of these, called the *Monument of Charity and Learning*, reminded spectators of that "famous and worthy Patriot" (l. 249) Sir Thomas White, founder of St. John's College, Oxford. White was the most prominent educational benefactor in the history of the guild; he had been Lord Mayor himself in 1553 (when he had participated in the trial of Lady Jane Grey) and had named his famous college for the patron saint of the Taylors. The pageant presented him seated under an elm tree in a flower garden decorated at its corners by "foure artificiall Bird Cages, with variety of Birds in them" (ll. 245–246). The elm signified the tree in White's dream that was said to have determined the college's site and that still grew on its grounds; the flowers and birds were to represent by visual and aural means "a Spring in Winter" (ll. 245–248). Flanked by Charity "with a Pellican on her head" and Learning with a book and laurel wreath, White was backed by the College of St. John Baptist "exactly modeled" (ll. 276–279). The whole pageant was surrounded by figures representing twelve of the cities that had especially benefited from White's philanthropy. After two cornets had exchanged fanfares, Learning humbled herself to the mayor and exhorted him in verse to emulate White as a patron of scholarship.

The final pageant, called the *Monument of Gratitude*, was another memorial to Prince Henry. An "Artificiall Rocke, set with mother of Pearle" was adorned with "foure curious Piramids" or tombs, each bearing the Prince's insignia and illuminated through "ovals and squares" from inside so as to glitter by night with simulated jewels. In the center on a golden pedestal stood the figure of the prince himself presiding over the riches, both spiritual and material, to which he had been born. He was canopied by "halfe a Celestiall Globe" from which hung "the Holy Lambe in the Sun-beames" (ll. 306–316) between angels; seated in niches around him were allegorical personifications of twelve appropriate virtues—Magistracy, Liberality, Industry, Chastity, Obedience, and the like. Verses delivered by a figure dressed as Amadeus V of Savoy, traditionally a rescuer of Rhodes from the Turks in 1315 and affiliated with the Taylors through his membership in the Society of St. John Baptist, bade Sir John Gore remember with gratitude and try to imitate the prince's finest qualities. It is characteristic of Webster and his age that even on this hopeful and festive occasion there should have been the inevitable philosophizing about death:

> *Such was this Prince, such are the noble hearts,*
> *Who when they dye, yet dye not in all parts:*
> *But from the* Integrety *of a Brave mind,*
> *Leave a most Cleere and Eminent Fame behind.*
> (ll. 359–362)[41]

This passage of course recalls Delio's final couplet at the end of *The Duchess of Malfi*: "*Integrity of life is fame's best friend / Which nobly, beyond death, shall crown the end*" (V.v.120–121). A dozen years after his burial Prince Henry could still serve Webster, like the heroes of his tragic masterpieces, as an embodiment of the stoic toughness that affirms human identity, a symbol of the courage and uniqueness that establish a man's fame in the teeth of the great leveler.

The entire spectacle was integrated, as its title suggests, by the theme of honor. Webster's plan was to show that his own guild, his native city, and his country at large all participated in a concept of honor that had geographical, historical, moral, and religious dimensions. The new mayor was to be symbolically reminded of a tradition that conceived London as the queen of cities, dominant equally over land and sea, and linked economically and spiritually not only to the major European seats of power, wealth, and prestige but also to races and continents beyond and especially to the Holy Land. Her unity was at once social, temporal, and eternal. She embraced in brotherhood all classes of men from apprentices to kings and all callings whether of tradesmen, educators, philanthropists, clergymen, writers, navigators, soldiers, or heads of state. Her present contained her past. Through the conceit of Troynovant her honor extended backward to classical Rome and through John the Baptist to the very fount of Christian civilization. The visual allusion to the Tudor myth with its representation of Lancastrian-Yorkist union in the person of Henry VII adumbrated the current reign, for the first Tudor sovereign was, of course, a prototype of the first Stuart, under whose scepter the whole island had been politically joined. All these radii met emblematically—one could almost say hagiographically—in the figure of Prince Henry, whose apotheosis in paint, carpentry, and verse as "*fames best president*" could be the more extravagantly transcendental because of his recent translation "*to a higher Court of Parliament, / In his full strength of Youth and height of blood*" (ll. 349–351). As Bergeron has suggested, Webster was re-erecting in more tangible form "the monumental column of honour"[42] that he had built more than a decade earlier with his elegiac verses on the prince.

Webster could neither begin nor end the description of his pageant without reminding readers that his literary and scholarly talents had only partially been tapped: "I could a more curious and Elaborate way have exprest my selfe in these endeavors, but to have bin rather too teadious in my Speeches, or too weighty, might have troubled my Noble Lord, and pusled the understanding of the Common People" (ll. 375–378). In his preface he had, in fact, already born witness to his fondness for history by mentioning what he might have included in the slender volume but for limitations of space—"the Original and cause of all Tryumphes" and "their excessive cost in the Time of the *Romans*," for instance, or "a survey . . . of the Triumphs of the precedent times in . . . *London*" (ll. 3–7). This last remark implies that he troubled to reacquaint himself with the details of former pageants so that, as Bergeron points out, he may well have drawn upon Munday's show of 1605 for his chariot of medieval kings or upon Squire's of 1620 for the figure of Oceanus.[43] Webster was obviously eager to please both the mayor and "my Worthy Imployers" (l. 379), and his dedication is pleasantly free of officiousness. He insists only upon his "quality of a Scholler" and promises, "I shall never either to your eare, or table presse unmannerly, or impertinently" (ll. 8–9).

* * *

The elegy on Prince Henry's death and the Lord Mayor's pageant established Webster firmly in London as a poet for public occasions. Some time after December 1624 (when the marriage treaty between Prince Charles and Henrietta Maria was ratified) and before the following March (when James I died), Webster translated and probably composed some brief verses of compliment as captions for the individual figures in a portrait of the royal family.[44] This was an engraving suitable for hanging, copies of which could be bought from William Riddiard "at the Vnicorne in Cornehill neare the Exchange." In theme it might serve as an illustration of James Shirley's great lyric written some years afterward:

> The glories of our blood and state
> Are shadows, not substantial things;

There is no armour against fate;
Death lays his icy hand on kings:
Scepter and crown
Must tumble down,
And in the dust be equal made
With the poor crooked scythe and spade.
(*The Contention of Ajax and Ulysses*, iii.1–8)[45]

King James holding a scepter sits on his throne in the center of the picture between memorial figures of the dead Queen Anne and Prince Henry, both of whom rest their hands upon skulls. At his feet sit two other reminders of death, a pair of deceased children. James's living offspring—the future Charles I with Henrietta Maria and Elizabeth with her husband the King of Bohemia and their numerous progeny—are likewise depicted. The only surviving copy of this engraving, now in the print department of the British Library,[46] is not the original (published a month or so before the end of the reign) but a later version (dating from after 1633) to which the portraits of more recent children and other death's heads, including one for King James himself, have been added. In both states the tradition of *memento mori* is obvious. The verse inscriptions, beneath one of which appear the identifying words "Haec composuit Ioannes Webster," are anything but remarkable. With their stale personifications of Fate, Death, and Fortune, they seem to derive from emblem books (a favorite genre with Webster), and they incorporate formulae from Martial, Virgil, and Ovid, at least two of which the dramatist had already employed elsewhere.[47] But their sheer conventionality suggests that by now Webster, indeed "much possessed by death," had acquired a special facility in funerary writing.

THE FINAL PHASE [II]

William Rowley's connection with Webster continued beyond the commendatory poem for *The Duchess* in 1623 and *Keep the Widow Waking* in 1624 into the
following year when the two friends collaborated on *A Cure for a Cuckold*. Like
Anything for a Quiet Life, this play was not printed until the collector and bookseller Francis Kirkman published it at the Restoration. Although the first quarto,
which advertises the play as "*Written by* John Webster *and* William Rowley," did
not appear until 1661, and although Kirkman's claim for Webster's part in the
drama has been questioned, both the joint authorship and the date (c. 1624–
1625) are now generally taken as established. Kirkman, as we have already had
occasion to notice, could sometimes be inaccurate, but Rowley's share has never
been seriously disputed, and the publisher would have little reason to lie or guess
about a second author. On internal grounds Thomas Heywood has been proposed as a third collaborator, but trustworthy evidence for his participation is so
slender that there is every reason for skepticism. Even this little suggests that
Heywood could hardly have taken more than a minor share.

Scholars have divided the play variously on various grounds—parallel
names, words, and phrases, stylistic traits, orthographical habits, linguistic
preferences, metrical tendencies, and the like.[1] What emerges from this confusing mass of argumentation is virtual unanimity on some sections of *A Cure for a
Cuckold*. Rowley is acknowledged to have written five scenes (II.i, II.ii, II.iii,
III.ii, and IV.iii), episodes that involve not only the "low" comic character Compass but also Rochfield, Annabel, Franckford, and others attached to the "high"
plot. There is equal agreement about Webster's responsibility for three of the
most dramatic parts of the action—Lessingham's meeting with Bonvile in France
for the supposed duel (III.i), Annabel's reaction to the suspected death of her
husband (III.iii.1–40), and the return of both men to Clare, the fountainhead of
all the misunderstandings (IV.ii). Authorship of the remaining sections, whether
individual or collaborative, can be specified less certainly, but the play as a
whole makes a remarkably unified effect. Webster's partnership with Rowley
(and perhaps Heywood) was obviously close.

The date of *A Cure for a Cuckold* could not be much later than early 1625,
for a particularly virulent epidemic of plague closed the London theatres from

mid-May until late December of that year.[2] Rowley died in February 1626, and the text contains several topical allusions that would have been impossible before 1624. Rowley was a popular comedian acting at this time with the King's Men, but he had earlier been a member of Prince Charles's Company at the Phoenix or Cockpit and had connections, as we have already seen, with the Red Bull. He seems to have regarded himself primarily as an actor rather than a writer, but he was certainly a member of Webster's inner circle, for he collaborated on plays with several of his partner's friends—Heywood, Dekker, Ford, and especially Middleton, for whose productions such as *The Changling* and *The Spanish Gypsy* he is thought to have provided important scenes, including, usually, the low comedy. Rowley was fat and specialized in clown roles. Since he clearly maintained relations with friends at both the Bull and the Cockpit, perhaps he invented the character of Compass as a vehicle for himself on one of these stages.

The main plot of *A Cure for a Cuckold*, with which Webster is usually credited, follows the modish school of Fletcher and is conceived somewhat after the manner of *The Devil's Law-Case*. With its unusually farfetched action, its protean characterization, and (despite notable exceptions) its comparatively lackluster verse, this tragicomedy may present the most formidable challenge to interpretation of any piece in the entire Webster canon. Although it is possible with Murray and others to read the drama as an elaborate morality on the educational progress of romantic lovers from selfishness to self-denial,[3] the initial impression that the play creates—and seems planned to create—is one of bafflement and psychological murkiness. It is not merely that Webster sacrifices consistency of character to improbable situations, surprise, and the requirements of an intricate plot; he appears to make the surface incredibilities of his intrigue a means of reflecting the obscure and unpredictable nature of the human heart. It is hard not to feel that in *A Cure for a Cuckold* Webster was writing against his natural tragic bent, for the web of misunderstandings, withheld information, verbal ambiguities, and shifting attitudes that holds the play together produces an effect dangerously close to moral absurdity. Good and evil alike seem to be bled of their intensity and even to lose definition. But the labyrinthine complexity of the dramatic procedure confuses us partly because it is meant to convey the experience of emotional and moral confusion. Some artistic consciousness of the issue appears in the word "lost," spoken repeatedly by characters at moments of stress and supported by the journey motif that pervades the play's imagery and action. (As will be remembered, "lost" figures prominently in the linguistic pattern of all three of Webster's unaided dramas.) It is typical of the tone, for instance, that one of the scenes should open with a lady abandoned on a road and the words, "I'm at doubt already where I am" (II.ii.1). The central narrative is built around a few strongly written key scenes and splendidly complemented by a broadly comic underplot—mainly Rowley's—from which the play takes its title. This simpler action comments significantly upon the "high" plot and helps to focus and clarify its meaning. The thematic cohesion of the work as a whole in conjunction with the more technical evidence of authorship would suggest that the collaborating dramatists divided the play, not exclusively by plots, but by sections in the method that Webster and Dekker had used in *Westward Ho* and *Northward Ho*.

The dominant situation, typical of the Jacobean taste for theatrical problem-mongering, pits friendship against romance and subjects both to the most sinister, unlikely, and irrational strains. The play opens on the wedding day of Annabel and Bonvile with a confrontation between the melancholy Clare and her frustrated suitor Lessingham, both of whom are guests at the festivities of the bride and groom. The emphasis on unaccountable depression against a backdrop of romantic happiness recalls Antonio at the opening of *The Merchant of Venice* and establishes at the outset a general atmosphere of psychic malaise. Lessingham has long been impatient to marry Clare, but, without giving her reasons, she continues to keep him languishing in an uncertainty that not only sets the tone of the succeeding action but also foreshadows its tortuousness:

> *Clare.*   with this Answer pray rest satisfied.
>   In all these travels, windings, and indents,
>   Paths, and by-paths which many have sought out,
>   There's but one onely road, and that alone
>   To my fruition; which who so findes out,
>   'Tis like he may enjoy me: but that failing,
>   I ever am mine own.
> *Lessingham.*   Oh name it, Sweet.
>   I am already in a Labyrinth
>   Until you guide me out.
>
>   (I.i.60–69)

Clare then compounds the mystery by withdrawing from her lover and sending him an ambiguous message:

> *Prove all thy friends, finde out the best and nearest,*
> *Kill for my sake that Friend that loves thee dearest.*
>   (I.i.118–119)

This letter plunges Lessingham into an agony of Hamletian pessimism as, "Distemper'd with a thousand fantasies," he wrestles with the ethical conflict it presents and laments "these last and worser times" in which "Justice [is] banisht th' earth" (I.ii.23–26). It is cruel enough to be obliged for love's sake to kill one's best friend, but who, in fact, is that? In order to find out, he manufactures a story that he must enter a duel on Calais sands in which the seconds as well as the principals are to fight, and sets about the testing of his friends to see which one is willing to risk his life for him. All make excuses except Bonvile, who, even at the sacrifice of deserting his bride without explanation and postponing the consummation of his marriage, insists on crossing to France immediately as the necessary second. Only when they reach the French shore and the supposed opponents fail to appear does Lessingham inform Bonvile that they two are to be the real duelists:

> You left your Bridal-bed to finde your Death-bed,
> And herein you most nobly exprest,
> That the affection 'tween two loyal friends
> Is far beyond the love of man to woman,
> And is more near allied to eternity.
>
> (III.i.52–56)

Bonvile first tries to talk Lessingham out of fighting by reinterpreting Clare's letter. It means, he says, that "you cherish in your breast / Either self-love, or pride, as your best friend, / And she wishes you'd kill that" (III.i.87–89). When this line of persuasion fails, Bonvile himself refuses to fight; he argues that Lessingham may claim already to have fulfilled Clare's instructions, since by valuing his best friend at a lower rate than his mistress, he has in effect killed their friendship. As they part, Bonvile says reproachfully, "may you finde a better friend then I, / And better keep him" (III.i.171–172).

Lessingham now returns to Clare with the story that he has done her bidding and killed Bonvile. Horrified instead of pleased, she berates Lessingham hysterically for misconstruing her intentions; then suddenly her grief shifts to exultation as she recalls that he has slain not only her "deerest friend" but also her "fatalest enemy" (IV.ii.53–54). She had doted on Bonvile "beyond reason," she explains, and having fallen "into despair" (IV.ii.70–74) because of his marriage to Annabel, really desired Lessingham to assist her in a kind of oblique suicide. The dark meaning of her letter had been that she herself was the "friend" referred to, and she had even planned that Lessingham should dispatch her "unwittingly . . . by poison" (IV.ii.78–80). But now that the death of Bonvile has removed all cause for jealousy, she will gladly marry Lessingham after all.

On hearing this, Lessingham understandably concludes that women are no more to be trusted than "*Lapland* Witches" (IV.ii.97); he rejects Clare "for ever," and, incensed with jealousy against his former friend, privately determines to "make as fatal breach and difference / In *Bonviles* love as mine" (IV.ii.120–124). No sooner has Lessingham strode angrily off the stage than Bonvile walks on— as it were, a ghost suddenly returned. Clare gives him a letter "which I meant to have sent you / An hour 'fore you were married" (IV.ii.158–159)—a letter that belatedly declares her love for Bonvile and construes the riddle of the earlier message sent to Lessingham. When Bonvile sees that Clare's passion is for him, he praises Lessingham to the lady, an act that she takes as proof of the two mens' friendship until Bonvile reveals insultingly that his purpose is to further the marriage of his enemy to "a Whore" (IV.ii.214). This marriage does, in fact, ultimately provide the necessary resolution, and the play ends, as it had begun, on a note of nuptial celebration. But further obstacles delay the benign conclusion. Bonvile and Annabel cannot be happily reunited until they have settled a painful quarrel and shown that Lessingham's vicious slanders on their sexual infidelity are lies. At one point Annabel charges Clare with being the first cause of all the unhappiness, whereupon, confessing her guilt and reverting to the imagery of the opening scene, Clare offers (at this late stage!) to "be the clew / To lead you forth this Labyrinth" (V.i.348–349). Although Clare finally repents of her "peevish will" and Lessingham admits that "wilde distractions" have "spilt the goodness" of his former self (V.i.441–448), Webster offers no satisfactory explanation for the extraordinary behavior of either character. He is content merely to dismiss the ethical questions with easy forgiveness all round and a gnomic couplet gleaned from his reading of Samuel Daniel:

> Cankers touch choicest fruit with their infection,
> And Fevers seize those of the best complexion.
> (V.i.351–352)[4]

Much of the unreality of this narrative can be attributed to elements that stem ultimately from the traditions of the folktale and the literary romance. Lessingham's "impossible task" (III.i.92), "A Task, / Hell till this day could never parallel" (I.ii.9–10), belongs to the familiar category of stories in which lovers must prove themselves by improbable means. The requirement that Helena obtain Bertram's ring in *All's Well That Ends Well* or that the prince guess Antiochus's secret in *Pericles* are obvious dramatic examples. Closely related is the even commoner device by which characters test their lovers or friends by subjecting them to painful choices. One thinks of the casket riddle in *The Merchant of Venice* or the various trials of the heroine in Dekker's *Patient Grissil*. Often the choice presented is between love and friendship. When Beatrice commands Benedick to "Kill Claudio" in *Much Ado About Nothing* (IV.i.287), she precipitates her suitor into a situation that is similar to Lessingham's. The notion of jealousy, envy, and malice as "Fevers" that attack their victims suddenly, cause endless pain and difficulty, and then disappear as swiftly as they had come is equally a characteristic of romance tradition that readers of *The Winter's Tale* will have no problem recognizing.

But Webster in some sense flies in the face of these conventions by introducing a spirit of skepticism alien to their usual operation. So much emphasis is placed upon the interpretation of puzzling words and actions that doubt becomes a prominent feature of the play's emotional landscape. The quartet of young lovers and their associates—those whose interrelations constitute the chief interest of the play—are oddly inscrutable to each other even in their intimacy and are given to speculating about one another's motives. At a loss to understand the indirection of his mistress, Lessingham wonders whether she is prompted by some "calumny and scandal" she has heard or by "perverse and peevish will" (I.i.55–57). Later it occurs to him that her riddling letter may be a test of his sincerity, although he is willing to act upon it without being certain. It remains for Grover, one of the wedding guests, to propose the theory of Clare's

"Emulation" and so hint at the attraction to Bonvile that proves in the event to be the heart of her mystery; Woodroff arrives independently at the same notion a bit later. But Grover speaks for all when he qualifies his explanation with a shrug: "who knows womens thoughts?" (I.i.97–102). Lessingham finds himself questioning "If such a thing there be" as friendship and, even if there is, whether it or love "claims the greatest right" (I.ii.28–30). Bonvile, who loves Lessingham enough to risk his life and his marriage for him, nevertheless questions "from Envy," whether Lessingham is not a "secret Rival" (I.ii.129–131) for Annabel's affection; and then at Calais the ominous evasions of his companion make Bonvile "begin to doubt" afresh the "goodness" (III.i.20–21) of the cause on which he has staked everything. Even when he knows the purpose for which he has been tricked, he continues to be suspicious of Lessingham's sincerity:

> What do I know but that thou lovest my wife,
> And faind'st this plot to divide me from her bed,
> And that this Letter here is counterfeit?
>
> (III.i.151–153)

Lessingham is able to stir up doubts in Annabel about her husband's faithfulness, and Woodroff, who correctly rejects the calumny, does so wholly because of admiration for a relative stranger. He can make sense of the situation only by echoing his son-in-law; he imagines that Lessingham secretly loves his daughter and has lured Bonvile into a duel "to divide" him from his bride (V.i.263).

Lessingham, Bonvile, and Clare each put a different construction on the ambiguous word "friend," and the lady herself has appeared so self-contradictory on the point to some readers that Webster's editor was driven to emend the text at one place in order to clarify the problem of whether Clare really intends Bonvile's death or her own.[5] Close reading makes it fairly certain that at the conscious level anyway she toys with the notion of suicide, but her approach is so circuitous that only the Delphic oracle could fathom it, and Webster seems to have raised the possibility that she knows her own mind as little as her suitor's. The playwright strengthens this impression by having Clare almost instantaneously change her allegiance from Bonvile to Lessingham when she believes the former to be dead; what "chills [her] heart with horror" one minute causes her to be "extasied with joy" the next. No wonder Lessingham is puzzled by her "strange changes" (IV.ii.28–52). Moreover, Clare withholds her love letter to Bonvile until long after it could have had its intended effect. Profound uncertainty both of self and others bids fair to being a premise of the action, nor does the conventional happy ending evoke the sense of providential wonder or transcendence that might hush our agnosticism and lift the play to a more visionary significance.

The story itself turns obviously on the most fantastic equivocations—equivocations typical of Webster's writing elsewhere but never before so essential to the fabric of an entire play. Francisco's letter to Vittoria in *The White Devil*

(IV.ii.16–39) and Ferdinand's missive to his sister in *The Duchess of Malfi* (III.v.28–37) both palter with their readers in a double sense, but the effect in each case is merely to heighten the sense of menace, not actually to misdirect action. The device of the deliberately ambiguous message had been used before in such plays as Udall's *Ralph Roister Doister*, Marlowe's *Edward II*, and, of course, *Macbeth*; Webster's attraction to it here and in other dramas may partly be explained no doubt as Jacobean love of manipulating words and playing wittily with multiple meanings. The tradition of casuistry, important to the techniques of Donne, clearly fascinated the dramatist as much as the metaphysical poet. But juggling and paradoxical language is so pervasive in *A Cure for a Cuckold* as almost to constitute a theme—as if Webster, like Pinter three and a half centuries later, were interested in the way words can dethrone reason, isolate persons from each other, and threaten their assurance, can block communication, obfuscate meaning, and fracture the security of shared assumptions.

The obsession with linguistic ambiguity and with the irrationality that it expresses and fosters in the play bespeaks a concern with the psychic conflicts that lie at the heart of intense relationships—with those shadowy corners of personality where love and hatred fuse. It is probably not an accident that Clare's phrase for Bonvile ("deerest friend") is the same that Ferdinand at an equally emotional moment had applied to his sister: "I bade thee . . . Go kill my dearest friend" (*The Duchess of Malfi*, IV.ii.279–280). Bonvile, whose very name is suitably oxymoric, makes the idea explicit in a scene in which he and Clare experience the most ambivalent feelings for each other and for Lessingham:

> *Bonvile.* I will love you now
> With a noble observance, if you will continue
> This hate unto me: gather all those graces
> From whence you have faln, yonder, where you have left 'em
> In *Lessingham*, he that must be your husband;
> And though henceforth I cease to be his friend,
> I will appear his noblest enemy,
> And work reconcilement 'tween you.
> *Clare.* No, you shall not,
> You shall not marry him to a Strumpet; for that word
> I shall ever hate you.
> *Bonvile.* And for that one deed,
> I shall ever love you. Come, convert your thoughts
> To him that best deserves 'em, *Lessingham*.
> It's most certain you have done him wrong. . . .
>
> (IV.ii.224–238)

The quibbling dialectic of this passage almost obliterates the traditional categories of lover, friend, and enemy.

Clare's equivocal letter, the first cause of all the verbal intricacy to follow, is the product of genuine emotional disturbance. Its shiftiness, not to mention that the message is in written form and delivered through an intermediary, seems to arise out of thwarted infatuation for Bonvile, jealousy of Annabel's happiness, and fear of Lessingham's addresses, to which are added guilt for these feelings and consequent self-hatred. Clare is presented as the sort of girl who desires a man precisely because he is unavailable. We learn that "many have pursued her Love," but that she is likely to "cast some more peculiar eye / On some that not respects her" (I.i.106–109). Her equivocation, which she herself refers to as "my fatal sport, this bloody Riddle" (IV.ii.30), may be seen as sadomasochistic, for it is a roundabout attack upon herself that nevertheless places the two men for whom she harbors the deepest feelings in positions of uncertainty and danger. Thus does love, when coupled with frustration and guilt, look like hostility and punish itself by punishing others.

This elaborately indirect response to pain immediately infects Lessingham, who begins to speak in "Riddles and Paradoxes" (I.ii.46) after the fashion of his beautiful tormentor. Although he loves Clare "madly" and is prepared to prove it by killing Bonvile, he can nevertheless compare her "malice" to "Deadliest Helle-bore" or the "vomit of a Toad" (III.i.76–78) and speak of friendship as "beyond the love of man to woman, . . . more near allied to eternity" (III.i.55–56). Les-singham's emotional confusion is now as radical as Clare's. The impetuous chal-lenger imagines that his mistress "loathes" him and has enjoined this "bloody" encounter upon him "For ever to be quit and free from" his attentions; his "affec-tion" for her is nevertheless of such "violence" that he can "fight in fury" and "kill . . . in cold blood," while protesting "heart-sorrow" for the victim (III.i.91–98). Moreover, he is as blind to the practical effects of his intended course as he is to the possibility that Bonvile may be right in suggesting that Clare's animus is directed against her own "self-love, or pride" (III.i.88). Ironically, Lessingham takes on the very willfulness that he had found so incomprehensible in Clare.

Webster now extends to Bonvile the irrational love-hate psychology that defines the feelings of both Clare and Lessingham. By declining to endanger his companion and by offering his own life as a sacrifice to friendship, Bonvile re-duces Lessingham to tears, then equivocates the affection into enmity with a speech as serpentine as any in the play:

> He wrongs me most, ought to offend me least,
> And they that study man, say of a friend.
> There's nothing in the world that's harder found,
> Nor sooner lost: thou camest to kill thy friend,
> And thou mayest brag thou hast don't; for here for ever
> All friendship dyes between us, and my heart
> For bringing forth any effects of love,
> Shall be as barren to thee as this sand
> We tread on; cruel, and inconstant as
> The Sea that beats upon this Beach. We now
> Are severed: thus hast thou slain thy friend,

And satisfied what the Witch thy Mistress bad thee.
Go and report that thou hast slain thy friend.

(III.i.131–143)

Having turned himself from friend to foe by sheer rhetoric, Bonvile now takes up his sword again; but this time Lessingham refuses combat, and the equivocations continue in a manner perilously close to the ludicrous:

> *Bonvile.* Will you advance Sir?
> *Lessingham.* Not a blow;
>   'Twould appear ill in either of us to fight:
>   In you unmanly; for believe it Sir,
>   You have disarmed me already, done away
>   All power of resistance in me—it would show
>   Beastly to do wrong to the dead: to me you say,
>   You are dead for ever, lost on *Callis-sands*,
>   By the cruelty of a woman; yet remember
>   You had a noble friend, whose love to you
>   Shall continue after death: shall I go over
>   In the same Barque with you?
> *Bonvile.* Not for yon town
>   Of *Callis*—you know 'tis dangerous living
>   At Sea, with a dead body.

(III.i.154–168)

In such a scene Webster dramatizes the power of ambivalent emotion to twist and sophisticate expression to the point where seriousness and absurdity meet. The recourse to cleverness and wit could be played by skilled actors as a nervous attempt to disguise or evade pain, and this might well be one of the subtleties intended. It is certainly clear that *A Cure for a Cuckold* attempts on the one hand to explore the relationship of words to complicated states of feeling and on the other to suggest how fluid and untrustworthy language is as a vehicle of truth or a guide to reality. The play touches on the epistemological question of the degree to which human utterance may be regarded as the subjective expression of a state of mind or an objective description of actuality.

Emotional conflicts half-perceived by those who suffer them, cloudy frustration, the interplay of love and hatred, of submissive and aggressive impulses—these are the stuff of which Clare, Lessingham, and Bonvile are concocted, and the playwrights elaborate the plot in order to complicate the cross relations among these characters to the fullest possible extent and in the most teasingly elusive way. Annabel, one of whose functions is ultimately to break up this triangle and resolve it quadrilaterally, remains unambiguously loyal to her husband throughout most of the action; by her sweetly reasonable temper she helps to place our response to the confusions and operatic extravagances of the other three. Yet by Act V, Lessingham's vengeful plot against Bonvile succeeds in converting even her from a devoted wife to a jealous vixen, so that love-hatred now disfigures the union of the married pair. The neurotic quarrel between Annabel and her husband—a dispute in which each suspects the other of sexual betrayal—is notable for the strain it places on the meaning of words. Not only are the double-entendres symptomatic of disappointment and hurt egos, but they become weapons of aggression as well.

When Clare praises Bonvile as "a Jewel" of manhood, Annabel twists the reference into an insult by playing bitterly upon the necklace and bracelets that her husband had earlier locked about her neck and wrists: "Wear it your self; / For these I wear are Fetters, not Favors" (V.i.267–269). In this jealous thrust, Annabel's jewels, originally emblems of fidelity and commitment given her by "a gentle Jaylor" (I.ii.214) and symbolic extensions of her lover's encircling arms, are wrenched from their first significance to suggest enslavement and humiliation. Also the word "Fetters" may remind us of Lessingham's compulsive feelings for Clare and of how he has been "fettered in a womans proud Command" (III.i.75). The wit is a means of concentrating and pointing an emotional reversal typical of the play as a whole—the ironic shift from love as trustful cherishing to love as dominance and constraint. Then Bonvile orders his wife to fetch the will he had devotedly sent her before embarking for France, and she responds sardonically, "I shall Sir, but leave your Self-will with you" (V.i.285). The pun connects egotism and self-assertion to the idea of death and reminds us of Clare's undisciplined "will," mentioned twice earlier. When Annabel hands the document to Bonvile, the aggressive double meanings continue to mount:

> *Annabel.* Look you, there's the Pattent
>   Of your deadly affection to me.
> *Bonvile.* 'Tis wellcome,
>   When I gave my self for dead, I then made over
>   My Land unto you—now I finde your love
>   Dead to me, I will alter't.
> *Annabel.* Use your pleasure,
>   A man may make a garment for the Moon,
>   Rather then fit your Constancy.
>
> (V.i.293–301)

From the omniscient perspective of the audience, the oxymoron "deadly affection" amounts to a triple pun, for it can suggest Bonvile's intention to provide for his wife if he dies, his unaffectionate willingness to imperil the marriage by risking death, or the deadly effect of his pretended affection to Annabel in the light of his supposed adultery. And the entire passage builds upon the ambiguous interrelation of love and death of which Webster was so fond and that constitutes a major theme of the play.

The "serious" plot of *A Cure for a Cuckold* draws the audience inexorably into an ever more complex entanglement of verbal trickery and emotional instability until the twists and turns of the final phase weary comprehension. The extraordinary obliquity of Lessingham's vindictive strategy against Clare for preferring Bonvile to himself is almost a paradigm of the play's dramatic method, for it illustrates once more the links between convoluted action and convolutions of character and language. Like Clare at the opening of the play, Lessingham is now a disappointed and guilt-ridden lover, and, like her also, he vents his frustration by projecting suffering upon others:

> Trust upon't.
> If I drown Ile sink some along with me;
> For of all miseries I hold that chief,
> Wretched to be, when none co-parts our grief.
> (V.i.128–131)

He even picks up the image of immersion that Clare had used to describe her feelings about the putative death of Bonvile:

> I stood
> As if a Merchant walking on the *Downs*,
> Should see some goodly Vessel of his own
> Sunk 'fore his face i'th Harbor. . . .
> (IV.ii.59–62).

Lessingham defames Annabel by telling her father that his daughter's husband is "dangerously wounded" (V.i.150)—an equivocation for "wounded in his Reputation" (V.i.160) as a result of Annabel's supposed unfaithfulness. At the same time he plants in Annabel the false notion that Bonvile is sexually involved with Clare. Although Woodroff believes that Lessingham is lying, he nevertheless relays the calumny about Annabel to Bonvile and so triggers the jealous quarrel between husband and wife. Lessingham has thus attacked Clare by trying to ruin the married happiness of the man he thinks she loves and by having Annabel attack her in jealous anger. No wonder the play produces an effect like being lost in the famous maze at Hampton Court. Since the term "labyrinth" occurs twice in the play, it is not impossible that the collaborating authors had in mind the example of the form at Theobalds, James I's favorite palace. But the source of the idea probably lay closer to hand. In *The Changeling* (1622), Rowley's collaboration with Middleton, the word "labyrinth" occurs in both plots (III.iv.71, IV.iii.107) in contexts that relate to moral, psychic, and sexual confusion.

The subplot of the play presents a refreshing contrast to this tale of refined bitchery. Its most delightful character is a gruffly affectionate, irrepressibly merry sailor called Compass, who after four years at sea returns to London to discover that his wife Urse is the mother of "a chopping Boy" (II.iii.35) only three months old. Franckford, the child's father, is married to a barren woman and has therefore lain with Urse in order to provide himself with a son. Far from being offended by his wife's loose behavior, the eccentric Compass is delighted with her and, blithely maintaining that he himself begot the child when he "came home in the Cock-boat one night, about a year ago" (II.iii.116–117), insists on claiming the bastard as his own. Compass wins a legal contest for custody of the child by recourse to logic-chopping and absurdly inappropriate analogies:

Is not the earth our Mother? And shall not the earth have all her children agen? I would see that Law durst keep any of us back, she'l have Lawyers and all first, tho they be none of her best children. My wife is the mother, and so much for the Civil-law. Now I come agen, and y'are gone at the Common-law: suppose this is my ground, I keep a Sow upon it, as it might be my wife, you keep a Boar, as it might be my adversary here; your Boar comes foaming into my ground, jumbles with my Sow, and wallowes in her mire, my Sow cryes *week*, as if she had Pigs in her belly—who shall keep these Pigs? he the Boar, or she the Sow?

(IV.i.172–181)

This victory with its reduction of the argument to barnyard fundamentals marks the climax of a long scene whose satirical point is the obfuscatory effect of legal jargon. After the litigants and their supporters have been happily reconciled, Compass divorces his wife to "cure" his cuckoldry, only to remarry her a few hours later. The remarriage, a humorous counterpart to the other weddings of the play, involves a whimsical charade in which the couple court each other as total strangers—he calling her "widow" (IV.iii.22) and comforting her for the "death" of her husband, she treating him as a widower and remarking on his curious likeness to her first spouse. Like Dickens's Sarah Gamp, Compass satisfies his needs by inventing a fantasy world and then living within it as though it were factual. Paradoxically, the fantasy is grounded in values so earthily robust and straightforward that Compass's approach to love makes the relationship between Lessingham and Clare seem almost factitious.

In a kind of pendant to the quasi-tragic material, Webster and Rowley supply additional comic interest with the lively character of Rochfield, an amiable gentleman who attempts to rob Annabel of her jewelry in an early scene but is then reclaimed for virtue by her kindness, taken into the family as a "kinsman" of her husband (II.iv.53), and much respected as the savior of her father's life in a naval battle against the Spanish. This "honest Thief" (II.ii.54) adds yet another paradoxical dimension to the play and contributes to its theme of equivocation by deliberately misleading Lessingham. Marrying "Craft with Cunning" (V.i.99), Rochfield reports that Annabel once gave him "Those Bracelets and the Carckanet she wears" (V.i.119), thus laying the foundation for Lessingham's slander; what he secretly means and later explains is that Annabel had given him not the jewels themselves but their value in money. His stated motive for this deception is the encouragement of Lessingham to entrap himself in his own machinations: "if he'l bite, / Ile give him line to play on" (V.i.99–100). The most obvious reason for it, of course, is the authors' desire for a further complication of the plot. Like Compass and the romantic lovers of the main action, Rochfield also touches upon the issue of how private subjectivities may alter or seem to alter external reality. As a man of decent instincts turned thief against his will, he soliloquizes vividly on the power of guilt to transform the harmless facts of nature into threats:

> It is the tremblingst trade to be a Thief,
> H'ad need have all the world bound to the peace;
> Besides the bushes, and the phanes of houses,
> Every thing that moves he goes in fear of 's life on.
> A furr-gown'd Cat, and meet her in the night,
> She stares with a Constables eye upon him;
> And every Dog, a Watch-man; a black Cowe
> And a Calf with a white face after her
> Shows like a surly Justice and his Clerk;
> And if the Baby go but to the bag,
> 'Tis ink and paper for a *Mittimus*. . . .
>
> (II.iv.101–111)

At every level of its action, *A Cure for a Cuckold* shows interest in the psychology of self-projection.

Although the two plots of the tragicomedy are structurally independent of each other,[6] a couple of casual links hold them together. Franckford, the father of Compass's "son" is also the uncle of Annabel and therefore loosely attached to the main action. Lessingham's shallow friends fill out the cast of the play as "gallants" at the wedding of Bonvile and Annabel and as witnesses to the "divorce" and remarriage of Compass and Urse. Raymond, the most conspicuous of these supernumeraries, demonstrates Clare's powers of attraction by making unrequited advances to her at one point; a little later he suggests to Compass the fanciful strategy for shedding his horns.

The thematic relationship between the plots is obviously closer than the structural. Physical death actually menaces the fulfillment of both marriages in the main action, for Bonvile is thought to be dead for a time and Clare's baffling demand that Lessingham kill his friend would apparently lead, if rightly understood, to her own extinction. To these dangers is added Lessingham's attempted revenge, which almost wrecks the reputations not only of his friend and his friend's bride but, when matters are finally laid bare, of himself and Clare as well. The capacity of love to survive its own most irrational manifestations, to endure the worst that its votaries are able to inflict upon themselves and others would appear, then, to be a dominant motif of the central story. Uncomprehending passion in Clare and Lessingham bring them and their friends to the brink of chaos; reason and repentance, even though not invoked until the eleventh hour, are asserted to be powerful enough to deliver them from self-destruction. However dubious its psychological foundations, the fable is one in which reality at last breaks through to snatch the victims of unreason from the disastrous consequences of their mania. The underplot comments ironically upon this idea by inverting it. Compass cures his wounded reputation and his wife's infidelity by a purely fictive death and resurrection. Passion is defeated not by heightened moral awareness and a return to reasonable behavior but by a comic denial of inconve- nient facts and an insistence on the supremacy of language over that to which language refers. A bastard son becomes legitimate and a philandering wife faith- ful merely by verbal fiat. The ritual of words, a kind of humorous sacramental- ism or essentialism, is all that is needed to annihilate the past and transubstantiate wishes into actualities. Compass delights us, as Clare and Les- singham fail to do, not simply by making irrationality so attractive but by mak- ing it socially viable. For if the Clare-Lessingham affair warns us sourly of the perils of unreasonableness, Compass's "cure" ebulliently demonstrates its tri- umph.

As Murray has pointed out, the play reinforces the contrast between the two plots as well as between extravagant and more realistic values by punning occasionally on the mariner's symbolic name.[7] Franckford's wife Luce is surpris- ingly indulgent with her husband's extramarital activities: "he may have a By- blow, or an Heir . . . Yet himself keep within compass" (I.i.197–201). Annabel speaks melodramatically of being "a Maid, a Wife, / And Widow in the com- pass of two days" (III.iii.23–24). Even more significantly, Bonvile describes Les- singham as a man who "bore his steerage true in every part, / Led by the Compass of a noble heart" before Clare "degraded him" from honor and "en- gaged him to an act / Of horror" (IV.ii.194–201). The nautical metaphor here ties in well with the theme of neurotic indirection, effectively contrasting the false "steerage" of Lessingham and Clare to the vitality of Compass's reunion with Urse: "Come, we'l eat and to bed, and if a fair Gale come, / We'l hoist sheets, and set forwards" (II.iii.155–156). For all the indecency of his wordplay, Compass in his "Cock-boat" is sure of his direction; Bonvile and Lessingham in their "Barque" are more divertible. Nor can it be entirely accidental that both plots make so much action depend upon strained argumentation and rhetorical sleight of hand, for in this play language often screens illusion from reality. In conception, then, the two plots are interestingly coordinated.

A Cure for a Cuckold is characteristically Websterian not only in the angu- larity and density of its style (though both features are less remarkable and more intermittent than in *The Devil's Law-Case*) but also in its fascination with the mysteries of the human ego. Once again Webster takes up the strong-willed fe- male who struggles to express her own individuality through the parodoxes of love, and whose confrontation with the self involves the perturbation of others. When Clare in the opening scene sends Lessingham to find the "one onely roade . . . To my fruition," promising, if he fails, to remain "ever . . . mine own," she embarks on a quest for identity whose perils she can scarcely foresee. Here, as in other plays, the dramatist studies the destructive potential in roman- tic fervor and the problem of dominance that so often shadows tense relations between the sexes. By appearing to command Lessingham to slay his friend, Clare usurps "a power" over him "Beyond all vertue . . . almost grace" (I.ii.11–12) and assumes an unnaturally assertive role. In their gossipy fashion, the gallants of the play underscore the inverted psychology of her "challenge" to Lessingham:

> *Raymond. Lessingham*
> Hath left us on the sudden.
> *Eustace.* Sure the occasion
> Was of that Letter sent him.
> *Lyonel.* It may be
> It was some Challenge.
> *Grover.* Challenge!—never dream it:
> Are such things sent by women?
> *Raymond.* 'Twere an Heresie
> To conceive but such a thought.
>
> (I.i.126–135)

Clare's willful control over Lessingham is defensive and must be taken in part as a confession of her failure to control herself.

Until she too becomes jealous late in the play, the more insipid Annabel does service as a foil, illustrating by her dependency on Bonvile the virtues of the passive and submissive wife. But even Annabel briefly becomes the focus of the play's interest in the subtleties of role reversal. In her encounter with Rochfield on the road to Dover, she persuades her would-be attacker to sheathe his sword by appealing to his gentle instincts and the sheer vulnerability of her position. Then, as he fumbles nervously with her locked-on jewelry, she takes full command of the situation and literally disarms him:

> *Rochfield.*   do I hurt you, Lady?
> *Annabel.* Not much, Sir.
> *Rochfield.* I'd be loath at all, I cannot do't.
>   *She draws his sword.*
> *Annabel.* Nay then you shall not, Sir. You a Thief,
> And guard your self no better! No further read?
> Yet out in your own book? A bad Clerk, are you not?
> *Rochfield.* I by Saint *Nicholas*, Lady, sweet Lady.
> *Annabel.* Sir, I have now a Masculine vigor,
> And will redeem my self with purchase too.
> What money have you?
> *Rochfield.* Not a cross, by this foolish hand of mine.
> *Annabel.* No money! 'Twere pity then to take this from thee:
> I know thou'lt use me ne're the worse for this,
> Take it agen, I know not how to use it. . . .
>
> (II.ii.55–68)

Annabel clearly embodies the self-possession that Clare lacks. By knowing how and when to yield, she masters her assailant, nor is her dignity as a woman purchased at the sacrifice of delicacy, softness, or feminine charm. In this most civilized of attempted robberies, the play offers an attractive exemplum of creative interchange between pride and humility and between threatener and threatened.

Webster betrays his interest in the crosscurrents of fear and affection through the paradoxical imagery of love and death already noticed earlier. He develops the tragic aspect of this idea by constantly linking romance with violence or reminding us of the skull beneath the skin. Lessingham speaks more than once not merely of killing his friend but of exchanging the bridal bed for the grave:

>   shall I be the man
> To rob you of this nights felicity,
> And make your Bride a Widow,—her soft bed
> No witness of those joys this night expects?
>
> . . . .
>
>   you may meet a grave,
> And that not amongst your noble Ancestors,
> But amongst strangers, almost enemies.
>
>   (I.ii.179–197)
>
> You left your Bridal-bed to finde your Death-bed. . . .
>   (III.i.52)

Having found in Bonvile "the greatest good" that life can offer, he "must make the womb where 'twas conceived / The Tomb to bury it" (I.ii.224–227), and his "cruel purpose" intensifies his feeling for his friend: "A Judge methinks looks lovelyest when he weeps, / Pronouncing of deaths Sentence . . ." (III.i.118–120). Later Lessingham associates fulfillment of desire with the murder of kings: "The ways to Love, and Crowns, lye both through blood . . ." (V.i.22). For a moment Clare indulges the romantic notion that Bonvile's death is synonymous with her own:

> *Clare.* Who is it you have slain?
> *Lessingham.* *Bonvile* the Bridegroom.
> *Clare.* Say?
>   Oh you have struck him dead thorough my heart. . . .
>   . . . oh I am lost for ever. . . .
>
>   (IV.ii.31–36)

Yet a second later she has reversed the paradox: "upon his grave / I will not gather Rue, but Violets / To bless my wedding strewings . . ." (IV.ii.38–40). Then when Bonvile turns up alive in the second part of the same scene, she wishes, were she a man, to drive her former idol "with my sword into the field, / And there put my wrong to silence" (IV.ii.219–220). Such is the play's "deadly affection."

Even Rochfield moralizes grimly on the ironic connection between sex and death when the indigent child grows up to be a highwayman: "our Mothers . . . love to groan, although the Gallows eccho / And groan together for us" (II.i.10–

12). And with his imagination still running on the scaffold, he can see in the love tokens that encircle Annabel's wrists and neck "Emblems / Of the combined Hemp to halter mine . . ." (II.ii.29–30). The macabre idea that love contains the seeds of death or is subject to violent interruption is balanced of course by the emergence of all the characters eventually from shadow into sunlight. The movement of Urse and Compass from separation to reunion and from symbolic death to a remarriage blessed by progeny obviously stresses the hopeful implications of romantic love without which the play would deny its tragicomic premise.

With its sophisticated approach to the ties between emotion and language and its obvious interest in ideas, *A Cure for a Cuckold* represents one of Webster's most ambitious and original experiments. Thematically the play is more cohesive than it first appears, and its best scenes, both comic and serious, are absorbingly and forcefully conceived. Despite these strengths, however, the drama as a totality leaves us with a sense of failure and disappointment. Webster and his collaborator toy with issues that are too profound, or at least too complex, to be satisfactorily explored within the Fletcherian framework. The detachment with which the main plot is conducted forbids much empathy yet fails to compensate with elegance, so that the personalities presented have something of the case study about them. The artificiality and self-consciousness of the genre with its tendency to satire and self-parody interfere with the psychological realism the narrative requires, and we therefore remain unsure as to where the confusion of the characters leaves off and that of the authors begins. Instead of the concentration and terseness that define Webster's style at its finest, we get too often a certain relaxed and diffuse effect.

Worst of all, the concern with love's confusions and perversities yields little in the way of moral insight. The most interesting characters fail to grasp the significance of their own predicaments and continually evade responsibility by uncostly appeals to psychological determinism. Lessingham equates his supine obedience to Clare with "the necessity of my fate" (III.i.116), and, believing himself "bewitched" (IV.ii.103), insists that she has destroyed his power to choose. At one point Clare forgets that she has prompted her suitor to commit murder and praises him for having misunderstood her letter: "you have done bravely, 'tis your Mistriss / That tells you" (IV.ii.86–87). Even when she embraces "blest repentance," admitting that she suffers "Deservedly," she nonetheless disdains accountability for all the trouble she has caused by invoking the image of the fickle goddess tossing coins:

> Fortune plays ever with our good or ill,
> Like Cross and Pile, and turns up which she will.
> (IV.ii.134–135)

Nothing illustrates the sentimental morality of the play so clearly as the general assault upon women that Lessingham releases when outraged by Clare's deception:

All that they have is feign'd, their teeth, their hair,
Their blushes, nay their conscience too is feigned,
Let 'em paint, load themselves with Cloth of Tissue,
They cannot yet hide woman—that will appear
And disgrace all. The necessity of my fate!
(IV.ii.98–102)

But the accuser here is no less guilty of feigning than the accused, for Lessingham knows that Bonvile lives and he has just led Clare to believe the opposite. Moral irony is hardly the point of the scene. Rather it is a case of ethical sense giving place to a rhetorical flourish. Webster and Rowley seem more interested in exploiting a succession of extreme situations and emotional crises for theatrical effect than in making a coherent moral pattern. The result is a tantalizing confection of paradoxes and ambiguities to which shallow, evasive, or purely conventional solutions are proposed. It is almost as though the playwrights had set out to illustrate the most exiguous connections between what an audience may accept on a stage and what actually governs life. We are forced therefore to conclude that Webster and his collaborator have fallen short of that integrity that we admire in both the dramatist and the characters of the tragic masterpieces.

No source is known for the tale of the returned seaman who blots out his wife's unfaithfulness by a temporary divorce, but there is evidence for thinking that Webster and Rowley may have been drawing on some incident or custom from the sociology of the London docks. Kirkman in his preface says that the "*Expedient . . . hath bin tried to my knowledge*" (ll. 24–25),[8] and in any case the idea had already been mentioned (apparently by Webster) in *Anything for a Quiet Life* (II.i.120–122). The collaborating dramatists may have derived their main action from Massinger's *Parliament of Love* (licensed for performance in November 1624), which also features a young man whose mistress bids him kill his best friend and who consequently lures that friend to a dueling ground under the pretext of enlisting him as a second, thereby causing him to put comradeship before romance. The priority of Massinger's play to Webster and Rowley's, however, remains in some doubt, and the influence (which there certainly must have been) could conceivably have flowed in the opposite direction.[9] That one of the two plays depends upon the other is the only point of which we can be reasonably confident. In any event, the motif of the woman who orders her lover to kill was not uncommon. One thinks, of course, of Shakespeare's Beatrice and Benedick.

Marston in *The Dutch Courtesan* had dramatized a similar story some twenty years before Massinger, and, earlier still, Bandello's tragic tale of the Countess of Celant, retold by Painter in his *Palace of Pleasure*, contained the germ of Webster and Rowley's situation.[10] Since Marston and Painter, as we have already noted, were important influences upon Webster, it is by no means out of the question that he knew all three possible sources. If so, he did not choose to imitate their clarity, especially as regards motivation. Whether intentionally or not, Webster appears to have repeated a few elements of plot from *The Devil's Law-Case* in *A Cure for a Cuckold*. Both plays contain two duels, actual or intended, of which the cause is a woman, and both make reference to Calais sands. One of the duelists in each play sends a will to his bride, and in each also a woman writes her lover a deliberately unclear letter. Both dramas make much of young men who are thought to be dead but who turn up alive to make possible the conventionally amorous resolution.

*   *   *

On 22 January 1625/26, shortly after the plague had abated and the theatres had reopened, the Master of the Revels, Sir Henry Herbert, licensed *The Fair Maid of the Inn* for production by the King's Men at the Blackfriars. To judge from its topical allusions, it was a new play, probably written later than the preceding March (when James I died),[11] but, at least in some part, before the end of August (when John Fletcher became one of the dread disease's notable victims). Herbert's record book mentions only Fletcher as author, and the play was not printed until 1647, when it appeared in the first Beaumont and Fletcher folio. While it is true that both Herbert and the publishers of the folio sometimes failed to name all the collaborators on a given play, Webster's connection with this drama, as in the case of *Anything for a Quiet Life*, remains dubious, for there is no external evidence. Nevertheless, scholars are virtually unanimous as to the collaborative nature of the play, and the case for Webster's share, although based entirely on stylistic data, is as difficult to dismiss out of hand as it is to embrace with assurance. Cyrus Hoy, who has analyzed the entire Beaumont and Fletcher canon with reference to the more or less involuntary linguistic habits of the various collaborators, has presented the most formidable argument for Webster.[12]

Hoy finds three distinctive patterns of usage in *The Fair Maid*—those of Massinger, Webster, and Ford as ascertained from their respective practices in unaided plays. Since there is little overlapping between patterns, since the patterns themselves are based upon thorough techniques of investigation, and since Hoy does not ignore the problems of scribal or compositorial intervention between the author's fair copy and the printed text, this evidence seems to carry considerable weight. Hoy believes that Fletcher worked briefly on the play, writing part of the first scene of Act IV just before his death, and that the other three dramatists were called in to complete the piece. Pointing out Webster's known preference for *you* (over *ye*), *them* (over *'em*), and for contractions such as *i'th'*, *o'th'*, and *'s* (for *his*), Hoy assigns Webster all of Act II, about half of Act IV, and most of Act V—in other words, nearly half the play. Murray, however, notes that the two longest scenes with which Webster has been credited (II.ii and IV.ii) contain contractions "that are rare" in the dramatist's other late work, and he is specifically "inclined to doubt" Webster's hand in episodes where we find an abnormally high incidence of *'em* and *hath*.[13]

With the assistance of David J. Lake's recent book on Middleton, I have been able to adduce a few new stylistic data that tend to corroborate Hoy's apportionment of *The Fair Maid*.[14] Lake's extensive word counts permit him to compare a wide range of Middleton's linguistic habits with those of each of the four dramatists who supposedly shared in our play. The scenes of *The Fair Maid* attributed to Webster exhibit most of the forms that characterize Webster's unaided work, especially the late *Devil's Law-Case*. These include (a) the contractions *'tis, of't, to'th', into'th', for't, on't, I'd,* and *I'le*; (b) preferences for *I am* (over *I'm*), for *between* (over *betwixt*), for *does* (over *doth*), for *has* (over *hath*), for *you are* (over *y'are* or *you're*), and for *yes* (over *ay*); (c) the use of the exclamations *marry* and *why*; and (d) a marked tendency to repeat the expression *I do protest* (or *I protest*), which occurs nowhere else in the play. This last habit (there are three instances in the putatively Websterian scenes of *The Fair Maid* and ten in the whole of *The Devil's Law-Case*) clearly distinguishes Webster's style from that of Massinger and Fletcher, who almost never use the phrase. Ford, it is true, does often write *I do protest*, but his idiosyncratic use of the contractions *d'ee* and *t'ee*[15] usually makes it impossible to confuse his hand with Webster's.

The evidence for Webster set forth earlier by scholars such as H. Dugdale Sykes and Lucas[16] is more suspect and consists chiefly of verbal parallels, borrowings from Sidney's *Arcadia* and the Overburian *Characters*—sources available, of course, to any dramatist of the period—and the name of Forobosco, which is the same as that of a minor figure from the cast list of *The Duchess of Malfi*.[17] Of itself the argument from parallel passages is flimsy, although several of Lucas's citations are very suggestive and the large number of Webster-like expressions is hard to ignore. One notices especially the lines, "Yet I have runne my sword quite through your heart, / And . . . hurt your sonne" (*The Fair Maid of the Inn*, II.i.99–100), which are almost certainly taken from *The Devil's Law-Case* ("You have given him the wound . . . Quite through your mother's heart" [III.iii.237–238]), from *A Cure for a Cuckold* ("Oh you have struck him dead thorough my heart" [IV.ii.34]), or from the passage in *Arcadia* (III,ii)[18] upon which both of these speeches in turn are based.

A few additional parallels not mentioned by Lucas or Sykes may be worth pointing out. In one of the so-called Webster scenes of *The Fair Maid*, the clown says of Forobosco that he "will never truly run himselfe out of breath, till he comes to the gallowes" (IV.ii.235–236). This macabre wit seems oddly close to a passage in *Sir Thomas Wyatt* in which Guilford Dudley greets the body of his newly executed wife: "Heres one has run so fast shee's out of breath . . ." (V.ii.172). In another such scene the clown of *The Fair Maid* speculates about a conjurer who might "fetch us back in a whirlewinde" (V.ii.59–60), a phrase that recalls Bracciano's remark to his wife, "I wonder much / What amorous whirlwind hurried you to Rome—" (*The White Devil*, II.i.148–149) as well as the Cardinal's reproof of his brother, "How idly shows this rage! which carries you, /

As men convey'd by witches through the air, / On violent whirlwinds" (*The Duchess of Malfi*, II.v.49–51). It is not easy to assess how common these ideas were in Webster's time and therefore the degree to which such similarities might be conscious or merely fortuitous. And it is theoretically possible, of course, as Baldini suggests,[19] that *The Fair Maid* merely shows Webster's influence rather than his authorship. Nevertheless, I find it hard to believe that verbal parallels from a variety of Webster's plays and prose characters, concentrated as they are in the very scenes that accord most closely with Webster's known linguistic usage, indicate nothing more than chance congruities or conscious imitation. And can it be mere coincidence that the phrase "a strange truth" (*The Fair Maid of the Inn*, III.ii.67), which later served as the subtitle for *Perkin Warbeck*, occurs in a scene that almost every scholar (on different grounds) has assigned to Ford?[20]

In the absence of any proof that Webster was writing for the King's Men in 1625, we must remain skeptical, although there is nothing inherently improbable in his having done so, since he had worked for this troupe earlier. Until some external evidence appears, there can be no certainty about Webster's participation in *The Fair Maid of the Inn*; but in the meantime there is sufficient warrant tentatively to include the play in Webster's canon.[21]

The play is another tragicomedy that combines the motif of the mother who falsely disowns her son (already familiar from *The Devil's Law-Case*) with typical folktale elements and a quarrel between families based upon Machiavelli's account of the notorious Neri-Bianchi feud in his *Florentine History* as translated into English by Thomas Bedingfield (1595).[22] Alberto and Baptista, wealthy naval commanders and sworn friends who reminisce about their "golden" days at sea together, are stirred to deadly enmity against each other in consequence of a horse race in which their sons contend. Baptista's son Mentivole accuses his rival of unsportsmanlike riding, and a quarrel between the two young men breaks out in which Alberto's son Cesario sustains a less than fatal wound. Baptista is so horrified at the possible effect of his son's act on the fathers' friendship that he orders Mentivole to apologize to Alberto for hurting Cesario and to beg for pardon. Mentivole reluctantly obeys, but the implacable Alberto, despite warnings and pleas, commands Cesario to have Mentivole's hand chopped off, whereupon the incensed old man (in response to an urgent summons from the Duke) immediately quits Florence for duties at sea and is shortly reported drowned. Cesario fulfills the letter rather than the spirit of his father's vengeful directive; he deprives Mentivole of his sword rather than his hand, and so, by a somewhat Webster-like equivocation, can claim to have "Tane away his use of fighting" (II.i.215). Baptista, shocked by Alberto's intended violence upon Mentivole, now swears "revenge on the whole Family" (II.iii.28) of Alberto.

At this point Mariana, Cesario's overprotective mother, is so fearful for her son's safety that she decides to shield him from the Baptisti by publicly disinheriting him and so putting him outside the pale of their vengeance. She trumps up the story that Cesario is really the son of a falconer palmed off upon Alberto at the time of the child's birth as the admiral's true offspring. At the hearing Cesario unprotestingly accepts this disinheritance, pointing out, like the loathly lady in Chaucer's *Wife of Bath's Tale*, that

> to be basely born,
> If not base-born, detracts not from the bounty
> Of natures freedom or an honest birth.
> Nobilitie claym'd by the right of blood,
> Shewes chiefly that our Ancestors deserv'd
> What we inherit; but that man whose actions
> Purchase a reall merit to himselfe,
> And ranck him in the file of prayse and honour,
> Creates his own advancement. . . .
>
> (III.ii.139–147)

The Duke is so impressed with Cesario's *gentilesse* and fortitude that he commands Mariana, the supposed widow, to marry the supposed foster son. The Duke, of course, is imposing a kind of test, and Mariana, by her lie about Cesario's humble birth, has nearly trapped herself into an incestuous union with the boy she has been trying so assiduously to preserve from harm.[23] The titillating difficulties of this ironic impasse are removed in the fifth act by the appearance of one Prospero—a friend of both Alberto and Baptista and, as his name suggests, a sort of deus ex machina. Having escaped from a twelve-year stint as a slave in the Ottoman galleys, he arrives at Florence in the company of a resurrected Alberto (whom he has freed from a Turkish prison) and of Juliana, Baptista's long-lost wife who has been languishing in "a *Greekish* Monastery" (V.iii.226). Former hatreds are dissolved in a congeries of reunions.

To the story of ruptured friendship and reconciliation the collaborating authors add the further complication of two love affairs conducted uncertainly between the four children of the quarreling fathers. Both of these apparently derive from a play by Lope de Vega entitled *La illustre fregona*, based in turn on one of the *Exemplary Novels* of Cervantes.[24] As in *Romeo and Juliet* the parental feud and the events that stem from it create various strains and frustrations in the lives of the lovers, but it is a double marriage at the end rather than a funeral that symbolizes the burying of the family grudge.

The first of these romances is between Mentivole and Cesario's sister, Clarissa. She secretly gives him a ring that her brother had made her promise not to part with, and Cesario, having discovered his sister's clandestine passion, maneuvers Mentivole into giving up the ring just before the hand on which he wears it is to be severed. The brother then confronts his sister with the token, throwing her off guard with his theatrical shock technique and a mode of indirection, amounting almost to psychological torture, that causes her to suspect for the moment that her beloved may be dead. Cesario's badgering of his sister (the play opens with a scene reminiscent of Laertes' pompous advice to Ophelia) reaches an effective climax in this emotional confrontation where Cesario's disgust for his sister overflows in a speech of Webster-like trenchancy:

> never more
> Shall a Womans trust beguile me; You are all
> Like Reliques: you may well be look't upon,
> But come a man to'th handling of you once,
> You fall in peeces.
>
> (II.iv.42–46)

Cesario's behavior to his sister in this scene distantly recalls Ferdinand's dark love-hatred for the Duchess of Malfi; the author gives the brother here a touch of the Duke's violent jealousy combined with his aristocratic pride of blood:

> Then shall I ever hate thee, oh thou false one;
> Hast thou a Faith to give unto a friend,
> And breake it to a brother? did I not
> By all the tyes of blood importune thee
> Never to part with it [i.e., the ring] without my knowledge?
> Thou might'st have given it to a Muliter,
> And made a contract with him in a stable
> At as cheap a price of my vengeance. . . .
>
> (II.iv.35–42)

And indeed this play more explicitly than *The Duchess of Malfi* deliberately insists upon the element of incestuous attraction, for Cesario has already told Clarissa that he loves her "With more then common ardour" (I.i.52) and would kiss her hand, "were it not my sisters . . . With too much heate" (I.i.135–136).[25] A little later she rebukes his attentions as "wanton" (I.i.342). When Cesario no longer believes that he and Clarissa are "pledges of one wombe" (IV.i.218), he proposes marriage to her—a move that drives his mother (who, of course, knows that they are brother and sister) to the brink of emotional collapse. Clarissa, however, despite her brother's interference, remains faithful to Mentivole throughout the play, and the possibility of incest is narrowly averted for the second time. But, just as all other obstacles to the wedding of Mentivole and Clarissa have been cleared away, the girl's father turns up to oppose it, and only the miraculous revelations of Prospero at the very end can persuade him to relent.

The second romance gives the play its title, dealing as it does with Cesario's attraction to Bianca, the fair maid of the inn. The tradition drawn upon is that of the *pastourelle* in which an aristocratic suitor courts a peasant maid.[26] She lives with her supposed parents, the Host and Hostess of "the grand Osteria" (I.i.94), in an environment of rustic simplicity, and is much courted by a whole parade of fools—a tailor, a dancer, a coxcomb, a mule driver, a pedant, and a clerk—the stage equivalents of Webster's satiric prose characters. The love scenes between Cesario and Bianca, which are delicately yet penetratingly written, constitute the most attractive feature of the play. The putative difference in social class creates a difficulty for the lovers, but this barrier seems trivial when Cesario's false parentage is announced, and the Duke decrees that the young man shall marry his mother.

The first interview between Bianca and Cesario establishes her at once as a maid of intelligence, sensitivity, and winsome virtue (she reminds us a little of Shakespeare's Perdita or Webster's milkmaid). Cesario is very conscious of "the unequall distance / Between my blood and thine" (III.i.160–161), but he argues wittily that his condescension, his wish to "raise thy lownesse to abundance" (III.i.212), is the best evidence of his affection and good faith. He is presented as somewhat smug and self-centered, but boyishly so in a manner that suggests the patrician undergraduate's sincere but irresponsible infatuation with a servant girl. Emotional immaturity and well-bred self-assurance meet convincingly in his character. For her part, she defends the unsophisticated life pertly but without arrogance, refusing to be dazzled by the prospect of "Gay clothes, high feeding, easie beds of lust, / Change of unseemly sights" (III.i.223–224). The entire dialogue is an elegant verbal sparring match not without touches of humor, a decorous facade partly to hide and partly to control deeper feelings. It ends with a chaste refusal of Cesario's addresses that nevertheless reveals Bianca's wish to encourage him:

> Sir, would you were
> As noble in desires, as I could be
> In knowing vertue. Pray doe not afflict
> A poore soule thus.
> (III.i.229–232)

At this point a messenger dramatically shatters the mood by summoning Cesario into court to hear Mariana's startling repudiation of him. When we next see Bianca, she has learned of Cesario's ill fortune and has come "To tender you the first fruits of my heart," "t'accept you for my husband, / Now when you are at lowest" (IV.i.94–96). The boy's reaction to this unexpected turn is spontaneous delight at first, then the pragmatist's hesitancy to commit himself. Unable to forget the advantages of a more aristocratic match, he affects to be astonished by her naiveté, and her disappointed withdrawal from the situation, once she has perceived her mistake, is the most poignant moment of the play. Hoy ascribes this scene to Fletcher and Ford;[27] if Ford had no part in its composition, the dramatist responsible at least possessed his characteristic skill in rendering the wounded sensibility of a woman with delicacy and tact:

> *Bianca.* Then I am lost againe—I have a suit too;
>   Youle grant it if you be a good man.
> *Cesario.* Any thing—
> *Bianca.* Pray doe not talke of ought what I have said t'ee.
> *Cesario.* As I wish health I will not.

Bianca. Pitty me,
    But never love me more.
Cesario. Nay now y'are cruell,
    Why all these teares?—Thou shalt not goe.
Bianca. Ile pray for yee
    That you may have a vertuous wife, a faire one,
    And when I am dead—
Cesario. Fy, fy—
Bianca. Thinke on me sometimes,
    With mercy for this trespasse.
Cesario. Let us kisse
    At parting as at comming.

                                [Kisses her.]

Bianca. This I have
    As a free dower to a virgins grave—
    All goodnesse dwell with yee.

                                      Exit.

Cesario. Harmless Biancha!
    Unskild, what hansome toyes are maids to play with!
    How innocent! but I have other thoughts. . . .

                                (IV.i.122–144)

The "other thoughts" concern Mariana, who enters at this point. Cesario immediately accosts her sexually: "my felicity, . . . lend me a lip / As soft, as melting as . . . old *Alberto* . . . tasted. . . . I will be Lord of my owne pleasures, Madame—" (IV.i.145–151). The instantaneous shift from delicacy to coarseness, from innocence to incest, is theatrical enough, but the sudden contrast carries a certain moral force. And after a prurient interlude during which both mother and sister refuse successively to be his "bedfellow," Cesario turns again to Bianca in a scene that finely balances their earlier encounter. This time, of course, it is she who rejects him—and no wonder, for he has as yet shed little of his complacent self-regard. The impulsive sophisticate is shown to be more naive than the innocent:

Cesario.   alas my pretty soule, I am come
    To give assurance thats beyond thy hope,
    Or thy beleife, I bring repentance 'bout me,
    And satisfaction—I will marry thee.
Bianca. Ha?
Cesario. As I live I will, but do not entertain't
    With too quick an apprehension of joy,
    For that may hurt thee, I have heard some dye of't—
Bianca. Do not feare me.
Cesario. Then thou think'st I faigne
    This protestation, I will instantly
    Before these testifie my new alliance,

> Contract my selfe unto thee—. . . .
>
> . . . .
> Entreat thy father to goe fetch a Preist—
> Wee will instantly to bed, and there be married.
> *Bianca*. Pride hath not yet forsaken you I see,
> Though prosperity has.
>
> . . . .
> Oh sir I did love you
> With such a fixed heart, that in that minute
> Wherein you slighted, or contemn'd me rather,
> I tooke a vow to obey your last decree,
> And never more looke up at any hope
> Should bring me comfort that way—and though since
> Your Foster-mother, and the faire *Clarissa*
> Have in the way of marriage despis'd you,
> That hath not any way bred my revenge,
> But compassion rather. I have found
> So much sorrow in the way to a chaste wedlock
> That here I will sit downe, and never wish
> To come to'th journies end. Your suite to mee
> Henceforth be ever silenc't.
> *Cesario*. My *Bianca*!
>
> (IV.ii.348–391)

Despite serious flaws of character in the suitor and various external pressures, the union of this couple seems both right and inevitable. Yet the way is not cleared for it until the final moments of the action, when Prospero reveals that Bianca is really the long-lost daughter of Baptista and Juliana, the Duke of Genoa's niece. As in Shakespeare's *Winter's Tale*, we are presented with the folkloristic convention that blood will tell, that nobility of character and nobility of descent ultimately coincide. If honest virtue is the true basis of gentility, as Cesario has earlier pointed out, it is at least poetically just that it should be crowned with the recognition of rank. And the world of the play is sufficiently make-believe to allow us to accept such a conclusion without demur.

But if Bianca comes to represent the symbolic union of high ideals with high birth, her lover, on a more realistic plane, embodies their tendency to diverge; indeed, it is the tension within Cesario that lends interest and complexity to his character. He presents two faces to the audience—on the one hand, that of the youthful idealist, charmed by Bianca and the pastoral values for which she stands, eager to embrace the "benevolent Fates" that have decreed his "fall / From a fair expectation" (III.ii.135–138); on the other, that of a sexually excitable materialist-snob prepared to rush into marriage with either of two women whom he has known all his life as mother and sister. The mechanics of tragicomedy, fanciful and plot-ridden as it usually is, tend to impose inconsistencies upon its characters or to make of them little more than puppets; but the schizophrenic doubleness of Cesario, which might at first be taken for mere confusion or expediency, is oddly lifelike. It projects the image of a mannered but nonetheless disoriented young man wavering, often semiconsciously, between his worse and better impulses. The marriage to Bianca is merely a signal rather than a dramatization of his moral victory, but the scenes that present his unresolved conflict, given the need for economy in so crowded a play, are not without subtlety.

The incest motif is, of course, a staple of Fletcherian sensationalism and is frankly intended in *The Fair Maid* to raise the specter of salacious horror. Yet it too can be defended—symbolically, if not psychologically—as a manifestation of Cesario's adolescent selfishness and hothouse isolation from reality. It may be seen, in other words, as merely the most melodramatic expression of the hero's tendency to blind overconfidence and self-absorption. We get a more amusing example of the same quality when he proclaims bumptiously at the beginning of one scene, "My fate springs in my owne hand" (IV.i.17), only to "curse / [His] fate" at the scene's end with such banalities as "I can but dye a Batchelor, thats the worst on't" (IV.i.300–306). Cesario, then, is well drawn, and his conduct throughout the action is appropriately described by one of his own remarks: "why heres a complement / Of mirth in desperation—" (IV.i.299–300). It is his mother, Mariana, who presents the most glaring weakness of characterization in the play, for, as Lucas points out,[28] she is given no credible motive for disinheriting her son. Her elaborate lie is an absurdly indirect means of insuring Cesario's safety, particularly as the need for it seems less than urgent by the time she takes action. The best that can be said for her improbable behavior is that it creates the impression of an unhealthy attitude of mother toward son, an attitude later reciprocated in his attempt to wed her.

Loosely attached to the main plot of *The Fair Maid* is the farcical comedy of Forobosco, a "great artist" (IV.ii.1) of dissimulation, and his clown. Forobosco's sole excuse for being, apart from entertaining the audience, is to cheat Bianca's simpleton admirers, "this gally-maufry of mans flesh" (III.i.12) as the Host calls them, out of their cash. The name has a certain suitability, for, as Lagarde points out, Florio defines it in his *New World of Words* as a "sneaking, prying, busie fellowe."[29] Forobosco, whose counterpart in Lope's play is the comic servant of one of the suitors, is compacted of familiar elements—conjurer, alchemist, musician, medical quack, showman, virtuoso of Senecan rodomantade, specialist in occult jargon, master of the "dark science" (IV.ii.309), and general confidence man. In these, of course, he recalls the staples of Jonsonian and Middletonian comedy. But in his function as a sort of dancing master to fools and exposer of their follies and pretensions, he also reminds us of characters and techniques from Marston.[30] One aspect of the satire brings Swift's academy at Lagado to mind, for the gulls (in addition to their common interest in Bianca) have "projects" upon which Forobosco instructs and advises them. Their senseless quests for novelty involve such schemes as "erecting 4 new sects of religion at Amsterdam" (IV.ii.89), "making a new Almanacke" with "9 dayes to the weeke"

(IV.ii.107–111), and traveling to the moon for "strange and exquisite new fashions" in dress (IV.ii.125).

The funniest episode of the play consists chiefly of an elaborate trick by which not only the silly onstage but the sophisticated in the audience are fooled. Forobosco beats his clownish servant, "A lump of ignorance" (III.i.79), for presuming to doubt his powers of conjuration, and the clown, parodying the stalest of conventions from revenge tragedy, responds by shouting "*vindicta, vindicta!*" (III.i.99). The "sweet vengeance" (III.i.91) that he seeks to exact consists of exposing the mountebank as a fraud before his victims. To this end he challenges Forobosco: "use all thy art, all thy roguery, and make me do any thing before al this company I have not a mind to, Ile first give thee leave to claime me for thy bond slave, and when thou hast done, hang me" (IV.ii.247–249). Forobosco agrees to the bargain; he then "*lookes in a booke, strikes with his wand*" and, to the accompaniment of music, produces four "*Boyes shap't like Frogs*" (IV.ii.277) with whom the clown, half naked, is magically compelled to dance. Terrified, the dancer begs to be released from the spell, implores forgiveness, retracts all his earlier charges, and then, as he is being dismissed in humiliation from the stage, makes it clear by a brief aside that the whole quarrel has been staged—that in fact we have witnessed a mere charade planned for the purpose of inspiring the suitors' trust. Thus the Fletcherian surprise technique is allowed to invade even the knockabout matter of the play, and here, at least, cleverly enlivens it.

The author of these scenes (probably Webster)[31] makes much of the balletic opportunities inherent in the material, and indeed the two high points of the whole sequence depend upon satirical effects that are more visual and musical than verbal. The six suitors (to music and choreography arranged by Forobosco) "*all make ridiculous conges, to* Bianca: *ranck themselves, and dance in severall postures*" (III.i.143) while the stage audience at the inn looks on; and the involuntary dance of the clown with the frogs in a later scene is obviously intended to provide even more in the way of bizarre spectacle. Both dances constitute a kind of nuptial antimasque and suggest a manic quality that, despite the important differences of tone, recalls the dance of lunatics in *The Duchess of Malfi*. There is perhaps even a verbal link at one point between the satiric comedy of *The Fair Maid* and the masque of madmen in *The Duchess*: both contain references to coaches equipped with feather beds the better to facilitate seduction.[32]

The low comedy barely intersects the main plot and could without difficulty be detached. It nevertheless bears a certain thematic relationship to the more serious matter. The mock quarrel between the two experts in cosenage (a mere confidence trick) echoes the foolish quarrel between the Alberti and the Baptisti and points up its essential unreality. The motive of revenge figures in both plots. In like fashion, the exaggerated overconfidence of the moronic suitors serves to parody Cesario's complacency and naiveté as a wooer. A balance of sorts is achieved at the end when the union of lovers and the mass reunion of friends and relatives in the high plot coincide with a falling out—this time in earnest—between the thieves. Forobosco and the clown are caught robbing Bianca's parents, and their punishment—imprisonment in the galleys—comes hard upon Prospero's deliverance from the same fate. The triumph of love, both social and romantic, is thus made neatly congruent with the banishment of fraudulency, betrayal, and greed.

The moral schematism of the play emerges perhaps more sharply yet in the symbolic contrast between Bianca (whose name appropriately suits her purity) and Forobosco, the dabbler in black arts. But, despite the appearance of a figure called Prospero, it would be mistaken to regard *The Fair Maid of the Inn* as a lesser *Tempest*, for its brittle surfaces cannot be made to sustain much metaphysical significance. Despite minor inconsistencies in the names of characters and a few anomalies in the plotting, possibly the effects of hasty and incomplete revision,[33] the play is skillful if deliberately shallow. Although the psychology of Cesario is interesting and the salty, sea-loving Alberto an effective creation, both plot and characterization obviously obey the conventions of the fairy tale rather than the dictates of reality. The whole performance is an exercise in the stirring of emotions disproportionate to the stimuli provided. We are not intended to be disturbed fundamentally by the repeated threats of incest or suicide. A happy ending is assumed from the outset, and the play engages us as much for its mannered articulation of solutions as for the dangers that make them necessary.

Only occasionally does this rather glossy drama suggest the art of *The White Devil* or *The Duchess of Malfi*. The verse, for the most part, seems smoothly un-Websterian. But there are moments in which the preconditioned ear can hear the faintest echo of the Italian tragedies:

> ô most noble sir,
> Though I have lost my fortune, and lost you
> For a worthy Father: yet I will not loose
> My former vertue, my integrity
> Shall not yet forsake me; but as the wilde Ivy,
> Spredds and thrives better in some pittious ruin
> Of tower, or defac'd Temple, then it does
> Planted in a new building—so shall I
> Make my adversity my instrument
> To winde me up into a full content.
> (V.i.115–124)

Thus Cesario at the nadir of his fortunes. Such a speech, although it lacks the compression, ruggedness, and intensity of the poet's most powerful verse, makes it tempting to accept majority opinion and ascribe the scene to Webster. When Clarissa "*offers to kill her selfe,*" exclaiming "Deaths the worst then / And hee shall be my bridegroome" (V.iii.161–162), we recognize a favorite idea of Webster; and Baptista's secret marriage to Juliana, discovered by an "incensed Duke" (I.i.275) and cruelly punished by banishing the husband and imprisoning the wife, is not dissimilar in situation to the outrage at Amalfi—particularly since the dangerous love appears to lead to the lady's death. The play's concern with dismemberment—a somewhat grotesque feature in so elegant a fabric—is also suggestive of Webster. In addition to Alberto's vengeful design that Mentivole should lose his hand, the stern old man enjoins his son to bravery at sea by invoking the image of a fighter who, in boarding an enemy vessel, would "hang by the teeth, / And die undanted," even after his "hands" had been "cut off" (I.i.195–196). The motif appears a third time with greater irony when the Duke of Florence insists that the two feuding houses must compose their differences:

> the petty brawles and quarrels
> Late urg'd betwixt th' *Alberti* and your family
> Must, yes and shall, like tender unknit joynts
> Fasten againe together of themselves:
> Or like an angry Chyrurgion, we will use
> The roughnesse of our justice, to cut off
> The stubborne rancour of the limbes offending.
>
> (III.ii.13–19)

This passage, based probably on Matthew 5:30 ("And if thy right hand offend thee, cut it off . . . for it is profitable for thee that one of thy members should perish, and not that thy whole body should be cast into hell"), forges a link between the severed hand as an emblem of unnatural ferocity and egotism and the sinful member of Christian tradition that corrupts the health of the body politic, subverting the law of love upon which civilized society depends.

Given the drama's shadowy connection with the Webster canon, such details are worth notice, but *The Fair Maid of the Inn* is a very derivative and conventional play. It contains almost no pervasive resonances of Webster that could not plausibly be explained by conscious—or perhaps even unconscious—imitation.

* * *

Webster's final play was probably the Roman tragedy *Appius and Virginia*, apparently written with Heywood, his long-time intimate. It was not published until 1654 and therefore takes its place beside *A Cure for a Cuckold* and the dubiously Websterian *Anything for a Quiet Life* and *The Fair Maid of the Inn* as the fourth posthumously printed drama of the playwright's canon. In their attempts to date the tragedy, scholars have agreed on almost nothing except that it belongs either to the early or to the late extreme of Webster's career. The arguments either way are far from conclusive and have tended to become intertwined with the question of collaborative authorship, but the weight of evidence, such as it is, seems to favor the later period.

Certain aspects of the play's style and characterization have prompted critics to associate it with Heywood's *Rape of Lucrece* (published in 1608) and to regard it as a complementary dramatization of a similar subject for a similar audience, perhaps at the Red Bull.[34] But Heywood's play with its unsophisticated hodgepodge of vaudeville and violence is very unlike Webster's dignified performance, even when we allow for some generic resemblance of the clowns. Dent suggests that the fairly extensive borrowing from Sir Thomas North's translation of Guevara's *Diall of Princes* (1557) may point to an early date, since the closest parallels to this source elsewhere in Webster tend to be more numerous in *The White Devil* than in later plays.[35] Yet George Pettie's rendering of *The Civile Conversation of . . . Guazzo* (1580) also appears to have been a source for *Appius and Virginia*, and Webster's debts to it extend to *The Devil's Law-Case* and, perhaps, to *The Fair Maid of the Inn*.[36] Moreover, it has yet to be shown that *Sir Thomas Wyatt* and the *Ho* plays borrow verbally from any of Webster's major sources. The dramatist's characteristic habits of imitation show up strongly only by 1612 with the major tragedies. Michael Payne Steppat has called attention to an allusion in Robert Anton's *Philosophers Satyrs* (1616) that conceivably refers to Webster's tragedy. Speaking of "our *lustfull Theaters*," the puritanical Anton mentions immodest subjects such as "*Virgineaes* rape" and "wanton *Lais*" with her "*Sirens charmes*" that characterize the contemporary stage.[37] This is suggestive, but the famous story of Appius and Virginia had been dramatized as early as 1567 and would have been a likely subject for almost any playwright with classical inclinations.

The case for a late date rests chiefly on the scenes that make much of the starvation of the Roman soldiers at their camp outside the city. Nothing of this appears in the known sources of the plot, and the concern would be effectively topical around 1624–1626 or later, when English sailors and troops on the Continent were undergoing similar privation and clamoring to the court for relief—like Virginius, unsuccessfully. Further support for a later date comes in the form of a possible allusion (V.i.163–166) to a disastrous fire that consumed Sir William Cockayn's flax warehouse along with neighboring buildings on 12 November 1623 and was described in the continuation of Stow's *Chronicle*.[38] It has been argued (more weakly) that Webster's failure to mention *Appius and Virginia* in his preface to *The Devil's Law-Case* (1623), where he refers to the two Italian tragedies and *The Guise* by name, also indicates lateness of composition, although Webster might, of course, have meant to include the play among the "others" of which he also speaks in the same sentence. Grasping at further negative arguments, Lagarde points to the absence of a ghost and the nonuse of the discovery space as evidence of delayed writing, and he seems to believe (with Clifford Leech) that the play's somewhat Fletcherian approach to character is equally a symptom of late Jacobean or Caroline style.[39] The possibility that the 1623 folio of Shakespeare, containing the first printed texts of *Julius Caesar, Antony and Cleopatra*, and *Coriolanus*, may have helped rekindle Webster's interest in Roman tragedy is worth considering as an additional point.

Speculative as such reasoning remains, there is a certain attractiveness to the notion that in his final dramatic effort Webster was returning to classical subject matter of the sort that had first challenged his pen in 1602, when he was working beside Munday, Middleton, and Drayton on *Caesar's Fall*. Lacking proof, we must content ourselves with probabilities, and these would seem to point to 1625–1634 as the period in which *Appius and Virginia* was composed. Heywood's reference in the past tense to his friend "Jack" makes a reasonable *terminus ad quem*, for, even if this is not taken to signify that Webster was dead in 1634, it surely implies that his literary activity had ceased by then.[40] Given the dramatist's involvement with *A Cure for a Cuckold* in 1624–1625 and perhaps with *A Fair Maid of the Inn* around 1625–1626, and considering also his usually sluggish pace of composition, it is tempting to assign *Appius and Virginia* to 1627; but the tragedy could have been written at any point during the final phase of Webster's career.[41]

The authorship of the play remains nearly as problematic as its date, although no one any longer doubts that Webster was the principal dramatist. The publisher Richard Marriot entered for his copy on 13 May 1654 "A Play called Appeus and Virginia . . . written by Iohn Webster," and, not surprisingly, the quarto title page of the same year echoes that designation. The text does not appear to derive from a copy that has seen theatrical use. How Marriot came by the manuscript we do not know, but he could hardly have profited in any way by misrepresenting the drama's parentage. This is the sum of the external evidence and the sum of all that can be relied upon with safety. Nevertheless, most students of the tragedy have detected Heywood's hand. Rupert Brooke, seconded by A. M. Clark, argued that Webster was little more than the reviser of Heywood's work;[42] then H. D. Gray and F. L. Lucas, each according to his own lights, divided the play between the two playwrights.[43] The ascription to Heywood, whether in large or small part, has tended to ignore or at least to undervalue Webster's imitative bent and his proved capacity to modulate his style at various times for various purposes. The occasionally recondite vocabulary of the play— the use of such Latinisms as "imposterous," "obdure," "infallid," "torvèd," and "strage"—is, however, strikingly Heywood-like and, with the possible exception of *A Cure for a Cuckold*, rather foreign to the Webster we know. Also Lagarde and Murray, the two most recent analysts of the play's colloquial contractions, have reached almost identical conclusions in support of Heywood's share, each working independently of the other.[44] The new statistical data do not eliminate doubt, especially considering that only two of Heywood's plays have been taken into account and that some overlapping of linguistic forms occurs between the two dramatists. It is still possible to argue for Webster's unaided authorship of *Appius and Virginia*. But something like a scholarly consensus seems to be emerging. This gives Webster credit for planning the play and for most of the writing, but it allows Heywood a minor share, most noticeably in I.iii–iv, II.i, III.i, IV.ii, and V.ii.

Coming, as it apparently does, after an extended period of experimentation with tragicomedy, *Appius and Virginia* represents a return on Webster's part to the stability of history, although, of course, the tale of the lustful judge and the virgin whom her father martyred in order to preserve her chastity had long since acquired the status of popular fable. It is interesting to observe that Webster did not rely on versions of the famous story that had been simplified for didactic or fictive purposes, such as he might have found in Chaucer's *Canterbury Tales*, Gower's *Confessio Amantis*, or even Painter's *Palace of Pleasure*. Nor does he seem to have consulted the old interlude written for boys by one "R. B." (possibly Richard Bowers),[45] which, with its jingling rhymes and cheerful Vice (Haphazard), richly deserves its published title of *A New Tragicall Comedie of Apius and Virginia* (1575).

Rather, Webster based his tragedy on the most detailed account available, that of Dionysius of Halicarnassus in Books X and XI of his *Roman Antiquities*. The Greek author in fact specifically defends the need "to report in accurate detail all the circumstances which attended the overthrow of the [decemviral] oligarchy" in 449 B.C.[46] Dionysius had been translated into Latin and published at Treviso as early as 1480 by Lapus Biragus; this text was thrice reprinted, once at Paris in 1529 and twice at Basel—in 1532 (as revised by Glareanus) and in 1549. Robert Estienne, the first editor of the Greek original (Paris, 1546), was followed by Friedrich Sylburg, who produced a new edition of the Greek with his own Latin translation (Frankfurt, 1586). A rendering into Italian by Francesco Venturi had already been printed at Venice in 1545. We cannot be sure that Webster was accomplished enough in even one of the three languages to make efficient use of any of these continental books, and one wonders perforce whether he did not lean upon some unknown version in English.[47]

Whatever volume he read, Webster obviously utilized elements that were to be found only in Dionysius, such as Appius's pretended reluctance to accept powerful office (dramatized in Act I)[48] and two debating points raised in opposition to Marcus Clodius's lie that Virginia is the daughter of his female slave (worked into the trial scene of Act IV). Why has Marcus waited fourteen years to claim possession of the girl and why would the wife of Virginius, if she had really meant to deceive her husband, choose a girl instead of a boy to present to him as his own offspring? Webster cleverly transfers the first of these arguments from Virginia's relatives in the source to Appius himself in the play, thereby adding an effective touch to the characterization of his chief villain and enhancing the effect of devious plausibility. He also imparts a measure of dignity to Appius in the final scene that significantly modifies our total impression of the character. The idea for this shift might well have come from Dionysius, who, unlike the other possible sources, lays some stress on Appius's sterling reputation before he became a decemvir, on his "most splendid words and deeds," his original "principles" that had been "honourable and inspired . . . great hopes of . . . virtue. . . ."[49] The playwright also builds up the contrast between the tyrant's aristocratic courage at the end and the agent's cowardice by having Marcus Clodius attempt to lay all the guilt upon his master (V.ii.162–164). This too must come from Dionysius, who alone reports that the subordinate escaped death "by putting the blame on Appius, who had ordered him to commit the crime. . . ."[50]

Webster appears also to have read Livy's version of the episode (available to him in Philemon Holland's translation of 1600), although it is not easy to cite details specifically attributable to this source. Several of Virginius's speeches sound as though they had been based on passages in Holland, such as the hero's momentary refusal of the generalship out of grief for the death of his daughter (IV.ii.184–188), his melancholy association of the death of his wife with Virginia's and his urging the soldiers to prevent outrages upon their own children in future (IV.ii.194–201), and his inclination to be lenient in punishing Appius (V.ii.66–80); perhaps this last was suggested by Livy's statement that Virginius offered to "pardon" the oligarch (cf. V.ii.72) for all tyrannies except the assault upon his daughter and that he also spared the life of Marcus, being unwilling to "take the extremitie" against a mere tool.[51] Webster's character of the nurse appears also to derive ultimately from Livy, for Dionysius merely refers vaguely to the girl's "governesses" whereas the Paduan historian mentions a specific woman who "cride to the Quirites for helpe";[52] the dramatic character likewise protests the seizure of her charge (III.ii.122–123).

Conceivably, Webster could have obtained these details from Painter, who in effect paraphrased Livy, but a few additional points not in Painter indicate that the dramatist must have gone directly to the original account in Holland's version. In the tragedy, for instance, Appius adroitly tries to save himself by appealing to Virginius not to imitate his own excesses:

> If in mine eminence I was stern to thee;
> Shunning my rigor, likewise shun my fall.
> And being mild where I shewed cruelty,
> Establish still thy greatness. Make some use
> Of this my bondage. With indifference
> Survey me, and compare my yesterday
> With this sad hour, my heighth with my decline,
> And give them equal ballance.
>
> (V.ii.58–65)

This reads distinctly like an elaboration of Holland's passage in which the fallen decemvir "would once againe call upon the Tribunes of the Commons for their help, and admonish them, not to follow and imitate them [i.e., the decemvirs], whom they would seem to hate."[53] And not surprisingly Webster picks up the *de casibus* emphasis of Holland's rendering; when Appius says to Virginius, "Fortune hath lift thee to my Chair, / And thrown me headlong to thy pleading-bar" (V.ii.56–57), or when Virginius answers, "I cannot chuse but pity and lament, / So high a rise should have such low discent" (V.ii.68–69), it is not difficult to imagine this staple irony of Renaissance tragedy being prompted by such moralizations as the following:

I see well (when all is done) there are Gods in heaven, and such gods as neglect not the affaires of mortall men. Pride and crueltie (although it bee long first) at length will surely have a fall, and thoroughly be punished. Lo, how he is now faine to appeale, who aforetime abolished and tooke away all appeale . . . and see how he is carried to prison, destitute and deprived of the benefit of libertie, who awarded and adjudged a free bodie to bondage and servitude. . . . so everie man was greatly troubled in spirit, to see so great a personage punished.[54]

Webster makes Icilius counter Virginius's lament for the fall of Appius by asking rhetorically whether the archvillain, if pardoned, would "Become a new man, a more upright Judge" (V.ii.75). The idea and phrasing for this detail probably derive from the sarcastic sentence in Holland's rendering where Livy condemns the politician's deceitful self-promotion: "He had so altered his nature, and became such a new man, that all on a suddaine, of a cruell and terrible persecutor of the commons, he proved a very *Publicola*, and courter of the Communaltie, and one that lay for to get every gale of popular love and favour that might be had."[55] Lucas, refining upon an observation of Rupert Brooke, clinches the argument for Webster's use of Holland as a secondary source by pointing out the curious use of the word "forthcoming" (III.ii.361–362) as a noun (in the technical sense of "bail" or "assurance that a person will appear in court"); this seems to be based on a miscomprehension of Holland's syntax, where the use is participial.[56]

As we should expect, the influence of other dramatists upon *Appius and Virginia* is obvious enough. Whether or not Webster's minor figure Calphurnia owes her name to the wife of the title character in *Julius Caesar* (it appears in none of the sources),[57] other reminiscences of Shakespeare's tragedy are unmistakable. Icilius refers to Appius as "The high Colossus that bestrides us all" (III.i.84), and Virginius, in a second probable echo, speaks of the fallen tyrant ("but yesterday his breath / Aw'd *Rome*" [V.ii.66–67]) in words that recall Antony's speech over his friend's corpse: "But yesterday the word of Caesar might / Have stood against the world" (III.ii.120–121). Icilius's persuasion of Virginius to avenge his daughter by publicly exhibiting her body also imitates an aspect of Antony's funeral oration, and the altercation over the propriety of sacrificing Virginia that erupts between the heroine's father and her lover has certain affinities with the quarrel between Brutus and Cassius in Shakespeare's play. The treatment of the crowds also suggests Shakespearean influence, for in the sources the Roman populace and even the soldiers are essentially liberty-loving and sympathetic victims of tyranny, whereas Webster, as Stoll suggests, tends to regard them as "fry" or "rabble" in the fashion of Shakespeare's Roman plays.[58] The scene in which Virginius quells the meeting of the Roman soldiers, for instance, powerfully resembles its counterpart in *Coriolanus*, where the hero cows the Roman citizenry. There is a clear imitation of *Othello* when the advocate in the trial scene makes reference to Virginia's "Jewells . . . More worth then all her Tribe" (IV.i.229–230).[59]

Apart from Shakespeare and a few incidental echoes from Marlowe's *Doctor Faustus* and Jonson's *Sejanus*,[60] the most notable stylistic influence upon *Appius and Virginia* was obviously Heywood. The number of Latinate or unusual words favored or coined by Webster's friend can hardly be accidental, and their presence in the text indicates that, if the dramatist was not actually collaborating with Heywood, he was deliberately copying his style. Whichever was the case, the subject called for a more elevated, austere, and "classical" vocabulary than had been usual with Webster, a diction that would help create the overall effect that Saintsbury, applying Sainte-Beuve, aptly characterized as "pale et noble."[61]

With or without Heywood's help, Webster followed his classical sources with some care, so that the general impression achieved, despite the comic interludes and the pathos, is one of dignified historicity. The dramatist could honestly have said with Chaucer's doctor, who relates a version of the story on his pilgrimage to Canterbury, "this is no fable, / But knowen for historial thyng notable."[62] He would also have been proud of the "truth of Argument" that Jonson in the preface to an earlier Roman tragedy had numbered among the "offices" that "a *Tragick* writer" should discharge.[63] No doubt Webster's natural penchant for creating effective villains partly explains the emphasis on Appius—the tendency to make him the most complex and interesting of the characters and to conceive the dramatic structure more in terms of his rise and fall than of Virginia's passive suffering or the cruel dilemma that the tyrant's lust forces upon her father. But both Dionysius and Livy show more interest in Appius as head of the decemviral oligarchy than in any of his victims, so that Webster in large measure was simply conforming to the pattern already established by the historians. It is worth noticing also that Webster resisted any temptation to deal with the tale purely as an exemplum of the virtues of chastity and the evils of lust, the approach taken by the interludist R. B. Livy, particularly, treats the episode of Virginia as merely the culminating outrage in a career of political egomania, as the final catalyst to the overthrow of the decemvirs and the re-establishment of traditional liberties.

Webster preserves some of this larger significance. He transfers the plea for freedom to address the Senate from Valerius in the historical accounts to Virginius in the tragedy (I.iv.49–51), thus keeping the issue central. Appius's lust for power is depicted as hardly less compelling than his lust for the girl, and early in the play we hear of "The rottenness of this misgovern'd State" (I.iv.81), of how Rome has "growne a most unnaturall mother" (II.ii.49), of how "the Camp pines, and the City smarts," indeed of how all society "fares worse for [Appius's] incontinence" (II.iii.94–95). Virginius warns the decemvir at the outset that, unless grievances are redressed and wants relieved, enemy forces will "Chase the gown'd Senate through the streets" and cover "brawns / Up to the elbowes" in his "traiterous bloud" (I.iv.74–77). We are therefore prepared to regard the tyrant's fall as considerably more than a personal defeat. By the end of Act I Virginia's father is already talking of the "universal businesse . . . That toucheth a whole people" (I.iv.162–163). Later, as Appius dies and as Marcus Clodius is dragged away to execution, Icilius can moralize about what has been gained:

> the life of the *Decemviri*
> Expires in them. *Rome* thou at length art free,
> Restored unto thine ancient liberty. . . .
>
> (V.ii.183–185)

And Webster in accordance with both his ancient authorities and a traditional association of long standing, enforces the inevitable parallel with Lucrece;[64] as the rape of that other pattern of chastity in 509 B.C. had resulted in the collapse of the Tarquin dynasty and the founding of the Roman republic, so Virginia's martyrdom sixty years later brought an end to the hated despotism of the decemvirate:

> Two Ladies fair, but most infortunate,
> Have in their ruins rais'd declining *Rome*—
> *Lucretia* and *Virginia*, both renown'd
> For chastity. Souldiers and noble Romans,
> To grace her death, whose life hath freed great *Rome*,
> March with her Corse to her sad Funeral Tomb.
>
> (V.ii.192–197)

The conception of Appius and Virginia as historical personages whose lives had real political importance did not, of course, prevent Webster, like any other dramatist, from taking certain liberties with the story, from introducing incidents and characters missing from the sources and altering emphases for his own ends. Most obvious of Webster's inventions, of course, is the famine and near mutiny of the Roman soldiers with Virginius's unsuccessful appeal to the Senate for their relief. This situation provides an effective confrontation between Appius and Virginius early in the action, establishes a natural antagonism between the two men apart from the issue of Virginia, and allows Webster to reveal the hero at the outset as a soldier of unquestioned probity, although undiplomatically emotional and outspoken. The quelling of the threatened mutiny shows Virginius to be a figure of impressive authority in his own sphere and therefore intensifies the effect of impotent frustration when he is dealing with supersubtle politicians rather than restive soldiers. The contrast between the commander's total control at the outset and his distraction later is not unlike the effect Shakespeare produces in the characterization of Othello.

The selfless payment of the men out of Virginius's own pocket is also Webster's innovation, as is Clodius's plot to impoverish the officer and so make easier the assault upon his daughter; the two complications mesh nicely, and they supply Icilius, the wronged lover, with an economic motive (he is concerned about the size of Virginia's dowry) that subtly modifies our response to his moralistic outburst in the interview with Appius. Indeed, the private quarrel between judge and fiancé is itself Websterian in origin, and its effect is not only to contrast the passion of the younger man with the icy self-possession of the elder but also to dramatize the point that deviousness and dissimulation may taint even the forces that oppose tyranny. (Shakespeare does something similar in the scene of *Macbeth* in which Malcolm feels out Macduff.) Icilius has intercepted the decemvir's letters to Virginia, a fact that he does not reveal to Appius until the judge tries to neutralize his interest in the girl by offering him an alternative marriage into his own family. Icilius both begins and ends this exchange with camouflage. He pretends that he has come only to plead in behalf of his father-in-law to be; then, after threatening his rival with a sudden explosion of "Lovers fury" (II.iii.107), he dissembles again by seeming to accept Appius's false denials.

Webster's emphasis on the Roman camp, then, sets up a contrast fundamental to the drama between the totally opposed realms of Appius and Virginius, the two worlds of ruthless intrigue (with its fleshly self-indulgence) and the Spartan life of the military (with its simple but robust virtues). But, lest the contrast between the realpolitik and the more forthright values of the play seem too artificial or schematic, Webster allows them to touch each other in the behavior of Icilius.

Apart from the playwright's symbolic enlargement of the soldierly domain, his most significant change affects the character of Appius. Dionysius describes him as a man "not by nature sound of mind" who is sometimes motivated by fear or anger and who misjudges popular reaction ineptly.[65] Webster's character is much cooler and more calculating—an ingenious Machiavel who functions well in crises and who preserves even to the death that audacious resolution Webster so admired. In the first scene of the play, it is true, Appius establishes himself as an overreacher in the Marlovian tradition:

> Had I as many hands
> As had *Briarius*, I'de extend them all
> To catch this office; 'twas my sleeps disturber,
> My dyets ill digestion, my melancholy
> Past physicks cure.
>
> (I.i.66–70)

But to this compulsive energy, Webster has added a blend of outward suavity and villainous self-congratulation that reminds us at times of Richard III, although Appius lacks the wit of Shakespeare's character. And the villain's obsession with Virginia is presented as the chilliest of lusts—all a matter of strategy, maneuvering, and "policy" that gives back a pale reflection of the Aragonian cardinal in *The Duchess of Malfi*. Appius is made to fulfill his wicked role compellingly enough, but the Machiavellian creed to which he so readily subscribes ("We should smile smoothest where our hate's most deep" [II.iii.197]; "Observe this rule—one ill must cure another" [III.iii.25]) robs him of sympathy and puts him unambiguously among the remorseless sinners of melodramatic tradition. Webster was clearly striving to endow the figure with a certain dark grandeur.

The playwright also developed the character of Marcus Clodius from the relatively minor figure of the sources, moving him closer to the center of interest. By transforming him from what Dionysius calls "a daring man"[66] to a sycophantic and craven "Secretary" (II.iii.106) who nevertheless conceives the elaborate plot to ensnare Virginia, Webster created an effective foil for Appius—a character who parallels his superior's Machiavellianism on a meaner plane at the same time that he contrasts with the decemvir's courage. In the histories Clodius is little more than the agent of Appius's villainy. Webster gives him a shady past (embezzlement), the initiative to concoct the tale of Virginia's concealed parentage, and the willingness to undergo public disgrace in the futherance of his superior's crime. With the death of Marcus, a dramatically and didactically necessary deviation from history, Webster exploited the same basic contrast that he had already used so successfully in the deaths of Cariola and the Duchess of Malfi. Appius, scorning to demean himself, embraces his fate with traditional stoic sangfroid:

> Learn of me *Clodius*,
> I'l teach thee what thou never studiedst yet,
> Thats bravely how to dy.
>
> (V.ii.138–140)

But the apprentice in vice, "one bred from the rabble" (V.ii.172), refuses to learn the lesson, pleads contemptibly for mercy, and is hauled off to the gallows like a common criminal. As Webster punishes Marcus more severely than history by changing banishment to execution, so he rewards Icilius and Virginius more generously by having them elected consuls instead of merely tribunes.

Here and there the relationship between the greater and lesser villain suggests once again an analogy to *Richard III*. One wonders whether Webster was conscious of it. For instance, when Appius, fixated upon Virginia, enters "*melancholly*" and internally "all in combat" (I.iii.1–8), Clodius irritates his master by intruding upon his self-absorption:

> *Clodius.* My Lord.
> *Appius.* Thou troublest me.
>
> (I.iii.1–2)

This is startlingly close—note the verbatim repetition—to the moment in Shakespeare's play when Buckingham breaks the meditation of his freshly crowned sovereign:

> *Buckingham.* My lord!
> *King Richard.* Ay, what's o'clock?
> *Buckingham.* I am thus bold to put your Grace in mind

Of what you promised me.

. . . .

King Richard. Thou troublest me. I am not in the vein.

(IV.ii.108–118)

In a less specific way the prearranged scene (III.ii) between Clodius and Appius when the underling first presses his counterfeit claim to Virginia and the judge makes a public show of resistance also parallels Shakespeare's history. The corresponding scene, of course, is the publicly staged episode in which Buckingham contrives to thrust the crown upon a Gloucester who, playing the maid's part, says no but takes it (III.vii). Nor should we forget Casca's cynical account in Shakespeare's Roman tragedy of how Caesar thrice refused a crown (*Julius Caesar*, I.ii.221–275). But Webster himself had already toyed with such devices. The Duchess of Malfi notices the rehearsed quality of the passage in which her brothers batter her homiletically on the subject of remarriage: "I think this speech between you both was studied, / It came so roundly off" (I.i.329–330). And in fact Webster even repeats the idea in a later scene of the Roman play. When the hired lawyer is arguing his fraudulent case before Appius, Icilius remarks, "I vow this is a practis'd Dialogue: / Comes it not rarely off?" (IV.i.142–143).

Given Webster's taste for trial scenes, we are not surprised at his handling of the tribunal over which Appius presides and at which Clodius formally claims Virginia as his bondslave. Not only does Webster remove the scene from the seething Forum that Dionysius describes to an undesignated location from which the general populace is apparently excluded, but he also invents a "spruce Orator" (IV.i.163) who argues in Clodius's behalf. Both innovations, of course, help concentrate attention upon the arguments and rhetoric of the speakers, but the addition of the lawyer gives Webster an opportunity to contrast the plainspoken Virginius, whose "Truth needs no Advocate," with the scheming Appius, who "Buyes up the tongues that travel with applause" (IV.i.66–67). Again, as in *The Devil's Law-Case* and *A Cure for a Cuckold*,[67] Webster indulged that penchant for antilegal satire long fashionable with such writers as Marston and Jonson. Such trial scenes of course would have an obvious relevance for audiences who could remember the unjust conviction of Sir Walter Raleigh for treason or the cynical pardoning of Lady Somerset for the murder of Overbury after her socially inferior accomplices had been executed.

The dramatist's final significant departure from the source material is, of course, the invention of the clown Corbulo, introduced as a bawdy companion to the nurse.[68] He speaks entirely in prose. The amusing badinage that is the character's sole excuse for being (the plot gives him nothing whatever to do) is made up of staple ingredients—dogged misunderstanding, indecent punning, traces of euphusistic rhetoric, choplogic, a tendency to anachronism, and the absurd reduction of almost every subject to physical terms. Such clowns are common enough throughout Renaissance drama, and nothing about Corbulo, despite the special pleading of Stoll and Brooke, is particularly or exclusively Heywoodian.[69] Indeed, the clown at one point jokes cynically about the typical behavior of widows in precisely the way that Webster had done in his character of *An ordinarie Widdow* and elsewhere.[70] No doubt the presence of this amiable comic improved the box office receipts, but the incidental levity is not without relevance to the play as a whole. Corbulo's general bawdry, somewhat stale to be sure, effectively localizes and syphons off irreverence of response, thereby preparing us to regard the virgin martyrdom with the seriousness required. By means of contrast, the clown helps to define the drama's standard of idealism; in this, of course, he parallels the function of such characters as Mercutio and the Nurse in *Romeo and Juliet* or Emilia in *Othello*. It is a mark of the dramatist's constructional skill that Corbulo is dropped at the end of Act III. By this time the clown's contrastive humor has done its work; like Lear's fool, the character would be unnecessary and inappropriate to the later movements of the tragedy.

Except for the quirky William Archer, who judged Webster's Roman piece "vastly superior" to the dramatist's other tragedies,[71] *Appius and Virginia* has excited only mild enthusiasm as a play. Hazlitt called it "a good, sensible, solid tragedy" containing "little to blame or praise,"[72] and few critics since his day have claimed more than mediocrity for it. Stoll spoke of its "frigidity and academic character," Brooke of its "forthright and unthinking simplicity," and Lucas of its "adequate handling of a not very brilliant theme."[73] Peter Haworth, although not unresponsive to its virtues, doubted, like Brooke, that the drama could be Webster's in any generative or fundamental way.[74] More recently, Melvin Seiden has applied such adjectives as "indifferent" and "insipidly sentimental," while Murray, assuming flawed coordination between Webster and Heywood, has even concluded that the tragedy "cannot be called a work of art."[75] Certainly, as T. S. Eliot perceived, *Appius and Virginia* is "a play far below Webster's best work, and in some respects dissimilar to it";[76] yet it deserves more sympathetic attention than it has customarily received.

Like Ford's *Perkin Warbeck* and Shirley's *Cardinal*, Webster's final drama represents a conscious attempt to revive an older and simpler mode, as though the playwright were at last weary of psychic complexities and grotesque or tragicomic ambiguities. The action of the Roman play, unlike *The White Devil*, *The Devil's Law-Case*, or *A Cure for a Cuckold*, can be summarized in a sentence. Its tone is cooler, its texture more uniform, its contours more readily apprehensible. The chief characters create a singleness and fixity of impression more akin to line drawings than to the florid and disturbing canvases that we think of as typically Websterian, and the play aspires to a generality and absoluteness surprisingly neoclassical for its author. One symptom of this tendency is the large number of parts assigned to unnamed speakers and figures differentiated only by function—two cousins of Appius, six soldiers who often speak in chorus as "Omnes," two petitioners, two lictors, two servingmen, a senator, an orator, a Roman officer, and the like. Another is the quasi-allegorical manner in which single characters are made to embody a familiar value or association of values. Virginia's name almost totally describes her character. Her father symbolizes the best traditions of Roman soldiership enlarged to heroic proportions:

> I will stand my self
> For the whole Regiment, and safer far
> In mine owne single valour, then begirt
> With cowards and with traitors.
>
> (II.ii.150–153)

This is grandeur, but the grandeur of a statue more than of a man. And Virginius is so unambiguously identified with the concept of death for honor (he tries to stab himself after stabbing his daughter) that he is made to violate psychological probability by offering the same dignified death to those who have ruined his life.

Appius, Clodius, and Icilius are somewhat more naturalistically presented, but even Appius, the most complex character in the cast, is psychologically transparent by mature Websterian standards, being a relatively simple compound of lechery, "the fire in hell" (IV.i.42) as Icilius calls it, and deceit—in other words of "a Divel" (II.iii.101) and a "Fox" (III.ii.166). Webster makes him reveal his ambition quite unconsciously, for instance, in the dispatching of a messenger:

> make as much speed
> As if thy father were deceas'd i'th' Camp,
> And that thou went'st to take th' Administration
> Of what he left thee. Fly.
>
> (III.iii.2–5)

The nurse and the clown are equally types rather than individuals. Webster seems to have suppressed his interest in particularity and striven instead for the generic in a way that forces us to modify Miss Bradbrook's generalization that "He was concerned with perfection of detail rather than general design. . . ."[77] With due caution, then, we might appropriate Eliot's comments on a related and equally anomalous tragedy, Marston's *Sophonisba* (1605–1606): "the play has a good plot, is well constructed and moves rapidly. There are no irrelevances . . . ; it is austere and economical."[78] Mentioning that work's "exceptional consistency of texture" and "underlying serenity,"[79] Eliot goes on to invoke the dramatic tradition of Daniel and Greville and even of Corneille and Racine as the spheres within which we might profitably confine our judgment. Webster's play differs importantly from Marston's in a variety of ways, but similar artistic impulses may have prompted both.

Webster of course had no wish or need to abjure the popular tradition altogether in *Appius and Virginia*. The low comedy and the impress of Shakespeare's and Jonson's tragedies have already been mentioned. Also the very subject with its mixture of political intrigue, sex, and violence offered sensational, not to say lurid, possibilities. As the analogy to *Sophonisba* suggests, Webster's play is a late addition to an established subgenre of tragedies with ancient, usually Roman, settings depicting threatened or violated purity—tragedies such as Heywood's *Rape of Lucrece* (1606–1607), Fletcher's *Valentinian* (1610–1614), and Dekker and Massinger's *Virgin Martyr* (1620). All these plays promote chastity as a moral absolute, "a dearer thing than life" in the words of Shakespeare's contribution to the tradition.[80] Like Sophonisba and her sister heroines (Lucrece, Lucina, Dorothea), Webster's Virginia is another "Wonder of Women," a secular saint in the theatrical hagiography of distressed maidenhood. By convention such dramas go in for essentially external conflicts between the vilest of evils and the most ideal of virtues.

Appius and Virginia is in no sense coterie drama, but, compared with its predecessors of similar kind, its handling of popular material is so restrained as to seem somewhat un-Jacobean. Except for the sudden climactic stabbing of the daughter, there is almost no exploitation of horror, physical suffering, shock, sensuality, or bloodshed. Indeed, the very chasteness of the dramaturgy (which obviously heightens the didactic effect) gives us further reason to doubt whether this tragedy could possibly be the staging of "rape" that Anton so deplored; for it is hard to imagine how even the sourest of Puritans could think that Webster's drama "would turne a modest *audience* / To *brazen-fac'et profession* of a *whore.*"[81] Of the three deaths in the play, only two occur onstage, and both are dignified by careful preparation. Virginia anticipates her fate when she begs her father to "take the life you gave me / And sacrifice it rather to the gods / Then to a villains Lust" (IV.i.33–35), and Appius is permitted to moralize with some eloquence on stoic resolution before he "Redeem[s] a base life with a noble death" (V.ii.121). Webster makes relatively little capital of the crowd scenes, preferring to center the most dramatic moments of the play in confrontations of a more or less private sort among the principals. Even the trial scene is removed from the Forum, where the sources place it, to a more restricted setting. Lucas remarks that in his Roman tragedy Webster "escapes from the influence of Fletcher."[82] In terms of plotting, this is undeniable, but in another sense *Appius and Virginia* is like Fletcher and unlike the Webster of the great middle period in its surface smoothness, its detachment, and the finite, absolutist, and frequently unspeculative clarity of the world it assumes—a world more concerned with morality than with metaphysics despite conventional references to "the gods." Appius may face death as courageously as Flamineo, but there is no confounding of knowledge with knowledge and, despite the reappearance of the word, no cosmic "mist"—only the recognition of corruption suitably punished.

The narrowing of focus and the turning away from psychology imply a compensatory concern with logical progression, with shapeliness and proportion. Archer's preference for *Appius and Virginia* over Webster's Italian tragedies seems to have been based not only on the play's avoidance of barbarous crudities, as that critic misunderstood these, but also on its greater approximation to the well-made play in the late Victorian sense of the term. The dramatic architecture of the tragedy is unexpectedly spare and orderly, its five acts building upon each other with a pleasing but unobtrusive sequaciousness. In the first, Appius achieves power, plots with Clodius to satisfy his lust, and rejects Virginius's plea for relief of the Roman troops. In the second, tension is gradually augmented by dramatizing the mutinous condition of the soldiers and by bringing the two rivals for Virginia into a contact with each other that is civil at first and then openly hostile. By the end of Act II, Webster has neatly defined both the political and sexual, the public and private antagonisms, and shown their interconnection. The third act raises both conflicts to the level of crisis with the arrest of Virginia and the frantic dispatching of contradictory messages to the camp, Icilius urging Virginius to hurry to Rome as Appius tries to arrange for his detention in the field. The climax of the drama with its staged tribunal, the stabbing of the girl, and the filicide's crazed return to the camp is thus effectively delayed until Act IV. The final movement of the tragedy can then be devoted to the aftermath—the re-establishment of Roman freedom (a direct consequence of the "freeing" of Virginia), the quarrel and reconciliation of the two men closest to the sacrificial victim, and the punishment of the two criminals, now conceived of as murderers.

The simplicity of this outline should not blind us to certain subleties of organization that a closer reading of the text discloses. Webster carefully undergirds the bold linear effect of the action with a system of anticipations and repetitions that not only tighten the play but also relieve its starkness with occasional touches of chiaroscuro. The meeting of Appius and Icilius (II.iii), already discussed in connection with Webster's departures from his sources, provides a convenient illustration.

The scene opens with two petitioners who are applying to Appius for redress of grievances, petitioners whom Clodius in his capacity as secretary puts off with sugary and apparently misleading assurances. We never see or hear of these men again, and their chief function (apart from the impression of popular dissatisfaction that they lend to the social background of the drama) is to set a paradigm for the segment of action that immediately follows: this begins with Icilius suing to Appius in behalf of Virginius's pay and ends with an insincere promise of favor at some indefinite future point. Before Icilius is admitted to the decemvir's presence, Webster briefly dramatizes the barely concealed enmity that the visitor and the secretary feel for each other so as to prefigure the ensuing quarrel between the principals. Icilius, for instance, insults Clodius by glancing at the practice of cropping a felon's ears (II.iii.20) only moments before Appius mentions the receptiveness of his own "suffering ears" (II.iii.37) and is then assaulted with "But suffer me, / I'l offend nothing but thine ears" (II.iii.104–105). Moving from lesser to greater concerns, the scene advances stepwise up the ladder of authority. The officious secretary summarily dismisses the petitioners in deference to Icilius, the more important applicant, only to be dismissed himself by Appius so that the lover and the judge may converse in private. Then after the explosive attack during which Icilius has threatened to "nail" his interlocutor "to the Chair" (II.iii.104), we hear Appius in a moment of vengeful excitement planning to dismiss his assailant "to [his] death" (II.iii.165).

Not content with a kind of preview of the quarrel episode, Webster also gives us a retrospect. In the scene that immediately follows, Icilius relates a version of the quarrel to Virginia, her uncle, and other members of their circle, telling how at first he dissembled his intentions, then "drew [his] Poinyard" and "took [Appius] by the throat" (III.i.90), finally how he parted from the judge as a friend "in outward shew," although he "perceiv'd his heart" (III.i.107–108). Icilius's narration of what we have just witnessed might seem dramatically redundant but for the fact that its details differ enough from the actuality to characterize the speaker as a youth eager to impress his betrothed, prone to exaggeration, and perhaps even to self-deception.[83] The repetition provides that contrast between a subjective and objective evaluation of events that heightens our sense of their complexity. Thus it adds a touch of realism to the relationship between the lovers at the same time that it serves as a somewhat biased gloss on the speaker's earlier behavior. By protracting tension beyond the confrontation proper, it also helps build up suspense. The atmosphere of suspicious privacy carries over from Icilius's session with Appius to the family council; the irresolute Numitorius conveys the sense of danger with nervous interruptions such as "Ha, who's that?" (II.iii.21) and "Keep fast the door there: Sweet Couz not too loud" (II.iii.98). Of course the entire quarrel episode with its false truce between the judge and his enemy balances the later quarrel of Icilius and Virginius that concludes in a genuine reconciliation.

In fact Webster delights in allowing different parts of the play to comment upon each other. He introduces the prison motif in the opening scene where Clodius remarks that if his master "Were . . . now / In prison, or arraign'd before the Senate / For some suspect of treason" (I.i.46–48), his opportunist relatives would quickly desert him; later we hear of plans to imprison both Icilius (II.iii.219) and Virginius (IV.ii.50) in addition to the latter's allusion to Rome as "yon prison" (IV.ii.198), so that, when we actually see the villains *fettered and gyved* (V.ii.1) in the final act, the irony of their downfall strikes us with greater impact. By the same token Clodius's timorous death reminds us of the deputy's earlier boast, "I am strong, / Fixt and unshaking" (I.iii.17–18). A rebellious soldier who threatens to "drag" Virginius "to the slaughter by his locks, / Turned white with riot and incontinence" (II.ii.93–94), gives us a verbal anticipation of the fate of Clodius, who is literally dragged to his death for abetting Appius's incontinence. When the toady soliloquizes on his readiness to sacrifice a daughter to the judge's appetite, he prepares us in ironic fashion for Virginius's ultimate sacrifice:

> Had I a wife, or daughter that could please him
> I would devote her to him, but I must
> Shadow this scorne, and sooth him still in lust.
> (II.i.84–86)

Employing musicians, Clodius woos Virginia in Appius's behalf with a "harmony" that the girl at first mistakes for the "kindnesse" (II.i.33–34) of her fiancé but that actually betokens the tragic discord to come. A hungry soldier rails against Rome as "a most unnaturall mother" (II.ii.49), and then, after the death of Virginia, Icilius attacks the man who has relieved the army at his own expense as "an unnatural Father" (V.i.111). Minutius relieves Virginius of his military tribuneship shortly before he yields his "full command" (IV.ii.183) as general. Perhaps the most effective of the play's structural ironies is the reversal of roles that Webster manages in the treatment of Appius and his accomplice. By prearrangement the judge heaps exaggerated obloquy upon his servant in order to dissociate himself publicly from the plot to ensnare Virginia; later, when the criminals have been brought to account, Clodius tries to dissociate himself from Appius by pleading that he merely acted out of compulsion.

The verbal ironies are sometimes more blatant and immediate than these examples might suggest. We are not far from the sardonic facetiousness of Shakespeare's Richard III when, in seeking to possess Virginia, Appius announces:

> And i'th' mean time I'l take the honoured Lady
> Into my guardianship, and by my life,
> I'l use her in all kindness as my wife.
> (III.ii.351–353)

And a similar effect is achieved when Clodius with tongue in cheek protests Appius's public denunciation of him:

> My Lord, it was some soothing sicophant,
> Some base detracting Rascal that hath spread
> This falsehood in your ears.
> (III.ii.269–271)

Perhaps Webster remembered Emilia's unwitting condemnation of Iago: "The Moor's abus'd by some most villainous knave, / Some base notorious knave, some scurvy fellow" (Othello, IV.ii.141–142). A more complex mingling of truth and falsehood occurs when Appius confesses his sexual obsession only to be surprised and annoyed by the laughter of his subordinate:

> *Appius.*   Can this my ponderous secresie
> Be in thine ear so light? seemes my disturbance
> Worthy such scorne that thou deridest my griefs?
> Beleeve me, *Clodius*, I am not a twig
> That every gust can shake, but 'tis a tempest

> That must be able to use violence
> On my grown branches. Wherefore laugh'st thou then?
> *Marcus Clodius.* Not that y'are mov'd—it makes me smile in scorne
> That wise men cannot understand themselves,
> Nor know their own prov'd greatnesse. *Clodius* laughes not
> To think you love, but that you are so hopelesse
> Not to presume to injoy whom you affect.
> . . . .
> Can you command Rome, and not countermand
> A womans weaknesse? Let your Grace bestow
> Your purse and power on me. I'le prostrate you.
>
> (I.iii.22–41)

The flattery is interesting here not only for the portents that it unconsciously contains but also for its hint of contempt imperfectly concealed.

Appius and Virginia reworks yet again the theme of love and death ironically conjoined. As will now be apparent, this is a persistent strain throughout Webster's art, and its centrality to the story of the Roman girl threatened by rape and killed for love must have had much to do with the playwright's choice of subject. It is scarcely too much to say that Virginia's sole function in the play is to serve as the magnetic point of three different attractions—physical lust, marital romance, and fatherly devotion. Such mythic power as the unadorned tale possesses springs from the tragic collision of all three forces. The paradox at the core of the fable is of course that Virginia's death results from the union of diametric opposites—of tyrannical aggression with loving protection—and that the second of these must express itself with a violence proper only to the first. The plunging of the knife into Virginia's body becomes ironically a symbolic usurpation of the ravisher's assault. Preservation and destruction thus coincide. In the ethical terms that the drama sets up, Appius's intended rape is equivalent to murder, and the violator's own death follows logically as a consequence. But the death of Virginia not only frustrates Appius and grieves her father to the point of distraction but also comes between Icilius and his bridal hopes. Without overstressing the point in a play much given to restraint, Webster touches once more on the idea of sudden death intruding upon human sexuality in both its legitimate and illegitimate forms. As the three "loves" all center upon the girl who must die, so the three "lovers" die or come near death. And all three too are seen at some point as dramatically opposed to each other. At first both the father and the fiancé are ranged together against the evil judge, but the sacrificial murder sets up a temporary opposition between the former allies. What Clifford Leech has called "a mere distraction"[84] is in fact part of the play's symbolic consistency.

As usual, Webster reinforces this pattern verbally at appropriate points of the action. Not for nothing does he place the most tenderly affecting speech of the tragedy—the father's reminiscence of his daughter's childhood—immediately before the stabbing:

> Farewel my sweet *Virginia*, never, never
> Shall I taste fruit of the most blessed hope
> I had in thee. Let me forget the thought
> Of thy most pretty infancy, when first
> Returning from the Wars, I took delight
> To rock thee in my Target; when my Girl
> Would kiss her father in his burganet
> Of glittering steel hung 'bout his armed neck;
> And viewing the bright mettal, smile to see
> Another fair *Virginia* smile on thee:
> When I first taught thee how to go, to speak:
> And when my wounds have smarted, I have sung
> With an unskilful, yet a willing voice,
> To bring my Girl asleep. O my *Virginia*,
> When we begun to be, begun our woes,
> Increasing still, as dying life still growes.
>
> . . . .
>   *Kills her.*
>
> Thus I surrender her into the Court
> Of all the Gods. And see proud *Appius* see,
> Although not justly, I have made her free.
> And if thy Lust with this Act be not fed,
> Bury her in thy bowels, now shee's dead.
>   (IV.i.321–347)

But not only at the moment of greatest intensity does Webster identify Virginius's affection and Appius's desire with death. He also repeats these linkages separately at later points in the play:

> *Virginius.*   and see still I wear
>   Her crimson colours, and these withered armes
>   Are dy'd in her heart-blood.
>
>   . . . .
>   But how? I lov'd her life. Lend me amongst you
>   One speaking Organ to discourse her death. . . .
> *Minutius.* How agrees this? love her, and murder her?
>   (IV.ii.130–138)

> *Icilius.* Speak damned Judg, how canst thou purge thy self
>   From Lust and blood?
>   (V.ii.51–52)

> *Minutius.*   we'l be just
>   To punish murdrous Acts, and censure Lust.
>   (V.ii.90–91)

    The motif appears elsewhere as well. As Icilius is courting his bride, Virginia and her uncle banter about the durability of amorous praise in terms of "wedding garments" soon outworn and "the funerall" of husbandly "kindnesse" (I.ii.22–24); the exchange presages the young man's charge to Virginius after the killing that he has "turned / [His] Bridal to a Funeral" (V.i.111–112). Finally, when Appius protests that he loves the girl's father, the old soldier equates the decemvir's hypocrisy with extinction:

> Love me?
> Thou lov'st me (*Appius*) as the earth loves rain,
> Thou fain wouldst swallow me.
>
> (IV.i.305–307)

Webster's treatment of the love-death theme is far shallower in *Appius and Virginia* than it had been in the Italian tragedies because the author rests content with using his polarities chiefly as moral signposts and stops short of plumbing the psychological contradictions inherent in their juxtaposition. But to have gone very far in this direction would, of course, have muddied the clarity and unbalanced the contrastive symmetry at which he was aiming in the Roman play.

The principle of symmetry extends beyond the obvious dichotomies of love and death, city and camp, lecher and virgin, liberty and tyranny, to small details of the dramaturgy and indeed to the rhetoric and imagery of the play. Webster's procedure announces itself in the first few minutes of the tragedy when Oppius presents Appius with a highly artificial and, by naturalistic standards, absurd choice between "two proffers"—"either to accept" absolute power on the spot "or be banished Rome / Immediately" (I.i.27–29). Bits of stage business also create the effect of balance:

> *Appius.*   Some pursue the villain,
>   Others take up the body.
>
> (IV.i.354–355)

> *1 Soldier.* Is our Hut swept clean?
> *2 Soldier.* As I can make it.
> *1 Soldier.* 'Tis betwixt us two. . . .
>
> (IV.ii.1–3)

> *Enter Icilius, Horatio, Valerius, Numitorius (at one door) with Souldiers; Virginius, Minutius, and others at the other doore.*
>
> (V.i.61)

> *Virginius.* Give me two swords. *Appius* grasp this,
>   You *Clodius* that.
>
> (V.ii.115–116)

Short speeches are juxtaposed with the stylization of opera or liturgy:

> *1 Soldier.* 'Tis false.
> *Omnes.* I, 'Tis false.
>
> (II.ii.58–59)

Appius. Mine, boy!
Icilius. Thine, Judg.

(II.iii.96–97)

Appius. Thou shalt not.
Icilius. Nay, I will not.

· · · · · · · · · · · · · · · · ·

Appius. Thou shouldst not.
Icilius. Nay, I would not.

· · · · · · · · · · · · · · · · ·

Appius. I will not.
Icilius. Nay, thou shalt not.

(II.iii.118–131)

Numitorius. How now, faire cozen?
Icilius. How now, Gentlemen?

(III.ii.136–137)

Clodius. A thousand Drachmas.
Orator. Good, a thousand Drachmas.

(IV.i.126–127)

1 Soldier. O villain *Appius.*
2 Soldier. O noble *Virginius.*

(IV.ii.157–158)

Syntactical and imagistic balance is a regular feature of the style. The following examples compose only a random sample:

partly with joy to see him,
Partly with fear for what his hast portends. . . .

(I.ii.30–31)

To give that man a Palace, whom you late
Deny'd a cottage?

(II.iii.215)

And she become your Strumpet not your Bride.

(II.iii.215)

If we fall
She cannot stand. . . .

(III.i.124–125)

In life they'l seem good Angels, in death divels.
(IV.i.260)

Did *Appius* right, or poor *Virginia* wrong?
(IV.ii.160)

Rather to die with honour, then to live
In servitude.
(V.i.129–130)

Better had *Appius* been an upright Judg,
And yet an evil man, then honest man,
And yet a dissolute Judg. . . .
(V.i.157–159)

They say there is *Elizium* and Hel,
The first I have forfeited, the latter fear.
(V.ii.154–155)

The language of *Appius and Virginia* contains an unusually large number of doublets, the second element of which often adds little to the sense but increases the feeling of weight and equipoise: "paine and industry" (I.i.109), "prescrib'd and taught" (I.iv.37), "Princely grace and clemency" (I.iv.43), "laziness and resty ease" (I.iv.115), "riot and incontinence" (II.ii.94), "Slaves and cowards" (II.ii.127), "Tokens and Presents" (II.iii.147), "eminence and state" (III.i.39), "place and sway" (III.i.44), "Daily and hourely" (III.i.63), "counsell and advice" (III.i.114), "penalty and danger" (III.ii.207), "form and shew" (IV.i.17), "bold and confident" (IV.i.20), "Madness and rage" (IV.i.355), "Prostitute and Paramour" (IV.ii.150), "Just and noble" (V.i.121), "unnatural and damnable" (V.i.124), "Law and Justice" (V.ii.85), "loud uproar, and confused noise" (V.ii.88), "place and Office" (V.ii.90). All such devices, coupled with the abnormally high incidence of rhyme and Webster's fondness for sententious repetition ("For they dy blest that dy in good report" [IV.i.83]; "*Appius* that sin'd, by *Appius*' hand shall fall" [V.ii.144]) contribute to the effect of stiffness, distance, and equilateral formality. It cannot be wholly fortuitous that the text contains at least four instances of the weighing metaphor. Virginius, for instance, protests at having the soldiers' "worths and merits ballanc'd in the scale / Of base moth-eaten peace" (I.iv.110–111), and Appius at his fall asks that his present be weighed against his past:

> With indifference
> Survey me, and compare my yesterday
> With this sad hour, my heighth with my decline,
> And give them equal ballance.
> (V.ii.62–65)[85]

The conscious striving for rhetorical symmetry accords well with a play whose atmosphere tends to be forensic—a play so deliberately conceived in the spirit of public utterance and, in its moral and aesthetic posture, so respectful of the Forum and the military base. Even scenes of private conversation—Icilius's interview with Appius or the recriminations of the two malefactors in prison, for example—contain speeches rather more impersonal and declamatory than the situations would seem to require.

As befits a tragedy that seeks to convey the impression of classicism, *Appius and Virginia* is relatively bare of arresting or highly colored imagery. Not that the play is without figurative language; but we search almost in vain for those startling flashes of illumination that concentrate emotion in the great Websterian manner. We find nothing comparable to speeches such as "Mark her I prithee,— she simpers like the suds / A collier hath been wash'd in" (*The White Devil*, V.iii.240–241), or "Fate's a spaniel, / We cannot beat it from us" (*The White Devil*, V.vi.177–178), or "thou hast ta'en that massy sheet of lead / That hid thy husband's bones, and folded it / About my heart" (*The Duchess of Malfi*, III.ii.112–114). The style of the Roman play is never so highly charged as this, and there is even a surprising paucity of classical allusions—less than a dozen examples in all. Inga-Stina Ekeblad has shown how effectively Webster reinforces the plot structure in a way that recalls his practice in the greater plays by the recurrent use of storm imagery.[86] Metaphors of rotten or falling trees tend to be associated with the tempest pattern and to be applied chiefly to Appius. The bird imagery also recalls Webster's former habits—swallows flying south invoked to suggest inconstancy (I.i.48–50), the lapwing to symbolize deviousness (I.i.127–129), quails and cocks to represent the bloodiness of combat (I.ii.39–41), the woodcock to embody insignificance and victimization (III.iv.29), the sparrow hatching the cuckoo to analogize monstrosity (IV.i.198–202), ravens and crows to stand for death (II.ii.81–87), and so on. And in like fashion, a number of references to animals dot the text—dogs, crocodiles, tigers, wolves, bloodhounds, monkeys, sharks, lions, bulls, bear-whelps, etc. Despite these, however, the language projects less sense of a vital or teeming world than might be predicted. Images of battle help to link the assailing of the heroine's "Virgin Tower" (I.iii.59) with the military and political conflicts of the play. The familiar image of mist to suggest uncertainty reappears twice in *Appius and Virginia* (III.ii.399; IV.i.88) but without the disturbing and metaphysical suggestiveness that it had carried in the earlier tragedies.

A few other characteristic signs of the more familiar Webster survive in the new context. We meet the idea of banishment again in *Appius and Virginia* (I.i.86–92) not only as enforced separation from society but also as self-alienation; Webster seems to be echoing a motif here that he had used with greater concentration and relevance in both *The White Devil* (I.i.1) and *The Duchess of Malfi* (III.v.1). He also repeats a sentence on mingled fear and desire, probably originally suggested to him by Sidney:

I have seen children oft eat sweet-meats thus,
As fearfull to devoure them. . . .

(I.i.20–21)[87]

To some extent the dramatist continued to use his old copybook method of composition. Also he was still capable of treating ugliness or horror with imagination and beauty:

> Come you birds of death,
> And fill your greedy croppes with humane flesh;
> Then to the City flie, disgorge it there
> Before the Senate, and from thence arise
> A plague to choake all Rome!

(II.ii.83–87)

And very justly Lucas admires the concluding lines of one of Webster's incorporated "characters" in which the playwright "recaptures his earlier, greater style":[88]

> The plague that in some foulded cloud remaines,
> The bright Sun soone disperseth; but observe,
> When black infection in some dunghill lies,
> There's worke for bells and graves, if it doe rise.

(III.ii.259–262)

We know nothing of the circumstances under which *Appius and Virginia* was written or produced. On 10 August 1639 the Lord Chamberlain issued an official document prohibiting any group but the King and Queen's Young Company at the Cockpit from acting this and other plays. The edict, which appears to list the entire repertory of the company, tells us merely that a manuscript of Webster's tragedy was then in the possession of William Beeston's troupe ("Beeston's boys" as they were popularly called) and that the manager was concerned to maintain exclusive right to it. If *Appius and Virginia* is too old-fashioned a play to have been written at the end of Webster's career (as some have argued), at least it was not so out of date as to be unplayable in 1639. How Beeston's boys came by the play we can only guess. William Beeston's father, Christopher, had organized the company for performances at court during the plague epidemic of 1636–1637 that forced the government to shut the London theatres temporarily. He appears to have recruited a miscellaneous group of actors, both boys and men, the core of whom had belonged to his old company, Queen Henrietta's Men, who had also played at the Cockpit. The Beestons were able to retain much of the repertory from the Queen's Company, but, since they also possessed plays that had previously belonged to other troupes, there is no way of telling where or by whom *Appius and Virginia* was originally acted.

That the play continued to be read in the seventeenth century is patent. The first edition of 1654 was reissued no less than four times (1654, 1655, 1659, 1679), in each case with a fresh title page. The final issue refers to a production at the Duke's Theatre under the name of *The Roman Virgin or Unjust Judge*. This was a version altered for Restoration audiences by Thomas Betterton, who himself played Virginius to his wife's Virginia. Betterton's adaptation, first played in the spring of 1669, was "very frequently *Acted* afterwards," according to John Downes.[89] Pepys attended the opening performance on 12 May and dismissed the revival as "an old play, and but ordinary," although he admits that he was sitting "in the side balcone over against the music" and so "did hear, but not see" what was happening onstage.[90]

PART III
THE MAJOR WORKS

De morte, & amore: Iocosum.

TO EDWARD DYER *Esquier.*

toachim. Belleius.
..*Mutarunt arma inter*
se Mors atque Cupido
Hic falcem gestat,
gestat at illa facem.
Afficit hæc animum,
corpus sed conficit illa:
Sic moritur nauius,
& moribundus amat.

WHILE furious Mors, from place, to place did flie,
And here, and there, her fatall dartes did throwe :
At lengthe shee mette, with Cupid passing by,
Who likewise had, bene busie with his bowe:
Within one Inne, they bothe togeather stay'd,
And for one nighte, awaie theire shooting lay'd.
The morrowe next, they bothe awaie doe haste,
And eache by chaunce, the others quiuer takes :
The frozen dartes, on Cupiddes backe weare plac'd,
The fierie dartes, the leane virago shakes :
Whereby ensued, suche alteration straunge,
As all the worlde, did wonder at the chaunge.
For gallant youthes, whome Cupid thoughte to wounde,
Of loue, and life, did make an ende at once.
And aged men, whome deathe woulde bringe to grounde :
Beganne againe to loue, with sighes, and grones;
Thus natures lawes, this chaunce infringed soe :
That age did loue, and youthe to graue did goe.
Till at the laste, as Cupid drewe his bowe,
Before he shotte : a younglinge thus did crye,
Oh Venus sonne, thy dartes thou doste not knowe,
They pierce too deepe : for all thou hittes, doe die :
Oh spare our age, who honored thee of oulde,
Theise dartes are bone, take thou the dartes of goulde.

Which

2. Geoffrey Whitney, *De Morte et Amore: Iocusum; To Edward Dyer Esquier,*
from *A Choice of Emblemes* (1586), p. 132.

DEATH meeting once, with *CVPID* in an Inne,
  Where roome was ſcant, togeither both they lay.
Both wearie, (for they roving both had beene,)
Now on the morrow when they ſhould away,
  CVPID Death's quiver at his back had throwne,
  And *DEATH* tooke *CVPIDS*, thinking it his owne.

By this o're-ſight, it ſhortly came to paſſe,
That young men died, who readie were to wed:
And age did revell with his bonny-laſſe,
Compoſing girlonds for his hoarie head:
  Invert not Nature, oh ye Powers twaine,
  Giue *CVPID'S* dartes, and *DEATH* take thine againe.

Hoc idem habet
Whitnæus in
Embl: quod bona
cum illius venia
ab Authore etiam
mutuatus ſum.

Latet

3. Henry Peacham, *De Morte et Cupidine*,
from *Minerva Britanna* (1612), p. 172.

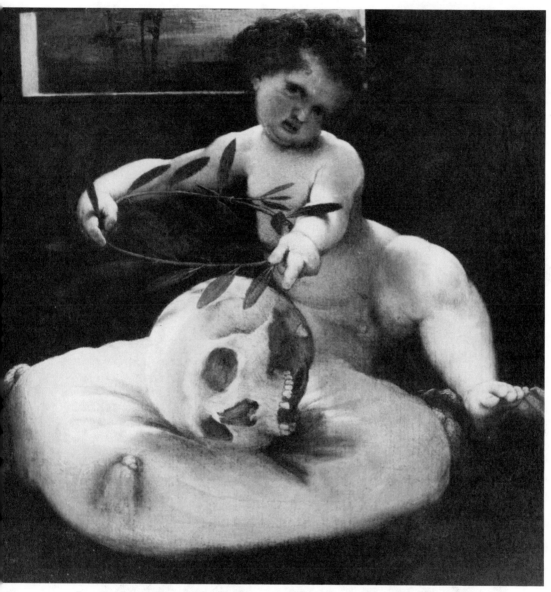

4. Lorenzo Lotto, *Putto with a Skull* (1520–25), from the private collection of the Duke of Northumberland. Reproduced by permission of the Duke of Northumberland.

5. Albrecht Dürer, *The Promenade, or Lovers Threatened by Death* (c. 1497). Reproduced by permission of the Art Institute of Chicago.

6. Master of Ulm, *A Bridal Pair* (c. 1470).
Reproduced by permission of the Cleveland Museum of Art.

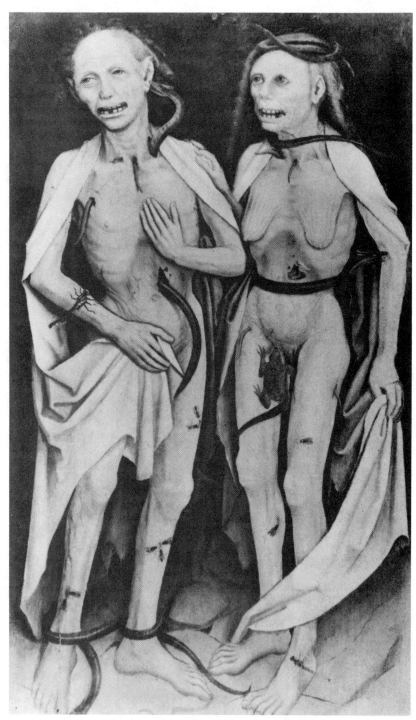

7. Master of Ulm, *Les Amants Tréspassés* (c. 1470). Reproduced by permission of the Musée de l'Oeuvre Notre-Dame, Strasbourg.

8. Abraham Bloemart, *Death and the Lovers* (c. 1620).
Reproduced by permission of the Courtauld Institute of Art, London.

THE LOVE-DEATH NEXUS
IN ENGLISH RENAISSANCE TRAGEDY

Death, death, O amiable, lovely death,
Thou odoriferous stench! Sound rottenness,
Arise forth from the couch of lasting night,
Thou hate and terror to prosperity,
And I will kiss thy detestable bones,
And put my eyeballs in thy vaulty brows,
And ring these fingers with thy household worms,
And stop this gap of breath with fulsome dust,
And be a carrion monster like thyself.
Come, grin on me, and I will think thou smil'st,
And buss thee as thy wife, Misery's love,
O, come to me!
                              (*King John*, III.iv.25–36)

Do I delight to die, or life desire?
    But now I liv'd, and life was death's annoy;
    But now I died, and death was lively joy.
"O, thou didst kill me; kill me once again!"
                              (*Venus and Adonis*, ll. 496–499)

                                        If I must die,
I will encounter darkness as a bride,
And hug it in mine arms.
                              (*Measure for Measure*, III.i.82–84)

                                        What will it be,
When that the wat'ry palates taste indeed
Love's thrice-repured nectar? Death, I fear me,
Swooning destruction, or some joy too fine,
Too subtle, potent, tun'd too sharp in sweetness
For the capacity of my ruder powers.
                              (*Troilus and Cressida*, III.ii.19–24)

"Love is as strong as death," wrote the poet of the Song of Songs, and the paradox that identifies the vital with the lethal, Eros with Thanatos, *l'amour* with *la mort* (as the punsters of medieval Provence might have it),[1] continues now, as then, to work its baffling fascinations, both mystical and horrific, upon our psyches. A novella in Marguerite of Navarre's *Heptameron* (first published in 1558) might serve for Renaissance readers as an emblem of this collocation. A young man of Cremona, frustrated by unrequited desire for a coy mistress, falls dangerously ill and is ordered by his doctors to be bled. Belatedly, the lady decides to relieve his sufferings by reciprocating his love. Then, during the consummation, the boy's sexual passion rises to such heights that the bandage on his arm loosens, the wound gushes forth, and he dies from loss of blood, whereupon his beloved commits suicide. The erotic fulfillment of the lovers not only implies their death but, in the case of the male participant, actually coincides with it. As the narrator puts it, "so great was his joy that not being able to grow more, it needs must grow less and come to an end."[2] The theme seems to have had a special force for Shakespeare and his fellow dramatists. Indeed, it became the basis for that entire genre that we call love tragedy, experimental and ill defined though this was even in Elizabethan times.

In Kyd's *Soliman and Perseda* allegorical personifications of Love and Death preside with Fortune over the tragic action of the play, inviting the theatre audience to judge for itself which of the three forces shall ultimately prove "greatest" (I.vi.38),[3] but the debate remains mysteriously unsettled. After a double climax in which Soliman, the rival lover, separates Perseda from her beloved Erastus and has him executed, only to become unwittingly both the agent of the lady's suicide and the victim of her revenge through a poisoned kiss, Love exits from the stage asserting defiantly that he "shall neuer yeeld to *Death*" (V.v.30). As is proper to tragedy, Kyd assigns the final speech to the gloomiest member of his choric trinity, but he does not permit Death to contradict the doctrine, at least twice reiterated, that "*Loues* workes are more then of a mortall temper . . ." (I.vi.11). Similarly, Marlowe in *Dido, Queen of Carthage*, a play that ends with three romantically induced suicides, allows his heroine, in words that anticipate Cleopatra's, to exclaim to Aeneas, "I never die, / For in his looks I see eternity . . ." (IV.iv.121–122).[4] As Kyd and Marlowe, among others, suggest, Love and Death are not only the cruelest of antagonists; they are also in some sense allies. The Duchess in Middleton's *More Dissemblers Besides Women* cries out in a moment of desire that "love and death / Are brothers" (I.iii.111–112).[5] Shirley allegorizes the ironic reciprocity of ostensibly opposite but "immortal" forces by making the title figures in his masque *Cupid and Death* unwittingly exchange their arrows on a hunting party. This familiar myth had already made its way into the iconography of popular emblem books (see figs. 2 and 3) such as Geoffrey Whitney's *A Choice of Emblemes* (1586) and Henry Peacham's *Minerva Britanna* (1612). Romances like those of Pyramus and Romeo and Guilford Dudley[6] are "death-marked" from their inception. Juliet half perceives this truth when she predicts after first meeting Romeo that "My grave is like to be my wedding bed" (I.v.136), and her lover confirms it by his allusion to "love-devouring death" (II.vi.7) and later to "the lean abhorred monster" of the tomb who is finally as "amorous" of his wife as he himself (V.iii.103–104). One of Ben Jonson's shepherds sums up the mysterious conjunction with lyric elegance:

> Though I am young, and cannot tell,
>   Either what Death, or Love is well,
> Yet I have heard, they both beare darts,
>   And both doe ayme at humane hearts:
> And then againe, I have been told
>   Love wounds with heat, as Death with cold;
> So that I feare, they doe but bring
> Extreames to touch, and meane one thing.
>   (*The Sad Shepherd*, I.vi.65–72)[7]

Although the love-death nexus amounted to something of a cultural obsession in the early seventeenth century and was variously employed by many Renaissance dramatists, Webster seems to have been especially drawn to the motif, touching upon it both early and late and exploring its potentialities most profoundly in the three unaided plays that constitute his finest and most distinctive achievement. Of course, it would be reductive to suggest that such complex dramas as *The White Devil*, *The Duchess of Malfi*, and *The Devil's Law-Case* can be adequately studied in relation to a single theme. Nevertheless, a concentration on this aspect of his work has broad implications and illuminates significances of form and content that other scholars have either neglected or approached differently. But we shall be in a better position to understand Webster's unique dramatization of the ironic interplay between love and death if we first survey what his contemporaries and successors did with similar material—that is, if we acknowledge the variety of activities and values of which the love-death conjunction could be made the dramatic vehicle. We may conveniently begin with Shakespeare and, after some associative excursions into the works of lesser playwrights, return to him at the end of this chapter, hoping (with Polonius) by indirection to find directions out.

* * *

The religious idealism of courtly love, embodied archetypically (as de Rougemont has pointed out) in the myth of Tristan and Iseult,[8] endowed erotic love with mystical transcendence. Death became the ultimate test of love's purity and intensity, for trammeled by earthly imperfections and hostilities, it could only free itself from anticlimax and fulfill its yearning for perfection through union with the absolute. Such is the love that is not Time's fool, though rosy lips and cheeks within his bending sickle's compass come—the love that Shakespeare inherited from Neoplatonism and the conventions of Petrarchan rhetoric. The Venetian painter Lorenzo Lotto (c. 1480–1556) endowed the idea with visual form in an allegorical picture that shows Love as a *putto* or Cupid crowning Death depicted as a skull (see fig. 4). *Romeo and Juliet* is, of course, the classic expression of this pattern in Elizabethan drama, and it stands as perhaps the most powerful refutation we could summon to the comic astringency of Rosalind's lesson that men have died from time to time, and worms have eaten them, but not for love. In debased, almost parodic, form, the pattern persists even into such domestic tragedies as *Arden of Faversham*, where Arden's servant Michael, by assisting his master's assassins, risks everything for his beloved's sake and exclaims in the final scene when both he and she are condemned, "Faith, I care not, seeing I die with Susan" (xviii.37).[9]

Yet to consider the erotic components of Renaissance tragedy in anything like their full range is instantly to overflow the confining singleness of the *Liebestod*, however richly Shakespeare orchestrated it in his play of star-crossed love. The involvement of eros with violence, terror, and revenge in the great majority of plays, its corrupting entanglements with realpolitik, ambition, lust, and murder, remind us that the self-destructive and tyrannical power of love was more variously usable by most tragedians, including Shakespeare, than its more idealized counterpart. When Burton speaks of erotic passion as a "*rabies insana*," a raging madness that "subverts kingdoms, overthrows cities, towns, families, mars, corrupts, and makes a massacre of men,"[10] we have no difficulty supplying illustrative titles from the repertory of the Globe and its rivals. John Ford, in fact, seems to echo Burton's view when he makes a court physician in one of his plays aver that

> Love is the tyrant of the heart; it darkens
> Reason, confounds discretion; deaf to counsel,
> It runs a headlong course to desperate madness.
> (*The Lover's Melancholy*, III.iii)[11]

No doubt one could argue—on the authority of Burton as well as of Freud—that nearly all tragic subjects are erotic *in posse* if not *in esse*, that most actions and emotions, pushed to their limit, imply an increment of passion. Yet it is difficult to regard the persistent association of the erotic with the violent in Shakespeare and his successors as unconscious. Richard III takes the Lady Anne into a marriage bed that becomes successively both rack and bier by trapping her in the cul-de-sac of her own hyperbole and thus converting her hatred into a kind of lust. Hamlet, joking bitterly about the fearful economy of a Denmark where death nourishes sensuality, where funeral-baked meats coldly furnish forth marriage tables, reduces innocent and incestuous lovers alike to the moral democracy of the grave. Lady Macbeth tries by diabolic prayer to unsex herself even as she enjoins her husband to "screw [his] courage to the sticking place" (I.vii.61)[12]—in fact to prove his manhood by sexualizing murder—and, as he moves toward Duncan's chamber, he goes "with Tarquin's ravishing strides" (II.i.56). Rape and regicide become metaphorically one. The ingratitude of unnatural daughters maddens Lear to confront the paradox of his having engendered monsters, and the Machiavel for whom both monsters lustfully compete pronounces their common epitaph: "All three / Now marry in an instant" (V.iii.232–233). Such unions are part of an ironic pattern in the tragedies: Othello sacrificing his wife in her wedding sheets only to join her minutes later in "the tragic loading of [their] bed" (V.ii.372); Antony and Cleopatra made one through a sword that he rushes upon "As to a lover's bed" (IV.xiv.101) and a "pretty worm of Nilus" (V.ii.243) that sucks its nurse asleep; Bianca and the Duke of *Women Beware Women* celebrating their nuptials by "Tasting the same death in a cup of love" (V.ii.221);[13] Giovanni in *'Tis Pity She's a Whore* grotesquely literalizing a Petrarchan metaphor by possessing Annabella's heart upon his dagger before himself "embracing" the death that he calls "a guest long looked-for" (V.vi.104).[14] One could multiply instances.

For the tragic dramatist, then, the subject of love or infatuation shadowed by death had its obvious utility. It could be the means of showing the isolation or vulnerability of happiness, "brief as the lightning in the collied sky," an idea to which Albrecht Dürer gave visual expression in his famous engraving of two lovers threatened by Death (see fig. 5). It could function to bring incompatible systems of value into poignant or devastating collision, at the same time embodying interior, psychic conflicts of almost every stripe. In homiletic tragedies such as *A Woman Killed with Kindness* it could be the occasion for dramatizing a pattern of sin, self-sacrificial suffering, and atonement, a way of reaffirming the supremacy of Christian *agape*. Contrastingly, in a chronicle play such as *Edward II*, Marlowe could make the king's homosexual love for Gaveston (a form of attraction that Burton calls "an inordinate passion even to death")[15] the focus of an almost nihilistic tussle between private desire and public power as well as a way of rendering intelligible the pathetic psychology of a royal figure in whom tenacity of will and emotional dependence were complementary elements. The climactic scene of Edward's degradation and murder recapitulates with uncompromising irony the contrarieties of politics and personality shown earlier, for the obscene manner of the monarch's death—pressing under the weight of a table and rectal penetration with a fiery spit (the "braver way" [V.iv.37][16] that must have suggested Lightborn's ironic name to the author)—unites the antitheses of cruelty and sexual passiveness, of retributive force and the need for love, that define both the central character and the action of which he is the cause and victim. Here is a love-death physically and psychologically horrible enough to call in question our traditional definitions of natural order. The weakling hero, unnatural both as king and as man, becomes in death a pitiable symbol of royalty desecrated and humanity violated, of helplessness savaged by the machinelike force of a nearly incomprehensible brutality.

Stories of disastrous love could explore the ambivalent relations between attraction and repulsion, commitment and doubt, freedom and bondage, elation and despair; they could address the contradictory needs for intimacy and separateness, for self-discovery and self-annihilation. No motive is so universal in Elizabethan tragedy as love or its frustration. Perceiving that romantic passion radically alters those whom it invades, playwrights could naturally locate the source of a character's energy at the place where joy and misery converge. They saw that love creates its own structures of order than which nothing is more frail or illusory, that where everything is invested everything may be lost. We think of Troilus and, more terribly, Othello:

> Excellent wretch! Perdition catch my soul
> But I do love thee! And when I love thee not,
> Chaos is come again.
> (*Othello*, III.iii.92–94)

* * *

In a large group of plays, especially the tragedies of revenge, love is either ranged against violence and death or else perverted into becoming their instrument. The prevalence of this pattern and the grotesque ironies that it is so often made to enforce suggest a more than casual interest in what a modern clinician might term psychosexual fear. We need look for no Freudian perversity in the threat of death that tears Romeo from his nuptial bed at dawn or the street brawls that twice shatter Othello's nocturnal privacy with Desdemona. Apart from special cases such as *Hamlet*, Shakespeare's treatment of sexuality is refreshingly wholesome. But violent intrusions upon the pleasures of romance recur in Renaissance tragedy—with increasing frequency and prurience in the Jacobean period—and it is worth noticing that the two dramas that frame the historical limits of the revenge play both make sensational use of it. In Kyd's *Spanish Tragedy* the arbor where Horatio and Bel-Imperia make love is converted before our eyes into a gallows; the two have been analogizing love and war in a playful duet of Petrarchan rhetoric, and the assassins enter with appropriate irony just as their victim puts the concluding flourish upon his amorous paradox:

> O stay awhile and I will die with thee,
> So shalt thou yield and yet have conquer'd me.
> (II.iv.48–49)[17]

In Shirley's *Cardinal* the rejected suitor murders his rival on his wedding night, threatening to "cut" whatever lover Rosaura should dare to take next from her "warm embrace, and throw his heart to Ravens" (IV.ii.72–73).[18]

Consummations devoutly to be wished are forever being disturbed in scenes that range from the satiric to the shocking: Guiszard of *Tancred and Gismund* discovered naked in his lady's arms by her jealous father, who then hales the young earl off to strangulation and presents the eviscerated heart to his daughter in a golden cup; Bassianus and Lavinia, the newlyweds of *Titus Andronicus*, intercepted in a forest by Aaron and Tamora, whose sons then stab the bridegroom that "his dead trunk" may serve as "pillow" for their rape of his wife (II.iii.130); Ferneze in *The Malcontent* surprised between the sheets with the duchess and impaled upon a sword as he flees in his nightshirt across the stage; Massinissa prevented from entering his own wedding bed in *Sophonisba* by the sudden entrance of a bleeding senator who summons him to battle; the defeated hero of *Caesar and Pompey* interrupted in a touching reunion with his wife Cornelia by political enemies who mercilessly cut him down with swords; Diaphanta in *The Changeling* literally fired from Alsemero's embraces and then shot. Most of these situations dramatize the deepest kind of sexual and psychological insecurity. They portray not only the sadistic forces that threaten love from without; they also hint at some dark component in sexual and romantic involvement that invites disaster. Gothic representations of human sexuality had already anticipated this idea. An anonymous German painter of the late fifteenth century depicts a pair of lovers repulsively transformed from their idyllic youth into a ravaged, emaciated couple (*Les Amants Trépassés* as a Strasbourg museum entitles the picture); shrouds hang from their shoulders, their otherwise nude bodies are covered with festering sores and insects, toads batten upon their genitals, and writhing snakes emerge from their open wounds (see figs. 6 and 7).[19] A modern biographer of Elizabeth I reminds us that the great queen herself probably suffered as a child from disturbing associations of sexuality with death. After her mother and stepmother had both been beheaded for adultery, the princess is reported to have told Leicester when she was only eight that she would "never marry"; moreover, her latent fears of eroticism must have been compounded in adolescence by the dangerous behavior of Thomas Seymour, who appears to have teased and molested her sexually, thus risking both their necks. To quote the modern account of Elizabeth's early years, "the events of her mother's death, and that of her mother's cousin, and the engaging of her own affections by Seymour's outrageous siege, seem to have done her nervous system and her sexual development an injury from which they never recovered."[20]

Even in dramas that end happily death can intrude upon or juxtapose itself with lovemaking in the most ironic and disturbing manner. Shakespeare cleverly contrives the plot of *Measure for Measure* so as to have Angelo's supposed bedding of Isabella coincide precisely with the supposed execution of Claudio for fornication. The head of the brother and the maidenhead of the sister are to fall at the same moment and to the same ravisher. Although neither of these cruelties actually occurs, their neatly paradoxical cross-positioning adds powerfully to the emotional and moral thrust of the play. Chapman builds his cynical drama, *The Widow's Tears*, on a more sustained junction of such incongruities. A husband, pretending to be dead, disguises himself as a soldier and exposes his "widow's" inconstancy by seducing her in the very tomb where she has been mourning over his ironically empty coffin. Then, while the soldier enjoys the woman sexually, a crucified body, which it was his responsibility to guard, is stolen from its cross, and, to save her new lover from death (the penalty for neglecting his watch), she urges him to open the coffin and substitute the body of her husband for that of the crucified robber. To complicate the irony still further, she presses for the substitution even after the soldier claims to be her husband's murderer. Thus does Chapman dramatize a disquieting, even shocking, idea— the overlapping of piety and lust through the circumstance of their having a common object, the same beloved. Middleton's tragicomedy *The Witch* commences with a wedding banquet at which the guests are made to pledge the bride's happiness with a cup fashioned from a human skull. This macabre and symbolic incident presages difficulties of a potentially tragic kind for two pairs of lovers, not to mention obscene trafficking with witches. In one case the horrible toast prompts a wife to undertake the murder of her husband; in the other, it foreshadows the misery that awaits newlyweds who do not know that the lady's previous fiancé is still alive and brimming with frustration. Robert Drue's extravagant melodrama *The Bloody Banquet* concludes even more gruesomely than Middleton's had begun. The tyrant of this crude play stages a Thyestean meal at which his adulterous queen is forced to eat from the dismembered body of her lover and to drink from his bloody skull.

The more sensationally morbid and grotesque ironies of the love-death nexus—what textbooks used to call the decadence of Jacobean drama—appear to be rooted, perhaps half-consciously, in the conflict of repression with desire.[21] The strong infusions of horror that subtend sexuality in the tragedies of Marston, Tourneur, Fletcher, Middleton, and Ford suggest an overwhelming burden of guilt coupled with the gloomiest of metaphysics. We can hear the Dies Irae reverberating through these plays. But the lesson that punishment is inescapable, that sin unwittingly hungers for the retribution that will devour it, takes on egotistical energy and relish. As love slides into lust, humanism gives way to satire. The deterministic theology of Marlowe's Faustus spreads and darkens like a stain to teach man that the Helen he hopes will make him immortal with a kiss is in truth a succubus who will suck forth his soul. Misogyny becomes a fashionable dogma in the visual arts as in the literary, and a painter such as Abraham Bloemaert (1564–1651) can depict woman emblematically as the gateway to death. One of his better-known pictures shows a beplumed gallant reaching under the skirts of a fashionable lady only to encounter the chill of the skeleton where he had expected voluptuous flesh (see fig. 8).[22] Sir John Suckling provides a kind of gloss on Bloemaert's drawing by perceiving the "deaths-head" beneath "that fresh upper skin" that attractive ladies show to the world:

> A quick corse me-thinks I spy
> In ev'ry woman; and mine eye,
> At passing by,

> Checks, and is troubled, just
> As if it rose from Dust.
> ("Farewell to Love," ll. 41–45)[23]

Eve's unique role in the Fall provided, of course, a theological excuse for the denigration of women. Donne invokes the typical justification:

> For that first marriage was our funerall:
> One woman at one blow, then kill'd us all,
> And singly, one by one, they kill us now.
> ("The First Anniversary," ll. 105–107)[24]

A medieval emphasis on chastity is revived so that a typical dramatic heroine of the period can describe her temptation to yield to a seducer as a desire to "run thus violently / Into the arms of death, and kiss destruction."[25] Calvinistic horror of the body unites opportunely with the vogue for antifemale satire, *contemptus mundi*, *memento mori*, and the *danse macabre*.

The symbolism of *The Revenger's Tragedy* underscores such attitudes with bizarre clarity. A lecherous duke, having murdered a virgin because of her chaste resistance to him, is himself murdered through the act of reseducing her. The poisoned lips of Gloriana's skull repay him for his sexual crimes with gruesome exactitude, thus uniting polar opposites in a ghastly embrace. Victim and criminal, chastity and lust, frustration and desire, appearance and reality, love and death fuse in a *seductio ad absurdum*, in a literal *mors osculi*. Nor should we forget that the revenger who sets up this mortal tryst is himself a thwarted lover, a monster of egocentricity whose fanatic rediversions of love into loathing recoil to ensure his own extinction.

Seventeenth-century dramatists were not slow to seize upon the titillating possibilities of necrophilia in their eagerness to equate both depraved and idealistic love with death. Nor was the taste for baroque horror limited to the drama. As early as 1598 one "L. B." published a lurid pamphlet about Henry Robson, a fisherman of Rye, who murdered his wife by introducing ground glass mixed with ratsbane "into her priuie parts" during intercourse.[26] A fictional account of the lecherous Queen Veneria, as told in an anonymous collection of related tales under the general title of *The Famous and Renowned History of Morindos* (1609), concludes with a didactic morbidity that is curiously parallel to Tourneur's celebrated *coup de théâtre*. The author of the prose tale relates how Veneria, having seduced a scullion from the palace kitchen, is taken unawares by her cuckolded husband, the King of Bohemia, as she lies asleep in the servant's arms. After sheathing "a short scimitar . . . in the breast of his wife's minion, whose blood with such fury gushed from his polluted bosom as it wakened the sin-stained queen," the enraged king

caused a large coffin to be brought, wherein he put the murdered body of the scullion; then to the same dead body, beginning now to putrefy and stink, he tied the live body of his queen, so in the coffin closed them up both together, that as she enjoyed his fellowship in life, so might she consume with him being dead, by which means the very worms that bred upon the dead carcass in a manner devoured up her live body. And thus were the sins of lust and adultery scourged with a plague but seldom heard of.[27]

The juicier forms of perversity were clearly becoming a literary fashion.

Marston in the opening lines of *Antonio's Revenge*, a play that antedates both *The Revenger's Tragedy* and *Morindos*, has his depraved duke, Piero Sforza, command an accomplice to bind Feliche's freshly stabbed body "Unto the panting side of Mellida" (I.i.2).[28] The heroine of the anonymous *Second Maiden's Tragedy* commits suicide to preserve her chastity, whereupon her lustful oppressor embalms the cadaver and dies making love to its poisoned lips; Massinger imitates this corpse-kissing scene in his *Duke of Milan* (V.ii) to similar effect, as does Shirley in *The Traitor* (V.iii). In the more Platonic and courtly vein of Ford's *Broken Heart*, Calantha weds the "lifeless trunk" (V.iii.100) of Ithocles before expiring of grief to the accompaniment of a song that she has expressly composed for the purpose:

> *Love only reigns in death; though art*
> *Can find no comfort for a broken heart.*
> (V.iii.93–94)[29]

The want of necroerotic action is sometimes supplied by imagery, and we find appropriate examples in the plays of Marston, Webster, and Jonson, among others. Marston appears to have been especially attracted to such grotesqueries and should perhaps be credited with popularizing them with his theatrical rivals and imitators. In addition to the offstage incident in *Antonio's Revenge* already mentioned, he resorts to necrophiliac ideas in two later plays: Herod Frappatore in *The Fawn* alludes to the tyranny of Mezentius, who bound "the living and the dead bodies together, and forced them so to pine and rot" (I.ii.198–199);[30] in *Sophonisba*, Syphax threatens to "use, / With highest lust" the "senseless flesh" of the heroine, should she kill herself to fend off rape, "And even then thy vexed soul shall see, / Without resistance, thy trunk prostitute / Unto our appetite" (IV.i.58–62).[31] Jonson in *Volpone* has Corvino threaten Celia in similar terms: "Death! I will buy some slave / Whom I will kill, and bind thee to him, alive" (III.vii.100–101); and he repeats the idea even more repellently in *The Sad Shepherd*, where Aeglamour imagines himself embracing the drowned body of Earine:

> I will love it still,
> For all that they can doe, and make 'hem mad,
> To see how I will hugge it in mine armes!
> And hang upon the lookes, dwell on her eyes:
> Feed round about her lips, and eate her kisses!
> Suck of her drowned flesh!
> (I.iii.67–72)[32]

Webster also employs such imagery, as for instance in *The White Devil*, where Francisco curses Vittoria and Bracciano ("Let him cleave to her and both rot together" [II.i.398]) and in *The Duchess of Malfi*, where the heroine desires that her persecutors "would bind me to that lifeless trunk [of Antonio], / And let me freeze to death" (IV.i.68–69).

The transmutation of sexual attraction into violence and death receives one of its most powerful explorations in *The Changeling*, where Middleton shows us the indissolubility of murder and lust in the fatal congress of Beatrice with De Flores. Regretting the rashness of her betrothal to one man in her infatuation with a second, Beatrice employs a third to liquidate the inconvenient fiancé only to discover that the price of her murderous naiveté is sexual union and death in the arms of the figure whom she thought she loathed the most. Middleton employs this plot to search the ironies of moral self-recognition: an overplus of disgust masks desire, repulsiveness is shown to be magnetic, and the servant becomes the master. Beauty is drawn into coalescence with the beast as a means of dramatizing to a shallow girl what beastliness she has already embraced. To be "the deed's creature" is also to be De Flores's paramour and, in fact, to have lusted for one's own death. Middleton's persistent punning on the word *blood* makes the ethical and psychological burden of the love-death pattern inescapable, as do the phallic symbolism of Piraquo's severed finger, which De Flores presents to his mistress, and the double connotation of the seducer's name.

Beaumont and Fletcher exploit such sadomasochistic ideas less intensely but not less theatrically. *The Maid's Tragedy* contains a scene in which the lustful king, awakening to find that his mistress has tied him to his bed, believes this prelude to his own assassination to be some "prettie new device" (V.i.47)[33] to enhance sexual pleasure. This pornographic murder is neatly contrasted with an almost equally sexual suicide: the chaste but rejected Aspatia fulfills her amorous desire by pretending to be her own brother and thus provoking her wished-for lover into running her through with his rapier. Lubricity and spotless frustration both invite the unsheathed blade.

Love Lies a-Bleeding, the suggestive subtitle of *Philaster*, provides still another example of the masochistic principle in operation. Fletcher and his collaborator so pattern the amorous relationships of this play as to contrast two feminine idealizations of virtuous love—one overt and passionate (the much calumniated Arethusa) and the other covert and Platonic (the selfless Euphrasia, disguised until her final speeches as the page Bellario). Both ladies are loyally devoted to the play's hero Philaster, and both, as an additional intricacy, are believed at the crisis to be libidinously involved with each other. The tragicomic mode of the drama offers us merely dangers, not deaths; but, significantly, all three principals of the romantic triangle sustain physical wounds, a fact that is symptomatic of a sophisticated taste for artful pathos and what might almost be called the luxury of suffering. When Philaster first threatens Bellario with his sword, the page offers to "love those pieces you have cut away, / Better then those that grow: and kisse those limbes, / Because you made um so"; and she can describe the death for which she begs as "A thing we all persue," the "giving over of a game, / That must be lost" (III.i.246–258).[34] The succeeding act reverses this situation with balletic symmetry to present Philaster offering the same sword to both ladies whom he now invites jointly to kill him. Of course they refuse, just as he had earlier refused to kill Bellario. Then, after the page has been dismissed, Arethusa reverses matters once more and persuades her aggrieved lover to give her "peace in death" (IV.v.65). He now stabs her only to be interrupted by a rustic who is horrified to see a man strike a woman, but this invasion of intimacy by a bumpkin so unschooled in emotional subtlety only elicits Arethusa's cry, "What ill-bred man art thou, to intrude thy selfe / Upon our private sports, our recreations?" (IV.v.89–90). Philaster himself is hurt in the ensuing struggle, and, in an effort to throw off his pursuers, he in turn wounds the sleeping Bellario whom he hopes they will take for Arethusa's assailant.

In this highly contrived and experimental play, the less-than-fatal stab wound becomes almost a metaphor for unrequited or unrecognized affection, a physical conceit for the displacement of psychic pain. As such, its recurrence serves as a kind of leitmotiv to exploit the ambivalences of creative and destructive love and to arouse complicated questions about the nature of selfhood. Nor is it accidental that Beaumont and Fletcher gain their elaborate and glossy effect in part by drawing upon the pastoral traditions of Sidney, Tasso, Montemayor, and others who had already treated romantic love in such a way as to suggest the interdependence of suffering and fulfillment.

*　　*　　*

As a form, romantic tragedy seems to have offered unique opportunities for probing the very paradoxes of identity that plays such as *Philaster* touch upon so tantalizingly. Questions of identity, of course, are central to a great variety of Renaissance tragedies as Shakespeare's Northumberland reminds us when he observes of Richard II that "The King is not himself" (II.i.241), or Webster's Ferdinand when he remarks to Bosola that the latter's "pity is nothing of kin" (IV.i.138) to the henchman he thought he knew. Yet romantic involvements under conditions of extreme pressure seem peculiarly apt to tease us out of thought. Do lovers win their precarious individualities *through* a great passion or merge into some higher synthesis? Do assertiveness or abnegation, aggression or surrender, selfishness or altruism lie at the roots of ardor? Donne, perennially fascinated by the mystical mathematics of love, could repeatedly argue that one plus one equals one, that two souls "endure not yet / A breach but an expansion," and that, like the Phoenix, they "die and rise the same, and prove / Mysterious"[35] by love. But Marvell could write with equal force of a love "begotten by Despair / Upon Impossibility," a love whose limits were defined by the grave—"a fine and private place," no doubt, "But none, I think, do there embrace."[36] Dramatists who sought to portray tragic love inevitably involved themselves in this dualism, and the greatest plays explore the unremitting ten-

246

sions between oneness and otherness, transcendence and finitude, sacrifice and defiance, hope and nihilism. By way of example, let me now suggest briefly two extreme cases—one from Shakespeare and one from Middleton—and then conclude with two tragedies, both Shakespearean, that in their different ways might be seen as intermediate.

Romeo and Juliet with its breathless idealization of romance seems to lie near the conservative, more medieval end of a historic spectrum. Although much is made of hostile destiny and feuding families, the love itself is free of all interior obstacles. The principals never quarrel or doubt each other, their union is sacramentally ratified, and they define their existences totally in relation to each other. In such circumstances a mutual suicide that tenderly, if ironically, re-enacts their sexual consummation, a "dateless bargain to engrossing death" (V.iii.115), is the ineluctable climax of the play's ecstatic teleology.[37] Juliet repeatedly refers to her lover's death at earlier points: in the orchard as Romeo descends from her window she observes, "Methinks I see thee, now thou art so low, / As one dead in the bottom of a tomb" (III.v.55–56), and then to her mother (with a double-entendre), "Indeed, I never shall be satisfied / With Romeo till I behold him—dead" (III.v.93–94). Only in Capulet's vault, where Tybalt lies in his bloody sheet and where Paris now keeps him company, can this couple fully satisfy the intensity of their need to be one, and Romeo unconsciously betrays his conception of death as at once end and beginning by referring to the charnel house in a single line as "detestable maw" and "womb" (V.iii.45). Even Friar Laurence, though characteristically he moralizes it, underlines the same paradox:

> These violent delights have violent ends
> And in their triumph die, like fire and powder,
> Which as they kiss consume.
>
> (II.vi.9–11)

But, as one critic has said, "Death is robbed of the greater glory; the ending is triumph, a transcending the limits of mortality by holding fast, in a union of suffering, to what is best in the mortal condition."[38]

At the other more modern and "realistic" extreme from *Romeo and Juliet* we might adduce Middleton's *Women Beware Women*. Leantio and Bianca commence the action of this play by eloping in a way that suggests at first that their desire for emotional fulfillment has overridden all considerations of safety, economic prudence, and family opinion. Leantio glories in the "noble" action of having won a lady of means who can "rejoice" in forsaking "friends, fortunes, and . . . country" for "a quiet peace" with a man of humbler station (I.i.37, 127–132). But it quickly becomes apparent that the romance is shallowly rooted and will be vulnerable not only to external pressure but also to internal weakness. Bianca has run off with a materialistic prig dangerously unaware of his own motives, a complacent *petit bourgeois* who might step with only minor alteration into one of Middleton's city comedies. While he congratulates himself on being free of desire for "this man's sister, or . . . that man's wife" (I.i.29), on "our quite innocent loves" that are "sealed from heaven" (I.i.45–52), he regards his wife jealously as a piece of property, referring to her in crassly mercenary terms as "the most unvalued'st purchase" (I.i.12), "my masterpiece" (I.i.41), "the best piece of theft / That ever was committed" (I.i.43–44), "a most matchless jewel" (I.i.162), and "a gem" to be "cased up from all men's eyes" (I.i.170–171). When business affairs force him to leave her for a few days, he tears himself away in a burgher's version of Romeo parting from Juliet, but with a disquieting and vulgar emphasis on the sexual deprivation that his absence will enforce: "'Tis e'en a second hell to part from pleasure / When man has got a smack on' t" (I.iii.5–6). By the end of the first act we recognize that this is a hasty union in which physical attraction and the illusion of romantic idealism provide the thinnest of veils for egotism, immaturity, and limited perception.

It comes, then, as no great shock that such a relationship should be easy prey to the cynical and sophisticated stratagems of an aristocrat like the Duke and a plausible hypocrite like Livia, characters who occupy the center of fashion and power and who are richer, more intelligent, and more corrupt than their younger and socially inexperienced victims. Leantio accommodates himself less gracefully to the Duke's seduction of his wife than the lady herself, but as both adjust to the affluence that their adulterous new roles as mistress and kept man have purchased them, they become increasingly impudent, coarse, bitter, and self-assertive. What had earlier seemed like "a happiness / That earth exceeds not" (III.ii.1–2) degenerates into an ugly antagonism in which injured pride, guilt, recrimination, spite, and obscene sarcasm are the dominant ingredients:

> *Leantio.* Y' are very stately here.
> *Bianca.*   Faith something proud, sir.
> *Leantio.* Stay, stay, let's see your cloth-of-silver slippers.
> *Bianca.* Who's your shoemaker? 'Has made you a neat boot.
> *Leantio.* Will you have a pair? The Duke will lend you spurs.
> *Bianca.* Yes, when I ride.
> *Leantio.*   'Tis a brave life you lead.
> *Bianca.* I could ne'er see you in such good clothes
>   In my time.
> *Leantio.*   In your time?
> *Bianca.*   Sure I think, sir,
>   We both thrive best asunder.
> *Leantio.*   Y' are a whore.
>   (IV.i.54–61)

Although Leantio vaguely threatens his wife, the Duke has him slain for indiscreetly boasting of his affair with Livia before he can take any action against her. Bianca hardens into a murderess, blindly trying to poison the Cardinal because he opposes her liaison with the Duke and killing her lover by mistake. Middleton pitilessly exposes the baleful effects of money upon love and shows the rapid slide of a flimsy romanticism, unsupported by integrity, self-knowledge, or spiritual depth, into selfishness, lust, and criminality.

Women Beware Women takes us a long way from the Petrarchan transcendence of Shakespeare's early success. Moral disintegration and squalor have replaced idealism. Rhetoric has been stripped of its aureate and inspirational fervor, and the interplay between darkness and light has been focused into a hard glare. The cosmic imagery of stars has given place to a mundane vocabulary of food and wealth, the emblems of sex and status. Middleton's play ends in a holocaust of death and alienation, gloomy with the despair that lies in store for those who live only for self-gratification:

> Lust and forgetfulness has been among us,
> And we are brought to nothing.
>
> (V.ii.146–147)

False commitments and temperamental differences between lovers are pessimistically stressed rather than the self-surrender and psychic oneness that unite Romeo and Juliet. And the plight of Isabella in the subplot symbolically replicates the frustrations to which romance is liable from both exterior and interior causes. Forced by her materialistic father into a degrading marriage with a mental defective, she is drawn for wholly emotional reasons into incest. Like Bianca and Leantio, Isabella and her seducer die apart, falling (like Guardiano upon his caltrop) into abysses of their own making. Death is the price of love in both *Romeo and Juliet* and *Women Beware Women*, but, if Shakespeare's lovers may be said in some sense to die into life, Middleton's only die out of it. Even when Bianca consummates her lustful union with the Duke, "wrap[ping] two spirits in one poisoned vapour" and "turn[ing] death / Into a parting kiss" (V.ii.194–196), she senses that ruin is the sole ultimate:

> Pride, greatness, honours, beauty, youth, ambition,
> You must all down together, there's no help for 't.
>
> (V.ii.218–219)

Othello and *Antony and Cleopatra*, Shakespeare's mature tragedies of love, fall somewhere between these two extremes. The noble Moor and his chaste bride take each other in what they conceive to be a marriage of true minds, a high and somewhat cloudy romance in which the sensual element is to be minimized. But, since Othello confuses his wife, a girl of some obvious independence, with the projection of his own ideal, he is more susceptible than a less inexperienced man would be to Iago's masterful infusions of distrust. Othello's idea of marriage is a romantic union with perfection, an alliance with a "young and rose-lipp'd cherubin" (IV.ii.63),[39] and, if a lower reality supervenes, his relief must be to loathe it. His image of the place where he has garnered up his heart, "Where either I must live or bear no life, / The fountain from the which my current runs / Or else dries up," changes with terrible completeness into "a cistern for foul toads / To knot and gender in" (IV.ii.58–62). Consequently, he sets about his appalling ritual of justice in a demented attempt to change the "cunning'st pattern of excelling nature" into the "monumental alabaster" (V.ii.5–11) of his own visionary rhetoric. We recall his premonition upon rejoining Desdemona at Cyprus:

> O my soul's joy!
> If after every tempest come such calms
> May the winds blow till they have waken'd death!
> And let the laboring bark climb hills of seas
> Olympus-high, and duck again as low
> As hell's from heaven! If it were now to die,
> 'Twere now to be most happy; for, I fear,
> My soul hath her content so absolute
> That not another comfort like to this
> Succeeds in unknown fate.
>
> (II.i.182–191)

When Desdemona tries to pacify rages in her jealous husband that she cannot comprehend, she tragically invites the death that is the psychological corollary of her husband's absolutism. She grants human imperfection in her spouse ("Nay, we must think men are not gods" [III.iv.149]), and her ill-timed intercessions on behalf of a man whose failure of duty she is eager to excuse only feed the rage of her husband's resentment for sublimity disfigured. *Othello* is the tragedy of an idealistic, potentially transcendental love in which the lovers fatally misconceive each other. Ultimately, each comes to a higher truth, a deeper self-realization through involvement with the other—she through self-sacrifice and he through the recognition of his terrible error—but, though their bodies are united upon the same bed of death, their souls transpire, Shakespeare suggests, to separate eternities.

Antony and Cleopatra, as everyone knows, is the most complex and profound portrayal of tragic love in English, for, in the developing relationship between its hero and heroine and through the incandescence of his poetry, Shakespeare somehow fused the comic with the heroic, the mundane with the exalted, the dung with the fire and air, in an amalgam so rich and various as to elude analysis. As many readers have been constrained to grant, the tone of the play, particularly in its final act, flies in the face of conventional expectations and will admit of no narrow moralism. One is led to speculate that Shakespeare may even have consciously chosen—though in a fully qualified and deliberately paradoxical way—to invert the orthodox hegemony of reason over passion and to explore the possibilities of a new kind of triumph. The triple pillar of the world and his Egyptian queen throw away greater earthly power than Bianca and the Duke of Florence ever possess, but the world that they purchase in exchange participates in none of Middleton's Medician bitterness and depravity.

Its richness redeems its corruption; its decay ministers to its ripeness and fertility; creativity springs from its disgrace. The affair between Antony and his regal courtesan involves mutual distrust and betrayal, and their crossings of each other—his Roman marriage, her flight at Actium, for instance—only serve to illustrate the principle that opposites attract. Selfishness mingles with generosity, the pettiest of weaknesses with the spirit of Renaissance magnanimity. Pride of self is the rock from which the oceans of emotional spending flow, and the lovers might finally say to each other as Juliet says to Romeo, "My bounty is as boundless as the sea, / My love as deep; the more I give to thee, / The more I have, for both are infinite" (II.ii.133–135).

Rushing to self-annihilation, Antony falls upon his sword as though he were about to consummate his passion for Cleopatra: "I will be / A bridegroom in my death, and run into 't / As to a lover's bed" (IV.xiv.99–101).[40] The sexual imagery that suffuses the play suggests a union that is at once fatally weakening and spiritually fortifying, a relationship that subsists upon a struggle of wills but in which resistance is the source that keeps appetite perpetually uncloyed, an interpenetration of personalities that, like the act of love that is its regnant metaphor, exhausts itself in the very process of creation. The truth of Madame de Staël's definition of love as "égoisme à deux" applies here, as perhaps also does Havelock Ellis's more clinical formula that love is "lust plus friendship."[41] Shakespeare patterns the physical separations so as to express the drama's psychic polarity more grandly—in order to endow the dynamics of the romance, its inherent conflict between dominance and submission, independence and union, with geographical extension. Yet, as physical as the attachment clearly is, it triumphs over distance, and the Herculean hero can reply to Cleopatra's protest, "O, my oblivion is a very Antony, / And I am all forgotten," with the paradoxical comfort that

> Our separation so abides and flies
> That thou, residing here, goes yet with me,
> And I, hence fleeting, here remain with thee.
> (I.iii.90–104)

The insights into each other that the lovers progressively acquire, and acquire fully only through death, reinforce their own solipsism; yet they continually become more like each other. Their growth toward a third identity is comically implied in the delightful symbolism of their exchanging clothes in a moment of alcoholic abandon:

> That time—O times!—
> I laugh'd him out of patience; and that night
> I laugh'd him into patience. And next morn,
> Ere the ninth hour, I drunk him to his bed,
> Then put my tires and mantles on him, whilst
> I wore his sword Philippan.
> (II.v.18–23)

Antony and Cleopatra sets out to define the limits of hedonism only to transcend these limits, to rise to a mystical love-death that "shackles accidents and bolts up change" (V.ii.6). Traditional discriminations between love and lust, subject and object, union and duality dissolve in the great climax of Cleopatra's luxurious suicide—a death as fully dignified and numinous as it is sexual and hedonistic. The gorgeous ritualism of "Give me my robe, put on my crown; I have / Immortal longings in me" melts into the sensual ecstasy of "Husband, I come! . . . I am fire and air . . . As sweet as balm, as soft as air, as gentle— / O Antony!" (V.ii.280–312).

Shakespeare's most ardent love tragedy, the tragedy whose hero Agrippa calls "thou Arabian bird" (III.ii.12), returns then to the paradox of self-annihilation and self-fulfillment that the dramatist had so cryptically and abstractly addressed in *The Phoenix and the Turtle*:

> So they loved, as love in twain
> Had the essence but in one,
> Two distincts, division none;
> Number there in love was slain.
> . . . .
> Property was thus appalled,
> That the self was not the same;
> Single nature's double name
> Neither two nor one was called.
>
> (ll. 25–40)

Antony and Cleopatra synthesizes the very principles of individuation and totality in an emotional fusion beyond the reach of reason, a fusion in which loss and gain are felt to be but aspects of the same truth. Iras expresses the heavy side of this insight when she laments that "the bright day in done, / And we are for the dark" (V.ii.193–194), but the lover's pinch that hurts and is desired annuls our rational categories. Distinctions between mirth in funeral and dirge in marriage, between immortal longings and oblivion, are assimilated into the mystery of art.

＊　＊　＊

The conjunction of love and death has always been a powerfully charged idea in Western civilization, but its force has lain essentially (as Shakespeare profoundly knew) in the kinetic ambiguities that radiate from its core. For to raise the topic at all is instantly to be concerned with fundamental questions about the nature and limits of human kind and hence to approach that murky territory where psychology, ethics, metaphysics, and religion shade imperceptibly into each other. It is therefore not surprising that tragic dramatists of the sixteenth and seventeenth centuries should have been attracted to such a subject and have tried to exploit its rich possibilities in language, character, and action. How better to evoke pity and terror for that continuing struggle between order and chaos that is one definition of the human lot? It is love as much as fear that makes Desdemona struggle so fiercely for life:

> *Othello.* Think on thy sins.
> *Desdemona.* They are loves I bear to you.
> *Othello.* Ay, and for that thou diest.
> *Desdemona.* That death's unnatural that kills for loving.
> . . . .
> *Desdemona.* O, banish me, my lord, but kill me not!
> *Othello.* Down, strumpet!
> *Desdemona.* Kill me tomorrow, let me live tonight!
> *Othello.* Nay, if you strive—
> *Desdemona.* But half an hour!
>
> (V.ii.42–85)

But love is also the power that drives the dagger so eagerly into Juliet's breast and applies the asp so luxuriously to Cleopatra's. Such mysteries were not lost upon Shakespeare or even the lesser dramatists of his age. How, indeed, could they be missed by playwrights who remembered Anne Boleyn or Catherine Howard or Mary of Scotland or Lady Arabella Stuart or the murderous Countess of Somerset? Clearly, these poets sensed that to bring love into meaningful contact with death was an effective way of rendering on the stage that "fierce dispute," as Keats was to call it, "Betwixt damnation and impassioned clay."

Webster's three most famous plays also probe the mysterious interconnections between love and death in ways that are intellectually and emotionally challenging. It will be the business of the following three chapters to examine these dramas in detail and to suggest, among other things, that the shifts of form and content that they disclose trace a progression in Webster's art. The theme is, of course, fundamentally tragic, but in choosing three different actions in which it is central Webster seems to have moved from a very dark and even nihilistic conception of human experience toward a somewhat more hopeful view of it.

THE WHITE DEVIL AND
THE AESTHETICS OF CHAOS

It has been customary to classify Webster's two Italian tragedies as revenge plays. Certainly they possess many of the expected features—smouldering hatreds, intricate stratagems that recoil upon their inventors, sensational cruelty, courtly depravity, madness (real, feigned, or both), a tone of cynical bitterness and gloom, and, perhaps most importantly, an obsession with mortality. T. S. Eliot evokes our popular image of Webster as a dramatist who "was much possessed by death / And saw the skull beneath the skin."[1] But both plays are equally tragedies of love, plays about romantic passion struggling to create and maintain its world of emotional intensity and sexual fulfillment in the face of hypocrisy, malice, brutality, and Machiavellian power. Webster's special contribution to the development of tragic form was a unique intermingling of conventions from tragedies such as Marlowe's *Dido* and Shakespeare's *Antony and Cleopatra* with those from the school of Kyd, plays such as *The Spanish Tragedy*, *Hamlet*, and *The Revenger's Tragedy*. The amalgam produced a hybrid genre that not only allowed love to be pitted against death in the most violent and terrifying fashion but could be made to promote unsettling doubts about the validity and safety of romantic emotion itself. Among the multiplying horrors of *The White Devil* one incident summarizes with cauterizing irony Webster's yoking of the two traditions: Lodovico and his fellow assassins strangle the most egregious romantic of the drama on his wedding day with "a true-love knot / Sent from the Duke of Florence" (V.iii.174–175). Such grotesque juxtaposition together with the suffering it implies is the very stuff of which Webster's first great tragedy is made.

* * *

The deliberate mixing of forms imparts to *The White Devil* a disorienting sense of fragmentation and uncertainty, a feeling that experience is puzzlingly discontinuous, its perspectives wrenched and shifting, its values unstable and self-canceling. Webster can therefore present the love between Bracciano and Vittoria as both a heroic passion and a sordid coupling of an ambitious "strumpet" with her lustful victim. One of the many patterns in the play allows us to regard the lovers as criminal descendants of Antony and Cleopatra—he a glamorous prince (unlike his gross original in history), a man of "able hand," "High gifts," and "prime age" who "Neglect[s]" his "awful throne" for "the soft down / Of an insatiate bed" (II.i.28–32); she a "famous Venetian Curtizan,"[2] outbraving "the stars with several kind of lights, / When she did counterfeit a prince's court" (III.ii.74–75), and seasoning her "beauty," "merry heart," and "good stomach to a feast" (III.ii.208–209) with "a most prodigious spirit" (III.ii.58). Like Cleopatra, Vittoria is the fatal siren for whom her renowned lover is content to sacrifice his honor and risk his life. As Cyrus Hoy has pointed out, both dramas present the death of the male lover first, reserving the heroine's tragedy for an even greater climax later.[3] It is even possible to see a rough analogy to Shakespeare's play in the treatment of supporting characters: Isabella, the insipid, "phlegmatic" wife, recalls Antony's "dull Octavia"; Flamineo, the self-appointed satirist, functions in some respects like Enobarbus, resolved upon detachment but drawn progressively into the tragic world upon which he comments; and the glacial Francisco, supreme master of power politics, has obvious affinities with Octavius Caesar. For instance, Webster's Medici duke, like Shakespeare's Roman emperor, would subject his defeated enemy to ceremonial mockery if he could.[4] Even Flamineo's pretended death, the seriocomic trick by which the brother tries to gain the upper hand over his sister, may owe something to Cleopatra's similar means of attempting to dominate Antony. In both plays the feigned deaths lead directly to the actual deaths of both deceived and deceivers.

But to mention *Antony and Cleopatra* and *The White Devil* in the same paragraph is instantly to call attention to differences more profound than any of the superficial resemblances. Webster not only shows passion ranged against politics, he shows it imbedded in a world of violent crime, terror, and madness. By invoking the Machiavellian deceptions, intrigues, and terrors of the revenge play, Webster darkens his effect more nihilistically than even the most skeptical of Shakespeare's dramas, let alone the Roman tragedy from which terror is virtually absent. A glance at the final scene of each play makes the point unmistakable. Whereas Cleopatra rises to a *Liebestod* of luxurious and transcendental serenity in a scene that converts suicide into art and creates its own supreme sense of wholeness, harmony, and radiance, Webster's corresponding scene almost disintegrates in a clutter of frenzied maneuverings and posturings, of shocking reversals, *coups de theatre*, and violent intrusions on a stage red with carnage and black with existential *angst*. If Shakespeare's characteristic image of love transmuted into death is the asp cuddled like a baby at Cleopatra's breast, Webster's is a "matachin" of thugs in monkish garb who trap and butcher the defenseless as they might "some sucking infant" (V.vi.233).

By building their relationship upon open defiance of the savage world that closes upon them, by tearing their pleasures with rough strife from the very jaws of death, Vittoria and Bracciano acquire a certain stature denied their persecutors. His amorous rhetoric is desperate, permeated with the imagery of doom, and it bespeaks a completeness of involvement that all but isolates him emotionally from everyone but Vittoria. When we first meet the duke, he is "Quite lost" (I.ii.3) in his infatuation, and Webster echoes this portentous quibble at three moments of high intensity. Approaching Vittoria a little later Bracciano begs,

> Let me into your bosom happy lady,
> Pour out instead of eloquence my vows,—
> Loose me not madam, for if you forego me
> I am lost eternally.
>
> (I.ii.205–208)

And when his love affair has brought him at last to a lingering death and the contemplation of what "horror waits on princes," his condition provokes Vittoria's desolate cry, "I am lost for ever" (V.iii.34–35). Finally, as she faces her own death at the hands of Lodovico, she exclaims once more, "O we are lost" (V.vi.174).

A residue of courtly love is perceptible in this corrupt relationship. She "is wondrous proud / To be the agent for so high a spirit," and he is "happy above thought" in being happy "'bove merit" of such a lady (I.ii.14–16). Bracciano is transfixed, consumed by his passion in the manner of a Petrarchan lover or of Othello greeting Desdemona on Cyprus:

> I could wish time would stand still
> And never end this interview, this hour,
> But all delight doth itself soon'st devour.
>
> (I.ii.202–204)

And, when Vittoria yields to him, he responds in the vocabulary of the sonneteer:

> Excellent creature.
> We call the cruel fair, what name for you
> That are so merciful?
>
> (I.ii.212–214)

Quickly she becomes the *summum bonum* of his existence, a source of joy who makes reputation, family, affairs of state, and morality itself inconsiderable:

> I'll seat you above law and above scandal,
> Give to your thoughts the invention of delight
> And the fruition,—nor shall government
> Divide me from you longer than a care
> To keep you great: you shall to me at once
> Be dukedom, health, wife, children, friends and all.
>
> (I.ii.263–268)

Bracciano's commitment is obviously blind, rash, and self-destructive; when Francisco and Monticelso urge him to abandon his "lascivious" attachment, he braves the man who will destroy him like a "lion" (II.i.83) roaring at a fox and heedless of the peril he is courting. His words are full of unconscious irony:

> were she a whore of mine
> All thy loud cannons, and thy borrowed Switzers,
> Thy galleys, nor thy sworn confederates,
> Durst not supplant her.
> . . . .
> 'Twere good you'd show your slaves or men condemn'd
> Your new-plough'd forehead—Defiance!—and I'll meet thee,
> Even in a thicket of thy ablest men.
>
> (II.i.60–79)

A violent quarrel with Vittoria, like a similar quarrel between Antony and Cleopatra in Shakespeare's play,[5] only strengthens her magnetic power over him: "Once to be jealous of thee is t'express / That I will love thee everlastingly . . ." (IV.ii.140–141). He can still call her his "dearest happiness" (IV.ii.130), speak of her "matchless eyes" (IV.ii.133) as having the brightness to "put out" his (IV.ii.164), and then crown the reconciliation by offering her "a duchess' title" (IV.ii.221). Even the hostile cardinal acknowledges the posture of chivalric romance by referring to Bracciano as Vittoria's "champion" (III.ii.180).

Participating fully in the treachery and evil of a world in which assassination is an art, Webster's lovers seem to fuel their passion for each other through acts of physical and verbal aggression. In her first close interview with Bracciano, Vittoria teaches him "in a dream / To make away his duchess and her husband" (I.ii.257–258). Then we do not see the couple in conversation again until their individual qualities of assertiveness and egoism have been separately revealed. Not content merely with having Isabella killed, Bracciano must villify his spouse, reject her from his bed, and curse both their offspring and "the priest / That sang the wedding mass" (II.i.190–191). As for Vittoria, she displays her fiery and "brave spirit" in the celebrated scene of her arraignment, overriding the question of guilt by sheer force of personality, by turning a diamond hardness to the "glassen hammers" (III.ii.140–145) of her accusers. Not once does Webster allow the lovers to be completely private onstage, and even in the relatively more intimate scenes he stresses the courageous inviolability of their separate identities. Their quarrel dramatizes a complex relationship of oneness and otherness. Bracciano may attack his lady for apparent disloyalty:

> Away.
> We'll be as differing as two adamants;
> The one shall shun the other. What? dost weep?
> Procure but ten of thy dissembling trade,
> Ye'd furnish all the Irish funerals
> With howling, past wild Irish.
>
> (IV.ii.92–97)

But she can respond with a grotesque metaphor that shows how much he has already become a part of her even as she asserts her willingness to be rid of him:

> Go, go brag
> How many ladies you have undone, like me.
> Fare you well sir; let me hear no more of you.
> I had a limb corrupted to an ulcer,
> But I have cut it off: and now I'll go
> Weeping to heaven on crutches.
>
> (IV.ii.118–123)[6]

A moment later he has "drunk Lethe" while she "weep[s] poniards" (IV.ii.129–132); as he tries to kiss her (at this point she *throws herself upon a bed*"), she speaks of biting off her lip rather than give it to him. The scene is meant to show internal stress, to illustrate a volatile romance in which repulsion and attraction are the two faces of a single coin. Bracciano's first greeting, "Your best of rest," together with her response, "The best of welcome" (I.ii.1–2), could scarcely begin matters more ironically.

Vittoria is both the cause of Bracciano's destruction and his only reason for survival. Jealousy makes him recriminate:

> Your beauty! O, ten thousand curses on't.
> How long have I beheld the devil in crystal?
> Thou hast led me, like an heathen sacrifice,
> With music, and with fatal yokes of flowers
> To my eternal ruin. Woman to man
> Is either a god or a wolf.
>
> (IV.ii.87–92)

But, when death by poison threatens a more permanent separation, he banishes his son from his side and wants only her:

> *Bracciano.* O I am gone already: the infection
>   Flies to the brain and heart. O thou strong heart!
>   There's such a covenant 'tween the world and it,
>   They're loth to break.
> *Giovanni.*   O my most loved father!
> *Bracciano.* Remove the boy away,—
>   Where's this good woman? had I infinite worlds
>   They were too little for thee. Must I leave thee?
>   What say yon screech-owls, is the venom mortal?
>
>   (V.iii.12–19)

Then in his final suffering he vacillates between guilty alienation from Vittoria and terrified need of her. In his feverish distraction he even fails to recognize her: "what's she? . . . Ha, ha, ha. Her hair is sprinkled with arras powder, that makes her look as if she had sinn'd in the pastry" (V.iii.116–118). But a dreadful clarity of vision returns when his torturers remind him that he will "stink / Like a dead fly-blown dog" and "be forgotten / Before [his] funeral sermon"; his final cry of desperation is directed not to God but to his fatal partner: "Vittoria? Vittoria!" (V.iii.165–168).

Clearly in *The White Devil* Webster draws upon the traditions of fatal eroticism that had informed the romantic tragedies of Shakespeare and others, but he uses them in such a way as to invoke the terrors of annihilation and despair, not transcendent reunion. Shakespeare's tragic lovers usually reach a point of wishing to sacrifice themselves for each other. Bracciano and Vittoria may be said in some subliminal way to race headlong toward the grave, but, consciously, they resist its encroachments and struggle valiantly for life. Extreme unction can offer Bracciano no solace: "On pain of death, let no man name death to me, / It is a word infinitely terrible,—" (V.iii.39–40). Vittoria can make a show of willingness to embrace suicide:

> I am now resolv'd,—farewell affliction;
> Behold Bracciano, I that while you liv'd
> Did make a flaming altar of my heart
> To sacrifice unto you; now am ready
> To sacrifice heart and all. Farewell Zanche.
> (V.vi.82–86)

But this is only a trick to prevent her brother from murdering her. Vittoria uses every wile, every resource of her explosive energy to evade death, and, when doom is not to be cheated, magnificent courage is her only mainstay. She has something of Cleopatra's regal composure, but, unlike Cleopatra, she has no thought of joining her lover. She fails even to mention him.

> *Vittoria.*   Yes I shall welcome death
>   As princes do some great ambassadors;
>   I'll meet thy weapon half way.
> *Lodovico.*   Thou dost tremble,—
>   Methinks fear should dissolve thee into air.
> *Vittoria.* O thou art deceiv'd, I am too true a woman:
>   Conceit can never kill me: I'll tell thee what,—
>   I will not in my death shed one base tear,
>   Or if look pale, for want of blood, not fear.
>   . . . .
> *Lodovico.*   Strike, strike,
>   With a joint motion.   [*They strike.*]
> *Vittoria.*   'Twas a manly blow—
>   The next thou giv'st, murder some sucking infant,
>   And then thou wilt be famous.
>   . . . .
>   My soul, like to a ship in a black storm,
>   Is driven I know not whither.
>   (V.vi.219–249)

The famous concluding lines of this passage play a dark and laconic variation on the familiar Petrarchan ship conceit in which the frustrated lover, after a storm-tossed interval, arrives ultimately at his haven. Perhaps Webster remembered Bel-Imperia's conventionally extended lines to Horatio in *The Spanish Tragedy*:

> My heart, sweet friend, is like a ship at sea:
> She wisheth port, where riding all at ease,
> She may repair what stormy times have worn,
> And leaving on the shore, may sing with joy
> That pleasure follows pain, and bliss annoy.
> Possession of thy love is th' only port
> Wherein my heart, with fears and hopes long toss'd,
> Each hour doth wish and long to make resort,
> There to repair the joys that it hath lost,
> And sitting safe, to sing in Cupid's quire
> That sweetest bliss is crown of love's desire.
>
> (II.ii.7–17)[7]

As presented by Webster the psychological relationship of the lovers is rooted in contradiction. If their attraction to each other spells death for themselves and others, it also affirms their vitality, their quest for self-realization in a world dominated—indeed defined—by hypocrisy, cynicism, loveless marriage, sadism, self-hatred, and casual promiscuity. Both have a flair for theatrical bravado. Bracciano intrudes unbidden upon Vittoria's trial, spreading "*a rich gown*" (III.ii.3), since no chair has been provided, and then, as he sweeps out of the room, leaves it behind in a gesture of princely contempt for Monticelso. Meanwhile, Vittoria grandly despises the cardinal, publicly daring him to condemn her:

> Find me but guilty, sever head from body:
> We'll part good friends: I scorn to hold my life
> At yours or any man's entreaty, sir.
>
> (III.ii.137–139)

Bracciano and his lady play not only to their enemies but to themselves in this scene, and each presumably glories in the other's virtuosity. But each also is self-centered, perhaps even warily concerned to protect himself first and the beloved second. Remaining silent throughout most of the hearing, the duke speaks up only once in Vittoria's behalf and then stalks out on a point of injured pride without waiting to learn her fate. Since we know him to be at least as guilty as she, this behavior can only trigger mixed reactions at best. As for the accused, she defends herself not only by displaying her "masculine virtue" (III.ii.136) but by disparaging Bracciano after he has left the court. Her simile implies that she has been no more than the passive and innocent occasion of *his* madness:

> Condemn you me for that the duke did love me?
> So may you blame some fair and crystal river

For that some melancholic distracted man
Hath drown'd himself in't.
(III.ii.203–206)

Vittoria waits until her lover is dying before she echoes his totality of commitment: "O my loved lord,—poisoned? . . . I am lost for ever" (V.iii.7–35). And the context is such that we cannot be entirely certain whether her cries convey desolation for the loss of her heart's desire or alarm for the loss of his husbandly protection and support.

Bracciano is capable of authentic concern for Vittoria: "Do not kiss me, for I shall poison thee" (V.iii.26); but a moment later her vocal grief repels and perhaps frightens him: "How miserable a thing it is to die / 'Mongst women howling!" (V.iii.36–37). While distracted he repulses her: "Away, you have abus'd me" (V.iii.82). Flamineo remarks on the "solitariness" that "is about dying princes" (V.iii.42), and, in fact, although she tries to comfort him, hoping that a crucifix "settles his wild spirits" (V.iii.133), Vittoria is not permitted to be present during her lord's final moments. The passionate relationship expires in a total breakdown of communication. A strong undertow of self-interest modifies the romanticism of both lovers, nor is it possible to exclude social ambition from Vittoria's tangle of motives, however "heavily" (V.iii.180) she may weep for Bracciano's death. After the duke's outburst of jealousy, she angrily refuses to continue as his mistress, but she leaves the way open for the status of duchess that is subsequently offered:

What dar'st thou do, that I not dare to suffer,
Excepting to be still thy whore? for that,
In the sea's bottom sooner thou shalt make
A bonfire.
(IV.ii.144–147)

The duke and his mistress risk much to live together, but they die separately, violently, *in extremis*, and the drama makes it clear that the forces of separation reside partly within. In the grotesque and terror-ridden universe the pair must inhabit (Vittoria justifiably calls it "hell" [V.iii.179]), grandeur and pettiness, devotion and selfishness, nobility and crime are somehow compatible. Darkened though their romance is by murder, lust, and arrogance, Webster nevertheless dramatizes it as the one existential experience through which two strong and lonely personalities may locate and preserve their integrities. The stoic postures and bitter denigrations of the tragedy are symptomatic of how far we have come from the Petrarchan formalism and Elizabethan exuberance of a play like *Romeo and Juliet*. Death defines the cost of love in both plays, but Shakespeare's lovers appear to transcend its boundaries spiritually, whereas Vittoria and Bracciano only expire with the courage of the trapped.

* * *

If the psychology of the lovers makes for ambivalence, the dramatic context in which their love is enmeshed complicates responses still further. In the commentary of other characters Webster gives us a persistent chorus of satirical deflation and hostile moralism. Generally speaking, this feeds our pessimism and discourages approval of the romantic values of the play, but it can also reflect negatively upon the detractors themselves, exposing their malice, their frustration, or their emotional and imaginative poverty. Flamineo arranges his sister's seduction with the voyeuristic relish of Shakespeare's Pandarus and the abrasive seaminess of Thersites. Within a minute of his first appearance Webster's go-between is busily puncturing Bracciano's "unwisely amorous" (I.ii.39) expectations. Like Iago defaming Othello, he sullies our image of Vittoria before her appearance onstage can correct the degrading cartoon: "what is't you doubt [i.e., fear]? her coyness? that's but the superficies of lust most women have; yet why should ladies blush to hear that nam'd, which they do not fear to handle? O they are politic, they know our desire is increas'd by the difficulty of enjoying; whereas satiety is a blunt, weary and drowsy passion. . ." (I.ii.17–23). When Vittoria does enter, Flamineo sneers (for the benefit of the duke as well as of Camillo) at those who take up idealizing or literary attitudes toward romance: "what an ignorant ass or flattering knave might he be counted, that should write sonnets to her eyes, or call her brow the snow of Ida, or ivory of Corinth, or compare her hair to the blackbird's bill, when 'tis liker the blackbird's feather. This is all: be wise, I will make you friends and you shall go to bed together. . ." (I.ii.115–121).

And Bracciano must prosecute his suit to Vittoria in the presence of no fewer than three disruptive commentators who distance audience reaction to the encounter and savagely undercut the exaltation that the duke feels. As the lovers exchange tokens of affection, Flamineo twists his master's earnest eroticism into the salaciousness of the brothel:

> *Bracciano.* What value is this jewel?
> *Vittoria.*   'Tis the ornament
>   Of a weak fortune.
> *Bracciano.* In sooth I'll have it; nay I will but change
>   My jewel for your jewel.
> *Flamineo.*   Excellent,
>   His jewel for her jewel,—well put in duke.
> *Bracciano.* Nay let me see you wear it.
> *Vittoria.*   Here sir.
> *Bracciano.* Nay lower, you shall wear my jewel lower.
> *Flamineo.* That's better—she must wear his jewel lower.
>   (I.ii.221–228)

The Moorish Zanche is also onstage pruriently to study the "happy union" of her mistress with a nobleman: "See now they close" (I.ii.214–215). Lastly we have the ominous Cornelia, a figure of nemesis like Shakespeare's Queen Margaret and a harsh moralist like Richard III's mother, who eavesdrops on the lovers, predicts disaster, and curses her own progeny:

> My fears are fall'n upon me, O my heart!
> My son the pandar: now I find our house
> Sinking to ruin. Earthquakes leave behind,
> Where they have tyrannized, iron, or lead, or stone,
> But—woe to ruin—violent lust leaves none.
>
> (I.ii.216–220)
>
> Woe to light hearts—they still forerun our fall.
>
> (I.ii.269)
>
> [*to Vittoria*] If thou dishonour thus thy husband's bed,
> Be thy life short as are the funeral tears
> In great men's,—
> . . . .
> Be thy act Judas-like—betray in kissing,
> May'st thou be envied during his short breath,
> And pitied like a wretch after his death.
>
> (I.ii.295–300)

Throughout the tragedy Vittoria is repeatedly referred to as a "whore" or "strumpet"—not always by those with a vested interest in her disgrace. Monticelso's "perfect character" of the courtesan (III.ii.79), his execration of "her black lust" (III.i.7), is as much a comment on the cardinal's bitterness as on his defendant's morals, but Flamineo, called "pander" even by the romantic duke (IV.ii.49, 62), does not hesitate to compare Vittoria to dogs that are tethered by day but "let loose at midnight" to "do most good or most mischief" (I.ii.199–200). When the lovers quarrel, Flamineo coarsely urges that his sister "be turn'd on her back" "as you take tortoises" (IV.ii.151–152), and even Bracciano notes that "all the world speaks ill of [her]" (IV.ii.102).

Such relentless disvaluing of the love between Orsini and Corombona creates a weary skepticism about the possibility of sexual or emotional happiness in the world of the play. The passionate love-hatred of a deeply flawed romance flames out against a background of unrelieved frustration, misery, and spiritual death in the other relationships. All of the institutions of a theoretically Christian society—family, palace, church, court of law—are seen to be in an advanced state of disintegration, honeycombed by viciousness, corruption, and hypocrisy. In this climate, those who seek to order or fulfill their lives through human bonds reap only cruelty and disaster. Symbolically, Bracciano himself invites his murderers to participate in his nuptial festivity, thus "invent[ing] his own ruin" (V.i.66). It is equally significant that, in addition to the self-destructiveness, not one but a trio of revengers range their forces against the lovers, and that all three spread their nets of death in the name of love.[8]

Francisco de Medici may feel a momentary pang for the murdered Isabella, but implacable commitment to the code of "honor" instantly replaces personal affection. He conjures up the image of his sister, not for love of a lost relative but to "fashion [his] revenge more seriously" (IV.i.98), spurred on by the visual aid. Hatred masquerades briefly as romance, and dissembled love, first for Vittoria, later for Zanche, becomes an instrument of policy and in fact the prelude to both women's destruction.[9] In one case his object is only to sow dissension, in the other to gather intelligence. The poisoning that he commissions is carried out by assassins who ironically disguise themselves as "Franciscans" (V.iii.37), who torture their victim by pretending to administer the spiritual comforts of the Commendatio Animae,[10] and then throttle him with a cord sent as by one great prince to another for a wedding present. The duke's own disguise as Mulinassar, an imposing Moorish soldier turned Christian, is emblematic of the barbarism that can present itself as "honourable service" (V.i.45) and be welcomed enthusiastically by those it has come to ruin. The lethal danger that he embodies is masked by a public bearing that matches his handsome "personage" and betokens international sophistication in "state affairs" and "rudiments of war," a presence that combines "a stern bold look" with "a lofty phrase" and advertises his reputation of having been "chief / In many a bold design" (V.i.6–35). That he shuns both flattery and self-praise, moralizing stoically on distinctions between a man's rank or appearance and his true merit, only intensifies the irony of his unique villainy.

Francisco is a kind of Vindice, cloaked for the final act as an Othello of sorts, but his most frightening attribute, lacking in both the Tourneur and Shakespeare figures, is detachment. He can relish the terror of Bracciano's "last gasp" (V.iii.213), but he is typically the looker-on, the apparently dispassionate observer of emotion. Affecting to be profoundly moved, he notes with almost scientific precision that grief has made Cornelia "a very old woman in two hours" (V.iv.54) and that Flamineo's visit to her will increase her tears. Even when physically present, he seems curiously removed from the action he initiates, and he leaves the stage entirely before the "glorious act" (V.v.9) of Vittoria's stabbing and the general slaughter that accompanies it. As Gasparo reminds Vittoria, "Princes give rewards with their own hands, / But death or punishment by the hands of others" (V.vi.188–189). Webster presents the Florentine duke as the ultimate horror—the spirit of carefully nurtured hatred, inhumanly Machiavellian and bloodlessly disengaged, a sort of death's-head who presides quietly, aloofly, efficiently, and invulnerably over the lives of virtually everyone in the play. The metaphor by which he commits himself to his sister's memory, "Believe me I am nothing but her grave" (III.ii.341), encapsulates an irony that defines the essence of Francisco.

Monticelso, the second great enemy of the lovers, makes a show of Christian virtue, officially condemning violence and pretending an inclination to "noble pity" (III.ii.259). But he reveals his true nature to Duke Francisco, whom he backs in everything until he achieves the papacy: "For my revenge I'd stake a brother's life, / That being wrong'd durst not avenge himself" (II.i.393–394). He not only urges the duke to "Bear [his] wrongs conceal'd . . . till the time be ripe / For th' bloody audit, and the fatal gripe" (IV.i.14–19), but he also lends him in aid of their common purpose his famous "black book" (IV.i.33). This antithesis to a work of devotion is "a list of murderers, / Agents for any villainy" (IV.i.89–90). The cardinal feels even less emotion for Camillo than Francisco feels for Isabella. His nephew's death is no more than an excuse for vengeance against the lovers, and he contemptuously sends his kinsman on a wild goose chase (an expedition against pirates) for the purpose of emboldening the adulterers and so creating a situation by which their reputations may be more easily poisoned. After becoming pope the churchman seems to shift course, insisting to Francisco's subordinate that revenge is "damnable" and moralizing about those who "slide on blood" (IV.iii.117–118).[11] But the new piety jars ostentatiously with the cynical portrait built up thus far, and, in any case, the pontiff does nothing to dissuade the duke from murders that he knows are in prospect. Like Francisco, to whom he allies himself, Monticelso is essentially a figure of death. He is the official face of a church that can excommunicate Vittoria and Bracciano but in which the aggrieved "ta[ke] the sacrament to prosecute" their "intended murder" (IV.iii.72–73).[12] If we could set aside the popularly antipapist response of a Jacobean audience, his ecclesiastical robes might suggest the law of love, but his actions disclose the power broker—a man absorbed by dissimulation, malice, and worldly ambition. It is hardly surprising that the penetrating Francisco refuses to trust him, and can so easily maneuver Lodovico into thinking that, privately, the new pope encourages revenge.

Count Lodovico, the henchman of Francisco and the executioner, so to say, of both Bracciano and Vittoria, also cites love as the pretext for his vengeance. In an almost parodic inversion of the rite of penance, he confesses his motive to the pope:

> Sir I did love Bracciano's duchess dearly;
> Or rather I pursued her with hot lust,
> Though she ne'er knew on't. She was poison'd;
> Upon my soul she was: for which I have sworn
> T'avenge her murder.
>
> (IV.iii.111–115)

But unrequited passion is but the peg upon which an embittered failure can hang his multiple frustrations and discontents. Lodovico's grief for the lady's death is objectively represented in dumbshow, and the conjurer tells Bracciano that the count "did most passionately dote / Upon [his] duchess" (II.ii.33–34); but everything that Lodovico says or does in the play confirms our impression of an unloving and unlovable solitary, a twisted outcast and sadist. His threat to "make Italian cut-works" in the "guts" of his enemies (I.i.52) and his scream against Vittoria, the "damnable whore" with whose blood he could "water a mandrake" (III.iii.111–115), typify his emotional imbalance. And his enraged "Banish'd?" not only opens the play on a note of personal violence and alienation; it also symbolizes a class—indeed, a whole society—that is fragmenting explosively. Deported for murder, profligacy, and debt—for having "in three years / Ruin'd the noblest earldom" (I.i.14–15), Lodovico turns pirate and ends humiliatingly as a courtly beggar and hired thug. He seems a composite of the "notorious offenders" (IV.i.31) in Monticelso's "general catalogue of knaves" (IV.i.63), for indeed most of the categories mentioned ("intelligencers," "pirates," "politic bankrupts," "murderers") apply literally to him.

Associated from the beginning with images of disruption (thunder, earthquakes, meteors, vomiting, butchery), Lodovico justifies the pope's designation of him as "a foul black cloud" threatening "A violent storm" (IV.iii.99–100). It is therefore richly ironic that this embodiment of chaos—emotional, moral, and civic—should specialize in the aesthetics of revenge. A connoisseur of the poisoner's art who especially favors prayer books, beads, saddles, looking-glasses, and tennis-rackets, he would have his plots "be ingenious" and "hereafter recorded for example" (V.i.75–76). Though he has been forced to become the duke's creature and is deceived into thinking he is also the pope's, his dying words are an assertion of psychic independence and a brag about his artistry as a revenger:

> I do glory yet,
> That I can call this act mine own:—for my part,
> The rack, the gallows, and the torturing wheel
> Shall be but sound sleeps to me,—here's my rest—
> I limb'd this night-piece and it was my best.
> (V.vi.293–297)

Lodovico is the third person of a mortal trinity that hunts the lovers to their gruesome deaths. Like Francisco and Monticelso, he may believe that he acts out of love for a deceased person, but the only face Webster shows us is the one his victims must confront—a face of pitiless hatred and death.

The revengers of *The White Devil* pretend to authorize or condone their savagery in retribution for injuries to love; but the marriages that Bracciano and Vittoria adulterously destroy are both presented as sterile relationships, emotionally arid and sexually incomplete. Webster portrays Vittoria's first husband as little better than the brainless wittol of city comedy, a deliberate caricature from whom sympathy is withheld. It is instantly clear that his wife is no more to him than a possession who might, if she were more favorably disposed, satisfy the "itch in's hams" (I.ii.138). Camillo, in truth, is a parcel of foolishness whose principal dramatic function is to serve as target for Flamineo's scarifying satire. Obsessive jealousy is the most salient trait, but he is also stupid, gullible, ugly, impotent, venereally infected, and a *parvenu*. Flamineo's characterizations of his brother-in-law are merciless, and, as they accrete, form a portrait of Over-burian grotesquerie: "The great barriers moulted not more feathers than he hath shed hairs . . . (I.ii.28–29); he is "So unable to please a woman that like a Dutch doublet all his back is shrunk into his breeches" (I.ii.32–34); "this fellow by his apparel / Some men would judge a politician, / But call his wit in question you shall find it / Merely an ass in's foot-cloth" (I.ii.48–51); he is "a lousy slave that within this twenty years rode with the black guard in the duke's carriage 'mongst spits and dripping-pans" (I.ii.130–133); he "hath a head fill'd with calves' brains without any sage in them" (I.ii.135–136); "when he wears white satin one would take him by his black muzzle to be no other creature than a maggot" (I.ii.140–142). It is hardly surprising that Camillo cannot "well remember . . . When [he] last lay with" his wife and that, when they did lie together, there always "grew a flaw between [them]" (I.ii.55–59).

It is also not surprising that a woman of beauty, passion, and intelligence such as Vittoria should find her "capon" husband (I.ii.129) so contemptible be-side the romantic duke; she readily tolerates her brother's verbal abuse of Ca-millo, and, when Flamineo is arranging the meeting with Bracciano, her only concern is how to "rid [her spouse] hence" (I.ii.161). Nor is the comic victim ca-pable even of suffering. Having accepted a military assignment that will separate him from Vittoria, he can shrug off the fear of "stag's horns" (II.i.363) with a joke about selling "all she hath" and a resolve "to be drunk this night" (II.i.370–374). Camillo is a foil to Bracciano, a parody of sexual desire, a burlesque of jealousy, and a travesty of death by violence. Flamineo pretends to work the reconcili-ation of the foolish husband with Vittoria ("I will make you friends and you shall go to bed together . . ." [I.ii.120–121]) by words and actions that actively promote the duke's cuckolding of him; then he murders him at the behest of the adulterers by pitching Camillo *upon his neck* when he leaps over *a vaulting horse* (II.ii.37)—a form of exercise often facetiously associated with sexual con-quest.[13] Camillo's love-death, a significant departure from the death by shooting that the historical Peretti suffered, is a tragicomic extension of his impotent frus-tration in life and a grim comment, made grimmer by the objective detachment of the dumbshow, on the hollowness of his relationship with Vittoria.

Bracciano's marriage is seen to be as unfulfilled and death-oriented as Vit-toria's, a point that Francisco acknowledges by implication when he reproaches his brother-in-law so bitterly for his unfaithfulness to Isabella:

> Thou hast a wife, our sister,—would I had given
> Both her white hands to death, bound and lock'd fast
> In her last winding-sheet, when I gave thee
> But one.
>
> (II.i.64–67)

The lusty Orsini is not only bored with his "phlegmatic" wife but openly and brutally hostile to her. When she arrives unexpectedly in Rome after a separation of two months, he taxes her with jealousy, refuses to kiss her on the lips, and puts the worst construction upon her movements:

> O dissemblance!
> Do you bandy factions 'gainst me? have you learnt
> The trick of impudent baseness to complain
> Unto your kindred? . . .
> Must I be haunted out, or was't your trick
> To meet some amorous gallant here in Rome
> That must supply our discontinuance?
>
> (II.i.171–177)

Riding rough shod over her protestations of affection, he rejects her in the cruelest and most absolute terms, literally unsaying his nuptial promises:

> Your hand I'll kiss,—
> This is the latest ceremony of my love,
> Henceforth I'll never lie with thee, by this,
> This wedding-ring: I'll ne'er more lie with thee.
> And this divorce shall be as truly kept,
> As if the judge had doom'd it: fare you well,
> Our sleeps are sever'd.
> . . . .
> Let not thy love
> Make thee an unbeliever,—this my vow
> Shall never, on my soul, be satisfied
> With my repentance: let thy brother rage
> Beyond a horrid tempest or sea-fight,
> My vow is fixed.
>
> (II.i.192–205)

Under this fusillade, Isabella can scarcely fail to come off as a figure of pathos, and, indeed, looked at simply, she impresses us as the martyred wife, a saintly woman who absorbs injury from her husband like a sponge, selflessly pardoning when pardon is not asked and praying for her wronger. At first appearance we see her urging Francisco to deal mildly with her husband, and almost everything she says from this point onward contributes to a general impression of purity, devotion, meekness, and Christian charity. But such unalloyed virtue in the jaundiced context of the play seems cloying and disconcertingly out of key. The posture of self-sacrifice becomes especially saccharine when Isabella goes so far as to feign a jealousy she has denied and to claim to have authored a divorce that she regards as the prelude to her death—both charades undertaken for the purpose of muting Francisco's wrath toward a man who accepts her gestures without gratitude. There is a touch of the self-deceiver as well as of the manipulator in Isabella, and she is less passive than she appears. Webster implies that she has indeed complained of Bracciano to her brother despite her disclaimer, for why else travel to the Medici palace without telling her husband? And she is determined, if she can, to control rather than be controlled by her wayward spouse:

> these arms
> Shall charm his poison, *force* it to obeying
> And keep him chaste from an infected straying.
> (II.i.16–18; italics added)

Moreover, her performance as the jealous woman, echoing, as it does, Bracciano's callous rhetoric of divorcement, is anything but halfhearted. Her words have a hyperbolical intensity about them that suggests a measure of genuine feeling. Francisco wonders indeed whether she has "turn'd Fury":

> Are all these ruins of my former beauty
> Laid out for a whore's triumph?
> . . . .
> O that I were a man, or that I had power
> To execute my apprehended wishes,
> I would whip some with scorpions.
> . . . .
> To dig the strumpet's eyes out, let her lie
> Some twenty months a-dying, to cut off
> Her nose and lips, pull out her rotten teeth,
> Preserve her flesh like mummia, for trophies
> Of my just anger: hell to my affliction
> Is mere snow-water: by your favour sir,—
> Brother draw near, and my lord cardinal,—
> Sir let me borrow of you but one kiss,
> Henceforth I'll never lie with you, by this,
> This wedding-ring.
> . . . .
> And this divorce shall be as truly kept,
> As if in thronged court, a thousand ears
> Had heard it, and a thousand lawyers' hands
> Seal'd to the separation.
> . . . .
> Let not my former dotage
> Make thee an unbeliever,—this is my vow
> Shall never, on my soul, be satisfied
> With my repentance,—*manet alta mente repostum*.
> (II.i.238–263)

Isabella's assumed role permits her, whether consciously or not, to release aggressions and compensate frustrations in a way that does violence to her self-image as the patient sufferer. It would be an overstatement to insist that she should be played as a hypocrite, but Webster (as so often) deliberately blurs the distinction between the mask and the face behind it so that a certain skepticism about her motives necessarily modifies our response. We might perhaps invoke Friar Laurence's precept, "Virtue itself turns vice, being misapplied . . ." (*Romeo and Juliet*, II.iii.21). As the pliable Camillo is foil to Bracciano, so the ostensibly supine Isabella is foil to Vittoria, but both women are actresses and both love the same man tenaciously, only to gain separation, suffering, and death as their ultimate guerdon. Isabella's love-death, in neat parallel with Camillo's, is a mute emblem of frustration and logically consistent with her wretched life. Again the irony of the dumbshow is pointed. The stifler of his wife's love "suffocate[s] her spirits" (II.ii.31) through the agency of Dr. Julio, and the lady, having tried to "charm his poison" (II.i.17) by returning love for hate, dies kissing a poisoned portrait: she "feed[s] her eyes and lips / On the dead shadow" (II.ii.27–28) of her murderer.

Apart from "romances" that on the male side are merely instruments of Machiavellian policy (Francisco's feigned attraction to both Vittoria and Zanche), the only erotic relationship of the play yet to be examined is that between Flamineo and his sister's Moorish servant. Webster makes this a scabrous, quasi-satiric illustration of the selfishness, fickleness, and cynicism that corrupt sexual mores in the tragedy as a whole. If Vittoria is conceived as the "white devil" of the title, Zanche complements her as a more obvious and less dignified figure of female depravity—the "black Fury" (V.vi.227) whose face matches "the black deed" of double murder in which—unlike her mistress—she confesses having "had a hand" (V.iii.249–250). Although the color symbolism is more ethical than racial, it has the effect (as in the case of Aaron in *Titus Andronicus*) of darkening the sexual ambience of the play almost hellishly. The language of diabolism is repeatedly invoked for Zanche: she is "that witch" (V.i.153) or "the infernal, that would make up sport" (V.iii.216), and, when Marcello tries to shame his brother into casting off the "devil" that "haunt[s]" him, Flamineo jests bawdily that the "cunning" required "To raise the devil" in female shape is less than that required "to lay him down" (V.i.86–90) in a man's codpiece.[14]

Zanche is both lecher and opportunist. She "claims marriage" (V.i.157) of Flamineo but quickly abandons him for Mulinassar, "a goodly person" (V.i.94) of her own race (as she believes) and of greater worldly importance. Her sexual gravitation from a lesser to the master villain of the tragedy is not without irony, for in this action, of course, she literally courts her own death. Again Webster underlines the concept of emotional engagement as a trap, as a dangerous exposure of what is most vulnerable in the self. Her declaration to the disguised duke, "Lovers die inward that their flames conceal" (V.i.230), brings her into direct contact with her nemesis. In furtherance of this new attachment, she is ready not merely to rob Vittoria of a large fortune but to betray both Flamineo and her by giving information about the murders. Yet she does die gamely beside her mistress with a loyalty that, in Webster, the imminence of death so often instills.

As for Flamineo, his involvement is a sour mingle of attraction and repulsion. He admits loving Zanche "very constrainedly," but he rightly fears her knowledge of his villainy: "I do love her, just as a man holds a wolf by the ears.

But for fear of turning upon me, and pulling out my throat, I would let her go to the devil." He adds that, "in seeking to fly from" his "dark promise" of matrimony, he "run[s] on, like a frighted dog with a bottle at's tail, that fain would bite it off and yet dares not look behind him." Webster shows us a "love" that "rather cools than heats" (V.i.153–162), a sexual experiment between a dyspeptic misogynist and a "gypsy" that degenerates fast into an intensity of loathing. Flamineo's irritable pride is such that it can prompt him to kill his younger brother for presuming to moralize and for daring to kick Zanche as "a strumpet" (V.i.189); yet he despises his sexual partner as much as Marcello does: "Lovers' oaths are like mariners' prayers, uttered in extremity; but when the tempest is o'er, and that the vessel leaves tumbling, they fall from protesting to drinking" (V.i.176–179). The mock-tragic episode in which the couple pretend suicide exposes the relationship in all its egotistical ugliness and defines its futility. They exchange romantic endearments to deceive each other ("my best self Flamineo"; "O most loved Moor!" [V.vi.88–89]), but their machinations are the product of mistrust, fear, and desperate self-interest. By shooting Flamineo, Zanche thinks she is saving herself and sending him "To most assured damnation" (V.vi.122); he in turn confirms his worst suspicions: "Trust a woman? —never, never; Bracciano be my precedent: we lay our souls to pawn to the devil for a little pleasure, and a woman makes the bill of sale. That ever man should marry!" (V.vi.160–163).

However limited or blinkered we may judge Flamineo to be, Webster forces us to grant a measure of assent to his pessimism, for there are no happy marriages in the play to confute him. Even such ambivalence as we are encouraged to feel about the love of Bracciano and Vittoria is negatively shaded by the antiromantic penumbra that surrounds it. *The White Devil* dramatizes a world in which sustained and peaceful mutuality seems impossible and in which attraction between the sexes is indissolubly wedded to psychic disruption and violent death. And what is true of the sexual relationships is almost equally true of the nonsexual ones as well. As in *King Lear*, which seems to have influenced *The White Devil* philosophically as well as stylistically,[15] love cools, brothers divide, and the bond is cracked betwixt parent and child.

*　　*　　*

Blood ties in Webster's tragic universe guarantee emotional *Sturm und Drang* as consistently as romantic or connubial attachments. All three of Cornelia's children give their mother extreme pain, and the dramatist makes of her pathetic collapse at their hands a domestic analogue to the social, moral, and political breakdown of the tragedy at large:

> see the curse of children!
> In life they keep us frequently in tears,
> And in the cold grave leave us in pale fears.
> (I.ii.280–282)

271

Flamineo and Vittoria reject Cornelia's traditional values in the most abrasive way, he having portentously broken off a limb of her crucifix while still a nursing infant. As an adult, Flamineo blames his mother for his poverty and sarcastically justifies the pandering of his sister on crass materialistic grounds:

> *Flamineo.* I would fain know where lies the mass of wealth
> Which you have hoarded for my maintenance,
> That I may bear my beard out of the level
> Of my lord's stirrup.
> *Cornelia.*   What? because we are poor,
> Shall we be vicious?
> *Flamineo.*   Pray what means have you
> To keep me from the galleys, or the gallows?
>
> . . . .
>
>   and shall I,
> Having a path so open and so free
> To my preferment, still retain your milk
> In my pale forehead? no this face of mine
> I'll arm and fortify with lusty wine
> 'Gainst shame and blushing.
> *Cornelia.* O that I had ne'er borne thee,—
> *Flamineo.*   So would I.
> I would the common'st courtezan in Rome
> Had been my mother rather than thyself.
>
>   (I.ii.311–335)

All semblance of decorum gives way when Cornelia strikes Zanche in court and her angry son rejoins that for such behavior she "should be clapp'd by th' heels" (V.i.186)—that is, put in irons.

The son's contempt for the mother is more than equaled by the mother's feelings of outrage toward the daughter. As we have seen, Vittoria's adultery provokes Cornelia to Lear-like cursing: "If thou dishonour thus thy husband's bed, / Be thy life short as . . . funeral tears" (I.ii.295–296). Moreover, the imprecation wounds Vittoria as few speeches in the play are capable of doing: "O me accurst" (I.ii.301). Obviously, the strain in both relationships stems from alienated affection, and, by way of orchestrating the interior conflicts, Webster typically associates sex with death, the most elemental forms of union and division, in the speeches of the quarrelers. Flamineo imagines hanging as the consequence of refusing to prostitute his sister; Cornelia compares Vittoria's adultery to Judas's kiss of betrayal and prays that it be punished by a life as brief as the weeping at the obsequies of the great.

When Marcello rashly and self-righteously quarrels with Flamineo over the liaison with Zanche, tension between Cornelia and her third child develops:

> *Cornelia.* I hear whispering all about the court,
> You are to fight,—who is your opposite?

The White Devil

```
                What is the quarrel?
Marcello.                         'Tis an idle rumour.
Cornelia.  Will you dissemble? sure you do not well
           To fright me thus,—you never look thus pale
           But when you are most angry. I do charge you
           Upon my blessing; nay I'll call the duke,
           And he shall school you.
```
                                              (V.ii.1–8)

The sudden, gratuitous, and Cain-like murder that immediately follows insures not only the mother's "perpetual sorrow" (V.ii.25) but also the disintegration of her mind. As his life ebbs away, Marcello points the obvious moral:

```
           O mother now remember what I told
           Of breaking off the crucifix: —farewell—
           There are some sins which heaven doth duly punish
           In a whole family.
```
                                              (V.ii.18–21)

The disturbing detail of Flamineo's infant blasphemy prefigures not merely his own sinful career (including the fratricide) but the violent disruption of the entire family and the dissolution of kinship itself.[16] Like Lear confronting the hanged Cordelia, the distracted mother tries to deceive herself about the reality of her son's death:

```
Cornelia.  Alas he is not dead: he's in a trance.
           Why here's nobody shall get any thing by his death. Let me call him again
           for God's sake.
Carlo.     I would you were deceiv'd.
Cornelia.  O you abuse me, you abuse me, you abuse me. How many have
           gone away thus for lack of tendance; rear up's head, rear up's head; his
           bleeding inward will kill him.
Hortensio. You see he is departed.
Cornelia.  Let me come to him; give me him as he is, if he be turn'd to earth;
           let me but give him one hearty kiss, and you shall put us both into one
           coffin: fetch a looking-glass, see if his breath will not stain it; or pull out
           some feathers from my pillow, and lay them to his lips,—will you lose
           him for a little pains-taking?
```
                                              (V.ii.27–41)

Here Webster not only transposes the love-death theme into a secular *Pietà*; he complicates the pathos still further by intensifying Cornelia's ambivalent feelings for the murderer, her one remaining son. Bracciano enters to discover Marcello's bleeding corpse, and, although Flamineo confesses his part in the "misfortune" of his brother's death, Cornelia vacillates between a desire to avenge the virtuous son and a need to protect herself against further loss. At first she tries to shield Flamineo from the consequences of his own candor: "He lies, he lies,—he did not kill him: these have kill'd him, that would not let him be better look'd to" (V.ii.47–48). Then, as the stage direction indicates, "*She runs to Flamineo with her knife drawn and coming to him lets it fall*" (V.ii.52). As her maternal instincts reassert themselves, she urges Flamineo to repent and predicts her own death:

> I have scarce breath to number twenty minutes;
> I'd not spend that in cursing. Fare thee well—
> Half of thyself lies there: and may'st thou live
> To fill an hour-glass with his mould'red ashes,
> To tell how thou shouldst spend the time to come
> In blest repentance.
>
> (V.ii.55–60)

Finally, she distorts the facts still more radically, trying desperately to salvage a remnant of life from the devastation of death:

> Cornelia. Indeed, my younger boy presum'd too much
> Upon his manhood; gave him bitter words;
> Drew his sword first; and so I know not how,
> For I was out of my wits, he fell with's head
> Just in my bosom.
> Page. This is not true madam.
> Cornelia.   I pray thee peace.
> One arrow's graz'd already; it were vain
> T'lose this: for that will ne'er be found again.
>
> (V.ii.62–69)

This psychic conflict between mother and son reaches lyrical climax in the episode, much indebted to Ophelia's mad scene, in which Cornelia winds Marcello's corpse and sings her famous dirge. Summoned to observe "the most piteous sight" (V.iv.51), Flamineo expects to hear only "superstitious howling" (V.iv.65), but the experience he confronts is poignantly, indeed threateningly, quiet. In her emblematic distribution of flowers, Cornelia reserves "rue" (sorrow or regret) for her son. At one painful moment in her ironic fantasizing, she takes him for "the grave-maker" (V.iv.80). The lyric itself is a superbly Websterian compound of motherly warmth and mortuary chill, of homely details from nature (the comforting "*robin-red-breast and the wren*," the "*ant, the field-mouse, and the mole*") and the disruptively macabre ("*the wolf . . . that's foe to men*" and digs up graves "*with his nails*" [V.iv.95–104]). Cornelia's distracted grief penetrates Flamineo's defensive cynicism as nothing else could and prompts a crisis of feeling and conscience in him:

> I have a strange thing in me, to th' which
> I cannot give a name, without it be
> Compassion.
>
> . . . .

>   I have liv'd
> Riotously ill, like some that live in court;
> And sometimes, when my face was full of smiles
> Have felt the maze of conscience in my breast.
>   (V.iv.113–121)

But, just as Flamineo awakens to a deeper sense of himself, moved by the filial love that he can no longer stifle, Bracciano's ghost appears to show him a *memento mori* ("A dead man's skull beneath the roots of flowers" [V.iv.137]) and to throw earth upon him. When tenderness rises to the surface for the first time in Flamineo, Webster imbeds the moment in a dramatic context that lays the heaviest possible stress upon mortality—his brother's, his mother's, his former master's, and his own.

The appearance of the ghost with its silent promise of doom short-circuits the impulse to self-regeneration that public disgrace, guilt, and his mother's dementia have aroused in Flamineo. So he catapults himself into a critical test of his relationship with his sister, "dar[ing his] fate / To do its worst" (V.iv.144–145) and forcing upon her in his desperation the role of either savior or victim:

>   Now to my sister's lodging,
> And sum up all these horrors; the disgrace
> The prince threw on me; next the piteous sight
> Of my dead brother; and my mother's dotage;
> And last this terrible vision. All these
> Shall with Vittoria's bounty turn to good,
> Or I will drown this weapon in her blood.
>   (V.iv.145–151)

Flamineo feels a terrible pressure to clarify his position and hence to resolve the wrenching conflicts that beset him. Deprived of Bracciano's tenuous protection through the latter's death (after the murder of Marcello, Bracciano had forced his dependent to sue daily for his life "or be hang'd" [V.ii.73–76]) and of young Giovanni's through dismissal from court, he must discover whether Vittoria spells hope or despair. From his lonely and half-crazed perspective, she represents in one person the cynical and "courtly" values to which he has long ago committed himself as well as the only remaining possibility of acceptance, affection, and emotional fulfillment. Thus does Webster modulate the moral and psychological tensions of Cornelia and her family into a final confrontation between brother and sister that gives full tragic expression to their prideful separateness as well as their need to draw together.

Thinking to bully Bracciano's "executrix" into providing a "Reward for [his] long service" (V.vi.7–8), Flamineo rudely interrupts Vittoria at her prayers. The book of devotions that she holds in her hand is the first hint Webster gives us that Vittoria has been troubled by compunctions similar to those that have been at work upon her brother. But challenged so presumptuously, Vittoria responds with contempt, calling Flamineo "ruffin" (devil) and bequeathing him not money but *"that portion . . . Which Cain groan'd under"* (V.vi.13–14). Uttered as it is by a murderess, this curse ironically underlines the moral kinship out of which their common hostility springs. And the operatic, semi-Fletcherian charade that the slur provokes is really a tragicomic struggle for dominance between two equally guilty and egotistical siblings.

Webster exposes us to a seemingly deadly but absurdly exaggerated contest between brother and sister that is designed to tighten suspense progressively in the manner of Russian roulette. And added to the genuine terror is a concatenation of self-conscious theatricalities—Flamineo's brandishing of pistols and rhetorically contrived threats, the triple suicide pact (which includes a servant), the stoic posturings in the face of imminent death, the double shooting, and the rush of the women in their frenzy to *"tread upon"* the fallen body (V.vi.118) and gloat over having outmanuevered their would-be destroyer. We may gauge by the survivors' ferocity not only the exhilaration of their release from a trap but the intensity of their former involvement (as sister and as lover) with their supposed enemy. Only after simulating death agonies and permitting Vittoria to prate to him of his incipient damnation does Flamineo rise from the stage unhurt to expose their treachery and seize the advantage of the shock he has just administered:

> O cunning devils! now I have try'd your love,
> And doubled all your reaches. I am not wounded:
> The pistols held no bullets: 'twas a plot
> To prove your kindness to me; and I live
> To punish your ingratitude,—I knew
> One time or other you would find a way
> To give me a strong potion,—O men
> That lie upon your death-beds, and are haunted
> With howling wives, ne'er trust them,—they'll re-marry
> Ere the worm pierce your winding-sheet: ere the spider
> Make a thin curtain for your epitaphs.
>
> (V.vi.148–158)

For the moment, lofty expressions of nobility, sacrifice, and mutual commitment have been proved hollow; independence and survival through guile have prevailed; "love" and "kindness" have been shown up as merely the hypocrisies with which the dying are consigned to the operations of the worm and the spider.

But Webster reserves his most powerful irony until the last, for Flamineo's smug triumph over his sister is almost instantly brought to nothing by the entrance of Lodovico and his professional assassins. Webster negotiates the transition from the staginess of feigned death to the grim actuality by means of a familiar convention—having Francisco's revengers intrude upon the scene as a "matachin" or group of reveling masquers with drawn swords who suddenly reveal their true identity and purpose. The mergence of theatrical show with genuine murder is at least as old as *The Spanish Tragedy*, but the sense of death becoming suddenly and ironically actual is a favorite of Webster's tragic effects. It is as though the dramatist had set out to stage the macabre point of Raleigh's well-known lyric, which develops the familiar conceit of life as "a play of passion" beginning in the womb or "tyring house" and ending with the "drawne curtaynes" of the tomb: "Thus march we playing to our latest rest, / Onely we dye in earnest, that's no Iest."[17] Significantly, the invasion from without, made possible by "false keys" (V.vi.168), occurs at the moment when, internally, trust has crumbled beyond repair. For a moment Flamineo regards Lodovico, his own nemesis, as a rival for the honor of punishing Vittoria: "You shall not take justice from forth my hands,— / O let me kill her" (V.vi.175–176); then, physically overpowered, he resigns himself with bitterest stoicism to his fate: "I am i' th' way to study a long silence, / To prate were idle" (V.vi.203–204). And, after a futile appeal to the "gentle pity" (V.vi.183) of her "death's-man," Vittoria bravely assumes the defiance of her brother and dies without "whining": "Yes I shall welcome death / As princes do some great ambassadors; / I'll meet thy weapon half way" (V.vi.219–221). Their common victimization converts brother and sister to admiration, respect, even love. Flamineo's words define the new solidarity that their final moments together confirm:

> Th'art a noble sister—
> I love thee now; if woman do breed man
> She ought to teach him manhood: fare thee well.
> Know many glorious women that are fam'd
> For masculine virtue, have been vicious
> Only a happier silence did betide them. . . .
> (V.vi.241–246)

Now both support each other rhetorically and in deed. Both accept the murderer's blade with a show of eagerness. Both, by glorying in their independence and refusing to be cowed, snatch a moral victory from their ruin. Both confess their faults as though they feared damnation, but, "confound[ing] / Knowledge with knowledge" (V.vi.259–260), anticipate only extinction and oblivion. Both assert their identities most courageously at the point of their dissolution—when they are facing the "black storm" (V.vi.248), the "mist" (V.vi.260), or the losing of their voices "Most irrecoverably" (V.vi.272). Having lived out their antagonism and selfishness to criminal extremes, they perish together with a panache that somehow transfigures what has gone before and suspends us mysteriously between condemnation and the emotional equivalent of applause. Deepened awareness of self is what brings brother and sister into closer rapprochement than they have ever known. But again Webster underscores the paradox that love and death in some sense nourish each other.

If the figure of Cornelia dramatizes isolation, exclusion, and dislocation in a parent, the orphaned prince, young Giovanni, exemplifies them (but more

ironically) in a child. Bracciano's pert son, like so many of Shakespeare's preco-
cious children, combines wit with innocence and therefore contrasts suggestively
with Flamineo, Vittoria, and Francisco, characters in whom intelligence is co-
terminous with corruption and self-interest. His two ostensible functions are to
evoke pathos on the occasion of his parents' deaths and to restore justice and order at the end of the tragedy. Gasparo's remark, "did you e'er see a sweeter
prince?" (V.iv.1), suggests the lad's advantages of feature. At one point he enters
in black, a kind of juvenile Hamlet, longing for the release of death, speculating
on the afterlife, and complaining that they have "wrapp'd" his mother "in a cruel
fold of lead, / And would not let [him] kiss her" (III.ii.334–335). Later, when his
father is also poisoned, he is brusquely shunted aside, as we have seen, in favor
of Vittoria.

But, in addition to stressing the boy's poignant devotion frustrated by death
or rejected by fear, Webster prepares us from the beginning for his future role as
successor to a throne. Our first impressions are anything but reassuring. Early in
the play Giovanni seems to heal a breach between his father and his uncle by in-
terrupting their quarrel: dressed in armor and prattling of martial ambitions, he
reminds his elders of their adulthood, and they agree for form's sake to compose
their differences "Like bones which broke in sunder and well set / Knit the more
strongly" (II.i.140–141). But the hollowness of this reconciliation is quickly
made plain, for the murders of Camillo and Isabella, suggested earlier by Vittoria, take place immediately, and Francisco soon learns from his nephew's
mourning dress that Giovanni is "all of my poor sister that remains" (III.ii.339).
The spirit of good humor that had hitherto obtained between uncle and nephew
evaporates directly. Reprisal is now the Grand Duke's sole obsession, and he
hustles the lad offstage ("Take him away for God's sake" [III.ii.340]) in a manner
that further emphasizes the child's systematic exclusion from the deeper sources
of power and emotion in the play.

Giovanni has been "taught to imitate" (III.ii.310) his uncle, who encourages
the boy's aggressive potential by giving him a horse and armor; not surprisingly,
upon inheriting Bracciano's authority, the prince uses it to cashier Flamineo. Flamineo, indeed, senses the insecurity of his position, suggesting caustically that
the boy's acquisition of a coronet more than compensates him for the loss of a father. Employing one of Webster's characteristic apologues, he likens the young
heir to an eagle—a "far fairer bird" than "the courtly peacock . . . not in respect
of her feathers, but in respect of her long tallants [that] . . . will grow out in
time . . ." (V.iv.4–9). And, when Giovanni piously rebukes him for commenting
that "the little boy that rode behind his father" is now "i' th' saddle" (V.iv.13–20),
Flamineo observes darkly that he "hath his uncle's villainous look already, / In
decimo-sexto" (V.iv.30–31). Again Webster presents affection in a context from
which the baser motives and more sinister potentialities cannot wholly be excluded. Although Flamineo's defensive cynicism reveals more about his own values than those of the youthful duke, his words disturb us by suggesting the ironic

gap between the child's conventional moralism and the barbarous atrocities of the adult world, whether past or in prospect, which take place outside his knowledge or control. Webster sharpens this irony acutely by having Giovanni arrive but seconds after the death of Vittoria and her brother, only to be pushed out of the way by the English ambassador, who commands the shooting of Lodovico. Giovanni does pronounce sentence on the "bloody villains" (V.vi.283), ordering them to prison and torture. But he learns too late that his uncle has authorized the massacre—that very uncle he has been "taught to imitate" and, as Lodovico mordantly points out, a "part of" himself (V.vi.286). More disconcertingly still, that same uncle, the most potent source of evil in the play, remains at large and presumably beyond his reach, so that the boy's rhyming apothegm,

> Let guilty men remember their black deeds
> Do lean on crutches, made of slender reeds,
> (V.vi.300–301)

sounds at best futile and at worst half-true. It is far from clear that "All that have hands in this, shall taste our justice . . ." (V.vi.292).[18] Giovanni, like the boy king at the end of Marlowe's *Edward II*, seems to preside over an erasure of wicked symptoms rather than a purgation of evil itself. But, of course, we cannot be sure. Webster leaves us, as he leaves Flamineo, "in a mist."

It will appear that almost without exception the personal relationships of *The White Devil* make up a world in which profound emotional commitment is difficult, dangerous, fatal, or perhaps only possible when the urgency of death promotes or activates it. Webster's play is diffuse in the sense that no single character predominates. This is because, like the plays of Pinter in our own century, Webster's drama addresses the tragic problems inherent in human relatedness rather than emphasizing the heroic stature of a unique figure such as Hamlet or Lear, who, by dwarfing the other characters spiritually, seems to establish himself as breathing a different air, inhabiting a more exalted world. When Vittoria and Bracciano and Flamineo engage our sympathy, they do so not because they are morally superior to their wretched context but because, within it, they define themselves with extraordinary courage and vitality. The paradox with which Webster grapples is that, however passionately or deeply human beings may need each other, they are driven asunder by an insuperable combination of internal and external forces—by frustrations, aggressions, and cruelties that they themselves express and therefore stimulate in others and by the degenerate institutions that such persons have collectively brought into being. Even the relatively blameless characters of the play who support the traditional unities of family and state behave in such a way as to estrange those whose good they seek and hence to exacerbate disruption. Thus Isabella, Cornelia, Marcello, and Giovanni all emerge as weakly or ineffectually virtuous and shallower, more self-deceived, than the "glorious villains" (V.vi.272) who consistently upstage them. In a way they call for their destruction as surely as Bracciano "calls for his" (V.ii.80).

Both the action and the language of the tragedy reinforce a sense of fragmentation and dispersion. Characters are drawn into relationship only to repel or be repelled. If they do not curse, insult, divorce, or quarrel with one another, they strike, kick, stab, shoot, strangle, poison, or break necks. The combat at barriers by which Bracciano elects to celebrate his wedding effectively symbolizes the spirit of division that seems to rule the stage even on occasions of putative harmony. Ironically, the poison he encounters there proves even more of a "flaw" than that which "grew . . . between" Vittoria and her earlier husband (I.ii.59). The play is studded with images that suggest unnatural violence—thunderbolts, earthquakes, storms, whirlwinds, explosions, beheadings, rackings, dismemberings, and the like. Webster's melancholy obsession with dissolution recalls Hamlet in the graveyard, but psychological and intellectual disintegration is even more emphasized than physical.

Poison and grief respectively destroy the minds of Bracciano and Cornelia, and, in the case of the duke, guilt compounds the madness; then to these obvious examples of mental breakdown Webster adds the convulsive frenzy of Lodovico and the half-feigned, half-genuine imbalance of Flamineo. *Quos Deus vult perdere prius dementat.* The psychic climate of the play is one in which focus and definition are easily lost. Camillo's jealousy is likened to spectacles that multiply an image twenty times (I.ii.100–107), and Bracciano's "brain-sick" mind "fastens / On twenty several objects, which confound / Deep sense with folly" (V.iii.73–75). Vittoria is accused of "loose thoughts" that "Scatter like quicksilver" (IV.ii.100–101). The high value that the tragedies of Webster place upon "integrity of life" reflects a pervasive fear of incoherence and loss of identity. Lodovico speaks of those who are "pash'd in pieces" by the "violent thunder" of their political masters (I.i.11–12), and he sees his own plight as that of a sheep ready "to be cut in pieces" (I.i.62). He thinks "fear should dissolve" his feminine victim "into air" (V.vi.222). Bracciano threatens to "cut" Vittoria "into atomies" (IV.ii.42). Flamineo speaks of "falling to pieces" and of being "pounded to death in a mortar" (V.vi.25–26). Such utterances only confirm the sense of a universe that is atomistic and governed, as Norma Kroll phrases it, "by an indifferent chain of random action and reaction."[19] By alluding to the twin gods of Democritus, "Courtly reward / And punishment" (I.i.3–4), Lodovico reminds us of a whole tradition of philosophical materialism as conceived by Democritus, adopted by Epicurus, synthesized by Lucretius, and quoted in Webster's age by the skeptical Montaigne. In at least one of its many aspects, *The White Devil* seems to depict the psychological equivalent of physical matter as described in *De rerum natura*: ". . . bodies are in many ways mutually hostile and poisonous; and therefore they will either perish when they have met, or will fly asunder just as we see, when a storm has gathered, lightnings and rains and winds fly asunder."[20] Chapman's Byron voices the same concept more poetically just before his execution when he rails upon the "Wretched world, / Consisting most of parts that fly each other, / A firmness breeding all inconstancy, / A bond of all disjunction" (*The Tragedy of Byron*, V.iv.62–65).[21] Indeed, the crazy quilt of Webster's verbal borrowings, documented so painstakingly by R. W. Dent,[22] suggests a technique of composition curiously analogous to the socio-emotional environment that his play records so vividly.

The term "integrity," which does not appear in *The White Devil* but which critics sometimes extend to Websterian drama generally by seizing upon Delio's concluding couplet in *The Duchess of Malfi*, has caused a certain confusion in Webster studies. Apart from Delio's aphorism,

> *Integrity of life is fame's best friend,*
> *Which nobly, beyond death, shall crown the end,*

Webster used the word only twice—both times in praise of "*Worthy Prince* Henry, *fames best* president" (*Monuments of Honor*, l. 349).[23] James I's eldest son seems to have become for the dramatist the apotheosis of heroic virtue of which a prominent component was "*the* Integrety *of a Brave mind*" that leaves behind it "*a most Cleere and Eminent Fame*" (ll. 361–362)—that same "Integrity" that forms the mainstay of Christian conscience and that, even in death, "*keeps /* *The safest Watch and breeds the soundest sleeps*" (ll. 371–372).[24] Henry Cockeram's *Interpreter of hard English Words*, the dictionary for which Webster composed a prefatory poem, defines "integrity" as "Soundnesse, right dealing," and a contemporary French-English lexicon adds the synonyms "honestie, sinceritie, innocencie, uprightnesse."[25] These definitions, implying as they do an orthodox standard of Christian rectitude, embrace the usual meaning of "integrity" in Shakespeare, Jonson, Middleton, Milton, and other Renaissance authors, and clearly they apply to Webster's usage as well. But Webster's association of the value with Prince Henry's "fame" and "brave mind," with his "*full strength of Youth and height of blood*" (l. 351), appears to lend it a special assertive or heroic force that stretches the concept somewhat beyond conventional religious and moral perimeters. Webster's "integrity" with its implications of psychic wholeness and physical audacity, would seem to include the humanistic grandeur, the "native noblesse" or "state of man / In his first royalty ruling" of which Chapman's tragic heroes are the flawed embodiments.[26]

Like so much else in Webster, then, integrity is a quality rooted in paradox. It is a value that daringly seeks to bridge—even to transcend—the contradictions between Christian virtue and pagan *virtus*, a word that, as Waith reminds us, derives from both *vir* ("man") and *vis* ("energy").[27] And ideally, at least, it also unifies that "*outward Fortitude*" or active valor (of which, for Chapman, Achilles in *The Iliad* was the literary prototype) with "*the Mind's inward, constant, and unconquered Empire*" (of which Ulysses in *The Odyssey* was the translator's chief exemplar).[28] Tragic heroism for Chapman, as to a lesser extent for his admirer Webster, had almost as much to do with personality as with ethics; it tended to glorify human possibility in the very process of insisting—and insisting grimly—on man's ephemerality and finitude. The heroic figure, somehow growing larger than life in the course of being crushed by it, compelled into integration, if only for a fleeting moment, a welter of incompatibilities—restless aspiration, stoical calm, majestic presence, invincible courage, Herculean self-sufficiency, intellectual and spiritual penetration, the grappling with existential terror, a mystical enlightenment borne of darkness, and, finally, the granitic capacity to stand firm, like Chapman's Chabot, "and look . . . destiny in the face at the last summons" (*The Tragedy of Chabot, Admiral of France*, V.i.29–30).[29] Millar MacLure has spoken of the typical Chapman hero as a "lonely figure, assured by inward powers, drawing his inspiration from secret and noble essences, and surrounded by ignorants, backbiters, misunderstanders, savages, baying monsters."[30] Although Webster's figures are more social than Chapman's and do not tower above their surroundings in the same epic manner, some of his characters—especially the women—do evince qualities of interior strength that suggest a kind of integrity in the extended or "heroic" sense of the term.

The Duchess of Malfi comes closer to this ideal (at least in its moral aspect) than the criminally willful Vittoria, but it is the nature of tragedy to stress achievement less than noble potentiality. Vittoria creates and maintains an integrated *image* of the self that serves her as a bastion against inner collapse. She resolutely imposes the *form*, if not the substance, of order upon a personality that would otherwise disintegrate under pressure, and her honesty to self, if not to the external world, allows us (and perhaps even her) to glimpse a vision of integrity that her actions have belied. This tenuous, subjective grasp on identity, Webster seems to suggest, may be all that is possible in so lost and irrational an environment as Francisco de Medici's Italy. The beauty and ugliness that modify each other so mysteriously in Webster's white devil finally evoke a divided response akin to that of Epernon's at the fall of Byron, Chapman's paradoxical traitor-hero:

> Oh of what contraries consists a man!
> Of what impossible mixtures! Vice and virtue,
> Corruption, and eternnesse, at one time,
> And in one subject, let together loose!
> We have not any strength but weakens us,
> No greatness but doth crush us into air.
> Our knowledges do light us but to err,
> Our ornaments are burthens, our delights
> Are our tormenters, fiends that, rais'd in fears,
> At parting shake our roofs about our ears.
> (*The Tragedy of Byron*, V.iii.189–198)[31]

At the core of this psychic division, as Chapman's passage implies, is the self-consciousness that allows man to perceive his own inconsistency even as he hankers nostalgically for the simplicity and unity of inner strength that the more settled, less protean values of an older civilization had seemed to foster. Surprisingly, then, "integrity" for characters on the Jacobean stage may be linked to the theatrical process by which it is dramatized, expressing itself as a kind of bravado in which authentic self-discovery and the sense of watching oneself perform a tragic role become indissoluble.

* * *

The contradictory impulses to union and division, to love and death, that Webster portrays in the human relationships of *The White Devil* define a psychology of *discordia concors*. Appropriately, the verbal texture of the play comprises a whole system of bizarre linkages—puns, juxtapositions, repetitions, macabre allusions and images, jolts of metaphysical wit—that reinforces our sense that attachment and estrangement, passion and mortality, are but shifting faces of the same perplexing truth.

The dramatist frequently pinpoints a larger irony not only through double meanings but through their placement and cross relation. Vittoria puns on "yew" and "you" (I.ii.233–234) when she broaches the murder of Camillo and Isabella to Bracciano, thus associating not only the destruction of two existing marriages with the graveyard but also, unwittingly, that of the new marriage that the killings are designed to promote. Then the same image reappears in a fresh but related context when Monticelso warns Lodovico about the dangers of avenging Isabella: "like the black, and melancholic yew tree, / Dost think to root thyself in dead men's graves, / And yet to prosper?" (IV.iii.120–122). The word "blood" crops up repeatedly in contexts that link it directly to both lust and murder. The meaning may be limited to a single denotation, as when Francisco commands at Vittoria's trial, "The act of blood let pass, only descend / To matter of incontinence" (III.ii.189–190), but her macabre wit in the final scene ("O my greatest sin lay in my blood. / Now my blood pays for't" [V.vi.240–241]) betrays the deeper indivisibility of the two significances. Camillo's jealous fear that Bracciano's "cheek . . . would fain / Jump with my mistress" (I.ii.66–68) anticipates the grotesquerie of his own sexually impotent death on the vaulting horse over which he "jump[s] into his grave" (III.ii.113). When Vittoria compares herself to a "fair and crystal river" in which her lover has passionately "drown'd himself," Monticelso expands her meaning to include not only the duke's public dishonor but the vengeance that lies in store for him: "Truly drown'd indeed" (III.ii.204–206).

A run of licentious double-entendres on "tilting" (III.i.16, 65–73) prepares for an enrichment of irony when Bracciano dies in "unfortunate revels" (V.iii.8) at the barriers and Flamineo impales his brother upon a sword, both deaths resulting from quarrels over sexual relationships. Flamineo's indecent pun on erection ("Tis not so great a cunning . . . To raise the devil: for here's one up already" [V.i.88–89]) intensifies the horror of Bracciano's death ravings about the devil's "great codpiece . . . stuck full of pins" (V.iii.99–100).[32] Indeed, the sexual meaning of "devil" may even be imbedded in Webster's title. The lovers' exchange of "jewels" at the beginning of the tragedy together with the sexual punning that accompanies it modulates at the end into the tense episode in which Flamineo and Vittoria trade puns about pistols, the "two case of jewels" (V.vi.20) that had formerly belonged to Bracciano:

> *Flamineo.* Look, these are better far at a dead lift
>   Than all your jewel house.
> *Vittoria.*   And yet methinks
>   These stones have no fair lustre, they are ill set.
> *Flamineo.* I'll turn the right side towards you: you shall see
>   How they will sparkle.
> *Vittoria.*   Turn this horror from me. . . .
>
>   (V.vi.24–28)

Less original but equally a part of the love-death pattern is Flamineo's use of the familiar pun on "die":

> *Vittoria.* Do you mean to die indeed?
> *Flamineo.*   With as much pleasure
>   As e'er my father gat me.
>
>   (V.vi.52–53)

The use of some image for rhetorical or figurative effect may adumbrate or echo a physical detail of the stage action. Dr. Julio's sinister reputation for being able, among other fantastic prodigies, to "poison a kiss" (II.i.301) leads directly to the mime in which we actually see him *wash the lips* of Bracciano's portrait and Isabella *kisses it thrice* (II.ii.23); then Webster recalls the lethal kiss once more when Bracciano forbids Vittoria to kiss him lest the death of his second wife replicate that of his first. The death of Camillo, which the audience likewise witnesses, involves the reverse process, for Hortensio's sententious couplet on the collusion of the revengers, "These strong court factions that do brook no checks, / In the career oft break the riders' necks" (V.v.14–15), employs a figure of speech to remind us of a literal fact. Francisco wishes that he had given his sister's "white hands" in marriage to death and bound them in "her last winding-sheet" (II.i.65–66) rather than to her faithless husband, and Isabella herself knows that she will need her "winding-sheet . . . shortly" (II.i.205–206); later the winding of Marcello's corpse is visually presented, and we see his grief-distraught mother seize the murderer's "white hand" and wonder how the blood-stains could "so soon be wash'd out" (V.iv.82–83). Marcello couches his disapproval of Vittoria's romance in what seems like hyperbole: "I would my dagger's point had cleft her heart / When she first saw Bracciano" (III.i.33–34). But the violence of his rhetoric finds its fulfillment in action when Vittoria is finally stabbed to death. In sentencing Vittoria for sexual enticement, the cardinal charges that she is "No less in ominous fate than blazing stars / To princes" (III.ii.262–263). Later, when she gloats over the fallen Flamineo whom she thinks she has fatally shot, she half-literalizes the same image: "This thy death / Shall make me like a blazing ominous star,— / Look up and tremble" (V.vi.131–133). Even abstract terms can contribute to this cross-patterning. At the arraignment Bracciano hypocritically explains that his motive for spending the night of the murders under Vittoria's roof was charity: "my charity, my charity, which should flow / From every generous and noble spirit, / To orphans and to widows" (III.ii.161–163). Later Webster puts the same reiterated word into the mouth of Gasparo as he is preparing to strangle the duke: "for charity, / For Christian charity, avoid the chamber" (V.iii.172–173). The same pretense to piety veils both the lust of the murderer and his cruel punishment.

The verbal surface of *The White Devil* is tirelessly roughened by abrupt shifts of imagery and reference that prevent the mind from relaxing into habitual or comfortable attitudes. Much of the play's psychic energy derives from a strenuous interplay between the unstable emotions of the characters and the audience's struggle to apprehend and adjust to the rapid mutations of their dialogue. The polarities and fusions of the love-death theme also play a part in this process and contribute further to the effect of disruption and imbalance. Sometimes the juxtapositions are yoked together by startling similitudes or antitheses in the manner of Donne. A sexual rapproachment with his wife will enable Camillo to "swoon in perfumed linen like the fellow was smothered in roses" (I.ii.155–156); by yielding to her lover Vittoria becomes his "sweet physician," for "cruelty in ladies" wrecks their reputations "as . . . many funerals" destroy the "credit" of doctors (I.ii.209–212); unlike earthquakes, which leave ruins in their wake, "violent lust leaves none" (I.ii.220); whores are like "flattering bells" that "have all one tune, / At weddings, and at funerals" and are "Worse than dead bodies . . . begg'd at gallows / And wrought upon by surgeons" (III.ii.92–97);[33] a politician hides his merriment under a "crabbed" face "as if some great man / Sate while his enemy were executed" and concealed the "very lechery" he secretly feels (III.iii.107–110); the content of a love letter is like the "fowl . . . coffin'd in a bak'd meat" (IV.ii.20); Vittoria's resistance to Bracciano's ardor is like that of young hares to pursuing hounds, a matter of "a quarter of an hour" before being cornered and "put to th' dead quat" (IV.ii.161–162); Monticelso's hypocrisy in inveighing against blood revenge is like that of "brides at wedding dinners" who feign modesty but dwell upon "those hot and lustful sports / Are to ensue about midnight" (IV.iii.145–149).

At other times Webster produces a similar wrenching association of love with death through mere juxtaposition. Flamineo defends his pandering of Vittoria by pointing out sententiously that "we seldom find the mistletoe . . . Without a mandrake by it" (III.i.50–52), thereby implying that the curative and the poisonous plants are mysteriously related in nature. Monticelso's striking image when he attempts to sound Francisco on his plans for taking vengeance invokes the erotic relaxation of the nuptial bedchamber in a context of menace:

Come, come my lord, untie your folded thoughts,
And let them dangle loose as a bride's hair.
Your sister's poisoned.

(V.i.1–3)

The Florentine duke dwells on "tombs," "death-beds," and "funerals" just before he pretends to be "In love with Corombona" (IV.i.114–121). The rhyming love letter, intercepted by Bracciano, promises that the duke's *love and care / Shall hang your wishes in my silver hair*," and Flamineo's "A halter on his strange equivocation!" underlines the macabre quibble on "hang" (IV.ii.32–34). Bracciano likens Vittoria's weeping to the "howling" at "Irish funerals," then remembers how often he has "wearied" her hand with "doting kisses" (IV.ii.96–99). Flamineo's sarcastic "We're blown up, my lord," immediately precedes Bracciano's protestation to Vittoria, "I will love thee everlastingly . . ." (IV.ii.139–141). In the same scene Vittoria throws herself upon the bed exclaiming how she wishes she could "toss [herself] / Into a grave" (IV.ii.126–127), but, as soon as her resentment softens, Bracciano "Stop[s] her mouth, / With a sweet kiss" (IV.ii.192–193). Bracciano's ghost holds a skull from which lily flowers (traditionally associated with Venus)[34] seem to grow, an emblem of love rooted in mortality; then Flamineo's guilty imagination is haunted by the superstition that the dead "hold conference / With their familiars, and many times / Will come to bed to them . . ." (V.iv.139–141).

Often the allusions of the tragedy, whether classical, biblical, or modern, support the pervasive ties between love and destruction. Flamineo urges Bracciano and Vittoria to "Couple together with as deep a silence / As did the Grecians in their wooden horse" (IV.ii.199–200). He compares his own sister to the "forty-nine" siblings of Hypernestra, who "cut their husbands' throats" (V.vi.163–165). In Monticelso's attack upon Vittoria she is like "those apples" that "grow where Sodom and Gomorrah stood"—"goodly fruit" to the eye but "soot and ashes" to the touch (III.ii.63–67). Accusing Bracciano of wife murder, Lodovico alludes to Leicester, who was reported to have had his countess "poison'd" and thrown "down the stairs" (V.iii.157–158).

It should be clear that this verbal forcing of love and death into uneasy conjunction is an important symptom of Webster's pessimism in *The White Devil* about hopes for moral or emotional steadiness. The technique partakes of the same restless, paradoxical mentality that produces the characteristic oxymora of the play ("white devil," "unsociably sociable," "politic ignorance," "glorious strumpet") and that verbalizes a world whose positive and negative values interpenetrate to such an extent that definition itself eludes the definer. The style comprises a matrix of startling, brief, and apparently disjunct images that combine animal with human, living with dead (or inanimate), fantastic with homely elements. The grotesque mixing of natural with unnatural or violent with peaceful connotations is designed to elicit the same sort of metaphysical *frisson* for which the phantasmagoric canvases of Hieronymous Bosch are noted. Fate becomes the affectionate "spaniel" that we "cannot beat" away "from us" (V.vi.177–178). A man dying of gunshot wounds feels that his liver is "parboil'd like Scotch holy bread" or that "a plumber" is "laying pipes in [his] guts" (V.vi.143–144). A "saucer / Of a witch's congealed blood" is imagined as the looking-glass by which one "set[s] one's face each morning" (III.iii.88–90). A pompous foreign ambassador "carries his face in's ruff" as a servant carries glasses, "monstrous steady for fear of breaking," and "looks like the claw of a blackbird, first salted and then broiled in a candle" (III.i.75–78). A courtier armored for the tournament "show[s] like a pewter candlestick fashioned like a man" (III.i.67–68). A revenger contemplates "play[ing] at football with [his enemy's] head" (IV.i.138). The "mould'red ashes" of the victim fill up his murderer's "hour-glass" (V.ii.58), and the criminal's death wound is acknowledged as the catching of "An everlasting cold" (V.vi.271). Vittoria's black serving woman "simpers like the suds / A collier hath been wash'd in" (V.iii.240–241). Hyperbole and understatement tend to modify each other in these examples, and nearly all tremble nervously on the verge of laughter, revealing how subtle and complex is Webster's continual engagement and disengagement of the emotions.

The White Devil is not lacking in more lyrical, sustained, or extended passages, but the overall linguistic effect is of almost ceaseless turbulence and strain punctuated at rare intervals by moments of haunting quiet—the moving silence, for instance, that follows Cornelia's distribution of flowers: "Now the wares are gone, we may shut up shop" (V.iv.111). Another example is Vittoria's response, after a pregnant pause, to her brother's "O I am in a mist": "O happy they that never saw the court, / Nor ever knew great man but by report" (V.vi.260–262). As John Russell Brown points out,[35] even the copybook *sententiae* with which Webster delights to weight the speeches of most of his characters constitute moments of fixity or imagined repose in the midst of bewildering turmoil. Ironically, they often seem to represent man's inadequate attempt to clarify or make sense of experience too contradictory and mysterious for such neat formulation. Flamineo's maxim, "Glories, like glow-worms, afar off shine bright / But look'd to near, have neither heat nor light" (V.i.41–42), is a fatuously oversimple means of expressing the subtle distinctions between appearance and truth in which the tragedy specializes—especially when we recognize that the speaker applies it to Mulinassar, the figure whose disguise he fails to penetrate and who will shortly have him assassinated. And we have already noticed that Giovanni's summary couplet at the end of the play on the manifest punishment of the guilty is similarly feeble. Webster's parables and apologues, which so often appear dragged in, misapplied, or otherwise inappropriate, assist our impression of man falling back upon proverbial or formulaic expressions in the face of realities too profoundly anarchic to accommodate received wisdom.

Perhaps the implied contrasts between hardness and softness (the imagery of diamonds, crystal, nails, steel, marble, iron, lead, and stone in a world of inevitable dissolution and flux) and between light and darkness (the momentary flashing of lightning, jewels, cannons, glowworms, ignited flax, comets, blazing stars, and meteors set against the encompassing blackness) give vesture to the same fundamental conflict.

* * *

The larger design of *The White Devil* reflects the same unstable relation of order to disorder that appears in its literary style. Critics have understandably judged the architecture of the play to be chaotic, crowded as it is with characters who, like Monticelso, seem to shift direction and double back upon themselves, and crammed with incidents that seem discontinuous, interruptive, tonally inconsistent with each other, even functionally gratuitous. The narrative line is so fractured that even editors and critics of the play who know it intimately find it difficult to recall the precise sequence of events. This is because causality in the ordinary sense is deliberately occluded or understressed. The tragedy is organized as a succession of sixteen scenes differing greatly in length (the longest is 398 lines, the shortest 15), and in the first half there is an odd tendency for scenes of similar duration to be arranged paratactically in pairs (I.ii and II.i are extremely long; II.ii and III.i are short; III.iii and IV.i are of medium length and in fact within three lines of being the same size).[36] If, however, such patterning has any significance, it dissolves into sheer randomness as the play approaches its conclusion, for the final six scenes are of inconstant lengths (232, 83, 270, 151, 15, and 301 lines respectively) and support the dynamics of evolving asymmetry. Act divisions were introduced only at the Restoration (in Q₃, 1665) and can therefore have no authority. Nevertheless, they confirm the impression of increasing disequilibrium, for the first three acts gradually expand in length (417, 455, and 557 lines respectively), whereas the fourth represents a slight decrease (539 lines) only to be followed by a wildly disproportionate fifth roughly twice the length (1,052) of the others. Even if this separation into acts reflects nothing more than the caprice of a Restoration printer, the attempt to impose a conventional structure upon the tragedy (as in the similar case of *Antony and Cleopatra*) only exposes its resistance to the strictures of neoclassical form. I do not mean to suggest that Webster counted lines or calculated scene lengths in an arithmetically conscious way, and, in any case, a good deal of irregularity is normal in Elizabethan plays. The statistics are only interesting as a reflection of his curiously shaped shapelessness in *The White Devil*, of a constructive technique that produced a drama dangerously close to a sprawling confusion of disparities, yet recognizably formed.

Webster's dramaturgy, moreover, involves a bizarre mingling of old-fashioned devices from popular tradition (dumbshows and visions conjured—in one instance by the use of a nightcap—ghosts, an emblematic skull, onstage combat, and a bloodbath of victims) with the more modish usages of the theatrical avant-garde (the satiric posturings and bitter mockery of the boys' companies, the intellectual knottiness of Chapman, the highbrow density of Jonson, the sensational surprises and eroticism of Fletcher). Along with characters, like Flamineo, who seem constantly to undergo a "varying of shapes" (IV.ii.246), Webster gives us a plot structure commensurate to a world of labyrinthine deceit, "winding and indirect" as the "subtle foldings of a winter's snake" (I.ii.352–354).

Motives and consequences often remain obscure. Webster withholds information, forcing the audience to reassess what it thinks it already knows in the light of later data. The precise degree of Vittoria's guilt is never explained, and her trial, though affording her a magnificent platform for self-dramatization, resolves nothing. Monticelso's role in the final revenges (if any) is concealed from us, and so is Francisco's fate. The time scheme of the play is nebulous. Camillo and Marcello are ordered away from court on a mission against pirates, but it is never clear whether they leave and return to be murdered or never get away in the first place. The relationships between Vittoria and Bracciano and between Flamineo and Vittoria are obviously complex but so volatile that their exact contours are impossible to fix with certainty. Sympathy for a character and moral judgment of him can seem almost unrelated. Amusement and horror are so intertwined in the play as to make an audience insecure about the mode of its response. Are the murders of Camillo and Isabella, huddled quickly together in dumbshow, meant to evoke dread, or are they expressions of black humor, the visual equivalents of Flamineo's cynical wit? The formal arraignment with its pageantry and Latin-speaking lawyer dissolves into a strident contest of wills at the end of which the supposed "whore" and accessory to murder is protesting about the "rape" of justice and crying out for "vengeance" (III.ii.267–274) against her accusers. The antiphonal Latin chanted over Bracciano as he is dying gives way to exultant joking when the assassins tighten the noose:

> The snuff is out. No woman-keeper i' th' world,
> Though she had practis'd seven year at the pest-house,
> Could have done't quaintlier. My lords he's dead.
> (V.iii.176–178)

The episode of Flamineo's false death seems calculated first to engage us in knuckle-whitening tension and then to release us in laughter when the supposed victim rises unwounded. But the genuine deaths quickly follow, ushered in by the "matachin" of "Churchmen turn'd revellers" (V.vi.169–170), so that still further adjustments of response are necessary.

From first to last Webster's staging is organized around a series of spectacles or ceremonies that suggest a kind of public order. Yet these ritualistic effects only supply the ironic backdrop for a display of psychic and social derangement and for the essential loneliness and egoism of individuals. A frenetic alternation between formal and informal (or even antiformal) elements becomes a principle of dramatic structure, but as the play gathers momentum the two sides of this distinction tend increasingly to encroach upon each other. Lodovico's explosion of rage to Antonelli and Gasparo in the first scene (a relatively personal episode) concludes with a "*sennet*" (I.i.60) announcing the grand entrance of Bracciano and his retinue; but within seconds the scene narrows again to a private conversation between the duke and Flamineo and then gradually re-expands upon the second appearance of Vittoria. The third scene opens with another court procession, this time led by Francisco and the cardinal, as Webster prepares the stage for a great public confrontation between the rival dukes with their respective attendants. Then Francisco orders the chamber voided, and the focus contracts to the testy exchange between Bracciano and his two chief enemies, Francisco and Monticelso. The entrance of Giovanni playing at soldiership alters the tone abruptly, and, after several more "private" interviews (Bracciano reviling his wife, Flamineo introducing Dr. Julio to his employer, Francisco and the cardinal dispatching Camillo on his naval enterprise, then deciding to recall Lodovico from banishment), the two dumbshows, a kind of stylized chaos, are presented against the commentary of Bracciano and the conjurer.

The three scenes that form what is now Act III consist largely of Vittoria's arraignment prepared for by a ceremonial "*passage of the lieger Ambassadors over the stage severally*" (III.i.64) and followed by a similar ambassadorial parade (III.iii.7–34). In both cases the pageantlike processions are met by the caustic utterances of Flamineo, and both also serve as preludes to bitter quarreling—the thrust and counterthrust of the trial scene itself in the first instance, the trading of insults and threats by Lodovico and Flamineo in the second. The early episodes of the fourth act (scenes viii and ix of the continuous sequence) present Monticelso furnishing Francisco with his secret "black book," the conjuring of Isabella's ghost, the planting of the fake love letter, and the quarrel between Bracciano and Vittoria that it precipitates. Then we get another procession of ambassadors in the habits of their various knightly orders and the ceremony of the papal election that culminates in the appearance of Monticelso "*in state*" (IV.iii.58) and the official excommunication of the lovers. Only the new pope's moralistic scolding of Lodovico separates us from still another "*passage over the stage*" (V.i.1), the wedding party of the Duke of Bracciano, his new duchess, and their entire household.

At this point Webster accelerates the rhythm of oscillation so as to enhance our sense of disruption invading and imposing itself upon ceremony in ever quicker and more violent fashion. A brief dialogue between Flamineo and Hortensio prepares the ritual entrance of the exotically disguised revengers, an attendant "*bearing their swords and helmets*" (V.i.43). After a private moment during which the conspirators ratify their plot against Bracciano and symbolically "*embrace*" (V.i.63), further cynical commentary by Flamineo and the bickering over his affair with Zanche occupy our attention. But a sense of courtly formalism returns in the midst of the desultory talk when an unnamed dandy with attendants enters to announce that "the lords are putting on their armour" (V.i.144) for the festival tourney at barriers. Then Flamineo's horrifying murder of his brother and Cornelia's chaotic reaction to it immediately usher in the stately procession of combatants, after which the crazed mother runs at her murderer-son with a drawn knife. The formal spectacle itself with its dancelike fighting, *"first single pairs, then three to three,"* is interrupted by the duke's screams of pain as he calls for an armorer to "Tear off [his] beaver" (V.iii.1–3), which in turn produces the appearance of the two physicians and then the stranglers *"in the habit of Capuchins"* (V.iii.37).

The episode with Bracciano *"presented in a bed"* (V.iii.81) is a grotesque compound of form and chaos, a deliberate wrenching of the ducal levee into a frightening parody of cross-purposes in which suffocation, ecclesiastical rituals for the consolation of the dying, and the irrational fantasies produced by guilt, madness, and high fever unite to suggest both corporate and individual collapse. This scene-within-a-scene is typical of Webster's dramaturgical method in *The White Devil*. It commences formally with many figures of the court assembled about the bed, but it rapidly breaks up into smaller groups and rearrangements, Bracciano becoming increasingly isolated and vulnerable, until only Lodovico and Gasparo "in private" (V.iii.170) hover menacingly above him. After Vittoria's emotional reaction to her husband's death, Webster lets the action trail off with apparent formlessness into sotto-voce commentary on the murder by Francisco, Lodovico, and Flamineo and the politico-sexual dalliance of Francisco with Zanche.

Flamineo formally greets the new child duke with his suite of retainers only to be banished from the royal presence, whereupon he is summoned to observe another combination of ceremony and chaos—his mother's insanity with its operatic aria on death and the ritualized preparation of Marcello's corpse for burial "discover[ed]" as a spectacle "behind the traverse" (V.iv.64). The experience provokes Flamineo's self-probing soliloquy and perhaps also the silent appearance of Bracciano's ghost. Then the play rushes on to the final crowded scene with its bizarre assemblage of feigned and actual deaths, of court masquing and bloodletting, of private hells and public speeches thereon. Formality and confusion fall together to blur if not almost to obliterate the line that traditionally divides them.

* * *

In 1924 T. S. Eliot referred to Webster as "a very great literary and dramatic genius directed toward chaos."[37] The features of *The White Devil* that I have been describing do indeed add up to an aesthetics of chaos—a structure of asymmetries and disproportions devised to convey the notion that, although humane or amorous commitment may be the only experience worth pursuing, it must be purchased, if at all, at the cost of oblivion and extinction, of "confound[ing] /

Knowledge with knowledge" (V.vi.259–260). The characters who at least intermittently command our pity or respect must come to terms with the omnipresent
menace of a world in which, as Flamineo puts it, "Man may his fate foresee, but
not prevent" (V.vi.180). This they try to do by inventing a unique self to shore up
some measure of dignity against inevitable catastrophe and dissolution, "scorn-
[ing]," as Vittoria says, "to hold" their lives at "any man's entreaty" (III.ii.138–
139).[38] Their constant role playing and showmanship represent in part a
response to fears of threatened identity. Isabella's pretense of jealousy, Bracciano's ostentatious bravado, Vittoria's "personation" of masculinity, Flamineo's contumely and elaborately staged suicide-recovery are all in some sense
"acts" of arduous, if risky, self-definition.

Not that Webster was unaware of the escapist impulse behind self-
dramatization. The feigned identities of the revengers (a Christian Moor devoutly committed to "honourable service 'gainst the Turk" [V.i.45]; knights of
Malta, "troubled in conscience," vowed "against the enemies of Christ" [V.i.18–
19], and turned "strict" monks) seem to be chosen not only for their deceptiveness but for their heroic theatricality, as though the murderers wished in some
subliminal way to fantasize their barbarities as a crusade against the infidel.
Apart from the circumstance that the imposters class themselves as Machiavellian "realists," the irony, of course, is that the savage facts of the play offer so
slender a footing for anyone's belief in Christian virtue or hope. The crucifix that
Flamineo damages as an unweaned baby would serve fittingly as an emblem of
the pessimism that seems to overtake the major characters almost from their
birth.

Webster puts such heavy emphasis on suffering, guilt, and punishment that
we naturally ask whether their contraries are even possible in the ethical super-
structure of the tragedy. Conventional preachment, to be sure, finds voices in the
warnings of Cornelia, in the admonitions of the new pope, and in the platitudes
of Giovanni, but such utterances, if they do not exactly fall on deaf ears, change
nothing. Retribution is the only significant action that claims virtue as its motive, and the revengers are clearly worse than their quarries. Moralism is pervasively associated with posturing—with Monticelso's "bitter" hypocrisy as
prosecutor and judge, with Vittoria's "innocence-resembling boldness" (in
Lamb's memorable phrase),[39] or with Francisco's lip service to piety: "Free me
my innocence, from treacherous acts: / I know there's thunder yonder . . ."
(IV.i.22–23).

Of course Webster does not entirely jettison Christian metaphysics. Some
recent critics have forgotten that no dramatist of the period would, or could,
have composed a play as radical in its nihilism as Beckett's *Endgame*. The vocabulary and rituals of religion remain, not necessarily as mere facade. Cornelia
prays that *"holy church"* will duly *"receive"* Marcello's body into consecrated
ground (V.iv.107); in his death throes Bracciano, officially excommunicated by
the pope, tries to "fix his eye" upon the image of the Savior (V.iii.131); Giovanni,

"threaten[ing] divinely," enjoins Flamineo to "Study [his] prayers . . . and be penitent" (V.iv.21–24); then as justicer, he wishes that the villains "shall taste" punishment as he himself "hope[s]" for "heaven" (V.vi.292–293); Vittoria, near the end, does apparently consult a book of devotion, though she, too, has been excommunicated; Lodovico and Gasparo obey revenge convention, a convention (despite Hamlet) especially popular with unsympathetic revengers,[40] in wishing not merely to kill but to damn Bracciano, thus implying (with a reflexive irony of which they seem unaware) that they accept the reality of hell. Later Gasparo, in an about-face, orders Flamineo to "Recommend" his soul "to heaven" (V.vi.196) before dispatching him into the "mist."

Even the spiritually calloused cannot dispense with the traditional categories of judgment. Flamineo, the disillusioned intellectual who has tried to shed the baggage of his Christian heritage, is unsettled by the sudden visitation of Bracciano's ghost and curious about the afterlife:

> In what place art thou? in yon starry gallery,
> Or in the cursed dungeon? No? not speak?
> Pray, sir, resolve me, what religion's best
> For a man to die in? or is it in your knowledge
> To answer me how long I have to live?
> That's the most necessary question.
>
> (V.iv.127–132)

But his urgent queries are answered only by silence and gestures that assure the asker of his mortality. The thinking characters of *The White Devil* seem to be profoundly agnostic, shackled to doctrines that they can neither believe in and live by nor wholly discard. Such faith as is evidenced in the play seems largely formulaic or prompted by desperation, and it is a faith in which the fear of damnation displaces all possibility of consolation and forgiveness.

In a world in which persons contrive to have their spouses killed and in which brother slays brother, appeals to human kindness are characteristically futile:

> *Vittoria.*   O your gentle pity!—
> I have seen a blackbird that would sooner fly
> To a man's bosom, than to stay the gripe
> Of the fierce sparrow-hawk.
> *Gasparo.*   Your hope deceives you.
>
> (V.vi.183–186)

The irreducible datum to which the play returns is that man is fundamentally solitary, driven back finally upon his own psychic resources, and worthy of respect only when he can confront death with courage and some degree of self-recognition. Vittoria and her brother are the only two figures who fully meet this criterion; for Bracciano dies in madness and terror, and Lodovico, though brave, can only continue to assert his blind will: "I do glory yet, / That I can call this act mine own . . ." (V.vi.293–294). Self-assertion and acknowledgment of guilt are important coordinates in the dying speeches of Flamineo and Vittoria. His life has been "a black charnel" that there is "some goodness" in ending, but he insists, in a final operatic flourish, that no church bells should knell his departure from the world: "Strike thunder, and strike loud to my farewell" (V.vi.269–276). Vittoria recognizes that her "greatest sin lay in [her] blood" (V.vi.240), but she insists grandly on the privilege of her rank:

> You shall not kill her [Zanche] first. Behold my breast,—
> I shall be waited on in death; my servant
> Shall never go before me.
>
> (V.vi.216–218)

If morality does not govern behavior in the play, neither is it totally absent. Conscience is never wholly suppressible.

It is probably significant that Webster should choose so corruptible a figure as Flamineo to serve as his nearest approximation to a chorus for *The White Devil*. Flamineo's final speeches, replete as they are with metaphysical gloom, sum up the deepest emotions of the tragedy and suggest both the grandeur and the necessity of self-conscious gesture in the face of destruction. (Richard Perkins, whom Webster singled out for praise when the play was published, must have been particularly impressive in these declamations.) Lodovico, just before "feed[ing] / The famine of [his] vengeance" (V.vi.200–201), would reduce Flamineo to a jelly of fright, but he succeeds only in prompting him to a splendid display of composure that nevertheless captures a central truth of the play:

> *Lodovico.*   What dost think on?
> *Flamineo.* Nothing; of nothing: leave thy idle questions,—
> I am i' th' way to study a long silence,
> To prate were idle,—I remember nothing.
> There's nothing of so infinite vexation
> As man's own thoughts.
>
> (V.vi.201–206)

After the wounding, his words become more plangent:

> We cease to grieve, cease to be Fortune's slaves,
> Nay cease to die by dying. . . .
> . . . .
>   I do not look
> Who went before, nor who shall follow me;
> No, at myself I will begin and end:
> While we look up to heaven we confound
> Knowledge with knowledge. O I am in a mist.
>
> (V.vi.252–260)

Here we get the sense of an identity fully achieved. Flamineo (like Vittoria) can accept the burden of the mystery but in a way that validates the self, endowing it with a magical imperishability in the very act of its perishing. The objective fact of death is made to coincide with the subjective uniqueness or individuality imposed theatrically upon it. Actor and role become one. Eloquence paradoxically transvalues negation into a kind of affirmation. Webster's most moving characters, like Marlowe's heroes, tend to fashion their own selves *ex nihilo*, but, as Susan Snyder has pointed out in a Shakespearean context, such creation is associated with divinity and produces its own kind of tragic exaltation.[41] Moreover, Webster's concentration on the overwhelming centrality of death implies that life, however evanescent, tortured, or evil, is infinitely valuable. Unlike most modern dramatists of the absurd, Webster insists upon the mysterious preciousness, intensity, and vigor of experience, which is why Rupert Brooke's image of "writing grubs in an immense night"[42] misses the mark. *The White Devil* is Webster's darkest "night-piece" (if we may borrow Lodovico's metaphor), but, as in all paintings of this genre, a certain amount of light is essential to the effect. Again the title of the play offers an insight, implying, as it does, that even the blackest diabolism may emit a certain radiance. Webster complained of the wintry conditions in which his tragedy made its debut, deploring the "open and black" auditorium of the Red Bull with its less-than-understanding patrons. But the vision that the play projects now, and doubtless projected then, is not without spiritual illumination. *The White Devil* may lead us to the edge of despair, but it stimulates enough pride in the depths and capacities of human nature to keep despair from being the obvious or easy course. Vittoria's aphorism, spoken so assertively to her sentencer, might apply appropriately to the drama of which she is the heroine: "Through darkness diamonds spread their richest light" (III.ii.294).

THE TRAGIC INDETERMINACY OF
THE DUCHESS OF MALFI

The Duchess of Malfi almost without exception has been acknowledged as Webster's "masterpiece" ever since Middleton and Ford applied that term to the play in their commendatory poems of 1623. Written for the most prestigious actors in the kingdom and played at the Blackfriars, the Globe, and later at court, the second of the two Italian tragedies was clearly more popular in its own day than the first. As we have noted, it appears to have been revived twice even before publication, and its re-emergence at the Restoration initiated a long chain of productions that have proved it more consistently stageworthy (particularly in the twentieth century) than any other of the dramatist's works. The greater centrality and more radiant portrayal of virtue in the title figure have always made *The Duchess* a more accessible and magnetic play than *The White Devil*, and the shift from a corrupt to a more innocent heroine altered the center of moral gravity significantly. The result is a tragedy of better balance between protagonists and antagonists, of sharper ethical clarity, and (partly because of the simpler plot) of greater coherence, of less interruptive and less cumbersome design.

The Duchess seems also to represent a refining and refocusing of both the psychological and philosophical insights of the earlier play—a somewhat more naturalistic, less strained, more satisfying integration of its contraries. Obviously, no sudden infusion of optimism is to be observed. Webster does not diminish the uncompromising power of evil to breed suffering, destruction, and chaos, but a more unselfish and fertile kind of love than was shown in *The White Devil* is now visible, and the overall effect is slightly to increase hope or the validity of hope. If wickedness in *The Duchess* is no less intense, at least it is allowed to run its full course and is seen finally to be self-consuming. No Francisco remains to disturb our sense of moral resolution and tragic closure. And if Vittoria regards her executioners as delivering her over to the formless terrors of "a black storm" (*The White Devil*, V.vi.248), the Duchess of Malfi sees her stranglers as "pull-[ing] down heaven upon [her]" (IV.ii.231). Perhaps the emblem of this realignment is the surviving child of the Duchess by her second husband who, in an important alteration of the source,[1] is established at the end of the play as a "hopeful gentleman / In's mother's right" (V.v.112–113). The boy who is to become the new Duke of Amalfi is the offspring of a loving marriage and symbolizes the continuance of the emotional and spiritual freedom for which his parents were sacrificed. The boy duke at the end of *The White Devil* is little more than a dispenser of punishments, and, though technically an upholder of right, seems to face a much more ambiguous and insecure future.

Obviously, this assessment assumes both our moral and emotional identification with the persecuted lovers, especially with the Duchess, whose protracted sufferings build to the tragic climax of Act IV. Such an assumption seems never to have been questioned in the theatre, either by actresses or audiences, and might, one feels, be too obvious to require debate. But a tradition of prim moralism has crept steadily into academic commentaries, stressing the Duchess's willful obsession with private happiness, her lack of sexual self-discipline, her violation of degree in marrying below her rank, her irresponsibility in abandoning her subjects, her secrecy and deceptiveness, her trifling with religious pilgrimage, and even her questionable piety in remarrying at all. Critics have pointed out that in his contrasting prose characters of widows, Webster idealizes the refusal to take a second husband and satirizes the eagerness to do so. They have also emphasized the didactic strictures of Painter, who at times condemns the secret marriage as "a Maske and couerture to hide [the Duchess's] follies and shamelesse lusts" and inveighs against Antonio as "a vile and abiect person" who "dare[s] to mount vpon a Princes bed."[2] Joyce E. Peterson is perhaps the most extreme proponent of the moralistic school, as the title of her book, *Curs'd Example* (Columbia: University of Missouri Press, 1978), reveals. Peterson regards the Duchess as a female King Lear who violates natural order by self-deceptively relinquishing a throne in order to indulge "private desire" (p. 66) and thinks Jacobean audiences would have looked upon her conduct with the same disapproval they presumably felt for the rash marriage of Mary Queen of Scots to Bothwell after the murder of Lord Darnley.[3]

Although it is undoubtedly true that some patrons of the Blackfriars might theoretically oppose the remarriage of a widow, particularly if such a marriage involved the clandestine union of a head of state with her social inferior, it is absurdly narrow to judge Webster's tragic heroine by such inflexibly pragmatic or pietistic standards. *The Duchess of Malfi* is neither a satiric caricature like Webster's own portrait of *An Ordinarie Widdow*, nor a cynical comedy like Chapman's *The Widow's Tears*, nor a cautionary tale designed to promote such religious ideals as Jeremy Taylor outlines under "Rules for Widows" in his *Holy Living*. Rather, it is a tragedy of erotic devotion in which the lovers, not unlike Romeo and Juliet, risk their lives for values that are shown to be healthier, richer, and more humane than those that they dare to flout. Aware of the fierce antagonisms that the forces of outraged conventionality, rigid class distinction, political expediency, or family hostility would inevitably unleash against such an irregular marriage, Webster incorporates these attitudes into the play, setting them in unflattering contrast to the life-affirming and courageous decision of the Duchess to be true to her own deepest need for completeness and self-realization.

Those inside the drama who condemn her for preferring emotional fulfillment with her steward to being "cas'd up, like a holy relic" (III.ii.139) or being
paired off lovelessly with "a mere stick of sugar-candy" (III.i.42) forfeit all claim
to our respect by reason of their cruelty and imbalance or because they are too
far removed from her true situation to understand it. Antonio may speak abstractly about the dangers of "Some curs'd example" (I.i.14) contaminating the
purity of princely courts, but it is the Cardinal, the most poisonous and unnatural of all Webster's villains, who calls his sister "Curs'd creature" and inveighs
against her "Unequal nature" (II.v.31–32). And Ferdinand, who moralizes fever-
ishly about women "luxurious" enough to "wed twice" (I.i.297–298), who later
calls the Duchess a "whore" (II.v.47) and Antonio a "lecher" (III.ii.100), behaves
so perversely toward his sister as to bring his own sexual motives under scrutiny.
If the "common rabble" also "say / She is a strumpet" (III.i.25–26), as Antonio
reports, or the pilgrims at Loretto disparage "her looseness" (III.iv.31) and misal-
liance, they respond predictably as outsiders who cannot know, much less judge,
the special quality of her relationships either with her lover or her brothers. Although the Duchess is not portrayed as flawless—and certainly she is not the
saintly paragon into which a few old-fashioned sentimentalists have tried to
metamorphose her—Webster makes ineluctably clear the fundamental goodness
for which she stands. The proof of this is what her murderers are finally compelled to acknowlege: Ferdinand, confessing that "the meanness of her match"
was of no true importance, regrets his pitiless "revenge" against "her innocence"
(IV.ii.278–282), and Bosola echoes his master's word, personifying her as "sacred innocence" (IV.ii.355). In such a context, observations about violated degree or the social pressures against remarriage seem almost irrelevant. Nor
should we forget that Webster wrote in an age of considerable social mobility.

By its very nature we expect tragedy to concern itself less with the commonplace than with the momentous or unusual. Even so, it is clear that remarriage,
especially among aristocrats, was ordinary in the Renaissance. It is also clear
that attitudes toward it could vary according to the particular circumstances and
almost as widely as they do today.[4] Mary of Scotland, who was married thrice,
may have been feared as a dangerous threat to England's virgin queen, but popular reprobation of her third marriage stemmed largely from rumors that she had
cleared the path to it by arranging to have her second husband assassinated.
Henry VIII's sister Margaret took a second husband after the death of her first,
James IV of Scotland, and then a third after divorcing her second. Two of Henry's six queens married more than once—Catherine of Aragon twice, Catherine
Parr four times. Henry's grandmother, Margaret Beaufort, married three times,
twice after Edmund Tudor, her first husband and father of Henry VII, died. The
formidable Bess of Hardwick, who at one point had held Mary Queen of Scots
prisoner under her roof, outlived four successive husbands. Lettice Knollys,
mother of the ill-starred Earl of Essex, married three times (her second husband
was Elizabeth's earlier favorite Leicester) as did Frances Walsingham, who was

first the wife of Sir Philip Sidney, then of Essex, and finally of Richard de Burgh, Earl of Clanricarde. Lady Margaret Hoby also took three husbands—first Essex's brother Walter, then Sidney's brother Thomas, and last Sir Thomas Posthumous Hoby, son of the translator of Castiglione. Closer to Webster's own circle was the widowed mother of his friend Thomas Middleton, who remarried (unhappily, as it turned out) within a year of her first spouse's death. Prejudice against such remarriages has been much alleged, but a popular manual of letter writing, Angel Day's *English Secretorie* (1586), shows that the attitude was anything but universal. This volume includes among its model letters "An Epistle Swasorie" (pp. 122–128) urging a young widow of good family to marry for her own protection and happiness. One sees the point in the Duchess of Malfi's self-defense: "I have not gone about, in this, to create / Any new world, or custom" (III.ii.110–111).

To be sure, widow hunting was a notorious subject for merriment in Webster's day, and his participation in *Keep the Widow Waking* reveals that, like most other dramatists, the playwright was far from unwilling to exploit it. Even lighthearted comedy, however, could present the remarriage of an intelligent and dignified widow with sympathy, as Fletcher does in *Wit Without Money*, a play almost exactly contemporaneous with *The Duchess of Malfi*.[5] Even the platitudinizing Painter, as Boklund observes, cannot withhold his implied assent in rendering the Duchess's protest: "What lawes be these, where mariage bed and ioyned matrimony is pursued with like seueritie as murder, theft and aduoutrie?"[6] Nor should we forget that even the implacable Ferdinand, as Webster portrays him, is himself inconsistent on the question of remarriage. After having stated flatly that he "would not have [his sister] marry again" (I.i.256) and having publicly forbidden her to do so, he announces Malateste as a candidate for her hand. Of course, this may partly be a stratagem to test her nerve, for her delivery of a "bastard" child has already been reported to him, but Ferdinand apparently knows nothing of her marriage at this point.

The correlative factors of the Duchess's secrecy and Antonio's humble birth of course complicate—and are intended to complicate—our response to her fatal decision to remarry. But here again critics have been too ready to assume a condemnatory attitude on the part of Webster and his audience. Clandestine marriages, usually contracted for emotional reasons, were understandable in an age when parents or higher authorities tended to think principally in political and financial terms. Such unions were often stringently punished, but it is unreasonable to believe that popular sympathy would be universally withheld. Catherine Grey, sister of the tragic Lady Jane Grey, secretly married Edward Seymour in 1560 with the result that both were imprisoned in the Tower; but the queen's harsh treatment was based on dynastic prudence, for the bride and groom were both descended from English kings. The situation was not dissimilar fifty years later, when Lady Arabella Stuart secretly married William Seymour (a grandson of Edward) and, after attempting unsuccessfully to elope with him to the Continent, was shut up for the rest of her unhappy life in the Tower. Arabella was James I's full cousin and, although she never pressed it, had a plausible claim to his throne. The king had good reason to fear her alliance with a family that also had royal blood in its veins. Nevertheless, James had earlier promised Arabella (in a careless moment, apparently) that she might marry whom she chose, and she had important friends at court (Queen Anne, Prince Henry, and Sir Robert Cecil among them) who were prepared to take a more indulgent attitude than His Majesty. Lady Rich, the "Stella" of Sidney's sonnets, offended King James by entering into secret marriage with her longtime lover Charles Blount; but James had earlier countenanced her adultery (she bore Blount's children and lived openly with him) and seems to have been displeased less by the secrecy of the union than by its violation of the ecclesiastical canon forbidding the remarriage of a divorcee.

Both the Earl of Leicester and Sir Walter Raleigh braved Elizabeth's fury by marrying secretly for love, and each paid the price of temporary confinement. John Donne too defied authority by secretly marrying Anne More, the niece of Lord Keeper Egerton, and was rewarded for his romanticism by imprisonment in the Fleet and dismissal from his post. But we are scarcely entitled to assume that private opinion in these cases would have sided wholly with a queen, jealous to the point of frenzy, or with Donne's outraged father-in-law. Egerton, who was genuinely sorry for Donne, mentions the "passionate petitioners" who interceded for the reinstatement of his ex-secretary, and Francis Walley, Egerton's stepson, offered the married lovers asylum in his manor house after the poet's release from custody.[7]

Nor were unequal marriages, despite official prejudice, inevitably deplored. Anne More's wedding had to be secret because the bride was still a minor and because her wealthy family would hardly have consented to a husband of Donne's relatively modest standing, but, even so, the lovers had influential and sympathetic friends. The Duchess of Suffolk, widow of Charles Brandon and famous victim of religious persecution under Queen Mary, married her servant Richard Bertie in 1552, and her story, told by Foxe, Holinshed, and Deloney, became popular. Thomas Drue's play on the subject (1623/24), influenced, incidentally, by Webster's tragedy and "sundry times acted with good applause," portrays the great lady as rejecting the King of Poland (among other noble suitors) in order to follow her heart:

> come worst of fate,
> *Bertie* I choose thyself my marriage mate,
> Upon this low foundation I erect
> The Palace of mine honors. . . .
> (I.i; ll. 196–199)[8]

The play unambiguously endorses the Duchess's decision to be "Queen of my rich desires" (I.i; l. 133), and even the disappointed suitors accept her choice with good grace. As the unsuccessful Duke of Northumberland puts it,

Consent I see is liberal to this match,
And offers frankly my applauding heart,
Wishing of heaven to smile upon your loves. . . .

(I.i; ll. 263–265)

But words spoken to the hesitant Bertie by Cranwell, a fellow servant, sum up Drue's romantic attitude. Cranwell urges that exalted rank is no necessary bar to emotional happiness:

She lessens not her honors in your choice,
But makes you Lord of her affections,
And them we serve not, but her royalties,
Which, as they are not lessened, why should we
Shrink from their service[?]

(I.i; ll. 255–259)

Drue's passage should remind us of a point too often forgotten about Webster's tragedy—forgotten, no doubt, because the Duchess of Malfi herself neglects to raise it—that, as a sovereign in her own right (not even her husband abandons the formality of her title) and no longer a minor, she presumably has the right to marry at her own discretion, even though she might be expected to seek counsel in the matter. If this is the case, the tyranny of her brothers not only offends against all canons of fraternal affection but constitutes an alarming intrusion upon her ducal prerogatives. That Webster makes so little of the issue of authority may surprise us, but the explanation would seem to lie in his stress on the overwhelming cruelties of power. In the Machiavellian jungle of Websterian realpolitik, fervent speeches against the violation of human, let alone legal, rights would be naive. Despite her technical hegemony, the Duchess is a virtual prisoner in her own realm long before she is physically incarcerated, and she herself appears to recognize this from the beginning. When a pilgrim at Loretto understandably asks how a foreign state may legitimately "determine of a free prince," the answer is simply that the pope, influenced by a report of "her looseness," has "seiz'd" her duchy "into th' protection of the church":

1st Pilgrim. But by what justice?
2nd Pilgrim.   Sure, I think by none.
     Only her brother's instigation.

(III.iv.29–35)

No wonder the Duchess feigns public conformity when her brothers insist with such menace that she remain single, while privately she embarks upon her own dangerous course. One of the many paradoxes of Webster's tragedy is that truth to self must not only disguise itself but be forced for defensive purposes to adopt the devious tactics of the enemy. Like Hamlet, the Duchess of Malfi can only survive either by yielding supinely to false authority or by fighting stratagem with stratagem. Hence the chain of dishonesties (she later invokes the principle of the "noble lie" or "magnanima menzogna" [III.ii.180] from Tasso) to which she feels she is driven.

However much we may debate the wisdom of the Duchess—and her strategies do at times seem shortsighted—the truth is that romantic alliances that run counter to political or social pressure have always provided strong dramatic appeal. While comedy accommodates this situation with less strain than tragedy, the myth of love struggling to overcome both natural and unnatural obstacles is equally available to both genres. No one raises problems about the unequal marriages with which *As You Like It*, *Twelfth Night*, *Friar Bacon and Friar Bungay*, and *The Shoemaker's Holiday* conclude. Rosalind and Celia, both daughters of dukes, may marry below their station in the first Shakespearean example as Orsino and Olivia, a duke and a countess, do in the second. And in *Twelfth Night* the steward Malvolio feeds his fatuous dream of wedding Olivia by mentioning a precedent—"the lady of the Strachy" who took to husband "the yeoman of the wardrobe" (II.v.38–39). In Greene's play an earl can marry a milkmaid without demur; in Dekker's the nephew of a peer can secretly wed a grocer's daughter and be forgiven for it, even though he is under charge of treasonable defection from military duty at the time and although elders in both families oppose the match. If protest arises in such plays, it is quickly silenced by a speech like that of Dekker's unnamed king:

> Dost thou not know that love respects no blood,
> Cares not for difference of birth or state?
> (xxi.105–106)[9]

Like sentiments had already entered the proverb lore of Elizabethan England.[10] This doctrine is of course less automatic in tragedy or tragicomedy, but in some plays it is no less apposite. Robert Wilmot's *Tragedy of Tancred and Gismund* dramatizes the conflict between a young widow in love and her tyrannical father who, having irrationally forbidden her to remarry, causes the death of both lovers when he discovers their secret union. Since Gismund is a princess and her beloved an earl, no disparity of class is involved, but the message that romantic passion rightly resists perverse expressions of authority comes through clearly. Even a problematic and "dark" comedy such as *All's Well That Ends Well* presents the social inequality of bride and bridegroom as an obstacle that true devotion not only can but should overcome. Nor must we forget Webster's considerable debt, even in his two major tragedies, to the traditions of tragicomedy.

The prose fiction of the Renaissance, to which so many English dramatists were indebted for material, seems to have interested itself especially in philosophical debates about the nature, priorities, and responsibilities of love. A case in point is Marguerite of Navarre's *Heptameron*, from which Painter drew extensively in *The Palace of Pleasure*—a collection of tales unified to some extent around the theme of romance in conflict with authority. Marguerite's twenty-first novel (tome I, no. 62 in Painter) evokes much pathos for Rolandine, kinswoman to a queen of France, who secretly marries a man of base origin and suffers cruel persecutions, including imprisonment, at the hands of both her father and the ruling house. A related story (Marguerite's novel 40) is even closer to Webster's tragedy in plot and in the humanism of its attitude toward forbidden alliances. In this tale a great lord loves his own sister (Rolandine's aunt) more dearly than his wife and children. When the sister falls desperately in love with a social inferior, her brother's dependent, rumors of her unchastity circulate; but in fact the lovers have been secretly married. The suspicious brother spies upon his sister, intrudes upon the wedded couple in bed, and, "beside himself with wrath," has the husband brutally slain and the sister cruelly imprisoned.[11] Although no evidence suggests that Webster knew the French story (it does not appear in Painter and was not translated into English until 1654), parallels with *The Duchess of Malfi* are striking. Marguerite's tale, like Webster's tragedy, includes the close relationship between brother and sister (with its hint of incestuous attraction), the secret marriage of the sister to a man who serves her, the lady's proposal to her lover (the heroine of the novella confesses that "he married me at my desire"), the brother's violent interruption of the lovers at a moment of intimacy, the killing of the husband after flight, the imprisoning of the wife-sister, her desire to follow her husband in death (although in Webster the Duchess is deceived into thinking Antonio dead), the brother's suggestion of an alternative marriage that the lady refuses, the brother's rage almost to madness, his subsequent attack of conscience, the sister's courageous defense of her marriage, and, finally, her religious faith in adversity.

In the *Heptameron* this narrative gives rise to an extended conversation about the propriety of secret marriage, and divergent views are expressed; but the case for approval in extraordinary circumstances is well developed. The leading character herself stresses her right to independence (she has "come to an age at which I can marry according to my pleasure"), and a listener in the frame story insists persuasively that "one who loves with a perfect love and in obedience to God's commandment knows not shame nor dishonour, save when it lessens or diminishes the perfection of her love." The debate does not ignore the lady's imprudence or violation of decorum, but the internal narrator (Marguerite herself under the persona of Parlamente) concludes the discussion by stressing the value of "a virtuous love" according to Christian principles of mutual affection "without regard to rank, or riches, or pleasure . . . as God and nature have ordained." Ideally, she points out, marriage should harmonize romantic fulfillment with "the goodwill of kinsfolk," but the story itself implies that such harmony is not always possible. Unlike Marguerite, Webster makes no attempt to debate these issues abstractly, but his attitude toward love in *The Duchess of Malfi* is implicitly as enlightened and humane as hers; and, ironically, he intends us to applaud the "excellent music" (III.ii.274) of Bosola's praise of the Duchess's choice and of her refusal "to examine men's pedigrees" before their "virtues" (III.ii.260). The tragic force of his play is predicated upon the noble suffering that devoted marriage must undergo when oppressed by cruelty, cynicism, and family arrogance at their most bestial and on the heroic resistance to evil that the forces of death can elicit from its victims.

*   *   *

Again, as in *The White Devil*, Webster focuses attention on the complex interrelationship of three siblings—two brothers and a sister—probing the inherent ironies and contradictions that their kinship and independence can be made in combination to exhibit. In Bosola he gives us a more fully developed, more richly imagined version of Flamineo the malcontented intellectual. And he returns also to a strong heroine who, despite her different moral orientation, controls the emotional temperature of the play by virtue of her psychic energy, her indomitable spirit, and her daring to confront her own nature under terrifying pressure without cowardice and finally without self-deception. Webster employs several types or roles that he had already utilized in the earlier tragedy—the female servant who functions as dramatic foil to her mistress, the corrupt and worldly cardinal who "should have been Pope" (I.i.163), the criminally deranged nobleman, the libidinous court lady, the supine cuckold, the child-survivor of the carnage, even the grotesques of doctor and lawyer. And, although the Duchess of Malfi dominates her play more consistently than the second Duchess of Bracciano dominates *The White Devil*, Webster once more constructs his drama upon an intricate system of cross relations that exploits the paradoxes of union and division, of attraction and repulsion, of love and death, of sexuality and murder involving five major characters and several lesser ones.

Beneath his vivid individualizations of personality—and these must be reckoned among his greatest strengths—the dramatist implants the disturbing notion that radical differences may spring from a common source. Commenting on the well-ordered state in the opening scene, Antonio observes that either "Pure silver drops" or poisoned water may flow from the "common fountain" of a "prince's court" (I.i.11–15). Webster stresses the blood relationship of Ferdinand, the Cardinal, and the Duchess not only to heighten contrasts between health and disease or between the natural and the unnatural in a single family (as in *King Lear*) but to suggest also that the three most powerful representatives of hatred and love in the play share each other's lives by means of strong, though ambivalent, ties that only death can sever. The Duchess and Ferdinand are biological twins while he and the Cardinal are morally allied—twins "In quality" (I.i.172). Like Cain and Abel, the persecutors and the persecuted are primordially linked. Antonio calls them "three fair medals, / Cast in one figure" but "of . . . different temper" (I.i.188–189). Fascinated by elements of sameness in diversity and by the threat to stable identity that such ambiguities imply, Webster builds the psychology of these relationships into the dynamics of his tragic structure.

A certain indefiniteness or ambiguity of motivation is thus a necessary part of Webster's scheme and may partly explain why commentators have judged the Duchess so harshly in some cases and so sympathetically in others, or why the causes of Ferdinand's bizarre cruelty to his sister have proved so debatable. We may take up the inevitable question of incest first. Although Webster seems to present a Ferdinand who is largely unconscious of his own sexual nature, and, although even Bosola with his characteristic alertness to human seaminess omits to comment on the subject, the language and action of the play persistently suggest incestuous jealousy on the duke's part without quite confirming it. Mulryne is surely right to notice that Webster's refusal to be explicit about this sexual involvement (so unlike Ford's procedure in 'Tis Pity She's a Whore) actually "helps to make the Duchess's tragedy [more] unnerving."[12] When Ferdinand deputes Bosola to spy upon his sister, he first insists (somewhat to the surprise of the spy) that he would not have the "young widow" remarry, then deliberately mystifies his interlocutor: "Do not you ask the reason: but be satisfied, / I say I would not" (I.i.255–258). What he conceals from Bosola he would also appear to be concealing from himself. From this point on Ferdinand betrays an obsession with the Duchess's body that neither the strictest, most Mediterranean conception of "attainted" family "honour" (I.i.296; II.v.21–23) nor the desire to inherit an "infinite mass of treasure" (IV.ii.285)—the stated motives for killing her—can possibly account for.[13]

Webster introduces "the great Calabrian duke" (I.i.87) in a context of bawdy double-entendres, appropriately associating his aggressiveness as a soldier with a marked tendency to quibble pruriently on the drawing and putting up of weapons (I.i.113–114) and a need also to suppress such punning in others, as when he silences his courtiers for laughing at the sexual implications of "reel[ing] from the tilt" (I.i. ~~0). Later in the same scene Ferdinand addresses the Duchess (for n the play) with the ambiguous line, "Sister, I have a suit to you—" nsibly, of course, he is recommending Bosola for the "provisorship (I.i.217), but the hint of a more personal and subterranean mean-self, and Webster quickly strengthens these early impressions by nd dwell embarrassingly on sex in his tirade against remarriage. e should "know already what man is," but she is nevertheless sus-ing her "high blood" (I.i.294–297) swayed by youth and other s. Those who "wed twice" are "most luxurious," their "livers . . . Than Laban's sheep," and potentially "Whores" (I.i.297–301) if, they should pass through more than one pair of hands. The court re" (note the animalistic implications) in which women who hide their "darkest actions" or even "privat'st thoughts" are like "witches" who "give the devil suck" (I.i.306–315). Ferdinand accuses his sister of craving "lustful pleasures," observing grossly, as he menaces her with his "father's poniard," that "women like that part which, like the lamprey, / Hath ne'er a bone in't," then claiming, when she protests, that he had referred only to "the tongue" (I.i.326–338). His parting epithet is "lusty widow" (I.i.340).

The duke's reaction to the news that his sister has borne a child is compounded of frenzy, horror, and sexual excitement. His imagination fluctuates wildly between exaggerated fantasies of her forbidden sex life and, more extravagantly still, of the fanatic punishments he would like to impose. In his febrile mind she becomes "a notorious strumpet," "a sister damn'd," who makes use of "cunning bawds" and other secret "conveyances of lust" (II.v.3–10); he envisions her partner "in the shameful act of sin" (it does not occur to him that at this juncture she might be married) as "some strong thigh'd bargeman," some athletic woodman who "can quoit the sledge, / Or toss the bar, or else some lovely squire / That carries coals up to her privy lodgings" (II.v.41–45). Sexual stimulation is self-evident. And Ferdinand would eradicate these intolerable images with the "sponge" of "her bleeding heart" (II.v.15), by "toss[ing] her palace 'bout her ears," rooting up her forests, blasting her meads, and laying waste "her general territory" (II.v.18–20). He would "purge" his sister's "infected blood" with "fire" and "cupping-glass" and, after having her "hew'd . . . to pieces," bequeath a handkerchief wet with his own tears to her "bastard" from which the child might fashion "lint for his mother's wounds" (II.v.24–31). He would "quench [his] wild-fire" with her "whore's blood" (II.v.47–48).

These ravings reach their climax in his vision of the amorous pair being consumed in the very act of lovemaking:

> I would have their bodies
> Burnt in a coal-pit, with the ventage stopp'd,
> That their curs'd smoke might not ascend to heaven:
> Or dip the sheets they lie in, in pitch or sulphur,
> Wrap them in't, and then light them like a match;
> Or else to boil their bastard to a cullis,
> And giv't his lecherous father, to renew
> The sin of his back.
>
> (II.v.66–73)

Although the duke is manifestly enraged by the idea of his sister's intercourse with an unknown lover, he can conceive of a revenge that would "renew" rather than extinguish that lover's passion. Act II ends with Ferdinand's admission that his sister's liaison has not only "put [him] / Into a cold sweat" but also engendered a kind of frustrated paralysis:

> Till I know who leaps my sister, I'll not stir:
> That known, I'll find scorpions to string my whips,
> And fix her in a general eclipse.
>
> (II.v.77–79)

Meanwhile he "bear[s] himself right dangerously" but is mysteriously "quiet" and "seems to sleep / The tempest out, as dormice do in winter" (III.i.20–22).

Clearly, Webster takes pains to underline the sexual component in what Antonio had described earlier as the duke's "most perverse, and turbulent nature" (I.i.169).

Critics have sometimes cited Ferdinand's delay in taking action against the Duchess until after two more children have been born to her as proof positive that Webster was incompetent in dramatic craftsmanship; but, as John Russell Brown points out in his edition (pp. 67–68), the lapse of years may be plausibly understood as further evidence of the deep-rooted nature of the duke's neurotic conflict, and particularly of his wrestling with both guilt and desire. The unfolding pattern of the final three acts would seem to corroborate Brown's insight, for Ferdinand's behavior toward his sister combines sadistic advance with timorous withdrawal. His first speech to the Duchess in Act III consists of two casual and superficially unrelated remarks—that he will go "instantly to bed" and that he is about to "bespeak / A husband" (III.i.38–40) for her. Although this juxtaposition may be fortuitous, it is nevertheless characteristic of Ferdinand's habit of dealing with his own emotions through displacement. Consciously he wishes to make his sister uncomfortable by reminding her that in taking a clandestine lover she has disobeyed him, but at a deeper stratum of his psyche he may be battling his own alarming attraction to her. When the Duchess attempts to defend herself from the "scandalous report . . . Touching [her] honour," he insists on remaining "deaf to't" and pretends to reassure her that, being "safe / In [her] own innocency," she has nothing to fear; but even as he backs off from confronting her openly with her potentially explosive secret, he mentions his "fix'd love," and "pour[s]" his misleading confidences into her "bosom" (III.i.47–55). Comforted by the mistaken belief that her immediate danger has passed, the Duchess leaves the stage to her brother, who observes, in the briefest of soliloquies, that "Her guilt treds on / Hot-burning coulters—" (III.i.56–57). Ironically, the words reveal more about his own precariousness, morally and psychologically, than about hers.

Having arranged to procure "a false key / Into [the Duchess's] bed-chamber," Ferdinand now challenges Bosola to "guess" (III.i.80–82) at his purpose, then retreats again into privacy without satisfying him. Meanwhile he has been struggling to reject Bosola's notion of sorcery as a possible cause of amorous attachment: can it be true that "potions" or "charms" can "make us love, whether we will or no?" (III.i.67–68). (Significantly, throughout the drama, Ferdinand associates sexuality with witchcraft.) The scene of the duke's sudden intrusion into his sister's bedroom draws even tauter the strain already established between his sexual revulsion (a manifestation of guilt) and his intense erotic fascination. Once more he produces his poniard—an instrument both lethal and phallic—and, handing the Duchess the naked blade, counters her brave assertion that whether "doom'd to live or die" she can "do both like a prince" with a sexually charged pun: "Die then, quickly!" (III.ii.70–71). His abrupt command that she kill herself (suggested probably by a similar episode in Marlowe's *Tam-*

burlaine, Part I [III.ii] in which Agydas is also presented with a dagger for daring to love Zenocrate) shows us a Ferdinand in whom aggression and self-destruction are two faces of the same disturbance.

Although the duke has expected to discover the identity of the Duchess's lover and has possibly hoped to interrupt their very embraces, he suddenly refuses to see Antonio, "now persuaded" that the revelation "would beget such violent effects / As would damn" (III.ii.93–95) brother and sister alike. He therefore charges her unseen partner to "Enjoy [his] lust still, and a wretched life, / On that condition" (III.ii.98–99) but to remain hidden and unidentified. He also announces that he will "never see [the Duchess] more" (III.ii.141), indeed, conducting all further communication with her either through the agency of Bosola or in darkness, as when he gives her the dead hand to kiss. The atmospherically—perhaps literally—darkened stage upon which so much of the central action takes place is obviously symbolic of the blackness that all but eclipses moral order in this tragedy, but the effects of "owl-light" (IV.ii.334) also speak volumes about the semiconscious lust, terror, and sadism that tangle so obscurely in Ferdinand's own psyche. The duke can scarcely bear to look upon his sister even after her strangling ("Cover her face: mine eyes dazzle: she died young" [IV.ii.264]), yet at the same time he cannot resist looking ("Let me see her face again—" [IV.ii.272]). And it is precisely at this point that he mentions their twinship and admits that in distraction he has ordered Bosola to "kill my dearest friend" (IV.ii.280). In Renaissance usage the term "friend" sometimes meant lover or paramour, as in Lucio's words about Claudio in *Measure for Measure*, "He hath got his friend with child" (I.iv.29). Thus does Webster present Ferdinand's self-alienation as an aspect of his claustrophobic involvement—indeed almost of his identification—with the image of his sister. The confused feelings of love-hatred that he expresses toward her are dramatized as a transference, in part, of inadmissible feelings about the self. And, just as the duke imposes a kind of artificial blindness upon his relations between himself and his victims, so he now orders Bosola, the agent of his villainy, "Never [to] look upon [him] more" (IV.ii.317). For Ferdinand, the full light of self-recognition is unendurable, but enough illumination has occurred not only to "dazzle" his eyes with tears but to make mental collapse nearly immediate. He becomes the creature of his own "deed of darkness" (IV.ii.335), a phrase that he himself applies to the murder but that Jacobeans more commonly used for copulation.[14]

Webster's Calabrian duke is an impressively sophisticated study in the psychology of a sadist, repressed by guilt and horrified to the point of self-delusion by the nature of his own erotic urges. The aristocratic pride and hope of wealth that he invokes to explain his behavior are not so much spurious as inadequate and superficial. It is his sister's secret "marriage" (especially to a social inferior who symbolically disrupts his essential closeness to a more acceptable image of the self) that draws "a stream of gall, quite through [his] heart" (IV.ii.286–287) and that impells him to retaliate in kind by intruding so destructively upon the competing relationship. And the obsession with image carries over logically into the revenge with its grotesque substitution of a dead and alien hand for Ferdinand's own living one and of wax effigies for actual corpses. The Duchess is "plagu'd in art" (IV.i.111) because the objective naturalness of her relationship to an outsider wrecks the indispensable private illusion upon which her brother subsists. Gruesome artifice is meant both to punish and to drive out the intolerable reality.

Three speeches in particular reflect the intimate nature of Ferdinand's pain and its rediversion into elaborately choreographed torment. When the trapped Duchess asks her brother why he is so irrationally opposed to her second union, he is incapable of answering directly; he responds instead with a threat and a cry of anguish:

> Thou art undone:
> And thou hast ta'en that massy sheet of lead
> That hid thy husband's bones, and folded it
> About my heart.
>
> (III.ii.111–114)

n to the burial of her first husband in such a context is revealing, for it
instinctively he identifies himself with her deceased sexual partner.
arsh and impenetrable metal that forever isolates the Duchess's dead
ff the living brother with equal finality, and, in doing so, murders his
hardly surprising, therefore, that Ferdinand responds by inflicting
ter so many emblems of death, including, of course, the coffin that is
ast presence-chamber" (IV.ii.171) and the noose, which is referred to (at least in Cariola's case) as a "wedding ring" (IV.ii.249). The ritual strangling and burying of his twin becomes a deviate means of self-repression, a way of twisting his need for forbidden intimacy into a kind of *danse macabre*.

But Webster has already brought out Ferdinand's difficulties with self-image earlier in the play. When first informed by letter of the Duchess's "strumpet[ry]" (II.v.4), the enraged duke, struggling for mastery over his emotions, betrays to his brother how closely he feels that his own identity is bound up with those of both the Cardinal and his sister:

> I will only study to seem
> The thing I am not. I could kill her now,
> In you, or in myself, for I do think
> It is some sin in us, heaven doth revenge
> By her.
>
> (II.v.62–66)

In his mechanistic term "thing" and in his fervent attempt to moralize what he cannot understand, we recognize Ferdinand's unsuccessful efforts to confront his deeper feelings. A later outburst—in response to Bosola's pleas for compassion upon the Duchess's "delicate skin"—again manifests the simultaneous feelings of identification and alienation that define the duke's relationship to his sister:

> Damn her! that body of hers,
> While that my blood ran pure in't, was more worth
> Than that which thou wouldst comfort, call'd a soul—
> (IV.i.121–123)

The complete disintegration of personality that finally overtakes Ferdinand is the logical result not merely of a murderer's guilt but of a psychic impasse—of his desire to love his twin and to hate himself through her for that same love. The symptoms of this malady, as Webster presents them, are remarkably close to those in certain modern descriptions of schizophrenia. John Vernon remarks that for the typical schizophrenic "areas of the personality are fragmented and mutually exclusive"; experience is characterized by "the simultaneous presence but absolute separation of a fantastic space and a real space."[15] Sufferers are often afflicted by a consciousness that selfhood somehow lies outside or is distinct from their own bodies, a problem for which they try to compensate by retreating into subjective fantasy, which then takes on a horrifying objectivity of its own. Schizophrenics are thus much given to hallucination and role playing as well as to obsessions with dismemberment (symbolic self-amputation or self-disposal) or with the merging of self into other identities. Ferdinand not only presents a ring and severed hand to his sister (his grotesque re-enactment of her betrothal and perverse literalization of giving her his hand in marriage) but also imagines himself to be a wolf, digs up corpses, and is observed at midnight "with the leg of a man / Upon his shoulder" (V.ii.14–15). The lycanthropy seems fittingly to dramatize the principle of Seneca (elaborated in his well-known moral epistle *On Wrath*) that man is never so near the beasts as when he is angry. But, as Elizabeth Brennan has suggested, Webster also seems to associate it with lovesickness. Treatises by Pierre Boaistuau and Jacques Ferrand both connect the jealousy of lovers with wolf madness,[16] and Ferdinand, in a curious anticipation of his own disease, compares his sister's confession of remarriage to "The howling of a wolf" (III.ii.88). He also speaks of her children by Antonio as "young wolves" (IV.ii.259). Subconscious identification with the Duchess and her offspring would appear to color his rejection of them. Webster portrays the crazed duke not only as doomed to relive the horror of his crimes ("Strangling is a very quiet death" [V.iv.34]) and to live in terror of discovery but as experiencing also the schizophrenic's appalling sense of being both inside and outside his own physique. Ferdinand believes he is at once a wolf and not a wolf—strangely "hairy . . . on the inside"—and he therefore demands to have his sensation verified by being "Rip[ped] up" with "swords" (V.ii.17–19). A moment later we see him falling upon his shadow in a futile attempt to obliterate the dreadful "otherness" that oppresses him, and he would "throttle" it (V.ii.38) just as he has already had his sister throttled.

Otto Rank in his study of the double as a literary and psychological archetype analyzes the obsession with one's twin or shadow as a well-known form of narcissistic self-projection. This motif, rooted in the myths and customs of many cultures, whether primitive or highly developed, became especially popular with the rise of continental romanticism (doubtless because of its applicability to questions of identity and self-consciousness), and Rank therefore draws his examples mainly from nineteenth- and twentieth-century works. His insights of course are equally relevant to earlier literature, even if Renaissance dramatists, for instance, did not formulate such configurations discursively or express them in a post-Freudian vocabulary. In fact, Ferdinand's love-hatred for his twin sister, as Webster dramatizes it, exhibits a pattern surprisingly close to the constellation of actions and feelings that Rank regards as central to the model:

Always . . . [the] double works at cross-purposes with its prototype; and, as a rule, the catastrophe occurs in the relationship with a woman, predominantly ending in suicide by way of the death intended for the irksome persecutor. In a number of instances this situation is combined with a thoroughgoing persecutory delusion or is even replaced by it [Ferdinand's fear of his own shadow], thus assuming the picture of a total paranoiac system of delusions.[17]

Ferdinand torments and finally kills in his twin sister a version of himself, a figure who symbolizes—simultaneously but irreconcilably—his infatuation with and revulsion from his own ego. Many of the narratives that Rank adduces involve savage jealousy on the part of the protagonist when his alter ego becomes involved with a rival lover. In addition, a late variant of the Narcissus myth establishes a significant identity of the beautiful youth with his twin sister, after whose death the boy assuages his grief by redirecting his love from her to his own image. In some of the stories, also, the hero's shadow represents his accuser or impending death. It can hardly be coincidental that Geoffrey Choice of Emblemes (Leyden, 1586), a book that Webster seems to , presents the image of a murderer terrified by guilt in the form of his .[18] The tragic constant in Rank's exploration of the Doppelgänger entral character's incapacity to love, a condition that leads to unbear- on, fear, self-loathing, and despair and that almost invariably ends iolence and some form of displacement and self-depersonalization. -acknowledged suggestions of incestuous passion with which Web- he character of Ferdinand are of course inseparable from other ele- s make-up—the painful loneliness, the savage aggression, the tility, the unhealthy fixation on the contamination of his bloodline, the tyrannical pride, the nightmarish imagination, the simultaneous self-absorption and fear of his own buried nature, the suicidal destructiveness, the almost child-like capacity for tears, the crippling remorse—and critics would perhaps be less inclined to doubt the sexual motive in his behavior if they did not consider it in isolation.[19] Every facet of Ferdinand's conduct and, characteristically of course, his discontinuous speech,[20] his "deformed silence[s]" (III.iii.58) punctuated by explosive laughter, reflects psychic incoherence and moral chaos. Together they exemplify by negation the quality, discussed in the previous chapter, that Delio praises in the stronger figures of the tragedy—namely, "Integrity of life" (V.v.120).

The passionate embodiment of wickedness in Ferdinand is partly, of course, the result of Webster's need to balance the equally passionate expression of goodness in his heroine. As their physical twinship implies, the two characters are complementary as well as opposed, each being defined primarily by means of intense emotional involvement with another human being. But it is the third member of the family, the Lord Cardinal, who furnishes the tragedy with a different and altogether more mysterious dimension of evil.

Like his sister, the "melancholy churchman" (I.i.157–158) is referred to throughout only by title. In the case of the Duchess, this emphasis on rank seems intended to establish her dramatically as a reigning princess and therefore to enhance her tragic stature; it in no way diminishes or limits her private sensibility, her magnetic individuality. But the anonymity of the Cardinal confers a shadowy remoteness upon him; and Webster seems deliberately to minimize particular traits in order to achieve something like the grandeur of generality. Like Duke Francisco in *The White Devil*, the prelate of *The Duchess of Malfi* tends to function behind the scenes and through the agency of subordinates, emerging as the most powerful but least knowable of the major figures—a cold character who in one way approaches the objectivity, even the absoluteness, of allegory yet who also in his opacity generates the fear peculiar to incomprehension. Webster's imagery suggests a man who is not only evil in himself but the source of evil in others. He is negatively creative: "the spring of his face is nothing but the engendering of toads . . ." (I.i.158–159); "That cardinal hath made more bad faces with his oppression than ever Michael Angelo made good ones . . ." (III.iii.51–52). The fire-immune "salamander" may live in the duke's violent "eye" (III.iii.49), but, as Bosola observes, the Cardinal "doth *breed* basilisks" in his, and therefore personifies death: "He's nothing else but murder" (V.ii.146–147). If Ferdinand portrays the chaotic and bestial in a specific individual, the Cardinal represents destruction made scientific, abstract, intellectual, and nihilistic. His allusion to Galileo's "fantastic glass" (II.iv.16) seems perfectly in character. He incarnates an evil rationalized to its first principles, elevated almost to the level of a metaphysical concept. Webster associates both brothers with the diabolical, but, whereas Ferdinand appears to be enthralled sexually by some personal demon, the Cardinal is the very spokesman for hell. Antonio remarks that "oracles / Hang at his lips" through which "the devil speaks" (I.i.184–186). According to Bosola, "Some fellows . . . are possessed with the devil, but this great fellow were able to possess the greatest devil, and make him worse" (I.i.45–47). At least Webster begins his characterization with some such distinction in mind. But then, typically, he blurs it in the final action, for the Cardinal forfeits his satanic dignity in the murderous scuffle that ends his life, wrecking the carefully wrought facade of icy control and dwindling in a trice to the cravenness of a "leveret" (V.v.45). Bosola speaks Webster's epitaph:

> Now it seems thy greatness was only outward;
> For thou fall'st faster of thyself, than calamity
> Can drive thee.
>
> (V.v.42–44)

As befits such a purposely distanced character, the play is all but silent about the Cardinal's motive. Of course the priest shares in his brother's revulsion for mingling "The royal blood of Arragon and Castile" (II.v.22) with that of a commoner, but he expresses no additional reason for implacable cruelty to the Duchess—cruelty that he not only approves but seems to initiate. He does not trouble, for instance, to plead the duke's excuse of desire for greater riches. We see him chiding his partner in revenge for "fly[ing] beyond [his] reason," for allowing idle "rage" and "intemperate anger" to "deform" his outward behavior; and he shrewdly perceives the incipient dementia of which the rabid emotionalism of his brother is a symptom: "Are you stark mad?" The Cardinal "can be angry / Without this rupture" (II.v.46–58)—that is, without raising his voice—and, with characteristic detachment, can distinguish between his own and the duke's attitude toward vengeance: "though I counsell'd it, / The full of all th' engagement seem'd to grow / From Ferdinand" (V.ii.107–109). This tranquil, slightly enervated villainy, especially in the earlier acts of the tragedy, comes close to denying the Cardinal human status, and we think of Coleridge's idea of "motiveless malignity" as though the churchman were a sophisticated mutant of the conventional Vice—a figure whose function is simply to stand for depravity but from whom the traditional wit, energy, and active control have been drained away. Although this formulation has its attractions, it is oversimple, for the diabolical mystique that the character projects proves to be more illusory than real. The interior feelings, which at length emerge, are all too human and anything but vicelike—tormented conscience and panic in the face of death and damnation. Underneath, the Cardinal is more like Ferdinand than we are led at first to suppose, for both are profoundly terrified of themselves. As the duke cannot rid himself of his alter ego, which pursues him relentlessly in the form of a shadow, so is the Cardinal haunted by his own hostile image, reflected as a threatening shadow in his "fish-ponds": "Methinks I see a thing, arm'd with a rake / That seems to strike at me:—" (V.v.5–7). The tortured conscience projects itself as a vision of eternal punishment.

Throughout most of the action Webster keeps the Cardinal in the background where, as a malign and inscrutable presence, he can evoke without explaining, the poisoned ethos in which all of the other characters must live. We hear more said about him than he tells us himself, and the churchman is notably absent from the entire fourth act, in which the sufferings of the Duchess mount to their tragic climax and resolution. But his influence is felt even when not seen. Politically, he appears stronger than his brother. Having already tested Bosola in villainous service before the action commences, he overrules Ferdinand's short-sighted inclination to appoint Antonio as intelligencer ("His nature is too honest for such business—") and easily installs the substitute, although he "would not be seen in't" (I.i.225–230). He is closer in touch with the military and diplomatic affairs of Italy, about which we hear only vaguely, and appears indeed the *éminence grise* of international intrigue. It is he who asks about naval strategy ("Are the galleys come about?" [I.i.149]) and the emperor's need for his commission ("Must we turn soldier then?" [III.iii.1]). It is also he who "solicit[s] the state of Ancona / To have [the lovers] banish'd" (III.iii.66–67), who persuades the pope to seize the dukedom of Amalfi, and who, by his letter, procures Antonio's con-fiscated property for Julia. The Cardinal is instantly apprised by Ferdinand of the Duchess's delivery of a son and, though just as guilty of her murder as his brother, wears the camouflage of passivity, pretending even to Bosola to know nothing of her death. Later, but only after Ferdinand has collapsed into guilty madness, we see him take more active charge of events, covering for his brother by inventing the apparition of "an old woman . . . murder'd . . . for her riches" (V.ii.92–94), ridding himself of his too inquisitive mistress with the poisoned book, and trying, though now unsuccessfully, to manipulate Bosola. It is ironic that Antonio naively places his hope for reconciliation in an appeal to the Cardi-nal and that the churchman prepares the stage for his own death by instructing the courtiers to ignore both the duke's and his own "mad tricks" (V.iv.15) or cries for help. But both ironies depend in large measure on a perception of the prelate as the chief source of Machiavellian power in the play.

Except in the final movement, then, when the mask falls from his face, the Cardinal contributes to the play's atmosphere of peril and uncertainty. Webster brings him into the foreground infrequently, and only then to fulfill one of two purposes, neither of which reveals the inner man. The first is to join Ferdinand in an antiphonal browbeating of the Duchess, to foist upon her the "terrible good counsel" (I.i.312) not to remarry that she herself recognizes as stagy and ar-tificial: "I think this speech between you both was studied, / It came so roundly off" (I.i.329–330). Here the Aragonian brothers speak, so to say, with a single voice, and the doubling is intended to create, as a chorus might, the effect of the same evil multiplied. As in Pinter's *The Birthday Party*, in which Goldberg and McCann similarly assault Stanley, Webster gives us a phalanx of oppression that cannot help but garner sympathy for the victim and underscore the isolation of her plight. But nothing of the Cardinal's individuality emerges here.

The second variation from pattern is, of course, the by-plot with Julia. The scenes that present the churchman with his mistress do provide a kind of close-up on the character, and these—especially the poisoning by means of a Bible—have sometimes been regarded as a melodramatic excrescence, a sensationalist departure from naturalism, that is part of the regrettable "caotica carneficina" of which Baldini speaks.[21] It is true that voluptuary and murderous prelates belong more to the conventional theatrics and anti-Catholicism of blood tragedy than to psychological verisimilitude, but Webster's rather gothic sideplay is not without structural and moral relevance. The entirely mechanical sexuality of the Cardinal's relationship to Julia shows us the thematic conjunction of love and death in yet another aspect—the seriocomic. Possessing neither the human warmth of the Duchess's commitment to Antonio nor the polymorphous perversity of Ferdinand's suppressed passion, the Cardinal's almost farcical entanglement with Julia is dramatized as merely a cynical and finally tedious experiment in physical gratification, an essentially casual and hypocritical affair devoid of passion and even of pleasure. She pretends affection only to secure privilege and to extract information. He loves her "wisely" (that is, "jealously") at first (II.iv.24–25), keeping her docile through dependency, then wearying of the encumbrance, regards her as his "ling'ring consumption" of whom he would "by any means . . . be quit" (V.ii.228–230). Total egotism and the absence of genuine attachment make the moral point and make it appropriately in the spirit of grim parody akin to the self-seeking automatons of *The Revenger's Tragedy*. Sexuality, whether fruitful and normative as with the Duchess or stifled and violent as with Ferdinand or cynically routine as with the Cardinal, is seen always to eventuate in murder, and the common dust to which the tragedy reduces such disparities suggests yet again that, in Webster's universe, physical death is the inexorable concomitant of erotic relationships irrespective of their psychological or ethical health.

Webster may have invented the Cardinal's lubricity as a polar contrast to the Duchess's "divine . . . continence," which, in the words of her most devoted admirer, "cuts off all lascivious, and vain hope" (I.i.199–200). Nevertheless, he treats these episodes with calculated superficiality as though to show us how dessicated and emotionally hollow the churchman fundamentally is. His keeping of a mistress accords with his other public accomplishments—playing tennis on wager, dancing, courting ladies, and fighting single combats—all of them "flashes" that "superficially hang on him, for form" and bear no significant relation to his "melancholy" and "inward character" (I.i.154–157). Webster's emblem of this space between the inner and outer selves is the ceremony at Loretto at which the Cardinal divests himself of his ecclesiastical regalia, puts on military armor, and banishes the Duchess and her family from Ancona.

This formal spectacle, presented in dumbshow but accompanied by the "*solemn music*" of "*divers* Churchmen" (III.iv.7) and the commentary of pilgrims, enacts the Cardinal's self-depersonalization as well as the Duchess's expulsion from a city state. The silence of the protagonists lends them, as in a *tableau vivant*, a special objectivity. The scene not only interposes maximal aesthetic distance between us and its focal character but also serves as a parallel of sorts to Ferdinand's ritual punishing of the Duchess. Both brothers make their violence ceremonial, imposing a masquelike artifice upon actions that stem from and encapsulate moral disorder. The Cardinal, for instance, symbolically annuls his sister's marriage by removing her ring; later, Ferdinand presents the Duchess with a wedding ring of his own but attaches a dead hand to the gift. The Cardinal's rite is intended, among other things, to deprive the Duchess of her true legitimacy as wife, mother, and ruler. As such, it must stress the disjunction between the poignant feelings of individuals and the harsh impersonality of officialdom as embodied in municipal pageantry. Public metamorphosis from priest to soldier institutionalizes the subversion of human and religious values in the play. As the sword replaces the pectoral cross and the accouterments of bellicosity those of pastoral concern, so mercy yields to retribution and love to death. One recalls Prince John's rebuke to the rebellious Archbishop of York in Shakespeare's 2 *Henry IV*, who, in donning armor at Gaultree Forest, has become "an iron man . . . Turning the word to sword and life to death" (IV.ii.8–10).[22] Webster's Cardinal thus gives shape to the darkest of cynicisms. He can condemn his sister for feigning a pilgrimage, for using religion as strategy (a "riding-hood / To keep her from the sun and tempest" [III.iii.60–61]), yet encourage Bosola to violate the seal of the confessional by bribing a priest for purposes of gathering intelligence (V.ii.135–137). In the public ceremony, at least emblematically, he abandons even the pretense of his sacerdotal office.

Although Webster obviously took pains to individualize the "Arragonian brethren" (V.v.82), he also insisted upon their complementarity. Bosola characterizes them as a pair—two "plum-trees, that grow crooked over standing pools," that, although richly "o'erladen with fruit," feed only "crows, pies, and caterpillars" (I.i.49–51); their twin "hearts are hollow graves, / Rotten, and rotting others," and their "vengeance, / Like two chain'd bullets, . . . goes arm in arm" (IV.ii.319–321). This imagery, of course, emphasizes their moral stagnancy, their mutual corruption and association with decay and death. Both brothers, being wifeless and childless, represent sterility in different guises and so contrast starkly with the natural fecundity and homemaking instincts of their sister. She produces children; they foster only "flatterers, panders, intelligencers, atheists, and a thousand such political monsters" (I.i.161–163). The shared destructiveness of the brothers is suitably embodied in their common commitments to soldiery. Both threaten enemies at moments of high anger with having them "hew'd . . . to pieces." Ferdinand, as noted earlier, applies the phrase to his sister (II.v.31); the Cardinal, late in the play, applies it to Bosola: "I'll have thee hew'd in pieces" (V.ii.292). The play would seem to bear out Castruchio's precept (though in an altered sense) that a "realm is never long in quiet, where the ruler is a soldier" (I.i.103–104). Ironically, Webster also makes the Duchess a soldier at one point—but, of course, metaphorically in order to stress not her malignant force but her quasi-masculine daring:

> as men in some great battles,
> By apprehending danger, have achiev'd

Almost impossible actions—I have heard soldiers say so—
So I, through frights, and threat'nings, will assay
This dangerous venture. . . .

(I.i.344–348)

Both Ferdinand and the Cardinal practice their corruptions in an ambience of secrecy and intrigue, a fact to which Webster calls attention by putting them both in possession of "master-keys" for gaining entry to private apartments: the duke obtains such a key from Bosola to enter the Duchess's chamber (III.i.80), and the Cardinal gives a similar one to Bosola so that he may secretly dispose of Julia's corpse (V.ii.327). The sexual suggestiveness of keys being inserted covertly into palace locks is disturbingly relevant to both contexts. Both brothers, of course, are practiced self-disguisers. As the Cardinal veils his interior gloom under an array of social or sporting activities, so Ferdinand "speaks with others' tongues" and "hears . . . With others' ears" (I.i.173–174).

The most important point in common is of course the remorse of conscience that both brothers suffer for their collaborative murder, although, like the protagonists of *Macbeth*, they suffer it in psychic isolation from each other. Also as in Shakespeare's tragedy, their doom is despair. Ferdinand goes to pieces before our eyes, actually becoming like the madmen whom he had set upon his sister and experiencing himself the agony of hopelessness to which he had sought to drive her. The Cardinal, although he too changes inwardly, maintains an uncanny reserve, "Bears up in blood" and "seems fearless" (V.ii.336), almost to the end. After the strangling, however, Bosola notices that the cleric has "grown wondrous melancholy" (V.ii.202), and Julia, observing that he is "much alter'd," tries (with results fatal to herself) to "remove / This lead from off [his] bosom" (V.ii.231–233). Both figures acknowledge the reality of their own damnation, which amounts to a kind of negative identity achieved in defeat. Ferdinand babbles wildly about carrying "a bribe" "to hell" (V.ii.41–42); his brother credits "the devil" with taking away all "confidence in prayer" (V.iv.27–28), is "puzzled" about the "one material fire" (V.v.1–2) that is said to burn the damned in distinct ways, and finally wishes only to "Be laid by, and never thought of" (V.v.90). Ferdinand moralizes his own death in a couplet that clearly includes his ecclesiastical accomplice:

Whether we fall by ambition, blood, or lust,
Like diamonds, we are cut with our own dust.
(V.v.72–73)

All-powerful in life, both brothers end as cyphers of their own fashioning, and Webster reinforces the irony of self-destruction by having the Cardinal cry out for assistance ("Help me, I am your brother"), only to be dealt his death-wound by a lunatic Ferdinand who thinks he is on a battlefield and facing his betrayer: "The devil! / My brother fight upon the adverse party?" (V.v.51–52). As one evil sister eliminates the other in *King Lear*, so with the wicked brothers of

The Duchess of Malfi. But, oddly, Webster complicates the relationship at the very last moment. Having consistently built up the Cardinal as the less human and more unfeeling of the pair, he imparts a touch of fraternal concern to the churchman in his dying utterance of which Ferdinand, even sane, would be incapable:

> Look to my brother:
> He gave us these large wounds, as we were struggling
> Here i' th' rushes. . . .
>
> (V.v.87–89)

This confirms Antonio's earlier hint that the churchman has done "Some good" (I.i.167). In addition, it may be worth noting that Webster suggests a link between the deaths of the prelate and his sister by having him echo her final word, "Mercy!" (IV.ii.353), just before Bosola runs him through: "O, mercy!" (V.v.41). But the verbal parallel only reinforces an ironic contrast, for whereas the Duchess had directed her final appeal to God, the churchman seems to address his to a human being, the threatening Bosola. The impenetrable mystery of the Cardinal's emotion is never wholly dispelled.

Webster seems to have conceived the vengeful siblings of *The Duchess of Malfi* in a way that, while intelligible in social and moral terms familiar to the Renaissance, also anticipated some insights of twentieth-century pathology. In his *Anatomy of Human Destructiveness*, Erich Fromm distinguishes two kinds of necrophilia: (*a*) an overt type that involves erotic or quasi-erotic attraction to dead bodies and often an obsession with graves, physical decay, the dismemberment of corpses, and the like; and (*b*) a more generalized type, sometimes manifested in political or military figures (Adolf Hitler is the principal example), that may be described simply as a deep-seated hatred of life, a desire to transform what is alive into its opposite, a love of destruction for its own sake, and an "exclusive interest in all that is purely mechanical."[23] Both types of necrophiliac personality may evince a considerable degree of sadism, but, in the second type, the cruelties tend to become bureaucratized and impersonal. Hitler, the murderer of millions, is said, for instance, to have evaded personal visits to the front during World War II because he was squeamish about seeing dead or wounded soldiers.[24] The typical necrophile is quintessentially self-destructive and often has strong impulses toward suicide. He also tends to overvalue the past as this is symbolically embodied in established institutions, rules, laws, castes, traditions, and family property. In his thinking, whether personal, philosophical, or political, "the past is sacred, nothing new is valuable, drastic change is a crime against the 'natural' [that is, the rigidly conservative] order."[25] Fromm derives his conception of necrophilia from Freud's dualistic opposition of the life and death instincts, even going so far as to hypothesize a causal link between the child's incestuous or Oedipal attraction to the mother and the transformation of this magnetism in certain autistic or narcissistic individuals into a desire for burial.

The child symbolically converts his mother, the life-giver and sustainer, into the smothering annihilator and bringer of death; the womb becomes the tomb.

Of course, we need accept neither Fromm's theories nor his assumptions to recognize in his clinical data a number of the symptoms or traits that Webster either invented or observed from experience in order to characterize his two savage antagonists. Obviously, Ferdinand with his incestuous fixation and his compulsive interest in artificial corpses, severed limbs, coffins, nooses, and the ritual details of execution, corresponds to Fromm's first model. The Cardinal, with his chillier, efficient, remote-control commitment to death, approximates the second type more closely. From Fromm's point of view such behavioral differences are less significant than examining the common sources from which they originate. What is clearest about the Aragonian brothers to a modern reader or theatregoer is their equally virulent hatred of natural vitality, of emotional freedom, of social flexibility, and of spiritual growth—the values with which their sister chooses to identify herself.

In characterizing the Duchess, Webster faced several related difficulties. First, he had to idealize her sufficiently to serve as a worthy counterweight to her depraved brothers without sacrificing the vulnerability—indeed, the fallibility—that would make her credibly human. He needed also to emphasize the private nature of a public woman, to show the personal charm and individuality that would not only explain but make emotionally acceptable the unusual relationship with her lover. At the same time, he could not compromise the dignity essential to an authentically royal and tragic, as opposed to bourgeois or merely pathetic and sentimental, heroine. Finally, since the facts of the Duchess's story cast her so prominently in the role of sufferer and victim, it was important to devise a means for avoiding the impression of abject helplessness and passivity and for making the character dramatically compelling. Obviously, no simple solution to such problems was available, but in adjusting a fundamentally strong, free, and commanding personality to a situation of extreme restraint, Webster had to suggest untapped reserves of stamina in the character and rely heavily on psychic conflict within her. By defying her brothers' wishes, the Duchess enters a pathless "wilderness" without "friendly clew" or "guide" (I.i.359–361). The tragic journey on which she embarks is largely solitary in both the physical and spiritual senses, and, ironically, this is true despite her romantic motivation. Her husband cannot protect her nor even be at her side in the crisis—a crisis that Webster dramatizes as a wrenching ordeal of self-discovery.

In addition, the playwright structured his drama so as to prevent, or at least to minimize, the damaging effect of resolute evil in simple black and white or melodramatic conflict with unexamined and untested virtue. The lady's marriage and its consummation constitute the primary events of the first act.[26] Here we are introduced to the Duchess in both her public and private spheres, the dramatist carefully establishing both her regal self-possession under pressure and her strength of will. The second act centers on her pregnancy and lying-in with its ominous aftermath—the brothers' nasty reaction to the news of the child-birth. Webster cleverly delays the face-to-face confrontation between the duke and his sister until Act III, the birth of additional children and Ferdinand's curious stasis having intervened. The duke's shocking intrusion then leads naturally to the flight of the lovers and the forced return of the Duchess to Amalfi. Such an arrangement allows the dramatist to devote the whole of the fourth act to the imprisonment, torture, and climactic death of his heroine, nevertheless keeping her atmospherically present in Act V by means of the echo scene and memorially so in Ferdinand's madness and in the rapid accumulation of deaths that directly or indirectly stem from her murder. By compressing the tragic career of his title figure into four acts and thereby placing the emotional catharsis early, Webster risked a letdown after her disappearance from the stage, but he knew the even greater risk of trying to prolong dramatic tension in a character who is the receiver rather than the initiator of the action.

Although Webster intends his audience to respond positively to the Duchess, he does not rob her behavior, particularly at the beginning, of a certain ambiguity. In this, of course, he shows her kinship not only to her brothers but also to the other major figures of the tragedy. She herself verbalizes the idea during her proposal to Antonio:

> as a tyrant doubles with his words,
> And fearfully equivocates, so we
> Are forc'd to express our violent passions
> In riddles, and in dreams, and leave the path
> Of simple virtue, which was never made
> To seem the thing it is not.
>
> (I.i.443–448)

Her point, of course, is that in a world of inequality—a world in which social station and political power govern human behavior more forcibly than romantic feeling—honest emotion and therefore the actions and language employed to express it must to some extent take on the protective coloring of the alien moral environment. Indeed, the Duchess employs some of the same "politic equivocation" in her own affairs that she later scorns in a Ferdinand who wants Antonio's "*head in a business*" (III.v.28–29). Forbidden love, however commendable by some higher standard, may involve a conscious deviation from "the path / Of simple virtue" as ordinarily or conventionally understood. Webster opens the play with Antonio's eloquent report of the French court, a court where the king is "judicious" and his council "provident," where nobility of character, genuine merit, and the pursuit of justice, truth, and other enlightened or humanistic ideals promote "a fix'd order" and "blessed government" (I.i.6–17). Strategically placed as it is, this passage defines by contrast the corruptions that the Duchess courageously opposes and by which she is also touched.

When the Cardinal alludes with some hostility to his sister's "high blood" (I.i.297), he himself enforces the double meaning of the phrase, correctly perceiving that aristocratic rank and sexual passion are correlative ingredients of her personality. Webster leaves us in no doubt about the sincerity of the Duchess's romantic feeling for her steward, but the play does raise questions about her prudence in selecting him, about her single-minded refusal even to consider the objections of her brothers, and about her devious means both of prosecuting her suit and of concealing it from the world. In his "character" of the lady, Antonio prepares the audience for her initial entrance by underlining her social graces— her "discourse," which is "full of rapture" yet not overvoluble, and the characteristic "look" that she "throws upon a man" causing him "to dote" upon her "sweet countenance." He quickly adds that these smiles, far from being flirtatious, bespeak "divine . . . continence" and "such noble virtue" as extends even to her "very sleeps." But his summary encomium, that she is the mirror of perfection in whom all other ladies should "dress themselves," elicits a skeptical laugh from Delio: "Fie Antonio, / You play the wire-drawer with her commendations" (I.i.190–206). The steward's praise is winning enough and wholly plausible in a future lover, but it is also hyperbolical. We think of Browning's injudiciously cordial Duchess of Ferrara, whose "looks went everywhere." When Cariola ponders in soliloquy "Whether the spirit of greatness or of woman" (I.i.504) predominates in her mistress, she speaks not only for herself but for us, for Webster insists strongly on the double-sidedness of the character and makes drama out of the tension.

The tenacious will with which Webster so often endows his major figures is evident in the Duchess from the start. Young, self-confident, and beautiful, she has already decided to take a second husband before the action begins, and we learn of her unshakable determination at an important dramatic moment—just after her brothers have pummeled her with sinister warnings and she has promised, or at least *seemed to them* to promise, "I'll never marry—" (I.i.302):

> Shall this move me? If all my royal kindred
> Lay in my way unto this marriage,
> I'd make them my low footsteps. . . .
>   (I.i.341–343)

These are brave but rash words. Although not unaware that she is inviting danger, the Duchess does betray signs of overconfidence, if not of naiveté. When Antonio during the betrothal asks in bewilderment about the ferocity of her brothers, she can answer,

> Do not think of them—
> All discord, without this circumference,
> Is only to be pitied, and not fear'd:

Yet, should they know it, time will easily
Scatter the tempest.

(I.i.468–472)

If Ferdinand and the Cardinal do not realize of what stuff their sister is made, she, equally, misestimates them. Bosola's praise of Antonio gains her trust too easily, and she worsens her plight disastrously by volunteering her husband's identity and by allowing her false confidant to determine the strategy of her escape to Loretto. She also exacerbates Ferdinand's rage needlessly by the glib tone in which she defends second marriages: "Diamonds are of most value / They say, that have pass'd through most jewellers' hands" (I.i.299–300).

Webster implants a few hints that in spite of her admirable resistance to tyranny, the Duchess is less than totally honest with herself. She may give her heart without restraint to Antonio, but she is willing to "let old wives report" that she "wink'd" (I.i.348–349) in choosing him; if this verb does not carry some slight feeling of guilt (as Brown's gloss suggests), it surely conveys a capacity for shutting her eyes to unwelcome realities. Nor does she consider that damaged reputation should be the price of her romantic unconventionality. In making Cariola witness to her legal contract *Per verba de presenti*," she stresses that concealment is everything: "To thy known secrecy I have given up / More than my life, my fame:—" (I.i.350–351). For all her courage and intelligence, the Duchess is unpracticed in court intrigue. Failing to foresee or provide in advance for emergencies, she is driven to improvise defensive measures that arouse more suspicion than they allay—wearing unfashionable gowns to disguise pregnancy, locking the palace guard into their chambers on a pretext of theft, arranging Antonio's departure for Ancona under color of his having mismanaged household accounts. Without detracting from her generosity and essential goodness, Webster manages to give the impression that danger heightens the Duchess's passion and lends it spice. Words that she puts into her husband's mouth at the tense moment when her brother has silently entered behind her back reflect an aspect of her own psychology: "Love mix'd with fear is sweetest" (III.ii.66).

The powerful effect that *The Duchess of Malfi* can make in the theatre results largely from the vitality of its heroine in the midst of so macabre and deadly a setting. What everyone remembers about the character apart from her impressive fortitude is her appetite for life. Webster of course associates her with nature and natural processes. She contrasts herself with those happy "birds that live i' th' field" that "may choose their mates" freely and "carol their sweet pleasures to the spring" (III.v.18–21); later in her prison she pursues the bird metaphor by observing darkly that "The robin-redbreast, and the nightingale, / Never live long in cages" (IV.ii.13–14). The Duchess is a free spirit in a world of stifling constriction. Strangling is the appropriate symbol of her doom, and her momentary revival, Desdemona-like, suggests the tenacity of her grip on survival. The play underlines her beauty but only as an aspect of moral character and humaneness.

Bosola mentions the "shape of loveliness" more perfectly discernible "in her tears, than in her smiles" (IV.i.7–8), a winsome presence that Webster sets in obvious antithesis to the repulsive cosmetic deformities of the grotesque Old Lady.

Royal bearing in no way undercuts the Duchess's healthy physicality. The drama does not spare us the clinical details of her pregnancy, allowing us actually to witness her "most vulturous eating of the apricocks" that Bosola offers both to confirm his suspicions that she is "breeding" (II.ii.1–3) and to degrade her with fruit ripened in "horse-dung" (II.i.140).[27] A by-product of this episode is the perception that her ready enjoyment of nature's "dainties" (II.i.143) overrides any fear of poison. The delightful scene in which she and Antonio prepare for bed shows us her lighthearted domesticity, combining it with both a sense of exalted rank and the verbal equivalent of erotic foreplay:

> *Antonio.* I must lie here.
> *Duchess.*   Must? you are a lord of mis-rule.
> *Antonio.* Indeed, my rule is only in the night.
> *Duchess.* To what use will you put me?
> *Antonio.*   We'll sleep together:—
> *Duchess.* Alas, what pleasure can two lovers find in sleep?
>   (III.ii.7–10)

Such warm and relaxed merriment provides the perfect context for Ferdinand's chilling invasion of her privacy, but the sense of humor thus revealed is all-important to Webster's effect of three-dimensional humanity. So, too, is the evidence of the Duchess's maternal instinct:

> I pray thee, look thou giv'st my little boy
> Some syrup for his cold, and let the girl
> Say her prayers, ere she sleep.
>   (IV.ii.203–205)

One of the ways in which Webster successfully conveys the impression of dual role in his title figure, insisting equally on her public image as regnant princess and on her private personality as wife and mother, is to define her internal struggle in terms of a dialectic between heroic self-assertion and religious humility. The Duchess never abandons her Christian faith *in toto*, but, in attempting to reduce her to despair, her persecutors bring her very close to the abyss into which they themselves have fallen. Her spiritual welfare requires the patience of a saint and martyr, but her role as tragic protagonist demands a more egoistic, less passive display of energy. Again, Webster does full justice to both emphases, mixing and alternating them fluidly enough to produce that mysterious amalgam of sympathy, sentiment, and awe essential to major tragedy.

Fundamentally Christian values inform both the attitudes and actions of the Duchess. She regards her secret union, despite its irregularity, as "a sacrament o' th' church" (IV.i.39) and clearly intends to have it publicly solemnized as soon as this should become feasible: "We are now man and wife, and 'tis the church / That must but echo this . . ." (I.i.492–493). Her belief in the afterlife is strong. She parts from her husband in the hope of rejoining him "in the eternal church" (III.v.71), she speaks of the "excellent company / In th' other world" that a condemned person "Know[s]" she will "meet" (IV.ii.211–212), and she greets death on her knees, confident of entering "heaven-gates" (IV.ii.232). Bosola is impressed by her willingness to die and by a quiet composure under duress that implies spiritual depth. He speaks of her "noble" behavior, of the "majesty" she lends "to adversity," and of "her silence" that "expresseth more than if she spake" (IV.i.5–10). She can ask pardon of her brother at one point (IV.i.31) and, with becoming piety, forgive her executioners. Webster suggests that her retention of sanity in the midst of howling madmen is "a miracle" and adds to the imagery of divine judgment ("molten brass" and "flaming sulphur") a distant echo from Isaiah that perhaps associates the Duchess with messianic sacrifice:

> I am acquainted with sad misery,
> As the tann'd galley-slave is with his oar;
> Necessity makes me suffer constantly,
> And custom makes it easy. . . .
> (IV.ii.23–30)[28]

But, of course, the religion of the Duchess is not free of conflict or inconsistency. Feigning a pilgrimage, what Cariola calls "jesting with religion," gives her conscience no pause, and she is impatient with her servant for objecting to the ruse: "Thou art a superstitious fool— / Prepare us instantly for our departure" (III.ii.317–320). She is torn between repudiating the tendency of her baser-born spouse to accept injustice too supinely ("Must I, like to a slave-born Russian, / Account it praise to suffer tyranny?") and the orthodox notion that earthly chastisement may be a necessary form of divine guidance:

> And yet, O Heaven, thy heavy hand is in't.
> I have seen my little boy oft scourge his top
> And compar'd myself to't: naught made me e'er
> Go right but heaven's scourge-stick.
> (III.v.76–81)

She questions whether identity, as human beings know it, continues after death ("Dost thou think we shall know one another, / In th'other world?" [IV.ii.18–19]), and her pessimism at its lowest ebb takes on a tone close to nihilism: "I could curse the stars . . . nay the world / To its first chaos" (IV.i.96–99). She threatens to teach her children to curse before they can prattle "since they were born accurs'd" (III.v.115), and she begs "heaven" to "cease crowning martyrs" long enough to "punish" her brothers (IV.i.107–108). At one juncture she seems ready to pervert penitence into suicide: "The church enjoins fasting: / I'll starve myself to death" (IV.i.75–76). She moves from a savage hostility toward Bosola

("Were I a man / I'd beat that counterfeit face into thy other" [III.v.117–118]) to an embrace of the death wish: "I long to bleed" (IV.i.109).

The dynamics of the fourth act—what might be called the "passion" of the Duchess—are built upon her psychic progression from outward control through frustration, rage, and near-despair to a deeper kind of serenity rooted in self-recognition, the tragic acceptance of evil, and quickened religious faith. As Sir Walter Raleigh, another great prisoner, wrote at about the same time that Webster was composing his play, "It is . . . Death alone that can suddenly make man to know himselfe."[29] First we hear of her sorrow in terms of its external manifestations—of her majestic bearing, of her tears, silences, and "melancholy . . . fortify'd / With a strange disdain"; but Bosola observes that this very "restraint" causes her to "apprehend / Those pleasures she's kept from" (IV.i.11–15) with emotional intensity. After the gift of the dead hand and her exposure to the wax corpses, the Duchess desires only to escape from life, to join her husband in death. Informed that she must continue to live, she begins to suffer mental "daggers," describing herself as having forfeited even her sentience, as "a thing so wretch'd / As cannot pity itself" (IV.i.89–90). At this point she comes near to losing her self-possession, and Webster marks her transition to a more precarious state of soul by her abandonment of prayer: "I'll go pray: no, / I'll go curse:—" (IV.i.95–96). Impotent anger follows as she thrashes out at the hostile stars, the seasons, the very universe, and as Bosola reminds her tauntingly that "the stars shine still" (IV.i.100). Ironically, his underlining of her cosmic helplessness also asserts a remote and mysterious order, suggests that, even in so black a world as Webster's Italy, light is not wholly extinguishable. In trying to loosen her hold upon coherence, Bosola unwittingly affirms that, in some sort, it exists.

The battery of torments to which the Duchess is subjected seems to shift emphasis from physical shock to mental disturbance—from mortuary and Grand Guignol horrors to the rout of madmen, conceived of as a means of forcing disintegration of the mind upon her. The protracted antimasque, made up of music, dance, lyric verse, and satiric prose, is an orderly representation of chaos, a grotesque ballet of rational collapse that not only puts the lady's psychic strength to its severest test but that, in doing so, also nerves her to combat fear in its most existential form, the threat to her very selfhood. Out of the proliferating references to physical dissolution in the tradition of *contemptus mundi*, out of the wild confusion of Bedlam identities and Bosola's protean disguises, the Duchess somehow plucks the fierceness to overpower despair and to recapture the sense of who and what she is. Her torturers try to shatter her inner core by surrounding her with a kaleidoscopic swirl of frenzied movement, sepulchral chatter, and macabre ritual, and so attempting to erase the boundaries that separate her from her enforced context. But in a person of the Duchess's independence the barrier between sanity and insanity is not so easily breached. They succeed only in prompting her to more resilient self-definition: "I am Duchess of Malfi still" (IV.ii.142).[30] She stands for a moment against staggering external and internal forces like a female Coriolanus, "As if a man were author of himself / And knew no other kin" (*Coriolanus*, V.iii.36–37).

This reaffirmation is more than a simple assertion of the self as dramatized earlier in the lady's defiance of marital conventions. It implies spiritual enlargement and growth, deepened perception, indeed a fundamental readjustment of values. Certainly it includes the readiness to face execution in an expanded frame of reference, for the Duchess no longer seeks merely to escape further suffering:

> tell my brothers
> That I perceive death, now I am well awake,
> Best gift is they can give, or I can take.
> (IV.ii.223–225)

Regal calm becomes the outward expression both of protest against injustice and of tragic acceptance of the inevitable. Perhaps some such ambivalence is to be inferred from her puzzling image of death's doors as double-hinged and opening "both ways" (IV.ii.222). At any rate, authority and dignified submission in about equal measure define the Duchess's voice as she approaches her end, and the two tones blend movingly in her death speech:

> Pull, and pull strongly, for your able strength
> Must pull down heaven upon me:—
> Yet stay; heaven-gates are not so highly arch'd
> As princes' palaces, they that enter there
> Must go upon their knees.— [*Kneels.*] Come violent death,
> Serve for mandragora to make me sleep!
> Go tell my brothers, when I am laid out,
> They then may feed in quiet.
> (IV.ii.230–237)

The Duchess does not go gentle into her good night, but in addition to the aristocratic poise there is a feeling of appropriate release from long struggle and a satisfying sense of tragic closure.

Like Gloucester in *King Lear*, Webster's heroine moves from limited awareness (with perhaps a touch of self-deception and complacency) through torture and despondency to a deeper comprehension of evil and to a more accepting and transcendent vision of reality. But Webster makes her seem sturdier than Gloucester by virtue of her vulnerability as a woman and by adding the stimulus to mental breakdown to which even Lear succumbs and to which she proves miraculously impervious. The sanity that the Duchess preserves even at the heart of her long nightmare lends her a special quality of heroism. It nullifies in a sense Cariola's earlier comment about the "fearful madness" (I.i.506) of marrying Antonio, and it also prepares the theatrical contrast to Ferdinand's lunacy after her exemplary life has been blotted out. The whole spectacle of the Duchess's suffering and death represents a dramatic verification in a profounder sense than Antonio could know of his distilled praise of his future wife: "She stains the time past, lights the time to come" (I.i.209). Indeed, the tragedy does characterize its title figure as a source of effulgence enclosed temporally and spatially by darkness. And Webster works this symbolism almost surrealistically into the tenebrous staging of the echo scene where Antonio, musing significantly on ruins, suddenly glimpses the image of his murdered wife as "a face folded in sorrow" illuminated by "a clear light" (V.iii.44–45).

Our complexity of response to the Duchess as a personality in whom egoism and religious submission are somehow coordinated would seem to be related, as so often in Webster, to her own consciousness of self as a tragic protagonist. This reflexiveness, like that of Shakespeare's Richard II (whom Webster might have recalled), may imply a tendency to solipsism. Somewhat indulgently, perhaps, she can regard herself—or enjoy being regarded—as an appropriate subject for the painter, the sculptor, or the tragedian:

> *Duchess.*   who do I look like now?
> *Cariola.* Like to your picture in the gallery,
>   A deal of life in show, but none in practice;
>   Or rather like some reverend monument
>   Whose ruins are even pitied.
> *Duchess.*   Very proper:
>   And Fortune seems only to have her eyesight
>   To behold my tragedy. . . .
>   (IV.ii.30–36)

But the Duchess's response to or use of these artistic and theatrical allusions also reflects an attempt (as is traditional in revenge tragedy) to objectify and therefore to understand and place her own experience. Silence is more threatening to her than noise because it throws her back upon the formless terrors of her own worst imaginings. Like Richard, she needs to hear sad stories of the death of kings as a way of enlarging and, in one sense, depersonalizing her situation:

> *Duchess.*   sit down;
>   Discourse to me some dismal tragedy.
> *Cariola.* O, 'twill increase your melancholy.
> *Duchess.*   Thou art deceiv'd
>   To hear of greater grief would lessen mine—. . . .
>   (IV.ii.7–10)

In spite of the obvious analogue to Shakespeare, this is a far cry from the sentimentalism of Richard's "Tell thou the lamentable tale of me / And send the hearers weeping to their beds" (*Richard II*, V.i.44–45).[31]

As a royal and necessarily ceremonial figure, the Duchess is by definition a player of roles; her acceptance of the tragic role forced upon her by her cruel brothers and by her own desire for emotional fulfillment is more a means of self-confrontation than a mawkish escape from reality: "I account this world a tedious theatre, / For I do play a part in't 'gainst my will" (IV.i.84–85). She has earlier complained of the topsy-turvydom of a state in which decency and genuineness must disguise themselves to the forces of corrupt power: "O misery! methinks unjust actions / Should wear these masks and curtains, and not we:—" (III.ii.158–159). By seeing herself as one of the numerous tragic "princes" with which "Fortune's wheel is overcharg'd" (III.v.96), the Duchess connects herself psychologically with a whole pattern of history and literature, at once establishing a traditional context for her fall and serving, for the moment, as her own chorus. Nor does Webster invoke the *Mirror for Magistrates* concept lazily or as a mere cliché. Antonio introduces the image of the looking glass, as noted earlier, when he suggests in his "character" of the Duchess that she is the model for lesser ladies (I.i.204–205). The familiar metaphor then comes alive in an unexpectedly dramatic way when "the glass" (III.ii.1) is imported as a stage property. We mark the downward acceleration of her ill fortune from the ironic moment that the Duchess, looking into her glass as she undresses, observes that her "hair tangles" and begins to "wax gray" (III.ii.53–59). It is this same glass, apparently, that a few seconds later reflects not only her own changing image but the freezing presence of her twin. A perception about identity is wedded to the sudden awareness of external danger, a link with which the tragedy in other respects is much concerned. (Both Ferdinand and the Cardinal, as we have noted, also have to contend with alien terrors in the form of self-images—shadows or reflections in water.) The Duchess of Malfi not only appropriates some of Richard II's tragic self-consciousness; she also has a "mirror scene" of her own—one as fully theatrical and thematically suggestive as his.

*   *   *

The intricately woven pattern of oppositions and convergences so remarkable in Webster's characterization of the Duchess and her brothers carries over into his treatment of Antonio and Bosola. Although the former is presented as a victim and the latter as a felon, Webster makes almost as much of their common ground as of their contrariety. The play sets up an ethical polarity between the two only to blur it by suggesting that, although each serves as dramatic foil to the other, each, too, participates—to some degree unwittingly—in a psychological cross-fertilization or interchange of values and perspectives that makes the relationship dynamic rather than static. Both are underlings, young, intelligent, traveled, and morally sensitive, in a world that encourages ambition even as it rewards, frustrates, or punishes it copiously. Both depend wholly on their social betters for recognition and advancement, and, notwithstanding that Antonio manages to preserve his integrity in a corrupt environment while Bosola fails to do so, Webster makes us suspect that in different circumstances the contrast might have been reversed. Ferdinand opines that Antonio would be "far fitter" (I.i.229) for spy work than Bosola before the Cardinal persuades him otherwise. Both are men of action and good horsemen, the one having won Ferdinand's riding contest and the other, "very valiant" (I.i.76) according to even his severest critic, being rewarded with the Duchess's "provisorship o' th' horse" (I.i.286). Both tend toward preachment and moralizing and, concerning each other, are notably acerbic. Both too attract female attentions without inviting them, although Bosola only feigns affection for Julia in order to use her as a source of information whereas Antonio responds genuinely to his lady's proposal of love. The roles of passive consort to a duchess and cynical toady to a duke are felt as alternative possibilities in a sycophantic court where probity and fortune stand in close but unstable relation to each other. Bosola's bitter comment that it is a "Miserable age, where only the reward / Of doing well, is the doing of it" (I.i.31–32) reveals the misanthrope, but it also contains a disturbing truth. If Bosola is a fallen Antonio, a satiric distortion of the faithful servant, Antonio represents to Bosola (and to us) an image of the cynic's potentially better self, a kind of alter ego who shows him his deformity.

Webster introduces the pair within the first thirty lines of the tragedy so as to emphasize at once both the contrast and the parallel. Their principal function in this opening is to serve as a sort of double chorus, announcing, as it were, two distinct outlooks—more and less idealistic—each with its recognizable voice. Antonio in his encomium of the French court and in his description of Bosola as a "court-gall" whose "railing" against the impieties of the time thinly veils his "lecherous," "covetous," "proud," "Bloody," and "envious" nature (I.i.23–27), establishes himself as a generally reliable and reasonably objective spokesman, a man who admires virtue for its own sake and who can tell the difference between genuine candor and hypocritical or self-interested carping. Antonio shows himself to be earnest and perceptive, but his goodness has yet to be tried in the forge of suffering. Bosola, though also repelled by corruption, proclaims himself the voice of jaundiced pessimism, and we immediately identify his animus as intense, obsessive, and more deeply colored by personal failure and self-hatred than by a desire for public reform. Then, as the drama unfolds, the two characters move ironically closer together.

Bosola's change is, of course, the more fundamental and dramatic, and Webster partly symbolizes the emergence of an altered identity through the various disguises or roles the character adopts in Act IV. Reluctant but growing admiration for both the Duchess and her spouse quickens his conscience, and his perception of Ferdinand's ingratitude pushes him one degree further into a radical reappraisal of himself and of his entire situation. Coming at length to revere the Duchess almost as devotedly as Antonio, he renounces allegiance to his cruel master and attempts to ally himself with the persecuted husband. What loving the Duchess had done for Antonio, torturing and killing her does for Bosola. After the execution, both men are similarly "haunted" (V.ii.346) by a sense of her presence, if not by an actual manifestation of it, although Bosola's "vision," unlike Antonio's, is prompted by guilt.

Antonio's shift is subtler and less obvious than Bosola's, but it, too, is perceptible. Marriage to a head of state draws Bologna, a stranger of sorts in his own country, from the innocent bewilderment of a more or less detached outsider into the double vortex of romantic love and power politics, awakening him in the process to the necessities of desperate and devious defense.[32] Like Bosola, he must pretend to be what he is not, even to the extent of feigning the malcontent's criminality and to taking up his characteristic complaint against "the inconstant / And rotten ground of service" (III.ii.198–199). The Cardinal, although we cannot trust him to report Antonio aright, suggests that the Duchess's lover, presumably grown cynical since his elevation, now "account[s] religion / But a school-name" and may attend mass merely "for fashion of the world" (V.ii.133–134). If Bosola at the end is moved to emulate Antonio's virtue, Antonio also takes on something of his counterpart's pessimism. As a dying man, he describes "all our quest of greatness" as a boy's pursuit of "bubbles, blown in th' air" and the "Pleasure of life" as "only the good hours / Of an ague" (V.iv.64–68). This is little different in tone from Bosola's own dying words that center on "this gloomy world" and the "deep pit of darkness" in which a "womanish and fearful mankind" (V.v.100–102) is condemned to live.

It is one of Webster's most theatrical ironies that the belated convert to Antonio's honorable ways should kill his would-be friend by mistake—"In a mist"; but the irony is reinforced when the crazed Ferdinand also stabs his ally, the Cardinal. The same irrationality seems to affect moral and immoral allegiances alike. Bosola's metaphor, "Such a mistake as I have often seen / In a play" (V.v.94–96), applies equally well to both confusions. And, lest we miss the curious way in which Antonio and Bosola become symbolically, even tragically, identified, Webster invokes the same phrase for both. After his agonizing crisis of conscience, Bosola wishes to "see that wretched thing, Antonio, / Above all sights i' th' world" (V.ii.144–145), and in their final encounter Antonio then describes himself to Bosola as "A most wretched thing" (V.iv.48). In the following scene, Malateste echoes these words again by applying them to Bosola: "Thou wretched thing of blood" (V.v.92). All these examples, of course, echo the words of the Duchess, who in a moment of despondency had described herself as "a thing so wretch'd" (IV.i.89) as to be incapable of pitying herself. Finally, the phrase is expanded to include the Aragonian brothers, those "wretched eminent things" (V.v.113) to whose bodies Delio points in the closing speech of the play. As the two pairs of corpses make graphic, Bosola has become Antonio's twin "in quality" as surely as Ferdinand and the Cardinal are also "twins," but tragedy fuzzes the moral distinctions, reducing them all, whether "eminent" or humble, whether wicked or good, to "wretched things." The basic truth that death is no respecter of persons is made powerfully visual.

Even with Antonio, the most transparent and least complex of the major figures, Webster promotes a certain ambivalence or uncertainty of response. Actors understandably find the role ungrateful, overshadowed as it is by the tragic prominence of the Duchess and by the greater weight, flamboyance, and volatility of the villains. Given the assumptions of Renaissance tragedy, it is far from easy to represent moral heroism, especially in a man, in a posture that combines social inferiority with political impotence. Nevertheless, even within the narrow frame imposed by his plot, the playwright does what he can to give Antonio the dramatic interest peculiar to his unusual situation, and he accomplishes this in part by forcing the audience to modify what they observe directly of the character in the light of statements and opinions about him that originate from other sources. Although some of this indirect characterization is unreliable and must be assessed according to the trustworthiness of the speaker or judged in relation to a particular dramatic context, the viewer cannot ignore it. Thus, the Antonio who finally emerges in the total consciousness of the playgoer is a compound of primary and secondary impressions that may seem inconsistent or even contradictory. Of course this is theoretically the case with nearly all dramatic characters, but Webster seems to rely upon the technique more heavily in Bologna's case in order to supply coloring to a person who is functionally less exciting than those with whom we must compare him. And the matter is complicated further by the fact that Webster uses Antonio neutrally at the opening of the play as a presenter to give thumbnail sketches or introductory "characters" of the other major figures who appear before us.

Accordingly, Antonio is a character to whom we react with greater or lesser detachment and with greater or lesser sympathy as the drama manipulates us. He comes off as the maker of choric statements about Bosola, Ferdinand, the Cardinal, and the Duchess that we are inclined to accept at face value, as well as a devoted husband, father, and friend. But, depending upon whether the speaker is the affectionate Duchess, the class-obsessed duke, or the sneering Bosola, he is also "an upright treasurer" (I.i.372) and "complete man" (I.i.435), a "slave" smelling "of ink and counters" who "ne'er in's life look'd like a gentleman, / But in the audit-time" (III.iii.72–74), and "this precise fellow . . . the duchess' bawd" (II.iii.65–66). And of course Bosola, the last speaker, is himself inconsistent on the subject of Antonio. On the one hand, the intelligencer seems merely to reflect vulgar opinion, as when, for instance, he advises the Duchess to "Forget this base, low fellow" (III.v.117). (A pilgrim at Loretto has recently referred to the Duchess's spouse as a "mean" [III.iv.26] person.) On the other hand, he offers the warmest and most extended praise of Antonio in the play: Bologna is "a most unvalu'd jewel," "an excellent / Courtier, and most faithful," "a soldier" who neither over- nor undervalues himself, a man whose "breast" is "fill'd with all perfection," a worthy and virtuous servant ruined by the changeability of "a prince's favour" and "the malice of the world," and, finally, "this trophy of a man" (III.ii.248–292). To be sure, this glowing tribute is partly a device of entrapment, for Bosola instantly betrays the Duchess to her brothers after drawing from her the knowledge that her steward is also her husband. But Webster does not permit us to discount such praise as mere trickery. Bosola, as his later behavior confirms, believes his own words and cannot help admiring the man he has been employed to expose and will later be commissioned to destroy.

Even if we could ignore everything but what Antonio himself says and does, our focus would still be blurred. Bologna, who has been abroad and would therefore presumably be out of touch with the great personages at the court of Amalfi, is the person to whom Delio applies for information about them. Antonio thus appears as both naive and sophisticated by turns. A certain innocence of the great world is implied by his astonishment in the wooing scene and by his attempt, in the face of Delio's justifiable skepticism, to work "A friendly reconcilement" with the Cardinal by means of a surprise midnight visit that "May draw the poison out of him" (V.ii.71–72). Yet he wears the punctilious "formal" dress of French fashion (I.i.3), is a shrewd observer of human nature, and is acutely (and humbly) aware of the "madness" (I.i.420) of ambition. When labor pains suddenly beset his wife, he is "lost in amazement" (II.i.173) and utterly dependent upon Delio for direction, but he can also be a competent deceiver when the even greater crisis of Ferdinand's sudden intrusion requires it. Delio suggests the increased strain by remarking (after an absence) that his friend's face looks "somewhat leaner" (III.i.10).

Antonio's views on marriage also seem a little unstable. In the wooing scene, Bologna speaks in favor of singleness as depriving a man of no more than "the weak delight" of seeing his child "ride a-cock-horse / Upon a painted stick" or hearing him "chatter / Like a taught starling" (I.i.400–403). But he has just advised his mistress to "provide for a good husband" and to "marry again" (I.i.387–392). After the secret wedding, when Cariola announces that she will never take a husband, Antonio launches upon an elaborate series of mythological exempla in support of marriage:

> O fie upon this single life! forgo it!
> We read how Daphne, for her peevish flight,
> Became a fruitless bay tree. . . .
>
> (III.ii.24–26)

His speech deprecating marriage is defensively modest, a rationalization of sorts and by no means irreconcilable with the two favorable ones, but the effect is nevertheless to raise a question in our minds about his true feelings.

More disturbingly, Webster suggests a curious combination of passivity and aggression in the Duchess's husband. When Ferdinand silently enters her private apartment, Antonio is offstage but within earshot of threats directed specifically to him. His failure to come to his wife's side until after the duke's exit smacks of timorousness, even though, when he does reappear, he comes armed with a pistol and a statement about his eagerness to confront the enemy. Moreover, Antonio follows his lady's lead when the couple are driven into exile. It is the Duchess who determines that for safety's sake they must go their separate ways, and he who meekly accepts her decision. But Antonio is not always so unassertive. He is actively hostile to Bosola, calling him "Saucy slave" and "impudent snake," and he threatens to "pull [him] up by the roots" (II.iii.36–38). Then, in rebellion against cautious inaction, he is willing to stake everything on his visit to the Cardinal:

> to live thus is not indeed to live:
> It is a mockery, and abuse of life—
> I will not henceforth save myself by halves;
> Lose all, or nothing.
>
> (V.iii.48–51)

Abjectly conscious of his "unworthiness" (I.i.430) at first, Antonio comes to believe later that his love is "warrantable" (III.ii.149), then greets separation from his beloved with stoical but essentially Christian resolve:

> since we must part
> Heaven hath a hand in't; but no otherwise
> Than as some curious artist takes in sunder
> A clock or watch when it is out of frame,
> To bring 't in better order.
>
> (III.v.61–65)

Webster portrays a rather solemn young man, so awed by the exalted rank of his wife that he never presumes, even in their most private moments, to call her by her Christian name. At the same time, the dramatist does not deny Antonio a strain of importunate levity. The concealed husband, a prisoner in his own wife's bedroom, can tease his Duchess (in the presence of Cariola) about the arduousness of satisfying her sexual desires and of being her ruler "only in the night" (III.ii.8).

If it is tempting to explain these apparent discordancies in Antonio's makeup as mere carelessness or inattention on the playwright's part, we must recall Webster's acknowledged interest in the mysterious unpredictabilities of personality and behavior. As is often the way in Websterian characterization, the general outlines of Antonio's identity are clear, defined, as they must be, by his function in the story as a sympathetic servant, lover, husband, father, friend, and victim. But Webster beclouds the portrait just enough to raise a few unsettling doubts about the man's weaknesses, limitations, and inconsistencies, and to remind us latently that no human nature, probingly observed, is ever susceptible of easy or merely sentimental delineation. A perception that underlies all of Webster's most compelling drama concerns the disequilibria, both within the psyche and outside it, that threaten a secure or fixed estimation of the self. And it is the tenuous hold on what Delio calls "integrity" that elevates the toughness to confront and resist brutal attacks upon self-confidence to such heroic stature in Webster's world. Compared to the more dynamic dramatis personae of *The Duchess*, Antonio exhibits a relatively settled nature, but he is no more immune to the unsettling conditions of a tragically uncertain universe than anyone else in the play. Appropriately, it is Bosola, in important respects Antonio's opposite, who embodies the protean aspect of human identity in an extreme form.

Ferdinand's tool-villain is Webster's classic example of the divided man. Indeed, he represents such a conflation of violent and reflective, repellent and sympathetic traits that he seems almost to approach Shakespeare's Hamlet in psychological complexity. Critics have been so impressed by the shifty turns and moral contradictions of the character and by his remarkable expansion from Painter that they have sometimes tended to make him, rather than the Duchess, the central figure of the play. The 1623 quarto, in a curious departure from the convention of listing noble personages before lesser ones, puts him at the head of the cast roster. Obviously, Bosola is essential to Webster's design, and, unlike the Cardinal, Antonio, or even the Duchess, he is prominently onstage in all five acts from the opening to the closing scene. Yet he is neither more nor less significant than the other major characters, with *all* of whom he interacts. At the deepest level Bosola is a man in quest of psychological and moral authenticity, but Webster presents his pursuit of identity as an intermittently conscious process involving much escapism and attempted self-deception. Because his fullest recognition of self coincides with his death, Bosola possesses tragic stature in his own right. But he is also the catalyst by means of whom the Duchess achieves her own tragic self-realization. In addition, Bosola is the play's most relentless and vitriolic commentator, a moralist deeply corrupted by vice and a criminal whose conscience no dedication to depravity can wholly anesthetize. More vulnerable to goodness than he believes possible, he is also an autodidact who cannot finally exempt himself from the condemnation with which he so readily scourges others. He has a certain self-awareness from the start: "Sometimes the devil doth preach" (I.i.291); but, ironically, he feels the sting of his own lash more acutely than those for whom he intends it.

Profound cynicism appears to govern Bosola from his first entrance, where we see him as a favor seeker, "haunt[ing]" the Cardinal (whom he has served in the past), voicing his typical discontent about being "slighted," and implying that even those who pursue "honesty" are "arrant knaves" (I.i.29–43) if necessity compels them to be. Experience has taught him that survivors in a politicized world cannot afford virtue, and that servitude as a galley slave is the characteristic reward of loyalty at court or crippled hobbling from hospital to hospital of bravery on the battlefield. When Ferdinand enlists him as a spy by giving him gold, he instinctively responds, "Whose throat must I cut?" (I.i.249). Bosola never manages to shake off his "melancholy" view of general human depravity, defensive though it is in great part. Even in Act V, after he has shed "penitent fountains" (IV.ii.365) of tears over the body of the Duchess and been unnerved by the "fatal judgement" that has "fall'n upon . . . Ferdinand" (V.ii.85–86), the old habit of mind persists. On discovering that the Cardinal has poisoned Julia, his initial reaction is to blurt out with almost comic indignation, "O foolish woman, / Couldst not thou have poison'd him?" (V.ii.286–287). Bosola may pluck a meager comfort from dying in "so good a quarrel" (V.v.100) as revenge for the death of the Duchess, but, although he claims that his own participation in her murder was "Much 'gainst [his] own good nature" (V.v.86), he neither asks nor expects reconciliation with anyone. Whatever the spiritual destiny of "worthy minds" such as Antonio and the Duchess, his "is another voyage" (V.v.103–105). The pessimism here is unrelieved, and the ship metaphor of course recalls the agnostic departure of Vittoria's soul "driven" to some unknowable destination "in a black storm" (*The White Devil*, V.vi.248–249). Bosola can find very little to hope for in the world. Even figures like Antonio and the Duchess who enkindle his respect seem to him exceptional—ephemeral pinpoints of light in the "shadow, or deep pit of darkness" (V.v.101).

But Webster encourages us to glimpse very different possibilities beneath this armor of negativism. Indeed, the very intensity of Bosola's alienation bespeaks not only personal disappointment but profound disgust with a system of patronage that victimizes altruism and promotes ruthlessness, hypocrisy, and fraud. Bosola is a man of fierce pride and independent spirit, expected to behave like a sycophant or "flattering pander" (I.i.52) to men less creative than himself. He reflects the plight of many university men in Webster's England, educated in classical literature and history, bred in a climate of liberal, antiauthoritarian, and frequently Puritan sympathies, endowed with a high opinion of their native capacities, and forced to compete for too few positions in church and state or to grovel for livings that they regarded as demeaning or otherwise unsatisfying. Marlowe gives us a vivid portrait of the type in *Edward II* when he makes the younger Spencer cynically advise Baldock, his fellow dependent, on how best to rise in the world of power politics:

> Then, Baldock, you must cast the scholar off
> And learn to court it like a gentleman.
> 'Tis not a black coat and a little band,
> A velvet-caped cloak, faced before with serge,
> And smelling to a nosegay all the day,
> Or holding a napkin in your hand,
> Or saying a long grace at a table's end,
> Or making low legs to a nobleman,
> Or looking downward with your eyelids close,
> And saying 'Truly, an't may please your honor,'
> Can get you any favor with great men;
> You must be proud, bold, pleasant, resolute,
> And now and then stab, as occasion serves.
>
> (II.i.31–43)[33]

335

This a lesson that Webster's hangers-on have learned only too well. At Padua, the "nursery of arts" as Shakespeare's Lucentio calls it in *The Taming of the Shrew* (I.i.2), Bosola would have been nourished on a humanistic curriculum committed to the doctrine that private virtue and civilized government are coextensive. To depend upon the Aragonian brothers could not but disillusion him bitterly. Delio ridicules Bosola as having aspired to be "a speculative man" (III.iii.47) by trivializing history (questioning the color of Achilles' beard or the symmetry of Caesar's nose), but this report is obviously a hostile caricature. Bosola is no fool, and Webster dramatizes him as a man whose genuine talent has been wasted, a spoiled idealist who has tried to suppress his finer nature in order to accommodate himself to the role of soldier of fortune, bully, spy, and murderer.

That Bosola rejects the stereotypical oiliness of the paid informer, even though he consents to serve as one, appears from the exaggerated scurrility and brusqueness of his speech. Like so many malcontents before him (Jaques, Malevole, Thersites, Apemantus, Vindice), he retreats to the pose of social critic partly as a means of assuaging his wounded ego. Nevertheless, Bosola's need to assert nonconformity has roots in moral outrage and goes deeper than facile affectation. The harsh attacks upon the Old Lady's painting and Castruchio's cuckoldom and social ambition are purposely excessive. The shallowness, hypocrisy, and stupidity of such figures deserve reproof, but Webster makes us feel that these particular targets are too easy and conventional and that Bosola wastes too much rhetorical energy on them. It is otherwise with the Cardinal and Ferdinand, whom Bosola also dares to satirize although his place depends on their favor. He can sneer at the prelate's "divinity" (I.i.41), insinuating, probably in his hearing, that the churchman is in no position to preach on the subject of honesty, and he is even less circumspect in standing up to Ferdinand, whom he punctures for boasting: "you / Are your own chronicle too much; and grossly / Flatter yourself" (III.i.87–89). Significantly, the duke, who is grudging of praise, acknowledges that his creature is friend enough not to flatter his master's defects. Bosola functions in some respects like a licensed fool, forever goading his betters, but more courageously than Lear's Fool or Feste, for he lacks their security and capacity for inspiring affection. Moreover, Bosola is incapable of a professional fool's detachment. Antonio's refusal to trust him he slurs as evidence of low "breeding" (III.v.52)—surely an instance of the pot calling the kettle black. For someone who pompously insists that "Man stands amaz'd to see his deformity / In any other creature but himself" (II.i.50–51), Bosola has curious blind spots.

A point often overlooked is Bosola's essential loneliness, his unsatisfied need for human attachment. In the nature of his calling, a professional intelligencer isolates himself from friendship, and Bosola feels the deprivation acutely. He cannot conceal his pain, for instance, on learning that the Cardinal, his former patron, withheld full trust ("He did suspect me wrongfully" [I.i.239]), and he warns Ferdinand not to make the same mistake:

> Yet take heed;
> For to suspect a friend unworthily
> Instructs him the way to suspect you,
> And prompts him to deceive you.
>
> (I.i.243–246)

After the murder of the Duchess, when Ferdinand announces his hatred for the accomplice, Bosola feels not only guilt but betrayal:

> Let me know
> Wherefore I should be thus neglected? sir,
> I served your tyranny; and rather strove
> To satisfy yourself, than all the world;
> And though I loath'd the evil, yet I lov'd
> You that did counsel it; and rather sought
> To appear a true servant, than an honest man.
>
> (IV.ii.327–333)

Bosola's so-called conversion to the side of Antonio represents not only a moral reawakening but a continuing and increasingly desperate search for someone worthy of his commitment. Much of the agony in Bosola's developing self-recognition comes from the knowledge that he not only invested his friendship in persons incapable of reciprocating it but that he killed—in one case involuntarily—the two people who might have done so. In denying his own better self he has destroyed the possibility of its being acknowledged by others, and Webster shows us a negative embodiment (the Duchess is his positive one) of the truth that self-respect is the only foundation upon which love can be built. In one of his dying speeches Bosola sums up his role as miscast "actor" in the evils of the play—"Much 'gainst mine own good nature, yet i' th' end / Neglected" (V.v.86–87). He takes his metaphor in part from Ferdinand's earlier rejection of him:

> For thee, (as we observe in tragedies
> That a good actor many times is curs'd
> For playing a villain's part) I hate thee for't:
> And for my sake say thou hast done much ill well.
>
> (IV.ii.288–291)

The sad word "neglected" is applied three times in the play to Bosola, once by Antonio and twice by the character himself. Clearly it implies more than scant material reward, although it obviously encompasses this meaning. Bosola dies as he had lived, unloved by himself and by others—"i' th' end / Neglected."

The need to be loyal, even if necessary to so depraved and undependable a figure as Ferdinand, goes far to explaining Bosola's ambivalent feelings toward all of the major characters. It accounts for the mixture of love and hatred the duke's half-willing servant feels for his master, and it suggests how he can continue to persecute the Duchess and her spouse even as his respect for them burgeons. Bosola is a man whose moral imperatives and emotional needs are fatally

337

at odds, and who can only live with the contradiction by foisting upon morality and feeling alike a spirit of acrid negation. Even such rewards and pleasures as the world affords are, for him, inseparable from contamination. He remarks cynically that his "corruption / Grew out of horse-dung" (I.i.286–287), implying that rottenness of character is the inevitable consequence of being appointed (through Ferdinand's procurement) to the Duchess's provisorship of horse; and later he cannot forbear to tell his mistress that the "delicate fruit" that she believes "restorative" was "ripen[ed]" in the same excrement (II.i.140–144). The dung-cured apricocks may have an emblematic significance that reaches beyond their immediate context, for the cross relationship, or even the interdependence, between beauty and ugliness, between the attractive and the repulsive, is a pervasively Websterian theme. The uneasy collocation of opposites fits the personal psychology of Bosola himself. It may also be read in an extended sense as a comment on the complex moral relationship between him and the Duchess.

Bosola begins with the more or less unexamined assumption that the masking of true identity is unavoidable if one would survive, let alone advance, in court politics. He may rail self-righteously against the face painting of ladies or the hypocrisy of judges who "smile upon a prisoner" and then "hang him" (II.i.9–10), but he seems also to accept the principle that only a fool would wear his heart on his sleeve in so treacherous an environment. When he learns that the Cardinal may have distrusted "some oblique character" in his own countenance, he expresses surprise at the implied naiveté of those who rely on "physiognomy," for "There's no more credit to be given to th' face / Than to a sick man's urine, which some call / The physician's whore, because she cozens him:—" (I.i.234–238). Bosola is the most consistent player of roles in the tragedy, and Webster suggests that he becomes so accustomed to the practice of deception that he is startled by simple honesty either in himself or in others. Even the scabrous satire, with its didactic tone betrays a self-conscious theatricality. But Bosola strikes postures and puts on masks, not only to protect himself against injury in the Machiavellian world but also to inure himself to that world. In becoming one of Ferdinand's "familiars," a "very quaint invisible devil, in flesh" (I.i.259–260), he must suppress his natural manhood and become, in a sense, "invisible" to his own conscience; after all, it is intolerable to be constantly reminding himself that his new allegiance makes him "an impudent traitor" and will ultimately "take [him] to hell" (I.i.265–266). The tragic irony that Webster dramatizes in Bosola is that the flight from selfhood through the conscious adoption of disguises brings him into sustained contact with the moral and psychological force of the Duchess. As he tries futilely to separate her through terror from a saving confidence in her own personhood, he calls forth the very strength of character that he had tried so assiduously to discard in himself. We might say that Bosola conducts a psychological experiment whose unexpected result prompts an upheaval in his own soul and hence a moral reorientation of major significance. His attempt to submerge identity in evil actually fosters its re-emergence. The *saeva indignatio* of Bosola's rhetorical question, "What thing is this outward form of man / To be belov'd?" (II.i.45–46), turns out to have implications for the speaker of which he only becomes aware when the Duchess, struggling with her own existential crisis, forces upon him a fresh and disquieting self-examination.

The change in Bosola is gradual, but it begins in Act II, where he waxes eloquent in praise of Antonio. We should notice here that he is motivated not only by the opportunity to inveigle the Duchess into trusting him but also by his genuine revulsion at hearing the palace guard debunk a man of spotless reputation the moment he is in trouble. In Antonio's "prosperity" these men would have suffered any indignity, would indeed "have prostituted their daughters to his lust," to secure his favor, and now they "drop off" like "lice" (III.ii.228–235). When the delighted Duchess reminds Bosola that Antonio "was basely descended," the spy warms to his subject, endorsing "virtues" over "pedigrees" (III.ii.258–260) in a manner that cannot help but betray personal feeling. In the soliloquy that ends this scene, Bosola announces that he is too far gone in corruption not to persist as a "politician . . . the devil's quilted anvil," and to "reveal / All" to the duke, but he is more uncomfortable in the "base quality / Of intelligencer" (III.iii.323–328) than ever before. Later, when he arrives to arrest the Duchess, Bosola may be masked, for he enters with soldiers who apparently wear "*visards*" (III.v.95), and the Duchess, who at length recognizes him, makes reference to his "counterfeit face" (III.v.118). Whether the disguise here is physical or merely metaphorical, it nevertheless suggests that Bosola retreats to an assumed identity in order to suppress the moral self that had surfaced earlier in his defense of Antonio.

Bosola now presides over the programmatic torture of the Duchess, but only after he has praised her noble and majestic response to suffering. He functions as presenter in showing his victim the gruesome tableau "*behind a traverse*" (IV.i.55), and then enjoins her to avoid despair, at the same time offering her false consolations: "Come, be of comfort, I will save your life" and "Now, by my life, I pity you" (IV.i.86–88). But Bosola, who has already been more deeply affected by his role than he had intended, now urges the duke to "go no farther in [his] cruelty," recommending that he "Send her a penitential garment" and "furnish her / With beads and prayer-books" (IV.i.118–121). More significantly still, he refuses flatly to appear before the Duchess again "in mine own shape" and insists that, even then, "The business shall be comfort" (IV.i.134–137). Ferdinand, with mild surprise, notices the shift in his servant: "Thy pity is nothing of kin to thee . . ." (IV.i.138).

As if to make good on his resolution, Bosola absents himself from the masque of madmen (an anonymous servant introduces it in his place), and he enters to the Duchess only as the lunatics leave the stage, now disguised as "*an old man*" (IV.ii.114). The aged figure, as in Chaucer's *Pardoner's Tale*, symbolizes human mortality, if he does not quite personify death, and Webster confirms the symbolism almost immediately by having Bosola represent himself as a "tombmaker" (IV.ii.148). His longest speech at this point is a curious hybrid of religious preachment on the vanity of the flesh (he echoes Donne on the body as the prison of the soul)[34] and of terror tactics aimed at the resistant composure of the Duchess: "Thou sleepest worse than if a mouse should be forced to take up her lodging in a cat's ear" (IV.ii.137–139). Bosola mingles the antithetical roles of spiritual counselor and specialist in psychological torture in a way that shows him struggling with profound internal divisions. The prolonged rumination on graves and tombs is "talk fit for a charnel," but it also serves as "dismal preparation" for the next phase of a continuing process, the entrance of the executioners with their grim "*coffin, cords and a bell*" (IV.ii.164–165). Here Bosola shifts his identity again to that of "the common bellman" traditionally "sent to condemn'd persons / The night before they suffer" (IV.ii.173–175).

These alterations of role—from old man to tomb maker to bellman—involve no change in costume. They represent subtle realignments of psychological perspective that shade into each other in an almost dreamlike sequence so as to suggest the inexorable drift toward death. In bringing the Duchess thus "By degrees to mortification" (IV.ii.177), Bosola also seems to induce a change in his own perspective, although this does not immediately produce a *volte-face* in his actions. Obviously, he allows the execution to proceed.

The ritual process of emergent identity reaches a crisis of emotional intensity in the great dirge, "*Hark, now everything is still,*" that Bosola recites, probably to the accompaniment of a tolling bell. This lyric produces a complex effect because it seems designed both to soothe and to frighten, and hence to reflect great uncertainty upon the speaker's motives. Bosola hints at the violence or "*hideous storm of terror*" (IV.ii.189) that awaits the Duchess, at the same time inviting her to embrace death as desirable release:

> 'Tis now full tide, 'tween night and day:
> End your groan, and come away.
> (IV.ii.194–195)

At the literal level he seems to draw upon the consolatory traditions of the *ars moriendi*, imaging death as the gateway from the "*long war*" that "*disturb'd*" the Duchess's "*mind*" to a state of "*perfect peace,*" a devotional sacrifice in which the purified and transfigured body will be made fit for its transpiring soul:

> Strew your hair with powders sweet,
> Don clean linen, bathe your feet,
> And (the foul fiend more to check)
> A crucifix let bless your neck.
> (IV.ii.190–193)

The tone is solemn, exalted, liturgical, and evocative of a medieval Christian metaphysic. But the lullaby quality of the verse, its lilting rhythm and rhyme, is also unsettling in the dramatic context. An instant reaction comes from Cariola, whom Bosola's words certainly do not relax:

The Duchess of Malfi

Hence villains, tyrants, murderers! alas!
What will you do with my lady? call for help.
(IV.ii.196–197)

This is not merely the vulgarity of a woman unattuned to spiritual refinement. It is a scream of alarm from the wide-awake world to remind us that a seductive meditation on the pains of life and luxuries of death must not be allowed to weaken our horror of atrocity. Cariola's outburst forbids us to tranquilize protest by entering too uncritically into the rhetorical spell of Bosola's poetry.

Assertive resistance to death (with its implication of ego strength and unconquerable individuality) and religious submission to the inevitable limit of human existence constitute the two familiar attitudes of tragic characters on the Renaissance stage. Webster gives full expression to both in *The Duchess of Malfi* without attempting to resolve the philosophical tension they define, but he focuses that tension brilliantly in Bosola's beautiful and disturbing lyric, giving it greater effect still by imbedding the poem in a highly ambiguous context. By voicing our outrage, Cariola embodies the natural will to survive (she must be physically subdued before she can be killed); but the Duchess, for whom the waiting woman is an obvious foil, meets her end in a way that satisfies our equally strong need to believe in death as more than simple extinction, in dignified resignation and the widening of horizons as a vital part of its meaning. Webster situates Bosola's dirge in such a way as to make the two responses possible in the same scene and, further, to cast the provoker of these responses in the puzzlingly double role of tormenter and comforter. The spiritual guide is superimposed upon the villain so that neither we nor even he himself can, for the moment, distinguish mask from man. Webster creates a kind of psychological mist as impenetrable as the *"mist of error"* (IV.ii.188) to which Bosola appeals in his own verses.

Our Pirandello-like insecurity as to the true identity of Bosola is an intermittent, not a sustained, effect of Webster's dramatic procedure. As hired murderer the character functions with great efficiency, dispatching Cariola and the children to their deaths tersely and without apparent qualm. But he is strangely fascinated, almost incredulously so, by the Duchess's freedom from terror:

> *Bosola.* Doth not death fright you?
> *Duchess.*   Who would be afraid on't?
>   Knowing to meet such excellent company
>   In th' other world.
> *Bosola.* Yet, methinks,
>   The manner of your death should much afflict you,
>   This cord should terrify you?
> *Duchess.*   Not a whit:
>   What would it pleasure me to have my throat cut

341

With diamonds? or to be smothered
With cassia? or to be shot to death with pearls?
(IV.ii.210–218)

Bosola, who is ironically less ready for death than the victim he has helped prepare for it, finds the contrast between himself and the Duchess burdensome indeed, but his full-front encounter with conscience does not occur until he has
violated it in the most radical way open to him—by eliminating the most re-
proachful embodiment of strength and innocence in his experience. It is the sight
of the dead bodies of the Duchess and her children that finally brings his moral
anguish to the surface:

> *Ferdinand.*　　　　　　Is she dead?
> *Bosola.*　　　　　　　　　　　She is what
> 　You'd have her: but here begin your pity—
> 　　　　　　　*Shows the Children strangled.*
> 　Alas, how have these offended?
> *Ferdinand.*　　　　　　　　　The death
> 　Of young wolves is never to be pitied.
> *Bosola.* Fix your eye here:—
> *Ferdinand.*　　　　Constantly.
> *Bosola.*　　　　　　　　　Do you not weep?
> 　Other sins only speak; murder shrieks out:
> 　The element of water moistens the earth,
> 　But blood flies upwards, and bedews the heavens.
> 　　　　　　　　　　　　(IV.ii.256–263)

The recriminations between master and servant ensue, the duke refuses
payment and banishes his accomplice to "some unknown part o' th' world"
(IV.ii.326), and Bosola rejects the Aragonian brothers as "hollow graves, / Rotten, and rotting others," thus separating himself from their moral influence as he
would from "the plague" (IV.ii.319–322):

> 　　　　　　　Why fare thee well:
> . . . .
> 　　　　　　　　I stand like one
> That long hath ta'en a sweet and golden dream:
> I am angry with myself, now that I wake.
> 　　　　　　　　　　(IV.ii.317–325)

Acting for the first time without ambivalence, he comforts the briefly resuscitated
Duchess with the magnanimous lie that her husband has been "reconcil'd"
(IV.ii.352) to her vicious brothers. Although Bosola continues to wear masks and
to be a politician, a role that necessitates new ties with the Cardinal as well as a
realistic appraisal of danger (he remarks later that the plan to ally himself with
Antonio is a "slippery" business in which a man "must look to [his] footing"

[V.ii.332–333] or else break his neck), he acknowledges his own true nature in the soliloquy that concludes Act IV:

> O sacred innocence, that sweetly sleeps
> On turtles' feathers, whilst a guilty conscience
> Is a black register, wherein is writ
> All our good deeds and bad, a perspective
> That shows us hell! That we cannot be suffer'd
> To do good when we have a mind to it!
> This is manly sorrow:
> These tears, I am very certain, never grew
> In my mother's milk. My estate is sunk
> Below the degree of fear: where were
> These penitent fountains while she was living?
> O, they were frozen up! Here is a sight
> As direful to my soul as is the sword
> Unto a wretch hath slain his father. Come,
> I'll bear thee hence:
> And execute thy last will; that's deliver
> Thy body to the reverent dispose
> Of some good women: that the cruel tyrant
> Shall not deny me. Then I'll post to Milan
> Where somewhat I will speedily enact
> Worth my dejection.
>
> (IV.ii.355–375)

He has finally come to terms with his own inner reality or, at least, as close to this as such a character can come in Webster's mist-filled world. The penitential tears flow, although tragically too late, and Webster gives the moral catharsis visual form by having Bosola bear the corpse of the Duchess offstage in his arms. The Judas figure of the play has been strangely transmuted into a Joseph of Arimathea. But, disturbingly, Bosola's conversion seems more a matter of feeling than of action. And, in any case, he appears already to be contemplating revenge—"somewhat . . . Worth my dejection [i.e., humiliation]." The blunders and violence of his behavior in Act V and the near-despair of his death force us to revalue, if not to question, the efficacy and depth of his moral experience.

* * *

Webster fills out the tragedy with six lesser characters who assist our perception of the major ones by showing them in a particular light. Delio, in addition to serving a choric function, establishes Antonio as a friend as well as a lover, husband, and father. He approaches being the Horatio of the play. The dramatist also uses him in the early episodes as a worldly foil to an Antonio as yet unschooled in the sophistications of the court amour. Certainly Delio's ambiguous, undeveloped, perhaps politically motivated wooing of Julia contrasts with his friend's heartfelt but inexperienced commitment to the Duchess. Julia, the ambitious courtesan who behaves in some respects like a more trivial Vittoria, reveals the gelidly controlled Cardinal in the unexpected role of lecher. Moreover, her casual adultery stands in stark opposition to the domestic fidelity of the title character. Her wooing of Bosola at pistol point parodies the Duchess's wooing of Antonio. Cariola plays the part of confidante to the Duchess, thus demonstrating what loyalty the great lady can inspire in a member of her own sex and balancing the similar relation of Delio to Antonio. But she also lends greater poignancy and dignity to the Duchess (as Emilia does to Desdemona) by embodying coarser and more commonplace attitudes. Her unpreparedness for death, her violent biting and scratching, enhance the effect of regal composure with which her mistress meets the same fate. Her almost comic lie that she is pregnant, perhaps a borrowing from Shakespeare's characterization of Joan of Arc in *1 Henry VI* (V.iv.62–64), recalls the actual pregnancy of the Duchess and invites us to remark the superior honesty and courage of the woman she serves.

Castruchio, a caricature of Websterian satire, personifies court mores in sex and politics at their most foolish and (together with the Old Lady) reflects Bosola in his seamiest and smuggest vein of mockery. Webster introduces the Marquis of Pescara as a good soldier and noble patron in obvious contrast to great aristocrats like Ferdinand and the Cardinal who use their power only to promote corruption. In teaching the dubious lesson that, since Antonio's properties have been ignobly "ravish'd" (V.i.42) from him, they should be ignobly bestowed (upon Julia rather than Delio), he at least symbolizes a concern for justice that the villains of the play never consider. Also, as a venerable figure of age in the play, he contrasts with such shallow and impotent old men as Castruchio. Count Malateste hardly has a character at all, but his very wateriness as the man Ferdinand proposes for the Duchess's hand lends a certain manliness and definition to her genuine lover by contrast.

Among the overall effects of this extensive cross-patterning is exposure to a spectrum of sexual and potentially sexual relationships that undermine our tendency to associate love with hope. The only fruitful and wholesome romance in the play is that of Antonio and the Duchess, but the violent oppression with which it must contend is such that only one child of the union survives its ravages. Against the centrality of this single tragic love affair the play shows us a range of "loves," all of which are even more unsatisfactory in quality or result— the impotency of Castruchio's marriage, the decadent ennui of the Cardinal's arrangement with his mistress, the incestuous sadism of Ferdinand's involvement with his sister, Julia's lust for Bosola (which indirectly brings about her murder), Delio's abortive attempt to seduce Julia, the merely pragmatic nature of the contemplated match between Malateste and the Duchess, the supposed contract with "a young gentleman" (IV.ii.249) that Cariola desperately invents to forestall the noose. In one form or another, Webster links all of the sexual relationships of the play, whether actual or imagined, to physical destruction or emotional death or some combination of the two.

We often assume that psychological consistency is the one sine qua non of a successful dramatic character. In spite of the great emotional upheavals that take place within them, we recognize Richard II, Othello, and Coriolanus for the same men at the end of their tragedies that we knew at the beginning. The profound internal changes that have occurred clarify rather than violate our sense of their identity. The Shakespearean principle holds true in *The Duchess of Malfi* also but with a signficant difference. Antonio and especially the Duchess deepen and expand the uniqueness that lies at their core without ever abandoning it. They remain fixed in their identification with noble and loving values just as the Cardinal with frightening single-mindedness holds his devotion to evil and death. The moral clarity of the action is never in serious doubt, whatever we may think of the Duchess's wisdom in remarrying, and this circumstance, as noted earlier, marks a shift from the greater perplexity, possibly the deliberate obfuscation, of *The White Devil*. But, without blurring the firm outlines of good and ill in his second tragedy, Webster also insists on the puzzling contradictions of behavior that make human personality surprising and unfathomable.

All of the major characters and some of the minor ones exhibit details that are disturbingly or inconveniently at variance with the person we thought we had understood. The Cardinal in his death throes betrays a flash of fellow feeling of which we would have judged him incapable. The emotionally calloused Bosola weeps, but is just as willing to shed blood *after* as before his "conversion." We are told that Antonio is less, not more, religious than Delio, information that tends to reverse the impression we otherwise derive from their actions. The Duchess's persecutors acknowledge the innocence that she asserts, but hints of guilt and touches of deviousness subtly becloud her image. Royal mein confirms her grandeur, and domestic, almost bourgeois, warmth her lovingness; but the two qualities seem slightly incompatible when we juxtapose them. It is as though Webster wished to support recognized moral and psychological norms while stimulating doubt about the absolutism and intelligibility that such norms imply. The major figures of *The Duchess*, like those of *King Lear*, fall neatly into the polar divisions of myth. The two wicked brothers are in clear opposition to their virtuous sister as the faithful servant is to the treacherous one. The lovers each have a loyal and sympathetic supporter whereas the two wicked antagonists ally themselves with the untrustworthy. But Webster undercuts this schematism with evidence of human and perhaps cosmic irrationality. Duke Ferdinand, now laughing, now raging, now shedding tears, a man metamorphosing before our eyes into a wolf, is the most obvious dramatic expression of incoherence, but Bosola's ever-shifting masks show us flux and relativity in another dimension.

If Antonio, the Duchess, and the Cardinal strike us as more or less stable identities, Ferdinand and Bosola suggest less reliable possibilities at the opposite extreme. Yet, on reflection, it is also possible to discern elements of unpredictability in the lovers and the prelate as well as predictable ones in the duke and his subaltern. Cariola, Delio, and Pescara may be regarded as mixtures of the formulaic and the surprising. Webster makes the relative fluctuation or stability of a character depend not only upon individual psychology but also upon the dynamic of that character's relationship to others. Antonio's Delio seems different from Julia's. Ferdinand is almost blind to the Duchess whom Antonio admires. In addition, the dramatist tends suddenly to alter or readjust the angle of vision from which the audience may form a judgment so that even the coordinates or points of reference are felt to be potentially in motion. Inga-Stina Ewbank has convincingly related Webster's puzzling vision of life to the "perspective" art of the sixteenth and seventeenth centuries, to paintings such as Holbein's *The Ambassadors* and the anonymous trick portrait of Edward VI in which apparent distortions or chaotic images "click into focus" when the observer discovers the correct position from which to view them. She also addresses a related tradition of satiric portraiture in which one face is superimposed upon another so as to produce an impression that, looked at in a particular way, can "change into its opposite." Such *trompe l'oeil* devices were apparently employed to express the moral dangers of false appearance or simply the equivocal and transient nature of reality itself.[35] Webster obviously accomplishes both purposes at once in his finest tragedy, building a kind of subjectivity into a medium that, by its very nature, calls for a high degree of objectification.

Although analogies between drama and the visual arts can be fruitful in understanding Webster, our sense of double or multiple images in his work undoubtedly has much to do with the increasing fascination with concealment and disguise that was becoming something of an obsession on the seventeenth-century stage. In an age when court life itself was highly theatrical and in which careers could be made or lost depending on the brilliance of one's self-created image, a concern with the encroachment of mask and face upon each other was probably inevitable. The plays of Marston, Tourneur, and Fletcher in particular are, among other things, experiments in the exploration of identity and in the related issue of manipulating audience response through various kinds of sensationalism. The author of *The Duchess of Malfi* was indebted to all of these playwrights and to the matrix of ideas and practices that they were helping to make fashionable. Whether or not we dare to invoke that notoriously vague term "baroque" in this connection, it is nevertheless true that such techniques could be used seriously, as indeed Webster uses them, to capture what Ewbank fittingly calls "the unreality of reality."[36]

* * *

As in *The White Devil*, Webster links up the theme of identity in *The Duchess of Malfi* with the psychological paradoxes of the love-death nexus. In some sense the Duchess completes and fulfills her own nature by taking Antonio as her lover, but, even as she does so, she also marries herself to Death. The tense scene in which Ferdinand invades the bedchamber of his sister as she prepares to sleep with Antonio underscores this macabre equivalence with powerful irony. The menacing brother with his drawn poniard suddenly replaces the erotic husband onstage in a paradigmatic *coitus interruptus*. The place of the Duchess's "private nuptial bed," what Bosola refers to as her "humble and fair seminary of peace" (III.ii.281–282), changes in a trice to a chamber of horrors. Positioned at the very center of the tragedy, this episode is pivotal, for it is full of echoes from the betrothal scene, which also contains foreshadowings of death, and it anticipates the scenes of torture and execution, which make up a ghoulish parody of courtship, marriage, and sexual union. The sadistic content is obvious enough, but the scene also says much about the fragile insecurity of love itself. Webster shows how quickly the forces of chaos may wreck man's feeble attempts at order, but, perhaps more tragically, he shows that order half betrayed from within. The Duchess can live and die like a prince, but, when she invites Antonio into her heart, she also invites her incestuous brother with his deadly key and even deadlier dagger. From the beginning the Duchess instinctively senses the ruinous consequences of her decision: "I am going into a wilderness, / Where I shall find nor path, nor friendly clew / To be my guide" (I.i.359–361). But formidable opposition, far from deterring her, seems to quicken her ardor and strengthen her resolve.

In the betrothal scene Antonio urges the Duchess to give her future husband "all" (I.i.388), and she complies almost immediately by proposing to him. Later Antonio reciprocates in kind: "I am all yours: and 'tis very fit / All mine should be so" (III.ii.206–207). In both instances the surface reference is to material goods, but the private significance of total commitment, of self defined in terms of the beloved, is unmistakable. As in *Othello*, it is absoluteness of affectional engagement that makes the love peculiarly vulnerable and, since it will admit of no compromise, produces an undertow of self-destructiveness. Furthermore, romantic surrender can both shape and obliterate individuality, becoming the supreme "all" as well as the "nothing" of emotional involvement. The filling of self with love for another implies a simultaneous emptying of self. Moreover, in the seventeenth century the negative side of this idea may have been strengthened by the common assumption that erotic activity by a kind of entropy steadily depleted the finite supply of human energy. The tragedy thus encourages us to speculate whether so ambivalent and irrational an antagonism as that between the loving sister and the hating brothers may not represent the dramatist's externalization of a subliminal conflict within love itself, a way of expressing the darker face of romantic impulse.

Antonio, parting for the last time from the Duchess, seems to perceive that the "all" they have so devotedly exchanged only pushes them faster toward some ontological void that will strangely comfort rather than oppress by reconciling the painful tensions and separations of their immediate experience:

> Do not weep:
> Heaven fashion'd us of nothing; and we strive
> To bring ourselves to nothing. . . .
>
> (III.v.81–83)

His lines anticipate a speech of the dying Bosola, who says of human life that it ends "like a huge pyramid . . . in a little point, a kind of nothing" (V.v.77–79). Earlier Antonio had spoken of his desperate decision to surprise the Cardinal in terms of "Los[ing] all, or nothing" (V.iii.51). The word "nothing," which Webster employs twenty-four times in *The Duchess*, echoes throughout the play with cumulative force and in contexts that keep us ever mindful of human weakness and uncertainty, of death and of the pathetic limits of our knowledge. At the risk of straining ingenuity beyond Webster's conscious intention, we might even discern a submerged pun in the "nothing" to which Antonio and Bosola refer, for in the Renaissance, as Hamlet indecently reminded Ophelia, the word could evoke "a fair thought to lie between maids' legs" (*Hamlet*, III.ii.116). Webster's grotesque juxtapositions are potentially of the kind that can treat both love and lust as encounters with nescience. Religiously, the lovers may regard their marriage as sacramental and hence as participating in a system of eternal order. But they also see it more existentially—as a transient mystery that makes possible a moment of sustaining significance between the unfathomable mysteries of birth and death, a brief candle threatened before and after by two vast blacknesses. As scholars such as Rosalie Colie and Robert Grudin have shown,[37] such paradoxical habits of mind were native to a variety of Renaissance writers and thinkers. In its complex but deliberately murky way, *The Duchess of Malfi* thus mingles moral, psychological, and philosophical perceptions to explore dramatically the age-old insight that romantic love is a *coincidentia oppositorum*, a force that simultaneously opens the gates to self-discovery and to self-annihilation, to enlightenment and to darkness, to life and to death.

The idea that love and death each contain their opposites is so elaborately worked out in *The Duchess*, so intricately woven into the texture of the tragedy, that it functions as a device for pulling disparate actions, characters, and language into organic relationship. Webster's technique may be illustrated by examining certain details of the play's language, some of which have already been mentioned for other reasons.

Even before the Duchess utters her first line, Antonio says that she can "raise" a dead man "to a galliard" simply by looking at him with her characteristic "sweet countenance" (I.i.196–198). No sooner have we been introduced to the major characters than the Aragonian brothers warn their sister against remarrying privately "Under the eaves of night." "Such weddings," says Ferdinand, "may more properly be said / To be executed, than celebrated" (I.i.318–323). A moment later (as we have noted) he reinforces this pun in an erotic way by pointing to his poniard. Lest the import be missed, Webster makes the Cardinal embroider his brother's image of execution: "The marriage night," says the churchman, "Is the entrance into some prison" (I.i.324–325). From the start, then, the very mention of marriage is made to carry the threat of doom. Only minutes later we see the Duchess disobeying her brothers; she proposes with delicate tact to her steward. But she is making her will as she does so, and she speaks of giving herself to him "In a winding sheet" (I.i.389). After Antonio has knelt to receive her wedding ring, the Duchess bemoans the "misery" of the high-born, who "are forc'd to woo, because none dare woo us" (I.i.441–442). In his gloss, Brown suggests that Webster puns on "woo" (pronounced in the Renaissance like "woe") and cites a Shakespearean parallel.[38] If this reading is correct, the double-entendre would further reinforce the conjunction of eros with disaster. Antonio hesitates nervously so that his lady urges him:

> Go, go brag
> You have left me heartless—mine is in your bosom,
> I hope 'twill multiply love there. You do tremble:
> Make not your heart so dead a piece of flesh
> To fear, more than to love me: sir, be confident—
> What is't distracts you? This is flesh, and blood, sir;
> 'Tis not the figure cut in alabaster
> Kneels at my husband's tomb.
>
> (I.i.448–455)

She works the language of mortality into her very proposal. The betrothal is sealed with a kiss, which the Duchess refers to in another pun, one that recalls Hamlet's musings on suicide: "here upon your lips / I sign your *Quietus est*" (I.i.463–464). And, after the marriage has been duly witnessed by Cariola, Antonio leads his bride offstage to a marriage bed that will contain as much fear as intimacy, a bed where sharp steel is fancied as a barrier to conjugation. Says the Duchess to her husband:

> (You speak in me this, for we now are one)
> We'll only lie, and talk together, and plot
> T'appease my humourous kindred; and if you please,
> Like the old tale, in Alexander and Lodowick,'
> Lay a naked sword between us, keep us chaste:—
> O, let me shroud my blushes in your bosom,
> Since 'tis the treasury of all my secrets.
>
> (I.i.497–503)

Webster has so contrived the context that the Duchess's allusion to a popular story, in which a man's best friend replaces him on the night of his wedding, mingles amorous whimsy and idealism with the symbolism of menace.

Antonio's newborn son, the first fruit of this fear-ridden marriage, is marked for violent death in his cradle, as Bosola learns when he discovers the child's horoscope. (Our discovery that this is the one child of Antonio who will

survive the carnage is delayed until the very end.) And, as the Duchess tries futilely to conceal her lying-in, the lubricious court, on which Bosola moralizes in
terms of "rotten and dead" bodies hidden under "rich tissue" fearful lest they be
"put . . . in the ground, to be made sweet" (II.i.57–60), buzzes with gossip about
a Swiss guard in the lady's bedchamber "With a pistol in his great cod-piece"
(II.ii.39). Ferdinand's wild response to Bosola's news that she has been delivered
of a child is to rave against her as "a notorious strumpet," "loose i' th' hilts"
(II.v.3–4), thus again associating weaponry with wantonness; and he proposes
to eradicate all consciousness of the deepest desires of his own heart by savaging
hers:

> here's the cursed day
> To prompt my memory, and here 't shall stick
> Till of her bleeding heart I make a sponge
> To wipe it out.
>
> (II.v.13–16)

When he knows "who leaps [his] sister," he'll "find scorpions to string [his]
whips, / And fix her in a general eclipse" (II.v.77–79).

Act III gives us the scene, already discussed in other contexts, in which Ferdinand interrupts the Duchess as she prepares for bed. Webster intensifies the
ironies of an already ironic situation by building an entire matrix of sex-death
associations into the texture of the dialogue. The conversation opens on a note
of charming intimacy, banter, and coquettishness. The Duchess calls her husband, in his impatience to bed her, "a lord of mis-rule" (III.ii.7), and Cariola,
who, like Juliet's nurse, takes vicarious pleasure in the anticipated union of others, jokes about her mistress's sleeping habits: "I know / She'll much disquiet
you . . . she's the sprawling'st bedfellow" (III.ii.11–13). After a kiss, which is the
Duchess's merry way of hushing her husband's pertness, she turns to comb her
hair. Antonio and Cariola, as a practical joke, secretly tiptoe out of the room,
leaving her to talk to her mirror:

> When were we so merry? —my hair tangles.
> . . . .
> Doth not the colour of my hair 'gin to change?
> When I wax gray, I shall have all the court
> Powder their hair with arras, to be like me:—
> You have cause to love me; I enter'd you into my heart
> Before you would vouchsafe to call for the keys.
>
> (III.ii.53–62)

The menacing brother, who has entered silently behind his sister's back, receives the
words intended for her spouse so that every detail of her love speech takes on a
dreadful, ulterior meaning. Her reference to the keys of her heart, which only Antonio can possess, makes the audience almost unbearably aware of the "false key"
(III.i.80) that has enabled Ferdinand to invade her privacy. The Duchess continues:

> We shall one day have my brothers take you napping:
> Methinks his presence, being now in court,
> Should make you keep your own bed: but you'll say
> Love mix'd with fear is sweetest. I'll assure you
> You shall get no more children till my brothers
> Consent to be your gossips: —have you lost your tongue?
>
> (III.ii.63–68)

Having finally sensed the alien presence, apparently with the aid of her glass, the lady wheels around to confront her brother, controlling her terror with princely courage. She can "welcome" the crisis to which her secret romance has committed her, whether it means that she is "doom'd to live or die." As already noted, Ferdinand instantly sexualizes her verb (by adopting the same play on words that Romeo and Othello use at the moment of their suicides) as he presents the naked blade of his dagger: "Die then, quickly" (III.ii.69–71). No wonder she feels "As if a mine, beneath [her] feet, were ready / To be blown up" (III.ii.156–157). The heroine's endearments to the "dying father" (III.v.88) of their children as the couple part for the last time provide a gloss on the love scenes that have gone before as well as a portent of future sufferings. Again Webster invokes the moral thrust of the *memento mori* tradition:

> your kiss is colder
> Than that I have seen an holy anchorite
> Give to a dead man's skull.
>
> (III.v.88–90)

Act IV perverts the rituals of marriage into a series of atrocities. Once the Cardinal has violently removed his sister's wedding ring, which he vows to "sacrifice / To his revenge" (III.iv.38–39), Ferdinand gives her another "for a love-token," and the Duchess finds herself "affectionately kiss[ing]" (IV.i.45–47) the hand of a corpse. After the Duchess has been shocked by what she believes to be the body of her husband, she desires to be bound "to that lifeless trunk" and allowed to "freeze to death" (IV.i.68–69). The masque of lunatics, a burlesque version of the genre fashionable in Webster's time at state weddings such as that of Princess Elizabeth to the Elector Palatine in 1613, contains references to love and death. These range from allusions to swans that welcome death with love songs to obscene remarks about "a snuffling knave" who hypocritically points out tombs, the obvious tokens of mortality, while groping with "his hand in a wench's placket" (IV.ii.101–102). The famous dirge that Bosola sings deliberately invokes hymeneal overtones (Jonson in his *Masque of Hymen* and Donne in his "Epithalamion at the Marriage of the Earl of Somerset" both, for instance, mention the bride's customary powdering of her hair). Several details of the execution episode also reflect back upon the betrothal and bedchamber scenes. When Bosola exults, for instance, over the Duchess's fear-haunted insomnia, his reference to her as an "unquiet bedfellow" (IV.ii.140) adds terrible new meaning to the salacious jocosity of Cariola's earlier statement that her mistress is "the sprawling'st bedfellow" (III.ii.13). The Duchess kneels to be strangled as she had earlier knelt to plight her troth, and just before the rope is pulled taut she again associates death with marriage:

> Go tell my brothers, when I am *laid* out,
> They then may feed in quiet.
>   (IV.ii.236–237; italics added)

Two familiar domestic ceremonies—the laying of the bride and the laying out of the corpse—are thus powerfully conjoined through another of Webster's brilliant puns.[39]

The equation of marriage with death is carried even further in the execution of Cariola, which, according to Webster's macabre decorum, must follow that of her superior in rank. As noted earlier, the maid, who tries to escape death by insisting that she is with child and "contracted" to be married, receives her "wedding ring" (IV.ii.248–249) in the form of the strangling noose. Even the sexual skirmishes of the fifth act continue the pattern. Julia wantonly threatens to shoot Bosola unless he will satisfy her desire and "kill [her] longing" (V.ii.161); when he seems reluctant, she likens him to those who "cannot sleep in feather-beds, / But must have blocks for their pillows" (V.ii.214–215). Then he appears to consent, but she compares herself to a "condemn'd" person whose "pardon" has been "promis'd" though not yet "seal'd" (V.ii.219–221). Later, of course, Julia dies from kissing the poisoned Bible after having extracted a confession of murder from her former lover, the Cardinal. But the idea of death is already implicit in the erotic fondling that leads up to this revelation. She offers to "remove" the "lead from off [his] bosom" (V.ii.232–233), a metaphor based on the practice of forcing confession from prisoners by pressing them to death. The Cardinal responds to her importunity with "Will you rack me?" (V.ii.247) and wonders whether her "bosom / Will be a grave, dark and obscure enough" (V.ii.271–272) for the secret he is about to disclose. Antonio imagines his wife peacefully "asleep" in their nuptial bed even as her voice in the form of an echo from her "*grave*" (he calls it "a dead thing") hints that he will "never see her more" (V.iii.39–42). In Webster's world the *ars amatoria* almost inevitably invokes the *ars moriendi*, the opposites frequently being yoked through paronomasia, antanaclasis, or other devices of rhetorical wit.[40]

* * *

To the great love-death oxymoron, which is so vital to the psychological substance of *The Duchess of Malfi*, Webster adds a third and complicating theme—that of fame or reputation, a subject about which no fewer than four of the major characters show earnest concern in the opening scene.[41] In fact, the three themes are formally associated in the little apologue on Reputation, Love, and Death by which Ferdinand moralizes to his sister after he has thrust himself so dramatically into her bedchamber (III.ii.122–135). The surface idea of Ferdinand's parable is that all human experience, be it loving or dying, forfeits its significance, fails to command respect unless honor and good name live on afterwards to enshrine it for posterity. Ferdinand, of course, is invoking that aristocratic tradition of the Renaissance that regarded fame or reputation—what Shakespeare's Iago calls "the immediate jewel of [our] souls" (*Othello*, III.ii.161)—as a kind of immortality. And doubtless Webster was aware of the traditional hierarchy, formally allegorized by Petrarch in his *Trionfi* and widely illustrated in woodcuts, paintings, and tapestries, by which Love, Chastity, Death, Fame, Time, and Eternity compose a progression of ascending value and significance. But the tragedy, without wholly negating the implications of this Christian-Platonic structure, tends to call them into question, and, in a sense, to collapse three of the Petrarchan strata into a vision of reality at once less certain, darker, and more disturbing. For the underlying irony of Ferdinand's apologue is that the speaker himself forfeits both love and reputation by his commitment to death. At the deepest level, the quest for fame and honor, at least of the hollow sort that Ferdinand insists upon, is another form of death both spiritual and physical. Delio's final comment on all of the deaths in the fifth act is significant:

> These wretched eminent things
> Leave no more fame behind 'em than should one
> Fall in a frost, and leave his print in snow;
> As soon as the sun shines, it ever melts,
> Both form, and matter. . . .
>
> (V.v.113–117)

It is the Duchess who dares to value love above fame—at any rate as her brothers and her subjects conceive the term—and who is almost naively content with her husband's promise to "remain the constant sanctuary" of her "good name" (I.i.460–461).

Finally, then, the tragedy builds on a three-way union of Love, Death, and Fame, a union as elusive of precise definition as the Christian Trinity, to which in its puzzling cross relations it suggests a certain analogy. All three elements are separate in one way—individuaized and contrasted with each other. Yet each, too, is by some mysterious alchemy an aspect of the others while, in another sense, containing them. Fame is represented in the play as proceeding from both Christian virtue and Machiavellian virtu; it is seen both as conventional ennoblement and as self-assertion, ambition, ruthlessness. It is a value that embraces both legitimate and illegitimate forms of human pride and may even point to their ultimate inseparability. Delio concludes the play (a little patly, perhaps) by telling us that

> *Integrity of life is fame's best friend,*
> *Which nobly, beyond death, shall crown the end.*
> (V.v.120–121)

But the very speech that ends with this gnomic couplet is also the one, quoted above, that compares fame to a vanishing impression in snow. Janus-like, Fame faces in two directions in Webster—toward grandeur and toward debasement. One thinks of Dalila's words, "Fame, if not double-faced, is double-mouthed / And with contrary blast proclaims most deeds . . ." (*Samson Agonistes*, ll. 971–972).

As we have already seen, love too has a terrible polarity about it, embodying self-fulfillment and even transcendence on the one hand and a certain willful and dangerous drive toward extinction on the other. Antonio refers to marriage as "locally contain[ing] or heaven, or hell" (I.i.394). Love becomes the reason for and the essence of the Duchess's spiritual independence, but, even as it isolates her from her brothers, it initiates the tragic movement that will unite her to them in a melting of all earthly barriers. Her true fame and supposed infamy as well as her brothers' dishonor in the name of honor are all rooted in the same paradox. Webster's strenuous dualisms constantly threaten to dissolve.

In this context, death becomes the ultimate mystery, for it subsumes love and fame; and it confronts us with the tragic dilemma between final meaninglessness, existential absurdity, the "mist" or "dark pit" of which Webster's characters speak, and some cosmic principle of order too obscure for human comprehension. Death in the play is not wholly negative, for even if, on final assessment, it seems to point to nothing beyond itself, it nevertheless provides the context for the deepest significances available to man. Death is the only crisis radical enough in Webster's universe to bring man to a perception of who and what he is, to awaken him to the limits of possible self-discovery. To revert to Webster's curious metaphor of the double-hinged door, we might say that death opens both upon psychic and spiritual order as well as upon possible chaos.

*   *   *

Predictably, Webster re-employs most of the stylistic and structural devices he had already used to good effect in *The White Devil*. Many verbal and thematic ideas he simply borrows from himself. The imagery of devils, mandrakes, whirlwinds, torture, poison, diamonds, stars, and birds (notably the robin redbreast) reappears, usually in a fresh context or with some altered resonance or twist of meaning. The notion of the whore as a white devil whose fair surface belies a corrupt interior, a whited sepulchre in human form, the playwright reapplies to the Duchess with an interesting difference: Ferdinand remarks of his sister that "her fault and beauty, / Blended together, show like leprosy, / The whiter, the fouler" (III.iii.62–64). Flamineo's homely image of death as "An everlasting cold" (*The White Devil*, V.vi.271) becomes merely a "catarrh, or cough o' th' lungs" (IV.ii.208) in the Duchess's deliberate depreciation of strangling. In the new tragedy Webster sometimes literalizes a metaphor from the earlier work or reduces to imagery what had originally been action. Thus, while Flamineo had spoken figuratively of his "varying of shapes" (*The White Devil*, IV.ii.246), Bosola actually alters his physical appearance onstage. Cornelia had referred in her dirge to "*the wolf*" who unearths corpses (*The White Devil*, V.iv.103–104), but we witness Ferdinand's lycanthropy and hear him speak of the "wolf" who will "find [the Duchess's] grave, and scrape it up" (IV.ii.309). Contrariwise, whereas Duke Francisco had impersonated a Christianized Moor during the latter action of *The White Devil*, Bosola merely refers at one point to the Duchess's marriage as so exemplary that it would make "Moors / Turn Christians" (III.ii.289–290). The ghosts of murdered characters (Isabella and Bracciano) had materialized before our eyes in the first tragedy; in the second we only hear of a ghost—that of the murdered woman who supposedly appeared to Ferdinand in the tale that the Cardinal fabricates to account for his brother's madness. The falsely reported ghost makes a subtler effect than the visually present apparitions, for the guilt that it symbolizes and that actually reduces the Calabrian duke to lunacy is infinitely more terrifying than any stage bogey could possibly be.

Webster did not like to waste pithy "sentences"; accordingly, he reuses some of his favorites in *The Duchess*. Antonio's dying admonition, "And let my son fly the courts of princes" (V.iv.72), obviously represents a reworking of Vittoria's "O happy they that never saw the court" (V.vi.261). The dramatist repeats "*Glories, like glow-worms, afar off shine bright, / But look'd to near, have neither heat, nor light*" (IV.ii.144–145), transferring the couplet from Flamineo to Bosola. In the first instance, Flamineo refers with ironic effect to the supposed wisdom of Mulinassar (*The White Devil*, V.i.41–42); in the second, Bosola seeks to loosen the Duchess's precarious grasp on self-esteem. Giovanni's rather smug preachment to Flamineo that "grief" is "nam'd the eldest child of sin" (*The White Devil*, V.iv.23) returns again with slight alteration in the Cardinal's self-condemnation: "*Sorrow is held the eldest child of sin*" (V.v.55). Webster's habit of introducing moralistic parables and sinister equivocations of course persists in *The Duchess of Malfi*. Flamineo's "tale" of the crocodile and the bird (*The White Devil*, IV.ii.222–241) has its counterpart in the Duchess's story about the dogfish and the salmon (III.v.124–140). Ferdinand's equivocal letter sending for Antonio's "*head in a business*" (III.v.28–36) represents the same kind of linguistic entrapment that marks Francisco's fake love letter to Vittoria.

Key words, phrases, and ideas associated with Webster's atmosphere of courtly vapidity, loneliness, alienation, and metaphysical uncertainty also recur. The hollow Malateste is satirically described as "a guarded sumpter-cloth" (III.iii.33) as Camillo's wit had been similarly likened to "an ass in's foot-cloth" (*The White Devil*, I.ii.51). Webster reintroduces a quibble on "devotion" (to God and to one's lover), transferring it from Isabella's feeling for Bracciano (*The*

White Devil, II.i.150–151) to that of Julia for the Cardinal (II.iv.5–6). "Banish'd Ancona!" (III.v.1), the phrase with which the Duchess commences a scene, recalls the startling "Banish'd?" that opens *The White Devil*; it may also remind us that *The Duchess* had begun with Antonio's return from "banishment" (I.i.396) as Lodovico returns from it in the first tragedy. When the Duchess sickens from eating green apricocks, Antonio moans to Delio, "O . . . we are lost" (II.i.160), an obvious echo of an often repeated expression in *The White Devil*. Then Webster reassigns the phrase to the trapped Cardinal ("I am assaulted! I am lost . . ."), combining it with a reminiscence of Richard III at Bosworth: "My dukedom for rescue!" (V.v.20–23). For her final line, "I go, / I know not whither" (V.ii.288–289), Julia lifts part of Vittoria's "My soul . . . Is driven I know not whither" (*The White Devil*, V.vi.248–249). In *The White Devil* Lodovico asks Flamineo before he stabs him, "What dost think on?" and receives the contemptuous answer, "Nothing; of nothing: leave thy idle questions—" (V.vi.201–202). Webster adapts the same exchange to the dialogue between Cariola and the Duchess in prison:

> *Cariola.* What think you of, madam?
> *Duchess.*   Of nothing. . . .
>   (IV.ii.15)

As already noted, the word "nothing" returns in other contexts to reinforce the pessimism of *The Duchess*. And of course Antonio is killed "In a mist" (V.v.94) just as Flamineo had died "in a mist" (*The White Devil*, V.vi.260).

Webster even repeats certain details of plot from *The White Devil*. The Duchess in wooing Antonio laments that she is "forc'd to express [her] violent passions / In riddles, and in dreams" (I.i.445–446), a clear reminiscence of the riddling dream by means of which Vittoria prompts the murders of Camillo and Isabella, thus, by implication, proposing to Bracciano. Later the Duchess, like her counterpart, actually relates a dream heavy with portent, but the effect is pathetic rather than sinister:

> Methought I wore my coronet of state,
> And on a sudden all the diamonds
> Were chang'd to pearls.
>   (III.v.13–15)

This surrealist metamorphosis symbolizes the dramatic shift from regal splendor and power to the tears of victimization—hence from public majesty to private sorrow. The jewel imagery imaginatively captures Webster's dual focus on royal and domestic tragedy and suggests a relation between them.

Sexual encounters for political purposes appear in both plays. Bosola's using of Julia and Julia's of the Cardinal to glean information repeat Francisco's feigning of love for Zanche; and, just as the latter's betrayal of Vittoria for the sake of her new attachment brings about her own death, so Julia's betrayal of the

The Duchess of Malfi

Cardinal for a similar reason has the like result. Insanity as a punishment for murder clearly interested Webster. Bracciano's ravings may be considered an early study for the more extended anatomy of madness in Ferdinand. Both instances are significantly based upon guilt for the murder of a woman to whom some unsatisfactory sexual relationship has been implied—a wife in one case, a sister in the other. At two points in *The Duchess* Webster makes a point of the heroine's graying hair (III.ii.58–59 and IV.ii.136). The effect is to add dignity and a touch of feminine poignancy to the themes of suffering and mortality, but Webster had already produced a similar, though less specific, detail in characterizing Cornelia who becomes "a very old woman in two hours" (*The White Devil*, V.iv.54) after the death of Marcello. The threatening with pistols in *The Duchess* also strikes a familiar note. Antonio brandishes such a weapon at Cariola when he suspects her of betraying him (III.ii.142–144) and Julia, as noted earlier, tries to force her affections upon Bosola at pistol point (V.ii.151–165). Both actions recall the theatrical ruse in which Flamineo threatens his sister with pistols and then seems to die at her hands. Even the "false keys" (*The White Devil*, V.vi.168) that enable Lodovico and his revengers to penetrate the locked chamber in which Vittoria and her brother quarrel reappear in *The Duchess*, for Ferdinand surprises his sister (III.i.80) and Bosola double-crosses the Cardinal (V.ii.327) by means of the same device.

As in *The White Devil*, so in *The Duchess of Malfi* Webster imposes a kind of artistic coherence upon the fragmentary and inconclusive universe of the play through a pattern of verbal and visual parallels that, individually considered, might seem almost fortuitous. They are, however, too numerous to be accidental. Usually the cross relationships intensify an irony or hint at complexities that the tragedy could not address directly or in detail. Bosola, for instance, defends himself against the charge of overweening ambition and taunts Antonio on his sudden ascendancy by moralizing that "when a man's mind rides faster than his horse can gallop, they quickly both tire" (II.i.92–93). By reminding us that both characters have been closely associated with horses from the beginning—Antonio for winning the duke's riding competition and Bosola for his recent elevation to the provisorship of the horse—the glib aphorism complicates our response to the whole question of courtly advancement in the play and causes us to compare and contrast the two men from a fresh perspective. Thus Webster forbids us to take too easy or too simple a view of either's career.

The verbal repetitions frequently have the effect of juxtaposing unlike dramatic contexts in the consciousness of the spectator, a technique that can surprise, unsettle, or even shock. From the beginning we are encouraged to think of Bosola as a cutthroat because he associates himself with throat-cutting twice in the opening scene (I.i.249 and I.i.285); later the Duchess scorns Bosola's attempt to terrify her with a strangling cord in a way that transfigures the violence of a thug into a strange kind of poetry: "What would it pleasure me to have my throat cut / With diamonds?" (IV.ii.216–217). The Duchess has acquired some

357

of her torturer's toughness and disdain but with a radiance and dignity beyond his reach. The Duchess at her dressing table jokes about having her court "Powder their hair with arras" (III.ii.60) so that silver hair might become fashionable; then the detail takes on a ritualisitic and sacrificial aspect in the lyric that Bosola intones before her execution: "*Strew your hair with powders sweet*" (IV.ii.190). The duke first threatens to "fix" his sister "in a general eclipse" (II.v.79), then asks her indignantly "what hideous thing . . . doth eclipse" her virtue (III.ii.72–73). Taken together, the two metaphors of eclipse (they occur less than two hundred lines apart) imply that the speaker himself, though unconsciously, is the great obliterator of light and goodness in the play.

In the proposal sequence, the Duchess puns, as noted already, on signing Antonio's "*Quietus est*" (I.i.464) when she kisses the man responsible for keeping her household accounts. Later, in order to protect him, she must pretend to accuse him of mishandling her affairs, but she repeats her earlier phrase in a way that reminds us of her secret commitment as wife to the figure she is publicly rebuking:

> I am like to inherit
> The people's curses for your stewardship.
> You had the trick in audit-time to be sick,
> Till I had sign'd your *quietus*; and that cur'd you
> Without help of a doctor.
>
> (III.ii.184–188)

A few lines later she reinforces the secret language of love, and Antonio consciously acknowledges it by repeating the key word "all" that had figured so significantly in their mutual giving of themselves to each other:

> *Duchess.*   We do confiscate,
> Towards the satisfying of your accounts,
> All that you have.
> *Antonio.*   I am all yours: and 'tis very fit
> All mine should be so.
>
> (III.ii.203–207)

Speeches of political false-seeming for the benefit of casual observers are made to contain an important element of romantic reassurance. Bosola's image of his own moral enlightenment as arousal from a dream ("I am angry with myself, now that I wake" [IV.ii.325]) repeats a phrase, perhaps unconsciously picked up from the Duchess, who had compared a different kind of awareness to waking up earlier in the same scene:

> tell my brothers
> That I perceive death, now I am well awake,
> Best gift is they can give, or I can take.
>
> (IV.ii.223–225)

358

The echoed language probably constitutes additional evidence of how deeply Bosola has been affected by the death of his victim.

Again Webster pursues his technique of preparing for some action onstage by introducing the idea first in a verbal and often apparently casual manner. For instance, when the Duchess slips her wedding ring on Antonio's finger, the steward covers his surprise and embarrassment with a moralistic speech on the dangerous madness of ambition. He mentions "the wild noise of prattling visitants" who are as common in the "fair lightsome lodgings" of the great house as in the "close-pent rooms" (I.i.420–424) of the asylum. Later, of course, the prattling visitants and close-pent rooms become an actual part of the Duchess's experience. By creating a verbal bridge between the marriage scene and the scene of imprisonment, Webster manages to suggest (as Middleton was later to do in *The Changeling*) that the entire court, particularly in its obsession with status, participates unwittingly in a kind of moral lunacy. Similarly, when Delio learns from his friend that the Duchess in labor is suffering "the worst of torture, pain, and fear" (II.ii.67), Webster seems to foreshadow the ordeal of her incarceration to which the same words in a different sense also apply.

Webster introduces the word "echo" in seemingly unrelated contexts twice before the scene in which echoing is the principal effect. Both are proleptic in different ways. In the first case, the Duchess hopes that the church will "echo" (I.i.493) her irregular marriage by giving it official sanction; in the second, Julia chides the Cardinal for temporarily refusing to confide in her: "Tell your echo this, / Or flatterers that like echoes still report / What they hear though most imperfect . . ." (V.ii.243–245). When it finally comes, the voice from the Duchess's grave actually *does* echo in several ways at once. It not only catches up the ends of Antonio's speeches, giving them an extended and ominously fateful meaning; it also calls to mind (if our memories are alert enough) two sexual relationships that, as the audience already knows, have ended in death.

The word "ruin," one of Webster's pervasive favorites, works in similarly intricate fashion. Critics sometimes praise Antonio's meditation on the ruined abbey, based on a passage from Montaigne, as though it were a beautiful but essentially detachable exercise in atmospherics. But it is considerably more than a romantic mood piece:

> *Antonio.*   I do love these ancient ruins:
>   We never tread upon them but we set
>   Our foot upon some reverend history.
>   And questionless, here in this open court,
>   Which now lies naked to the injuries
>   Of stormy weather, some men lie interr'd
>   Lov'd the church so well, and gave so largely to't,
>   They thought it should have canopy'd their bones
>   Till doomsday; but all things have their end:

> Churches and cities, which have diseases like to men,
> Must have like death that we have.
> *Echo.*   *Like death that we have.*
> (V.iii.9–19)

The moving effect that this speech makes in the theatre depends in great part on the many resonances it picks up from earlier speeches and episodes, blending them into a nostalgic and generalized threnody on loss, decay, and mutability.

Hardly a major character fails to say something in the course of the tragedy that does not funnel into or out of this carefully placed aria. Ferdinand ironically praises Bosola for checking "*a great man's ruin*" (III.i.92) by refusing to flatter him. Antonio observes gloomily, after the Duchess's servants have deserted, that fair-weather friends shrink from "decay'd fortunes" and that "Men cease to build where the foundation sinks" (III.v.10–11). Anticipating her fate when arrested, the Duchess is almost relieved at what seems like a breaking of the tension: "I would have my ruin / Be sudden" (III.v.97–98). In prison, perhaps glancing back to "the figure cut in alabaster" that the Duchess has mentioned as a feature of her first "husband's tomb" (I.i.454–455), Cariola tells her mistress that she looks "like some reverend monument / Whose ruins are even pitied" (IV.ii.33–34). Antonio must look on helplessly while his confiscated lands, now in Pescara's gift, enrich others: "How they fortify / Themselves with my ruin!" (V.i.36–37). Such scattered and miscellaneous references gather a kind of force by accumulation and finally come into rich association with each other in the late scene where physical ruins become the setting for a theme that Webster has been building all along. Nor does the dramatist drop these related ideas after the echo scene. Bosola knits together the images of graves, ruins, and echoes in his final speech:

> —O, I am gone!—
> We are only like dead walls, or vaulted graves,
> That ruin'd, yields no echo: —Fare you well—
> (V.v.96–98)

And Delio, gesturing toward the collection of corpses that now litter the stage, speaks tellingly of "this great ruin" (V.v.111).

Additional linkages are also suggestive. Delio tries to calm Antonio's fears when the Duchess goes suddenly into labor by mentioning various omens, including "Bleeding at nose" (II.ii.77), that he regards as mere superstition. Then in the following scene, after his son has been born, Antonio's nose does bleed, staining his own initials embroidered on a handkerchief and causing the father to drop the horoscope that presages "*a violent death*" (II.iii.63) for the baby:

> My nose bleeds:
> One that were superstitious would count
> This ominous; —when it merely comes by chance.
> Two letters, that are wrought here for my name,

Are drown'd in blood!
Mere accident:—
    (II.iii.41–46)

By calling our attention twice to a so-called superstition, Webster promotes rather than allays doubts about the mysterious workings of fate in the play. The nosebleed accurately portends the bloody death of Antonio by the unintentional hand of Bosola, and, more immediately, it enables Bosola to read the dropped horoscope, thereby exposing the whole family of the Duchess to increased danger. Still, the horoscope itself, also a superstition in some sense, turns out to be unreliable, for its gloomy predictions about the child's doom do not come to pass. The whole question of the relation between chance and destiny is raised only to be begged.

Another kind of audience uncertainty arises when Cariola objects to "this jesting with religion," the feigned pilgrimage that covers the escape from Amalfi. Since the emergency is acute, we are inclined to sympathize with the Duchess when she overrules her maid as "a superstitious fool" (III.ii.317–319). But Webster has already sown seeds of skepticism in the earlier scene in which Julia, "a witty false one" in the Cardinal's phrase, explains to her illicit lover that she has escaped to Rome without her husband under color of "visit[ing] an old anchorite . . . for devotion" (II.iv.4–5). Julia's trifling with religion almost parodies the Duchess's in advance, necessarily complicating our response to both Cariola's protest and to the unquestioning decision of her mistress to depart instantly for Loretto.

Some of Webster's cross-related details deepen the impression of psychological pressure or turbulence in the characters. We observe the unstable mixture of laughter and menace in Duke Ferdinand almost from his first entrance. Then, when he fantasizes about the Duchess's hidden sexual adventures, he projects his own perverse trait upon his sister: "Methinks I see her laughing— / Excellent hyena!" (II.v.38–39). The Duchess does in truth laugh, but Ferdinand's bestial distortion of her natural happiness serves to reveal with peculiar force the unconscious identification that is part of his psychosis. Bosola's letter informing the duke of his sister's childbirth is described by a servant as "put[ting] him out of his wits" (II.iv.69). Ferdinand himself feels that he has "grown mad" with the news as though he had had some mysterious contact with "a mandrake" (II.v.1–2). These early references to madness are at least partly metaphorical, but they prepare us for the duke's actual derangement that quickly follows the murder of the Duchess. In prison the heroine cries out that she is "full of daggers" (IV.i.90). The phrase vividly captures her sense of torment coming from all directions, but of course it also brings to mind the specific dagger with which her brother has threatened her in two previous scenes. When the Duchess kneels to receive the executioner's rope, she assumes the posture of prayer because "heaven-gates are not so highly arch'd / As princes' palaces" (IV.ii.1232–233). The penitential gesture is moving enough in itself, but Webster gains a significant increase in pathos by reversing a physical action from the betrothal scene that would be unforgettable to any audience. There the Duchess had raised her steward from his knees with a similar architectural image in a symbolic equalization of their stations and with an implied assertion of her need for greater psychological space:

> Sir,
> This goodly roof of yours is too low built,
> I cannot stand upright in't, nor discourse,
> Without I raise it higher: raise yourself,
> Or if you please, my hand to help you: so.
> (I.i.415–419)

*   *   *

Lest it be supposed that Webster makes his tragedy more coherent by attention only to the minutiae of language and action, we should note certain larger parallels on the level of plot. The unusual situation of a woman's wooing a man, with which the first act concludes, is echoed in a semiparadoxical way by Julia's unsolicited advances to Bosola. Obviously, Webster introduces the lustful behavior of the courtesan as a counterweight to the more idealistic action of his heroine. The dramatist makes the breaching of privacy an important theme by exemplifying it in no fewer than three differing contexts. Cariola witnesses the betrothal from behind an arras, startling Antonio by her sudden appearance. Then Ferdinand, a far more alien presence, overhears the Duchess expressing endearments to her husband in the undressing scene. This time terror is added to surprise. Finally, Bosola spies upon the "intimate" interview between Julia and the Cardinal, emerging from his hiding place at the moment when she kisses the lethal Bible, thus precipitating a tense confrontation with the churchman. The Duchess has herself locked into her private apartments and the palace officers confined to quarters that she may conceal her lying in. The Cardinal adopts a similar stratagem—having himself barricaded against intrusion in order to screen the removal of Julia's body. Love, fertility, and death are all represented as being artificially enclosed, temporarily sealed off in vacuums that reality abhors and will inevitably penetrate.

The staging of the play thus relates closely to its thematic, imagistic, and psychological substance. It can be no accident that the entire fourth act takes place in a prison—an unnaturally darkened and confined space that represents isolation and constraint in their most far-reaching senses, metaphysical no less than emotional, moral, and political. A prison is the appropriate locus for a tragedy whose action and imagery are loaded with ideas of darkness, obscurity, entrapment, unfathomed terrors, and emotional stricture. Even the uncaged madmen who howl, gambol, and chatter so bizarrely before the Duchess may be thought, as Ralph Berry has suggested,[42] to analogize several of the characters in the main action. Ferdinand in particular seems to dance or "fetch a frisk" (V.ii.73) in his scene with the charlatan doctor, thus re-enacting the grotesquerie of the prison antimasque. The implication would seem to be that at least half the court of Amalfi are like escapees from a madhouse and require locking up.

Despite Webster's regular use of the open stage, *The Duchess* projects an atmosphere of greater privacy and emotional subtlety than *The White Devil*. John Russell Brown has speculated that the enclosed auditorium and smaller audience of the Blackfriars theatre for which Webster was writing may have partly conditioned these effects.[43] The darkened stage with the sudden revelation of "Hah! lights! —O, horrible!" (IV.i.53), the disclosure "*behind a traverse*" of "*artificial*" wax corpses (IV.i.55), and the crepuscular ruins with their grave that returns a deadly echo and presents a mysterious face suddenly irradiated by light, have no parallel in the more boisterously public earlier tragedy. Ferdinand's hushed line, "Strangling is a very quiet death," followed by his "whisper, softly" (V.iv.34–36), conveys the new emphasis on feeling internalized or repressed and the more eerie and haunted quality of the play's tone.

Pauses and pregnant silences contribute to the greater intimacy between spectators and performers upon which Webster seems to count. Even apart from the claustrophobic setting of the fourth act, most of the tensest episodes appear to take place in private quarters or behind locked doors. These include the betrothal and marriage, the lying-in (though it occurs offstage), Ferdinand's insane reaction to the news of the childbirth, the preparation for bed, the entire by-plot between Julia and the Cardinal, and the final carnage in the Cardinal's apartment. Much of Bosola's action, the reading of the horoscope by a dark lantern and the mistaken killing of Antonio, for example, is presented in semidarkness, a condition that almost inevitably draws the audience emotionally closer to the stage. The more formal court assemblages, when they occur, quickly fragment into smaller groups or duologues that narrow our focus. The Duchess speaks of the "deadly air" (III.i.56) of her brother's presence at court, but the sense of suffocating enclosure prevails almost throughout. As is usual in Renaissance drama, some scenes are unlocalized, but the only three that unambiguously take place outdoors are the brief ones at Ancona (III.iv-v) and the episode at the Duchess's grave (V.iii), two of which (the Cardinal's ceremony and the echo scene) are obviously included for their special effects.

The word *grotesque*, so frequently applied to Webster's style, probably derives from the Italian *grotto*, meaning cave. This etymology can be useful if it cautions us that what we tend to regard as unnatural or sensationally odd has its roots in a fairly ordinary and natural phenomenon. But more than this, the original word with its dark and subterranean connotations may remind us that the playwright supports his outlook on human happiness as perpetually shadowed and threatened by means of a pervasive symbology that is atmospheric and visual as well as verbal. Much in the tragedy invites us to regard life as a succession of experiences in necessarily dark and closed places, as a fitful passage from womb to tomb in which the bedroom and the chamber of horrors are alarmingly contiguous. The setting of *The Duchess of Malfi* is one in which love and personal freedom must express themselves in the same airless prison where death and destruction preside, and the bars may be either physical or psychological. Paradox reigns here as elsewhere in the play because the fact of enclosure suggests the need for shelter and refuge from the storm as well as the confining oppression of the storm itself. When Ferdinand invades the Duchess's apartment (significantly, at night), he symbolically melts the partition between a secret world of private freedom and another of public tyranny. Both worlds, though in differing senses, are cavelike in their darkness, and Webster seems to imply that at some deep level of the psyche the two may be inseparable. A place of human warmth modulates so suddenly into its dramatic opposite that we cannot help speculating on the interconnections between love and death. What if, like the brother and sister who focus these opposites so theatrically for us, they should have sprung from the same source?

One common understanding of the grotesque in art sees its defining characteristic as a conscious superimposition of incompatible emotions upon each other, a yoking of laughter with tears, of the absurd with the pathetic, or the mechanical with the natural, of that which alienates our sympathies with that which engages them. The genius of Webster's greatest play lies partly in its subtle balancing and blending of these contraries so that our experience of extraordinary horror does not annul our pride in human strength or our pity for human suffering. Webster's grotesque techniques in *The Duchess of Malfi* are brilliantly conceived to make us aware of the skull beneath the skin even at moments of intense vitality without permitting too easy escape into a premature or reductive cynicism. Any performance of this tragedy alive to its emotional depths and complexities must not shrink from exploiting the sensationalism and theatricality for which it is justly famous. But neither should it portray its unique amalgam of tenderness and violence as a Jacobean farce of cruelty or a Brechtian cosmic joke.

* * *

Not surprisingly, Webster's most popular play has prompted a greater number and diversity of interpretations than his others. Most of these have tended to cluster into two opposing camps, represented, on the one hand, by critics eager to deny that the tragedy possesses any solid moral foundation or intelligible framework of values, and, on the other, by those who discover some kind of traditional Christian order embodied, however tentatively or gloomily, in its puzzling configurations. Gunnar Boklund thinks that Bosola's nihilistic comment late in the play, "We are merely the stars' tennis-balls, struck and banded / Which way please them" (V.iv.54–55), comes near to summarizing the dramatist's final stress on futility in *The Duchess*.[44] But Peter B. Murray argues that "Webster's vision greatly transcends that of . . . Bosola,"[45] referring to the heroine's much vaunted "integrity," to her faith, hope, and capacity for unselfish devotion, and to an essentially religious, if not necessarily orthodox, outlook on Webster's part. Variations of such views, though differing importantly in emphasis, are legion in Webster criticism, and the persistence of disagreement, as with the plays of Shakespeare, at least testifies to the vitality and richness of response that the tragedy continues to elicit. The difficulty, of course, is that both Christian and agnostic attitudes find powerful expression in Webster's text— sometimes in the mouth of a single character—and that these attitudes, far from being static or fixed, are presented as fluctuating elements in the dynamics of a dramatic organism greater and more complex than its analyzable components.

In *The White Devil*, Webster had overwhelmed our sense of a viable Christian metaphysic, not by eliminating it from consideration but by rendering its apparent irrelevancy with such cruel power. But *The Duchess of Malfi* alters this balance by building religious belief into its strongest and most magnetic character. The result is an unresolved tension or philosophical dualism in which uncertainty and contradiction become the generative sources of tragic emotion. The Duchess seems as sure of the eternity of her soul "In th' other world" (IV.ii.212) as her brother is of the oblivion of his: "let me / Be laid by, and never thought of" (V.v.89–90). Even the most wicked characters are plagued by bad conscience, but, although they consciously accept responsibility for the evils they commit, thus by implication acknowledging their freedom of will, they seem unable to act upon their own knowledge, shackled apparently to some opaque necessitarian force that makes them the playthings of chance. Bosola may weep "penitent fountains" over the body of the Duchess, but the drama does not satisfy us (or him) as to why these same tears "were frozen up" (IV.ii.365–366) while the lady still lived or why he should plunge onward into further murder and despair after his obviously sincere contrition.

Such austere Christianity as the play embodies puts far heavier stress on guilt and damnation than on the salvific power of God; and the worldly disorders and depravities that it depicts make belief in a loving and just deity necessarily more fideistic than rational. Death pulls good and evil together down into the same "deep pit of darkness" (V.v.101), and even the virtuous and presumably religious Antonio dies not looking forward to a heavenly reunion with his spouse but backward upon "the good hours / Of an ague" that define his sole "Pleasure of life": for Bologna, the endurance of "vexation" amounts to little but "a preparative to rest" (V.iv.67–69). Webster seems to insist on the profoundly solitary nature of the human struggle. Consequently, the play, to the extent that it is Christian at all, offers no consolations of communal solidarity or of a spirituality that transcends individual perception or private experience.

As in *The White Devil*, the most admirable posture is stoical. In its pessimism and quasi-deterministic tone, the tragedy would appear to reflect a certain Calvinist bias. But, equally, we can detect the traditions of late medieval Catholicism with its ritualistic emphasis on the imminence of and preparation for death, the ubiquity of sin, and the individual soul at perpetual war with the World, the Flesh, and the Devil. D. C. Gunby even argues with some plausibility that "the faith upon which Webster's world-view rests" in *The Duchess* is "that of Jacobean Anglicanism"; read by the light of the established church's teachings "on providence and free will, grace, security, and despair, the limitations of evil and the sovereignty of God," the tragedy emerges, in his view, as "essentially a world of theodicy."[46] Robert Ornstein, in contrast, asserts just as confidently that "Webster has no interest in philosophical issues or metaphysical ideals" and that both his major tragedies present "the skeptical, pragmatic nominalism of the late Renaissance, the weariness with meaningless abstraction and endless debates over words"; for Ornstein these plays bespeak an intellectual climate in which "the Elizabethan faith in didacticism—in the moral power of words—is blown away by the first gust of violence."[47] Can Boklund, Murray, Gunby, and Ornstein all be talking about the same play? Are faintness of hope and the plangency of despair in *The Duchess of Malfi* intended to damage beyond repair our traditional assumptions about moral and metaphysical coherence? Or are they meant only to show us how fallen the world has become, how egregiously man has separated himself from Grace through willfulness, blind egotism, and sin?

That both answers are possible, although logically contradictory, is surely an index of the play's power to disturb and engage us. The paradoxical effect of Webster's characterization and the multifarious grotesqueries and ironies of his poetic and structural technique have already been discussed. These, too, point to a view of reality in which polar opposites modify or complicate our perspective without forcing us to abandon one set of possibilities for another. The clash of unlikes, whether of emotions or of ideas, has the effect of shocking or jerking us into a livelier apprehension of the elusiveness of truth. Bosola's assertion that "the stars shine still" (IV.i.100) embodies both hope and despair depending upon whether we choose to invest his image with the notion of galactic radiance in a dark world or with the idea of cosmic indifference and remoteness. Both readings make sense of a dramatic context that refers to "winter," "chaos," and illimitable distance as well as to the "three smiling seasons of the year" (IV.i.97–99). More importantly, we can scarcely choose between the two meanings (a subtle actor might preserve the ambiguity) without simplifying the complex relationship between the Duchess and her torturer, let alone the weltanschauung of the play as a whole. In different senses, Bosola is both the destroyer and savior of the Duchess just as she is at once his savior and destroyer. His ministrations help prepare her for a Christian death, but he presides impassively as her executioner. Her innocence and courage enlist his admiration and prick his hardened conscience, but he dies violently in her cause, in "Revenge, for the Duchess of Malfi" (V.v.81).

In the fifth act Webster reverses likelihood or predictability so consistently that he undermines all usual conceptions of causality. The miscarrying of intention, what Boklund calls a "complete confusion of success and failure,"[48] seems almost to emerge as a philosophic principle in the tragedy. The noble Pescara refuses Antonio's property to Delio, bestowing it instead upon an undeserver, but justifies his act on moral grounds. Julia threatens to kill Bosola but does so in the name of loving him. The courtesan hears the confession of the priest, is shocked by what she learns, then does a kind of deadly penance by swearing (on a poisoned Bible) not to violate the seal of secrecy. Bosola prays that he may "taste" the "cup" of "Penitence" (V.ii.348), but then murders the man he hopes to save by a "direful misprision" (V.iv.80). The Cardinal orders his servants not to rescue him just before he needs them most, so that his cries for help go unheeded. The crazed Ferdinand stabs his brother and closest ally, then turns lucid at the moment of death. The prelate becomes unpredictably compassionate in his final seconds. Antonio's son lives to inherit his mother's duchy, not only violating primogeniture but apparently proving the dismal horoscope false.

It is possible, of course, to endow these actions with ethical significance and perhaps even to see a kind of providential pattern in them. The evil forces eliminate themselves in the process of working their calamities or as a direct result of them, and remnants of virtue endure in the child duke and in Delio. The boy, it is hinted, can begin the painful work of rebuilding, and Delio is left to moralize upon "*integrity of life*" in a generalization that seems to invite application to the Duchess and perhaps to her husband—"lords of truth" whose example in adversity should inspire and who "*nobly, beyond death, shall crown the end*" (V.v.119–121). Earlier, Antonio has explained human weakness and ineffectuality by placing them in religious perspective, under the aspect of eternity, as it were: "Heaven fashion'd us of nothing; and we strive / To bring ourselves to nothing" (III.v.82–83). Bosola had also noted that affliction, in his particular case penitential sorrow, "throws men down, only to raise them up" (V.ii.349).

But Webster compels us to weigh Antonio's earlier conception of "nothing" against Bosola's statement about the Cardinal's career, begun "like a huge pyramid . . . upon a large and ample base" but ending "in a little point, a kind of nothing" (V.v.77–79). Fame may stabilize integrity of life, conferring a kind of eternity upon it, and Heaven may be ordinant in man's affairs, however mistily apprehended. But human aspiration and identity may also end in nullity as the grandeur of the pyramid diminishes upward to the vanishing point. Antonio compares man's "quest for greatness" to the futility of "wanton boys" pursuing "bubbles, blown in th' air" (V.iv.64–66), and Delio likens fame to the melting of a footprint in the snow, a natural dissolution of both "form and matter" (V.v.117). In suspending us between alternative perceptions, both of which the experience of the individual characters and the larger patterns of the play appear to validate, *The Duchess of Malfi* finally projects a vision of tragic indeterminacy.

Epicurus, a follower of Democritus, was able to incorporate a theory of free will into his materialistic conception of natural process by proposing that individual atoms spontaneously swerve from their logically determined course through the undisturbed void. Thus necessity and contingency, intelligible plan and randomness, could be made to coexist within the same frame of reference. Pietro Pompanazzi (1462–1525), the famous Christian Aristotelian who studied and lectured at Bosola's own University of Padua, separated philosophy from theology in order to contend that apparently contradictory conclusions stemming, on the one hand, from reason and, on the other, from faith could together constitute a so-called double truth. Perceiving conflicts between the rationalistic formulations of Aristotle and divine revelation, Pompanazzi denied that the immortality of the soul could be demonstrated on the basis of reason alone and argued indeed that the opposite could be more strongly supported by logic and probability. He nevertheless accepted immortality as an article of faith. Pompanazzi also took up the vexing issue of fate, free will, and predestination, concluding, according to a leading authority, that "the Stoic doctrine of fate, on purely natural grounds," is "relatively free from contradictions": "Yet since human wisdom is subject to error, [Pompanazzi] is willing to submit to the teaching of the Church, and to accept the doctrine that God's providence and predestination are compatible with man's free will."[49] Robert Grudin, in a discussion of contrariety in Shakespeare, has drawn attention to the writings of Paracelsus (c. 1494–1541), whose dualistic thinking bears a striking analogy to that in such plays as *Romeo and Juliet* and *Macbeth*. These dramas, like Paracelsus, "seem to suggest the simultaneous existence of fluid and determined causalities—of freedom and fate."[50]

To shift ground from a sense of contradiction in philosophy to its counterpart in aesthetic perception, we might invoke Norman Rabkin's well-known essay on *Henry V*.[51] Rabkin accounts for the notoriously divided response to Shakespeare's monarch, some praising him as a chivalric hero and others condemning him as a ruthless Machiavellian, by appealing to E. H. Gombrich's analysis of illusion in the visual arts. Gombrich instances a trick drawing that looks equally like a rabbit and a duck, depending on how one perceives the shape at a given moment. Even if the viewer cannot experience the two likenesses simultaneously, he can shift back and forth between them with such rapidity that both come to coexist as valid in his mind. Like the drawing, Shakespeare's drama thus generates a dual response, which in turn produces feelings of mysterious complexity or "complementarity." I do not suggest that Webster was a student of Epicurus, Pompanazzi, or Paracelsus, or that their ideas impinged upon him in any direct fashion. Nor do I believe that Webster necessarily read *Henry V* with Rabkin-like ambivalence. It is enough simply to re-emphasize what Rosalie Colie[52] and others have demonstrated, that paradoxical thinking and a fascination with felt contradiction were endemic to the intellectual climate of Webster's age.

The Duchess of Malfi, like other great Renaissance tragedies, moves us in part because it heightens by emotional and artistic means our sense of unresolved dissonance between knowledge and belief, between fears of spiritual impermanency or meaninglessness and hopes of eternity or universal signficance.

Webster allows us to affirm with Bosola that "worthy minds" need not "stagger in distrust / To suffer death, or shame for what is just." But the drama also frightens us with contemplation of "another voyage" (V.v.103–105), of identity dissolved and annihilated, of the great void on the other side of consciousness and of the ultimate *horror vacui*. From one point of view the tragedy reflects the darker side of a perplexing but finally coherent universe; from the other it records the pathetic and courageous attempts of confused human natures to cope existentially with chaos. Either perspective divorced from its contrary would, at least theoretically, offer a measure of assurance, for even the abandonment of hope implies a relaxation of sorts, a settling of the protracted and wearying irresolutions of life. Such exaltation as Webster's greatest drama affords embraces the uncertainty and sees in it the measure of man's tragic dignity.

THE DARK AFFIRMATION OF
THE DEVIL'S LAW-CASE

Unlike the two Italian tragedies (especially *The Duchess of Malfi*), which have accumulated an impressive record of performances in the theatre, the third of Webster's major plays can claim almost no stage history at all. Even in its own day *The Devil's Law-Case* seems to have been neglected. No edition after the first (1623) appeared until Alexander Dyce collected Webster's plays in 1830. Apart from the quarto title page (which tells us that the drama "was approouedly well Acted") and the dramatist's own praise of the original actors in his preface ("A great part of the grace . . . lay in action"), we have only the undocumented assertion of David Erskine Baker in 1764 that the tragicomedy "is a good Play, and met with Success."[1] Seventeenth-century allusions to the drama are scarce. Although John Cotgrave included twenty-three passages from it in his 1655 florilegium of quotations from the English stage (*The White Devil* is represented thirty-six times, *The Duchess of Malfi* forty times),[2] and although compilers such as Edward Phillips, William Winstanley, Gerard Langbaine, and Charles Gildon included it in their surveys of Webster's works,[3] the play seems to have aroused scant enthusiasm. A note in Abraham Wright's commonplace book (c. 1640), despite the author's admiration for the episode of Romelio's attempted murder and the trial scene, judges the whole drama to be "But an indifferent play": its "plot is intricate enough, but if rightly scannd will be found faulty, by reason many passages doe either not hang together, or if they doe it is so sillily as noe man can perceiue them likely to bee euer done [that is, acted]."[4] An anonymous Puritan controversialist, writing a dozen years after the public theatres had been shut, is even more dismissive. In an appendix to Thomas Hall's *Histrio-Mastix* (1654)—an attack on John Webster of Clithero (1610–1682), the nonconformist preacher and author of *Academiarum Examen*—this "Learned Pen" either deliberately or ignorantly confuses his enemy, the educational critic, with the dramatist. His allusion to the tragicomedy is predictably sarcastic: "This Mr *Webster* (as I suppose) is that Poet, whose Glory was once to be the Author of Stage-plaies, As the Devils Law-Case. . . ."[5] Of course, Hall and his nameless friend (despite a respectful mention of Jonson's dedication of *Volpone* to the two universities) would have condemned the theatre in general, so that the singling out of this example has more to do, one suspects, with the superficially unholy title of the play than with any sense of its demerits as a work of art.

After its debut in 1617 (or 1618) *The Devil's Law-Case*, so far as we know, had to wait over three and a half centuries for a professional revival. Even then, responses were mixed and uncertain. Michael Winter, who directed the Theatre Royal production of 1980 at York, appears to have underlined the farcical aspects of his script in the belief that Webster was intentionally satirizing tragicomic conventions that the taste of his era had inconveniently thrust upon him. Robert Beaumont, the *Yorkshire Evening Press* reviewer, accepted this conception as valid,[6] while Robert Cushman, who covered the same production for the *Observer*, tended to see the play as a tragedy *manqué*—at least insofar as "its central character" is "cheat[ed]" of "a tragic finish": "This is frustrating; nothing but death should really stop Romelio and the playwright has [had] simply to fade him out" in the service "of a kind of happy ending."[7] Nicholas de Jongh of the *Guardian* thought that the courtroom scene failed to realize the "stinging urgency and irony" that, in view of its weighty cause and probable effects, it deserved to produce, and, while he commended the "farci[c]al 'game' of honour" between the rival suitors, "which suddenly slips into tragedy," was disappointed by the dispassionate characterization of Leonora and Romelio whose overpolite performances turned an emotionally full-blooded play into "a dry and diminished thing."[8] Ned Chaillet, reviewing for the *Times*, summed up the York production as "a literate and comic romp"; delighted by the "very funny" lines and the "sense of wry mockery that seems to be Webster's own intention," he nevertheless observed that the actress who played Leonora turned a potentially "grotesque" character into a "pleasantly perverse" one. Chaillet would appear to have spoken for most spectators in questioning whether *The Devil's Law-Case* is "a major Jacobean treasure" while at the same time noting that "if [the play's] reputation grows, as I expect it will, this production will be the main reason."[9]

Two obvious but related truths emerge from the experiment of remounting Webster's long-neglected work—first, that the play contains conflicting signals that make audience response especially problematic, and, second, that the coherence of the text itself depends to an unusual degree—even for a tragicomedy—on interpretive decisions made in the theatre. Much of this ambivalence, as Baldini and others have noticed, derives from the way in which psychology and plot seem to pull apart from each other in *The Devil's Law-Case*. But added to this difficulty is Webster's troubling instability of tone—his tendency to shift fitfully back and forth between tragic and comic emphases, between engagement and detachment, and between ethical seriousness and something akin to flippancy.

The most memorable example of this technique occurs at the end of the play when the arrogant Romelio openly spurns religious admonition, then seems suddenly to humble himself—awakened at long last to spirituality by the emblems of mortality that his mother ritually presents to him as he is preparing to enter upon a duel. In a spirit of valedictory resignation and accompanied by "*Soft music*" (V.iv.134), he recites one of Webster's most affecting lyrics to produce an almost mystical effect on stage. But the moment is short-lived. Romelio's penitential emotion turns out to be nothing but a ruse by means of which the pseudo convert locks Leonora and the Capuchin friar "*into a closet*" (V.iv.167) so as to be rid of her "howling" and his tedious "preaching" (V.iv.173–178). Then after the trumpets have actually summoned the combatants to battle, Romelio shifts again and sends a key to unlock the prisoners, smitten "at the last gasp" (the phrase is his own) by the need "To have some churchman's prayer" (V.vi.10–11). Presumably Romelio now repents in earnest, but no eloquence like the earlier dirge attends the genuine contrition, so that it is hard to know from the printed page whether Webster is offering us a travesty on the shallowness of a comic convention that dismisses even villains to happiness in the final minutes of a play or the actual reclamation of a hardened and resistant heart at the eleventh hour by the fear of death and the inscrutable operation of divine Providence. Both interpretations are possible and both even seem half right, but it requires a subtle director with a gifted actor in his troupe to make sense of so radical an ambiguity. The open-endedness of Webster's conclusion is only the most blatant evidence of a conceptual dubiety that the play seems to pursue more or less programmatically. It is as though the dramatist's purpose were somehow to embarrass his audience into a kind of emotional impasse by manipulating it at one moment toward astringent iconoclasm and the next toward rooted conviction. Disengaged skepticism and didactic orthodoxy struggle with each other for dominance.

Although such volatile dramaturgy may be extreme in the case of Webster's play and although signs of it had already been perceptible in the tragedies, the uncommitted tendency of *The Devil's Law-Case* is partly an inheritance from the genre that Fletcher had done so much to encourage. Conditioned by the often quoted preface to *The Faithful Shepherdess* (1608–1609) in which Fletcher defines tragicomedy, we are likely to think of the form principally in terms of plot: "A tragie-comedie is not so called in respect of mirth and killing, but in respect it wants deaths, which is inough to make it no tragedie, yet brings some neere it, which is inough to make it no comedie: which must be a representation of familiar people, with such kinde of trouble as no life be questiond, so that a God is as lawfull in this as in a tragedie, and meane people as in a comedie" ("To the Reader," ll. 20–26).[10] *The Devil's Law-Case* fits this description in essentials, containing, as it does, both aristocratic and meaner characters, dangers rather than deaths, and confining its focus to what may be called "realism"—that is, to the "representation of familiar [or recognizable] people" and "such kinde of trouble" as is conceivably within the experience of the ordinary spectator. Implicit, of course, is a happy ending somewhat unexpectedly issuing from difficulties that might be presumed to lead irretrievably to disaster. But tragicomedy at its best is neither mutant tragedy nor an unsatisfying hodgepodge of mirth and near-killing.

Guarini, in his famous defense of the genre, had insisted that "he who makes a tragicomedy does not intend to compose separately either a tragedy or a comedy, but from the two a third thing that will be perfect of its kind and may take from the others the parts that with most verisimilitude can stand together."[11] Art "alters" these contraries "before they are joined in order that they may be able to exist together and, though mixed, produce a single form." For Guarini, moreover, "the mingling of tragic and comic pleasure . . . does not allow hearers to fall into excessive tragic melancholy or comic relaxation."[12]

Tragicomedy assumes a high degree of randomness and, hence, of insecurity in the world it seeks to mirror and counts upon the sophisticated pleasure of its analytical audience in confounding and unconfounding appearance with reality. It caters to the taste for permitting oneself to be caught up in a storm of competing subjectivities that only gradually take on the firmness of an objectifiable pattern. These are among the attributes that the academic William Cartwright (himself an author of tragicomedies) admired in Fletcher's plays and that, with due allowance for differences of emphasis and texture, may be said to describe Webster's puzzling drama also. Cartwright's central point has to do with an almost scientific arrangement of dramatic elements in such a manner as constantly to surprise and mislead the playgoer without finally violating his sense of achieved design:

> No vast uncivill bulke swells any Scene,
> The strength's ingenious, and the vigour cleane;
> None can prevent the Fancy, and see through
> At the first opening; all stand wondring how
> The thing will be untill it is; which thence
> With fresh delight still cheats, still takes the sence;
> The whole designe, the shadowes, the lights such
> That none can say he shewes or hides too much:
> Businesse growes up, ripened by just encrease,
> And by as just degrees againe doth cease,
> The heats and minutes of affaires are watcht,
> And the nice points of time are met, and snatcht:
> Nought later then it should, nought comes before,
> Chymists, and Calculators doe erre more:
> Sex, age, degree, affections, country, place,
> The inward substance, and the outward face;
> All kept precisely, all exactly fit. . . .
> ("Vpon the Dramatick Poems of Mr John Fletcher," ll. 35–51)[13]

The Devil's Law-Case may be far removed from the lacquered smoothness and finish of Fletcher's style, but however granular the play's surface and however "metaphysical" its admixtures of wit and passion, Webster's toying with audience reaction for purposes more ambitious than mere frivolous theatricality can be traced to Fletcherian precedent.

* * *

An important symptom of Webster's hesitancy to abandon tragedy in *The Dev-il's Law-Case* appears from the many elements of character and situation that the playwright retained from the earlier dramas. Romelio in many respects is a refashioning of the depraved cynics, Flamineo and Bosola. He possesses their hubris, assertive energy, jaundiced outlook, contempt for social betters, and half-strangled conscience, although, unlike them, he is rich, self-sufficient, and almost wholly impelled by mercantile values, treating even members of his family like currency to be invested. The secret passion of a widow for a young man is as critical to *The Devil's Law-Case* as to *The Duchess of Malfi*, and Leonora, like her more virtuous counterpart in the tragedy (I.i.302), promises a close relative, "I will never marry again" (*The Devil's Law-Case*, I.ii.88). The widow of the tragicomedy combines some of Vittoria's concealed malice and some of the Duchess of Malfi's sexual desire with the dominance and independence of both. As Webster's title and subtitle (*When Women go to Law, the Devil is full of Business*) both imply, Leonora is as much a "white devil" in her way as the lover-murderess of the first tragedy. All three plays are set in Italy and radiate that air of floridly sophisticated evil that Webster and his tradition loved to associate with Machiavelli. All three, too, show romantic relationships leading to confusion, unhappiness, and death—or at least the appearance of death.

As in the case of *The White Devil* and *The Duchess of Malfi*, so in the tragicomedy the relationship between siblings becomes important; and two suggestions of incest even arise, one of which involves Jolenta's report that her brother is the father of the unborn child she pretends to be carrying. Her sudden claim of pregnancy also, of course, brings Cariola to mind. Leonora's attempted vengeance upon her son—an action that contains a typically Websterian component of self-destructiveness—presupposes an element of the love-hate psychology that informs Cornelia's complex relationships with her children. Again we have the mother's cursing of her daughter, for Leonora's fury at Jolenta for wishing to marry Contarino recalls Cornelia's similar harshness to Vittoria over the alliance with Bracciano. The two reactions are also parallel: Jolenta's anguished "Your imprecation has undone me forever" (I.ii.110) has the same wounded fatefulness about it as Vittoria's "O me accurst" (*The White Devil*, I.ii.301). Disintegration of the family is as central here as in the preceding dramas.

The two corrupt surgeons in the tragicomedy seem like more broadly comic versions of the two physicians whom Bracciano scorns when he is dying (*The White Devil*, V.iii.19–22) or blood brothers of the quack who attends Duke Ferdinand in *The Duchess of Malfi* (V.ii). Once more lawyers come in for theatrical scourging. The "spruce" Contilupo and the legal clerk Sanitonella represent lighter embodiments of the same pretentious insincerity that we have already met in the speeches of Monticelso and the anonymous prosecutor at Vittoria's arraignment. Webster even repeats his tragic heroine's point about the obfuscatory effect of Latin in court, for Leonora's maid Winifrid (in an unlikely request) hopes to cloak the immodest content of her perjury by being examined in the learned language. Of course, the trial itself (Contilupo significantly protests that it "deserves / Rather a spacious public theater / Than a pent court for audience . . ." [IV.i.107–109]) marks an important climax in *The Devil's Law-Case* as in *The White Devil*—and (although the proportions of levity and seriousness are different) with something of the same blend of pervasive vice and wry mockery.

The ceremonial pageantry of death returns also in the final play of the major three. The macabre furniture of Jolenta's mourning (a table with tapers and a death's head) is a clear holdover from the mortuary atmospherics of the tragedies, and Webster now combines elements from the winding of Marcello's corpse (*The White Devil*, V.iv) with others from the Duchess of Malfi's ritual execution (particularly the bringing of a coffin onstage in IV.ii) to produce the eerie *memento mori* impression at the end of *The Devil's Law-Case*: "*Enter* Leonora, *with two coffins . . . and two winding-sheets. . .* (V.iv.125). Romelio's much anthologized aria at this point on the transitoriness of life ("All the flowers of the spring . . .") amounts to yet another dirge in the style of "*Call for the robin-red-breast and the wren . . .*" (*The White Devil*, V.iv.95) and "*Hark, now everything is still . . .*" (*The Duchess of Malfi*, IV.ii.178), chanted or intoned to similarly haunting effect. The two bellmen and the Capuchin whose entrance ritualizes the church's sorrow for the "excommunicate" duelists "Denied Christian burial" (*The Devil's Law-Case*, II.iii.94–103) suggests Bosola's fearsome ministrations to the Duchess of Malfi as "the common bellman . . . sent to condemn'd persons" (IV.ii.173–174). Ironically, Romelio also mentions "the common bellman" just before the ecclesiastical procession for Ercole and Contarino enters—but, characteristically, in a commercial context, for he takes the offstage tolling of bells to be an advertisement for "the sale of goods" (*The Devil's Law-Case*, II.iii.86–87). Webster gives us an altered version of a sensational shift from pretense to actuality in Romelio's false repentance followed by his authentic one. Flamineo's feigned death, resurrection, and genuine murder (an earlier example of this surprise technique) necessitate the same rapid readjustments of emotion from gravity to laughter and back to gravity again.

Nor does this list exhaust the parallels to the earlier plays, although most of the others consist mainly of incidental details. Jolenta's disguise as a Moorish nun in the last scene of the tragicomedy reminds us of Francisco's impersonation of Mulinassar at the end of *The White Devil*, and the cast list describes her suitor Ercole as a Knight of Malta, the same order, apparently, to which the two Hungarian noblemen who attend the soldierly Moor are said to belong (*The White Devil*, V.i.18–20). Capuchins, of course, appear in both plays, although in the tragedy they are actually disguised revengers, not savers of souls. The "precontract" of marriage between Jolenta and Contarino (*The Devil's Law-Case*, III.iii.53) that Romelio plans to announce as a means of legitimizing his bastard and that Ercole is prepared to credit because only "the ceremony o' th' church was wanting" (III.iii.349) invokes the device of marriage "*Per verba de presenti*" that had figured so importantly in *The Duchess of Malfi* (I.i.478–479). Romelio's "Absolute matrimony" (*The Devil's Law-Case*, III.iii.57) even echoes the Duchess's "absolute marriage" (I.i.479). Furthermore, Jolenta's veiled words of affection to her suitor recall the Duchess's proposal to Antonio, for the girl speaks of leaving him "all that's mine" in "a deed of gift," to which he rejoins, "That's done already; you are all mine" (*The Devil's Law-Case*, I.ii.234–237). The Duchess also makes a will in the presence of her lover, and he later puns on the possession of property in similar fashion: when she pretends to "confiscate . . . All that you have," Antonio replies, "I am all yours: and 'tis very fit / All mine should be so" (*The Duchess of Malfi*, III.ii.206–207).

Jolenta's feigning of pregnancy with the "qualms and swoundings" of "a great-bellied woman," the "quilted preface" to her "petticoat," and the eating of "unripe fruit" (III.iii.186–191) represents the inverse of the Duchess of Malfi's behavior. The tragic character blames her "cold sweat" and swollen stomach on "green fruit" (*The Duchess of Malfi*, II.i.154–156)—the apricocks that Bosola has given her—and wears a "loose-body'd gown" (II.i.149) to hide her condition; in addition, Ariosto has already mentioned "apricocks" as a likely delicacy "to pleasure a friend at Court with" (II.i.197–198). Romelio and Leonora lecture Jolenta in concert on the folly of her marriage plans (I.ii.70–92) as the Aragonian brothers browbeat their sister in a similar manner and on a similar theme in *The Duchess of Malfi* (I.i.292–328). Later on in *The Devil's Law-Case* (II.i.174–189), Ariosto and Romelio bait Julio in like fashion on the vices and irresponsibilities of youth. The motif of twins, so vital to the symbolic relationships of the Duchess of Malfi and her siblings, surfaces briefly in the tragicomedy when Romelio proposes that Jolenta pass off her own unborn child together with that of Angiolella as a double parturition—"two at a birth" (III.iii.80). Contilupo's farfetched testimony at the trial that his client had pretended to deliver her child prematurely as the result of fright induced by a servant's arson (IV.ii.222–229) may have been suggested by the Duchess of Malfi's early labor pains brought on by eating indigestible fruit (*The Duchess of Malfi*, II.i.161–162).

As a revenger, Leonora glories in her "unimitable plot," "a subtle combination" of diabolism, litigiousness, and "one woman's wit" (*The Devil's Law-Case*, III.iii.426–431). Her mixture of gusto and malevolent artistry resembles that of Lodovico, who would have his "plot be ingenious" (*The White Devil*, V.i.75) and who murders "quaint[ly]" (V.iii.178). Like her male counterpart, Leonora also uses the church to back up her villainy, swearing Winifrid to secrecy with the assistance of her "ghostly father" (III.iii.426); Lodovico seals his unholy bargain with Francisco by taking "the sacrament to prosecute . . . murder" (IV.iii.72–73). The waiting woman's cynical suggestion to her mistress that the best means of ensuring trust between accomplices is through the exchange of guilty secrets (*The Devil's Law-Case*, III.iii.389–392) echoes the similar episode in *The Duchess of Malfi* when Julia inveigles the Cardinal into revealing the strangulation of his sister by reminding him that he has long possessed the knowledge of the confidante's secret sins (V.ii.250–257). Ercole's sudden access of "compassion" for Jolenta (*The Devil's Law-Case*, III.iii.340), on revealing himself to Leonora and misinterpreting her strange grief to mean that her daughter is pregnant by Contarino, recalls Flamineo's equally sudden attack of "Compassion" in *The White Devil* (V.iv.115) after observing his mother's crazed lament over the body of Marcello. The two spectacular combats of *The Devil's Law-Case*—especially the second in the "lists" with its ceremonial trappings—represent stage effects similar to the elaborate "barriers" of *The White Devil*. In all three cases the symbolism of profound emotional and moral confusion against a background of punctilious "honor" and social order comes through forcefully. In the tragicomedy Webster once more invokes his habit of imbedding a set character sketch in mid-scene as he had done with Monticelso's portrait of a whore (*The White Devil*, III.ii.79–101) and with Antonio's descriptions of the royal family at Amalfi (*The Duchess of Malfi*, I.i.156–205). Perhaps it is not entirely fortuitous that the rivals for Jolenta's hand reveal that they have been "students . . . together" (*The Devil's Law-Case*, II.i.240–241) at Bosola's university, Padua, and that the foolish Julio ends by going to sea "Against the pirates" (*The Devil's Law-Case*, V.vi.71), the same activity assigned to Camillo and Marcello in *The White Devil* (II.i.359–362).

Not surprisingly, the language of *The Devil's Law-Case* is replete with images, "sentences," turns of thought, and other stylistic hallmarks from the tragedies, often significantly altered by a change of context or reapplied in a fresh way. Webster, for instance, associates mathematics with physical movement as in his preceding play, but in the tragicomedy with less grotesquerie: Romelio speaks of the body's "rare and curious pieces / Of mathematical motion" (*The Devil's Law-Case*, I.i.70–71) whereas Bosola had referred to the locomotion of disabled veterans on crutches as "a kind of geometry" (*The Duchess of Malfi*, I.i.61). Romelio, contemplating the murder of Contarino, soliloquizes upon his own danger with the maxim that "pyramids o' th' top are still most weak" (*The Devil's Law-Case*, II.iii.195), a totally changed use of the pyramid figure that Bosola had invoked for the Cardinal whose life ended "in a little point, a kind of nothing" (*The Duchess of Malfi*, V.v.79). Delio's moving comment on the temporary eminence of evil men, its "form and matter" melting like a "print in snow" when "the sun shines" (*The Duchess of Malfi*, V.v.113–117), modulates in the tragicomedy into a caustic remark by Romelio on one of his beggarly competitors in merchandizing—a man who has "melted" himself "to snow water / With toiling" all his life for a mere "fifty thousand ducats" (*The Devil's Law-Case*, I.i.22–24). Webster's potent word "mist" to suggest tragic confusion, particularly the confusion of death (*The White Devil*, V.vi.260; *The Duchess of Malfi*, IV.ii.188, V.v.94), changes in *The Devil's Law-Case* to the more socially oriented "court-mist" (I.ii.68), a metaphor to signify Jolenta's misguided preference for the more aristocratic of her two suitors. The "bitter" speeches of Monticelso at Vittoria's trial (*The White Devil*, III.ii.107) and the "flashes" that "superficially hang" on the Aragonian cardinal (*The Duchess of Malfi*, I.i.156) seem to recombine in the "bitter flashes" that Jolenta utters when her brother disillusions her about Contarino (*The Devil's Law-Case*, III.iii.182). The "black storm" (at sea) of Vittoria's metaphysical despair before her death (*The White Devil*, V.vi.248) becomes "a storm . . . more terrible than a sea fight" (*The Devil's Law-Case*, V.iv.119–120), an image used to describe Romelio's ultimately affirmative struggle with unbelief.

Of course more straightforward repetitions occur as well. Ariosto borrows the Duchess of Malfi's joke on Count Malateste (*The Duchess of Malfi*, III.i.42–43) for a rebuke to Julio: "You are a mere stick of sugar candy: a man may look quite through you" (*The Devil's Law-Case*, II.i.150–152). Webster reappropriates the figure of an overcharged cannon flying in pieces, applied earlier to the heroine's emotional extremity in *The Duchess of Malfi* (III.v.105–106), for Leonora's passionate soliloquy of vengeance (*The Devil's Law-Case*, III.iii.289). Antonio's line, "The devil, that rules i' th' air, stands in your light" (*The Duchess of Malfi*, II.i.95), is given with the change of only a pronoun to the Capuchin of the later play (V.v.23). A favorite sentence from the *Arcadia*, used already for the Duchess of Malfi's brave confrontation with her brother in the tragedy (III.ii.70–71), Webster now reassigns to Contarino preparing to fight his rival: "whether our time calls us to live or die, / Let us do both like noble gentlemen . . ." (*The Devil's Law-Case*, II.i.316–317). Duke Ferdinand's unconsciously charged line to his sister, "I have a suit to you" (*The Duchess of Malfi*, I.i.213), reappears in *The Devil's Law-Case* (the pun on "suit" is even clearer in the tragicomedy) when Contarino approaches Leonora about his interest in Jolenta (I.i.150). The word "lost" reverberates through *The Devil's Law-Case* as through *The White Devil*, and Leonora's "O, I am lost forever!" (II.iii.102) on the report of her beloved's death is an exact quotation of Vittoria's cry after Bracciano has been poisoned (V.iii.35). The expression "part of yourself" (*The Devil's Law-Case*, I.ii.296), used to convey the sense of the indissoluble blood-relationship between Jolenta and her brother, is virtually the same as that adopted in *The White Devil* to describe the tie between Giovanni and his sinister uncle (V.vi.286); the theme of identification thus sounded is similarly disquieting in both contexts. Webster also appears to borrow from *The White Devil* (perhaps unconsciously) several other details of the tragicomedy. Winifrid's aside on the amorous attraction between Contarino and Jolenta, "How they grow together!" (*The Devil's Law-Case*, I.ii.265), is a somewhat more discreet version of Zanche's remark on the openly sexual interview between Bracciano and Vittoria, "See now they close" (*The White Devil*, I.ii.214). Also Romelio's exclamation just before commencing his duel, "I do not well know whither I am going" (*The Devil's Law-Case*, V.vi.9) echoes Vittoria's "My soul . . . Is driven I know not whither" (*The White Devil*, V.vi.248–249) and Julia's "I go, / I know not whither" (*The Duchess of Malfi*, V.ii.288–289), both spoken at similar moments of existential crisis.

This chain of incidental resemblances to the tragedies could be extended, for Webster mosaicked *The Devil's Law-Case* with images and associations that keep the earlier dramas close to the forefront of our consciousness almost perpetually. The tomb maker (I.ii.3–4), screech owls (II.iii.82), the impermanence of monuments (II.iii.137–140), the mortal danger of "security" (II.iii.192, V.iv.121), the shadow's pursuit of the body (III.ii.2, V.i.48, V.iv.70–72), the mirror as a model to dress by (III.iii.15–16), the rottenness of graves (III.iii.25), the poniard in the heart (III.iii.94), visits of Franciscans (III.iii.226), rapid aging as an effect of grief (III.iii.235), the heatless fire of glowworms (IV.ii.116–117), mushrooms springing from dunghills (IV.ii.128–129), the winding of dead bodies (IV.ii.326), and Toledo sword blades (V.iv.64) all show up in the text. Even the names of Julio (Crispiano's son) and Francisco (Romelio's deceased father) are duplications from the cast of *The White Devil*. This regular appropriation of material from the tragedies or—which is often the case—from the same commonplace book that served them also as a source testifies irrefragably to Webster's continuing preoccupation in *The Devil's Law-Case* with themes and ideas that had already energized his poetic imagination so individually. The most interesting features of the new play have to do with the dramatist's subduing of old and seemingly refractory components to a lighter, and finally, comic form. The success with which Webster met this daunting challenge may be less than total, but his attempt at least produced one of the most distinctive and unusual dramas of the seventeenth century. Literary criticism as well as the professional theatre appear at last to be ratifying this judgment.

* * *

The disjunctive tendencies of Webster's dramaturgy seem to threaten cohesion in *The Devil's Law-Case* even more radically than in *The White Devil*. Wright's complaint, penned within living memory of the play's publication, that a number of its passages fail to "hang together" would gain ready assent from many—perhaps most—modern readers. As has been suggested already, the mixed genre that Webster chose to exploit presupposes an audience that can enjoy the witty activity, stimulating both emotionally and intellectually, of watching a plot evolve in which sudden surprises, mysterious behavior, hidden motives, and baffling or apparently inconsistent feelings are progressively shaped by the dramatist into an intelligible whole. Dryden speaks of how "infinitely pleasing" it is "to be led in a labyrinth of design, where you see some of your way before you, yet discern not the end till you arrive at it," and he includes Beaumont and Fletcher's popular *Maid's Tragedy* among his examples of dramas that satisfy this criterion of excellence. For Dryden "variety" of plot is much to be desired so long as "the variety become not a perplexed and confused mass of accidents."[14] The plotting of *The Devil's Law-Case*, although sufficiently labyrinthine, is more irregular and nervous than Beaumont's and indeed seems to court the very perplexity and confusion against which Dryden cautions. Raising as many questions as it answers, the drama gives an impression of having been conceived as a group of separate episodes or emotionally entangling situations that were only later spliced together into a play—the family pressure on the sister, the mother's concealed passion for the daughter's intended, the duel between boyhood friends, the "murder" that effects a miraculous cure, the mother's public dispossessing of her son through a false confession of adultery, the getting of a nun with child, the feigned pregnancy of the sister, the trial by combat, the tricking of the mother and friar into confinement by a pretended repentance, the separate resurrections of the "dead" suitors, and the last-minute submission of a callous and stubborn individualist to religion.

Not that *The Devil's Law-Case* totally wants logical sequence. Looking backward over Webster's mainly unborrowed narrative, we can discern the larger outline of its movement. Romelio's unfeeling scheme (with the help of his mother) to force his sister to marry Ercole results (through a duel and an attempted murder) in the apparent killing of Contarino, Jolenta's choice and Leonora's secret beloved. The supposed death then generates a two-phased countermovement, Leonora's litigatory revenge upon her son and former ally, and the second duel in which Romelio's own life is put at risk. A comic resolution becomes possible when it transpires that both rivals for Jolenta's hand are alive and when the two obsessive schemers, Leonora and Romelio, undergo religious conversions (she through exposure as a liar in court, he through exposure to near-death in combat) and can then be paired off (with Contarino and Angiolella respectively) as co-participants in a triple marriage. Family differences have apparently been composed and the tension between bourgeois fortune building and aristocratic profligacy eased. Selfishness, cynicism, and greed give way before the delayed force of spirituality, intended death eventuates in life, hatred changes to compassion, and tragic potentialities are seemingly transmogrified into parallel weddings, the traditional symbol of personal fulfillment, social connectedness, and future hope. Observed from on high—as it were, under the aspect of eternity—the twisted intentions and would-be crimes of Romelio and Leonora may even be regarded as a composite *felix culpa*, the necessary transgression of Christian myth that brings death and chaos into being, awakens man to his dependence on God, and thus prepares the way for a deliverance from self more profoundly beneficent than his original and untested innocence could ever have merited.

That Webster had such significances at the back of his mind and wished to give them symbolic expression in a story of sin, suffering, and moral clarification is far from dismissible, but the didactic simplicity and even the factual clarity of this summary do violence to much that is psychologically puzzling and satirically deflationary in the actual working out of the conflicts. Such a neatly moralistic overview clashes uncomfortably with the play's density of detail; it belies the pea soup of mystification and the ethical quagmire through which any reader or viewer is required to find passage, even supposing (and this itself is questionable) that he emerges from obscurity into light.

Almost from the beginning Webster immerses us in a world of multiplying uncertainties—a world in which the slipperiness of language and the ambiguity of action make the apprehension of reality frustratingly elusive. Romelio, in his opening speech, smugly compares the "strange confidence" of his "way of trading" to the certainty of "gain / In erecting a lottery" (I.i.15–17). Thus the character who claims a more unlimited control over money and people than any other, who rejoices in the appellation of "Fortunate Young Man" (I.i.13), ironically chooses a simile that telegraphs the dangerous unpredictability of Fortune. This amounts to somewhat more than the dramatization of Marlovian pride in naive flirtation with its own fall. A significant by-product of the remark is our disconcerting awareness that lotteries are either certain or uncertain, either profitable or unprofitable, depending upon whether we operate or patronize them, upon whether they are honestly or dishonestly run, and upon whether we belong to the tiny minority on whom Fortune smiles. The image reminds us, in short, that much in life rests on the shifting relation of facts to our perception of those facts and of both to the uncertainties of human character and the vagaries of chance. To wrestle with all these variables at once is perhaps to consider too curiously, but it is just this kind of problem with which the unfolding action of *The Devil's Law-Case* confronts us. In some respects the actual experience of the play resembles a bewildering passage through a long sequence of mirrored chambers.

In the opening act (the quarto contains no scene divisions) Webster introduces all five of the principals, the most commanding of whom are, of course, the overweening merchant-prince Romelio and his dignified and more subtle mother Leonora. The foolish overconfidence and contemptuous cynicism of the former establish themselves immediately. Romelio boasts untowardly of his vast wealth (did Webster remember Marlowe's "infinite riches in a little room"?), of his international connections, and of his imperviousness to "loss at sea" (I.i.12), then imputes wholly mercenary motives to "the great Lord Contarino" (I.i.30), who courts Jolenta, as he believes, in order to repair "ancient riches . . . pitifully in the wane" but who visits the house under "color" of "sell[ing] land" (I.i.41–43). Romelio, it would appear, cares only for money and power, scorning Contarino's title of nobility and "ancient house" as merely "a superstitious relic of time past" (I.i.37–39). As he tells Prospero, his "most trusted friend," he intends to "break the alliance" (I.i.33–34): let the blue-blooded "venturer" hope "to catch a gilt-head"; he will more likely "draw up a gudgeon" (I.i.50–52).

But, surprisingly, when Contarino enters, Romelio dissembles, pretending to have no inkling of the romance that the suitor (with some embarrassment) now confesses. Then, albeit sarcastically, he encourages him to pursue the union, hiding his intention to thwart the peer's "over-confident purpose" (I.i.117) in a brief aside at the end of the speech:

Believe me, sir, as on the principal column
To advance our house. Why, you bring honor with you,
Which is the soul of wealth. I shall be proud
To live to see my little nephews ride
O' th' upper hand of their uncles; and the daughters
Be rank'd by heralds at solemnities
Before the mother: all this deriv'd
From your nobility. Do not blame me, sir,
If I be taken with't exceedingly;
For this same honor with us citizens
Is a thing we are mainly fond of, especially
When it comes without money, which is very seldom.
But as you do perceive my present temper,
Be sure I am yours—[aside] fir'd with scorn and laughter
At your over-confident purpose—. . . .

(I.i.103–117)

The motive for this elaborate insincerity (apart from Romelio's general dislike of aristocrats) is never entirely clear, although we gather it may have something to do with Leonora who, Romelio assumes, will be delighted by the prospect of a titled son-in-law. And Webster adds another slightly disorienting touch to this interview—a moralistic lecture by Romelio on the "virtue" of action "for a man of great spirit" (I.i.67–72), whether he be soldier, scholar, or merchant—for there is no indication that Contarino fits any of the categories mentioned. The visitor nevertheless is impressed by Romelio's "worthy parts," however "blasted" these may be "By insolent vainglory" (I.i.121–122).

The dramatist also beclouds the nobleman's true intent by forcing us to weigh Romelio's cynical assumption about his quest for a rich wife against Prospero's statement that Contarino surely "loves [Jolenta] entirely, and she deserves it" (I.i.46). For the moment, at least, Webster has given the suitor (according to Prospero, "There lives not a completer gentleman / In Italy" [I.i.36–37]) the aspect of a seventeenth-century Morris Townsend, and the Jamesian ambiguities proliferate immediately in the colloquy between Contarino and Leonora. Considering that he has already obtained the brother's consent, Contarino now seeks "The mother's approbation to the match" (I.i.123), but he pauses (in a soliloquy) to describe the matron so glowingly that we may wonder whether the older or younger woman attracts him the more:

[Leonora] is a woman of that state and bearing,
Though she be City-born, both in her language,
Her garments, and her table, she excels
Our ladies of the Court. She goes not gaudy,
Yet I have seen her wear one diamond
Would have bought twenty gay ones out of their clothes,

And some of them, without the greater grace,
Out of their honesties.

(I.i.124–131)

At the very least, this speech, although it mentions Leonora's jewelry, compares favorably in warmth with Contarino's earlier allusion to Jolenta as the "wealthy" object of his "voyage," a "mine" to be "got . . . In mine own possession" (I.i.93–95)—words, by the way, that, however romantic their true meaning, might easily be taken to confirm Romelio's assessment of the speaker as a fortune hunter.

Alone finally with the mother, Contarino now seems to apply a strange test to discover "How she stands affected" to him (I.i.133). The necessity of a test is anything but patent, since Romelio has already predicted her approval of the marriage and since, as we quickly learn, the suitor is already "bound to [her] for many special favors" (I.i.138). He nevertheless proceeds with mysterious indirection, praising the "sweet[ness]" of her "breath" (I.i.140–141), mentioning the "suit" (I.i.150) he is about to make to her, asking for her "picture" (I.i.154), and adding that the "latter spring" of her autumnal beauty

shows in my eye
More fruitful and more temperate withal,
Than that whose date is only limited
By the music of the cuckoo.

(I.i.158–161)

The mention of the "cuckoo" with its associative ties to cuckoldry suggests a certain sexual ambience in the relationship, but, more importantly, Webster causes several possible meanings to hang on the suggestive word "picture," and the misunderstandings because of it mount like arithmetic.

Does Contarino consciously intend merely to flatter his fiancée's mother before broaching the delicate matter of his precontract with her daughter by begging a likeness of the older woman that he can treasure as "a most choice object" (I.i.166)? Or does he mean Leonora (and Webster the theatre audience) to take "picture" and "object" as metaphors for Jolenta? If this latter is Contarino's intention, it sorts oddly with his apparent surprise, expressed later, that the mother has somehow got wind of his plan to marry the girl and with the implication that a figurative understanding of his words would require ingenuity. Leonora, who privately adores Contarino, is of course only too willing to see in the request for a picture a veiled declaration of romantic love. But then, after Leonora's offer of "forty thousand crowns" (I.i.205) and her equivocal statement,

I would not have you come hither, sir, to sell,
But to settle your estate. I hope you understand
Wherefore I make this proffer . . .

(I.i.209–211),

Contarino misinterprets her misinterpretation. Or does he? He believes, he says, that Leonora cleverly understood the word "picture" in a purely figurative sense, although it is hard to think that her coy reaction to his request could have left any such impression:

> She has got some intelligence, how I intend to marry
> Her daughter, and ingenuously [i.e., ingeniously] perceived
> That by her picture, which I begged of her,
> I meant the fair Jolenta.
>
> (I.i.214–217)

Contarino's curious reading of this episode, let alone his part in it, seems rather more strained than Leonora's. Moreover, the extended discussion of portrait painting (with its complex implications about appearance and reality) that has preceded Contarino's dubious inference adds further to the audience's sense of disorientation. Only with the advantage of hindsight can we see that Webster has been subtly preparing the ground for his coupling of Contarino and Leonora in the denouement by dramatizing a mutual attraction the true nature of which is suppressed, or at least goes unacknowledged, by one of the parties involved. Nor does the psychological murkiness stop here, for the scene ends with Contarino's revelation of a puzzling letter from his betrothed that raises still further queries. He is to visit her ominously at midnight:

> "Fail not to come, for 'tis a business
> That concerns both our honors.
> *Yours, in danger to be lost, Jolenta.*"
> 'Tis a strange injunction. What should be the business?
> She is not chang'd, I hope. I'll thither straight;
> For women's resolutions in such deeds,
> Like bees, light oft on flowers, and oft on weeds.
>
> (I.i.220–226)

That Contarino's only means of accounting for this cryptic summons is to suspect Jolenta of fickleness may constitute further preparation for the amorous realignments of the comic ending, but at this point the immediate effect is to create still further uncertainty and suspense.

The bringing of Jolenta and Ercole onstage in the second scene also complicates our sense of how matters stand, for now additional incongruities and dissonances accumulate. Romelio introduces the rival suitor to his sister with a royal testimonial that Jolenta rudely suggests may have little to do with the worthiness of its subject. For his part, Ercole feels insulted that Romelio should have misled him about Jolenta's intentions, threatening to call him to "strict account" for "unmanly dealing" (I.ii.64–65); but then he passively allows Leonora and her son to badger the girl cruelly into what looks like reluctant acquiescence. As part of the heavy persuasion, Leonora announces (most ironically in view of her passion for Contarino and the final outcome) that for her childrens' sake she "will never marry again" (I.ii.88). Ercole, apparently mollified, takes his leave with the assertion that he loves Jolenta "entirely" and will, if necessary, "depart from life / To do [her] any service" (I.ii.161–167), while she, surprisingly, promises to "pray for" him (I.ii.169). Romelio (like the jealous husband of humours comedy) orders Winifrid to "bar [his sister] / All visitants" (I.ii.182–183) and, on pain of death, to guard her like a criminal, but Contarino gains access without difficulty, and Winifrid (in the vein of Juliet's nurse) is soon urging the lovers to go "instantly to bed together" (I.ii.286).

When Jolenta reveals that she is "forespoken / To be married to another" (I.ii.242–243), Contarino proposes that he and she "instantly be married" (I.ii.285) to prevent the alliance to Ercole, and Jolenta consents, but only on condition that he promise not to quarrel on grounds of wounded honor with her relatives or the rival. Contarino agrees to the proviso because Jolenta has defended Ercole as "guiltless" (I.ii.295) and praised his "true compassion" and "worthy / Demeanor" (I.ii.257–259), but he also pardons the wrongdoing of Romelio and his mother simply on account of their blood-relationship to his sweetheart. Although Webster offers us no explanation, the plan for a private marriage is aborted, for the next time we see Contarino (in Act II after the subplot has been launched), he is not only unmarried but in the process of breaking his word to Jolenta—that is, challenging Ercole to a duel. If the riddles and unpredictabilities of the play's opening do nothing else, they at least establish a world in which illogicality is the rule rather than the exception and in which the characters appear to understand their own motives as little as those with whom they interact. The strong-willed Romelio and Leonora may know—or think they know— what they want out of life, but their perception of others is shown to be myopic, and Jolenta, Contarino, and Ercole appear, in their different ways, to grope their way along as though half blind. Even the loyalty of Winifrid, whether to Romelio or Jolenta, seems unreliable. Webster introduces us to a tangle of relationships in which hypocrisy, solipsism, impulsiveness, and shifting allegiances command the stage.

As *The Devil's Law-Case* gathers momentum, its characters and actions continue to generate uncertainties of response. The lawyer Crispiano disguises himself as a merchant, partly that he may spy undetected on his spendthrift son; yet he genially tolerates Julio's "course of riot" (II.i.22), arguing with bizarre logic that the accumulation of money is more pleasurable than the spending of it:

> neither wine, nor lust, nor riotous feasts,
> Rich clothes, nor all the pleasure that the devil
> Has ever practic'd with to raise a man
> To a devil's likeness, e'er brought man that pleasure
> I took in getting my wealth: so I conclude.
> If [Julio] can out-vie me, let it fly to th' devil.
>
> (II.i.87–92)

Crispiano takes the comic position that since money offers the devil special opportunities to tempt a man, there is a kind of mad justice in letting it revert as
quickly as possible to its diabolic origins. Nevertheless, the taking of fees has
been the chief delight of the lawyer's energetic career. Of course, Crispiano's attitude toward wealth is too jocosely paradoxical to bear much ethical scrutiny,
but his view of getting and spending as a sportive contest between two different
forms of personal gratification obviously contrasts with Romelio's arrogant ac-
quisitiveness. Romelio's materialism invites condemnation, whereas Crispiano's
encourages bemused acceptance. No doubt Webster presents this opposition
partly as a means of relating the subplot to the central action (another example is
the obvious parallel between the baiting of young Julio and the earlier baiting of
Jolenta), but the effect is also to raise questions about the proper attitude toward
amassing riches and, beyond this, about the didactic or amoral foundation upon
which the whole drama is presumably to stand.

The quarrel between the play's two aristocrats is similarly unsettling. Contarino approaches his rival in a tone of injured friendship, bending over backwards to deliver his challenge with an elaborate display of gentlemanly courtesy
and emotional sensitivity. Ercole responds in kind: "You deal fair, sir" (II.i.269).
But Contarino has a nagging "doubt," namely whether Romelio was "a main instrument" (II.i.270–273) in Jolenta's change of marriage plans, and, unaccount-
ably, Ercole now denies (with a defensive show of veracity even more elaborate)
what has clearly been shown to us in Act I:

> *Ercole.* If I tell truth, you will not credit me.
> *Contarino.* Why?
> *Ercole.* I will tell you truth,
>   Yet show some reason you have not to believe me.
>   Her brother had no hand in't: is't not hard
>   For you to credit this? For you may think
>   I count it baseness to engage another
>   Into my quarrel; and for that take leave
>   To dissemble the truth. Sir, if you will fight
>   With any but myself, fight with her mother;
>   She was the motive.
>
> (II.i.275–285)

Is Ercole blatantly lying to his friend here? He knows that Contarino will find his
explanation hard to accept. Or is he honestly deceived about Romelio's selfish
reasons for preferring him over Contarino? Ercole, after all, was present when
Romelio exerted pressure on Jolenta and when she bitterly resisted, and we have
heard him in the same scene charge Romelio angrily with fostering the "vain confidence that I should marry / Your sister" (I.ii.58–59). Is Ercole so foolish as to
regard Romelio as merely the agent of his mother's designs? Or are we dealing
here with another example of myopia? Since nothing else in the play consists
with a conception of Ercole—the future spouse of the heroine—as willfully men-

dacious, we are more or less compelled to conclude that he does not know whereof he speaks; but almost any audience might be pardoned for thinking that Webster had gone out of his way to sow confusion.

This impression is compounded by the contradictory attitude toward Italians that the dramatist manages to work into the same episode. Appealing to the values of chivalry, Contarino couples "noble gentlemen" and "true Italians" (II.i.317–318) as virtually synonymous, but a few lines earlier, in reference to his openness in challenging Ercole, he implies the very opposite: "I have not ta'en the way, / Like an Italian, to cut your throat / By practice . . ." (II.i.265–267). When the two enemies embrace, the uncertainty persists:

> *Contarino.* Methinks, being an Italian, I trust you
> To come somewhat too near me;
> But your jealousy gave that embrace to try
> If I were armed, did it not?
> *Ercole.* No, believe me,
> I take your heart to be sufficient proof,
> Without a privy coat; and, for my part,
> A taffety is all the shirt of mail
> I am armed with.
> (II.i.320–328)

Does Webster mean to suggest in Contarino an unresolved struggle between aristocratic magnanimity and pragmatic suspicion, or has he simply forgotten within the space of a single scene that his play is set in Italy and that his characters would be most unlikely to share the prejudices of Jacobean Protestantism?

The duel appears to be predicated on a kind of knightly absolutism, as though the most rigid and archaic code of honor were the only value to be considered. Yet Webster riddles his presentation with the sort of ambiguity that makes it impossible to ignore human complexity. The combatants are torn between affection and enmity, between trust and wariness, and larger truths have been concealed or unconsciously suppressed in the service of an ideal that seems partial, oversimplified—perhaps even foolhardy—and is certainly incommensurate with the actualities of their situation. Nor is it insignificant that so grandiose an action as a contest to the death should end so inconclusively, each figure injuring but failing to eliminate the other. The tragicomic conventions of the plot are obviously at work here, but it is wholly typical of this play that its conflicts should refuse to resolve themselves neatly or schematically. Webster even involves the audience in these insecurities, for at the end of the fight Ercole, apparently *in extremis*, must be carried offstage, and Contarino's life, too, is in grave peril. Then in the following scene the Capuchin (with his bellmen) bemoans the "sad fate" of both and pronounces them canonically "guilty of their own death" (II.iii.93–98). Probability would appear to have become fact. But only a hundred or so lines brings us to the startling revelation that Ercole has been "preserved beyond natural reason" (II.iv.1) and the opinion that "There is hope of life / In Contarino" (II.iv.18–19). We have entered a world in which appearances onstage and reports of actions offstage are, at best, only provisionally true and, at worst, false.

Events now begin to modify and therefore to complicate our first impression of Romelio. In the opening episodes he had come off as a Marlovian overreacher, single-mindedly committed to self-aggrandizing action—his own enrichment and the domination of his sister toward that end. Now with the news of his calamitous losses at sea, Romelio reveals an introspective side, philosophizing with barbed stoicism and caustic wit on the hypocrisies and futility of received opinion—particularly religious opinion. He spurns the "superstitious" doctrine that the "devilish names" of his ships (II.iii.65–69) could account for their wreckage. He ridicules Ariosto's counsel of Christian patience by pointing out that the law's delay is such as to convert three quarters of the world to the recommended virtue and insisting that only cuckolds have been sufficiently tested by adversities to be qualified preachers of it. He intones a Hamletian "meditation" (II.iii.111) in rhymed couplets on funeral ostentation and the impermanence of graves, remarking on the outrages to which human bones are subjected—an oddly discordant aria on the theme of Ecclesiastes: *vanitas vanitatum*. His view of the married state is so negative and his misogyny so virulent (he greets even his own mother with the epithet "screech owl" [II.iii.82]) that we are brought up short by his spontaneous expression of tenderness for his sister when he believes her lover to be dead:

> Poor Jolenta! Should she hear of this,
> She would not after the report keep fresh
> So long as flowers in graves.
>
> (II.iii.156–158)

This unselfish impulse—the cynic's momentary but unguarded manifestation of a better nature—points to the softer, more humane Romelio that emerges, however tentatively, at the end of the play, but, in context, it seems out of character. By the end of the scene, after Prospero has shunted the story in a fresh direction with news that Contarino still lives and has made Jolenta his heir, we see a Romelio "full of thoughts"—simultaneously plotting to recoup his "losses" through murder and moralizing on the corruptibility of a world "made insolent with riches" (II.iii.187–193). If Romelio's conscience is too weak to restrain him from homicide, at least his awareness has been stretched. Through Leonora's intense but disguised interest in Contarino's survival, her "cruelty appareled in kindness" (II.iii.186) as he calls it, Romelio appears to feel intimations, however inexplicitly, of his mother's secret passion. Now he sees the effect of greed and knows, as he did not before, the danger of "security" (II.iii.192)— that is, of a naive faith in his own invulnerability. Webster would seem to have superimposed the affectionate brother upon the misanthropic individualist, the philosopher upon the criminal, and the conscience-plagued moralist upon the callous opportunist.

A suddenly changed Ercole also strains our grasp of character. The gallant who, earlier in the act, was so committed to Jolenta that he had hazarded his life and tried to kill his best friend rather than give her up, now reverses position with the same conviction of unshakable rightness that had originally impelled him:

> *Capuchin.* Look up, sir. You are preserved beyond natural
> reason; you were brought dead out o' th' field, the sur-
> geons ready to have embalmed you.
> *Ercole.* I do look on my action with a thought of terror;
> To do ill and dwell in't, is unmanly.
> *Capuchin.* You are divinely informed, sir.
> *Ercole.* I fought for one in whom I have no more right
> Than false executors have in orphans' goods
> They cozen them of; yet though my cause were naught,
> I rather chose the hazard of my soul,
> Than forgo the complement of a choleric man.
>
> (II.iv.1–11)

This, too, may be taken as proleptic of the improbable ending—a dramatic precedent, so to say, of the unpredictable conversion (often in response to a brush with death) that comes with the overwhelming force and speed of St. Paul's blinding light near Damascus. But the *dramatic*, as opposed to the structural, point is again to underline the inconsistency of human behavior and to place its deeper motivations almost beyond the range of common understanding or observation. Humility is claimed miraculously to have subdued pride, probity underhandedness, and friendship sexual desire—virtues that now, paradoxically, make Ercole a worthier mate for Jolenta than the conventionally proprietary claimant of the earlier scenes.

But the new absolutism proves no more reassuring than the old. Ercole wants "the report of [his] death" (II.iv.12) to remain in force so that, if Contarino recovers, he can marry the girl unopposed; to the argument that his friend may then be charged with murder, Ercole replies that an automatic pardon, hereditarily guaranteed for anyone who "should chance / To kill . . . in a noble cause" (II.iv.33–34), would shield him. A certain queasiness about means seems unavoidable: the living out of a lie and a special exemption from the law are invoked to advance friendship and promote what the speaker assumes to be true love. And, furthermore, doubts about just how "noble" Contarino's "cause" is have never quite been laid. Moreover, Ercole now puts upon Romelio the "guilt" (II.iv.39) for his wound, thus contradicting his statement before the duel that the merchant "had no hand" (II.i.279) in the quarrel over whom Jolenta should marry; and he adds the charge that Romelio "has got a nun with child" (II.iv.41), a new bit of information sensational not only for itself but for the reassessment of character that it instantly necessitates, for we have so far had no indication of lustful proclivities in the villain. Also, since the speaker has just barely escaped embalming, we wonder where and how he could have obtained his information. No explanation is forthcoming. When the Capuchin remarks that Romelio's "crimes" are damnable unless speedily repented, Ercole's strangely opaque reaction is to express "much compassion" for the wrongdoer and to speak of "violence" as the only means of sundering "sin and shame" (II.iv.42–47), as though violence (unless suicide is being foreseen) bore much logical relation to a sinner's struggle with his conscience. Webster presents us with a character (his name is a variant of Hercules) in whom physical bravery, high religious principle, personal loyalty, factual inconsistency, privileged knowledge, misplaced sympathy, and a certain moral astigmatism seem to be bafflingly mingled. No wonder we have trouble keeping Ercole in focus.

Act III functions as the fulcrum of the play, raising Romelio's villainies to their apex and gradually transferring the focus of attention to Leonora, the second diabolic activist of the drama. In this process—through a staccato succession of errors, revelations, untruths, deceptions, and counterdeceptions, Webster keeps his audience perpetually off balance. Ironies proliferate vertiginously, spawned by the twists and turns of plot and by the "giddy and uncertain changes" (III.iii.203) of the characters. The climate of intrigue and distrust is quickly made international by the disclosure that Crispiano has disguised himself not only in order to spy on his son but also to serve as informer to the King of Spain about Romelio's financial dealings and what he ominously refers to as the "mad tricks . . . play'd of late by ladies" (III.i.10). A collection of antifemale generalizations by Ariosto darkly prepares the ground for Crispiano's role in the law case to follow, for the disguised jurist reponds to them in these words:

> Well, I have vowed
> That I will never sit upon the bench more,
> Unless it be to curb the insolencies
> Of these women.
>
> (III.i.27–30)

Romelio, dressed as "a rare Italianated Jew," seems now to cloak the moral and psychological complexities developed earlier under the habiliments of the stage Machiavel, reveling, like a self-parodist, in the fantasy of "as many several changes of faces / As I have seen carv'd upon one cherry stone" and a list of farcically irrelevant outrages, including "Betray[ing] a town to th' Turk" (III.ii.3–13), that identifies him temporarily with Marlowe's revenger-farceur, Barabas. Disguise, whether physical or behavioral, starts to become nearly everyone's stock-in-trade. The "murder" scene is presented as a seriocomic crosshatching of unnatural acts and purposes mistook designed to alter our perception of reality almost momently even as it darkens our view of human motivation.

To gain entrance to the bedside of Contarino, now pronounced by the attending surgeons to be "past all cure" (III.ii.23), Romelio corrupts the doctors to the tune of ten thousand ducats and invents the improbable tale that he, too, is a physician and has been sent by a Roman kinsman of the sick man to persuade him to change his will: the kinsman will supposedly replace Jolenta as Contarino's heir, and Romelio, with the help of his fellow physicians, will then smother the nobleman. The Jew, of course, pretends to be working against Romelio, so that the paramount irony (from the audience's point of view) consists in the villain-hero's having created for himself a villainous alter ego who will actually advance his real interests but appear to be defeating them. Yet appearance and reality also coincide in a way, since both true and false identities are as one in purposing the same man's death. Romelio, true to his fantasy image of duplicity, does indeed "play with [his] own shadow" (III.ii.2) in this episode. But as he approaches the wounded Contarino, a fresh irony quickly surfaces, for the would-be murderer rationalizes his action as "revenge" for the "untimely death" (III.ii.85–86) of Ercole, who, as we know, remains alive.

At this point also Romelio's moral complexity suddenly re-emerges from behind the farcical mask. The soliloquist pauses to remind himself as he prepares to kill Contarino that the Machiavel's "desperate stiletto," small enough to "be worn / In a woman's hair," is "a most unmanly weapon" (III.ii.93–98); and the contemplated action prompts him to muse upon the treachery of Julius Caesar's assassination. The merchant, "horribly angry" with himself for causing a noble enemy to die "scurvily" (III.ii.106–107), wrestles with the conscience of which, but minutes earlier, he had appeared to be disburdened, and can finally strengthen his resolve only by reassuring himself that a death by stabbing is preferable to the shameful execution for the murder of Ercole that might be Contarino's fate in the event of his recovery. That the stab wound, unbeknown to Romelio, should ultimately bring about the healing of the nobleman rather than his death makes all the preliminary ironies of the scene laughable, but Webster has first to pursue his witty pattern of discrepant perceptions to its utmost.

The surgeons, whom Romelio mistakenly characterizes as "credulous fools" (III.ii.82), also play a double game. Suspecting "some trick" (III.ii.80), they confront Romelio with being a "rogue mountebank" (III.ii.117) after he thinks he has murdered their charge, whereupon the "Jew" instantly "turn[s] Christian," discloses himself as "Romelio the merchant" (III.ii.120–124), and attempts to buy their silence with "a bag of double ducats" (III.ii.138). The most prominent manipulator of the drama has been exposed and trapped by a pair of pettier charlatans. They gleefully point out that murder was unnecessary, since, in the course of nature, Contarino would have died of his wounds within "two hours" (III.ii.132). Then, after promising to keep his guilty secret, they privately prepare to extort money from Romelio "every eight days" or "peach" (III.ii.152–153). By the end of the scene the terms "Christian" and "Jew" have been reduced absurdly to alternative labels for the same absence of scruple, and we must therefore take with some reservation both the sincerity and the validity of the first surgeon's religious explanation for Contarino's revival:

> The hand of heaven is in't,
> That his intent to kill him should become
> The very direct way to save his life.
> (III.ii.164–166)

Profit is still uppermost in the physicians' minds, and the new situation doubles the opportunities of the old by making "reward / On both sides" (III.ii.169–170) possible: Romelio, even when he discovers that his violence has failed of its object, will continue to pay for silence, and Contarino will suppose that he owes his life to the medical expertise of his physicians.

Webster's tortuous plot requires a yet thicker profusion of ironies. In the presence of a skull (the tragedian's emblem of mortality) Jolenta grieves for the premature death of Contarino, while her brother (who, for a different reason, also believes the young lord dead) cruelly augments her pain by depreciating the loss: "Why, I pray tell me, / Is not the shortest fever the best. . . ?" (III.iii.6–7). Hostile wit abrades pathos, and mercantile arrogance sneers at hereditary privilege. One form of pride dismisses another:

> I must tell you, sister,
> If th' excellency of the [court] could have wrought salvation,
> The devil had ne'er fall'n from heaven; he was proud.
> (III.iii.16–18)

Then, cutting off Jolenta's escape from such bitter sayings, Romelio proposes a conspiracy to "breed . . . advancement" (III.iii.22–24) out of the deaths of the rival noblemen—namely, the cynical scheme of passing off his unborn bastard (begotten upon the nun Angiolella) as the fruit of a precontract of marriage between Ercole and his sister. In this way Jolenta can inherit from both her former suitors, and Romelio, who can dominate her, will have gained control over two fortunes instead of one. The grief-stricken girl, suddenly more aggressive than we would have thought likely, now turns the tables on the manipulator by announcing without the slightest warning, and in direct contradiction of her claim to be "a virgin" (III.iii.35) only a moment earlier, that she is "with child already" (III.iii.67) by Contarino. We have moved very quickly indeed from the gloom of the *memento mori* tradition to the comedy of sexual license and legal trickery. Brother and sister are now competing in a contest of ingenuity, the apparently weaker player having nearly checkmated her opponent through the strategy of surprise. The audience, like Romelio, is temporarily taken in by the new datum—"strangely puzzled" (III.iii.76), to borrow his phrase—but, of course, Jolenta is only feigning pregnancy, as we are to learn in a few minutes.

Meanwhile, Romelio tries in desperation to salvage his original plot by suggesting that Angiolella's and his sister's children could be claimed as twins, while Jolenta counters by raising the problems of dissimilar appearance and the resulting damage to her "fame" (III.iii.88). When she decides to reveal that her news was only a trick—a test of Romelio's love through the measuring of his attitude toward her reputation—she refers to her "fatal purpose" (III.iii.91) and seems to return us uncertainly to the ethos of tragedy:

> If you had lov'd or tender'd my dear honor,
> You would have lock'd your poniard in my heart
> When I nam'd I was with child; but I must live
> To linger out, till the consumption
> Of my own sorrow kill me.
>
> (III.iii.93–97)

Jolenta, apparently without mockery, asks her brother and us to regard her deception as a failed, if circuitous, attempt at suicide, casting herself in the role of a violated heroine (such as the Virginia of Webster's Roman drama) whose dishonor only death at the hands of a loving relative could expunge. Apart from the contextual absurdity, the test itself seems ludicrously superfluous, for the treatment she has already suffered at her brother's hands should leave little doubt about the depth of his "love" for her.

Romelio's aside, "This will not do . . ." (III.iii.97), comically understates both his response and ours, and the male player in this game of wits, immediately recovering the initiative, now improvises an even more farfetched plot to manipulate his sister and draw revenue from the supposed death of Ercole. It is the brother's turn to prevaricate. Accordingly, Romelio invents "a most unnatural falsehood" (III.iii.99) designed to blacken Contarino's character so indelibly in the eyes of Jolenta that, in negative reaction, she will be attracted to the memory of the rival suitor whom before she had spurned. Again Webster makes a lie serve truth in the indirect sense that the calumny against Contarino helps prepare the heroine for her alliance with Ercole at the end of the tragicomedy by weaning her away from an immature and rather ill-considered first choice. But however false in fact and intention, Romelio's story contains an element of truth, for it rests upon Leonora's genuine feeling for Contarino. His outrageous claim is that Leonora only pretended to oppose her daughter's marriage to Contarino as a blind; privately she had wished to see the wedding go forward as a cover for her own incestuous passion for the bridegroom, since all three would be living under the same roof. As for Contarino, he had cynically planned to take both women to his bed—Jolenta "For his lust," Leonora "for her money" (III.iii.148–149).

Romelio pretends that he can scarcely "whisper" this scandal "without horror" (III.iii.115), but Jolenta, disconcertingly matter-of-fact, cooly begins cross-examining him like a witness in court. If Contarino had designs on the mother, why did he make the daughter his heir? Why, if he really wanted Leonora, was he willing to "lose / His life" (III.iii.130–131) in a duel over Jolenta? And how could Romelio possibly have learned these shocking secrets? The inventive answer to this last question—that one of the surgeons overheard Contarino's deathbed confession and, doubly violating the sacrament of penance, passed it on—epitomizes the operatic unreality of the whole report and more than prepares us for Jolenta's skeptical line, "Can this be truth?" (III.iii.143). Her brother answers by equivocating the word "falsehood" (III.iii.144) from its plain meaning (a lie) into a strained synonym for Leonora's incestuous plan (her immoral behavior). Then, appearing to discard much of the intelligence she has just displayed in the cross-examination, Jolenta collapses into a state of emotional "conflict / Between apparent presumption and unbelief . . ." (III.iii.154–155). Romelio's strategy has succeeded. Jolenta, railing against the "inconstancy" of men with the same abandon that had characterized her brother's condemnation of women, now protests that she "affect[s] the Lord Ercole's memory / Better than the other's" (III.iii.159–162), would refuse Contarino even if alive, and will consent to "mother" her brother's child to "beguile part of [her] sorrow" (III.iii.170–171), although she is bitter about the necessity to "dissemble dishonesty" (III.iii.183).

Again, ethical questions make the action problematic. Jolenta not only pretends "dishonesty" (in the sense of unchastity), she also *practices* dishonesty. Her willingness to connive in the concealment of her brother's lust and in his acquisition of Ercole's wealth not only is morally irresponsible in itself but also bears only the most tangential relation to the supposed infidelity of Contarino. Romelio, who is in no position to moralize, implies that her motive is "jealousy" (III.iii.207) and seems to associate it with diabolic possession. Yet the play at this point presents Jolenta chiefly as the victim of Romelio and appears to invite only the mildest judgment against her. Webster has deliberately minimized the rights and wrongs of her decision in order to move his plot forward. But again he succeeds in producing a climate of emotional confusion (offstage as well as on) that approaches mental breakdown. Jolenta might almost be speaking for the audience in her exit lines:

> O, my fantastical sorrow! Cannot I now
> Be miserable enough, unless I wear
> A pied fool's coat! Nay worse, for when our passions
> Such giddy and uncertain changes breed,
> We are never well, till we are mad indeed.
> (III.iii.200–204)

Lest Leonora undeceive her daughter, Romelio determines to play his mother and sister off against each other, and unwittingly foreshadows the diabolical "law-case" (III.iii.210) against him by commenting on the lengths to which jealousy can drive women. After the "supposed childbirth," he intends to sequester Jolenta in a nunnery so as to prevent her marriage and become official "guardian / To her estate" (III.iii.214–217); he plans further to secure his safety by shipping the two surgeons off to the East Indies. When Leonora enters, a kind of black comedy ensues, Romelio cheerfully pressing upon her the "strange news" (III.iii.222) of Jolenta's pregnancy while she struggles to absorb the fresh misfortune without slackening her eagerness for news of Contarino's health. Romelio comments acerbly on her emotional gymnastics: "Strange that you can skip / From the former sorrow [i.e., her daughter's disgrace] to such a question!" (III.iii.229–230). Then he delivers the coup de grâce by confessing that he has killed Contarino "in a trice" (III.iii.232), thereby saving him from the lingering death that would otherwise have been his fate at the hands of the bungling doctors. Once more Webster expoits the dramatic irony of cross-purposes. Romelio interprets his mother's agony after the dreadful news as an expression of jealousy, based on the assumption that Contarino is the father of Jolenta's child: Leonora "would have him live" (III.iii.240), presumably to bring him to account not only for disgracing her daughter but also for preferring the younger woman to herself as a romantic partner. But when Romelio insists that Ercole is the father, a statement that he thinks will "heal" his mother's "sorrow" (III.iii.239), he only makes it worse, for she now realizes that she might have had Contarino for herself, her daughter being no true rival after all.

This convoluted situation is typical of Webster's dramatic method in *The Devil's Law-Case*, for it involves the misreading of character on both sides of a theoretically intimate relationship—in this case between mother and son. Romelio brazenly deceives his own parent out of greed but at the same time misjudges her reaction. She in turn accepts his lie for truth but is prompted, partly because of it, to manufacture an even more baroque plot against him—her grotesque revenge at law for the murder of her beloved. Both plots depend on lies as a means of victimization (Jolenta's pregnancy, Ercole's fatherhood, Leonora's adultery, Romelio's illegitimacy), but of course Webster envelops these specific untruths in the more general irony, grasped only by the audience, that both contestants in the tussle of deception are united in their shared ignorance of what *we* know—namely, that Ercole and Contarino survive. Both structures of extravagant cunning rest on the shifting sands of misapprehension.

The long soliloquy in which the idea of revenge against her son germinates in Leonora's mind brings the complicated widow into full definition for the first time in the play. Thus far she has remained shadowy, mysterious, and psychologically ambiguous—a confection of hints, hesitations, and fascinating inscrutabilities. Now she steps forward as a disappointed lover, aging but sexually frustrated, who reproaches herself for oversubtlety and lack of directness, attributing Contarino's death with both conscious and unconscious irony to her solicitude (through the agency of her son) for his recovery. Her phrase, "precise curiosity" (III.iii.266), applies not only to her own self-destructiveness but also to the ironic ways in which the drama as a whole twists and turns back upon itself. But for our knowledge of what Leonora cannot know—that Contarino still breathes—we are squarely back in Webster's high tragic mode:

> Never was woe like mine. O, that my care
> And absolute study to preserve his life
> Should be his absolute ruin! Is he gone then?
> There is no plague i' th' world can be compared
> To impossible desire, for they are plagued
> In the desire itself. Never, O never
> Shall I behold him living, in whose life
> I lived far sweetlier than in mine own.
> A precise curiosity has undone me: why did I not
> Make my love known directly? 'T had not been
> Beyond example for a matron
> To affect i' th' honorable way of marriage
> So youthful a person. O, I shall run mad!
> For as we love our youngest children best,
> So the last fruit of our affection,
> Wherever we bestow it, is most strong,
> Most violent, most unresistable,
> Since 'tis indeed our latest harvest-home,
> Last merriment 'fore winter; and we widows,
> As men report of our best picture-makers,
> We love the piece we are in hand with better
> Than all the excellent work we have done before.
> And my son has depriv'd me of all this. Ha, my son!
> I'll be a fury to him; like an Amazon lady,
> I'd cut off this right pap, that gave him suck,
> To shoot him dead. I'll no more tender him,
> Than had a wolf stol'n to my teat i' th' night
> And robb'd me of my milk; nay, such a creature
> I should love better far. —Ha, ha, what say you?
> I do talk to somewhat, methinks; it may be
> My evil genius. Do not the bells ring?
> I have a strange noise in my head: O, fly in pieces!
> Come, age, and wither me into the malice
> Of those that have been happy; let me have
> One property more than the devil of hell,
> Let me envy the pleasure of youth heartily;
> Let me in this life fear no kind of ill,
> That have no good to hope for.
>
> (III.iii.258–295)

As Lamb (who quoted part of it in his *Specimens*) knew, this is one of the richest and most powerful speeches of the play—a tense orchestration of discordancies that evokes empathy for the speaker's grief and sexual unfulfillment even as it creates revulsion for her translation of these emotions into unnatural loathing for the fruit of her own womb. Webster embodies the depth of her conflict in the imagery: Leonora first draws a parallel between her romantic passion and the love a mother feels for her youngest child, then conjures up the figure of a wolf nursing at her breast to release resentment for the son who, as she believes, has forever destroyed her happiness. And the rhetoric is remarkable too for its balancing of nervous incoherence—a state of mind close to madness—against a wild kind of concentration, self-conscious envy, and malicious rationality. Leonora at this moment can claim only the most tenuous hold upon sanity, yet there is more than a suggestion of unholy method in her raving that tends to reverse her dramatic role, transposing her from victim to nascent villainess. Her allusion to the tragic frustration of Elizabeth over Essex as she falls to the ground (like Othello in his fit) nicely suits her double function as deadly activist and helpless sufferer.

The sudden appearance of Leonora's confessor at this juncture reminds us of the moral and religious threads in her make-up so that the dramatist compels us to walk the knife-edge between regarding the widow as a female devil and as a tortured soul in need of priestly counsel. The Capuchin chooses to interpret her prone position as the self-abasing posture of the contemplative, but his conventionally pietistic words only elicit one of Webster's most trenchantly understated and hauntingly memorable lines: "I am whispering to a dead friend" (III.iii.310). And now with the reappearance of Ercole, who waits in shadow until the friar can prepare Leonora for the shock of seeing him, the scene reverts once more to its characteristic wavering between comic and tragic irony. The Capuchin's "tidings of a friend . . . Restored to life again," of a "son-in-law, miraculously saved" (III.iii.312–318), which Leonora misunderstands as applying to Contarino, briefly restore her faith in divine Providence; then Ercole walks into view, dashing her hopes and plunging her once more into despair:

> O, I am dead again! Instead of the man,
> You present me the grave swallowed him.
>
> (III.iii.329–330)

Ercole, shattered by the unexpected revelation that Romelio has murdered Contarino and that Leonora wishes his rival alive rather than himself, desperately attempts to retrieve the situation by resorting to macabre wit—by identifying himself (as a living penitent) with the corpse of his friend:

> There cannot be a nobler chronicle
> Of his good than myself: if you would view him dead,
> I will present him to you bleeding fresh,
> In my penitency.
>
> (III.iii.333–336)

Ercole's rhetorical fusion of himself with Contarino, of the living with the "dead" suitor, again hints at the protean, almost surreal, concept of identity that so permeates the characterization and dramaturgy of *The Devil's Law-Case*. But a new moral issue has been broached, for Ercole and the Capuchin now know (or rather *think* they know) about Romelio's murder of Contarino, and do nothing to expose the crime or the criminal. Again the complexities of plot create ethical confusions for the audience, but, as we have already seen, Ercole's character eludes moral definition at more than one point in the action.

When Leonora impeaches Ercole (on the basis of Romelio's lie) for the "vild sin" (III.iii.339) of getting Jolenta pregnant, Ercole jumps to the false conclusion that the older woman has misjudged the situation and that Contarino is the true father. Once again ignorance and misperception on both sides of the exchange make for a complex intersection of ironies. And further complexity develops when Ercole, in compassion for Jolenta's endangered "fame," offers to "preserve her credit," marry the girl, and claim the child as his own, while making Leonora his emissary to the lady lest, by appearing suddenly before her (a ghost, as it were, from the grave), her "fright" or "shame" might "blast the fruit within her" (III.iii.342–358). Webster has now maneuvered two of the romantic partners of his conclusion into proper position for union, but he has done so by ironically possessing each of them with the grossest kind of misinformation about the other. Jolenta still believes Ercole to be dead and only gravitates favorably to his memory in revulsion from Contarino, whose good name her brother has besmirched. Ercole, having given up all claim to Jolenta as a result of his conversion experience after combat, now reoffers himself to the lady by way of rescuing her reputation and in homage to his wronged friend, with whom, as he thinks, she has consummated a true marriage "But that the ceremony o' th' church was wanting" (III.iii.349). For her part, Leonora is hugely impressed by Ercole's "loyalty" to his beloved. Within the space of twenty lines her contempt for a man who supposedly debauched her daughter has shifted to admiration for a "most noble fellow" (III.iii.365); but, ironically again, her improved opinion of Ercole causes pain, for she is made more miserable than before by the thought of what similar devotion she has forfeited through the untimely death of "dear Contarino." As she says, laconically summarizing her plight, "all adds / To my despair" (III.iii.367–368).

Webster ends this intricately configured act with a semicomic episode between Leonora and her maid, between two dishonest and distrustful characters seeking to establish a basis for trusting each other. While Winifrid (who represents deceit on a lower social plane) is sent to fetch a mysterious portrait from her mistress's "inner closet" (III.iii.369), Leonora meditates cooly on the artful form of her revenge, preferring to reduce her son to ignominious poverty and disgrace rather than see him suffer violent death as a murderer. The picture, given her "Forty years since" (III.iii.376) by a donor whose name she omits to mention, apparently has the property of inspiring mischievous stratagems in those who gaze upon it; but Webster introduces this object tantalizingly as a clue to future complications and deliberately keeps both Leonora and the theatre audience baffled as to its true import. We do not even know whose likeness Leonora has been carefully preserving, or why. For her part, she "was enjoined" by its original owner to consult it when "vex'd," but does not grasp the mysterious "meaning" (III.iii.375–378) of this instruction. The portrait therefore creates suspense, while also reinforcing the play's themes of uncertain perception and identity, and, of course, recalling Contarino's equivocal request for Leonora's picture in Act I.

As Leonora shrewdly recognizes, Winifrid—both a confidante and potential accomplice—is as necessary to the success of her revenge plot as she is dangerous. By proposing that the servant suggest some means by which her mistress may be sure of her discretion, Leonora reveals a surprising dependency upon her woman that joins the poignant to the ludicrous. The schemer's instinctive fear of sharing a guilty secret gives way before the widow's need for companionship, assistance, and emotional support. The wish for human connection overbears distrust. But at the same time Leonora has entered into a contest of devious wit matching, only to invite her opponent and social inferior to dictate the terms of play, so that the unexpected reversal of roles brings intrigue close to parody. Winifrid's clever response is to point out that an exchange of guilty secrets on the part of both women would endow each with the power of blackmail over the other, and Leonora applauds this cynical idea, acknowledging that "intelligence of one another's shame" has historically "wrought far more effectually than the tie / Of conscience, or religion" (III.iii.398–400). Winifrid gives a further twist to the guilty badinage by insisting that Leonora impute to her no sin against her lady, for if Winifrid had been false in the past, her mistress would be "a fool" to "trust [her] / In the least matter of weight" (III.iii.404–405). The dialogue has quickly become brittle, moving almost to the level of comedy of manners.

Then Webster once again shifts the tone abruptly, showing Leonora in the dejected light of emptiness, futility, and plaintive self-recognition:

> Thou hast lived with me
> These forty years; we have grown old together,
> As many ladies and their women do,
> With talking nothing, and with doing less.
> We have spent our life in that which least concerns life,
> Only in putting on our clothes; and now I think on't,
> I have been a very courtly mistress to thee:
> I have given thee good words, but no deeds. Now's the time
> To requite all. . . .
>
> (III.iii.406–414)

As Elizabeth M. Brennan observes, this passage is strikingly Prufrockian, a seventeenth-century equivalent of "I have measured out my life with coffee spoons."[15] Weary of testing, feinting, and guarded maneuvering, Leonora decides to impart her secret plan as an overdue reward for loyal service. But it is entirely typical of the opaque world of *The Devil's Law-Case* that even when honesty replaces lying, the verbal form of the communication should be liable to misapprehension; for when Leonora speaks metaphorically of the "poison" she is "brewing" for Romelio (meaning her law case against him), the more literal-minded Winifrid automatically assumes that her mistress is plotting murder and can caution her to administer the potion "with all privacy" (III.iii.418–419). Still suspicious of her capacity to keep counsel, Leonora hustles Winifrid offstage to swear her to silence before the priest and to involve her zestfully in "such a subtle combination" of cozenages as to require "Four devils" and "five advocates" to match "one woman's wit" (III.iii.429–431). Farce and the conventions of revenge tragedy come together to provoke a grim but amused anticipation of catastrophe.

Legal preparations for the trial of Romelio and the courtroom proceedings themselves make up the entire fourth act of the play, bringing Webster's serpentine plot to its major turning point and portending (though by no means guaranteeing) its comic resolution. By the end of the trial scene Leonora's calumny against her son, with its basis in her self-destructive claim to be an adulteress, has been exposed as a vicious fraud; the mysterious portrait has been presented in evidence, thus disclosing the true identity of Crispiano (to whom Leonora seems long ago to have been attracted); and Ercole, who has sat through the testimony and cross-examination "*muffled*" and "unseen" (IV.ii.1–4), has shown himself (although unwittingly) to Contarino, who had believed him dead. A route out of the labyrinth, if not yet mapped, at least seems possible.

Here Webster's dramaturgy follows the technique of Fletcher even more obviously than elsewhere. At the start of the act—and indeed well into it—nothing of Leonora's plan to ruin her son has yet emerged apart from her general intention to work her mischief "In open court" (III.iii.421). The playwright thereby places his audience in the disadvantaged position of Romelio who is "wholly ignorant of what the court / Will charge [him] with" (IV.ii.64–65) until he actually stands at the bar. Moreover, the elaborate perjuries that Leonora has invented to discredit him are presented almost totally through agents. Leonora, veiled in black not only out of pretended shame but for reasons of semiconcealment, maintains virtual silence, speaking briefly and only when directly addressed. The case against the merchant comes through the mouths of the pettifogging lawyer Contilupo (to the tune of comic interjections by the simpleton clerk Sanitonella) and of the bawdy Winifrid. Their premanufactured "facts" are fed piecemeal to the stage audience; these accumulate entertainingly like parts of a puzzle falling into place and, in combination, have a patently rehearsed and factitious quality. Then, when Crispiano steps down from the bench, announcing that he is "made a party" to the quarrel just when everyone expects him to pronounce a "definitive sentence," the "fine cross tricks" (IV.ii.476–479) of the episode reach their comic peripety. With the revelation that the judge himself is anything but disinterested, that he is, in fact, the very man whom Leonora has charged with impregnating her, the vengeful mother's house of cards collapses about her, and her brief career as a Machiavel ends in foolish embarrassment, which she attempts to cover by announcing suddenly that she will herself undertake "a severer penance" than the "court / Can impose" by "enter[ing] into religion" (IV.ii.557–558). In the interests of plot articulation and theatrical surprise, Webster has temporarily deprived Leonora of her psychological and moral complexity. If we cannot take her instant decision to join a convent as a bride of Christ without smiling, at least we are assured that her short-lived marriage to the Prince of Darkness has been dissolved as impulsively as it had been contracted. And, in any case, a Protestant audience would be well aware of the convention (already familiar from Shakespeare and other dramatists) by which nunneries become convenient refuges for women who eventually end as romantic spouses.

The trial scene also has the effect—and again temporarily—of diminishing the opprobrium that had earlier attached to Romelio, despite the prosecutor's essentially true remarks about his overweening presumption and social-climbing. Since the death of Contarino is not the central issue (indeed the supposed corpse is present as a silent and unrecognized spectator) and since Leonora's charge of bastardy is absurdly wide of the mark, the trial unexpectedly casts the master villain of the play into the role of innocent victim. Truth here has a double face, for the accused is criminally guilty but not of what his mother accuses him. The point, of course, is that moral passion—notwithstanding the hits at legal chicanery, the mockery of formal justice, the grotesque display of devilish litigation on the part of a woman, and Romelio's past criminality and present complacency—is at a low ebb in Act IV. Webster's emphasis falls on the giddy turns and clever debating points of the courtroom process, as the argument is plausibly constructed and then ingeniously dismantled, rather than on didactic power. As in *The White Devil*, the corruption of the legal and social institutions is such that equity for anyone seems almost irrelevant. Manipulative skill, verbal facility, and quick thinking, rather than commitment to virtue, are the values that matter as Ariosto trips Winifrid up in the tangles of her own mendacity. Appropriately, the tone is detached, humorously cool, almost Middletonian in its bemused treatment of monstrosity. At the end of the act, violence still threatens happiness as Ercole and Romelio face off in anticipation of their trial by combat—both accused of responsibility for the death of Contarino. But even here levity undermines the tragic potential. The challengers, after all, are about to fight over the death of a figure who stands (still unrevealed) beside them on the stage, and who offers himself as Ercole's second.

Julio makes the comedy of Contarino's position symmetrical by stepping forward as his counterpart on Romelio's side (the better to rehabilitate himself in his father's eyes), and proceeds to threaten his opposite in ridiculously visceral and antichivalric terms, giving Contarino "the lie in the stomach— / That's somewhat deeper than the throat—" and offering to "scour" his sword "in the gravel of [his] kidneys" (IV.ii.629–634). Ercole's summation of the whole trial (addressed to Ariosto) might perhaps, if it stood alone, re-establish the mood of tragic seriousness:

> You have judged today
> A most confused practice, that takes end
> In as bloody a trial; and we may observe
> By these great persons, and their indirect
> Proceedings, shadowed in a veil of state,
> Mountains are deformed heaps, swell'd up aloft,
> Vales wholesomer, though lower and trod on oft.
>
> (IV.ii.653–659)

But it is the fatuous Sanitonella to whom Webster assigns the final word before the stage is cleared:

> Well, I will put up my papers
> And send them to France for a precedent,
> That they may not say yet, but for one strange
> Law-suit, we come somewhat near them.
>
> (IV.ii.660–663)

This facetious termination of the specific action from which *The Devil's Law-Case* takes its title may serve to remind us of how prevalent comedy and satire are allowed to become in the penultimate act. As a kind of introduction to the trial, Webster devotes an entire scene to travestying the ignorant pretensions of the law clerk (presented as the dramatized equivalent of *A Puny-clarke* from the *Characters*) and the deeper-dyed cynicism of Contilupo (a stage version of the related sketch, *A meere Petifogger*). These two figures, caricatures of all that is venal, pedantic, and pompously obfuscatory in the Jacobean legal system, are ranged against Ariosto, a lawyer as honest and direct as they are fraudulent and devious. Together with Leonora, Sanitonella and Contilupo form a triple butt for the excoriations of Ariosto, who represents the moral sanity from which all three have so obviously diverged and of which *A Reverend Judge* is Webster's counterpart among the *Characters*. But Sanitonella, in particular, convicts himself so obtusely out of his own mouth that it is hardly necessary for Ariosto to waste much wit reproving him. When Contilupo picks out the Latin phrase "*vivere honeste*" from Sanitonella's ill-written and long-winded "brief" (Webster makes a joke out of the implied oxymoron), the silly clerk, with Dogberry-like unawareness of the moral implications, insists that his reader should cancel the offending phrase wherever it appears in the document by drawing a line through it (IV.i.89–92). Before the lawsuit gets underway Sanitonella mentions to Winifrid that he is duly forearmed against too long a pleading by reason of the "very lovely pudding-pie" concealed in his "buckram bag" (IV.ii.39–46), and further slapstick details punctuate the formal presentation of evidence: Sanitonella, for instance, prompts Contilupo not to forget a point in his speech by offering to "pinch by the buttock" (IV.ii.207), and Winifrid makes much of such risible ir-relevancies as the "tennis-court woolen slippers" that Crispiano supposedly wore "For fear of creaking" (IV.ii.393–394) when he crept to Leonora's bed.

Another feature of the long trial episode that lends it an operettalike unreal-ity is the preponderance of disguises. Here, of course, Webster expands upon the device of Romelio's impersonation of a Jew. Obviously the motif of undisclosed or altered identity supports the pervasive theme of circumscribed knowledge and clouded perception, but the sheer number of disguised persons onstage at one time, not to mention the matrix of dramatic ironies that their cross-relations produce, inevitably assures a degree of mirth, even allowing for the Elizabethan convention of impenetrability in disguise. No fewer than seven characters are in-volved. Leonora sincerely wears the veil of mourning (for the "death" of Conta-rino), but at the same time feigns contrition for her supposed sexual misconduct as well as physical illness. Truth and falsehood, genuine grief and calculated de-ception, meet in her changed appearance, to which Ariosto adds yet another meaning when he mordantly quips that her refusal to show her face accords well with her insane machinations against her own flesh and blood: "She's mad, my lord, and would be kept more dark" (IV.ii.57). Ercole, Contarino, and the two surgeons, though little more than spectators, all wear borrowed garb. Ercole muffles his face, occupying "a closet" on the periphery (IV.ii.3), while Conta-rino, unrecognized in the costume of a Dane and also presumably at the side of the stage, whispers to the surgeons, who have disguised themselves in some un-specified way so as to prevent Romelio from knowing that they have *not* taken ship for the East Indies as he supposes. No one save the doctors knows about Contarino's recovery, nor does Contarino know that Ercole is alive. The audi-ence, which perceives the genuine identity of both, thus enjoys the piquant spec-tacle of seeing them onstage together, each ignorant of the other's existence.

Ercole's self-revelation late in the scene astonishes both Ariosto and Con-tarino (characteristically, Romelio maintains a remarkable sangfroid), but the two react very differently to the same information: Ariosto is pleased to be able to arrest the supposed killer of Contarino, while Contarino himself is relieved to learn that he cannot be guilty of having slain his friend. The lawyer Crispiano, it will be remembered, has been "habited" like a merchant throughout the play, al-though his legal skills have somehow catapulted him (we are not told how) into the role of judge. His assumed mask falls away only when Leonora's picture makes it clear that her putative former lover and the presiding officer at the trial are one and the same. Thus within two lines of verse Leonora is caught prepos-terously off guard, "confounded" by the recoil of her own gin, and Julio blurts out comically, "This is my father" (IV.ii.502–503), a moment that recalls Lucio's ludicrous recognition of Duke Vincentio in the finale of *Measure for Measure*. Like Leonora, Crispiano presents both a true and false identity simultaneously. As judge, he functions in his actual profession (he has been described earlier as "one of the most eminent civil lawyers in Spain" [II.i.4]), but he remains unrecognizable to Leonora and his own son until the disclosure. Finally, Winifrid wears a disguise, having whitened her hair "with bean-flour" (IV.ii.535) at the behest of her mistress in order to appear to be a woman of forty-five. Only after Crispiano exposes her testimony as an elaborate lie, does she reveal her true age of less then twenty-five:

> May it please the court, I am but a young thing,
> And was drawn arsy varsy into the business.
> (IV.ii.530–531)

Winifrid apparently tells the truth here, although her confession seems to contradict Leonora's earlier statement that the two women have lived under the same roof for "forty years" and "have grown old together" (III.iii.406–407).

It should be stressed that these revelations, however comic or seriocomic their effect, do not wholly dispel the factual and psychological fog so typical of the drama as a whole. It is never entirely clear, for instance, whether Romelio's failure to express surprise at the courtroom reappearance of Ercole is the result of icy self-control or of some offstage communication between him and his sister or mother. Contarino and the surgeons remain puzzlingly hidden under their assumed identities for reasons that are less than transparent or convincing. At one point, when Contarino is about to reveal himself to the court, following the example of Ercole, the physicians pull him back, persuading him to "keep in [his] shell a little longer" (IV.ii.565). Earlier he has justified the continuance of his disguise on grounds that the "rumor'd" pregnancy of Jolenta "by noble Ercole" might come to "a violent issue"; he mentions that Romelio is already arranging to marry off the unborn child (depending on its sex) either to "the Duke of Austria's nephew" or to a girl from "the noble ancient family / Of the Palavafini" (IV.ii.15–23). The surgeons presumably wish to remain incognito lest the revelation of Contarino's cure wreck their chances for blackmail or bring to light their complicity in the murder conspiracy, although, so long as Contarino is presumed dead, they would have as much to fear as to gain from Romelio. Earlier in the play, they have voiced their fear of his poisoning them (III.ii.154). As usual in *The Devil's Law-Case* motives and logic remain obscure, although the most plausible explanation for these uncertainties lies in Webster's need to keep the plot boiling for another act. General knowledge of Contarino's resurrection at the end of Act IV would, of course, make the remaining complications unnecessary.

In his final act (a group of four very short and two medium-length scenes), Webster manages to perplex his narrative skein still further before quickly—indeed almost perfunctorily—untangling its major strands. As in the immediately preceding action, we get a sense of manic acceleration—of new events and readjustments of attitude or perspective coming too fast upon each other's heels to be easily absorbed. The breathless motion and crowded press of incident are of course appropriate to comedy and might, in fact, suggest the prestidigitatory conclusion of a Jonson or Middleton play but for the arresting pauses for psychological speculation, for metaphysical reflection, and, especially, for the contemplation of death that so profoundly inform all the greatest Webster. The nun Angiolella makes her first appearance onstage, thus providing a partner for Jolenta (we learn that they were childhood "playfellows" [V.i.2]) in a relationship that is structurally parallel to the friendship between Ercole and Contarino. And the Capuchin moves from being a peripheral figure to one at center stage, a change that lays new stress on the philosophical and religious implications of the story and that further complicates our judgment of the principal characters.

Nowhere in the entire drama does the strain between comic manipulation of the audience and tragic engagement of it become more acute, so that the resultant mixture of near-absurdity and pathos makes for a peculiarly suspended and indeterminate sense of the play's ending. The pageantlike scene in which Romelio recites his dirge on mortality contains perhaps the most riveting verse in the play as well as what may arguably be the finest lyric of the canon; but this section is embedded in a sequence of episodes written in a more mundane style (it includes prose) for purposes of driving the plot forward and of providing comic byplay. Laughter and a kind of tragic gloom seem to contend for dominance at the end. Even after it is clear to everyone that no lives have actually been lost and after the romantic couplings, however dubious, have somehow been achieved, our mental image of a skull presiding at the feast sours what ought conventionally to have been a more holiday ethos. The fragility and tenuousness of joy, given the selfishness, perversity, and blindness of the human condition, prevail disturbingly over emotional fulfillment and social unity. Yet at the same time Webster exploits the theatricality of his conclusion, as though laughing over his shoulder at the very conventions that make such unpredictable endings possible. An odd mixture of hilarity and grimness, of the enjoyment of artifice and the consciousness of the intractable vexations that must underlie it, conditions our reaction not only to present solutions but also, retrospectively, to the embroilments of plot and character that have led up to them. A prominent symptom of this emotional and conceptual dividedness appears in Webster's introduction of ceremonial, emblematic, and masquelike elements into the final movement—elements that the playwright incongruously juxtaposes with more naturalistic and satiric features of the dramaturgy.

The act begins with a striking visual contrast between the fallen woman and the technically chaste heroine—between Angiolella, now *"great-bellied"* (V.i.1), and Jolenta, not pregnant, who welcomes her sympathetically. What might appear at first like a quasi-allegorical opposition between guilt and innocence, between lust and virginity, refuses to resolve itself schematically. Instead we have the reunion of friends who have more in common than meets the eye and whose dialogue generates uncomfortable ironies. Jolenta, whom gossip has reported to be with child by Ercole and who has earlier agreed (for Romelio's benefit) to counterfeit pregnancy in the belief that her first love (Contarino) was "false" (III.iii.169), now confronts the actual victim of her brother's seduction and enlightens her about the true state of matters:

> *Angiolella.* 'Tis reported you are in the same taking
>   [i.e., also pregnant].
> *Jolenta.* Ha, ha, ha! So 'tis given out;
>   But Ercole's coming to life again has shrunk
>   And made invisible my great belly; yes, faith,
>   My being with child was merely in supposition,
>   Not practice.
> *Angiolella.*   You are happy: what would I give
>   To be a maid again!
> *Jolenta.* Would you? To what purpose?
>   I would never give great purchase for that thing
>   Is in danger every hour to be lost. Pray thee, laugh:
>   A boy or a girl for a wager?
> *Angiolella.*   What heaven please.
> *Jolenta.* Nay, nay, will you venture
>   A chain of pearl with me whether?
> *Angiolella.* I'll lay nothing;
>   I have ventur'd too much for't already—my fame.
>   (V.i.15–29)

The tone here—and hence the moral attitude conveyed—is characteristically mixed. Jolenta treats maidenhood lightly, even cynically—jesting about how the revival of Ercole has made her own simulation of pregnancy needless, offering to bet on the gender of a nun's fetus, and refusing, in any case, to put much store by something as vulnerable and impermanent as virginity. Perhaps her motive is partly kindness, as though she hoped to cheer Angiolella's drooping spirits or mitigate her guilt. But the nun is in no mood for jokes. Rather she is genuinely grieved by her transgression and can scarcely repress a touch of envy of her friend's less embarrassing condition: "what would I give / To be a maid again!" Earlier in the scene she has veiled her face (an ironic echo of Leonora's action at the trial) because "There's nought more terrible to a guilty heart / Than the eye of a respected friend" (V.i.8–9). Whatever we may think of Jolenta's moral character as revealed thus far, it is hard not to question whether Angiolella's guileless respect is fully justified, for Romelio's sister seems worldly indeed beside her cloistered companion. And the result of juxtaposing penitent gravity with a sort of knowing frivolousness is to draw our sympathy away from the latter and toward the former. Yet even this ironic reversal, supposing that Webster intends it, does not quite clarify the pattern of characterization in the scene, for Jolenta, with puzzling inconsistency, betrays a hint of naiveté as well. The same wag who can pun bawdily on Angiolella's being "tumbled" (V.i.41)—on shipboard by rough seas and in Romelio's bed—can be so ignorant of matronly experience as to ask her comrade whether quickening in the womb is the first sign of pregnancy (V.i.12–13).[16] This is immaturity indeed, and it seems to agree with Jolenta's consciousness of being very young: in reference to her and Angiolella's recent childhood, she confesses, "We are neither of us wise yet" (V.i.4).

The "intended combat" (V.i.31) between Ercole and Romelio strains the loyalties of both ladies. Jolenta feels torn between her "sweetheart" and her "brother" (V.i.32), although neither (despite Ercole's willingness to save her good name by marrying her) has done much to deserve profound loyalty. Angiolella fears that the duel will end in the death of her seducer whom she nevertheless refers to as a "friend" (V.i.33). The ironic "good counsel" (V.i.33) that the more passive Angiolella begs and gets from Jolenta is simply to run as far away from this combat as possible in her company—apparently to Rome. Evasion of moral and emotional difficulties becomes palpable through physical escape, but not before Webster has sounded a further note of mystification by having Jolenta dispatch a letter to Ercole, the content of which he temporarily withholds from us by keeping it also from Angiolella, who remains onstage. Since we recall Jolenta's earlier cryptic missive to Contarino, this action at least establishes her penchant for sending ominous communications in writing to her suitors.

In another abrupt shift of tone, Webster ushers in Prospero and Sanitonella for a brief satiric interlude, in prose, on legal mores, such as laughing at clients behind their backs or making them overfriendly by getting them drunk. Then, a bit of bizarre pageantry covers the dismissal of the lawyers from the stage and conducts us back to the solemnity of verse. Contarino and Ercole appear onstage, both *"in friars' habits, as having been at the Bathanites, a ceremony used afore these combats"* (V.ii.14). Their similar dress, of course, stresses their closeness as friends, even though Ercole believes Contarino to be dead. No one has been able to explain either the reference to Bathanites (is it a corruption of Bethlemites or Bethanites?) or the obscure ceremony, presumably religious, that may have preceded duels in Italy; but it is quickly obvious that, once again, the dramatist is about the business of creating more doubt and mystery than the action resolves. According to the roster of dramatis personae in the quarto, Ercole is a Knight of Malta, that is, a Knight Hospitaler of St. John of Jerusalem, theoretically vowed (as a monastic soldier) to poverty, chastity, and obedience. The ecclesiastical garb might be meant to hint at this connection (St. John was the patron of the Merchant Taylors), although clearly Webster forgets or ignores the special restrictions of Ercole's order, and, in any case, the dialogue nowhere even mentions it. But why has Contarino, who has no affiliation with a religious order, abandoned his Danish dress for that of a friar? The new identity seems to be symbolic only, for Ercole still recognizes the anonymous second who sprang to his aid at the trial without knowing that he is Contarino. In both cases, the religious garments seem more emblematic than naturalistic—a visual signal that the characters have somehow experienced a heightened awareness of eternity in the face of impending battle and likely death. As such, they prepare us for the later appearance of Jolenta and Angiolella as nuns in a scene of some spiritual weight, and for the Capuchin, who becomes the major spokesman for transcendence in the play. But all this is merely preliminary to the posing of two major questions that Webster seems determined to raise rather than to settle.

The first has to do with Contarino's "obstinacy" (the word is his own) in refusing, even at this late hour, to disclose himself, realizing, as he does, that "all the blood which will be shed" in the duel—Ercole's, Romelio's, Julio's, and possibly his own—"Must fall upon my head" (V.ii.16–19). Contarino puts this problem to himself in an aside, then, without reaching any conclusion, evades the moral issue by asking Ercole how he can love Jolenta enough to marry her and father her illegitimate child, yet be willing to kill her brother in combat. The answer to this alternative puzzle—that Ercole will fight out of devotion to Contarino, whom Romelio killed, and to punish Romelio for his shocking mistreatment of his sister—simply raises the dramatic irony to an almost unendurable pitch, since Ercole is justifying his participation in the duel as revenge for a murder that his interlocutor and we know did not occur.

The unresolved question of why Contarino continues his disguise when it obviously causes so much danger and misunderstanding is directly linked to the second principal question, namely the reason for Jolenta's strange letter to Ercole. We now learn the contents of the message that had aroused our curiosity in the previous scene, but, perversely, the fresh knowledge only generates greater mystery than if there had been no letter at all. Ercole, we discover, has written to his intended to find out who was the true father of her unborn child, supposing that this was Contarino. But Jolenta's letter, a reply to Ercole's query, turns out to be another equivocation.

According to Ercole's paraphrase, his sweetheart "writes . . . that the shame she goes withal / Was begot by her brother" (V.ii.36–37). Interpretation, of course, hangs on the double significance of "begot." Jolenta really means that her whole unfortunate situation as a pretended mother has been engendered (caused) by Romelio's sexual misconduct with Angiolella, while Ercole, taking the word literally, assumes that Romelio and his sister have committed incest. As at the play's opening, with its confusion over the meaning of "picture," we are back in a world where language does more to impede than to facilitate the communication of truth. Contarino, in a further extension of the irony, shares Ercole's misreading of the letter and turns in disgust from any lingering interest he may have had in Jolenta, covering his inner thoughts by pretending to be musing upon a parent:

> *Contarino.* I will no more think of her [Jolenta].
> *Ercole.* Of whom?
> *Contarino.* Of my mother—I was thinking of my mother.
> (V.ii.42–44)

(The mention of "mother" in this context seems to glance obliquely at Leonora, the mother whom Contarino eventually marries in lieu of her daughter.) Why Jolenta should deliberately mislead her future husband by planting the horror of incest in his mind remains obscure, despite the surgeon's statement in the following scene that she is rumored to be "a little mad" (V.iii.31). Webster's major point in the case of both Contarino's and Jolenta's motives would appear to be inscrutability (at the least) or psychosis (at the worst). The theatre audience, of course, is involved in the more fundamental irony of knowing that Jolenta is chaste, while she herself and others have promoted, or believed, conflicting reports about three men (Contarino, Ercole, and Romelio) each of whom becomes a candidate for the father of her supposed child.

The irrationality that so informs the twists and turns of *The Devil's Law-Case*—increasingly as the play nears its end—appears revealingly in the device Webster invents to transmit to the central characters the all-important fact that Contarino has survived. Since the character himself seems doggedly unable to come forward to those most vitally concerned, the knowledge that he is alive must rise to the surface by comic indirection. One of the surgeons offers to marry Winifrid—a coupling, however improbable, that at least yokes together two of the more disreputable members of the cast. The doctor imparts the secret to his new fiancée and hopes to reclaim her reputation for dishonesty by having her relay a piece of valid information for once—to Leonora. But Leonora happens to be the one impossible recipient of the news, having ironically sworn her maid "by oath" (V.iv.17) never to mention Contarino's name; and Ariosto, the suggested alternative, is almost as unsuitable because he has heard Winifrid's lies exposed in court and could hardly be expected to credit so implausible a tale from her lips. Only by a process of elimination is the Capuchin selected to be told the facts about Contarino's recovery, so that the very plotting, like the equivocal language of the characters, is made to call attention to the obstacles that encumber the communication of truth. Reality is so deeply buried under false appearances in the world of this drama that unearthing or even recognizing it is far from easy. Significantly, impersonation once more enters the action, for the surgeon, in order to arrange the return of the runaway Jolenta, contrives to assume Romelio's discarded disguise as a Jew, to pretend to be the victim of robbery, and thereby to have all travelers brought back to Naples as suspect fugitives. This mechanism for getting Jolenta and Angiolella onstage at the denouement may be laughably artificial and indirect, but it fits the thematic pattern admirably.

The three remaining scenes of the tragicomedy possess a unity of their own, embracing a long step-by-step prelude to the trial by combat, the chivalric contest itself, and Ariosto's pell-mell distribution of rewards and punishments upon the Capuchin's disclosure that Contarino lives. The closely related episodes form a continuous, almost seamless, movement with its own rising action, climax, and aftermath, so that the conclusion of the play resembles a miniature drama-within-a-drama. After the obscurities, disjunctions, and asymmetries that converge at this point, the clarity of the final pattern might seem refreshing, but its very neatness is paradoxically unsettling, for, again, Webster would appear to impose a fairy-tale artifice upon the psychological nuances and unfathomable complexities of his material. Nor does the inconsistent tone of this last segment quite match the shapeliness of its dramatic contours, comprehending, as it does, such a mixture of incompatible ingredients—humor, melancholy, pageantry, violence, religious homily, cynicism, and what at least passes for romance.

The long scene of preparation for the duel commences with low comedy, exploiting Julio's reluctance to fight (somewhat in the vein of Sir Andrew Aguecheek) and dragging in the legendary joke of how to make a cowardly Welshman bolder in fencing—that is, by tipping his opponent's foil with toasted cheese. At bottom, Julio cares only for physical survival, and his antiheroic fears provide occasion for easy laughter. Nonetheless, the prospect of sudden death has been made nervously present to our consciousness. Then the entrance of Romelio, "*very melancholy*" (V.iv.43) and in the company of the friar, suddenly turns the levity to something much darker. As Julio's fellow combatant against Ercole, the merchant-villain also faces possible extinction and is at once deeply depressed and fearful about his plight, however much he may try to hide his fear under a mask of cynical bravado. The Capuchin, who has now been informed of Contarino's recovery, is withholding the fact from Romelio in order "To sound [his] penitence," although we know that he intends to "end these errors" (V.iv.47–48) once he has brought the man to his spiritual senses.

This situation sets up a partly comic, partly serious, sparring match between the churchman and the sinner in which they fail utterly to communicate because of widely divergent priorities: Christian supernaturalism collides head on with a kind of pagan humanism, inviting a typically Websterian mixed response. The friar tries to bring Romelio to contrition through an awareness of approaching judgment; Romelio worries about the temper of sword blades and treats the preachments of the church as weakening and coward-making. To the direct question, "Did you murder Contarino?", Romelio can only pose another, "Did you ask it as a confessor, or as a spy?" (V.iv.82–84); and, in fact, he never explicitly repents the attempt to kill the nobleman anywhere in the drama. Webster dramatizes the root conflict between Romelio's agnostic and the friar's religious point of view by making the former call for nourishment before he enters the duel and receive it in the form of theological sustenance:

> *Romelio*. Get me some good victuals to breakfast—I am hungry.
> *Capuchin*. Here's food for you.
>
> *Offering him a book.*
> (V.iv.92–93)

Here, even the physical action underlines the pervasive theme of linguistic doubleness by incorporating the split between literalism and metaphor into a stage direction.

Resisting the predictable and somewhat tiresome ministrations of the cleric, Romelio retreats to a moral and psychic stance that recalls the tough and bitter stoicism of a Flamineo or a Bosola when Fate is not to be cheated. Again the theme of intestinal fortitude or irreducible "integrity" (in Webster's special sense) makes its appearance, and the playwright gradually draws the opposition between Romelio and the Capuchin to a tautness that returns us to the emotional intensity and metaphysical "mist" of *The White Devil* or *The Duchess of Malfi*:

> *Romelio.* I am to fight, to fight, sir, and I'll do't
>   As I would feed, with a good stomach.
> *Capuchin.* Can you feed, and apprehend death?
> *Romelio.* Why, sir, is not death
>   A hungry companion? Say, is not the grave
>   Said to be a great devourer? Get me some victuals.
>   I knew a man that was to lose his head
>   Feed with an excellent good appetite,
>   To strengthen his heart, scarce half an hour before.
>   And if he did it, that only was to speak,
>   What should I, that am to do?
> *Capuchin.* This confidence,
>   If it be grounded upon truth, 'tis well.
> *Romelio.* You must understand that resolution
>   Should ever wait upon a noble death,
>   As captains bring their soldiers out o' th' field
>   And come off last. For, I pray, what is death?
>   The safest trench i' th' world to keep man free
>   From Fortune's gunshot; to be afraid of that
>   Would prove me weaker than a teeming woman,
>   That does endure a thousand times more pain
>   In bearing of a child.
> *Capuchin.* O, I tremble for you!
>   For I do know you have a storm within you
>   More terrible than a sea fight, and your soul
>   Being heretofore drown'd in security,
>   You know not how to live, nor how to die.
>   But I have an object that shall startle you,
>   And make you know whither you are going.
> *Romelio.* I am arm'd for't.

(V.iv.96–125)

Here we have the famous style—at once flinty, arresting, and deeply felt, wittily grotesque yet humane, homely of vocabulary but mind-stretching—that entitles

The Devil's Law-Case to be considered in this section of the book under major works. But we must not forget the ironic context. The superbly heightened and controlled emotion of these lines, achieved through a subtle blend of the bizarre and the ordinary and through a fine instinct for combining understatement with the imagery of tragic situations (a land battle, an execution, a storm, a sea fight), is enclosed within a broader and more comic arch; for *we* know, as Romelio cannot, that the experience of confronting death is somehow to become the condition of his survival and the key to the righting of what the Capuchin has earlier referred to as the play's "errors." The friar is submitting his fault-prone advisee to a test (as in earlier episodes Contarino had tested Leonora, and Jolenta her brother), but this time we can project, however indistinctly, the outlines of a fortunate issue.

The scene reaches its highest pitch of emotional solemnity with the prechoreographed procession of Leonora and her servants, the silent presentation of the coffins and winding sheets to Romelio and Julio, and the affecting dirge (quoted in an earlier chapter [pp. 132–133] in connection with *A fayre and happy Milke-mayd*) that the macabre gifts elicit from the villain-hero. The Capuchin and Leonora have created a kind of masque to allegorize the transcience of life, into which the principal spectator suddenly steps as the dominant performer. Romelio could hardly speak more to the purpose than if the friar had written his lines, and the moment is all the more theatrical for the sudden quietude and simplicity that contrast so markedly with the knotted and noisy complexities that surround it. The famous lyric seems to give eloquent voice to the most distilled wisdom of the play, and hence to suggest a kind of emotional breakthrough of genuine significance for everyone onstage as well as for the theatre audience. With seeming effortlessness and a liquidity of movement precisely suited to their message, Webster gathers up into these delicate tetrameter couplets a cluster of favorite and traditional themes—impermanence or flux, the recurring cycle of natural process, the coincidence of beginnings and endings, the dangerous glitter of courts, the "bewitching" enticement of the senses, the association of sexual desire ("Sweetest breath, and clearest eye") with extinction, the futility of ambition, the folly of trying to perpetuate "a living name" through earthly memorials ("trophies and dead things"), and the depth of human frustration ("weav[ing] nets to catch the wind"). The last-quoted phrase is, of course, proverbial (Tilley cites numerous parallels),[17] but it may also faintly echo Ecclesiastes 5:16 ("and what profit hath he that hath laboured for the wind?"). In any case, the entire poem can be read as an imaginative gloss on the familiar scriptural contrast between the brevity of earthly life and the endurance of divine truth, although its second term is present only by contextual implication:

For all flesh is as grass, and all the glory of man as the flower of grass. The grass withereth, and the flower thereof falleth away.

But the word of the Lord endureth for ever.

(I Peter 1:24–25)

When Romelio shockingly turns his own profoundest insights into a *coup de théâtre*, cynically using the apparent "miracle" (V.iv.144) of his religious conversion as a trick to lock up Leonora and the Capuchin in a castle turret, the sudden shift from moral weight to travesty is particularly difficult to accommodate, even in a play predicated on such shifts. Webster seems to present us with two Romelios in rapid and contradictory juxtaposition—the moral philosopher whose noble words spring from a "heart of adamant" suddenly "melt[ed]" by a fresh recognition of human transience (V.iv.144–145) and the icy scoffer-manipulator for whom the attitude of penitence is just another useful (if derisory) disguise. The very abruptness of the reversal is both comic and unsettling, for again it promotes doubt about the true moral identity of a major character. Is Romelio's brash, almost clownish treatment of two authority figures (his only remaining parent and his ghostly father) a genuine expression of his cynicism? Or is this behavior as theatrically artificial for him as the Jewish gaberdine (and, possibly, the fake nose) he had worn as a would-be murderer, or as false to his deeper emotions as the masquerade of penitence that he has seemingly just thrown off? (It is worth notice in this scene that Romelio seems to play consciously to Julio, who obligingly occasions his sharpest satiric retorts and serves as an appreciative onstage audience.) As so often in the play, the dramatist makes capital out of our uncertainty, but the stagy quality of Romelio's master-joke and the vitriol with which he gleefully tips his shafts at his irritating prisoners ("So much the better; / I am rid of her howling . . ." [V.iv.177–178]; "Let him knock till his sandals fly in pieces" [V.iv.180]) suggest an impetuous and guilty flight from self as convincingly as a wish to enter upon a settled despair by silencing "divinity" (V.iv.163).

Significantly, ironies of self-destructiveness operate from both sides of the conflict, creating a half-threatening, half-funny impasse; for the action dramatizes how both Romelio and the Capuchin—one through his cynical trick, the other through his penitential test and a heavily moralistic dumbshow—work reciprocally against their own good fortune. The friar, armed with the secret of Contarino's recovery, has the power to make the risk of a duel needless, but gets himself imprisoned through complacency and the failure to speak soon enough. Romelio arrogantly hustles the man who could save his neck, let alone help him to salvation, off to a place removed where his special knowledge cannot be imparted. Webster further intricates the irony of failed communication by having Julio catch just enough of the Capuchin's message (shouted almost out of earshot from his prison) for Romelio, in the depth of his anticlericalism, to misinterpret:

> *Julio.* Ha! What says he? Contarino living?
> *Romelio.* Ay, ay, he means he would have Contarino's living
>   Bestowed upon his monastery; 'tis that
>   He only fishes for. So, 'tis break of day;
>   We shall be call'd to the combat presently.
>   (V.iv.181–185)

Again, the dual meaning of a word ("living") directly affects plot. Nor can we miss the point that Romelio's characteristic trait of imputing the worst motives to everyone rebounds here to push him to the brink of death. In a lighter vein, Julio, who mimics his partner's attitude, also affects to think as ill of the monastic as he may:

> *Julio.*   Well, if the young Capuchin
>   Do not talk o' th' flesh as fast now to your mother
>   As he did to us o' th' spirit! If he do,
>   'Tis not the first time that the prison royal
>   Has been guilty of close committing.
> *Romelio.* Now to th' combat.
>
>   (V.iv.189–194)

The scene remains precariously suspended between near-tragedy and jest to its very end.

The short dialogue between Leonora and the friar, spoken *"above at a window"* (V.v.1), forms a kind of coda to the preceding action and comments chorically upon it. Only now does the cleric rekindle the woman's passion for Contarino by revealing that her lost beloved is alive and about to undergo dangerous battle against her son and Julio. Webster's staging is symbolic, for the contrast between high and low, between frustrated inaction in a small turret and the nervous preparation for combat below, reinforces another aspect of the tension between the religious and antireligious attitudes embodied in the characterization and plotting. The spatial relationship obviously carries theological overtones. The Capuchin and widow now possess a kind of heavenly knowledge in a stage location appropriately near "the heavens," but their confinement and distance from the arena of human activity make their higher truth maddeningly unavailable to those it might benefit. The cleric attributes the locking up to diabolic influence:

>   Some evil angel
> Makes [Romelio] deaf to his own safety. We are shut
> Into a turret, the most desolate prison
> Of all the castle; and his obstinacy,
> Madness, or secret fate has thus prevented
> The saving of his life.
>
>   (V.v.3–8)

When Leonora, more interested in delivering Contarino than Romelio from death (she exclaims hysterically that her son's life is "worth nothing" [V.v.10]), offers to commit suicide by leaping from the battlements as a means of stopping the duel, the Capuchin again matches his speech to the staging in language that sums up the central irony of the entire play:

>   O, look upwards rather:
> Their deliverance must come thence. To see how heaven
> Can invert man's firmest purpose! His intent

Of murdering Contarino was a mean
To work his safety, and my coming hither
To save him is his ruin. Wretches turn
The tide of their good fortune, and being drench'd
In some presumptuous and hidden sins,
While they aspire to do themselves most right,
The devil that rules i' th' air hangs in their light.

(V.v.14–23)

This passage contains the kernel of Webster's tragicomic vision in *The Devil's Law-Case*, underscoring, as it does, the depth of "presumptuous and hidden sins" and the incomprehensible nature of causation, the ironic chasm in human consciousness between intention and effect. As Romelio's attempt to kill Contarino miraculously brought about his recovery, so the friar's attempt to save Romelio's soul will apparently result in his destruction. The lesson would appear to be that deliverance, if and when it comes, is the work of God, not of man, and that, although God may work His divine will through human agency, His means and final purposes must remain bafflingly obscure to mere rationalism. Our only refuge from infernal misdirection and despair lies in a blind trust that God understands the welfare of his creatures better than they can know it themselves and that His beneficent order, however mysterious and painful it may be from the circumscribed vantage point of human perception, will ultimately prevail. If we identify Webster's vision of reality with the Capuchin's, such is the dark affirmation that the play propounds—a dramatic illustration, as it were, of Tertullian's "*Credo quia impossibile.*"[18]

Yet the frustrations of Leonora and her confessor, the seeming impotence of the friar's lessoning, and the philosophical dilemma in which their actions and present situation have placed them make it possible to invert the fideism of the cleric's words, and to see the multiple confusions and uncertainties of the drama as cumulative evidence for the kind of skepticism expressed by Montaigne in his famous epigram, "nothing is so firmly beleeved as that which a man knoweth least."[19] If we interpret the action in this way, Webster might seem to embody a most distressing paradox—namely that, as a consequence of the Fall, man's will has become so deeply "infected" (to use Sidney's term)[20] as to be virtually unresponsive to the dictates of his "erected wit," but that this very waywardness has led man, in turn, to trust in and passionately to affirm what he cannot know. His depravity has predetermined him, so to speak, to an epistemological vicious circle in which the fallen will not only separates the mind from light but prevents it even from knowing what and where light is.

Thus, *The Devil's Law-Case* leads us to its crisis, the trial by combat, by inviting us to contemplate opposing attitudes toward intellectual limitation. We may "look upwards" with the Capuchin, "exercis[ing our] faith," as Sir Thomas Browne phrases it, "in the difficultest point" and "pursu[ing our] Reason to an O *altitudo,"* or relapse into the quasi-Calvinist despair suggested by Leonora's near-suicide. One thinks of Edgar's half-literal, half-metaphoric "Do but look up" (*King Lear,* IV.vi.59), spoken to the despondent Gloucester, and of his later "Look up, my lord" (V.iii.317), addressed to the dying king.[21]

Webster's concluding scene may be said both to resolve and to sidestep the many complexities of plot, character, and meaning so assiduously cultivated in all that precedes. The ritualism connected with the *"set[ting] up"* of the *"lists,"* the double fanfare *"by several trumpets,"* the formal entrance of "the knights" with their "weapons," and the ceremonial formula, *"Soit la battaile, et victoire à ceux qui ont droit!"* (V.vi.1–8), all establish an ambience of heroic grandeur and medieval tradition strangely alien to the middle-class sociology and mercantile realism that the play as a whole projects. The pageantry asserts an altogether simpler, older, and more comforting kind of order than any of the conflicts to which we have so far been exposed would permit us to assume. Nevertheless, the very concept of a trial by combat also implies that justice is inaccessible to human reason: "heaven," after all, must "Determine the right" (V.vi.6–7) *because* mere mortals are unable to do so on their own. The high ceremonial of the battle, then, serves to symbolize the play's religious and metaphysical fideism, combining the reassuring appearance of a settled order with disturbing implications of blind helplessness. Romelio's change of heart at this point, the unpredictable suddenness with which impending death shatters the carapace of his unbelief, shifts the focus dramatically from a philosophical puzzle to a psychological one—from an abstract issue to the inner workings of a major character. By calling for the prayers of the Capuchin and by sending a key to free his prisoners, Romelio demonstrates in an external gesture the urgency of his own longing for release: "Bid them make haste, and pray; / I may be dead ere he comes" (V.vi.14–15).

Ironically, the beginnings of spiritual regeneration in Romelio coincide with the moment of his greatest physical peril. Webster could hardly have been unaware of the theatrical advantages of an onstage fight, *"continued,"* as the stage direction informs us, *"to a good length"* (V.vi.16); but the motive behind Contarino's continued silence and the needless risk of his own life as well as that of his closest friend is puzzling indeed, for it raises even more difficult questions of psychic and moral identity than those posed by Romelio's startling *volte-face* a moment earlier. Only with the deliberately delayed entrance of Leonora and the friar is the saving presence of Contarino disclosed. And even then, the young lord seems less than eager to make himself known, for the Capuchin must force him to unmask with his exclamation, "Behold him living" (V.vi.22). In fact, Contarino says nothing until he responds to Leonora's expression of devotedness by announcing (again surprisingly and without explanation) that he has "entirely vowed [his] life" (V.vi.26) to the lady. All the unanswered questions, of course, suggest a world in which truth is typically buried and stubbornly resists being disinterred. Ariosto, who presides as judge at the lists and whose public

duty is to see that guilt and innocence are revealed, would instinctively silence
the very truth he seeks:

> What are these that interrupt the combat?
> Away to prison with them.
>
> (V.vi.18–19)

The undisguising of Contarino—the play's brief but climactic epiphany—
renders the few remaining actions of the plot mechanical or, at least, comically
routine. In order to skirt cumbersome explanations of what the theatre audience
already knows, Webster makes Leonora, most improbably, supply a written account of past confusions:

> Cease here all further scrutiny; this paper
> Shall give unto the court each circumstance
> Of all these passages.
>
> (V.vi.56–58)

The pairing off of the three couples (Winifrid and one of the surgeons have already been joined) is oddly joyless and so unadorned by poetry or romance as to
seem imposed—more like a convenience of the playwright than a psychologically
valid, much less inevitable, harmonization of dissonance. An arranged rather
than a felt or emergent symmetry is what Webster offers us at the end—a state of
affairs made obvious by the fact that the couples say so little to each other and
must make their unions clear to an audience through stage gestures rather than
through speech. Passion dwindles almost to the vanishing point. Leonora, referring to herself in the third person, proposes to Contarino in eight words and is
accepted in a manner almost as laconic and impersonal. The widow, after all,
can provide her youthful nobleman with financial advantages, and Webster has
never quite dispelled suggestions of the fortune hunter in his makeup. Or does
Contarino now feel that any woman who would go to such lengths for one man
deserves him? Ercole, having been formally "contracted" (I.ii.127) at the behest
of Romelio and Leonora, apparently joins hands with Jolenta (there is no stage
direction to confirm the action)—but only after she has returned from her escapist travels with Angiolella in the disguise of a Moorish nun and has delivered a
moral speech in tetrameter couplets on the difference between the outward appearance of sin and the chastity that this may cloak.

The allegorical technique of this masquelike presentation (the white nun
being emblematic of sexual transgression, the black nun of virtue) also distances
emotion by rendering Ercole's choice of a mate in terms of an ethical abstraction
rather than of personality.[22] Rather than a white devil, we have a black saint:

> Like or dislike me, choose you whether:
> The down upon the raven's feather
> Is as gentle and as sleek
> As the mole on Venus' cheek.

417

> Hence, vain show! I only care
> To preserve my soul most fair;
> Never mind the outward skin,
> But the jewel that's within;
> And though I want the crimson blood,
> Angels boast my sisterhood.
> Which of us now judge you whiter,
> Her whose credit proves the lighter,
> Or this black and ebon hue,
> That, unstain'd, keeps fresh and true?
> For I proclaim't without control,
> There's no true beauty but i' th' soul.
>
> (V.vi.34–49)

Serving as a companion piece of sorts to Romelio's lyric, which had also touched upon the idea of deceptive appearance, these formal lines make explicit a theme with broad relevance for nearly all the relationships of the drama. Nevertheless, the black and white simplicity of the moral contrast, made simpler still by the visual effect and the jingling rhymes, falsifies the characters of the two friends, as dramatized earlier, by recasting them as personifications of shame and innocence; and the heavy-handed didacticism therefore invites more laughter than assent. The "Jewish" surgeon who ushers the nuns onstage seems to expect a comic reaction by referring to them facetiously as "A couple of strange fowl" (V.vi.30).

The marriage between Romelio and the pregnant Angiolella is as much a punishment as a reward. The philandering merchant is sentenced to make the sister of Saint Clare an honest woman, a destiny he embraces "Most willingly" (V.vi.77); but the nun devotes her final speech not to reconciliation with her new husband but to moralizing upon her painful situation:

> O sir, you have been unkind;
> But I do only wish that this my shame
> May warn all honest virgins not to seek
> The way to heaven, that is so wondrous steep,
> Through those vows they are too frail to keep.
>
> (V.vi.78–82)

No sense of deepened or fulfilled understanding attends any of these unions, and preachment rather than festivity sets the tone despite Ariosto's summation of the plot as "these so comical events" (V.vi.63). Distinctions between victims and criminals are disturbingly blurred, at least insofar as justice is concerned. Leonora is treated no more harshly than Jolenta, and Romelio comes off almost as unscathed as the man he had intended to murder. It is indicative, too, of the play's astringency that all three sets of brides and grooms are saddled with financial penalties more suitable to city than to romantic comedy. The men must pay for keeping anti-Turkish galleys on the seas for seven years whereas the women are to "build a monastery" (V.vi.88) in recompense for their breach of vows to religious orders. (It is not clear whether Jolenta has briefly taken the veil in Rome or merely offended a convent by pretending to do so.) Like the couples at the end of *Love's Labor's Lost*, Webster's lovers (if that is the word) still have to earn or grow into happiness.

Ariosto, after he has sentenced all offenders, concludes the play didactically, summarizing its action in words that might be taken as Webster's epilogue to the audience:

> So we leave you,
> Wishing your future life may make good use
> Of these events, since that these passages,
> Which threaten'd ruin, built on rotten ground,
> Are with success beyond our wishes crown'd.
> (V.vi.91–95)

The miraculous "success" of the outcome, given the "rotten ground" of human frailty that would seem to guarantee disaster, points by implication to the incomprehensible mercies of God. As in *Measure for Measure*, sin is mysteriously deflected from its own worst purposes and uneasy marriages replace the severities of tragedy. But Webster's language is much less theological than Shakespeare's, and his final tone remains more secular than religious. It can hardly be fortuitous that in a slightly earlier speech Ariosto borrows the words of the skeptical Montaigne to comment upon the extraordinary convolutions of plot and character that have led up to an ending more arduous and strange than explicable and, in important ways, more perturbatious than reassuring:

> Rareness and difficulty give estimation
> To all things are i' th' world.
> (V.vi.60–61)[23]

Webster's emphasis, like Montaigne's, may finally be more aesthetic and psychological than moral. It is therefore possible to read *The Devil's Law-Case* as a dramatic experiment in stimulating and intensifying our desire for order by showing it to be difficult to attain and not even wholly within our ken.

* * *

It will, I hope, be obvious to anyone who has persevered to this point that *The Devil's Law-Case* is treacherous terrain—difficult to map, beset with interpretive traps, puzzles, surprises, and inconsistencies, and formidably resistant to comfortable generalization. Like its principal characters, the play seems perpetually to shift its shape, change its direction or tone, and alter its angle of vision, so that taking a fix on it may recall Polonius's comic insecurity about the cloud: from moment to moment it may assume the aspect of a camel, a weasel, or a whale depending on immediate stimuli and the suggestibility of the viewer. Even for tragicomedy—a mixed genre by definition—Webster's drama aspires to an unusual degree of inclusiveness. Most of the familiar comic modes are represented—cynical city comedy (with its urban setting, its tension between citizens and aristocrats, its obsession with money, sex, and social status, its gullers gulled); humour comedy (with its passionate excoriation of folly and vice, its caricatures, its relentless satire on the professions—medicine, law, the church); romantic comedy (with its idealization of chastity and gentlemanly virtue, its disguises, its providential resurrection of characters thought dead, its ending in multiple marriages); problem or "dark" comedy (with its strain between ethical seriousness and fictional improbability, its difficult tests of character, its soiled idealists, its intended but unaccomplished crimes, its disturbing or unclear treatment of motive); and Fletcherian tragicomedy (with its witty, ironic, and labyrinthine plotting, its withholding of information, its sensational surprises, its prurient suggestiveness, its interest in abnormalities such as incest, its conflicting absolutes such as love and honor). We can recognize here a collection of elements from such diverse plays as *A Mad World, My Masters*, *Volpone*, *The Merchant of Venice*, *Measure for Measure*, and *A King and No King*.

Then, in addition to or overlapping the comic subspecies, we have materials from revenge tragedy, pageant, masque, lyric, dumbshow, morality play, and chronicle history. The dwelling on mortality, the existential conflict between terror and resignation in the face of death, and the tussle between nihilism and transcendence or between cruelty and tenderness are recognizable features of the Italian tragedies. So, too, are the haunting dirge and the elements of pantomime, procession, and emblem. But it seems odd to combine (and within a single scene) a trial by combat as medieval in atmosphere as its counterpart in *Richard II* with a modish allegory as Jacobean in technique as Jonson's *Masque of Blackness*. Ancient and modern are made to coexist. Archaic codes and rituals of honor inform a play that images disturbing social change and conflicts of class, and that fairly teems, as Pearson has observed,[24] with allusions (especially during the trial when chronology becomes important) to the disruptive events of recent or contemporary affairs—the tragic relationship of Elizabeth to Essex (III.iii.295–300), skirmishes over spices between the British and the Dutch in the East Indies (IV.ii.11–13), the Gunpowder Plot (IV.ii.314–316), the Battle of Lepanto (IV.ii.366–367), notable frosts and plagues (IV.ii.433), the loss of Calais (IV.ii.434), and so forth. In a drama like *The Devil's Law-Case* that betrays such "artistic greediness," that hankers so shamelessly after "every sort of effect together" (to borrow words from Eliot),[25] thematic interconnection becomes the indispensable agent of unity and cohesion. Accordingly, Webster cements his disparate ingredients of character, action, and genre into something like an aesthetic whole through the linkage of related ideas or motifs. Most of these have been mentioned already, since they are inseparable from the developing action, but a summary and exploration of the more prominent themes may serve to clarify the larger significance and overall effect of the play.

The most obvious of these, incorporated into both the title and subtitle, is of course diabolism. Devil imagery suffuses all three of Webster's masterworks, nor dare we forget that in Jacobean England the devil was considerably more than a mere metaphor for evil.[26] James I believed fervently in demonic possession (the third edition of his *Daemonologie* is exactly contemporaneous with *The Devil's Law-Case*) and in 1603 issued a new statute prescribing savage penalties (usually death) for a wide range of offenses having to do with witchcraft, conjuration, and familiarity with evil spirits. Webster's audience would certainly know the scriptural teaching that "the Devil rangeth abroad like a roaring lion, still seeking whom he may devour" (I Peter 5:8), and would understand, as Burton puts it (quoting St. Cyprian), that

"all his study, all his endeavour is to divert [us] from true religion . . . and because he is damned himself, and in an error, he would have all the world participate of his errors, and be damned with him." The *primum mobile*, therefore, and first mover of all superstition, is the devil, that great enemy of mankind, the principal agent, who *in a thousand several shapes, after divers fashions, with several engines, illusions, and by several names* [italics added] hath deceived the inhabitants of the earth, in several places and countries, still rejoicing at their falls.[27]

The play contains no fewer than thirty references to devils, fiends, and witchery, thus encouraging the notion that human depravity not only imitates traits of the devil but may actually embody, incarnate, represent, or extend his hellish power on earth.

Webster repeatedly identifies both major villains with supernatural evil. Contarino calls Romelio "a subtle devil" (IV.ii.23), Julio thinks he may be "a witch" (II.i.192), and the Capuchin speaks of "Some evil angel" (V.v.3) that stops the merchant's ears against the words that would save him. What Ercole calls Romelio's "crimes," that is, his ultimate responsibility for the near-fatal duel and his impregnating of Angiolella, will, if not repented, "make work . . . for the devil" (II.iv.42–43). Romelio's inspiration can also be diabolic. According to Ariosto, the names of his ships are "devilish" (II.iii.65), and the trader himself reacts to the news of their loss as though he had just "met the devil in villainous tidings" (II.i.336). The "wicked world bewitches" Romelio (II.iii.192) as he contemplates the murder of Contarino, and "The devil" suddenly "furnish[es]" him with the "unnatural falsehood" (III.iii.98–99) with which he deceives his sister—namely the tale of Leonora's plan to commit incest with her prospective son-in-law. Moreover, like a devil, he encourages evil in others: "craftily" he "nourish[es]" the "fiend" of jealousy (III.iii.211) between his mother and Jolenta, and the latter accuses him of aging her before her time (she mentions "this frosty age in youth, / Which you have witch'd upon me" [III.iii.86–87]) with his scheme to have her mother his bastard child. Finally, when the Capuchin tries to preach divinity to Romelio, "As one that fain would justle the devil / Out of [his] way" (V.iv.85–86), the merchant turns the figure back upon the religious, arrogantly, if wittily, implying that he has himself experienced personal contact with the devil:

> Um, you are but weakly made for't.
> He's a cunning wrestler, I can tell you,
> And has broke many a man's neck.
> (V.iv.87–89)

Given the wide streak of antifeminism that runs through *The Devil's Law-Case* (we hear of the "mad tricks . . . play'd . . . by ladies [III.i.10], of "their game . . . all i' th' night" [III.i.21], of "the insolencies" [III.i.29] and "violencies of women" [IV.ii.316], of their being "compounded / Of all monsters, poisoned minerals, / And sorcerous herbs" [IV.ii.317–319]), it is hardly surprising that Leonora is even more strongly associated with the nether world than her son. Indeed, her very name may glance at the familiar passage from St. Peter that compares the devil to a lion. Her unnatural law case against her own offspring, of course, gives the play both its titles—an emphasis that Webster reinforces at least seven different times in the dialogue. Ariosto, who serves more consistently than any character as a chorus for the play, suggests openly that "lunacy, or else the devil himself / Has ta'en possession" (IV.i.69–70) of Leonora, thus (with Burton and other theorists) relating madness as well as certain kinds of melancholy to diabolic invasion of the body. Romelio marvels in soliloquy how often violent jealousy, "especially in women," has "rais'd the devil up / In form of a law-case" (III.iii.207–210), a sentiment that he later echoes at the trial when he avers that "this suit of hers / Springs from a devilish malice" (IV.ii.311–312). Crispiano also believes that Romelio is "practic'd upon most devilishly" (IV.ii.279). But the real force of Webster's link between Leonora and the devil lies in her own words. Even before her strategy against Romelio has taken shape in her mind, she is intent on "be[ing] a fury to him" (III.iii.281) and prays to outdo the archfiend in malice, blasphemy, and despair: "let me have / One property more than the devil of hell. . . . Let me in this life fear no kind of ill, / That have no good to hope for" (III.iii.291–295). And later she tells Winifrid that in addition to female wit and a handful of "advocates," she will "require, to make the practice fit, / Four devils" (III.iii.430–431). In an age much given to belief in infernal possession, Webster deliberately raises in the audience's mind the possibility that, temporarily at least, Leonora may be a witch.

But the sense of diabolical influence is by no means confined to the two chief malefactors. Webster portrays a society so ungodly, a world so stained by corruption, that one may expect to find telltale traces of Satan or the odor of sulphur almost anywhere—at court, in pleasures and luxuries, in law, in romantic relationships, in language, and even in the frustration of good intentions. Romelio remarks mordantly to his sister that if Contarino's social orbit, the court, "could have wrought salvation, / The devil had ne'er fall'n from heaven" (III.iii.17–18). Crispiano insists that the pleasure of making money exceeds that of wine, food, sex, rich dress, or any other "pleasure that the devil / Has ever practic'd with to raise a man / To a devil's likeness" (II.i.88–90). Romelio associates Ariosto, one of his judges, with "The devil," seeing him as a diabolical aid "To prompt the . . . memory [of the devilish prosecutor] when he founders" (IV.ii.153–154); and Ariosto himself, reacting to the suggestion that Latin be spoken to veil unseemly testimony, exclaims, "Here's a Latin spoon, and a long one, / To feed with the devil!" (IV.ii.402–403). (In this last comic detail, Webster connects the operation of malignant powers with another pervasive theme, the dangerous property of language to conceal, mislead, or obfuscate.)

At the beginning of the drama Jolenta tells Contarino that she is "bewitch'd" in being "forespoken / To be married" to Ercole, and when Contarino lays claim to "all" of the lady, Winifrid interjects bumptiously, "Yes, but the devil would fain put in for's share, / In likeness of a separation" (I.ii.237–244). Despite the malevolent imagery, Jolenta's forced cleavage from her first admirer and reluctant alliance with his rival may work ultimately toward the greater happiness of all three characters; but our sense of the devil's making mischief in amorous affairs is nevertheless acute, and Webster can tinge the inscrutability of supernatural influences, even if these turn out in the end to be beneficent, with the coloration of hell. Furthermore, as the Capuchin points out, human nature is so deeply flawed that, blinded by pride and "drench'd / In . . . presumptuous and hidden sins," people unwittingly "turn / The tide of their good fortune": "While they aspire to do themselves most right, / The devil that rules i' th' air hangs in their light" (V.v.19–23). Satanic powers abound in both the metaphysics and psychology of the play to an extent that suggests the gloomy doctrine of Calvin. Grace may somehow operate upon the souls and actions of the selfish, but when this happens, it appears sudden, miraculous, playlike, and contrary to what one might rationally expect or hope for.

The idea of possession by the devil, whether intended as theological reality or rhetorical figure, points logically to the more comprehensive theme of uncertain identity that touches virtually all aspects of *The Devil's Law-Case*. Questions of identity are peculiarly central to tragicomedy: indeed it is difficult to think of the major Jacobean examples—those, for example, by Marston, Shakespeare, Beaumont and Fletcher, or Middleton—without fastening immediately on the obsessive way these plays probe, worry over, or toy with the concept. Disguise is obviously crucial here, and, as we have noticed already, Webster's plot not only requires a large number of disguised characters (nine in all) but also delights to blur the line between altered appearance and the actual concealment of identity. After his recovery, Contarino dresses like a Dane so as to hide his existence from almost everyone including Ercole, but before the tourney, the two men garb themselves as friars—a symbolic shift of identity that suggests spiritual self-questioning but that apparently involves no deception. Leonora plays the role of a penitent adulteress by wearing a veil, Jolenta at least plans to affect pregnancy by padding her gown, and Winifrid tries to pass herself off as an elderly servant by whitening her hair; but each of these women keeps her true name. These are half disguises intended to mislead without totally abandoning recognizability—mixtures, so to say, of truth and falsehood. At the end of the play, Angiolella and Jolenta allegorize their identities for didactic purposes, and Ercole asks why his fiancée has "eclips'd" herself (V.vi.51) as a Moorish nun, but he nevertheless knows who she is in the physical sense. As judge, Crispiano goes unrecognized by Leonora and Julio, having earlier disguised himself as a merchant in order to spy on his son, but the portrait that Leonora has treasured for many years strangely reveals to the court what it has apparently concealed from her. In the world of *The Devil's Law-Case*, blindness and vision, even at the level of identifying other human beings, can be disturbingly subjective.

Romelio dons the stagy costume of a Jew to cloak his murder; then he is forced to disclose himself to the surgeons, who, in turn, disguise themselves from him; finally, one of the surgeons, in order to control Jolenta's movements, redisguises himself in Romelio's discarded Jewish habit, thus identifying himself in a symbolic way with the man whom he wishes to deceive. This playfully ironic but nevertheless unsettling motif of metamorphosis or shape-shifting raises serious, even tragic, questions. If personhood is so fluid and unstable as such action would imply, who can know himself, let alone be sure of anyone else? Inevitably one begins to ask with Lear, "Who is it that can tell me who I am?" (*King Lear*, I.iv.226). And the logical extremity of such uncertainty about selfhood is total dissolution or loss of identity. Romelio, when he thinks that the loss of his ships has ruined him, agonizes in one of Webster's most arresting metaphors:

> O, I am pour'd out like water! The greatest
> Rivers i' th' world are lost in the sea,
> And so am I! Pray leave me.
>
> (II.i.338–340)

Physical disguise, of course, is merely symptomatic of the elusive substitutions and superimpositions of role that make all the principal characters so hard to pin down. The sexually frustrated widow, the dignified matron, the jealous lover, the witch, the implacable revenger, the alienated parent, the religious convert, and the dedicated wife all represent aspects of Leonora's character; but some of these are merely latent or emerge briefly and intermittently, only to be replaced by or absorbed into new psychological emphases, patterns, and combinations. Jolenta is both ingenue and bitch, both virgin and pretended sexual partner outside formal marriage, both accomplice in cynical deception and moralist on false appearances, depending on which of her actions or speeches we choose to stress. Contarino looks successively like an improvident marrier of money (*contare*, the Italian verb for counting or reckoning, is embedded in his name), a passionate suitor, an upholder of chivalric honor, an idealistic friend, and a kind of voyeur upon the complicated troubles that his supposed death has generated. Romelio (his name, a possible derivative of Romeo, suggests a pilgrim or wanderer) presents a baffling kaleidescope of evanescent personae as diverse as Jonson's Volpone, Marlowe's Barabas, Massinger's Sir Giles Overreach, Webster's own Bosola, and (at the end) a fusion of Shakespeare's Angelo and Vincentio. *The Devil's Law-Case* reflects a world in which simple or primal values, despite a certain nostalgia for them, have almost been swept away and in which character is at least partly at the mercy of shifting economic and social pressures rather than defined by metaphysical absolutes.

The world Webster portrays is nervously insecure, relativistic, and self-consciously theatrical—a world in which the mask and the face behind it become increasingly difficult to pry apart. And at the heart of personality, Webster seems to suggest, may lie the ineradicable and frightening sense that a man's own deepest self is protean, mutable, subject to currents of inexplicable and unpredictable transformation. When Romelio, wearing the semifarcical costume of an "Italianated Jew," refers to "play[ing] with [his] own shadow" (III.ii.2–3), he conveys more than the conventional self-congratulation of the stage Machiavel. He touches upon a concept of identity that profoundly informs the psychology of the whole drama. Here we glimpse a man in the role of self-conscious audience to his own performance, trapped in a society where one must perpetually re-invent the self. In fact, the motif of the shadow, with its plain relevance to the problem of identity, pervades *The Devil's Law-Case*, as it had *The Duchess of Malfi*. Leonora puns on the word in the senses of cooling shade and portrait when Contarino asks for her "picture" ("O, sir, shadows are coveted in summer, / And with me, 'tis fall o' th' leaf" [I.i.154–156]), thus enhancing the ambiguity of whether he has referred to the mother or the daughter. Crispiano plays on the word again at the trial when he reveals himself to be the same man, now aged, of whom Leonora owns a portrait: "Behold, I am the shadow of this shadow" (IV.ii.505). Angiolella suggests her dependency on Jolenta—indeed her emotional kinship with her friend—when she follows her in flight: "I, like your shade, pursue you" (V.i.48). And the term (again as in *The Duchess*) takes on the mixed connotations of Christian conscience, alter ego, and the threat of death when the Capuchin warns Romelio before he takes up his sword, "Were I in your case, / I should present to myself strange shadows," only to be answered with stiff-necked mockery: "Turn you, were I in your case, / I should laugh at mine own shadow" (V.iv.69–72). Finally, Romelio's lament for the passing of all things, which vanish "As shadows wait upon the sun" (V.iv.139), links the fascination with identity to ideas of dissolution, flux, and insubstantiality. And in this connection it may be relevant to note that the two most complex figures of the tragicomedy are both middle-aged and therefore more conscious of the brevity of life. Romelio is thirty-eight and his mother, as Pearson phrases it, "fights desperately against society, time, and her own daughter" to experience one "Last merriment 'fore winter" (III.iii.276).[28]

Insecure feelings about identity, whether these have to do with the true nature of the self or of others, imply an unstable society in which people are likely
to distrust each other or become easily estranged—a society in which emotional
commitments are saddled with difficulty, confusion, and misperception, and in
which doubts and frustrations make for neurosis, psychic distress, and even
madness. It can hardly be accidental in an environment where integrity and self-
definition are so problematic that so many characters in the play come close to
distraction themselves or are accused by others of being mad. Leonora, at the
climax of her distraught soliloquy after hearing that Contarino has been slain, is
aware of the links in her own psyche between interior division, extreme emotional disorder, and the mysterious wellsprings of malignity:

> Ha, ha, what say you?
> I do talk to somewhat, methinks; it may be
> My evil genius. Do not the bells ring?
> I have a strange noise in my head: O, fly in pieces!
> (III.iii.286–289)

Later at the trial, Ariosto regards her behavior toward Romelio as nothing less
than medically abnormal:

> Woman, y' are mad, I'll swear't, and have more need
> Of a physician than a lawyer.
> The melancholy humor flows in your face;
> Your painting cannot hide it.
> (IV.i.61–64)

Webster has already prepared us for this judgment by having Crispiano refer earlier to the "mad tricks" (III.i.10) of women. Typically, Leonora returns the compliment, referring to Ariosto as insane: "Sure the old man's frantic" (IV.i.73).

Jolenta also is associated with madness. We have noted earlier in another
context the surgeon's statement that she is said to be "a little mad" (V.iii.31), but
her brother twice suggests that she shows signs of mental imbalance by resisting
his plans for her marriage. First he cries out reproachfully, "You are not mad?"
(I.ii.16); then when she asks hyperbolically for "some potion to make [her] mad"
so that she may "consent" to be contracted to Ercole, "happily not knowing
what I speak," he retorts, "Come, you are mad already . . ." (I.ii.94–97). Later,
in reaction to Romelio's plan to have her feign pregnancy, she can exclaim: "O,
my fantastical sorrow! . . . We are never well, till we are mad indeed"
(III.iii.200–204). Even Romelio, by refusing to accept the judge's offer of ad-
journment (the better to prepare his defense against his mother), incurs the
charge of being "more mad than she" (IV.ii.81). Later on, when Romelio has
locked up his mother and the Capuchin in the turret, the churchman attributes
his action to possible distraction: "his obstinacy, / Madness, or secret fate has
thus prevented / The saving of his life" (V.v.6–8). All three members of this fa-

426

therless family regard each other or are regarded as dangerously irrational: in Ariosto's words, "the lunacy runs in a blood" (IV.ii.80).

Suspicions of one family member for another, indeed the coldness, alienation, and sense of being cut off or isolated from one's own kin, relate madness to the family unit and, beyond it, to the disintegrative forces in society at large. The cynicism and hostility that Webster dramatizes, whether between siblings or between child and parent, accord exactly with Lawrence Stone's findings with regard to the affectional distance and emotional deprivation of the typical upper- or middle-class family of the seventeenth century—attitudes that Stone suggests are traceable to such factors as the early loss of a parent, the high rate of infant mortality, the relegation of children to wet nurses, and a consequent anxiety about one's true parentage.[29] The comic counterpart to the "mad" behavior of Leonora, Jolenta, and Romelio appears, of course, in the antics of Julio, the youthful prodigal, and of his strangely indulgent but nevertheless eavesdropping father Crispiano. Until the disclosure at the trial, Julio supposes that his father is dead and wastes no filial sentiment on his parent: "He died in perfect memory I hope, / And made me his heir" (II.i.119–120). Then in his final speech the wag announces his plan to go to sea, where he intends to furnish himself "with a rare consort / Of music" (a traditional cure for madness)[30] and listen, apparently with a quibble on the judge's name, to a theatrical or musical version of Ariosto's *Orlando Furioso*: "when I am pleased to be mad, / They shall play me *Orlando*" (V.vi.72–74). (Earlier in the drama Julio had referred to the lawyer as "a mad fellow" [II.i.212].) Even the parody lawyer Contilupo is comically associated with madness, for he is presented as delirious with joy at the prospect of arguing Leonora's case: "I am struck with wonder, almost ecstasied, / With this most goodly suit" (IV.i.103–104). The playwright thus comes close to suggesting that most litigation is a form of moral insanity.

Madness in *The Devil's Law-Case* therefore covers a range of significances—everything from criminal dementia to folly, from near-tragic irrationality to mere silliness and self-indulgence. Moreover, one man's sanity is another's lunacy. Indeed, we are not far from the paradoxical situation that elicits Vindice's wry comment:

> Surely we are all mad people, and they
> Whom we think are, are not; we mistake those:
> 'Tis we are mad in sense, they but in clothes.
> (*The Revenger's Tragedy*, III.v.80–82)[31]

But Webster is at pains to suggest the serious implications of madness not only for the inhibiting of self-knowledge but also for the fracturing of fundamental family and social harmonies. Prospero (and again the name of the character is suggestive) hints at these deeper meanings in his choric statement on the self-destructiveness of the rival suitors, whom Julio, after they have almost killed each other, calls "Brave valiant lads" (II.ii.47):

> Come, you do ill, to set the name of valor
> Upon a violent and mad despair.
> Hence may all learn, that count such actions well,
> The roots of fury shoot themselves to hell.
>
> (II.ii.48–51)

As in the major tragedies, so in the tragicomedy Webster explores the paradox of union in division and division in union not only within characters but also between them. If, through the motif of madness, he suggests the isolating, separative, and disintegratory aspects of human identity, he also employs the motif of companionship and emotional attachment to convey suggestions of fusion or even obliteration. Renaissance ideals of friendship and romance fostered the notion that close personal alliances could express themselves symbolically in terms of physical as well as spiritual identification. Likeness of temperament and common interest could imply, as frequently in Donne, an interpenetration of souls and sometimes even bodily interchangeability. In *The Merchant of Venice* Portia speaks of the relationship between Antonio and Bassanio as a kind of identity:

> for in companions
> That do converse and waste the time together,
> Whose souls do bear an egall yoke of love,
> There must be needs a like proportion
> Of lineaments, of manners, and of spirit;
> Which makes me think that this Antonio,
> Being the bosom lover of my lord,
> Must needs be like my lord.
>
> (III.iv.11–18)

But Webster instinctively knew, with Wallace Stevens, that "Both in nature and in metaphor, identity is the vanishing point of resemblance,"[32] that likeness, whether in art or in life, can lead to vexed and confusing notions of emotional involvement as a species of psychic absorption or eclipse. *The Devil's Law-Case*, being finally comic, refrains from pursuing this dimension of the identity puzzle as searchingly as, say, *The Duchess of Malfi*, but the theme is nevertheless observable.

We have already noticed that Contarino echoes the earlier play when he asseverates his dedication to Jolenta as a form of possession: "you are all mine" (I.ii.237). A little later Winifrid reinforces this sense of a single organism in the making with her prurient comment, "How they grow together!" (I.ii.265). Contarino also identifies Jolenta with Romelio when he reassures her that he could hardly quarrel with her brother—a person who by definition is an extension of her, "part of yourself" (I.ii.296). Angiolella, as has already been pointed out, invokes the image of a "shade" (V.i.48) or shadow to express her inseparability from Jolenta. For the most part, these are conventional metaphors of devotion that would ordinarily or in isolation from each other imply nothing sinister. But the idea of one personality blending with or superimposing itself upon another takes on a certain negative coloration in a play like *The Devil's Law-Case*, so charged, as it is, with the notion that a stable sense of self is difficult to discover or create and precarious to sustain.

Perhaps Webster's most unsettling application of the concept of alter ego emerges in his dramatization of the love-hate psychology that develops between the rival suitors. During the duel in Act II, Ercole protests bizarrely that because of his own wounds he is "now unfit / For any lady's bed"; then he lunges at Contarino to give his opponent what he supposes will be his death wound: "take the rest with you" (II.ii.25–26). One mortally injured friend supposedly kills the other, inviting him to take what remains of the other's body with him across the barrier that divides the living from the dead. (Ercole puns on the word "rest," meaning "peace" or "relaxation" as well as "remnant.") The stage direction specifies that "Contarino *wounded, falls upon* Ercole" (II.ii.26), and both men, now prone, struggle with each other until they lose consciousness. The staging here is revealing because it adds visual emphasis to the concept, already embodied in the dialogue, of friends fighting to preserve their separateness even as they fall together in a physical union emblematic of their sameness. Later, a remorseful Ercole embroiders the idea of identification with Contarino when he says fancifully to Leonora, "if you would view him dead, / I will present him to you bleeding fresh, / In my penitency" (III.iii.334–336). Webster continues the symbolism of identification in the later duel, where the disguised Contarino serves as Ercole's second—as a kind of duplicate or shadow-version of Romelio's opponent. When Contarino at long last reveals himself, Ercole explicitly underlines this point: "You were but now my second; now I make you / Myself forever" (V.vi.23–24).

It is an easy step from uncertain or confusing identity in persons to its equivalent in speech, namely, equivocation. Webster's fascination with double meanings, with the property of ambiguous words to endanger, threaten, corrupt, or destroy relationships, persists throughout his work; but in two of the tragicomedies, *The Devil's Law-Case* and *A Cure for a Cuckold*, the dramatist makes equivocal language a significant element of plot and character. In the unaided drama duplicitous wordplay and the witty distortion of plain sense become so dominant as to constitute a sort of combined villain in their own right. Bacon calls equivocation "the great sophism of all sophisms," applying his censure especially to "such words as are most general and intervene in every inquiry."[33] Jonson stresses the social destructiveness of verbal obscurity:

Wheresoever manners, and fashions are corrupted, Language is. . . . *Speech* is the only benefit man hath to express his excellencie of mind above other creatures. It is the Instrument of *Society*. . . . In all speech, words and sense are as the body, and the soule. The sense is as the life and soule of Language, without which all words are dead. . . . Whatsoever looseth the grace, and clearenesse, converts into a Riddle; the obscurity is mark'd, but not the valew. That perisheth, and is past by. . . . Our style should be like a skeine of silke, to be carried, and found by the right thred, not ravel'd, and perplex'd; then all is a knot, a heape. . . . *Language* most shewes a man: speake that I may see thee.[34]

Shakespeare, of course, had associated misleading language with the powers of darkness—with the prophesies of the wicked spirit whom Margery Jourdain and her confederates conjure up in *2 Henry VI* (I.iv) or with the "juggling" hags of the Scottish tragedy who practice "th' equivocation of the fiend / That lies like truth" (*Macbeth*, V.v.43–44). In the latter instance, he seems to have been influenced by the Gunpowder Plot (to which Webster also alludes) with its trial of Father Garnet, who familiarized all England with the Jesuitical doctrine (to quote Sir Edward Coke) "wherein under the pretext of the lawfulnesse of a mixt proposition to expresse one part of a mans mind, and retaine another, people are indeed taught not onely simple lying, but fearefull and damnable blasphemie."[35] In *The Devil's Law-Case* Webster implicitly invokes these moral, even religious, attitudes toward ambiguous or deceptively figurative language, dramatizing what Puttenham calls "abuses or rather trespasses in speach," which "deceiue the eare and also the minde, drawing it from plainnesse and simplicitie to a certaine doublenesse, whereby our talke is the more guilefull & abusing."[36]

But at the same time the playwright never loses sight of the amusement that double meanings can afford when the intention is mainly to be playful. Punning (*paronomasia*), whether meant wittily by a speaker or uttered ignorantly by a dramatic character and therefore intended by the author to delight hearers only, is an ancient literary game. For the Elizabethans—Shakespeare first among them—it could be "the fatal Cleopatra for which [they] lost the world, and [were] content to lose it,"[37] however much Augustans might repine. Rhetoricians such as Puttenham, Wilson, and Carew endorsed the double-entendre, properly used, and could enjoy wrenched meanings, mistaken significances, and verbal fallacies as much as Hamlet when, in response to the brilliant nonsense of the gravedigger, he cautions Horatio facetiously, "We must speak by the card, or equivocation will undo us" (*Hamlet*, V.i.137–138). Quintilian, who defined the "essence of all wit" as lying "in the distortion of the true and natural meaning of words,"[38] recognized that our pleasure in mistaking them or becoming suddenly aware of ulterior and unexpected significations derives from a willingness, for the sake of entertainment, to absolve language from its usual function of clarification. To quote one recent analyst, "Wit is thus sophistry rescued from the ignorant and villainous, intended not to convince but to delight."[39]

The Devil's Law-Case pursues the game of semantic ambiguity relentlessly with the purpose, on the one hand, of presenting deviousness, isolation, self-absorption, mania, perversity, and the breakdown of mutual trust, while, on the other, seeking cleverly to exploit one of the standard resources of wit. In some cases the contrary functions are easily separable, but in others the two overlap, creating for the audience genuine puzzles as to the proper mode of response.

Thus Webster gives us a language of doubleness not only equivalent to the psychological and sociological problems of the action but also appropriate to both the serious and lighter concerns of his play. When the two kinds of wit are fused or unsuccessfully combined, we approach linguistic anarchy—the kind of uncertainty that confuses audiences as much as it confuses persons within the fiction. But when the mixed functions are intelligible, Webster daringly forges a verbal medium designed to express, sometimes simultaneously, the divided emphases of his mixed genre—tragicomedy. In *The White Devil*, Duke Francisco had spoken of his plot to entrap the lovers as having its amusing side: "My tragedy must have some idle mirth in't, / Else it will never pass" (IV.i.119–120). At its most complex, Webster's equivocation in *The Devil's Law-Case* strives to elicit both fear and laughter at once—to disturb by the miasma of emotional and moral confusion it implies and to please by its vermiculate inventiveness and display of fancy.

A number of the play's double-entendres seem to be mainly serious in effect—intended to unsettle the audience by occluding motivation, by showing the readiness of characters to mislead or misconstrue, and even to portray a symptom of ambivalence or psychological dividedness—one of the means by which persons may evade responsible confrontation with the darker face of their own natures. The semantic ambiguities of the opening scene, in which Leonora and Contarino tease us with the alternative meanings of "suit" (I.i.150), "picture" (I.i.154), "a most choice object" (I.i.166), and "settle your estate" (I.i.210), are of this kind. So, too, are Romelio's twisting of "falsehood" (III.iii.144) so as to infect Jolenta with the lie that Leonora intended to commit incest with her future son-in-law, and Jolenta's equivocal "begot" (V.ii.37), which also raises the specter of incest—this time in Contarino's mind. And, like most Renaissance dramatists, Webster is attracted to the quibble that intensifies tragic emotion. Contarino's words to Ercole when one friend wounds the other ("You are hurt" [II.ii.15]), the Capuchin's lament when the duelists have seemingly ended each other's lives ("let fall a bead / For two unfortunate nobles" [II.iii.92–93]), and Romelio's line to Leonora just after the merchant has confessed to murdering her beloved ("You are troubled with the mother" [III.iii.250]), are good examples. Here the secondary meanings (wounded feelings as well as a physical wound, a tear as well as the bead of a rosary, the mothering of a killer in addition to hysteria) simply deepen our sense of reality in a painful way as Shakespeare characteristically does when, for instance, he makes Romeo pun on "rest" ("O, here / Will I set up my everlasting rest . . ." [*Romeo and Juliet*, V.iii.109–110]) or Othello play on "light" ("Put out the light, and then put out the light" [*Othello*, V.ii.7]). Even Leonora's plan to wreak vengeance on her son, "To let him live and kill him" (III.iii.373), exemplifies a verbal doubleness more proper to tragedy than to comedy.

But of course *The Devil's Law-Case* also employs puns in the traditionally comic mode. Contarino picks up Leonora's reference to the Exchange, the principal place of business for merchants, wittily reapplying it to the courtly exchange of gossip and "new fashions" among women (I.i.144–150). Julio plays bawdily on "the prick" (a sword point and a penis), which may "spoil" men "for women's sakes" (II.i.352–354). The jesting on "brief," the legal document that contains "some fourscore sheets of paper" (IV.i.11–12) and weighs as much as a package of cheese or figdates, has already been mentioned, as has also Jolenta's indelicate pun on the "tumbl[ing]" (V.i.41) of Angiolella, both on shipboard and in Romelio's bed. At the trial Ariosto chides the defendant, "an East Indy merchant," with having "a spice of pride in [him] still" (IV.ii.86–87); and the surgeon plays humorously on the two meanings of "honest" (chaste and truthful) when he proposes to marry Winifrid and help her "recover [her] good name" (V.iii.7–12).

The most interesting and characteristic duplicities of language in the drama, however, fall neither on the tragic nor comic side but hover tremulously between. This kind of verbal ambiguity usually resonates too openly with tragic potential and is too deeply ingrained with moral significance to be be taken superficially as mere cleverness or a display of verbal gymnastics; yet it nevertheless tends to elicit a smile, if not downright laughter. When Julio refers to the fallen duelists, one of whom he assumes to be dead, as "perfect lovers" (II.ii.40), he jests impudently on their foolhardy commitment to honor almost as Falstaff might; but his phrase also carries a more deeply emotional meaning for an audience that has just been engaged in the conflicts of romance with friendship and of affection with egotism that have defined the relationship of the combatants before and during their deadly contest. If we laugh here, we must do so uneasily. Similarly, when Jolenta puns on her brother's plan to pass off his illegitimate child as her offspring, we feel a combination of flippancy and bitterness, a strained and nervous quality about her wit, that makes it at once less than tragic but more than simply ludicrous: "So. Then I conceive you, / My conceived child must prove your bastard" (III.iii.58–59). Having shocked his sister with the idea that their mother was planning to conduct an incestuous affair, he counsels her cynically simply to erase the scandal from her mind: "Throw the fowl to the devil that hatch'd it . . ." (III.iii.151). Romelio wittily embeds the secondary meaning of "foul" in his metaphor, but, again, the situation is too tense and the context too repugnant to make merriment the obvious response.

Sometimes Webster brings us close to an explosion of laughter. Winifrid's assumption that her mistress's "poison" (III.iii.418) refers to murder rather than to bastardy, the Capuchin's insistence that Romelio's call for food before the tournament should mean a devotional manual rather than "good victuals to breakfast" (V.iv.92), and Romelio's comic misinterpretation of the friar's word "living" (V.iv.181) as a noun rather than a verb—money rather than a life-preserving revelation of Contarino's survival, are all cases in point. Each of these misunderstandings contains a strong element of absurdity. But in each case, too, the context overshadows the joke with the threat of death or of serious injury. The mistakes, whether deliberate or unaware, are funny only in an immediate or restricted sense, and, on reflection, dilate to touch or encompass the more momentous concerns of the play.

We experience a sense of tragicomic disquiet when Leonora reacts nervously to the news that Jolenta is pregnant:

> I do look now for some great misfortunes
> To follow, for indeed, mischiefs
> Are like the visits of Franciscan friars:
> They never come to prey upon us single.
> (III.iii.224–227)

The pun on "prey" neatly encapsulates the drama's characteristic tension between religious and antireligious perspectives, also highlighting the villainess-heroine as simultaneously a satiric commentator and prototragic sufferer. But the speech as a whole does more than this: in the act of wittily disparaging friars, Leonora anticipates the greater disasters and painful complications to ensue. And the doubleness of her language generates further mixtures of response, appropriate to the tragicomic mode of the action. Later in the same scene, the lady learns of Contarino's supposed murder, an emotional blow that occasions another of her wry ulterior meanings, for she speaks of making Romelio "chief mourner" (III.iii.257) for the nobleman's death. Then, when the Capuchin (a coweled Franciscan like those to whom she earlier referred) arrives with what he believes to be good news—news calculated to change her tragic notes to comic— she expresses her disappointment at seeing not Contarino *redivivus* but Ercole, with another tragicomic quibble:

> O, I am dead again! Instead of the man,
> You present me the grave swallowed him.
> (III.iii.329–330)

Leonora's conceit for Ercole—a grave that has buried Contarino by being the agent of his wounding and therefore, in an extended sense, the root cause of his death—forces the audience to negotiate the awkward leap from a literal to a figurative use of words, and then to relate this disparity to the ironic situation that the plotting has just obtruded upon our consciousness. Leonora's figure of speech is tragic from her own point of view within the fiction, and Webster permits us to share her bitter emotion to some extent. But her language is also comic to those who know that Contarino is alive and who cannot help smiling—both at her frustrating surprise and at her failure to grasp the secret reality that no one is really dead.

Webster's equivocal language, then, may help to bridge the troubling hiatuses that tragicomedy sets up between the conflicting emotions, ironies, and responses of its own double mode—a mode that seeks to incorporate comic and tragic impulses within the same form and to make sophisticated drama out of their complex interaction. A final example may help to clinch the point. Before the trial gets underway, Sanitonella jokes bawdily about the secret testimony of Winifrid, which the Register is about to record: "Take her into your office, sir. She has that / In her belly, will dry up your ink, I can tell you—" (IV.i.1–2). Again Webster toys with the mingling of literal and figurative meanings to produce, at a single stroke, both laughter and a vague suggestion of dire consequences to follow; for the ambiguous word "belly" encourages us to invest the speech with a range of associations—physical and abstract, ludicrous and sinister. Winifrid's own loose morals, the humorous but ugly lies the servant is about to disgorge or give birth to in court, the story of Leonora's adultery, the secret hatred of the mother for her own child, and the pregnancies (feigned and actual) of Jolenta and Angiolella are all somehow present here—*in utero*, as one might say. The effect is simultaneously funny and disturbing—but not only because the language is equivocal. The calculated ambiguity, achieved through rhetorical technique, points beyond the words themselves to a radical ambivalence about the subject matter, which happens in this case to be sex. *The Devil's Law-Case*, like many Jacobean plays, treats sexuality as a matter both for laughter and for tears, but Webster's special kind of linguistic duality in this play suggests an attitude uncomfortably divided between the two. If reality itself is double, equivocation, in a way, becomes the logical medium of expression.

The mixed response to sexuality leads us back inevitably to Webster's pervasive concern with the relatedness of love and death, a theme that touches *The Devil's Law-Case* at nearly every significant point of its plotting and characterization. In his major tragedies, the playwright had explored the dark recesses of romance and passion in such a manner as to suggest that, ineluctably, death was not only the effect of love but also, in some sense, its concomitant. Not inappropriately, the tragicomedy inverts this emphasis, offering us a drama that educates its characters in the value of love by taking them through a confrontation with their own mortality or by forcing them, temporarily at least, to undergo an experience of loss that painfully rearranges or radically alters their view of themselves and of their world. Again Webster expands his concept of love to encompass more than merely sexual or romantic relationships, extending it to include also ties between a brother and sister, between a parent and her children, between friends, and, finally, between man and God. *The Devil's Law-Case* thus dramatizes how vital love is to survival—that is, to our hopes for the emotional, social, and metaphysical connectedness without which life, in any meaningful sense, can scarcely be sustained. At the same time, the play insists that such hopes are somehow grounded in and inseparable from an acute awareness of the brevity of existence and of human frailty—that they must be won (if won at all) through a deracinating struggle with pride, uncertainty, doubt, and fear. Webster's play, then, ends in marriages that not only illustrate the formidable dangers (internal and external, psychological and situational, subjective and objective) that may threaten happiness, but that also teach Montaigne's lesson (elaborated from Cicero) that "to philosophize is to learn to die":

434

Ammiddest our bankets, feasts, and pleasures, let us ever have this restraint or object before us, that is, the remembrance of our condition, and let not pleasure so much mislead or transport us, that we altogether neglect or forget, how many waies, our joyes, or our feastings, be subject unto death, and by how many hold-fasts shee threatens us and them. So did the Aegyptians, who in the middest of their banquetings, and in the full of their greatest cheere, caused the anatomie of a dead man to be brought before them, as a memorandum and warning to their guests.[40]

From the beginning Webster reticulates the emotional relationships of the play with the language of mortality or associates them in some way with the danger or fact of death. Jolenta, for instance (in a typically Websterian juxtaposition), speaks of her enforced marriage to Ercole as though it were tantamount to being buried:

> *Romelio.* O sister, come, the tailor must to work
>   To make your wedding clothes.
> *Jolenta.* The tomb-maker, to take measure of my coffin.
> *Romelio.* Tomb-maker?
>
> (I.ii.1–4)

Later in the same scene she expresses her attraction to Contarino in words that also hint at her imminent demise: sorrowfully, she takes inventory of her jewels in order to make her beloved a bequest, "a deed of gift" (I.ii.236). Thus, through imagery as well as action, the dramatist builds the motif of the skull beneath the skin into Jolenta's feelings, both negative and positive, for her two suitors. Webster then makes the same association part of the rivalry between the two men, friends of long standing. When Contarino discovers that Ercole has supplanted him as a candidate for Jolenta's hand, he exclaims impetuously, "I'll make his bravery [i.e., his fine clothing] fitter for a grave / Than for a wedding" (I.ii.251–252). This, in turn, elicits a partial reversal of attitude from the girl, who suddenly admires the noble character of the man she is being forced to wed. Accordingly, she begs Contarino to moderate his murderous hostility and to replace it with affection. If he should kill his friend for the sake of love, he "will beget / A far more dangerous and strange disease / Out of the cure"; and she adds, "You must love him again / For my sake" (I.ii.253–256). As for Ercole, he is only too eager to prove his devotion to Jolenta by exposing himself to death: he will happily "depart from life / To do [his betrothed] any service" (I.ii.166–167). Clearly, Webster defines the romantic triangle with which the play opens in terms that imply the mingling and interdependence of love and death.

Even Romelio and Leonora are drawn tangentially into the love-death pattern. Contarino feels that Romelio has betrayed a friendship by seeming to promulgate his suit while actually favoring Ercole, and he tells Jolenta that her brother, "He that vows friendship . . . and proves / A traitor," deserves "to be hang'd" (I.ii.273–275). Moreover, Romelio himself perceives that, by shifting his sister from Contarino's arms into Ercole's, he risks death at the hands of the disappointed rival. Her resistance, of course, only exacerbates the danger, as he makes plain when he darts an angry aside at his sister: "Do you long to have my throat cut?" (I.ii.66). Leonora's romantic inclinations are too ambiguous at the start of the play to allow Webster to make much of the love-death nexus in her case, but he nevertheless associates her subtly with both sides of the same thematic polarity. She herself emphasizes her widowhood and insists upon her declining years ("with me, 'tis fall o' th' leaf" [I.i.156]) even as she flirts with Contarino; and her intense jealousy of her daughter (embodied in a withering curse if Jolenta should marry the object of her mother's passion) suggests a metaphorical "death" between parent and child that fuses ominously with half-concealed feelings of sexual desire.

Webster's intricate entanglements of plot often grow out of or further exploit these ironic linkages between love and death. Contarino prevents Ercole's putting to sea for reasons of "love" (II.i.230), a word that, in context, seems to refer not only to their incipient (and deadly) quarrel over Jolenta but also to their abiding affection for each other. As challenger in the duel, Contarino repeatedly underscores his "love" for his friend, even as he reproves his "unkindness," speaking of "two that have dearly loved, / And fall'n at variance" (II.i.237–252). Torn between devotion to Jolenta and his rival, he would willingly "divide" the lady between them, if that were possible, and "give [Ercole] half" (II.i.293–294):

> But since 'tis vain to think we can be friends,
> 'Tis needful one of us be ta'en away
> From being the other's enemy.
>
> (II.i.295–297)

An embrace follows—an expression of love on Ercole's part, as noted elsewhere, that also tests whether his opponent is concealing a weapon. This ambiguous encounter leads directly to the duel itself, a combat in which "perfect lovers" (II.ii.40) are apparently "slain" as well as "guilty of their own death" (II.iii.98–101). A conflict between romance and friendship has very nearly destroyed three different loves (Jolenta's for Contarino, Ercole's for Jolenta, and the two rivals' for each other) although, as is proper in tragicomedy, Webster tips the scales ever so slightly in favor of survival.

The victory of love over death, however, remains anything but clear at this point, for the play withholds the fact of the double preservation itself. Julio remarks tartly that "none love perfectly ideed, / But those that hang or drown themselves for love," adding that Ercole and Contarino "have chose a death next to beheading" by "cut[ting] one another's throats" (II.ii.43–46). The tolling of bells, the mention of "screech owls" (II.iii.82) and "a soft requiem" (II.iii.92), and Romelio's protracted disquisition on graves, funerals, monuments, bones, and charnels, darken the ambience even further before we are permitted to learn that the two suitors have been "preserved beyond natural reason" (II.iv.1). Even then, death plays a subversive role in the advancement of eros and in the masking of sexual passion. The mortally wounded Contarino makes Jolenta his heir, a circumstance that Romelio tries to bend to his own greed and that prompts him to publish his sister's pregnancy by the putatively deceased Ercole as a pretext for concealing his lustful treatment of Angiolella. Leonora pretends that her interest in the survival of Contarino (actually erotic, of course) stems from her desire to see him punished—that is, legally put to death—for murdering her daughter's fiancé. Even the comic subplot touches upon the love-death theme, for Julio blithely pursues a career of spendthrift "whoring" (II.i.137), secure in the belief that his father has "died i' th' Indies" and made him "heir" to a large fortune (II.i.118–120).

The central emblem of a "death" that preserves life and that therefore indirectly promotes romantic fulfillment is, of course, the attempted assassination of Contarino. Webster highlights this structural and thematic paradox by having the first surgeon report that "to make incision" upon the body "were present death" (III.ii.27–28) and by making explicit in Romelio's motivation the desire to prevent the victim from altering his will in case the "great man" should live but "not enjoy my sister" (III.ii.88–89). That only an intended murder should be capable of bringing about the miraculous recovery of a man who is "past all cure" (III.ii.23) exemplifies the inscrutable causation upon which tragicomedy, as a genre, tends to subsist. But, characteristically, Webster invests the irony with his special brand of macabre imagery: the "intent to kill" that becomes the "direct way to save" is likened seriocomically to being "cured o' th' gout by being rack'd" (III.ii.165–168) in the Tower of London. Furthermore, Webster embroiders this sensational reversal with other ironic junctures of love and death. Romelio claims for his lethal act a "most merciful" effect, since it will save Contarino "From dying on a public scaffold" (III.ii.112–114). Jolenta makes her brother's willingness to stab her "in [the] heart" the test of his "love" (III.iii.93–94) for her honor, when she claims to be with child. Romelio "wound[s]" Leonora "Quite through [her] heart" (III.iii.237–238) when he announces his "charity" (III.iii.232)—the killing of Contarino; and she expires metaphorically ("O, I am dead again!") when the Capuchin unexpectedly presents Ercole—not her true love but rather "the grave" who has supposedly "swallowed" him (III.iii.329–330). The effect of the mother's rage against her son then becomes her attempt to "kill him" (III.iii.373) emotionally through her deadly law case. A series of minor love-deaths becomes the dramatic means of intensifying emotional crises and marking points of sudden deflection or ricochet in the action.

It is clear, then, that Webster associates both villains of the tragicomedy with sexual misconduct as well as with the attempt to destroy others, linking the two activities obliquely. Romelio's worst outrages—the seducing of a nun and the stabbing of Contarino—meet curiously in his scheme to manipulate his sister as pretended mother and heiress. The "violence of [Leonora's] love" (IV.ii.587) for the young nobleman results in her attempt to avenge his death by "killing" her son—that is, by disinheriting him through a public confession of adultery, an act that Contilupo ironically protests will allow her to "go unto a peaceful grave, / Discharg'd of such a guilt as would have lain / Howling forever at [her] wounded heart" (IV.i.112–114). And, lest we forget it late in the play, the dramatist reminds us again of the love-death in which the duelists have involved themselves by making Ercole, now arrested for murdering the man he had loved and once more facing death, reflect upon the quarrel:

> I begun to love him
> When I had most cause to hate him; when our bloods
> Embrac'd each other, then I pitied
> That so much valor should be hazarded
> On the fortune of a single rapier,
> And not spent against the Turk.
>
> (IV.ii.604–609)

The playwright's disentangling of love from death after having shown their disquieting interconnection not only accompanies but also, in some sense, becomes the basis of the tragicomic resolution. The return to life of three characters supposed dead (Crispiano, Ercole, and Contarino) and the finding of spouses (however perfunctorily) for all four women represent the symbolic triumph of love over death—love now conceived, of course, as embracing divine Providence and the imponderable operations of Grace upon human depravity. But the final deliverance of the drama's remarkably unlovely characters to a qualified and contingent happiness seems to involve not the skirting of death so much as a vicarious passage through it. Leonora undergoes a kind of moral death when infatuation turns to self-destructive vengeance; then she must die to self when her shameful lies against Romelio are at last exposed and she "enter[s] into religion" (IV.ii.558). The painful movement from false to genuine penitence implies an almost revolutionary reorientation of values. The four combatants of the chivalric contest at the end also must come very close to death—in this case physical death—before liberation seems possible. It is no accident that Romelio's last-minute request for prayers (after he has contemptuously rejected the urgent ministrations of the Capuchin and the pageant on mortality presented by his mother) immediately precedes the release of the prisoners from their tower and the salvific disclosure that Contarino lives. Romelio's spiritual conversion, even though Webster presents it through a kind of dramatic shorthand, requires a change from despair—from a pagan stoicism that regards death as merely "The safest trench i' th' world to keep man free / From Fortune's gunshot" (V.iv.113–114) to the humbler fortitude of a Christian, to the recognition that true courage is fear that has said its prayers. Even Jolenta participates symbolically in this progress through death to love, for the deceptive blackness of her features, compared in her lyric to the color of the bird of death (she refers to "The down upon the raven's feather" [V.vi.35]), becomes an allegory of deep as opposed to lighter or merely sexual love (conveyed in her verses by the contrasting image of "Venus' cheek" [V.vi.37]). Ariosto's "epilogue" summarizes this movement from merely secular love through apparent death, spiritual death, or near-death to richer kinds of fulfillment in his image of a complicated series of events "threaten[ing] ruin" and "built on rotten ground" but "crown'd" ultimately "with success beyond our wishes" (V.vi.94–95).

It must be granted, nevertheless, that Webster shades the emergence of love as the reigning value of the play in ways that continue to invite skepticism; for such social and spiritual harmony as the action may imply is not only minimal in terms of its psychological probability but also minimally dramatized. The emotionally disengaging conclusion of *The Devil's Law-Case*, for instance, is especially unreassuring about the possibilities of renewed family unity. If the egotistical and disintegrative forces that have defined relations between Leonora and her two children and between the children themselves have somehow been softened by unselfishness and familial affection, the dramatist gives no hint of it in the final speeches. Actors, of course, might do much through stage gestures, but the silence of the text is almost clamorous. Webster indeed seems to imply that the harmonies of love owe as much to theatrical contrivance as to moral and psychological actuality. One recalls the rather styptic comment of Francis Bacon on the subject: "The stage is more beholding to love than the life of man. For as to the stage, love is ever matter of comedies, and now and then of tragedies: but in life it doth much mischief; sometimes like a siren, sometimes like a fury."[41]

In addition to his focus on diabolism, problems of identity, madness, linguistic ambiguity, and the usual intersection of love with death, Webster weaves several subsidiary themes into the thickly textured fabric of *The Devil's Law-Case*. A concern with dueling (the structure of the play rests heavily upon the parallel but contrasting onstage combats) is obviously significant here. Defense of one's personal honor had become something of an obsession by the reign of James I and was hotly debated by courtiers, soldiers, and lawyers as well as by clergymen and moralists. Numerous private affrays and armed quarrels attracted public attention, partly because the king himself so detested physical violence. In 1614 Sir Francis Bacon prosecuted the test case of Priest and Wright in Star Chamber, expressing His Majesty's negative views on dueling in a published charge to the court—views that James quickly reinforced by issuing two royal proclamations forbidding challenges and private combats under the strictest penalty. Gervase Markham of Dunham (not to be confused with the dramatist of the same name) challenged Lord Darcy in 1616, an affair that also occasioned a Star Chamber prosecution, while Middleton and Rowley's *A Fair Quarrel* (acted the same year and alluded to in *A Cure for a Cuckold* [IV.i.120–124]) gave dramatic expression to the problematic relationship of gentlemanly honor to unjust, foolish, or unreasonable quarreling.[42]

Webster's play, too, sets the artificial code of honor with its excessive tenderness about family reputation and injured pride against the bourgeois pragmatism of figures like Julio on the one hand and against Christian absolutism about humility on the other. Contarino and Ercole are judged by the church to be guilty of suicide, murder, or both, and are therefore technically "excommunicate" (II.iii.94). Romelio regards Contarino as the murderer of Ercole, while Leonora later ascribes a similar culpability to Ercole for his part in the supposed death of Contarino. Yet the final combat paradoxically exposes four men to mortal wounding—with legal sanction—in a primitive, if highly formalized, attempt to establish the guilt of a single person for the slaying of Contarino. Hindsight and privileged knowledge render both quarrels absurd, for the rivalry of the two noblemen for the same girl's affection proves false to the true natures of all three persons, and the trial by combat is to be fought over a nonissue, a "murder" that has never occurred. Nevertheless, the two duels have an important function in the drama for they serve as tests of valor and as mechanisms by means of which more sensible and more Christian values are recognized and embraced. If *The Devil's Law-Case* condemns the morality of the *duello* by implication, it does so in a curiously indirect and backhanded manner.

Since the theme of "fame" or reputation, which Webster had already developed powerfully in *The Duchess of Malfi*, relates closely to concepts of personal honor, it is hardly surprising to find it woven into the tragicomedy as well. The word "fame" occurs ten times in the play, being applied successively to the worldly standings of Contarino, Angiolella, Jolenta, Leonora, and Romelio, in addition to its use in connection with the notoriety of the law case itself (IV.ii.33). The dramatist employs the term most often to convey the strictures that society imposes upon the sexuality of women: Angiolella feels genuine remorse for her loss of "fame" (V.i.29), Jolenta is acutely conscious of the danger of having her "fame" poisoned (III.iii.88) by her brother's plan to have her pretend pregnancy, Ercole hopes to "preserve [Jolenta's] fame to' th' world" (III.iii.342) by marrying her, and Leonora admits that her passion for Contarino was strong enough to cause her to act "'Gainst [her] own fame" (IV.ii.542) by concocting the tale of adultery. Even Winifrid is offered the opportunity "To recover [her] good name" (V.iii.12) by making amends for past lies with present truth. But the value of moral and social credit in the world's eyes extends to the men also. Leonora, for instance, is attracted to Contarino in the first place partly because his "fame renders [him] most worthy" (I.i.139). Webster seems to underscore the mundane standards of fame—chastity, integrity, family honor, knightly valor—not to deny their importance or validity but to suggest that they become shallow, inhumanely limited, and merely conventional unless rooted in a deeper, humbler, and more spiritual understanding of virtue.

The religious values of the play, of course, find their explicit spokesman in the Capuchin, but Webster dramatizes their force more potently—in a way less tarnished by clichés—through the prideful negation of metaphysical realities on the part of Romelio and his mother, both of whom, incidentally, defy Christian principle by casting themselves in the role of revengers. The operative word here is "security," a term that Bosola had identified with "the suburbs of hell" (*The*

Duchess of Malfi, V.ii.337) and that the dramatist twice applies to the arrogant merchant. The character himself recognizes the peril of being "Lost in security" (II.iii.192), and later the friar echoes him: "Being . . . drown'd in security, / You know not how to live, nor how to die" (V.iv.121–122). G. K. Hunter observes that "security" had a special significance in Renaissance moral theology, meaning (according to the *Oxford English Dictionary*) "a culpable absence of anxiety." This is the meaning encapsulated in Hecate's ominous jingle, "you all know, security / Is mortals' chiefest enemy" (*Macbeth*, III.v.32–33), and allegorized in a lost Elizabethan morality play entitled *The Cradle of Security* (c. 1570) wherein a wickedly overconfident prince, attended by three ladies called Pride, Covetousness, and Luxury, is lulled into a state of deceptive well-being until frighteningly summoned, when he is least expecting it, to face the Last Judgment.[43]

As with the protagonist of the lost play, pride, greed, and lust are also among the defining features of Romelio's character. The merchant preens himself on his "strange confidence" (I.i.15) in trade and tempts Fortune by giving his ships hubristic names such as *The Storm's Defiance* (II.iii.61). Contarino remarks on his "insolent vainglory" (I.i.122). Romelio is ready to frustrate his sister's happiness, assassinate her beloved, and endanger her reputation for chastity—all to enrich his own coffers; and Webster presents his seduction of the nun as little better than lecherous self-gratification. Contemplating his armed encounter with Ercole, Romelio agnostically scorns prayer, having, as he says, "not made up [his] account" (V.iv.54) with the world as yet. When the friar warns him solemnly that he has "a dangerous voyage to take" in the duel, the merchant answers haughtily that he "will be [his] own pilot" (V.iv.57–58). This is "security" indeed, and the priest can only comment ominously, "This confidence, / If it be grounded upon truth, 'tis well" (V.iv.107–108). When time has almost run out, Romelio finally learns the truth of the Capuchin's teaching—that "He that is without fear, is without hope, / And sins from presumption" (II.iii.154–155); but, quasi-tragically, the lesson not only comes very late, it comes also through the agency of physical danger rather than through the traditional wisdom of the church. Romelio seems deaf to all instruction but the most visceral of experiences.

Leonora, in her way, behaves almost as presumptuously as her son. The tissue of lies on which she founds her unnatural prosecution of Romelio is itself evidence of the most arrogant self-absorption and of virtual obliviousness both to her own spiritual peril and to the moral realities of the normal world. The veil that she wears in court suggests (apart from her deceptive intentions) the self-generated blindness of her moral state and the treacherous "security" in which she envelops herself—until (as with Romelio) painful experience awakens her to a healthier and humbler frame of mind. The theme of culpable presumption even touches other characters as well. Jolenta sometimes appears selfishly manipulative and assertive in her treatment of both suitors (her misleading letter to

Ercole is a case in point); Romelio, who believes that Contarino is pursuing his sister chiefly for her money, mentions the impoverished lord's "over-confident purpose" (I.i.117); and Ercole, "divinely informed" after his near-death in the first duel, confesses that it was pride—the desire to be reputed "a choleric man"—that impelled him to fight for a sweetheart to whom he had no "right" (II.iv.6–11).

As in many of Webster's plays, satire on the legal profession is indispensable to the total effect of *The Devil's Law-Case*. The trial itself affords much of the play's best comedy, but, as Berry has noticed, this scene also contains serious moral ideas.[44] The jaundiced light in which the processes of civil law are presented helps to illuminate the contrasting values of natural and divine law that the drama also embodies. The tragicomedy illustrates the vast gulf between the corrupt justice of man's law and the supreme justice of God's law. Between these poles, however, lies the law of nature, symbolized by the fact and pretense of bastardy. (It is, of course, one of the trenchant ironies of the play that Romelio, who has begotten a bastard, should be falsely accused of being illegitimate himself.) Divine law condemns bastardy as a violation of marriage, and human law debars from inheritance those born outside wedlock, as Leonora attempts to do by proclaiming her own adultery. But, as Crispiano wisely points out (in lines that contain a quotation from Richard Hooker),

> We observe
> Obedience of creatures to the law of Nature
> Is the stay of the whole world; here that law is broke,
> For though our civil law makes difference
> 'Tween the base and the legitimate,
> Compassionate Nature makes them equal, nay,
> She many times prefers them.
> (IV.ii.263–269)

Webster's treatment of the legal theme in the play becomes a means of defining different kinds of social and moral disorder and of examining these from both worldly and philosophical perspectives. The time-serving Contilupo, the tolerant Crispiano (together with Ariosto, his replacement on the bench), and the metaphysically oriented Capuchin function partly as voices to discriminate three distinct levels of law—civil, natural, and divine. As Crispiano tries to bring civil law into alignment with nature and as Ariosto argues that "Such vild suits" as Leonora's unnaturally "Disgrace our courts, and . . . make honest lawyers / Stop their own ears whilst they plead" (IV.i.64–66), the friar attempts to bring a merely human understanding of law within the orbit of "divinity" (V.iv.163).

The final theme to be mentioned here will be equally familiar to students of Webster—namely the tendency of the characters to see experience in theatrical terms or to behave self-consciously as actors in a drama. Play metaphors on the Elizabethan stage often call attention to the complex relationship between illusion and reality, but in *The Devil's Law-Case* the principal thrust of such imagery is to expose moral distortion and falsehood. Jonson, citing the commonplace that "our whole life is like a *Play*," remarks that "every man, forgetfull of himselfe, is in travaile with expression of another," thereby risking the loss of his true nature: "wee so insist in imitating others, as wee cannot (when it is necessary) returne to our selves."[45] Webster makes this concept of deviation from reality an important part of the moral framework of the tragicomedy. We have already noted the proliferation of disguises and the revealing comment of the fraudulent Contilupo that the law case is the stuff of entertainment and "deserves . . . a spacious public theater" (IV.i.107–108) to do it justice. But, of course, *injustice* is the point; and there is a symbolic correlation between the comic show (which the trial becomes) and the shaky structure of perjury and pretense that is built up only to fall of its own weight when truth emerges.

In addition to being actors, both Romelio and Leonora function as internal playwrights who try to redirect life in accordance with their private scripts and cast others manipulatively in specific roles to this end. Romelio obviously treats his sister in this way, first by dictating her marriage and then by forcing her to play the role of mother. Typically, he gives a stage direction to Ercole when he tells him to "kiss" the "doggedness" out of his resistant sister: "Nay, continue your station [i.e., keep your present position onstage], and deal in / Dumb show [i.e., make a kiss do the work of verbal persuasion]" (I.ii.125–126). When Leonora is fashioning her elaborate plan to frame Romelio by suborning Winifrid, she announces in soliloquy, "Here begins / My part i' th' play" (III.iii.380–381). Leonora returns to herself (in Jonson's sense) when her unnatural attempt to enact the revenger in court fails so abysmally; but Romelio must play a whole succession of artificial or quasi-artificial roles (including infallible master of international trade, Machiavellian revenger, Jewish surgeon, cynical atheist, desperate swordsman, and religious convert) before he "comes home," admits his need of prayers, and accepts the pregnant Angiolella for his wife. Unwittingly (with an irony that applies to both speaker and dramatist), Romelio predicts his own self-reclamation as a response to the threat of death in his epigrammatic line, "O, look the last act be the best i' th' play . . ." (II.iii.129), when he meditates on mortality after the supposed deaths of Ercole and Contarino. Jolenta and the two noblemen also arrive at a truer sense of self. Both the men wear alien garb for much of the action, Webster's symbolic means of suggesting that they, too, wander from their genuine selves. Jolenta's Moorish appearance at the end constitutes a semidisguise for explicitly didactic purposes, but the nun's habit nevertheless belies the marital direction in which she is actually moving.

The artificialities of emotion and behavior that *The Devil's Law-Case* presents as simultaneously dangerous and comic make their impact more through elaborations of plot and the conventions of an overtly stagy genre than through a sustained pattern of theatrical imagery and allusion. Such specific references to the stage as the play does contain nevertheless support the pattern suggested above. Just before Romelio involves Jolenta in his scheme to profit from the putative deaths of her suitors, he attempts to abbreviate her grief by a strained analogy to the theatre: "are not bad plays / The worse for their length?" (III.iii.7–8). Romelio suggests cruelly, but not entirely without truth, that his sister's ostentatious mourning for Contarino contains an element of self-delusion by comparing it to the false sentiment of an inferior drama. Ariosto also associates pretentiously fraudulent conduct with theatricality in his rebuke to Sanitonella:

> Methinks you prate too much.
> I never could endure an honest cause
> With a long prologue to't.
>
> (IV.i.17–19)

Webster makes the very medium in which he works serve the import of his ethical design.

* * *

Although most recent commentators acknowledge the importance of *The Devil's Law-Case* in Webster's canon, few have found the play wholly satisfactory. Lee Bliss, despite her admiration for the tragicomic emphasis in Webster generally, denies that this drama is "a felicitous successor to [the] tragedies"; Berry speaks of its "bad" and (until lately) "attenuated . . . press" (perhaps with statements in mind such as Ornstein's "The rest should have been silence . . ."), while Madeleine Doran, in a much respected assessment, censures the ethical confusion and "disjointedness" of the tragicomedy:

Webster does not let the findings of the trial govern the outcome of the play. He winds it up with a solution of affairs directly athwart every sympathy he has created, all sense of justice, and what might be called the "leading" of the plot. Instead of the double ending one expects from such a plot, with the virtuous rewarded and the abductors and traducers at least shamed if not punished, there is an obviously contrived and anticlimactic "happy" ending. Everyone gets a mate; even Leonora is rewarded with the man she had tried to take away from her own daughter, and the unoffending daughter has her second and less favored suitor fobbed off on her.[46]

Peter Haworth, in a similar vein, judges "Much of the last act" to be "beneath criticism."[47] Not all scholars have been so harsh. The drama receives an imaginatively cordial reading from Gabriele Baldini and its structure a painstaking and sympathetic analysis by Ingeborg Glier.[48] But Doran's statement nevertheless typifies reaction to *The Devil's Law-Case* and fairly conveys the disappointment and disquiet that the play has usually evoked—a disquiet not unrelated in most cases to a fundamental distaste for the hybrid genre in which Webster chose to write.

Serious criticism has tended to resolve itself into two antithetical schools—the Christian and the skeptical. David Gunby sees the Webster of *The Devil's*

Law-Case as "a didacticist," as the dramatist of "a thesis play," who sets out, by presenting the progressive reclamation of Romelio, to justify the ways of God to man.[49] Peter Murray also reads the play as a theodicy, as a drama that undertakes "to show how love and peace may triumph" in an evil world and that illustrates "the religious belief that happy endings occur only by Contrivance, by the intervention of God."[50] Berry, too (though less single-mindedly than Gunby or Murray) regards the dramatist of this play as "a moralist," a writer, "Tempermentally . . . of Jonson's stamp," who was "fascinated with the problem of calibrating punishment to offence."[51] To the opposite camp belong writers such as Jacqueline Pearson, Robert Beaumont, and Lee Bliss. Pearson sees Webster's "tragicomic world" as "relativistic," the "solid Christian assumptions" of the Capuchin as "ironically undercut," and the "newly formed relationships" of the comic resolution as "surrounded by question marks."[52] Beaumont, reacting to the 1980 stage production, thinks that Webster not only "satirise[s] his earlier, heavier plays" in *The Devil's Law-Case*, but also "gives us a . . . panoramic, tongue-in-cheek view of contemporary . . . Jacobean drama."[53] Bliss goes further still in the direction of iconoclasm: the relationship between the two suitors, for instance, comes close to "sophisticated hypocrisy," and indeed the entire dramatic structure encourages us to "enjoy observing self-important fools [Romelio chief among them] outwit themselves." "*Contemptus mundi*," she stoutly insists, "is *not* the play's motto or goal."[54]

The difficulty, of course, is that the text supplies warrant for both approaches. Let us consider the conservative argument first. It is unlikely that Webster, let alone Jacobean audiences, could take the preachments of the Capuchin (despite the anticlerical humiliation to which Romelio subjects him) and the spiritual implications of the lyric on transience (despite the trickery that it masks) with total disregard. The playwright's contrast between the merchant's smug worldliness and the friar's transcendentalism comes painfully close to a truth repeatedly emphasized in scripture and in Anglican liturgy:

There be some that put their trust in their goods: and boast themselves in the multitude of their riches.

But no man may deliver his brother: nor make agreement unto God for him. . . .

For he seeth that wise men also die, and perish together: as well as the ignorant and foolish, and leave their riches for other.

And yet they think that their houses shall continue for ever. . . .

This is their foolishness. . . .

They lie in the hell like sheep, death gnaweth upon them, and the righteous shall have domination over them in the morning: their beauty shall consume in the sepulchre out of their dwelling.

(*The Book of Common Prayer*, Psalms 49:6–14)

And I will say to my soul, Soul, thou hast much goods laid up for many years; take thine ease, eat, drink, and be merry.

> But God said unto him, Thou fool, this night thy soul shall be required of thee: then whose shall those things be, which thou hast provided?
>
> So is he that layeth up treasure for himself, and is not rich toward God.
>
> (Luke 12:19–21)

> Let no man deceive himself. If any man among you seemeth to be wise in this world, let him become a fool, that he may be wise.
>
> For the wisdom of this world is foolishness with God.
>
> (I Corinthians 3:18–19)

> Who is a wise man and endued with knowledge among you? let him shew out of a good conversation his works with meekness of wisdom.
>
> But if ye have bitter envying and strife in your hearts, glory not, and lie not against the truth.
>
> This wisdom descendeth not from above, but is earthly, sensual, devilish.
>
> (James 3:13–15)

The consciousness of mortality that haunts the entire final movement of *The Devil's Law-Case*—and especially the ritual presentation of coffins and winding-sheets—finds an obvious parallel in Donne's last sermon, "Death's Duel," preached at court during the Lent of 1631:

> But then this *exitus a morte*, is but *introitus in mortem*, this *issue*, this deliverance *from* that *death*, the death of the *wombe*, is an *entrance*, a delivering over to *another death*, the manifold deathes of this *world*. Wee have a winding sheete in our Mothers wombe, which growes with us from our conception, and wee come into the world, wound up in that *winding sheet*, for wee come to *seeke a grave*. . . .[55]

We can hardly exclude Christian values from Webster's play without doing it violence.

Neither, on the more skeptical side of the debate, can we ignore the damaging glibness of tone, the shrugging off of moral responsibility, and the quasi-cynical fillips of plot that push the ending of the drama dangerously close to parody. Scarcely any subject that the play takes up escapes satire; romantic love, aristocratic improvidence, bourgeois social climbing, Jacobean marriage arrangements, the system of inheritance, dueling, monastic institutions, merchandizing, law, medicine, and religion all come in for a certain amount of ridicule, whether implicit or explicit. And, as others have observed, Webster seems to revel in the conventions of a mode that positively forbids too much solemnity and that makes its special effects by self-consciously alerting its audience to provocative disparities between art and life and between form and content. Nor is it difficult to find cultural and intellectual support in Webster's own age for the philosophic and moral uncertainties that the ending of *The Devil's Law-Case* may be taken to reflect. In his study of *King Lear*, William Elton amply documents "the skeptical disintegration of providential belief" and "the progressive distancing of God from man" that increasingly characterized much European

446

thinking in the Renaissance.[56] Montaigne, for instance, whom Webster had read, writes in his "Apologie of Raymond Sebond" that

we, and our judgement, and all mortall things else do uncessantly rowle, turne, and passe away. Thus can nothing be certainely established, nor of the one, nor of the other; both the judgeing and the judged being in continuall alteration and motion. We have no communication with being; for every humane nature is ever in the middle between being borne and dying; giving nothing of it selfe but an obscure apparence and shadow, and an uncertaine and weake opinion. And if perhaps you fix your thought to take its being; it would be even, as if one should go about to grasp the water. . . .[57]

The parallel between Montaigne's metaphor for futility (grasping water) and Romelio's ("weav[ing] . . . nets to catch the wind" [V.iv.143]), although both are proverbial, may be more than mere coincidence.

What Boklund refers to as "the baffling neutrality" that Webster and other writers of bitter comedy "prefer to maintain to the very end"[58] seems to relate partly to the mixing of dramatic kinds of which *The Devil's Law-Case* is such a puzzling example. Rosalie Colie conceives of literary genres as a set of recognizable frames or fixes upon life and their mingling as the expression of an unconscious desire to render the totality of experience, to reach for forms that include rather than exclude, unite rather than divide, and that minister to our hunger for apprehending culture as unitary, all-embracing, and universal.[59] The questionable resolutions of tragicomedy may indeed speak to this need for emotional and philosophical fence-sitting—to a refusal to come down too positively on either the tragic or comic, the pessimistic or optimistic, side of serious issues.

John Danby discusses the problem of unresolved conflicts of value in tragicomedy from a more unflattering angle—by analyzing the plays of Beaumont and Fletcher as elaborate theatrical conceits that portray a world of irreconcilable absolutisms, expressed by compulsive "self-galvanizations of the will" or "adolescent intensities" on the part of major characters. Danby characterizes this world as "violent, extreme, arbitrary, sudden, and wilful . . . ready at any moment to be inverted, or to swing from one contrary to another."[60] We might account for the wavering focus of Webster's play in this way too, for there is a sense in which its central figures adopt stances that convert them into quasi allegorizations of chivalry, honor, romantic love, chastity, and penitence, or, conversely, of money, trade, power, litigiousness, and revenge.

Uncertainty of value is also a function of the protean characterization and the deliberate mystifications of the plotting, which are intended to become a basis for aesthetic delight in *The Devil's Law-Case*. Indeed Webster seems to transfer the metaphysical "mists" of his tragic vision to the very events of his tragicomedy. Through the conventions of an uncertain form, then, Webster invites his audience to participate in its own deception. The idea is not entirely revolutionary; Bacon notes that in certain kinds of entertainment "the deceiving of the senses is one of the pleasures of the senses"; he also points out that a traditional "use" of fiction or feigning in poetry "hath been to give some shadow of satisfaction to the mind . . . in those points wherein the nature of things doth deny it. . . ."[61]

The rapid and imperfectly explained surprises of the comic ending, with its near-arbitrary couplings and the evasions of serious ethical judgment that attend them, occasion our greatest discomfort in *The Devil's Law-Case*. Unexpected endings, of course, have a venerable lineage in Western drama. Euripides' *Andromache*, a tragedy that concludes with divine intervention of a sort that might be compared to the "miracle" of Romelio's sudden shift toward divinity, defines life (in the words of its final chorus) as essentially unpredictable: "Many are the shapes of Heaven's denizens, and many a thing they bring to pass contrary to our expectation; that which we thought would be is not accomplished, while for the unexpected God finds out a way. E'en such hath been the issue of this matter."[62]

Comedy, too, may traditionally accommodate the unexpected or violate the very harmonies its form would seem to require. Bertram in *All's Well That Ends Well* is "dismissed to happiness" (in Dr. Johnson's arch phrase) even though he has done little to deserve Helena or to suggest that he could ever be a suitable husband to her; and his final promise to "love her dearly" is hedged with an "if" (V.iii.313–314). It is scarcely surprising that Johnson could not "reconcile [his] heart" to a romantic protagonist "noble without generosity, and young without truth."[63] Duke Vincentio's pardoning of Angelo and marriage to Isabella in the final moments of *Measure for Measure* neatly tie up dangling threads of the story but put a heavy strain on moral propriety and psychological verisimilitude. Shakespeare also mars the propitious denouement of *The Tempest* by refusing to provide us with any reassurance that Sebastian and Antonio, the most "unnatural" characters of the play, have been awakened to any sense of sin by Prospero's gracious leniency toward them. Robert Hunter has illuminated these problematic endings by suggesting that they grow out of a theological tradition of Christian forgiveness embodied in the nonbiblical miracle plays of the Middle Ages and then secularized in the sixteenth century: man forgives his brother (as God forgives man) because his sins have already been paid for by Christ's sacrifice on the cross.[64] As in Shakespeare, similar feelings of psychological incompleteness and of moral dubiety also trouble the hurried ending of *The Devil's Law-Case*; but, despite the religious implication of Leonora's and Romelio's "conversions," Webster shows us almost nothing of the contrition that would make their forgiveness theologically appropriate or their marriages symbolic of new spiritual enrichment or social awareness.

Perhaps the most fruitful way to take account of our mixed response to both the affirmed harmony at the end of Webster's play and the stubborn dissonance that seems to repudiate it is to apply Kermode's distinction between myths and fictions:

Myth operates within the diagrams of ritual, which presupposes total and adequate explanations of things as they are and were; it is a sequence of radically unchangeable gestures. Fictions are for finding things out, and they change as the needs of sense-making change. Myths are the agents of stability, fictions the agents of change. Myths call for absolute, fictions for conditional assent. Myths make sense in terms of a lost order of time . . . ; fictions, if successful, make sense of the here and now. . . .[65]

The peripeties of the play's resolution belong to the *mythos* of comedy—a form that perennially confers happiness upon those whom its plot has tested. In other words, the genre that Webster has adopted presupposes a teleology in which, for stage purposes, the motion of the story must ultimately come to rest and in which the characters, symmetrically paired off in the traditionally accepted way (in marriage), cease to exist once they have aroused and then satisfied our need for aesthetic closure. The fable, which it is the business of a play to dramatize, depends upon our confidence of an end in the same way that musical compositions set up the expectation of a cadence that will retrospectively confirm the validity and meaning of the pattern that led up to it. To be more specific, the general felicity in which the stage careers of Romelio and Angiolella, Contarino and Leonora, and Ercole and Jolenta conclude offers us a version of what Kermode calls "naive apocalyptic."[66]

But the very need for such consolations of artistic form implies that reality, honestly scrutinized, might disconfirm the traditional paradigm of which myth, in a way, is a wish-fulfilling expression. Webster's ending also recognizes (through its slapdash and psychologically unconvincing unions) the way in which the conventions of art can falsify or oversimplify the untidy actualities of life. The dramatist therefore configures the more "fictional" or verisimilar aspects of *The Devil's Law-Case* in such a way as to acknowledge that immediate solutions—especially those depicted in the theatre—are necessarily contingent, aleatory, and dependent on a sense of futurity that extends beyond the artificial confines of the five-act structure. Webster qualifies the guarded optimism of the play (an optimism to some extent dictated by tragicomedy as a form) by subjecting his audience to an uncomfortably split response between the pleasures of aesthetic closure and the disturbing consciousness of anticlosure, of a chronicity or open-endedness that will not submit to the archetype of fixed points of commencement and finality.

There is general agreement that *The Devil's Law-Case* is less powerful aesthetically and morally than the two great tragedies on whose themes and techniques it may be regarded as an experimental variation. For all that, it is a comparably challenging and complex play. But its successes and failures as a work of art have much to do with Webster's attempt, imperfectly realized, to serve conservative moral and religious ideas without closing off the hesitations and doubts of an increasingly modernist perspective and without muzzling the kind of laughter that the clichés of an unleavened didacticism tend to invite. Added to this is the play's tireless reflexiveness about its own theatricality and its thematic underscoring of the untrustworthiness of words—the primary medium of poetic drama. Webster's artificially closed ending, which paradoxically communicates such a failure of genuine closure, may be regarded as a final confession of the epistemological chasm that separates felt reality from the conventional means available to the playwright for representing it. If the author of *The Devil's Law-Case* were here to defend his own procedure, he might say, with the Eliot of "East Coker," "That was a way of putting it—not very satisfactory: / A . . . study in a worn-out poetical fashion. . . ." Webster, without altogether jettisoning a concept of religious and moral order as the basis of civilized life, could also be aware that man's formulation of that order may constitute "a receipt for deceit."[67] One of the reasons that Webster's drama has begun to excite fresh interest among professionals in the theatre as well as among literary critics is its implicit address to the dilemma of subjectivity, to the problem of sustaining belief in an age of unbelief, and to the search for absolutes in a world of encroaching relativism. Wallace Stevens wrestled eloquently with the same issues:

> to speak of the whole world as metaphor
> Is still to stick to the contents of the mind
> And the desire to believe in a metaphor.
> It is to stick to the nicer knowledge of
> Belief, that what it believes in is not true.
> ("The Pure Good of Theory," III, 17–21)[68]

PART IV
THE POSTHUMOUS REPUTATION

Taken as a whole, Webster's career—as much of it, at least, as we know about—seems inconveniently, not to say depressingly, shapeless. It is all but impossible to make the final pattern yield much in the way of meaningful development. No clear process of artistic maturation emerges. Instead, the half-dozen or so years of the dramatist's greatest and most memorable work (roughly 1612 to 1618) rise suddenly, sui generis, above the relative flats of his apprenticeship on the one side and the uncertain experimentation and more routine achievements of his late period on the other. Webster appears to have been a more than ordinarily dependent writer, a dramatist who required not merely a particular confluence of stimuli to help him to his finest efforts, but who also was ever ready to subordinate his most distinctive talents to the design or tone of other writers. When he assisted Dekker in the early city comedies, he wrote in a style that very few readers have managed to distinguish from that of his mentor. There is, of course, nothing startling about a beginner's imitation of an established and successful practitioner—especially in the theatre—but later on, after he had succeeded massively in his own right, Webster reverted to copying the fashions and genres invented by others and less suited to his bizarre genius. Modifications, naturally, were inevitable; but when he was working with Rowley on *A Cure for a Cuckold*, and probably with Middleton on *Anything for a Quiet Life*, and probably with Fletcher, Massinger, and Ford on *The Fair Maid of the Inn*, and perhaps with Heywood on *Appius and Virginia*, he seems to have suppressed a great deal of the dramatic and poetic intensity that we think of as uniquely Websterian.

The iteration of "probably" and "perhaps" in the preceding sentence expresses more than the nagging uncertainties of canon with which any student of Webster must continue to wrestle; for even when his authorship of at least part of a play is universally acknowledged (as in the case of *A Cure for a Cuckold* and *Appius and Virginia*), the poet's characteristic voice is sometimes difficult to identify and, even then, not consistently sustained. No doubt Webster's chameleon tendencies can be accounted for in part on grounds of commercial pressure. We do not expect to hear the accents of *The Great Gatsby* or *Tender Is the Night* in the film script of *Gone with the Wind*, to which Fitzgerald (together with in-

453

numerable other writers) contributed his indeterminate share. But theatrical fashions, however significant, do not explain enough.

Webster had the creative stamina to resist such pressure when he wrote *The White Devil* for an audience accustomed to more superficial fare, and he was able, after the disheartening reception of that tragedy, to write *The Duchess of Malfi* for a company that, so far as we know, had never played anything in a style like it before. In any case, since he was heir to a citizen of means, mere profit-mongering was probably not foremost among his considerations; and the spacing of his plays suggests that he may not have needed to depend exclusively upon the box office for a living. For a few brief years Webster managed to find the time, pertinacity, and subject matter appropriate to his special gifts, and to combine these in the service of art that had depth, originality, and fire—that offered an unflinchingly dark but nevertheless luminous vision of the human condition. *The Devil's Law-Case* and the prose characters—perhaps also *The Guise*—retained some of the superb force and complexity of language that is the glory of the Italian tragedies, but already Webster's hand had begun to falter. The lapse into tragicomic cleverness, psychological and moral unsteadiness, or mere ingeniousness of plot and rhetoric were already incipient. The thinning out of texture had already commenced. After this his self-confidence failed him, and he lent himself to the whirligig of city farce, to the twists and turns of Fletcherian romance, or to the black and white simplicity of Roman tragedy. Never again were we to get the stabbing concision of "Cover her face: mine eyes dazzle: she died young" (*The Duchess of Malfi*, IV.ii.264) or the music of the superb dirges, which show that Webster, with Donne and Jonson, might have become one of the finest of Jacobean lyricists.

The assertively rugged style and individual tone of the dramatist's independent work contrast markedly with the more self-effacing quality of his collaborative efforts. Yet, paradoxically, Webster could create the unique and precariously achieved style we most admire, like a mosaic, only from the shards and fragments of other (and often lesser) writers. His sensibility seems to exemplify a sort of aesthetic schizophrenia in which impulses toward the hazardous, the unusual, or the experimental clashed with those toward the conventional or the safely derivative. The masterpieces were apparently written at a point in his career when these conflicting forces were equally enough poised to stimulate and modify each other creatively. Some such hypothesis seems needful to account not only for the astonishing fluctuations of style, both early and late, but also for the unpredictable shifts in moral or philosophic emphasis. But, as R. G. Collingwood has pointed out, expectations of progress or steady advance, either in the career of a single artist or in the history of art generally, are apt to be naive:

The artist's life is one of singular instability; it overreaches itself, bursts its own bonds, fails him at every turn. . . . The artist is an artist only for short times; he turns artist for a while, like a werewolf, and for the rest of the time he only carries marks by which the instructed may recognize him. . . .

The same instability which affects the life of the individual artist reappears in the history of art taken as a whole. To the historian accustomed to studying the growth of scientific or philosophical knowledge, the history of art presents a painful and disquieting spectacle, for it seems normally to proceed not forwards but backwards. In science and philosophy successive workers in the same field produce, if they work ordinarily well, an advance; and a retrograde movement always implies some breach of continuity. But in art, a school once established normally deteriorates as it goes on. It achieves perfection in its kind with a startling burst of energy, a gesture too quick for the historian's eye to follow. He can never explain such a movement or tell us how exactly it happened. But once it is achieved, there is the melancholy certainty of a decline. The grasped perfection does not educate and purify the taste of posterity; it debauches it. The story is the same whether we look at Samian pottery or Anglian carving, Elizabethan drama or Venetian painting. So far as there is any observable law in collective art-history it is, like the law of the individual artist's life, the law not of progress but of reaction. Whether in large or in little, the equilibrium of the aesthetic life is permanently unstable.[1]

Even if the brief equipoise of Webster's greatest period be seen as merely an extreme case of what Collingwood takes to be a general tendency in cultural history, we are nevertheless left with the suggestion that the dramatist's hold on artistic integrity was more than ordinarily insecure—that the playwright won his greatest triumphs at considerable cost. If we knew more about his private life, we might perhaps be tempted to regard the arrogance of his prefaces and dedications and the bitterly denigratory strain in his work as self-protective, or to see the courage and indomitability of his characters under stress as imaginative projections of a desire to be more strongly independent than circumstances or his nature allowed him to be. That his emotionally strongest figures are so often women might betoken a special fascination with heroic attitudes and behavior under conditions of enforced restraint or passivity. But the paucity of facts cuts short such speculation, and the complex personality behind the plays disappears in the mists that tend to enshroud his dying characters on the stage.

Webster's work as a body submits most uneasily to generalization. The playwright seems to have worked almost exclusively to please popular taste and yet to have scorned much in the very traditions that nourished his art most richly. He was obviously attracted to the sinewy texture and labored obscurity of Chapman, to the ostentatious learning of Jonson, and to the satiric acridness of Marston. These men and the fashions they represented helped form his taste for stylistic shock effects, for a curt and sententious rhetoric, for contemptuous posturing, for the insistent abuse of courts, for the cynical disenchantment with lawyers, and so on. But salient as such features are in Webster's plays, they sometimes seem more like self-conscious mannerisms than the instinctual centers of his deepest feeling or concern. For all its coterie pretensions and surface artiness, Websterian drama is rooted firmly in the traditions of popular entertainment—in chronicle history, in the tragedy of violence and revenge, in the staging of frustrated love, in the broadly guaged comedy of bourgeois London, in the theatrical excitements of dramatic romance.

The canon in its entirety exhibits a truly Elizabethan variousness and range of modes, styles, tones, and dramatic forms. Webster seems to have been willing to try almost anything that might find favor or advance him professionally. To this end he drew upon the most diverse traditions, taking up ideas, fashions, and attitudes from fellow dramatists almost as readily as he appropriated the language of Sidney, Montaigne, Guazzo, Matthieu, Sir William Alexander, and others. To read through every play with which Webster is associated from *Sir Thomas Wyatt* to *Appius and Virginia* is to be confronted with something like an anthology of Renaissance drama or, more precisely, a composite of the major dramatists. At different places and in various combinations we recognize Marlowe's preoccupation with the tenacious will, Dekker's middle-class robustness, Heywood's appeal to sentiment and Christian piety, Middleton's psychological realism and concentrated irony, Tourneur's exploitation of grotesque horror, and Fletcher's operatic sensationalism and salacious toying with sexuality. The spectacular formalism of the court masque as well as its tendency to fracture or dissolve (perhaps an influence from Webster's experience at the Middle Temple) are equally observable. Less specifically but more profoundly, we sense in Webster at his best that generous commitment to humanity, even at its ugliest or most depraved, that marks the characterizations of Shakespeare.[2]

Although most of these influences have been noted before, the impress of Marlowe upon Webster deserves special emphasis, if for no other reason than that it has tended to be minimized or ignored. Points of contact between the two dramatists are surprisingly numerous, and I have treated some of the more specific similarities and indebtednesses in my commentary on individual plays—such details as the presentation of a naked dagger to threaten a victim with death, (*1 Tamburlaine* and *The Duchess of Malfi*), the character of an "Italianted Jew" (*The Jew of Malta* and *The Devil's Law-Case*), the ominously equivocal message (*Edward II* and *The Duchess of Malfi*), and the probable influence of *The Massacre at Paris* on the lost *Guise*. But a more pervasive Marlovian impact upon Webster seems likely as well, partly, perhaps, because of theatrical connections. Henslowe, for whom Webster began writing, was the father-in-law of Edward Alleyn, the player who had made Marlowe's heroes famous on the stage and who at one point owed money to the playwright's father. Moreover, Richard Perkins, whom Webster particularly admired, acted the roles of both Barabas and Flamineo. But probably more significant than these ties are several themes and characteristic attitudes that link the two dramatists.

Both playwrights were attracted to history—especially foreign history that could be dramatized to exhibit extremes of ruthlessness, cruelty, and political force. Marlowe's fascination with characters who in some way are cut off or isolated from their communities carries over into Webster, and their adamantine refusal to bend to or accommodate a world for which they express a glorious kind of contempt finds parallels in the Jacobean playwright also. The Marlovian overreachers are sometimes heroic in ways that have little to do with conventional assessments of virtue and vice. Their hallmark is supreme egocentrism—a stubborn or grandiloquent assertiveness that appals or horrifies even as it excites wonder. Tamburlaine, Barabas, the Guise, and Mortimer may be thought of in certain respects as the spiritual ancestors of commanding individualists like Vittoria, Bosola, and Romelio. The bleakness and cruelty of Marlowe's moral universe also replicate themselves in Webster's Italian settings, begetting a cynicism with quasicomic effects not unrelated to the element of savage farce that Eliot saw as the defining attribute of *The Jew of Malta*. The ending of Marlowe's play, especially, has a good deal in common with the horrible absurdities that conclude *The Duchess*. And the realpolitik of *The Jew*, in which the agent of justice (Ferneze) is as corrupt as the vanquished (Barabas), may remind us of the ending of *The White Devil*, in which the worst of the murderers (Francisco) goes unpunished simply because he is wilier and more powerful than his subordinates.

Nor is the intense pity we feel for such doomed figures as Faustus and Edward denied to characters like Vittoria and the Duchess of Malfi, characters who can face their ultimate terrors without illusion. In Marlowe, as in Webster, the evaporation of selfhood may seem more terrible than physical death. Barabas, even in desperation, shuns suicide lest he "vanish o'er the earth in air, / And leave no memory that e'er I was" (*The Jew of Malta*, I.ii.264–265).[3] One thinks of Delio's similar comment about the Aragonian brothers, whose terrible fate is to "Leave no more fame behind" than a snowprint when "the sun shines" (*The Duchess of Malfi*, V.v.114–116). Perhaps unconsciously, Webster may also have been moved by Marlowe's penchant for enclosed and restricted places, for the psychological equivalent of "Infinite riches in a little room" (*The Jew of Malta*, I.i.37). As Marjorie Garber has noticed, the Elizabethan poet explores a dialectic between unboundedness and limitation, between the need to grasp infinity and the trammels of cage, study, countinghouse, cauldron, or castle vault.[4] Webster seems to transpose this kind of conflict into the desire for emotional and sexual freedom in persons confined by sealed rooms, locked bedchambers, airless dungeons, and finally by nooses and coffins. Lastly, of course, Marlowe richly exploited the ironic interconnections between love and death that Webster was later to explore so imaginatively. Dido and Aeneas, Tamburlaine and Zenocrate, Faustus and Helen (Marlowe's "white devil"), Edward and Gaveston, and Mortimer and Isabella are all presented as couples whose relationships link romantic desire, frustration, the quest for identity, and politics to the irreducible fact of mortality. Marlowe, too, saw the skull beneath the skin and was profoundly interested in "that love that hatcheth death" (*Edward II*, IV.v.24).[5] It could be argued, then, that the plays of Marlowe constituted as formative a pressure on Webster as those of Kyd, Shakespeare, Dekker, Marston, Chapman, or Jonson.

With all these strains in his work, Webster emerges as a curiously hybrid dramatist, a writer who took whatever he could use from the traditions of both the public and the private stages, who appears to have mingled heterodoxy and orthodoxy, skepticism and belief—sometimes derivatively, to be sure, but in the finest plays with commanding originality and power. If his entire canon represents "a challenge to our powers of assimilation," so do the individual masterpieces themselves; nor is it entirely accidental that I borrow the quoted phrase from an essay on *The Jew of Malta*.[6] In the Italian tragedies, for instance, Webster may push well beyond the conventional pieties of Jacobean officialdom to confront a moral order trembling on the verge of collapse, but he does so without totally abandoning the time-honored absolutes to which his audiences at the Red Bull and the Globe probably clung—or tried to cling—retentively. If Websterian tragedies, like *King Lear*, put humanistic conceptions of good and evil to a severe test, like *Lear* also, they place a high value on human dignity and recognize the need, if not always the efficacy, of faith, hope, and charity. It is worth noting with Alfred Harbage, for instance, that Webster shares Shakespeare's tendency to alter the material of his sources in the direction of greater idealism and moral elevation.[7] Although Webster clearly aspired to association with the elitist fashions of the "private" theatre, his deepest values seem to have been firmly rooted in the traditions of the popular drama.

* * *

The use that seventeenth-century contemporaries and successors made of Webster's work seems to have outdistanced their active praise. Many dramatists, whether consciously or not, echoed and imitated his plays in specific and unspecific ways (see the Appendix), but allusions to Webster in the period are surprisingly sparse. Hemminge's mention of to Webster in his *Elegy on Randolph's Finger* (c. 1632) and Heywood's in *The Hierarchie of the Blessed Angels* (1635) have already been discussed in connection with the dramatist's biography. More impressive than any other tribute is that of John Cotgrave in *The English Treasury of Wit and Language* (1655). This miscellanist (who, unlike others of his type, confined himself to excerpts from the drama) quoted Webster 104 times— oftener than any other playwright besides Shakespeare, Beaumont and Fletcher, Jonson, Chapman, and Greville, and substantially more often than Webster's collaborators, Middleton, Marston, Dekker, Ford, and Rowley. Curiously, Heywood is missing altogether. Among the eighteen favorite plays of Cotgrave (that is, those of the two hundred forty-six identified in the volume from which he drew sixteen or more passages), all three of Webster's unaided dramas are prominent: *The Duchess of Malfi* and *The White Devil* come third and fourth in the list of frequencies, while *The Devil's Law-Case* ranks twelfth. Inasmuch as the 1,686 extracts in Cotgrave's collection represent at least forty-nine different dramatists, Webster's showing is remarkable indeed.[8] Edward Pudsey about 1615 was sufficiently struck by *The White Devil* to jot down a few brief excerpts from the preface "To the Reader" and the second scene of the tragedy into his commonplace book,[9] but similar evidence of Webster's popularity among non-dramatic writers is hard to come by.

A later copybook in which quotations from Webster appear is that of Abraham Wright, entitled *Excerpta Quaedam per A. W. Adolescentem* (c. 1640). Wright, an Anglican priest, quotes from twenty-eight plays by nine different authors. Later, he seems to have used these excerpts for instructional purposes in the education of his son James, a Middle Templar and the author of *Historia Histrionica*. Again, all three of Webster's major dramas are represented—a higher number than for any of the playwrights (including Shakespeare and Jonson) except Shirley, with ten plays, and Beaumont and Fletcher, with six. Even more interesting than the incidence of plays and dramatists, however, are the opinions of each play that Wright also wrote down in his notebook. Not surprisingly, perhaps, he preferred *The Duchess* to Webster's other works, but since the final act of that tragedy has provoked a certain amount of censure by modern critics, we should note that Wright admired this "good play, especially for ye plot at ye latter end." He must be the first in a long chain of commentators, however, to note the problem of elapsed time in the tragedy, even though he gets his details slightly askew: "And wch is against ye lawes of ye scene ye businesse was 2 yeares a doeing as may bee perceaued by ye beeginning of ye 3d act; where Antonio has 3 children by ye Dutchess, when in ye first act hee had but one." Wright rated *The White Devil* "But an indifferent play to reade, but for ye presentments I beeleeue good." He also approved of the episode in which Lodovico and Gasparo strangle Bracciano while engaging in a religious ritual and indeed of all of the final act for its "maine plot." Wright's ill opinion of the too "intricate" and obscure plotting of *The Devil's Law-Case* has been quoted already in the chapter on that play, but his view of the tragicomedy was nevertheless mixed. The "strange accident" of Contarino's healing, effected unintentionally by his would-be murderer, and the characterization of the lawyer Contilupo both elicited his respect.[10]

The most enthusiastic early appreciator of Webster was undoubtedly Samuel Sheppard (fl. 1646), the poet, pamphleteer, and romancer. Sheppard's collection entitled *Epigrams, Theological, Philosophical, and Romantic* (1651) includes a rhapsodic encomium "*On Mr.* Websters *most excellent Tragedy, Called the White Devill*," which singles out most of the principal characters for praise and makes Webster a seventeenth-century reincarnation of the Greek tragedians:

> Wee will no more admire *Euripides*,
> Nor praise the Tragick streines of *Sophocles*,
> For why? thou in this Tragedie hast fram'd
> All reall worth, that can in them be nam'd:
> How lively are thy persons fitted, and
> How pretty are thy lines!—thy Verses stand
> Like unto pretious Jewels set in gold,

459

> And grace thy fluent Prose; I once was told
> By one well skil'd in Arts, he thought thy Play
> Was onely worthy Fame to beare away
> From all before it—*Brachianos* Ill,
> Murthering his Dutchesse, hath by thy rare skill
> Made him renown'd, *Flamineo*['s] such another,
> The Devils darling, Murtherer of his brother:
> His part—most strange!—(given him to Act by thee)
> Doth gaine him Credit, and not Calumnie:
> Vittoria Corombona, that fam'd Whore,
> Desp'rate Lodovico weltring in his gore,
> Subtile Francisco—all of them shall bee
> Gaz'd at as Comets by Posteritie:
> And thou meane time with never withering Bayes
> Shalt Crowned bee by all that read thy Layes.
>
>   (*Epigrams*, V.27)[11]

Sheppard also gave Webster a place in his "Hall of Fame" (along with twenty-three other figures of English literature) in Book V, canto 6, of his unpublished imitation of Spenser, *The Fairy King* (1648–1654). Only seven other playwrights (Shakespeare, Chapman, Jonson, Fletcher, Goffe, Cartwright, and Randolph) appear in this pantheon, and Sheppard sounds slightly defensive about his inclusion of Webster. It is barely possible that this praise might have been influenced by some personal contact with the dramatist, although Webster had long been dead when *The Fairy King* was composed and Sheppard (who was born about 1624) could not have been more than a boy in the waning years of the dramatist's life:

> WEBSTER the next, though not so much of note
> nor's name attended with such noise & crowd
> yet by the Nine & by Apollo's vote
> whole Groves of Bay are for his head allow'd,
> most Sacred Spirrit (some may say J Doate)
> of thy three noble Tragedies, bee as proud
> as great voluminous Johnson, thou shallt bee
> read longer, & with more Applause then hee.[12]

The mention of "three noble Tragedies" has understandably puzzled scholars, for one wonders if Sheppard intended to include *The Guise*, *Appius and Virginia*, or perhaps even *The Devil's Law-Case* as the third play in his trilogy. The French tragedy may never have been published, and the Roman play probably reached print too late for Sheppard to have seen it; but, of course, the reference need not have depended upon printed versions of all the plays despite Sheppard's prediction that Webster would "bee read longer" than Jonson.

The verses contributed by Webster's friends, Middleton, Rowley, and Ford, to the 1623 quarto of *The Duchess of Malfi* (noticed earlier in this volume) almost exhaust the contemporary or near-contemporary praises of the dramatist. All three commendatory poems seem to establish *The Duchess* as Webster's most popular play in his own lifetime, and Middleton and Rowley in particular stress the vivid characterization of the heroine ("lively body'd" is Rowley's phrase for her). As noted earlier, Edmond Howes numbered Webster among "Our moderne, and present excellent Poets which worthely florish in their owne workes" in his augmentation of Stow's *Annals* (1615), although most other chroniclers of the period omit him.[13] Nathanael Richards imitated at least two passages from the final scene of *The White Devil* to enrich the imagery of his devotional poem, *The Celestial Publican* (1630)—Vittoria's comparison of her foundering soul to a storm-driven ship (V.vi.248–249) and Flamineo's of his brief revival before death to a "spent taper" (V.vi.263–264).[14] An anonymous royalist pamphleteer quoted "the excellent Tragedian Webster" in *A City Dog in a Saint's Doublet* (1648), invoking a couplet from *The White Devil* ("Divinity, wrested by some factious blood, / Draws swords, swells battles, and o'erthrows all good" [IV.i.96–97]) to attack the Puritan habit of "beat[ing] Religion into mens brains with a Poleax."[15] The same year another royalist, Marchmont Nedham (under the pseudonymn of Mercurius Pragmaticus), invoked the name of *"famous WEBSTER"* in an attack on the Lord Protector (*The Second Part of Crafty Cromwell*); later Samuel Holland assigned Webster, with Shakespeare, Fletcher, Massinger, Dekker, Suckling, Cartwright, and Carew, to the "Elizian Shades" in Book II, chapter 4, of his *Wit and Fancy in a Maze* (1656).[16]

Milton's nephew, John Phillips, the apparent editor of *Wit and Drollery* (also 1656), alluded in his preface to Webster's praise of Perkins as an actor; the same preface reappeared in a second edition (1661), now signed not "J. P." but "E. M."[17] James Wright, the son of Abraham, profited by his father's admiration for Webster to the extent of quoting the famous passage on ruins from *The Duchess of Malfi* in his *Country Conversations* (1694); interestingly, the younger Wright cites Webster in a discussion of the value of ruins to painters.[18] Robert Baron, a seventeen-year-old student at Gray's Inn, plundered *The Duchess of Malfi* for numerous passages in his amateur pastoral romance, *The Cyprian Academy* (1647)—especially in the interpolated playlet *Gripus and Hegio*—and again in *Pocula Castalia* (1650).[19] One of the most ironic seventeenth-century plagiarisms of Webster (if it is one) is Thomas Adams's quotation of *The White Devil*, not in his sermon of the same name (preached at Paul's Cross in 1612, the same year as the play's publication), but in his *Diseases of the Soul* (licensed 29 November 1614). Webster himself borrowed from the Puritan preacher on several occasions, but Adams, despite his execration of the theatre, seems to have been sufficiently impressed by Vittoria's characterization of Bracciano as a "melancholic distracted man" who "Hath drown'd himself" in a "fair and crystal river" (III.ii.204–206) to appropriate the words for his description of a man consumed by lust.[20]

The early historians of literature and the stage of course listed Webster as a poet and dramatist, usually without significant comment. Edward Phillips, Milton's other nephew, mentioned "Joan. Websterus" with numerous other playwrights in his *Compendiosa Enumeratio Poetarum*, appended to the seventeenth edition of Johann Buchler's *Sacrarum Profanarumque Phrasium Poeticarum Thesaurus* (1669), going on to include the dramatist again, this time with a list of his "not wholly to be rejected Plays," in *Theatrum Poetarum* (1675) under "Eminent Poets Among the Moderns."[21] William Winstanley in his *Lives of the Most Famous English Poets* (1687) also recorded the titles of Webster's dramas, remarking that the collaborations with Dekker "pass'd the Stage with sufficient applause," while Gerard Langbaine in *Momus Triumphans, or the Plagiaries of the English Stage* (also 1687) claimed to expose the "originals," whether in English or in foreign languages, from which many dramatists (including Webster) "Stole their Plots."[22] Langbaine treated Webster more extensively in his *Account of the English Dramatick Poets* (1691), noting that he had been thought "an Excellent Poet" in the reign of James I and giving information, some of it collected from title pages, on the acting history, dates, and sources of individual plays, "which have even in our Age gain'd Applause." Charles Gildon both abridged and extended Langbaine's *Account* in his *Lives and Characters of the English Dramatick Poets* (1699), a book that has become infamous among Webster scholars because of its unsubstantiated and almost certainly untrue statement that the dramatist "was Clerk of St. *Andrews* Parish in *Holbourn.* . . ."[23] The *Historia Histrionica* (also 1699), another volume by James Wright, mentions the unusual feature of printing the names of actors in play quartos, citing *The Duchess of Malfi* (1623) among the exceptions: "some few Old Plays there are that have the Names set against the Parts. . . ."[24] John Downes in his *Roscius Anglicanus, or an Historical Review of the Stage* (1708) recorded that *The White Devil* was one of a group of "Old Plays . . . Acted but now and then" at the Restoration, which, "being well Perform'd, were very Satisfactory to the Town." He went on to point out that when *The Duchess of Malfi* was revived by Sir William Davenant's company at the Duke of York's Theatre in Lincoln's Inn Fields in 1662, it was "so exceeding Excellently *Acted* in all Parts, chiefly Duke *Ferdinand* and *Bosola*, It fill'd the House 8 Days Successively, it proving one of the Best of Stock Tragedies."[25]

This last production, in which Thomas Betterton played Bosola, Henry Harris Duke Ferdinand, John Young the Cardinal, William Smith Antonio, and Mary Saunderson (subsequently Mrs. Betterton) the Duchess, was attended on 30 September 1662 by Samuel Pepys, who judged the play "well performed"; Betterton and his leading lady, he thought, acted "to admiration." Four years later (2 November 1666) Pepys had begun to read the tragedy, "which seems a good play," and on 6 November was further into it, finding it "pretty good." But in two years' time the inveterate playgoer had totally changed his mind: on 25 November 1668 another performance of *The Duchess* occasioned the observation that it was "a sorry play," the diarist adding that he "sat with little pleasure, for fear of my wife's seeing me look about."[26] Pepys thought even worse of *The White Devil*, performances of which (acted by the King's Company) he attended at the Theatre Royal in Vere Street on 2 and 4 October 1661. The first of these evenings Pepys and his wife arrived late and were forced to sit "in an ill place": "I never had so little pleasure in a play in my life; yet it was the first time that I ever saw it, *Victoria Corombona*—methinks a very poor play." The following day Pepys heard Mrs. William Batten, the wife of a Gray's Inn barrister and a member of the same audience, speak of the play "with admiration, like a fool." On his return journey to the same theatre he "saw a bit of *Victoria*, which pleased me worse then it did the other day." He therefore "stayed not to see it out but went out and drank a bottle or two of China-ale, and so . . . home."[27] On 2 May 1669 at the Duke of York's playhouse (Lincoln's Inn Fields) Pepys saw Betterton's adaptation of *Appius and Virginia*, now retitled *The Roman Virgin*, judging it "an old play, and but ordinary," although Downes records that this version was "*Exactly* perform'd," "lasted Successively 8 Days," and was "very frequently *Acted* afterwards."[28]

An anonymous disputant of 1698, replying to Jeremy Collier's *Short View of the Immorality and Profaneness of the English Stage* (published the same year), defended some flexibility in the handling of time and place on the stage, particularly in plays on historical subjects; he nevertheless cited Shakespeare's *Henry VIII* and Webster's *Duchess* as egregious examples of violated probability because they both show marriages and the subsequent birth of children within too short a compass. Thus even the author of *A Defence of Dramatick Poetry* regarded Webster as demanding more willing suspension of disbelief than was acceptable to turn-of-the-century audiences:

the Audience shall be almost quite shockt at such a Play as *Henry* the 8th. or the *Dutchess of Malfey*. And why, because here's a Marriage and the Birth of a Child, possibly in two Acts; which points so directly to Ten Months length of time, that the Play has very little Air of Reality, and appears too much unnatural. In this case therefore 'tis the Art of the Poet to shew all the Peacocks Trains, but as little as possible of her Foot.[29]

Obviously, the scattered and scrappy references to Webster that have come down to us from the seventeenth century are hardly more than the desultory reactions of particular individuals at discrete moments—a handful of friendly notices from colleagues and later writers (Heywood, Middleton, Rowley, Ford, Nedham, and Holland), a few satirical detractions from literary amateurs or Puritans (Stephens, Fitzgeffrey, and Hall), the manuscript jottings of play collectors and readers (Pudsey and Abraham Wright), copious extracts by an anthologist (Cotgrave), the two appreciative outbursts from a genuine admirer (Sheppard), an incidental joke from a mock funeralizer (Hemminge), the silent pilferings of verbal borrowers and imitators (Adams, Richards, and Baron), the more distanced praise of historians (Howes, Phillips, Winstanley, Langbaine, and Downes), the mercurial opinions of an incessant playgoer (Pepys), and the censure of a neoclassical critic on stage time. Nothing like a school of thought or consensus of views emerges from all this, and indeed early entertainers—especially playwrights—could hardly lay claim to a literary reputation at all in the modern sense of that term. Webster's dramas were revived at the Restoration, like those of many other Renaissance dramatists, but they were regarded chiefly as theatre pieces, as vehicles for talented and popular performers such as the Bettertons. Nothing illustrates this attitude more clearly than the radically doctored and "regularized" versions of Webster that were characteristic of the early eighteenth-century theatre.

*　*　*

Nahum Tate's adaptation of *The White Devil* (1707), according to its title page, was "Design'd to be Acted at the Theatre Royal" but apparently never staged. The title, *Injur'd Love, or the Cruel Husband, a Tragedy*, conveys the undisguised didacticism and moral simplification that the reviser sought to father upon Webster's ruggedly complex drama. Tate gives no credit whatever to Webster, allowing himself to be advertised as the presumably well known "Author of the Tragedy call'd *King Kear*" (his earlier mutilation of Shakespeare). In the fashion of the time, he furnished the play with an inappropriately chatty prologue and epilogue, the functions of which were to moralize about "*our wicked Husband and wrong'd Wife*," to make clear the "Reforming" purpose of the drama, and to wink coyly at the "Virtuous Ladies" and "*Wits*" of the audience, smugly congratulating them on the absence of Italinate barbarities in their own culture. The prologue speaks of a "Pious Court" where "English *Principles*" and "*Morals, Piety, and Hymen reign*."[30] The epilogue does contain a single veiled admission that the play is not wholly Tate's invention: the author "*chose a Vessel that would bear the shock / Of Censure; Yes, old Built, but Heart of Oak*."[31] Tate would hardly have dared to let Webster's original go unmentioned unless he believed *The White Devil* to be too archaic and *démodé* for anyone to remember.

Injur'd Love totally alters the character of Vittoria by making her an essentially "good" woman. No longer an impassioned spitfire possessed of ruthless, sexually charged, and ambiguously disturbing aggressions, she has been softened, feminized, and rendered decorous—readied indeed, for the charms of a post-Restoration actress. While Isabella is still alive, Tate's Vittoria praises her rival's virtues at length and hopes "to quench and stifle" Bracciano's "hopeless Passion";[32] at her arraignment she is the picture of calumniated innocence and certainly no murderess, although she does suffer death at the denouement, somewhat at variance with Tate's usual application of "poetic justice." The adapter has not succeeded, however, in expunging every trace of her Websterian original, for she still treads vehemently on the supposed corpse of her brother. Striving for an increase in pathos, Tate enlarges the role of Isabella in the tradition of she-tragedy. He also deletes many of Flamineo's bitter and bawdy asides, extirpates Vittoria's criminally suggestive dream, omits the cuckolding of Camillo and Cornelia's mad scene, transfers the Moorish disguise from Francisco to Lodovico, excises the papal election and the Latin of Bracciano's stranglers, and presents the plotting of the revengers against the background of a masked ball. The subtleties have been eliminated, the play shortened, and the plot line simplified, although not without a certain troubling inconsistency. Even the final scene commences with a song, although no text is supplied. Tate also purges Webster's language of its profanity and sexual explicitness, modernizing the diction and smoothing out the "metaphysical" texture by deleting such features as Flamineo's emblematic tale of the crocodile and the bird (IV.ii.222–235). Tate's version must have been familiar enough for Fielding to travesty (along with other plays) in *The Tragedy of Tragedies, or the Life and Death of Tom Thumb the Great* (1731), making no distinction, incidentally, between Webster's language and that of the reviser.[33]

The eighteenth century also saw two modifications of *The Duchess of Malfi*, both of which reached the boards. The first deserves only brief mention—a revival entitled *The Unfortunate Duchess of Malfy, or the Unnatural Brothers*, credited to "Mr. Webster" and performed on 22 July 1707 at the Queen's Theatre in the Haymarket with Mary Porter as the heroine, John Verbruggen as Ferdinand, John Mills as Bosola, Theophilis Keene as the Cardinal, and Barton Booth as Antonio. A quarto printed the following year lists the cast of the production and marks some, though not all, of the acting cuts—frequently expurgations or passages considered too obscure. The play was shortened by omitting the scene of the Cardinal's arming (III.iv), and also the parables of Reputation, Love, and Death (III.ii.119–135) and of the salmon and the dogfish (III.v.124–141). The anonymous reviser deleted the reference to the Duchess's son by her earlier marriage (III.iii.69–71), thus making Antonio's eldest child the logical heir to his mother's title; in many places he neoclassicized Webster's irregular meter and Jacobean vocabulary. But these alterations were certainly less radical than those of Lewis Theobald, who published his version of the play in 1735 under the title of *The Fatal Secret*.

This adaptation had been staged two years earlier (on 4 and 6 April 1733), and, in fact, Theobald had begun to work on the play as early as 1731. In a letter to Dr. William Warburton, dated 18 December of that year, Theobald wrote that he had "a Design upon the Ladies Eyes, as the Passage to their Pockets." Here he outlined the plot of the Duchess's clandestine marriage opposed by her "two haughty Spanish Brothers," apparently assuming (for he fails to mention Webster) that even so great a scholar as Warburton, the editor of Shakespeare and friend of Pope, would fail to spot *The Duchess of Malfi* as his source. The letter to Warburton also includes two sample soliloquies—one each for the Duchess in her bedchamber and for Ferdinand wrestling with his conscience—that draw upon Webster's poetry here and there but that inflate the characters with much emotional wind and sentimentalize them outrageously.[34] By the time the play was in production, Theobald had come to believe in the necessity of confessing his dependence on an earlier play, for a prologue was now devised by Philip Frowde, plainly stating that the new author was "*tr[ying] his Strength in* Webster's *nervous Bow.*"

Frowde's facile couplets make the need to recast Webster's tragedy for the more refined tastes of the age of reason only too obvious. Having discovered a wilderness, Theobald left it a garden:

> *A waste, uncultivated, Soil he found*
> *O'er-run with Weeds; yet in the fertile Ground*
> *Some Flowers, almost impervious to the View,*
> *Fragrant and Fair, irregularly grew.*

These Websterian "*Flowers*" Theobald now desires "*to display / In comely Order . . . With decent Grace.*" Not only had Webster neglected the neoclassical "unities," he had also permitted himself embarrassing liberties offensive alike to morality and decorum:

> *The rude, old Bard, if Critick Laws he knew,*
> *From a too warm Imagination drew;*
> *And, scorning, Rule should his free Soul confine,*
> *Nor Time, nor Place, observ'd in his Design.*
> *This Wild Luxuriance our Chaste Muse restrains,*
> *Binds him indeed, but 'tis with friendly Chains;*
> *Such as the prudent Parent, soft and mild,*
> *Tho' griev'd, yet forc'd, puts on a Frantick Child.*[35]

The play was mounted at the prestigious Theatre Royal, Covent Garden, by a distinguished cast. Mrs. Hallam acted the Duchess, Lacy Ryan Ferdinand, Thomas Walker the Cardinal, James Quin Bosola, and William Milward Antonio. In addition Theobald had created a few new characters such as Flavio, tutor to the Duchess's son, and Urbino, secretary to Duke Ferdinand; but the most important of these (indicative of Theobald's bid for pathos) was a twelve-year-old Duke of Amalfi (Antonio's stepson), intended to be played affectingly by "Miss Binckes." Theobald's effort, which closed after two performances, seems to have met with indifference, if not hostility. An anonymous playwright, disappointed by having had his own tragedy rejected, wrote to the *Grubstreet Journal* on 26 April 1733 (number 174) to complain about the fare being provided by the manager of Covent Garden, mentioning Theobald's play as typical of the theatre's bad entrepreneurial judgment. The theatre column of the *Gentlemen's Magazine* picked up the devasting item the same month, apparently agreeing that "King Log's [i.e., Theobald's] *Fatal Secret* met with the Reception it merited."[36] And when Theobald published his script, he not only disclaimed any "*Intentions of disguising from the Publick that . . .* John Webster *had preceded [him],*" he also felt compelled to blame the play's failure on extraneous factors: "*But such was its Fate then, that, appearing at a Season when the Weather was warm, and the Town in a political Ferment, it was prais'd and forsaken; and I had this choice Comfort left me, of hearing every body wonder that it was not supported."*[37]

Theobald's preface, like Frowde's prologue, speaks volumes about the typical eighteenth-century response to Webster: *"When I first read his Scenes, I found something singularly engaging in the Passions, a mixture of the Masculine, and the Tender, which induced me to think of modernizing them. . . ."*[38] Hoping to enrich his version, Theobald consulted what he took to be Webster's sources (Goulart, Bandello, and Lope de Vega), finding the Spanish playwright's Thyestean meal at the close of *El Mayordomo de la Duquesa de Amalfi "a Piece of Cookery, as extraordinary as it is shocking"*; and he adds that Webster's *"Incidents of* Horror" are *"almost as extravagant as those of the* Spaniard." Webster *"had a strong and impetuous Genius, but withal a most wild and indigested one,"* sometimes *"conceiv[ing] nobly,"* but *"not always express[ing] with Clearness."* He *"often rises into the Region of Bombast"* and *"his Conceptions were so eccentric, that we are not to wonder why we cannot trace him."* Webster's anachronisms and his pell-mell handling of sequence distress Theobald: *"when any Poet travels so fast, that the Imagination of his Spectators cannot keep pace with him, Probability is put quite out of Breath."* And Theobald ends revealingly by touting his improvement as more palatable to women than Webster's original: *"If the Piece has any Praise, it is, in my Opinion, that it had Power to draw Tears from fair Eyes. The Poet, who writes for the Stage, should principally aim at pleasing his female Judges: for the best Proof, whether he can draw a Distress, is, how far their Nature and Virtues are touch'd with his Portrait."*[39]

Theobald's play emasculates, moralizes, and prettifies Webster's in much the way that Tate's *Lear* had neutered the cosmic intensities of Shakespeare's drama and Dryden's *All for Love* had domesticated *Antony and Cleopatra.* But Theobald goes further than Dryden and Tate: since the Duchess is innocent, she must survive her brothers' cruelty, being reunited with Antonio and her son by the first marriage. Bosola, also a figure of virtue, employs a wax image of her corpse to persuade Ferdinand that his order for her execution has been carried out. The amorous couple produce no offspring, thus solving the notorious problem of telescoping the years between the heroine's marriage and the birth of three children, and avoiding the awkwardness of Ferdinand's delayed vengeance. Webster's visceral horrors, clearly embarrassments to Theobald, are mostly avoided: no dead hand surprises the Duchess (a ring only is presented), no spine-chilling corpses appear behind a traverse, and no madmen and strangling onstage are allowed to disturb our composure. Antonio takes a more aggressive role—a compensation of sorts for the softening of the Duchess—and the Cardinal and Ferdinand kill each other in a symbolic purging of evil that balances the survival of virtue in the persons of Bosola, Antonio, the Duchess, and the young Duke of Amalfi. Antonio becomes the boy duke's Lord Protector. Theobald's

Duchess is allowed no sexual intimacy with her husband (Webster's wooing and undressing scenes are expunged); the wicked duke has been afflicted with lycanthropy in the past so that his sudden attack will seem more explicable; there is no Julia to clutter up the action with a by-plot or scandalize us by her improper relationship with a prelate; and Antonio returns to Amalfi (where the entire action takes place), disguised as a religious pilgrim.

These changes, of course, are all in the direction of greater simplicity, sequential logic, propriety, poetic justice, and, above all, of pathos. Even when Theobald retains Webster's verbal ideas, he relaxes their tenseness and deadens their spark, even reducing the staccato of Ferdinand's most admired line to "Cover her Face; my Eyes begin to dazzle."[40] Ironically, the attempt to equip Webster's tragedy with a plain, unvarnished message resulted in a trivialization of its true moral force. In her epilogue, the Duchess, far from confirming our desire to regard her as a heroic champion against unfathomable evils, ludicrously teaches her female spectators that a woman should take as many husbands as opportunity and her physical charms will permit her:

> Our gen'rous Poet some good Conscience shew'd,
> Scorning to make my Wedding Sheets my Shroud;
> And tho' my Brothers sware they'd ne'er forgive it,
> He let me marry twice, and yet out-live it.
> His lesson, then, is "Each fair Offer seize,
> While you have Beauties, and the Pow'r to please."[41]

These lilting rhymes epitomize the shallow, socially comfortable optimism with which Theobald has replaced Webster's dark and lonely view of the human predicament.

The eighteenth-century adapters of Webster illustrate not merely a failure to appreciate his unique gifts as a tragedian and poet but also the massive shift in cultural sensibility that increasingly governed taste after the return of Charles II. As Clifford Leech in part suggests, Webster had written in an age before the mysteriousness of nature, the cruelty of pain, religious vision, cynical humor, the comic and frightening aspects of the body, and the unpredictabilities of the psyche had been totally split apart—before experience was wholly divisible or subject to scientific categorization.[42] Pity and terror, sex and death, mockery and awe, laughter and tears, good and evil, were all parts of a cosmic pattern vaster than social institutions or moral conventions, however little that pattern could be intellectually grasped or however much the contemplation of its shadows on the half-lit walls of the mind might disturb, threaten, or amuse. When the dark web of moral, psychological, and metaphysical connections gave way to the more rationalistic attitudes of "the enlightenment," men of the theatre such as Tate and Theobald inevitably tried to accommodate the old plays to the new environment. But Webster, even shorn of his complexities, did not really suit the times, and both of his finest tragedies dropped out of the repertory.

The Duchess of Malfi had to wait until 1850 for a revival—again in an adapted version (this time by R. H. Horne, the author of the "farthing epic" *Orion*), much expurgated and coarsened in the manner of Victorian melodrama. Samuel Phelps, the manager of Sadler's Wells, where the production opened, played Ferdinand himself. For the first time Webster's great lady had a name in addition to her title; but that Horne chose to call her Marina, apparently borrowing from the virginal heroine of Shakespeare's *Pericles* or of Lillo's rewriting, *Marina* (1738), only shows how little he grasped—or was willing to accept—the full-bodied sensuality and assertive grandeur of Webster's conception. In Horne the strangling occurs in silhouette, after which the Duchess rushes back onstage to die. An alternative adaptation by George Daniel, which capitalized upon the staging of Horne's version (and is therefore sometimes confused with it), but is closer to Webster's language, was published sometime in the 1850s in Cumberland's British Theatre series; there is little evidence, however, to confirm that Daniel's more conservative revision ever reached actual production.[43] After mid-century, Webster's tragedy, usually much altered, became a standard vehicle for leading ladies of the nineteenth century. Isabella Glyn had starred in Horne's adaptation, and the role of the Duchess was later taken up by prominent actresses such as Emma Waller, Alice Marriott, and Mary Rorke. In versions usually closer to Webster's intention, the play has established itself as part of the classic repertory of our own time.

After more than two centuries of neglect, *The White Devil* was reintroduced to London audiences in 1925, and, although less popular than *The Duchess*, has enjoyed several notable productions since then. Webster's two Italian masterpieces still present formidable challenges to directors, actors, and audiences, but they have clearly reclaimed their position among the great plays of the past that the modern theatre can no longer ignore.

* * *

The failure of Tate and Theobald to make Webster live on the eighteenth-century stage seemed to prove the obvious, namely, that, even tidied up, moralized, and pruned of its uncouth excesses, such tragedy was, after all, not for all time but for an age only. In consequence, Webster's reputation lapsed into a torpor from which it would take the Romantic enthusiasm of Charles Lamb in his *Specimens of the English Dramatic Poets* (1808) to resuscitate it. A certain antiquarian interest in Webster did begin to emerge somewhat earlier, but chiefly on the part of literary archeologists for whom any of Shakespeare's contemporaries were relevant, merely for the light they might shed upon their infinitely greater coeval. In 1738 Thomas Hayward compiled *The British Muse*, a three-volume anthology of extracts, largely from the drama, designed to exhibit "Thoughts Moral, Natural, and Sublime" under alphabetically arranged headings such as Adultery, Cruelty, Jealousy, Peace, and Sin. A later edition of this work appeared under the title of *The Beauties of the English Drama* (1777). Webster was well represented, for in addition to numerous passages from *The White Devil*, *The Duchess of Malfi*, and *The Devil's Law-Case*, several from *Westward Ho*, *The Malcontent*, *Anything for a Quiet Life*, and *The Fair Maid of the Inn* were also included. Edward Capell subtitled the third volume of his *Notes and Various Readings to Shakespeare* (1779–80) *The School of Shakespeare*, reprinting "authentic *Extracts from divers* English *Books*" of "*that Author's Time*," including some from *The White Devil*, *Anything for a Quiet Life*, *Appius and Virginia*, *A Cure for a Cuckold*, *Westward Ho*, and *The Malcontent*—passages that the compiler considered illustrative or significant, not for their own sake, but for "*a due Understanding*" of the Bard.

Robert Dodsley, the first anthologist of complete Elizabethan dramas, reprinted *The White Devil* (essentially without commentary) in volume III of his twelve-volume *Select Collection of Old Plays* (1744), a second edition of which appeared in 1780. The quartos of Webster's plays were now mainly to be found only in great libraries, but at least one of the tragedies had been made available to the general reader. In his *Biographia Dramatica, or a Companion to the Playhouse* (originally compiled in 1764), David Erskine Baker recorded the names and dramas of the early playwrights, noting with evident lack of excitement that Webster had been "accounted a tolerable poet, and was well esteemed by his contemporary authors, particularly Decker, Marston, and Rowley, with whom he wrote in conjunction," while Edmond Malone, the greatest Elizabethan scholar of the age, referred occasionally to Webster in the apparatus of his 1790 edition of Shakespeare.[44] The Jacobean tragedian was becoming the stuff of learned footnotes. But, popularly speaking, Webster had all but been forgotten.

The romantic movement naturally brought with it an enthusiasm for the Elizabethans in their own right. No longer so much antiquarian furniture to set off Shakespeare, the old dramatists began to be valued as individual talents worth taking seriously. Not only did they embody an important part of England's heritage, they also manifested a tangible link between the literary past, acknowledged now as possessing standards proper to itself, and modern taste. Marlowe, Webster, Ford, and the others could now be enlisted as allies in the revolt against a sterile neoclassicism, in the promulgation of imaginative freedom, and in the legitimation of a personal vision. It is therefore no surprise that names such as Lamb, Hazlitt, Shelley, and Swinburne are prominently associated with the rehabilitation of Webster's standing as a major figure of English literature. And since none of these men was primarily a dramatist, it is also worth observing that their interest was usually more heavily concentrated upon Webster the poet than upon Webster the practical playwright. Even for the most vocal admirers, Webster tended still to be the author of great scenes or of magnificent passages. And when Phelps revived *The Duchess of Malfi* for performance at Sadler's Wells, he did so in a mutilated and heavily carpentered version that betrayed the persistent refusal to take the play whole.

As everyone knows, Lamb's marginal comments in his *Specimens of the English Dramatic Poets Who Lived About the Time of Shakespeare* (1808) must be credited with restoring Webster to critical respectability, or (to be more precise) with beginning that uncertain process. The extracts that Lamb reprinted were generous, embracing passages from *The Devil's Law-Case* and *Appius and Virginia* as well as from the two more famous tragedies. Lamb admired the great moments in Webster, the points of high poetic and dramatic intensity such as Vittoria's trial, Cornelia's grief-stricken dirge, and the Duchess's torture and execution; he was also attracted by the quaintness of Webster's interpolated fables or apothegms, a quaintness that his own mannered style partly reflects. His method is, of course, impressionistic and highly personal. He points to particular "beauties" in the same way that earlier anthologists had done, but, unlike them, with a view to illustrating a unique effect or particular emotional coloring rather than a moral sentiment aptly captured in words. In an often-quoted remark, he rhapsodizes over Vittoria's arraignment: she "sets off a bad cause so speciously, and pleads with such an innocence-resembling boldness, that we seem to see that matchless beauty of her face which imspires such gay confidence. . . ." He compares Cornelia's "*Call for the robin-red-breast and the wren* . . ." (V.iv.95) with its counterpart in *The Tempest*, "Full fathom five thy father lies . . ." (I.ii.399): "I never saw anything like this Dirge, except the Ditty which reminds Ferdinand of his drowned Father. . . . As that is of the water, watery; so this is of the earth, earthy. Both have that intenseness of feeling, which seems to resolve itself into the elements which it contemplates." Lamb's praise of the Duchess of Malfi's death is typical of his approach and became justly influential:

To move a horror skilfully, to touch a soul to the quick, to lay upon fear as much as it can bear, to wean and weary a life till it is ready to drop, and then step in with mortal instruments to take its last forfeit—this only a Webster can do. Writers of an inferior genius may "upon horror's head horrors accumulate," but they cannot do this. They mistake quantity for quality, they "terrify babes with painted devils," but they know not how a soul is capable of being moved; their terrors want dignity, their affrightments are without decorum.[45]

Lamb's friend Hazlitt, infected by the same rage for native vitality and force that inspired the *Specimens*, launched into a series of *Lectures Chiefly on the Dramatic Literature of the Age of Elizabeth* (delivered in 1819, published in 1820), in which Webster figured prominently. For Hazlitt the great Elizabethans, far from being "the spoiled children of affectation and refinement," especially *foreign* refinement, were "a bold, vigorous, independent race of thinkers, with prodigious strength and energy," who "savoured of the soil from which they grew," and who more than made up in "natural grace" and "heartfelt . . . delicacy" for what they lacked in "tinsel" art and sophistication.[46] Somewhat unprofitably, Hazlitt pits Webster against Dekker, finding in the latter "more truth of character, more instinctive depth of sentiment, more of the unconscious simplic-

471

ity of nature," and in the former, "more scope" for the rendering of changeability in character, "a wider arc of oscillation" in the passions, and the tendency to carry "terror and pity to a more painful and sometimes unwarrantable excess." Less focused and more prolix than Lamb, Hazlitt nevertheless asserted, though not without qualification, that Webster "upon the whole perhaps" came "the nearest to Shakespear of any thing we have upon record. . . ." Like Lamb, he loved the character of Vittoria, whom Webster had "made fair as the leprosy, dazzling as the lightning" and had "dressed like a bride in her wrongs and her revenge"—a white devil whose self-possession in the teeth of death defined "the sublime of contempt and indifference."[47]

In the companion tragedy, the heroine's plucky "I am Duchess of Malfi still" (IV.ii.142) shows a similar grandeur of response to suffering—"as if the heart rose up, like a serpent coiled, to resent the indignities put upon it . . ."; and Ferdinand reacts to the murder of his sister not with "the bandying of idle words and rhetorical commonplaces, but with writhing and conflict, and the sublime colloquy of man's nature with itself."[48] In 1826 Hazlitt again invoked this passage from *The Duchess* (IV.ii.260–269) as a stick to poke at the inadequacies of modern tragedy, in which the poet (here exemplified by Byron) "fills his page with *grandes pensées*," giving his audience "the subtleties of the head, instead of the workings of the heart."[49]

Implicit, of course, in the comments of Lamb and Hazlitt was a profound discontent with the nineteenth-century stage, with the typically flat, unpoetic, and derivative fare of the popular theatre. Bored with "correctness" and conventionality in literature and starved for energetic feeling, originality, color, and "the sublime," it was natural enough that those of romantic sensibility should gravitate to a more muscular and aesthetically less fettered age. But Lamb and Hazlitt would have preferred Webster in the study to Webster on the boards even if they had been able to choose. The talents of actors, designers, and producers would, after all, fall pitifully short of what the charged imagination could create in its own private domain, and, in any case, dramatists like Webster were diamonds in the rough. One had to pick and choose among their splendors, ignoring or refining away the dross. To Hazlitt, "the occasional strokes of passion" in *The Duchess* were wonderful indeed, but the story was "laboured" and the "horror . . . accumulated to an overpowering and insupportable height": the episodes of the madhouse and dead hand, for instance, "exceed, to my thinking, the just bounds of poetry and tragedy." Even if merit be allowed here, it is "of a kind, which . . . we wish to be rare." "Such exhibitions . . . must tend to stupefy and harden, rather than exalt the fancy or meliorate the heart."[50] Ironically, in the very act of promoting Webster, one of the chief enthusiasts had expressed reservations that adumbrate the nature of the debate about the dramatist's true excellence that would dominate literary and theatrical discussion throughout the century. Although Webster's great passages might be excerpted and admired, his unevenness, his flaws of structure, and his questionable taste—especially the sensational horrors—continued to attract negative commentary. And even to-day, although Webster's reputation is now secure, such caveats have yet to be completely stilled.

Lamb's extracts and appreciative notes, if they did not instantly re-establish Webster as a giant, at least compelled serious attention. Now readers wanted whole plays, not merely swatches of the dramatist. Consequently *The Ancient British Drama* (1810), perhaps edited by Sir Walter Scott, reprinted *The Duchess of Malfi*; and Charles Dilke's *Old English Plays* (1814–15), a continuation of Dodsley's enterprise, included *Appius and Virginia*. Finally, in 1830, the Reverend Alexander Dyce published his four-volume edition of Webster with scholarly introduction and notes, assembling the meager biographical information then known and making the entire canon (as understood at the time) available. Dyce instinctively anticipated modern scholarship by implying that Webster's environment and experience must somehow have impressed the dramatist with the grim realities of prison, funeral, and tomb:

His imagination had a fond familiarity with objects of awe and fear. The silence of the sepulchre, the sculptures of marble monuments, the knolling of church bells, the cerements of the corpse, the yew that roots itself in dead men's graves, are the illustrations that most readily present themselves to his imagination. If he speaks of love, and of the force of human passion, his language is,—

> "This is flesh and blood, sir;
> 'Tis not the figure cut in alabaster,
> Kneels at my husband's tomb"—

and when we are told that

> "Glories, like glow-worms, afar off shine bright,
> But look'd to near, have neither heat nor light,"

we almost feel satisfied that the glow-worm which Webster saw, and which suggested the reflection, was sparkling on the green sod of some lowly grave.[51]

Lamb's book and, later, Dyce's edition, began also to stimulate discussion in the periodicals, some of it inevitably denigratory. An anonymous writer in the *Annual Review* of 1809 (Lamb thought he was Coleridge) took exception to the influential anthologist's enthusiasm for *The Duchess*, pronouncing the praise twice as "fine" as its object, a drama "as absurd as it is monstrous."[52] John Wilson, writing on both the Italian tragedies in *Blackwood's Edinburgh Magazine* for 1818 under the initials "H. M.," also implies that Lamb had preposterously exaggerated Webster's merits. Although he acknowledges that "single scenes" are superb and quotes many splendid passages, he censures the dramatist for inconsistent character portrayal, for "extravagance," for failure to sustain an interest once he has aroused it (particularly in Act V of *The Duchess*), for the indecorous mixture of the comic with the tragic, and for certain episodes that "altogether revolt and disgust." Webster gives too much prominence to "mean, abandoned, and unprincipled characters": "scene follows scene of shameless profligacy, unredeemed either by great intellectual energy, or occasional burstings of moral sensibilities."[53] All these Websterian failings, in Wilson's two essays, become symbolic illustrations of how high Shakespeare towered above his contemporary dramatists. And the condemnation on ethical grounds (Wilson was a professor of moral philosophy at Edinburgh) began a trend in Webster criticism that would gather momentum in the Victorian period.

Interest in Webster continued to manifest itself in a succession of articles for the intellectual journals. Following the lead of *Blackwood's*, the *European Magazine* published a series of essays on the "English Dramatists," commencing in 1820 with Webster. The anonymous author linked long quotations from *Appius and Virginia* and *The White Devil* in illustration of the "faults" and "excellencies" of the early playwrights, admitting, in the case of the latter drama, "the irregularity of the fable" but lauding the poet's "impassioned and inspired verse."[54] Another nameless writer, even more favorably disposed than his predecessor, singled out Webster's plays in the *Retrospective Review* of 1823 as "much better calculated for representation than most of our early dramas" without offering a shred of evidence.[55] Considering that there had been no public performances of Webster for almost a century, the statement is arresting, but at least it points to the first stirrings of a desire, not merely to read, but to see Webster.

Barry Cornwall, the minor poet and dramatist, anonymously reviewing a pair of contemporary tragedies in the *Edinburgh Review* (also in 1823), used the occasion to rank the Elizabethan dramatists. Although he assigns Webster a lower station (after Shakespeare) than Beaumont and Fletcher, Jonson, or Massinger, he nevertheless commends him warmly as a playwright "full of a gloomy power" and touched by "profound sentiment," whose "pen distilled blood." Like others, he responded to the breathtaking moment in *The Duchess* when Ferdinand confronts the corpse of his sister; the essay is also interesting for the contrast between Marlowe and Webster that it draws: "The one rose to the stars, the other plunged to the centre."[56] Finally, an essay of 1833, signed "J. M." in the *Gentleman's Magazine* (in part, a review of Dyce's edition), opined that, although Webster is in several respects inferior to Jonson, Fletcher, and Massinger, he nevertheless "far . . . surpasses them . . . in the depth of his pathos, his tragic powers, and his command over the sublime, the terrible, and the affecting." Webster's famous horrors are much stressed. But, surprisingly, this writer finds fault with the generally popular scene of Vittoria's trial, which "is too long coming to the point" and which obtrudes irrelevancies upon us. Less surprisingly, he is moved to "tears" by Bracciano's rejection of Isabella, the "most powerful and . . . pathetic scene" of *The White Devil*. He finds the wax effigies of *The Duchess* "childish and disgusting," however, and the play's final act "but coarse and common butchery."[57] Victorian prudery, sentimentality, and moralism had already begun to condition reactions to Webster.

Meanwhile, as early as 1817 the essayist-physician Nathan Drake had re-marked Webster's "genius" by citing the two Italian tragedies as "striking" if "ec-centric proofs of dramatic vigour"; and the poet Thomas Campbell had imitated Lamb in 1819 by including three samples of Webster in his own anthology of English verse, at the same time dissenting from Lamb's high estimate of the dra-matist. Campbell speculated, most unhistorically, that the cool reception of *The White Devil* at its initial performance (which he confused with that of *The Duch-ess of Malfi*) had probably been due to the play's extravagant terrors. He noted further, with undisguised contempt, that, in *The Duchess*, the heroine "is mar-ried and delivered of several children in the course of the five acts."[58]

In 1839 Henry Hallam brought out his massive four-volume survey, an *In-troduction to the Literature of Europe in the Fifteenth, Sixteenth, and Seven-teenth Centuries*, which devoted a few pages to Webster. Hallam was writing more as a historian than a critic, but he did not scruple to record his opinions. In *The Duchess*, for instance, Webster was "tainted . . . with the savage taste of the Italian school," "scarcely leav[ing] enough [people alive] on the stage to bury the dead." But Hallam also defends the playwright, noting that "he is seldom ex-travagant beyond the limits of conceivable nature" and admiring especially the wooing of Antonio: no "dramatist after Shakespeare would have succeeded bet-ter in the difficult scene where [the Duchess] discloses her love to an inferior." The historian also endorses Dyce and disagrees with Lamb on the character of Vittoria at her arraignment: rather than "innocence-resembling boldness," Vit-toria displays "desperate guilt, losing in a counterfeited audacity all that could seduce or conciliate the tribunal." A decade later Thomas Budd Shaw produced his *Outlines of English Literature* (1849), a manual for students, fancifully iden-tifying Webster's muse with "the hideous skeleton of the monkish imagination, the 'grim anatomy,' with his crawling blood-worms, and all the loathsome hor-rors of physical corruption." In a later edition he compared Webster to Dante, noting erroneously that *The Guise* has survived, and pointing to the "extraordi-nary union of complexity and simplicity" in the playwright's language.[59] 1857 saw an alternative but inferior edition of Webster's plays, produced by Hazlitt's grandson, W. C. Hazlitt, and heavily dependent upon Dyce.

Creative writers, as well as editors, historians, critics, anthologists, and re-viewers, were also drawn to Webster in the age of romanticism. Shelley ac-knowledged no indebtedness to the Jacobean dramatist in *The Cenci* (1819), but this somewhat anamolous play betrays his reading of Renaissance drama in sev-eral respects. Herbert Read unjustly accuses it of being little more than "a pas-tiche of Elizabethan drama, of Webster in particular," denying the tragedy any of the originality proper to Shelley's best work.[60] However misleading Read's statement may be (I have found no verbal borrowing from Webster), influence of a general nature there surely must have been. Set in sixteenth-century Italy, the play phosphoresces with a tyrannical evil, sexually motivated and cosmically significant, not unlike that of Webster. The incest theme, explicit in Shelley, is powerfully implicit in *The Duchess of Malfi*, and the climactic episode of Beatrice's trial for murder before corrupt judges, a trial in which we are intended to sympathize with the courageous, though technically guilty, defendant, has obvious affinities with the arraignment scene of *The White Devil*. Shelley's biographer Thomas Medwin confirms the importance of Webster's impress on the imagination of the romantic poet: "Among English plays he was a great admirer of *The Duchess of Malfy*, and thought the dungeon scene . . . equal to anything in Shakespeare; indeed he was continually reading the Old Dramatists—Middleton and Webster, Ford and Massinger, and Beaumont and Fletcher, were the mines from which he drew the pure and vigorous style that so highly distinguishes *The Cenci*."[61]

Lord Byron in a letter to John Murray of 4 January 1821 pretended to dismiss most of the "mad old dramatists" in vogue with his fellow romantics, labeling them "turbid mountebanks"; but he read Lamb's *Specimens* that year and confessed to Medwin that he was amazed to discover a passage from *The Duchess of Malfi* "astonishingly like one in [my] *Don Juan*"—amazed enough to worry about being thought a plagiarist.[62] Even across the channel Webster was beginning to be recognized. Stendhal (probably via Lamb) used Cornelia's crazed sentence over the body of Marcello ("if he be turn'd to earth; let me but give him one hearty kiss, and you shall put us both into one coffin" [*The White Devil*, V.ii.36–38]) as the epigraph for the final chapter of his novel, *Armance* (1827). One of the most effusive admirers of Webster in the period was George Darley, mathematician, moody poet, and neo-Elizabethan dramatist. Writing to his friend Allan Cunningham, the art critic, on 22 May 1831, Darley asked, "Have you ever read *Webster*? Why . . . there are passages in *Vittoria Corombona* almost worthy of the Angel Gabriel." Cunningham was advised to ignore the acerbities of Thomas Campbell and embrace Webster without reservation: "Shakespeare & Milton excepted, there is poetry in Webster *superior* to that of any other English Author. If you have not *The White Devil* by heart, get it."[63]

With the 1850 production of Horne's ruthlessly adapted *Duchess of Malfi* at Saddler's Wells, Webster—or at least a castrated and heavily draped remnant of him—could once more be seen in the theatre. The event could not help but make the playwright more widely known beyond the academy and the small circle of writers, antiquarians, and intellectuals who had hearkened to the call of Lamb and Hazlitt. Response, however, was anything but undivided. In general, Horne was praised for his noble attempt, and the production itself (particularly Isabella Glyn in the title role) garnered much applause. But the critics were by no means convinced that Webster, even substantially bowdlerized and reshaped, could be made playable on the Victorian stage. Horne's published preface reveals much. The adapter speaks of having "exhumed" the play "from its comparative obscurity"; he thinks of *The Duchess* as a ruined "abbey" in desperate need of rebuilding—"with as much of its own materials" as it was possible or appropriate to use, but "asking pardon for the rest." Horne wanted to preserve Webster's "majestic halls and archways," his "loftiest turrets," his "most secret and solemn chambers, where the soul, in its hours of agony, uplifted its voice to God."[64] The religioarchitectural language, of course, bespeaks Horne's object of tidying up Webster's plot and of expunging anything that might be thought to interfere with a Victorian understanding of high seriousness. The rewriting was necessarily extensive.

The journals of the day reacted to the new production with a skepticism about Webster's worthiness that has persisted—at least in the professional theatre—well into our own era. The London *Times* pronounced Webster "barbarous" despite the play's "pristine strength," warning readers not to expect "anything beyond a curiosity": "the revolting nature of the story and the anti-climax of the fifth act . . . are beyond the reach of the reformer's skill." This reviewer nonetheless felt bound to report that "the applause" at the final curtain "was loud, continuous, and unanimous."[65] The *Athenaeum* reviewer spoke of the tragedy's "clumsy structure," despite Horne's labors, and concluded unequivocally that "Webster is wholly unfitted for the modern stage"; but he added that "the beauties of the dialogue seemed to be appreciated by the pit."[66] A writer for the *Spectator* was perhaps even harsher. He thought *The Duchess* "a sorry work, showing equally the strength and the untutored condition of the mind that produced it"; the characters, far from possessing any psychological subtlety, are "so many lumps of moral deformity." He also believed that Horne with "his fine poetical mind" might have spent his time more profitably on a wholly original drama.[67] But it was for the philosophical essayist and drama critic George Henry Lewes to bring the sledge hammer of iconoclasm down upon Horne's Webster. He began by confessing that in the flush of naive youth and stimulated by Lamb, he too had been seduced by the siren song of the Elizabethans—playwrights that, upon maturer reflection, he now considered to be "a fatal obstruction to the progress of the drama," misleading "many a brave and generous talent." *The Duchess of Malfi* he judged to be "a feeble and foolish work," its mediocrity "irredeemable," its effects "wearisome" and "ludicrous" by turns: "If Shakespeare [was] a great dramatist, Webster and company [were] not dramatists at all. . . ." The play was "a nightmare, not a tragedy," and, as for the quality of the verse, one could hardly tell where Horne began and Webster left off "unless [one were to] have the two books side by side." Horne, who could have written a better tragedy on his own, should not have "wast[ed] his faculties in the hopeless task of making falsehood look like truth."[68] Lewes's antagonism to Webster and the entire tradition of drama that he represented anticipated that of William Archer, who was to edit his fellow derogator's critical essays (including the present review) at the end of the century.

It was, of course, Horne's *Duchess*—or at least a text similarly altered—that took the stage intermittently both in England and in the United States during the latter part of the century. This was the tragedy, in Horne's words, "shorn and abated" of all "excesses," denuded of anything "like a shocking *reality*," and "softened by stage arrangements."[69] Webster's irregularities of plot and language were doctored by omitting most of the satire, muting the physical and psychological terrors, simplifying and clarifying the motivation (often through self-explanatory soliloquies), rearranging the character relationships, and adding much fluent but listless iambic pentameter. Most disastrously, Webster's effects of moral and philosophical chiaroscuro were resolved into blatant antitheses of black against white. George Daniel, who anonymously implied that Horne had gone much too far as a reviser, claimed in the preface to his alternative version to be preserving "every grain of gold" from Webster's original; but, however much he might scorn "the presumptuous pen of interpolation" and the "mock-modest, mealy-mouthed" hypocrisy of Horne's text, he nevertheless felt it imperative to rewrite Webster's lines on occasion.[70] Both Horne and Daniel expurgated sexual indelicacies, seeking, of course, to forestall the blue pencil of official censorship.

The following versions of a speech by Ferdinand characterize the authors' general practice as adapters and illustrate the comparative degrees of their candor in the treatment of sex:

> In, in; I'll go sleep—
> Till I know who leaps my sister, I'll not stir. . . .
> (Webster, II.v.76–77)

> In, in—I'll go sleep,
> Till I know who is the companion of my sister's shame;
> Until I know who hath our sister wrong'd
> I'll stir not. . . .
> (Daniel, p. 26)

> So much, I must first sleep and dream of it.
> Ay, let me rest and freely breathe once more,
> Before I act.
> (Horne, p. 29)[71]

Horne's version of *The Duchess* was more popular with British audiences, including several outside London, than the negative strictures of the professional critics would suggest. And its success was just as notable in America as in Britain; in productions even more elaborately staged than in England, theatregoers in San Francisco, New York, New Orleans, Philadelphia, Pittsburgh, Cincinnati, Chicago, and other cities seem to have received it enthusiastically.

As the century wore on, division of opinion about Webster's significance tended to center upon the apparently unrelated issues of his questionable stagecraft and dubious morality. Dissenters on both grounds wanted a neatness, clarity, everyday naturalism, and ethical simplicity that *The White Devil* and *The Duchess of Malfi* could never pretend to offer—at least in their original versions. Beneath the surface, of course, ambiguous characterization, sanguinary violence, and gothic plotting might be taken as refracting a concept of life unwilling to be confined within polite or "civilized" norms and evocative of the darker, less reassuring aspects of the human psyche. Those who sought vainly for acceptable moral preachment in Webster, or who longed for more sprucely tailored stage-pieces, would doubtless have thought themselves of widely differing camps; but their objections sprang subliminally from a common source—a rejection of that irrational and fearful side of human impulse that conventional institutions and beliefs find it pleasantest to ignore. In 1924 T. S. Eliot would define Webster as a "literary and dramatic genius directed toward chaos."[72] The disturbing intensities and configurations that Eliot was to regard as Webster's greatest gift looked like chaos in dramaturgy to convinced turn-of-the-century Ibsenites and like chaos in the heart and soul to a Victorian evangelist.

Probably the most forceful and articulate of the mid-Victorian anti-Websterians was Charles Kingsley, Canon of Westminster, novelist, and guardian of public morals. His essay "Plays and Puritans" (originally written in 1856 for the *North British Review*) unleashed a torrent of condemnation against Elizabethan drama in general, raising the same kind of objection that had characterized Puritan attempts to repress the theatre in Webster's own day:

> The tragedies of the seventeenth century are, on the whole, as questionable as the comedies. That there are noble plays among them here and there, no one denies—any more than that there are exquisitely amusing plays among the comedies; but as the staple interest of the comedies is dirt, so the staple interest of the tragedies is crime. Revenge, hatred, villany, incest, and murder upon murder, are their constant themes, and (with the exception of Shakspeare, Ben Jonson in his earlier plays, and perhaps Massinger) they handle these horrors with little or no moral purpose, save that of exciting and amusing the audience, and of displaying their own power of delineation, in a way which makes one but too ready to believe the accusations of the Puritans (supported as they are by many ugly anecdotes), that the play-writers and actors were mostly men of fierce and reckless lives, who had but too practical an acquaintance with the dark passions which they sketch. This is notoriously the case with most of the French novelists of the modern "Literature of Horror," and the two literatures are morally identical. We do not know of a complaint which can be justly brought against the School of Balzac and Dumas, which will not equally apply to the average tragedy of the whole period preceding the civil wars.[73]

Kingsley went on to observe that the Italian subject matter and settings of the revenge tragedies were enough to make them dangerous fare for a high-minded Protestant nation. His attack on Webster, however, goes well beyond the "sin and horror" that that playwright delighted to portray. Kingsley contends that Webster's plays are a collection of effects and that (except for Bosola) his characters are untrue to life; they "exhibit" no "development of the human soul," for "the study of human nature is not Webster's aim."[74] This account of the dramatist discloses nothing so much as the critic's insensitivity to any rendering of experience that falls outside the literal, the nonsymbolic, or the conventionally moralistic.

Sir William Watson, a later poet-critic of the old-fashioned school, was content, like Kingsley, to elevate Shakespeare by depreciating Webster and his fellows. Watson sees Webster as merely derivative of the master without being truly like him; he inveighs against the lesser dramatist's "gross melodramatic horrors, irredeemable by any touch of saving imagination," against a "twilight" world of "lust and blood," where "virtue . . . is merely wasted, honour bears not issue, [and] nobleness dies unto itself"; Webster's fatalism, unlike that of the Greek tragedians, has "its root in a conception of existence as essentially anarchic."[75] But the loudest gun of all was to be fired by William Archer, the influential critic and promulgator of the plays of Ibsen and Shaw.

Not only did Archer lack sympathy with the conventions of Elizabethan staging and play construction, he was also woefully uninformed about them. Both of his blasts against Webster were touched off by recent productions, the first by William Poel's historically important Independent Theatre Society revival of *The Duchess* in 1892 (Horne's text had by now been abandoned), the second by a later production of the same play in 1919 that involved, among other absurdities, a Ferdinand who died standing on his head. Archer was willing to grant (with Lamb) that Webster was a great poet from time to time, but his rationalistic and realistic aesthetic prevented him from recognizing Webster's merits as a dramatist: both the major tragedies, in Archer's view, were "not constructed plays, but loose-strung, go-as-you-please romances in dialogue" marked by vulgar lapses of taste and horrors that were "frigid, mechanical, brutal." (Misled by Dyce's text of *The Duchess*, Archer believed that Webster had intended the children as well as the adults to be strangled onstage.) In his second outburst, the confirmed disciple of Ibsen was even less kind to Webster, analyzing the construction of *The Duchess* act by act, and finding it badly motivated, "brokenbacked," "childish," "ramshackle," and "barbarous."[76] George Bernard Shaw, the friend and ally of Archer, dismissed Webster in a line, dubbing him "the Tussaud laureate" and referring to "the opacity that prevented" him "from appreciating his own stupidity."[77]

Defense of Webster in the late Victorian period was just as passionate as the castigation, but the champions tended to be *fin de siècle* essayists ("decadents" to their enemies) whose attachment to the Jacobean drama was a function of their emancipation from the ponderous moralism of the Kingsley school. The major names here are Algernon Charles Swinburne and John Addington Symonds. It is hardly fortuitous that Havelock Ellis, the pioneer sexologist (and another lover of the "Tussaud laureate"), was also the founder of the popular Mermaid series of Elizabethan dramatists that gave Symonds the chance to edit and assess Webster. Swinburne stands out as the most extravagant and verbose of Webster's supporters. A lineal descendant of the school of Lamb (he had read Campbell's *Specimens* of *The Duchess* at age twelve), Swinburne tried to imply that dramatic structure and poetic imagination in a dramatist were critically inseparable; but it was the beauty, terror, pathos, and "fancy" of Webster's plays that mesmerized him. Typically, he attempted to catch the peculiar tone and atmosphere of the playwright in one of his several *Sonnets on English Dramatic Poets* (1882):

THUNDER: the flesh quails, and the soul bows down.
  Night: east, west, south, and northward, very night.
  Star upon struggling star strives into sight,
Star after shuddering star the deep storms drown.
The very throne of night, her very crown,
  A man lays hand on, and usurps her right.
  Song from the highest of heaven's imperious height
Shoots, as a fire to smite some towering town.
Rage, anguish, harrowing fear, heart-crazing crime,
  Make monstrous all the murderous face of Time
  Shown in the spheral orbit of a glass
Revolving. Earth cries out from all her graves.
Frail, on frail rafts, across wide-wallowing waves,
  Shapes here and there of child and mother pass.[78]

Swinburne's prose encomium (originally published in 1886 as a contribution to *Nineteenth Century*) is almost as impressionistic as his poem. Here Webster becomes not only "a limb of Shakespeare" but his "right arm," the second greatest tragedian of England and a more moral one than Euripides. Far from depending for his fame upon "a casual passage here or there," and certainly more than a mere "artist in horrors," Webster possesses an "infallible . . . sense" of the fine line that "divides the impressive and the terrible from the horrible and the loathsome." He is the dramatist who can render the "deep truth of natural impulse" and convey "passionate austerity and prophetic awe." Webster delineates character with "incomparable power": Flamineo and Bosola, for instance, are "Bonapartes in the bud, Napoleons in a nutshell, Caesars who have missed their Rubicon and collapse into the likeness of a Catiline." Swinburne counters the charge that Webster violates "what is now called naturalism or realism" by insisting that poetic drama *must* do so by definition. Swinburne's Webster, then, is the poet of a more exalted reality, of the "latent mystery of terror which lurks in all the highest . . . beauty" that only "the crowning gift of imagination" can express; and Shakespeare alone possessed this quality in equal degree.[79]

As might be expected, J. A. Symonds, the devout student of Renaissance Italy and the translator of Michelangelo and Benvenuto Cellini, was another strong proponent of Webster's excellencies. In a rhapsodic essay published in *Italian Byways* (1883), "Vittoria Accoramboni and the Tragedy of Webster," he offered a colorful account of the history behind Webster's first major play, going on to praise both the Italian tragedies as the work of "a vigorous and profoundly imaginative playwright." Like Swinburne, Symonds was struck by the lurid power of Webster's characters and language. Vittoria "blaz[es]" throughout her trial "with the intolerable luster of some baleful planet," her "malice and her energy are equally infernal," and she shows herself "a magnificent vixen, a beautiful and queenly termagant." A "mysterious man of genius," Webster "penetrated the secrets of Italian wickedness with truly appalling lucidity," and "deeper than any poet of the time, deeper than any even of the Italians, he read the riddle of the sphinx of crime." In the companion play, "when Bosola presents the body of the murdered Duchess to her brother, Webster has wrought a scene of tragic savagery that surpasses almost any other that the English stage can show."[80]

Symonds reworked some of the same material into the briefer and less hyperbolic introduction of his Mermaid edition of *Webster and Tourneur* (1888). Here, to some extent falling back upon criteria like Archer's, he acknowledged the dramatist's tendency to constructional weakness and mechanical characterization, but saw Webster as the great master of dramatic situations, particularly those that blend "tenderness and pity with the exhibition of acute moral anguish" and that "reveal the struggles of the human soul with sin and fate." Symonds also anticipated twentieth-century "new criticism" by noticing the intricately compressed, detailed, and conceited nature of Webster's style: "He is not a poet to be dealt with by any summary method; for he touches the depths of human nature in ways that need the subtlest analysis for their proper explanation." Symonds also understood (as Kingsley and Archer did not) that the bizarre, the grotesque, and the shocking could be legitimate subjects for great art:

[Webster] was drawn to comprehend and reproduce abnormal elements of spiritual anguish. The materials with which he builds are sought for in the ruined places of abandoned lives, in the agonies of madness and despair, in the sarcasms of reckless atheism, in slow tortures, griefs beyond endurance, the tempests of sin-haunted conscience, the spasms of fratricidal bloodshed, the deaths of frantic hope-deserted criminals. . . . Yet his firm grasp upon the essential qualities of diseased and guilty human nature, his profound pity for the innocent who suffer shipwreck in the storm of evil passions not their own, save him, even at his gloomiest and wildest, from the unrealities and extravagances into which less potent artists—Tourneur, for example—blundered.[81]

Symonds ended by endorsing Swinburne's dictum, "There is no poet morally nobler than Webster."

William Poel, although the son of an ardent pre-Raphaelite, was tempermentally very different from Swinburne and Symonds. He was a practical man of the theatre—an actor, manager, and person of historical bias, who led the movement of attempting to restore the old dramatists to something like the original theatre for which they had written. Poel in his 1892 revival of *The Duchess of Malfi* at the Opera Comique aimed to demonstrate the validity of taking Webster (with comparatively modest tampering) more or less on his own terms, although a "Dance of Death" (a group of dancers suddenly assuming the appearance of skeletons) was added, and emphasis on the madmen was lessened. The play had not been seen in central London for almost a quarter century.

Poel's experiment produced mixed reactions. The usual protests about dramatized horror surfaced in the press, and the *Times* thought that "an ordinary audience" would find the play too long, "oppressive and tiresome."[82] Swinburne, on the other side, was enraptured and wrote to Poel on 27 October 1892, congratulating him "on the benefits you have conferred upon all lovers of English dramatic poetry at its best and highest" and offering to show him his personal copy of the 1623 quarto.[83] Swinburne later wrote a prologue for the play, originally published in *Nineteenth Century* (1899) and reprinted in *A Channel Passage and Other Poems* (1904). Again Webster was seen as the worthiest successor to Shakespeare:

> Half Shakespeare's glory, when his hand sublime
> Bade all the change of tragic life and time
> Live, and outlive all date of quick and dead,
> Fell, rested, and shall rest on Webster's head.
> Round him the shadows cast on earth by light
> Rose, changed, and shone, transfiguring death and night.
> Where evil only crawled and hissed and slew
> On ways where nought save shame and bloodshed grew,
> He bade the loyal light of honour live,
> And love, when stricken through the heart, forgive.
> Deep down the midnight of the soul of sin
> He lit the star of mercy throned therein.
> High up the darkness of sublime despair
> He set the sun of love to triumph there.
> Things foul or frail his touch made strong and pure,
> And bade things transient like to stars endure.
> Terror, on wings whose flight made night in heaven,
> Pity, with hands whence life took love for leaven,
> Breathed round him music whence his mortal breath
> Drew life that bade forgetfulness and death
> Die: life that bids his light of fiery fame
> Endure with England's, yea, with Shakespeare's name.[84]

Apart from his restoration of *The Duchess* to the stage, Poel's contribution to the controversy about Webster took the form of a reply to Archer's destructive review ("Webster, Lamb, and Swinburne"), which Poel published in the *Library Review* of 1893. Significantly entitled, "A New Criticism of Webster's *Duchess of Malfi*," Poel's essay refuted Archer's contention that the dramatist, though studded with "poetic jewels," was primitive and "valueless" as a playwright; he asseverated baldly what others had already implied—namely, that "Webster's poetry . . . cannot be separated from its dramatic interest." Poel emphasizes the importance of context to the great anthology pieces and points to the "imperfect historical knowledge" in which Archer's prejudices are rooted. If the events of *The Duchess* appear absurdly and cheaply artificial to a late Victorian rationalistic Englishman, let him read the history of Renaissance Italy and exercise his "historical imagination" more actively.[85] Poel's approach to Webster thus marked the beginning of a modern and historically aware understanding of

Elizabethan dramatic aesthetics and of the theatrical conditions in which they were grounded.

A few other nineteenth- and early twentieth-century writers made some impact on Webster's reputation. The American essayist and lecturer, Edwin P. Whipple, lecturing at the Lowell Institute in Boston in 1859, spoke appreciatively of the dramatist. He was especially impressed by *The White Devil* in which the "moral confusion" of the major characters "is traced with more than Webster's usual steadiness of nerve and clearness of vision." The playwright "lifts . . . wickedness . . . from the region of the senses into the region of the soul, exhibits its results in spiritual depravity, and shows the satanic energy of purpose which may spring from the ruins of the moral will."[86] William Minto, Professor of Logic and English Literature at the University of Aberdeen, defended Webster's worthiness for the stage in his *Characteristics of English Poets from Chaucer to Shirley* (1874), while Adolphus William Ward, later a co-editor of *The Cambridge History of English Literature*, compiled a two-volume *History of English Dramatic Literature to the Death of Queen Anne* (1875), in which he found Webster somewhat deficient in moral uplift but endowed with "flashes of genius which seem to light up of a sudden a wide horizon of emotions." Ward perceptively notices the surpassing "elaborateness of [Webster's] workmanship" and, unlike most earlier commentators, points out his "satirical powers," directed especially at lawyers.[87]

That proper Bostonian, man of letters, and diplomat James Russell Lowell included a discussion of Webster in his hastily composed *Lectures on the Old English Dramatists* (read before the Lowell Institute in 1887). Lowell's sympathy with Webster was less than total, and the most striking of his observations often have a guarded, even grudging, tone. He speaks of the improbability and "gratuitous miscellaneousness" of the plots—of Webster's presenting crime "as a spectacle" rather than "as a means of looking into our own hearts." Lowell compares Flamineo unfavorably to Iago, "but for [whom, the Websterian character] would never have existed," and he concludes by invoking Victor Hugo, who, in his opinion, shares a number of Webster's failings:

There is the same confusion at times of what is big with what is great, the same fondness for the merely spectacular, the same insensibility to repulsive details, the same indifference to the probable or even to the natural, the same leaning toward the grotesque, the same love of effect at whatever cost; and there is also the same impressiveness of result. Whatever other effect Webster may produce upon us, he never leaves us indifferent. We may blame, we may criticise, as much as we will; we may say that all this ghastliness is only a trick of theatrical blue-light; we shudder, and admire nevertheless. We may say he is melodramatic, that his figures are magic-lantern pictures that waver and change shape with the curtain on which they are thrown: it matters not; he stirs us with an emotion deeper than any mere artifice could stir.[88]

The final names to be mentioned in the late Victorian and early post-Victorian phase of Webster criticism are Edmund Gosse, the author of *Father and*

Son, and Rupert Brooke, the romantic poet of World War I. Both in their different ways had an abiding interest in the theatre. Gosse's father, a man of rigid puritanical piety and a friend of Kingsley, had unwittingly prepared his son for the excitements of Webster by forbidding him all access to imaginative or "worldly" literature as a boy. It is scarcely surprising, however, that the adult Gosse, a devotee of Ibsen like Archer (with whom he collaborated in a translation of *The Master Builder*), perceived an almost unbridgeable gap between Webster's brilliant talents as a poet and his constructional inadequacies as a playwright. Gosse even propounded the highly dubious theory that "in another age, and in other conditions" the dramatist "would have directed his noble gifts of romantic poetry to other provinces of the art." Gosse's discussion of Webster in his *Jacobean Poets* (1894) reminds us how persistently doubts about the theatrical viability of a play like *The Duchess of Malfi* continued to disturb even the most sympathetic of the poet's admirers. From Gosse's perspective, Webster had "sacrificed" coherence or "the movement of the whole" to "an extraordinary brilliancy" of detail: although *The Duchess* "has again and again been attempted on the modern stage, each experiment has but emphasized the fact that it is pre-eminently a tragic poem to be enjoyed in the study." Obviously, the ghost of Lamb still walked abroad. Moreover, Gosse, who was himself a writer of verse, found Webster metrically "lax."

But these imperfections, in Gosse's opinion, were a small price to pay for the transcendental vision of greatness that Webster offered. *The Duchess* was "the finest tragedy in the English language" next to Shakespeare: in the characterization of the heroine, "All is original, all touching and moving, while the spirit of beauty, that rare and intangible element, throws its charm like a tinge of rose-colour over all that might otherwise seem to a modern reader harsh or crude." Gosse's earlier and more diffuse essay on Webster (originally written in 1874 for *Fraser's Magazine* and revised in 1883 for his *Seventeenth Century Studies*) is marked by the same enthusiasm for Webster's characters, for his visionary eye for what lies beyond "the common world," and for his rich canvas, "lurid with the colour of a thunder-cloud, and red with blood and flame."[89]

As one of the founders of the Marlowe Society while still an undergraduate at Cambridge, the handsome young Rupert Brooke took an early and active role in the reviving of Elizabethan plays, acting himself in a production of *Doctor Faustus*. His *John Webster and the Elizabethan Drama* (1912)—the dissertation with which Brooke won his fellowship at King's College in 1913, published posthumously in 1916—is written in a boyishly conversational and sometimes complacent style; but, except for E. E. Stoll's rather Teutonic monograph, *John Webster: The Periods of His Work* (1905), it constituted the most sustained treatment of Webster's canon theretofore attempted.

Brooke inherited the "passage worship" of the older enthusiasts, but he saw Webster as a true playwright, not merely as an assembler of fiery and lyric splendors clumsily imbedded in baggy monsters. Not that he fails to reprove Webster's "occasional dramatic insensibility," his habit of tossing in "childish" apothegms or smugly gnomic irrelevancies; but he analyzes the choric purposes in the dramatist's technique and perceptively defends his pastiche of verbal borrowings: " 'Originiality' is only plagiarising from a great many. . . . Webster reset other people's jewels and redoubled their lustre."

A man tends to collect quotations, phrases, and ideas, that particularly appeal to and fit in with his own personality. If that personality is a strong one, and the point of his work is the pungency with which it is imbued with this strong taste, the not too injudicious agglutination of these external fragments will vastly enrich and heighten the total effect. And this is, on the whole, what happens with Webster. The heaping-up of images and phrases helps to confuse and impress the hearer, and gives body to a taste that might otherwise have been too thin to carry. Webster, in fine, belongs to the caddis-worm school of writers, who do not become their complete selves until they are incrusted with a thousand orts and chips and fragments from the world around.

And Brooke, too, has a fine perception of the energetic irrationality of the Websterian ethos:

The world called Webster is a peculiar one. It is inhabited by people driven, like animals, and perhaps like men, only by their instincts, but more blindly and ruinously. Life there seems to flow into its forms and shapes with an irregular abnormal and horrible volume. That is ultimately the most sickly, distressing feature of Webster's characters, their foul and indestructible vitality.[90]

With Dyce's 1830 edition of Webster (later revised and several times reprinted), with articles by Sir Sidney Lee in the *Dictionary of National Biography* (1899) and by Swinburne in the famous eleventh edition of the *Encyclopaedia Britannica* (1910), and with the book-length studies of Stoll and Brooke, Webster had become academically respectable. The foundations had now been laid for F. L. Lucas's magisterial edition of 1927. Nor was Webster any longer the exclusive possession of British and American culture. Friedrich Martin von Bodenstedt had translated *The Duchess of Malfi* and other parts of Webster into German in 1858. Robert Prölss followed with a German rendering of *The White Devil* in 1904. Ernest Lafond published French versions of both the Italian tragedies in 1865, and Georges Eekhoud made a second French translation of *The Duchess* in 1893. *The White Devil* was done into Russian by I. A. Aksenov in 1916 and *The Duchess of Malfi* into Spanish by Enrique Díez-Canedo in 1920. Camille Cé published another French translation of the two major tragedies in 1922. A German version of *Appius and Virginia* was made by F. A. Gelbke in 1890. Notable translations of Webster, especially in Italian, have followed.

* * *

T. S. Eliot's endorsement of Webster as an author of the first rank and the developing taste for Donne and the metaphysicals that served as critical corollary to the changing literary aesthetics of the nineteen twenties, thirties, and forties, greatly accelerated, if they did not quite begin, what we must now call the Webster industry. The result is that one can no longer avoid meeting Webster in the standard university syllabi for degrees in English (regardless of whether one likes or dislikes sex and violence on the stage), and that articles and books on all aspects of the subject pour forth every year in a profusion exceeded by those of no other dramatist of the period save Shakespeare. The present volume is merely the latest in what is becoming a Websterian avalanche. Inevitably, modern scholarship has involved itself in numberless eddies and crosscurrents, ranging from the most precise kinds of historical and bibliographical investigation to highly theoretical techniques of interpretation—Freudian, Marxist, linguistic, phenomenological, poststructuralist, and the like. A full analysis of these trends would require a book in itself. I can only hope that the reader will have encountered some of them in the chapters (and accompanying documentation) that precede this one.

A few major lines of continuing critical inquiry, however, may be summarized by way of conclusion. Eliot's influential remarks on Webster and the other dramatists of his age opened up the challenging but interpretively fruitful problem of mixed modes—that is, of the mingling of naturalistic with artificial (or conventional) elements in Elizabethan-Jacobean dramaturgy. This combination is especially radical in Webster, who seems both old- and new-fashioned by turns, and who liked to use outmoded or even archaic devices in puzzling and experimental ways. Although Eliot tended to regard this kind of impurity as artistically damaging, others have seen in it a theatrical means of fusing or yoking together disparities in human experience and of eliciting ambivalent, even multivalent, responses to the subjects presented. Tragic involvement and comic detachment may thus be viewed as complementary aspects of a single dramatic complexity. Travis Bogard's *The Tragic Satire of John Webster* (1955), a stimulating account of the playwright's drawing simultaneously upon traditions of Renaissance tragedy and satire, is a case in point.

A further extension of this line of thought concerns itself with another kind of mixture in Webster—the hybridization of genres. I have emphasized the combining of love tragedy with revenge tragedy in the major plays, but other kinds of generic mixture are equally significant, particularly the superimposition of comic upon tragic structures and the drift toward tragicomedy (already incipient in *The White Devil* and *The Duchess of Malfi*) that reaches fuller definition in *The Devil's Law-Case*. Jacqueline Pearson's *Tragedy and Tragicomedy in the Plays of John Webster* (1980) and Lee Bliss's *The World's Perspective: John Webster and the Jacobean Drama* (1983) have both taken this path with enlightening results. And the open-endedness of tragicomedy, its resistance to the teleological satisfactions of closure, is additionally relevant to the notorious Websterian uncertainties and contingencies of form.

An important implication of the tragicomic approach is the vexed question of self-consciousness in Webster's characters and the degree to which they stage their own tragedies or parody the dramatic conventions of which they are themselves a part. Most students of the great plays have discerned a compelling depth and emotional complexity in figures like Vittoria, Bosola, and the Duchess of Malfi; but the undeniable effects of psychological realism are by no means continuous or unaffected by countervailing flatnesses and deliberate stereotyping— stereotyping reinforced by the stylized acting of the children's theatres and by the humour comedy, city farce, and prose character-writing so close to Webster's own professional career. It can hardly be an accident that *The Duchess*, Webster's most popular work, has spawned at least one historical-psychological novel (David Stacton's *A Dancer in Darkness*, [1960]), a seamy television play set in the twentieth-century Caribbean (Kingsley Amis's *A Question of Hell* [1964]), and two operas—Stephen Oliver's *Duchess of Malfi* (first performed in Oxford, 1971; then in Santa Fe, New Mexico, 1978) and Stephen Douglas Burton's piece of identical title (first given at Wolf Trap Farm Park for the Performing Arts near Washington, D.C., in 1978).[91] It may be significant, too, that Oliver's music is uncompromisingly spare, forward-looking, and discordant while Burton's is contrastingly lush, conservative, and romantic. Nor should we forget that as early as 1840 Ludwig Tieck could write a German romantic novel, inspired in part by Webster, *Vittoria Accorombona: ein Roman*, and that Clifford Bax followed exactly a century later with a popular historical account of the same characters and incidents in *The Life of the White Devil* (1940).[92] Clearly Webster's tragedies contain much to inspire both the symbolic and the literalist, the avant-garde and the more traditionalist styles of art. Indeed, the historical novel and the contemporary opera might be taken to demarcate the very margins of psychological realism on the one hand and of self-conscious artifice on the other.

Webster's much debated horrors, at least theoretically, no longer excite the same outrage that they once did. The most highly acclaimed production of *The Duchess* in our century (with John Gielgud as Ferdinand, Cecil Trouncer as Bosola, and Peggy Ashcroft in the title role) was mounted in London in 1945, just when the unspeakable enormities of the Nazi holocaust were coming fully to light. What had seemed like fantastic and tasteless excesses to the more sheltered audiences of earlier generations suddenly took on a frighteningly new credibility. The rapid piling up of corpses can still trigger nervous giggling in the auditorium when the acting or direction are insufficiently skillful, but Auschwitz, Belsen, Buchenwald, and Dachau, the gulags of Soviet Russia, the atrocities of Idi Amin, and the repressive obscenities of Latin American dictatorships have prepared us to react to Webster's extreme savagery in an altered frame of reference. Historical parallelism can, of course, be detrimental as well as advantageous, as was the case in 1979 when the Acting Company of Washington, D.C., directed by Michael Kahn, produced an execrable *White Devil* in "Punk Rock" style with obvious allusions to the drug-crazed world of Charles Manson and the Sharon Tate murders. Artaud's theatre of cruelty has offered insights beneficial to Webster, but the results—especially in the implied denial of human greatness and of moral dignity—have also entailed some loss. Obsessively "relevant" interpretations of Webster—often the pitfall of contemporary directors—tend to forget that our bureaucratized, remote-control age of nuclear threat is emotionally a pole away from Webster's world of intense personal relationships and heroic suffering.

The issue of whether the tragic centers of Webster's dramas betoken a coherent or meaningful purpose in the cosmos—or whether indeed a tragic center exists at all—is perennial and no doubt dependent, in large measure, on the value systems of the particular commentators. Webster criticism has been rife with interpreters (Ellis-Fermor, Jack, Leech, Boklund, and Ornstein, for instance) who fail to detect any consistent or definable vision of the moral life beneath the multiple cruelties and mutable utterances of the characters.[93] For many, the copybook sententiae are merely intrusive or irritatingly out of key with the actions to which they are applied, and so represent a hollow or smug mouth ethic that has little to do with behavior or reflect the simpler codes of an earlier time, now fallen into an advanced state of decay. Others, (such as Ribner, Murray, Gunby, and Berry) discern, however obscurely, patterns of human depravity and potential or actual virtue that only come into focus through the search for ethical and religious universals, universals at least implicitly affirmed by the plays.[94] For some of these scholars, the nodes of gnomic wisdom represent an attempt—usually inadequate—to take a moral fix on the uncertain mutations of a baffling world. Any true advance in our understanding of Webster's larger meanings will have to find ways of coping with both the skeptical and affirmative valences in his texts and of reconciling the existential crises that the plays dramatize with our glimpses of a more objective reality behind them.

Questions about the moral and cosmic dimensions of Websterian drama return us again to considerations of aesthetic form. Patterns of imagery and speech and the rhythms of repetition, featuring parallel and contrasting episodes, can be surprisingly intricate in Webster and do much to vitiate the conclusions of critics, like Archer, who are blind to logic and design in the dramatist. Such matrices, even if they can only be appreciated in the study or absorbed subliminally during a performance, are in some sense metaphors for an ultimately intelligible universe, or at least for the powers of the human mind to discover and reveal a design in the carpet. Hereward T. Price's impressive essay on "The Function of Imagery in Webster" (1955) goes some distance (though only by implication) in this direction.[95] And Webster's complex mosaics of verbal borrowings, taken from such a dispersion of sources, also suggest a vision of aesthetic order imposed upon multiplicity, which, in turn, may adumbrate some higher concept of order. Similar inferences (although perhaps unintended by the writers themselves) can also be drawn from the work of critics such as Ekeblad, Calderwood, and Hurt, who emphasize the fracturing or inverting of ceremony.[96] The ritual elements of Websterian dramaturgy serve partly by way of foils to show up the disintegrative forces of disruption and collapse; but they also work in a reverse way to make us aware of norms (or *potential* norms) that are being so grotesquely violated.

Still another paradox of Websterian technique is that the dramatist simultaneously decenters (or breaks up) and holds together his dramatic fabric by abandoning the older principle of a single commanding character or pair of characters. No matter that the titles of both his greatest plays would seem to refer to an individual. The "white devil" of the first tragedy is not merely a sobriquet for Vittoria but a generic term that, in different senses, applies to other characters as well. The Duchess of Malfi gives her title (not her name) to the play in which she suffers, but the tragedy as a whole is built upon the complex interrelationship of five major characters, all of whom play off and upon each other. This diffusion of interest makes it possible for Webster to dramatize the psychic isolation of the individual in the group and to show that claustrophobic closeness and cosmic loneliness may be aspects of each other. Moreover, the relational emphasis of Webster's approach to characterization suggests the importance of social and family cohesion through the very denial of it. A coordinate theme here is the breakdown of language as an instrument of communication. Webster's famous penchant for equivocation, at the surface level a device of wit, forges an important link between the spoken word (the medium of drama) and human responsibility in both the smaller and larger units of society.

Finally, Webster's greatest plays are rich in psychosexual insight and tell us much about the dark places of the human soul where attraction and repulsion, relatedness and separateness, love and hatred, touch. But his interest in the obscure connections that relate the groin to the head and the heart, and all three to the pervasive consciousness of mortality, is imaginative, not clinical. Webster's great achievement was not to produce the poetic equivalent of the insights of a Krafft-Ebing or a Kinsey but to make us care deeply for a vulnerable humanity, even at its ugliest, most confused, and most brutal. Webster was much possessed by death because he set the highest possible value on life.

Appendix

Notes

Index

APPENDIX

Webster's Influence on Seventeenth-Century English Drama

Webster's imitation of contemporary or near-contemporary drama is pervasive, and David L. Frost, for example, has conveniently summarized the most notable debts to Shakespeare.[1] But Webster's influence on the other playwrights of the century, although not widely recognized and virtually unacknowledged by those who borrowed, was nearly as multifarious as theirs upon him. Even Shakespeare may owe something to his younger coeval. In *Henry VIII* (a "new" play when it was performed at the Globe in June 1613), Queen Katherine insists that Wolsey drop his pretentious Latin and deal with her more plainly in his native language: "A strange tongue makes my cause more strange, suspicious; / Pray, speak in English" (III.i.45–46). *The White Devil*, which almost certainly antedates Shakespeare's chronicle play by a year or more, contains a striking parallel: Vittoria at her arraignment not only insists, like Katherine, that her accuser speak "his usual tongue" (III.ii.13) instead of Latin but also does so for the same reasons—because it sounds more honest, is less subject to misinterpretation ("I will not have my accusation clouded / In a strange tongue"), and because she would have all hearers, whether lettered or not, be able to follow the proceedings. Shakespeare, it is true, found Katherine's preference for English in his Holinshed source, but Webster's scene might well have illustrated for him the dramatic effectiveness of a tiff based on the formal pomposity of entrenched authority versus the vernacular testiness of the accused. Both episodes involve an embattled woman and a hostile cardinal, and, although the phrase is common enough, Shakespeare could be echoing Webster's words, "a strange tongue" (*The White Devil*, III.ii.18–19).

John Ford expresses the typical attitude of the age toward this sort of borrowing in his prologue to *The Lover's Melancholy* (1628):

> Our writer, for himself, would have ye know
> That in his following scenes he doth not owe
> To others' fancies, nor hath lain in wait
> For any stol'n invention, from whose height
> He might commend his own, more than the right
> A scholar claims, may warrant for delight.[2]

As we know from Webster's own practice, such disclaimers did not deter dramatists from imitating each other, either with the deliberate aim of alluding to popular plays that at least some members of the audience might remember or simply in the exercise of "the right / A scholar claims" to appropriate effective ideas, metaphors, or turns of phrase. Ford himself was of course a great borrower. His indebtedness to Webster hardly compares with his highly visible bow to Shakespeare's *Romeo and Juliet* in *'Tis Pity She's a Whore* or to *Othello* in *Love's Sacrifice*, but the younger dramatist admired his older colleague's style enough to echo it repeatedly.

In *The Lover's Melancholy*, for instance, Thamasta falls in love with Eroclea disguised as a boy, and Amethus, her disapproving brother, remarks that

> Women, in their passions,
> Like false fires, flash, to fright our trembling senses,
> Yet in themselves contain nor light nor heat.
>
> (IV.i [I,69–70])

This comparison seems to be based on one of Webster's favorite *sententiae*, "Glories, like glow-worms, afar off shine bright / But look'd to near, have neither heat nor light." After having used this couplet in one of Flamineo's speeches (*The White Devil*, V.i.41–42), Webster repeated it verbatim as a comment on Bosola in *The Duchess of Malfi* (IV.ii.144–145) and again with some variation in *The Devil's Law-Case* (IV.ii.115–117). More importantly, the entire episode of Ford's play in which the court physician presents a masque of madmen before Prince Palador in order to cure his love melancholy (III.iii) was clearly suggested by the cruel entertainment that Ferdinand devises for the Duchess of Malfi. In Webster's tragedy a servant announces to the heroine:

> Your brother hath intended you some sport:
> A great physician, when the Pope was sick
> Of a deep melancholy, presented him
> With several sorts of madmen, which wild object,
> Being full of change and sport, forc'd him to laugh,
> And so th' imposthume broke: the self-same cure
> The duke intends on you.
>
> (IV.ii.38–44)

The grotesques in Ford's "Masque of Melancholy" are similar to those of Webster's corresponding scene, but the clinching evidence is the first figure to appear who suffers, like Ferdinand, from lycanthropy, who howls like a wolf and feeds upon corpses dug up in churchyards at midnight. For this and other medical lore Ford in effect acknowledges Burton, but Webster's dramatic treatment of insanity in *The Duchess* has obviously played its part as well.

Love's Sacrifice (1633) also betrays the influence of Webster. The tragedy begins with an abrupt "Depart the court?" that recalls the startling effect of Lodovico's "Banish'd?" at the opening of *The White Devil*; and the villain Ferentes, dying of stab wounds like Vittoria, says, "My forfeit was in my blood; and my life hath answered it" (III.iv [II, 72]), in clear imitation of her words, "O my greatest sin lay in my blood. / Now my blood pays for't" (V.vi.240–241). One suspects yet a further echo of *The White Devil* when Fernando, soliloquizing about the hopeless love he feels for his friend's wife, says, "I am quite lost" (II.ii [II, 36]), a phrase that recalls Bracciano's fatal attraction to the already married Vittoria: "Quite lost Flamineo" (I.ii.3). Ford's tragedy also seems to draw upon the episode in *The Duchess of Malfi* (I.i.404–415) in which the title character proposes to her steward, for in the later play the duke's widowed sister Fiormonda woos

Fernando (as the Duchess woos Antonio) by trying to press upon him a ring that her first husband had once bade her "never part / With . . . but to the man [she] lov'd as dearly / As she lov'd him" (I.ii [II, 23]).

In *The Broken Heart* (1633) Ford again levied upon Webster. Orgilus expires in language based directly on Flamineo's famous "O I am in a mist" (*The White Devil*, V.vi.260): "A mist hangs o'er mine eyes. The sun's bright splendour / Is clouded in an everlasting shadow" (V.ii.152–153).[3] And Ferdinand's terrifying invasion of his sister's private apartment with a naked poniard (*The Duchess of Malfi*, III.ii) may have suggested Bassanes's similar intrusion upon Penthea in Ford's play (III.ii). Apart from the drawn dagger, both contexts involve suddenness, fanatic jealousy, and overtones of incest.

It is scarcely surprising to find echoes of Webster in *'Tis Pity She's a Whore* (1633), certainly in plot and style the most Webster-like of all Ford's tragedies. Giovanni in his incestuous passion for Annabella elaborates Bracciano's "Quite lost," the words, as we have seen, that Ford also copied in *Love's Sacrifice*: "Lost, I am lost; my fates have doomed my death" (*'Tis Pity She's a Whore*, I.ii.144).[4] That Ford was again imitating *The White Devil* seems even surer when we note a still clearer reminiscence of Webster's play in the subplot. Vasques poisons Hippolita, the woman who has trusted in his love, with the words, "Foolish woman . . . thy vain hope hath deceived thee" (IV.i.72–74). This of course is nearly a direct quotation of Gasparo's response to Vittoria when she tries to talk her assassins out of their mortal resolution: "Your hope deceives you" (V.vi.186). Annabella's courageous resistance to her enraged husband when he discovers her pregnancy also seems to echo Webster's tragedy: "No, be a gallant hangman, / I dare thee to the worst, strike, and strike home . . ." (IV.iii.69–70). The tone here again recalls the final encounter between Vittoria and Lodovico, for Webster's heroine also refers contemptuously to her attacker as "a hangman" (*The White Devil*, V.vi.211), daring him to do his worst. Moreover, Lodovico commands his murderers with a similar repetition of the verb *strike*: "Strike, strike, / With a joint motion" (V.vi.231–232).

'Tis Pity probably contains other specific debts to Webster as well. Annabella's father Florio urges his daughter to send Bergetto a ring that she has already given to Giovanni but that her "mother in her will bequeathed, / And charged [her] on her blessing not to give . . . To any but [her] husband" (II.vi.36–38). Again Ford appears to have recalled the incident in *The Duchess of Malfi* (imitated more closely in *Love's Sacrifice*) in which the heroine proposes to Antonio by giving him her "wedding ring" that she has vowed "never to part with . . . But to [her] second husband" (I.i.405–407). In *'Tis Pity*, unlike *The Duchess of Malfi* and *Love's Sacrifice*, the wedding ring is not introduced to remind us of a widow's earlier marriage, but the giving of it does serve in true Websterian fashion as a gesture of female independence and so dramatizes the conflict between a strong private commitment to love and the cruelties of family pressure. *The Duchess of Malfi* apparently suggested additional details of Ford's play. Grimaldi's mistaken killing of Bergetto is suspiciously like Bosola's unintended slaying of Antonio, especially since both dramatists specify the use of "a dark lantern" (*'Tis Pity She's a Whore*, III.vii.1; *The Duchess of Malfi*, V.iv.43). Ford's Hippolita is referred to as "This thing of malice" (IV.i.77), a phrase that recalls Webster's "thing of blood" (V.v.92), applied to Bosola. The contexts are not dissimilar, for both characters are suffering the throes of death. Only a few minutes later in *'Tis Pity*, Richardetto moralizes on Hippolita's fate, predicting the death of Soranzo also: "he will fall, and sink with his own weight" (IV.ii.6). Al-

though Ford's language is his own, we recall Bosola's similar statement about the death of the Aragonian cardinal: "thou fall'st faster of thyself, than calamity / Can drive thee" (V.v.43–44). Even the scene in which Giovanni first declares his passion to Annabella has Websterian overtones, for he "*offers his dagger to her*" (I.ii.209). Giovanni's gesture is a youthful expression of romantic sincerity (he invites his sister to rip open his chest and examine his heart) whereas Duke Ferdinand's presentation of a dagger to the Duchess of Malfi (III.ii.71) is an act of persecution. Nevertheless, in both contexts the giving of an unsheathed weapon signals the dangerous and unhealthy implications of a sexual relation between siblings and ironically foreshadows the violent cruelty to ensue. Incidentally, Ford's imitation of the dagger episode in so explicitly an incestuous situation may well indicate that seventeenth-century audiences and readers would have been prepared to regard the ambivalent relationship between the Duchess of Malfi and her brother in a similarly disturbing light.

The emphasis that Ford places in so many of his plays on the fortitude and psychic stamina of unfortunate lovers, especially women, is perhaps the most noticeable and pervasive of his ties to Webster. Even in so apparently un-Websterian a drama as *Perkin Warbeck* (1634), we have the example of Lady Katherine Gordon, who in typical Webster fashion accepts disaster in love as a challenge to her resilience:

> It is decreed; and we must yield to fate,
> Whose angry justice, though it threaten ruin,
> Contempt, and poverty, is all but trial
> Of a weak woman's constancy in suffering.
> (V.i.1–4)[5]

Although stoical attitudes are common currency in Stuart drama, the terms of Lady Katherine's sentiment are remarkably similar to those of a speech by Antonio after the death of his wife in *The Duchess of Malfi*:

> Though in our miseries Fortune have a part,
> Yet in our noble suff'rings she hath none—
> Contempt of pain, that we may call our own.
> (V.iii.56–58)[6]

Like Ford, Middleton also paid Webster the compliment of verbal imitation. The most obvious instances occur in *The Changeling* (1622). De Flores, for instance, draws the reluctant Beatrice into his loathsome embrace with "Come, rise, and shroud your blushes in my bosom . . ." (III.iv.167),[7] which clearly echoes the Duchess of Malfi's address to her husband at the end of the marriage scene: "O, let me shroud my blushes in your bosom, / Since 'tis the treasury of all my secrets" (I.i.502–503). For anyone who might recognize the borrowing, Middleton's alteration of the original context would add an extra twist to the psychological horror.[8] Again, when Beatrice's father approaches Tomazo de Piraquo, brother to the murdered suitor, he apparently echoes a question that Julia puts to the Cardinal in *The Duchess of Malfi*:

> Unless you be so far in love with grief
> You will not part from't upon any terms,
> We bring that news will make a welcome for us.
> (*The Changeling*, V.ii.54–56)

> Are you so far in love with sorrow,
> You cannot part with it?
> (*The Duchess of Malfi*, V.ii.235–236)

The Changeling may contain yet a further borrowing from *The Duchess* (probably an unconscious one) in the scene where De Flores, startled by the ghost of his murder victim Alonzo, tries to dismiss his "mist of conscience" (V.i.60). Bosola's memorable dirge contains the related phrase *"mist of error"* (IV.ii.188) in a context of penitence, and Webster was especially fond of the word *mist* in the somewhat unusual sense of confused or uncertain knowledge. Flamineo's kindred image, "maze of conscience" (*The White Devil*, V.iv.121) may also have influenced Middleton.

Likewise in *Women Beware Women* (c. 1621) Leantio's cynical comment about his preferment at court, his being "raised from base prostitution, / E'en like a sallet growing upon a dunghill" (III.iii.50–51),[9] was probably suggested by Bosola's similar remark upon being promoted: "say then, my corruption / Grew out of horse-dung" (I.i.286–287). It has often been observed of course that in setting, characterization, plot, and general atmosphere, the major tragedies of both Ford and Middleton owe a clear debt to their Websterian predecessors. Dorothy Farr has pointed out, for instance, that the dance of madmen and the dead man's finger in *The Changeling* probably owe something to similar details from the torture episode of *The Duchess of Malfi*.[10]

Even Middleton's comedy seems to betray occasional touches of Websterian characterization or language, hardly a surprising circumstance in the light of Middleton's probable collaboration with Webster in *Anything for a Quiet Life*. Farr argues plausibly that the destructive commentary of Allwit in *A Chaste Maid in Cheapside* and of De Flores in *The Changeling* both spring from a technique for which Webster's Flamineo was the likely model. Moreover, in his late play *A Game at Chess* (1624), Middleton continued to appropriate Websterian phraseology and imagery. Two memorable speeches from *The Duchess of Malfi*, the heroine's "I stand / As if a mine, beneath my feet, were ready / To be blown up" (III.ii.155–157) and Delio's concluding aphorism, *"Integrity of life is fame's best friend"* (V.v.120), both reappear in Middleton's satiric allegory:

> Methinks I stand over a powder-vault
> And the match now a-kindling.
> (*A Game at Chess*, II.i.158–159)[11]

> Integrity of life is so dear to me. . . .
> (*A Game at Chess*, III.i.274)

John Fletcher with his popularization of tragicomedy obviously helped chart new directions for the Webster of *The Devil's Law-Case* and *A Cure for a Cuckold*, nor is it improbable that in his *Wit Without Money*, a comedy about widow hunting, he supplied certain elements of plot and theme to Webster and his collaborators in *Keep the Widow Waking*.[12] But a few clues suggest that influence also flowed in the reverse direction. Fletcher's comedy *The Chances* (c. 1617, slightly revised in 1627) makes light entertainment out of a situation from which Webster had extracted the last measure of dramatic menace—a brother's vengeance against a sister who is thought to have sullied her family's good name and against the lover with whom she is believed to be lasciviously involved. Disaster is quickly averted when the supposed lecher (a duke) reveals that he is secretly married to the lady and that he would have "long since" obtained "the Churches approbation, / But for [the brother's] jealous danger" (III.iv.55–57);[13] the implication therefore is that their child is not a bastard but a legitimate son. Our suspicion that Fletcher was recalling *The Duchess of Malfi* here and deliberately introducing a piquant tension predicated on audience familiarity with that tragedy increases greatly when we recognize a couple of verbal echoes from the Webster play. Constantia, the heroine of *The Chances*, is tempted, like Webster's Duchess, to "curse those starres, that men say governe us" (II.iii.1), and is later accused, as Ferdinand accuses his sister, of being "loose ith' hilts" (II.iv.75). Webster's words are very close: "I could curse the stars" (IV.i.96) and "she's loose i'th' hilts" (II.v.3). Both phrases, it is true, have a proverbial ring, but Webster was apparently original in applying the latter image to lust, clearly the significance that Fletcher appropriated.[14]

Webster's influence upon Massinger is less easy to particularize, largely because of the problem, mentioned in an earlier chapter, of whether *The Parliament of Love* (1624) borrowed from the plot of *A Cure for a Cuckold* or *vice versa*. Philip Edwards, the most recent editor of *The Parliament*, argues forcefully that Massinger, not Webster, is the debtor.[15] M. C. Bradbrook has suggested that Cleora's sufferings in *The Bondman* (1623) have a few affinities with those of the Duchess of Malfi.[16] A conscious relationship to the earlier play does indeed seem probable, for at the point where Leosthenes is reunited with the lady, Massinger slightly varies a figure of speech that Webster had used to express his duchess's happiness with her lover:

> And pray excuse me,
> If like a wanton Epicure I desire,
> The pleasant taste these cates of comfort yeild me,
> Should not too soone be swallow'd.
> (*The Bondman*, IV.iii.99–102)[17]

> I have seen children oft eat sweetmeats thus,
> As fearful to devour them too soon.
> (*The Duchess of Malfi*, I.i.466–467)

Massinger's fondness for amorous relationships between aristocratic ladies and men of more humble station could also be a legacy from Webster's most popular tragedy; both *The Bondman* and *The Roman Actor* (1626) make much of such attachments. In *The Duke of Milan* (1621–1622) and *The Unnatural Combat* (1624–1625) Massinger continued the tradition of the romantic revenge plot with a Mediterranean setting that Webster had done so much to make popular, but the prurient treatment of sex, the deliberate mystification of the audience, and the surprising reversals of plot in which these plays delight suggest that Fletcher was a stronger pressure upon their author than the Webster of the Italian tragedies.

Since *The Duke of Milan* is a highly derivative performance, containing clear reminiscences of *Othello*, *A Midsummer Night's Dream*, Jonson's *Catiline*, Tourneur's *The Revenger's Tragedy*, and the anonymous *Second Maiden's Tragedy*,[18] the play may also bear the impress of *The Devil's Law-Case*. In the final and most sensational scene of the play, the villain Francisco gains admittance to Marcelia's corpse and the two physicians who attend it by disguising himself as a Jewish doctor; before he can proceed to the poisoning of the cadaver (his means of ensnaring the duke), he insures privacy by insisting that "The art I vse / Admits no looker on . . ." (V.ii.152–153).[19] This incident is suspiciously close to that in Webster's tragicomedy where Romelio, also bent upon murder, insinuates himself into Contarino's bedchamber by disguising himself as a Jewish physician and rids himself of the two attending surgeons by protesting "I must use my art singly" (III.ii.72). Also, since the Duke of Milan's friend, the Marquis of Pescara, has no counterpart in Massinger's major source, the dramatist may have taken the name from Duke Ferdinand's ally in *The Duchess of Malfi*.[20] Finally, Massinger seems to echo Webster in at least two additional places. Beaumelle, condemned to death for adultery in *The Fatal Dowry* (1615–1620), says, "my lust / Is now run from me in that blood, in which / It was begot and nourished" (IV.iv.152–154),[21] another apparent reworking of Vittoria's famous lines, "O my greatest sin lay in my blood. / Now my blood pays for't" (*The White Devil*, V.vi.240–241). And, as T. S. Eliot noticed, *The Roman Actor* contains a reference to "tand gallie-slaues" eager to be "redeeme[d] . . . from the oare" (IV.i.75–76) that undoubtedly borrows from *The Duchess of Malfi*: "I am acquainted with sad misery, / As the tann'd galley-slave is with his oar" (IV.ii.27–28).[22] Since they occur in close proximity to the galley-slave simile, Massinger's lines on the spy Aretinus may also owe something to Webster's tragedy: "Here he comes / His nose held vp; he hath something in the winde . . ." (*The Roman Actor*, IV,i.51–52). Eliot detected here an echo of the sinister description of the Aragonian cardinal: "he lifts up's nose, like a foul porpoise before a storm—" (*The Duchess of Malfi*, III.iii.52–53).[23]

Of all the Caroline dramatists whom Webster influenced, Shirley seems to have borrowed more extensively from him than any other. As Collier and Dyce noted long ago,[24] *The Cardinal* (1641)—with its courageous but deceptive duchess thwarted in love and driven to the brink of madness, its passive and doomed lover, its mysterious prelate-villain, and its lower-born avenger—looks very much like a late reworking of material from *The Duchess of Malfi*. This seems the likelier, since no determinative source for the plot of Shirley's tragedy has been found. Moreover, Shirley takes over some of Webster's metaphoric and stylistic habits with a consistency that makes deliberate imitation virtually certain. Both *The Duchess* and *The Cardinal*, for instance, contain passages that identify the nuptial bed with the winding sheet (*The Duchess of Malfi*, I.i.387–389; *The Cardinal*, I.ii.242), that speak of "shrouding" blushes (*The Duchess of Malfi*, I.i.502; *The Cardinal*, II.iii.162–163) or of eyes so fiery that they contain salamanders (*The Duchess of Malfi*, III.iii.49–50; *The Cardinal*, II.ii.30–33), and that mention perspective glasses that induce flame by concentrating the rays of the sun (*The Duchess of Malfi*, IV.ii.73–75; *The Cardinal*, II.iii.76–78). Nor did Shirley neglect *The White Devil* in composing *The Cardinal*. The dying words of his title character ("the mist is risen, and ther's none / To stear my wandring bark" [V.iii.284–285]) imitate Vittoria's much admired lines, "My soul, like to a ship in a black storm, / Is driven I know not whither" (V.vi.248–249), while Rosaura's "My Heart is in a mist" (I.ii.239) seems clearly indebted to Flamineo's "O I am in a mist" (V.vi.260).[25] It is not unlikely that Webster derived his favorite "mist" image from Marlowe, who had referred to Zenocrate in *Tamburlaine, Part II*, as "All dazzled with the hellish mists of death" (II.iv.14);[26] if so, the Jacobean playwright was probably a significant link between the Elizabethan and the Caroline tragedian. At least it is evident that Shirley was striving to endow his final tragedy (in his dedication he calls it "the best of my flock") with some of the textural density of Webster's finest achievement by adopting a compositional method that Webster himself could scarcely have faulted.

The Traitor (1631), Shirley's earlier revenge tragedy, does not evince the same linguistic dependence upon Webster as *The Cardinal*; nevertheless, it contains a few details reminiscent of *The White Devil*. By way of comic contrast, the later dramatist introduces a fantasy trial at which a page arraigns and convicts his foolish master of high treason. This mock tribunal might well be Shirley's attempt at a parody of Vittoria's arraignment, a possibility made likelier by the mention of villainies (III.i.104–126)[27] for which Webster's play was probably the source—the poisoning of a hunting saddle and prayerbook and the readying of a case of pistols for homicide. Lodovico names the first two crimes as he conspires to assassinate Bracciano (*The White Devil*, V.i.69–70), and later in the same act Vittoria and her servant try to murder Flamineo, using "*two case of pistols*" (V.vi.23) for the purpose. *The Traitor* also contains a scene in which Sciarrha pretends to pander his sister to the Duke of Florence in a way that elicits vigorous protest from Sciarrha's younger brother Florio. Although Shirley undoubtedly based all four of these characters on some history of Florence as yet unspecified, he may well have been influenced in a secondary way by the antagonism between Flamineo and Marcello over the pandering of their sister to the Duke of Bracciano in *The White Devil* (III.i.32–63).

It is characteristic of Shirley's use of Webster that the later dramatist should imitate the style of the Italian tragedies not merely in plays of like genre but also in comedy and tragicomedy. His comedy *The Brothers* (1641?) contains echoes from both *The White Devil* and *The Duchess of Malfi*. A more diffuse rendering of Vittoria's comparison of herself to "a ship in a black storm . . . driven I know not whither" (Shirley also imitated the passage in *The Cardinal* and probably in *The Young Admiral* [1633])[28] reappears in the comedy as

> My heart is in a storm, and day grows black;
> There's not a star in heaven will lend a beam
> To light me to my ruin. Felisarda!—
> That name is both my haven and my shipwreck.
> (*The Brothers*, IV.i [I, 242])

And in the same play Shirley converts the Duchess of Malfi's

> wish me good speed
> For I am going into a wilderness,
> Where I shall find nor path, nor friendly clew
> To be my guide.
> (*The Duchess of Malfi*, I.i.358–361)

into the weaker

> Sir, with your pardon,
> You lead me to a wilderness, and take
> Yourself away, that should be my guide. . . .
> (*The Brothers*, II.i [I, 210])

Shirley also copied twice from Webster in *The Gentleman of Venice* (1639). In that drama Florelli, threatened with death, confronts his adversary in words obviously suggested by Vittoria's remark to Lodovico just before he kills her ("Thou hast too good a face to be a hangman . . ." [*The White Devil*, V.vi.211]):

> Thou hast
> Too good a face to be a mercenary
> Cut-throat. . . .
> (*The Gentleman of Venice*, III.iii [V, 45])

Later in the tragicomedy Cornari menaces Florelli with a loaded pistol and a rapier, referring to the weapons with mordant irony:

> These are the jewels
> Which you must wear, sir, next your heart. How do you
> Affect the lustre of this toy? 'tis bright;
> But here's a thing will sparkle.
> (*The Gentleman of Venice*, V.ii [V, 72])[29]

This language also derives from *The White Devil*—from the passage in which Flamineo and his sister spar bitterly with each other about a pair of pistols:

> *Flamineo.* My lord hath left me yet two case of jewels
> Shall make me scorn your bounty; you shall see them.
> . . . .
> Look, these are better far at a dead lift
> Than all your jewel house.
> *Vittoria.*   And yet methinks
> These stones have no fair lustre, they are ill set.
> *Flamineo.* I'll turn the right side towards you: you shall see
> How they will sparkle.
> *Vittoria.*   Turn this horror from me. . . .
> (V.vi.20–28)

Valerio's dying speech in another tragicomedy, *The Duke's Mistress* (1635/36), also seems to borrow from the same play:

> I am rewarded;
> And that which was the rank part of my life,
> My blood, is met withal; and 'tis my wonder
> My veins should run so clear a red, wherein
> So much black sin was wont to bathe itself.
> I would look up, and beg, with my best strength
> Of voice and heart, forgiveness; but heaven's just:
> Thus death pays treason, and blood quencheth lust.
> (V.i [IV, 257–258])

This is obviously an embroidering, more elaborate than the parallel examples by Ford or Massinger, of Vittoria's much imitated "O my greatest sin lay in my blood. / Now my blood pays for it" (*The White Devil*, V.vi.240–241). It is probably safe, although a little surprising, to conclude that after the work of Fletcher and Shakespeare none of the hundreds of dramas to which Shirley was indebted touched his glossy style more significantly than Webster's rugged tragedies of bloodshed and revenge.

Minor dramatists of the mid-seventeenth century, courtly or academic amateurs as well as professionals, continued to echo Webster's arresting phrases and images. Not surprisingly, tragedies of sex, murder, and revenge are among the clearest examples. In

Osmond, the Great Turk (1622–1638) Lodowick Carlell copied the same speech from *The White Devil* that Ford, Massinger, and Shirley had all appropriated. Melcoshus, Emperor of Tartary, stabs his beloved Despina in order to prove that he is capable of putting his honor and the welfare of his subjects above his passions; this situation allows the lady to exclaim (in imitation of Vittoria), "Oh me, my fault lay in my blood, let that expiate my sin against heaven . . ." (V.i).[30] Davenant's *Albovine* (1626–1629) contains an equally striking recollection of *The White Devil*. Valdaura commits a kind of suicide by tricking her adulterous husband into stabbing her; as she expires, he begs her in words that echo Flamineo's death: "O speak, ere thou dost catch an everlasting cold, / And shalt be heard no more" (IV.i).[31] Nathanael Richards, equally impressed by the same speech, plucks another flower from it to adorn his tragedy of lust, *Messalina* (1634–1636). At the end of this melodrama, Silius, the empress's favorite, dies in the arms of his wronged wife: "Like a spent Taper onely for a flash, / I doe recover to embrace thee sweet . . ." (ll. 2410–2411).[32] This of course is a somewhat forced appropriation of Flamineo's "I recover like a spent taper, for a flash / And instantly go out" (*The White Devil*, V.vi.263–264). Even though the comparison of a dying person's final moments to a lightening candle was proverbial, Richards's phrasing is too close to Webster's to be fortuitous. Indeed, Richards was here merely reusing an image that he had already borrowed in his long religious poem *The Celestial Publican* (1630).[33] Silius's speech continues with a reminiscence from *The Duchess of Malfi*: "Take from my lippes (deare heart) a parting kisse / Cold as the dead man's Skull" (ll. 2413–2414). This is a clear echo of the Duchess's parting words to Antonio at Ancona: "your kiss is colder / Than that I have seen an holy anchorite / Give to a dead man's skull" (III.v.88–90). The lecherous Messalina herself dies in a "dimme black fogge" (l. 2606), an image that suggests a conflation of Webster's famous "mists" with the "black storm" (*The White Devil*, V.vi.248) in which the dying Vittoria imagines her soul to be foundering.

William Cavendish, Duke of Newcastle, probably alluded to Webster's first Italian tragedy in his comedy *The Country Captain* (1639–1640), acted by the King's Men at Blackfriars. Newcastle's play contains a drinking song that praises "Renish *wine and Devills white*" to which Captain Underwit responds by pointing out to the singer that "a white Devill is but a Poeticall fiction" (IV.i).[34] The phrase, of course, was proverbial, and the Anglican divine Thomas Adams had preached a sermon at Paul's Cross the very year Webster's tragedy was printed on the theme of "The White Devil, or the Hypocrite Uncased,"[35] but it seems likely that the "Poeticall fiction" Newcastle had in mind was that of his predecessor in the theatre, John Webster.

In *Aglaura* (1637), a fashionably dilettante drama of love and vengeance, Sir John Suckling implies a certain creative depletion by comparing plays to "Feasts" in which "everie Act should bee / Another Course": he virtually confesses his indebtedness to earlier playwrights:

> in good faith provision of wit
> Is growne of late so difficult to get,
> That doe wee what wee can, w'are not able
> Without cold meats to furnish out the Table.
> (Epilogue to the tragicomic version)[36]

Webster's tragedies were certainly among the leftovers that contributed to Suckling's "varietie" of fare. In the first act Suckling offers a softer version of the tense scene from *The Duchess of Malfi* in which Ferdinand suddenly interrupts his sister as she prepares for bed with Antonio: the blunt soldier Zorannes similarly intrudes upon Aglaura and Thersames just as they are about to consummate their marriage. His purpose is to inform the lovers that the king must have the lady for his mistress. To the sensationalism of *coitus interruptus*, Suckling adds another Websterian irony, a night scene (V.i) in which Aglaura mistakenly stabs her beloved whom she is trying to protect in the belief that she is killing her great enemy, the king. One thinks immediately of the murky episode of *The Duchess of Malfi* in which Bosola stabs Antonio, "The man [he] would have sav'd 'bove [his] own life" (V.iv.53).

Aglaura also contains some verbal reminiscences of Webster, including references to the unreliability of "Glow-wormes fire" (II.iii.83) and to the "first *Chaos*" (V.i.9),[37] the comparison of a dying queen to "a sickly Taper" that "but made / One flash, and so expir'd" (V.iii.173–174), and a conception of suffering that focuses on the torturer's prolongation of life. In the tragicomic version of the play Thersames simplifies Flamineo's remark about the "tormenter" giving "hot cordial drinks to one three-quarters dead o'th' rack, only to fetch the miserable soul again to endure more dog-days" (*The White Devil*, V.i.139–142): "It will be with mee, but as 'tis with tortured men, / Whom States preserve onely to wrack agen" (V.i.231–232).

Suckling's dramatic fragment, *The Sad One*, also displays a few Websterian touches—not surprisingly, inasmuch as the play centers on revenge, resembles *Aglaura* in numerous respects, and owes a clear debt to the tradition of plays such as *Hamlet* and *The Revenger's Tragedy*. Scholars have noted that the unfinished play contains a rather old-fashioned dumbshow in the style of those in *The White Devil* and *The Duchess of Malfi*.[38] Moreover, Florello's condemnation of ambition,

> Oh!—how happy is that man, whose humbler thoughts
> Kept him from Court, who never yet was taught
> The glorious way unto damnation. . . .
>
> (IV.iv.7–9)

reads like an elaboration of Vittoria's dying apothegm:

> O happy they that never saw the court,
> Nor ever knew great man but by report.
> (*The White Devil*, V.vi.261–262)

Incidentally, this couplet immediately precedes Flamineo's "spent taper" simile that Suckling used in *Aglaura*, and our suspicions of Websterian influence are further confirmed by Clarimont's cry, "How cunning is the Devil in a Woman's shape!" (V.ii.28). It seems clear that Suckling admired Webster almost as much as he did Shakespeare.

The Fatal Contract (c. 1630–1642) by William Hemminge is mainly a pastiche of quotations, paraphrases, and plot motifs from Shakespearean tragedy. But this highly derivative revenge play seems to be indebted to *The Duchess of Malfi*. Brisac, recognizing a ring that belongs to his daughter, reveals her vow that "she'd never part with it / But when she ment to wed" (II.i).[39] This detail probably derives directly from the wooing scene in Webster's play (I.i.405–407) or else from Ford's imitation of the same lines (noted above) in *Love's Sacrifice* or *'Tis Pity*. It is possible also that King Clotaire's likening of the putatively adulterous Aphelia to "a Christal well" that "Has her spring poyson'd . . . For which it's death . . . to tast" (IV.i)[40] is a more specific application of Antonio's comment that

> a prince's court
> Is like a common fountain, whence should flow
> Pure silver drops in general: but if't chance
> Some curs'd example poison 't near the head,
> *Death, and diseases through the whole land spread.*
> (I.i.11–15)

We know that Hemminge knew *The Duchess of Malfi* because of his allusion to the tragedy in the lines on Webster's brother in his *Elegy* (c. 1632) on Randolph's finger.[41]

Samuel Harding's never acted university play, *Sicily and Naples* (1638?–1640), was an attempt, as one of its many introducers phrased it, to "out-blaze bright *Aglaura's* shining robe."[42] Since this tangle of vengeance, treachery, and incest contains echoes from Shakespeare, Fletcher, and Shirley, among others, it is not improbable that the author also picked up a few hints from Webster. The most likely of these is the disguising of the revenger Zisco as a Moor, an element for which Francisco's assumed identity as Mulinassar in *The White Devil* may well have been the model.

Even so didactic and pedestrian a play as Thomas Drue's *The Duchess of Suffolk* (1623), licensed for production at the Fortune within months of the publication of *The Duchess of Malfi*, shows signs of Webster's influence. Both plays contain early scenes in which a widowed duchess flouts convention by wedding her servant. Although Drue took the essential facts of his story from Foxe's account of the lady's persecution and flight for religious reasons, nothing in the sources corresponds as closely as Webster's parallel episode to the scene in which the noblewoman proposes marriage to her kneeling gentleman-usher. Both scenes play verbally on the role of husband and repeat the word several times. Both also invoke bosom imagery in similar ways. Webster's Duchess addresses Antonio:

> O, let me shroud my blushes in your bosom,
> Since 'tis the treasury of all my secrets.
> (I.i.502–503)

Drue's corresponding speech for his heroine is

> Into thy bosom all my thoughts I send.
> (I, 125)

The Duchess of Malfi uses architectural language as she raises Antonio (socially as well as physically) from his knees:

> This goodly roof of yours is too low built,
> I cannot stand upright in't, nor discourse,
> Without I raise it higher: raise yourself,
> Or if you please, my hand to help you: so. [*Raises him.*]
> (I.i.416–419)

The Duchess of Suffolk speaks in like fashion to her servant Bertie:

> Upon this low foundation I erect
> The Palace of mine honors, on this knee
> I place the head of mine authority;
> Let hand from hand exchange their offices. . . .
>
> (I, 198–201)

Both ladies ratify the betrothal with a kiss:

> And 'cause you shall not come to me in debt,
> Being now my steward, here upon your lips
> I sign your *Quietus est:* —   [*Kisses him.*]
> (*The Duchess of Malfi*, I.i.462–464)

> What's mine is thine, thine mine, seal'd with this kiss.
> (*The Duchess of Suffolk*, I, 202)

And Drue may possibly have echoed Webster in having his heroine say to her husband, "*Bertie*, I am so us'd to misery, / That it seems nothing" (III, 1250–1251).[43] The Duchess of Malfi speaks in a similar vein:

> I am acquainted with sad misery . . .
> Necessity makes me suffer constantly,
> And custom makes it easy. . . .
> (IV.ii.27–30)

That major dramatists such as Ford, Middleton, Fletcher, Massinger, and Shirley as well as lesser ones such as Carlell, Davenant, Richards, Cavendish, Suckling, Hemminge, Harding, and Drue should evince the influence of Webster in their plays is not wholly surprising. Most of these writers, however different from each other, were to some degree imitators of Elizabethan revenge tragedy, the very tradition to which Webster had contributed so materially. Moreover, most of these playwrights shared with Webster a taste for bizarre or arresting imagery, for pithy moralization, and for extreme situations charged with violence and erotic passion. No matter that their dramas were frequently softened by heavy infusions of Fletcherian contrivance and sentimentalism. Conscious or unconscious appropriations from Webster's major tragedies were entirely natural, especially since, as Suckling pointed out, originality of plot, character, theme, and phrase—what the Caroline poet called "provision of wit"—was becoming ever more difficult for later practitioners of a nearly exhausted form.

With the closing of the theatres during the Interregnum Webster's popularity inevitably declined, only to be enthusiastically revived at the Restoration. A public hungry for dramatic excitement naturally looked back to what had proved successful before. That certainly included Webster. *A Cure for a Cuckold* saw print for the first time in 1661. New editions of *The White Devil* came out in 1665 and 1672, and of *The Duchess of Malfi* in 1678 and 1708; reissues of *Appius and Virginia* appeared in 1659 and 1679. The lack of new plays together with the novelty of actresses eager to exploit intense female roles stimulated the revival of Webster's tragedies on the stage. In 1669 Thomas Betterton, the actor, altered *Appius and Virginia*, retitling it *The Roman Virgin, or the Unjust Judge* and casting his wife in the title role. *The White Devil* was successfully remounted in 1661, 1665, and probably 1671, while *The Duchess of Malfi*, again with the future Mrs. Betterton in the starring part, made its appearance on the boards in 1662. Later performances of *The Duchess* were given in 1668, 1672, and 1686 (the last at court). Joseph Harris's *The City Bride, or the Merry Cuckold*, an adaptation of *A Cure for a Cuckold*, was both acted and published in 1696. Except for the curiously neglected *Devil's Law-Case*, which was apparently neither reprinted nor performed after Charles II came to the throne, conditions were auspicious for continued imitation of Webster's major works by the new writers for the stage. Such influence is hardly to be wondered at in an age that went in so extensively for rewritings, adaptations, and "improvements" of Shakespeare, Fletcher, Massinger, and other Renaissance dramatists.

Most of the Websterian imitation shows up quite predictably in the stream of exotic tragedies (or rather melodramas) of bloodshed and horror that entertained audiences almost continuously throughout the last four decades of the century. Webster or at least the theatrical traditions and themes with which he was strongly identified influenced these plays in several respects. Most obvious was the taste for a "gothic" atmosphere of gloom and morbidity with heavy emphasis on physical agony and death—a penchant for darkened stages and mortuary props such as death's heads, coffins, vaults, and dismembered or mutilated corpses. Closely related was the popularity of characters, often women, who are motivated by sexual jealousy and who grieve inconsolably or run mad from guilt or frustrated love. Incest and poison are frequent motifs, and depravity is sometimes portrayed as having the same implacable dedication as that of Webster's "glorious villains." But what had been devices in Webster's originals for emblematizing psychological or metaphysical complexity already present in the language and characterization of the play usually got simplified in the Restoration to mere Grand Guignol or operatic clichés that make no claim to represent genuine experience. Sentimental morality and rhetoric heightened to the pitch of a scream replace Webster's penetrating and tersely understated ironies. Emotional excess virtually takes the place of intellect. By the end of the seventeenth century, the horrific effects had become so common that what seem to have begun as deliberate borrowings from the Jacobean tragedian ended in many instances as a set of conventions upon which any dramatist of the period might improvise variations. Specific episodes or scenes from Webster's tragedies and certain touches of characterization as well as the macabre atmosphere were occasionally imitated, but most such elements were added casually and, usually because of the altered context, have a quite un-Websterian effect.

The second most pervasive evidence of Webster's influence was of a kind that Webster himself would have appreciated—the incidental borrowing of phrases and sentiments. Some playwrights, as their Caroline predecessors had done, simply plagiarized language or imagery directly from Webster's tragedies, no doubt having read them or heard them performed. Others, eschewing the details of his highly compacted style, nevertheless reworked or extended ideas and comparisons to be found in his plays. The atmospheric and thematic kind of influence has been remarked more frequently than the verbal, but neither has been very specifically or comprehensively documented, and both (for they often occur in the same play) are revealing. We may begin by noting that scarcely a major tragedian of the Restoration failed to draw upon Webster in some manner, whether directly or indirectly, and that the two finest tragedies of the period, Dryden's *All for Love* (1677) and Otway's *Venice Preserved* (1682) both were indebted to him.

The first tragedy by a Restoration author to betray a hint of Webster's influence was Thomas Porter's *The Villain* (1662). This play is a blatant imitation of Shakespeare's *Othello*, whose title character, "honest Maligni," is a heartless schemer clearly modeled on Iago. But Porter punishes his criminal with a sensationalism that owes more to Webster than to Shakespeare. Maligni is suddenly *"discover'd peirc't with a stake"* (V.i.)[44] in a manner that recalls the grisly figures of Antonio and his children in *The Duchess of Malfi* "discovered . . . as if they were dead" (IV.i.55). Such gruesome spectacles were to become typical of a whole class of unheroic tragedies in the period. Moreover, Porter appears to take a verbal suggestion from *The White Devil* when it is remarked that "slander fly's back in the slanderers face . . . like a man that pisseth against the Wind" (IV.i).[45] Vittoria at her arraignment confronts her accusers with similar language: "for your names / Of whore and murd'ress they proceed from you, / As if a man should spit against the wind, / The filth returns in's face" (III.ii.148–151). The idea of urinating or spitting against the wind was, of course, proverbial, but Tilley cites no examples other than *The White Devil* that apply to the notion of slander.[46]

The Marriage Night (1663) by Henry Cary, Viscount Falkland, resembles *The Villain* in its essentially unheroic mode and in its concentration on a mélange of sex and violence, but here Webster rather than Shakespeare seems to have prompted the playwright less casually. The bafflingly intricate plot includes a criminal duke who attempts to disguise his passion for a widowed duchess, a malcontent hanger-on who serves him, and a cluster of revenges, the most shocking of which entails an intrusion into the duchess's bedchamber by means of a false key and the murder of both her and her husband in their nuptial bed. The relationship between the evil duke and his melancholy henchman clearly suggests that of Ferdinand and Bosola, and the menacing invasion of the duchess's privacy seems to derive from the same play. In addition, the murderer of the heroine, not unlike Vittoria, spiritedly outfaces his judges and then manages to die of stab wounds with a characteristically Websterian image: "Oh—whither must I wander in this mist?" (V.i).[47]

Sir Robert Howard's *The Great Favourite, or the Duke of Lerma* (1668) carries on the genre that Porter and Cary had found so profitable, and, indeed, if Harbage is correct, Howard was merely revising a manuscript play by John Ford (now lost) entitled *The Spanish Duke of Lerma*.[48] Direct indebtedness to Webster in this drama is less easy to verify than the reappearance of conventions that he had done so much to make current. Nevertheless, the Howard-Ford play contains imagery and rhetorical effects strongly suggestive of the Jacobean dramatist. The title character, for instance, anticipates his future greatness in terms of rising "To be a Pyramid," having "laid a large foundation" (II.i),[49] which reminds us of Bosola's mordant rebuke to the Cardinal: "I do glory / That thou, which stood'st like a huge pyramid / Begun upon a large and ample base, / Shalt end in a little point, a kind of nothing" (*The Duchess of Malfi*, V.v.76–79). Medina remarks of the king's sudden passion for Maria, "He's lost" (II.ii),[50] in what could well be an echo of Bracciano's infatuation with Vittoria: "Quite lost, Flamineo" (*The White Devil*, I.i.3). Later on the king utters a gnomic couplet that is stylistically close to Webster's often repeated glowworm simile:

> But all pure Love, like glow-worms heatless fires
> Lives where it shines, and with that life expires.
>
> (V.ii)[51]

Glowworm images, of course, were fairly common, but Webster seems to have been one of the very few to stress the heatlessness of the insect's fire.[52] Finally, *The Great Favourite* sounds a typically Websterian chord when some friars in procession with crucifix and tapers sing a funeral dirge for Caldroon as he is being led to execution (V.i). *The White Devil*, *The Duchess of Malfi*, and *The Devil's Law-Case* are all famous for their dirges, but the two last-named plays both feature the same sort of ceremonial and *memento mori* accompaniment to the lyric that Howard (or Ford) employs. Bosola, disguised as a bellman, ritually ushers in executioners to offer the Duchess of Malfi the symbols of death, *"a coffin, cords and a bell"* (IV.ii.165); Leonora in the tragicomedy enters *"with two coffins borne by her servants, and two winding-sheets"* (V.iv.125) to be presented to Romelio and Julio in the presence of a Capuchin. An earlier scene in *The Devil's Law-Case* in which Jolenta mourns the supposed death of her lover features a *"table set forth with two tapers"* and *"a death's head"* (III.iii.1).

Webster's fondness for lugubrious settings and macabre physical details shows up unmistakably in Sir William Killigrew's(?) *The Imperial Tragedy* (1669). Not content with one or two symbolic coffins as in Webster, Killigrew opens his drama with a stage *"fill'd with empty Coffins"* and a ghost who commands in the manner of Duke Ferdinand, "Let dismal blackness now the Scene obscure" (I.i).[53] The end of the play fulfills the promise of its beginning by showing *"a dismal Vault, set round with Coffins, in each a dead corps . . . a small Lamp burning . . ."* (V.i).[54] Killigrew's tragedy is the crudest of tyrant plays, but its rant is replete with screech owl imagery, a favorite of Webster's, and contains as well the exclamation, "Horror / Dazels my eyes, or else, among the dead, / I see *Longinus* in that next Coffin" (V.i),[55] a prosaic imitation of part of Ferdinand's famous line, "Cover her face: mine eyes dazzle: she died young" (*The Duchess of Malfi*, IV.ii.264). Even Webster's interest in dismemberment makes an appearance. After an execution scene during which *"a false head . . . is cut off,"* Killigrew literalizes one of Webster's ironical equivocations. In *The Duchess of Malfi* Ferdinand writes to his sister requesting that she send Antonio to court: *"I want his head in a business"* (III.v.28). In *The Imperial Tragedy* the decapitated head, one of many in the play, provokes this baroque elaboration:

> *Souldier.* I am conducting this head to Council.
> *Officer.* Do heads consult after they are cut off?
> *Souldier.* Yes, the rest of his Cabal attend him.
> *Officer.* But where, I pray, does this great Council meet?
> *Souldier.* Zeno [the emperor] has appointed them the high Tower
>   Upon the *Western* wall; thence to survey
>   The Country, which their wisdoms thought to sway.
>
> (V.i)[56]

The Websterian imitations of Porter, Falkland, Howard, and Killigrew in the sixties released a flood of such practices in the succeeding decades, although much of the borrowing was incidental and, since in some cases it was at several removes from the original, probably unconscious. In *The Forc'd Marriage, or the Jealous Bridegroom* (1670), for instance, Mrs. Aphra Behn simply persisted in the fashion for mortuary atmosphere that had so inspired Killigrew by setting her denouement in "*a Room hung with Black, a Hearse standing in it with Tapers round about*" (V.v).[57] Later in *Abdelazer, or the Moor's Revenge* (1677) she actually quoted the Jacobean poet. The Moorish revenger of that tragedy laments his frustration at one point by simply lifting a line from *The Duchess of Malfi* and characteristically weakening its effect by adding a relative clause: "Oh, I cou'd curse the Stars, that rule this night" (III.i).[58]

John Dryden's extensive indebtedness to Shakespeare is so often studied that his use of Webster has all but escaped notice. It is interesting in this connection that Webster receives no mention in "MacFlecknoe" (1862), the satiric poem in which Dryden referred to a number of Webster's fellows, including Heywood, Shirley, Fletcher, Jonson, and Dekker. Dryden may have been partly motivated in the hasty completion of *Tyrannick Love, or the Royal Martyr* (1669) by Betterton's successful adaptation of *Appius and Virginia* at a rival theatre several weeks earlier.[59] Both tragedies are based on classical history, although Dryden's period is post- rather than pre-Christian, and both also exploit the taste, then current, for austere Roman settings and unambiguous characters of exemplary villainy and virtue. More importantly, both tragedies center on the pathetic conflict between despotic power and lust on the one side and virginal purity and defenselessness on the other. There appear to be no verbal imitations of Webster in Dryden's play, unless a reference to St. Catherine's "golden dream" (IV.i.102),[60] a not uncommon phrase, be taken as a reminiscence of Bosola's moral awakening in *The Duchess of Malfi*:

> I stand like one
> That long hath ta'en a sweet and golden dream:
> I am angry with myself, now that I wake.
> (IV.ii.323–325)

The two contexts are disparate, but Dryden later imitated the same speech more closely in *All for Love* when Antony expresses his disillusionment:

> My whole life
> Has been a golden dream of love and friendship;
> But now I wake. . . .
> (V.i.204–206)[61]

Another speech in Dryden's most celebrated play paraphrases language from *The White Devil*, an indication, by the way, that Dryden discerned a parallel of sorts between Vittoria and Cleopatra. Bracciano had described his disastrous attachment to Vittoria in terms of pagan religion:

> Thou hast led me, like an heathen sacrifice,
> With music, and with fatal yokes of flowers
> To my eternal ruin.
> (IV.ii.89–91)

In the more neoclassical drama Ventidius accounts for Cleopatra's destruction of Antony in similar terms:

> Oh, she has decked his ruin with her love,
> Led him in golden bands to gaudy slaughter,
> And made perdition pleasing.
>
> (I.i.170–172)[62]

And for the death of the Egyptian queen, Dryden employs Webster's characteristic mist imagery: "my eyelids fall, / And my dear love is vanished in a mist" (V.i.496–497).

A few other probable recollections of Webster crop up in Dryden's later plays—in *Oedipus* (1678) and *The Duke of Guise* (1682), both written in collaboration with Nathaniel Lee, and perhaps also in *Don Sebastian, King of Portugal* (1689). In the neo-Sophoclean tragedy, Oedipus, after his blinding, soliloquizes about his failure to commit suicide:

> thou, Coward, yet
> Art living, canst not, wilt not find the Road
> To the great Palace of Magnificent Death;
> Tho' thousand ways lead to his thousand doors. . . .
>
> (V.i.284–287)[63]

This passage, which derives ultimately from a Senecan commonplace and can be paralleled in Marston and Montaigne,[64] might be a recasting of the Duchess of Malfi's lines before her strangling:

> I know death hath ten thousand several doors
> For men to take their exits. . . .
>
> (IV.ii.219–220)

The Duke of Guise, which could conceivably have owed something to Webster's lost *Guise*, as it certainly does to Marlowe's *Doctor Faustus* and Shakespeare's *Tempest*, also echoes *The Duchess of Malfi* at a few points. The necromancer Malicorne, horrified by the appearance of an infernal spirit who reminds him of his impending damnation, reacts in words that recall Ferdinand's speech over his dead sister: "Do my Eyes dazle?" (V.ii.68).[65] Another of Ferdinand's lines to the Duchess, "I will never see you more" (III.ii.136), reappears twice with slight alteration in the same scene. Marmoutier rejects the Guise's love with "I tell you, I must never see you more" (V.ii.185, 193). Finally, Malicorne's line, "Then I am lost forever" (V.ii.74), as well as Almeyda's similar "I am lost forever" (*Don Sebastian*, V.i.432)[66] upon her discovery that she has been guilty of incest, both may derive from an exclamation dear to Webster—either from *The White Devil* when Bracciano sighs out his passion for Vittoria ("I am lost eternally" [I.ii.208]) or from *The Devil's Law-Case* when Leonora is told that her beloved Contarino has been slain ("O, I am lost forever" [II.iii.102]). These last similarities are admittedly slight, but the lines all occur at moments of great dramatic tension in Webster, and are therefore memorable. Furthermore, it can hardly be accidental that the three Websterisms in *The Duke of Guise* all cluster in the same scene within a hundred and twenty-five lines of each other.

We hardly expect to find much connection between Websterian tragedy and Restoration comedy. The leading French authority on Webster has nevertheless suggested that William Wycherley knew *The White Devil* well enough to imitate certain of its details in three of his four comedies.[67] Lagarde warns us that Wycherley's approach to Webster was that of a practical dramatist who possessed a sharp sense of formula and situation rather than that of a self-conscious plagiarist, and that we must necessarily expect reminiscences to be imprecise.[68] Whether such parallels between the two playwrights as Lagarde detects are to be explained merely in terms of shared traditions or because of specific indebtedness on Wycherley's part is difficult, perhaps impossible, to say with assurance. In any case, some interesting similarities of situation and thought are certainly observable.

Wycherley's earliest comedy, *Love in a Wood, or St. James's Park* (1671) presents Sir Simon Addleplot, a coxcomb ever in pursuit of wealthy marriages, as remarking that "a promise to a Widow is as seldome kept as a Vow made at Sea" (I.i).[69] This is fairly close in thought, if not in wording, to Flamineo's more picturesque statement that "Lovers' oaths are like mariners' prayers, uttered in extremity; but when the tempest is o'er, and that the vessel leaves tumbling, they fall from protesting to drinking" (*The White Devil*, V.i.176–179). Wycherley may indeed be imitating Webster here, but the comparison has proverbial overtones and has precedents other than him.[70]

The Gentleman Dancing-Master (1672), Wycherley's next play, contains more convincing ties to *The White Devil*, for twice in the comedy, as in the tragedy, female characters report that they have dreamed as a means of revealing, yet half disguising, their true purposes. In Webster's play, Vittoria proposes the murder of Camillo and Isabella by claiming that she had had a "foolish idle dream" (I.ii.231) in which a grave, a yew tree, and a rusty spade became the emblems of death. Wycherley uses the same device more lightheartedly when Hippolita, the romantic heroine of the play and also Formal's cynically restricted daughter, pretends that she has "dream't all night of . . . the new Song against delays in Love" (II.i).[71] Hippolita's transparent fabrication serves as a humorous means not only of suddenly introducing a new singer and song into the comedy but also of expressing, without awakening her father's alarm, the girl's frustration and rebellion against his crassly materialistic view of marriage. Webster's Vittoria is as unhappy with her present spouse as Wycherley's Hippolita is with her prospects. Later in the action Hippolita's maid Prue flirts with the foppish Monsieur de Paris, pruriently encouraging him with the story that in a dream "methoughts you came to bed me" (IV.i).[72] The episode, even to the phrasing, is strikingly like that of another scene in *The White Devil* in which Vittoria's black maid Zanche makes sexual advances to Francisco when he is disguised as a Moor: "My dream most concern'd you. . . . Methought sir, you came stealing to my bed" (V.iii.225–227).

Further evidence that Wycherley admired Webster's tragedy appears in *The Plain-Dealer* (1676). Not only does Manly, the title character, vent his hatred of flattery and court mores like Webster's satiric commentators, but he also speaks of places where "downright Barbarity is profest . . . where they think the Devil white . . ." (I.i).[73] Also Olivia regrets the day that she married Vernish in a speech that suggests *The White Devil*:

wretched Woman that I was! I wish I had then sunk down into a Grave, rather than to have given you my hand, to be led to your loathsom Bed.

(V.i)[74]

Francisco expresses the same thought when he repines at having married his sister to Bracciano:

> would I had given
> Both her white hands to death, bound and lock'd fast
> In her last winding-sheet, when I gave thee
> But one.
>
> (II.i.64–67)

And it is possible that Wycherley knew both *The Duchess of Malfi* and *The Devil's Law-Case* in addition to *The White Devil*. The foolish Novel of *The Plain-Dealer* praises Olivia by asserting extravagantly that "she stands in the Drawing-room, like the Glass, ready for all Comers to set their Gallantry by her: and, like the Glass, too, lets no man go from her, unsatisfi'd with himself" (IV.ii).[75] Although Lagarde overlooks the point (probably because such mirror images—in Shakespeare and elsewhere—are very traditional), these lines might be an elaboration of Antonio's encomium of the Duchess of Malfi: "Let all sweet ladies break their flatt'ring glasses, / And dress themselves in her" (I.i.204–205). Both passages contain the notion of the viewer's self-admiration as well as of the lady as a model. Wycherley's comedy also contains an element of plot that recalls Webster's best-known tragicomedy, for the widow Blackacre, with a view to disinheriting her son, announces publicly that she has conceived him out of wedlock. This is the very tactic that Leonora uses in *The Devil's Law-Case* when she tries to disown her son Romelio. Of course the same motif had been used in other plays. Indeed, as noted earlier, Webster himself may have been influenced by a similar situation in the anonymous *Lust's Dominion*.[76] Nevertheless, given the attraction of Wycherley to *The White Devil*, it seems likely enough that he had also read (or seen) other plays by Webster.

Returning to tragedy, we may note three dramatic productions of the early seventies that, although different from each other in many respects, continued to draw inspiration from what by this point in theatrical history may be called the Webster tradition: Henry Nevil Payne's *The Fatal Jealousie* (1672), Elkanah Settle's *The Empress of Morocco* (1673), and Thomas Shadwell's *The Libertine* (1675). Dryden, who ridiculed both Settle and Shadwell, could at least have approved of his rivals' attraction to Webster. Payne's *Fatal Jealousie*, like Porter's *Villain*, is fundamentally a reworking of materials from *Othello* (there is a clear debt to *Hamlet* as well), but the atmosphere and tone are quite unlike *The Moor of Venice*. Jealousy is here defined as "love lost in a Mist" (II.i),[77] and, when the insanely suspicious husband stabs his sister-in-law, mistaking her for his supposedly adulterous wife, the accident suggests Bosola's blind killing of Antonio "in a mist" (*The Duchess of Malfi*, V.v.94) rather than Othello's ritualistic sacrifice of Desdemona.

The Empress of Morocco, Settle's hugely popular but factitious mixture of heroic and melodramatic features, seems also to take part of its design from *The Duchess of Malfi*. The play is crammed with operatic effects and stage conventions that stem from Elizabethan revenge tragedy—among them, a lustful queen, a Machiavellian usurper, and a court masque during which real blood is spilled. Princess Mariamne, one of the suffering heroines of the piece, is persecuted by the villain Crimalhaz whose creature Hametalhaz oversees her imprisonment and is directed to have her beheaded. The cynical henchman develops a romantic passion for his victim, and in a paroxysm of conscience is suddenly converted from evil to virtuous courses:

> *Mariamnes* Head presented by my Hand!
> I'd first strike his that gives me that Command.

> For since that Beauteous Prisoner was my charge,
> Her charming Image did my Soul enlarge.
> At the approach of so Divine a Guest,
> I've shook my late familiars from my Breast;
> The thoughts of Mischeifs, Villany and Blood,
> By her fair Eyes inspir'd I dare be good.
>
> (V.i)[78]

Later Mariamne can say of Hametalhaz, as her "best of Converts" decorously relinquishes her to a lover of royal station, "A Nobler Passion Story never writ, / That turn'd a Traytor to a Proselyte" (V.ii).[79] The relationship of the characters recalls that of Ferdinand, Bosola, and the Duchess, but it is entirely typical of Settle's more sentimental bent that Hametalhaz's conversion should be prompted by the lady's "charming Image" rather than by the complex moral, psychological, and political factors (including the Duchess's courageous death) that awaken Bosola to himself. Settle ends his play with a spectacle of horror quite beyond anything Webster would or could have managed—a scene that displays the body of Crimalhaz "*cast down on the Gaunches*" and "*hung on a Wall set with spikes of Iron*" (V.ii).[80] An illustration in the original edition shows a collection of hideously contorted and impaled bodies with skulls, bones, and dismembered limbs to garnish the effect. The severed hand and wax effigies of *The Duchess of Malfi* seem restrained by comparison.

Shadwell's *Libertine*, the earliest dramatization in English of the Don Juan story, is an odd compound of tragical, mock epic, and even farcical ingredients. Among many echoes of Shakespeare we find at least one detail that may have been influenced by *The White Devil*. In Act III, Leonora, a former mistress of the Don, pursues him in spite of all his cruelties only to be rewarded for her devotion with death by poison. As she dies, the callous murderer experiences a moment of sympathy for his victim and then quickly stifles it:

> This is the first time I ever knew compassion.
> Poor Fool, I pity her, but tis too late—
> Farewell all sensless thoughts of a remorse,
> I would remove what e'r wou'd stop my course.
>
> (III.i)[81]

Flamineo has a similar moment in Webster's play when he observes his mother's grief for the younger brother whom he has just brutally slain:

> I have a strange thing in me, to th' which
> I cannot give a name, without it be
> Compassion. . . .
>
> (*The White Devil*, V.iv.113–115)

Then, like the Don, Flamineo resists the moral impulse and before long reverts to his cynical ways.

Nathaniel Lee, almost exclusively a writer of tragedies, seems to have been more consistently influenced by Webster than any of his contemporary dramatists. One detects Websterian elements—verbal as well as situational echoes—in no fewer than nine of his thirteen plays; nor do these nine include the two mentioned above, in which Lee was Dryden's collaborator. Often Lee's borrowings are so minor and incidental as to suggest the unconscious use of phrases or metaphors that had been thoroughly assimilated to his own style; sometimes, however, they are too salient to be accounted for on any ground other than deliberate imitation. It is worthy of remark that Lee's plays on ancient and classical subjects are often no less indebted to Webster's two major tragedies than those set in Renaissance France or Italy.

The *Tragedy of Nero* (1674), Lee's earliest work, seems in several details to bear the impress of *The White Devil*. Agripina cries out, "Oh me accurst!" (I.i.121)[82] as she is being led to execution at the behest of her tyrant son—an obvious recollection of Vittoria's "O me accurst" (I.ii.301) spoken in reaction to her mother's denunciation of her union with Bracciano. Later Britanicus responds to an ominous tale related by Cyara with "Thou raisest something in me, which as yet / I cannot give a name to" (III.i.45–46), a sentiment almost certainly based on Flamineo's attack of unaccustomed compassion, which he calls "a strange thing in me, to th' which / I cannot give a name . . ." (V.iv.113–114). There may be further reminiscences of *The White Devil* in Otho's mention of "a thousand Devils, / In Chrystal forms" (II.ii.21–22) and in the funeral dirge for Octavia (III.i.7–25). Bracciano refers to "the devil in crystal" (IV.ii.88) when he is voicing disillusionment with Vittoria, and Cornelia sings a famous dirge over the body of Marcello (V.iv.95–110). These last details are of course partly conventional,[83] but in view of Lee's known attraction to Webster, *The White Devil* would be a likely origin. *Nero* also contains a clear, though contextually regrettable, borrowing from *The Duchess of Malfi*. Cyara, in a couplet based upon the Duchess's desire to "curse the stars . . . nay the world / To its first chaos" (IV.i.96–99), acknowledges the power of the emperor to wreak destruction upon Rome:

> You can do all things, Sir, both drown and burn;
> Nay, the whole World to its first Chaos turn.
>
> (IV.i.63–64)

Britanicus's exclamation in the same scene, "Some whirl-wind snatch me headlong through the Ayr . . ." (IV.i.13), appears to conflate images from Shirley's *Cardinal* and Webster's tragedy: "a whirlwind / Snatch me to endless flames" (*The Cardinal*, IV.ii.287–288), and "men convey'd . . . through the air, / On violent whirlwinds" (*The Duchess of Malfi*, II.v.50–51).

Lee's next play, *Sophonisba, or Hannibal's Overthrow* (1675), deals in exactly such macabre subject matter as brings Webster (and of course Marston, who had also dramatized the story) to mind. Here the verbal indebtedness is less blatant than it was in *Nero*, but all the same we recognize a few Websterian preoccupations. King Massinissa, contemplating the double suicide of himself and Sophonisba by poison avers that he will "in winding-sheets embrace my Bride" (V.i.293), an apparent reminiscence of the proposal scene in which the Duchess of Malfi and her husband-to-be speak quibblingly of giving themselves to each other in "a couple" of winding sheets (I.i.389). The sudden death of Trebellius also carries a suggestion of Webster about it:

> Just Scipio will revenge my death, beware,
> I feel I'm going, though I know not where. [*Dies.*]
>
> (IV.i.243–244)

Here Lee seems to have combined the phrasing of Shakespeare's Claudio in *Measure for Measure* ("to die, and go we know not where" [III.i.117]) with the blood-darkened despair of Vittoria, whose soul "Is driven I know not whither" (*The White Devil*, V.vi.249). The superimposition of sources is entirely typical of Lee.

Gloriana, or the Court of Augustus Caesar (1676), another of Lee's pseudohistories, may again levy upon Webster for a couple of phrases, although other precedents for both could be adduced. Marcellus mentions "death's mist" (IV.i.4), by now of course a cliché, and Gloriana parallels words from Bosola's speech on evil as a "sweet and golden dream" (*The Duchess of Malfi*, IV.ii.324); she prepares to "awaken" the lustful Augustus to reality by plunging a dagger into the man who will lean "upon my Virgin-breast, / In golden dreams expecting boundless bliss . . ." (V.ii.12–13). An impossibly exaggerated variant of the tornado image reappears as well:

> Whirlwinds shall bear thee hot all reeking o're,
> And sweating drops of blood, and round thee blow,
> Then plunge thee in th' Abyss of Ice and Snow.
> (I.i.181–183)

Again in *The Rival Queens* (1677) Lee works into the drama Webster's fascination with extremes of sexual jealousy and with the horror of death as the consummation of desire. Roxana contemplates the attachment of Alexander to her rival Statira with frustrated malice:

> I could behold you kiss without a pang,
> Nay take a Torch, and light you to your Bed:
> But do not trust me, no, for if you do,
> By all the Furies, and the flames of Love,
> By Love, which is the hottest burning Hell,
> I'le set you both on fire to blaze for ever.
> (III.i.312–317)

Although no phrasal borrowing is involved, Lee probably derived the idea of turning erotic heat into literal fire from Ferdinand's fevered ravings about the Duchess of Malfi and her secret lover: "dip the sheets they lie in, in pitch or sulphur, / Wrap them in't, and then light them like a match . . ." (II.v.69–70).[84] And Alexander's death by poison seems to have been partly inspired by the similar mortal agonies of Bracciano, for the great conqueror in his final distraction cries out, like Webster's duke (*The White Devil*, V.iii.167–168), "Victoria, Victoria, / Victoria" (V.i.352–353). In Lee's case the repeated word, taken literally, seems to be a cry of triumph, for Alexander is undergoing hallucinations about his defeat of Darius at this point, but the similarity to Webster's scene is too striking to be accidental.[85]

Lee confessed in the dedication of his next tragedy, *Mithridates, King of Pontus* (1678), that he had "endeavour'd . . . to mix Shakespear with Fletcher";[86] William Van Lennep, discussing the "neo-Elizabethan manner" of the play, suggested that for the incest theme Lee had quite likely been prompted by Ford.[87] Webster, too, may take his place among the contributing influences, though, again, in a very incidental fashion. In a proud statement that recalls the famous "I am Duchess of Malfi still" (IV.ii.142), the Asian emperor of the title asserts his identity as an enemy of the West: "In spight of Rome, I'm Mithridates still" (I.i.228). After a disturbing omen suggests on his wedding day that marriage to Monima is "not pleasing to the Gods" (I.i.287), the lady responds by mingling familiar speeches from two plays by Webster. The mere title of queen, she insists, will be hollow,

A senseless sound, except I am your Love:
I find, I find that I am lost for ever.
I have but slept, charm'd with a golden Dream,
And now am wak'd to beggery again.

(I.i.311–314)

As we have noticed earlier in this account, the "golden dream" image (possibly prompted, despite its proverbial nature, by Bosola's speech of conversion) and "lost for ever" as an expression of devotion (possibly lifted verbatim from *The Devil's Law-Case* or modified slightly from *The White Devil*) had already become popular with both Dryden and Lee. At the catastrophe, Mithridates's son Ziphares stabs his beloved Semandra by mistake in the dark, thinking her to be an enemy (V.ii.280). This Bosola-like situation with its heavy freight of tragic irony had also become something of a favorite in later drama; it will be recalled that Suckling had helped to make it popular by using it in his enormously prestigious *Aglaura* and that Payne had made it the climax of his *Fatal Jealousie*. When Ziphares in turn dies a few minutes after Semandra, we are not surprised to hear him echoing Flamineo: "Death's Myst comes fast upon me" (V.ii.322). *Mithridates* serves as an excellent example of how thoroughly Webster's style had permeated Lee's and how it had become part of the stock-in-trade of a practicing man of the theatre.

Despite the likelihood of influence on account of its subject matter, *The Massacre of Paris* (written in 1678–1679 but not produced until 1689) shows only a few traces of Webster. The most probable debt is the scene in which the Duke of Anjou is assaulted psychologically by being shown the mangled body of his dearest friend, the youth Ligneroles, which is "*held up all bloody*" (IV.i.1). One thinks, of course, of Ferdinand's similar torturing of the Duchess of Malfi by displaying the apparent corpses of her husband and children. Coligny's courageous death may also owe something to Webster. First the admiral enjoins a dying companion to stoic resolve:

stand fixt, and look on Death
With such Contempt, so Masterly an Eye,
As if he were thy Slave.

(V.iv.23–25)

Then he relinquishes his own grasp on life with the same tenacious reluctance as Bracciano in *The White Devil*: "My Soul so likes her house, she's loth to part . . ." (V.iv.44). Webster's duke says something close to this when he is expiring:

O thou strong heart!
There's such a covenant 'tween the world and it,
They're loth to break.

(*The White Devil*, V.iii.13–15)

Nowhere in Lee's dramas is the influence of Websterian tragedy so pervasive as in *Caesar Borgia, Son of Pope Alexander the Sixth* (1679). Since the story Lee chose to dramatize is a gruesome tale of frustrated passion, jealousy, degeneracy, and wholesale murder based on Italian sources that have much in common with Webster's, and since one of the author's purposes was to feed the rabid anti-Catholicism that the affair of Titus Oates had recently aroused, the tapping of the earlier dramatist should cause little surprise. Indeed, Van Lennep, without going into much detail, long ago noticed that, generically at least, Lee was "following in the footsteps of Webster."[88] The play reflects obvious Shakespearean influence as well, particularly that of *Othello* and *King John*, but the depraved world that Lee's characters and situations are meant to convey is clearly more evocative of Webster's than of Shakespeare's Italy. The play is in fact loaded with elements that suggest Lee's intimate knowledge of *The Duchess of Malfi*.

Superficially, many of the characters are parallel. These include a murderous and lustful cardinal, a tool villain of whom it is said "Murder's thy Trade, and Death thy Livelihood" (III.i.14) but who then suffers qualms of conscience, a pair of more or less innocent lovers who are persecuted and killed by an insanely jealous brother, an icy Machiavellian, a guileless child who is cruelly used, and a woman whose tongue is hushed by a gift of poisoned gloves.[89] The incest motif, which Webster had treated subtly and by implication only, becomes explicit in Lee's play where Lucretia is referred to as having excited "with incestuous Fires" (I.i.266) both her father, Pope Alexander, and her two brothers, Caesar and Palante, Duke of Gandia. The historical Machiavelli, who aided Cesare Borgia in his conflict with the Orsini, becomes (as the character Machiavel) a malign controller of the intrigue, a cold, cynical, egotistic blend of wickedness and loyalty. The major emphasis falls on the inflamed struggle between Borgia and his brother Gandia for the love of Bellamira, the fictional daughter of Paul Orsino, and it is here that Webster's masterpiece seems to have had the strongest impact.

Borgia's wild fits of jealousy as he fantasizes about Bellamira's supposed union with his brother resemble the insane speeches of Ferdinand about punishing the Duchess and Antonio:

> I'll joyn 'em Breast to Bosom, stab 'em through,
> And clinch my Dagger on the other side.
>
> (IV.i.155–156)

Earlier Borgia has been warned to control such emotions ("Master this Gothick Fury in your blood" [I.i.563]) just as the Cardinal in Webster's tragedy similarly admonishes his brother: "there is not in nature / A thing that makes man so deform'd, so beastly, / As doth intemperate anger: —chide yourself" (II.v.56–58). And Machiavel arranges for Borgia to surprise the lovers (as Ferdinand surprises his sister) by offering to bring him "With a false Key into the Bridal Lodging" where he may "gaze upon their curst incestuous Loves" (IV.i.230–232). Borgia tortures Bellamira before her execution, as Ferdinand tortures the Duchess, by showing her the corpses of those dear to her—in this case her father and his adherents:

> *Borgia.* Go, draw the Curtain; glut her eyes with Death,
>   And strangle her: my Veins are all on Fire,
>   And I could wade up to the eyes in blood.
>   Draw, draw the Curtain.
>   [*Orsino, Vitellozzo, Duke of Gravina, Oliverotto, appear disguised.*]
> *Bellamira.*   Gorgon, Medusa, Horror;
>   Yet I will shoot through Daggers, rush through flames
>   To clasp him in my armes, O wretched Paul,
>   O noble Orsin, what quite cold? pale, dead?
>   And you, dear Images, will you not give
>   One gasp of breath, one groan, one last farewell?
>
> (V.i.150–158)

Bellamira, like Webster's Duchess, kneels to be strangled and thinks serenely of her final destination:

> if my tortur'd vertue merits glory,
> Pardon my frailties, see with what joy
> I leave this life, and bring me to perfection.
>
> (V.i.180–182)

After the strangling, Borgia, again like Ferdinand, is seized by remorse and, like him also, expresses love for his victim:

> I swear I have been cruel to my self,
> For that I lov'd her, is as true, as she
> Is past the sense on't: she is cold already—
> . . . .
> Her lips are lovely still;
> The Buds, tho gather'd, keep their Damask Colour:
> Yes, and their odour too! haste, Machiavel,
> Rush to my aid: I grow in Love with death.
>
> (V.i.194–202)

The murderer also recriminates with Machiavel as Ferdinand does with Bosola:

> why did I trust thee then?
> Had any softness dwelt in that lean bosom,
> My Bellamira now had been alive. . . .
>
> (V.i.227–229)

Finally, Borgia anticipates madness as the penalty of guilt, the terrible punishment that does indeed overtake Ferdinand:

> no more of Woman tell;
> Name not a Woman, and I shall be well.
> Like a poor Lunatick that makes his moan,
> And for a time beguiles the lookers on;
> He reasons well; his eyes their wildness lose,
> And vows the Keepers his wrong'd sense abuse:
> But if you hit the Cause that hurt his Brain,
> Then his teeth gnash, he foams, he shakes his Chain,
> His Eye-balls rowl, and he is made again.
>
> (V.i.260–268)

Curiously, Lee relies very little on Websterian phrasing in *Caesar Borgia*, possibly because he had so worked himself into the desired idiom that it was unnecessary. When verbal reminiscences do crop up, they seem mostly to come from plays other than *The Duchess of Malfi*. Gandia, for instance, swears vengeance in words that recall Webster when Caesar crosses his romance with Bellamira by forcing the lady into marriage:

> I will revenge the honour thou hast lost:
> Nor shalt thou pass to Bellamira's Arms,
> Till through my heart thou cutt'st thy horrid way.
>
> (III.i.135–137)

Ironically, Gandia's speech echoes an earlier one by Caesar in which the tyrant declares his single-minded desire for his brother's lady:

> the subtle God [of Love] has made his entrance
> Quite through my heart: he shouts and triumphs too,
> And all his Cry is Death, or Bellamira.
>
> (II.i.343–345)

Both passages appear to derive in part (and probably unconsciously) from a speech in *The Devil's Law-Case* ("You have given him the wound . . . Quite through your mother's heart" [III.iii.237–238]) or from a similar one in *A Cure for a Cuckold* ("Oh you have struck him dead thorough my heart" [IV.ii.34]).

A few probable traces of *The White Devil* are also discernible, first when Machiavel rejects the strangling of Adorna in favor of poisoning her with "perfumed" gloves because "this is quainter" (IV.i.305), and, second, when Borgia's death is described in terms of a candle's expiring flame: "The Taper's spent, and this is his last Blaze" (V.iii.335). Bracciano relishes Camillo's murder on the vaulting horse as "quaintly done" (II.ii.38) and then is poisoned and strangled himself by means of a stratagem to which Lodovico applies the same adverb (V.iii.178). The candle metaphor may well be a variation on Flamineo's much quoted "I recover like a spent taper, for a flash / And instantly go out" (V.vi.263–264). The taper simile was, however, by no means unique to Webster in the seventeenth century, and Lee's use of it here does not echo the dramatist's phrasing in the telltale manner of the earlier passages by Richards and Suckling.[90] Whirlwind images, which occur at least twice (III.i.622; IV.i.34) and the thematic juxtaposition of sex with death (for instance, "I will wait you, / To Death or to your Bed—O ill compar'd!" [III.i.601–602]) are further evidences of Websterian imitation. Of course Lee had not Webster's power of ironic understatement or his capacity to probe the psychological complexity of his characters so that *Caesar Borgia* ends by having the furniture of Webster without the sustaining spirit. Nevertheless, Lee was striving as never before for Webster's dark grandeur. That he did not wholly fail may be illustrated by some resolute words of the poisoned Borgia that at least approach Webster's special quality:

> *Machiavel.* Is't possible that you can bear the pangs
>   Of violent poyson, thus unmov'd?
> *Borgia.*   'Tis little
>   To one resolv'd: No let the Coward States-man,
>   Women, and Priests, whine at the thoughts of death;
>   For me, whose mind was ever fierce and active,
>   Death is unwelcom, only for this reason,
>   Because 'tis an Eternal laziness—
>
> (V.iii.235–241)

After *Caesar Borgia*, Lee's attraction to Webster appears to have fallen off. Neither *The Princess of Cleve* nor *Theodosius* (both 1680) show notable similarities to the Jacobean dramatist, and in *Junius Brutus, or the Father of his Country* (also 1680) Lee, by his own admission, had Shakespeare's *Julius Caesar* and Jonson's *Catiline* in mind as models. One possible reminiscence of Webster in Lee's play about the founder of the Roman republic may be mentioned. Brutus alludes to Lucrece's desolation after being raped by

Tarquin: she wept "As if she had lost her wealth in some black Storm" (I.i.98). Lee perhaps remembered the "black storm" (*The White Devil*, V.vi.248) in which the dying Vittoria imagines her soul to be foundering. The only other possible evidence of Webster's influence in the play is a horrific scene of human sacrifice, based on Plutarch, that is certainly Senecan, if not Jacobean, in its sensibility: "*The Scene draws, showing the Sacrifice; One Burning, and another Crucify'd: the Priests coming forward with Goblets in their hands, fill'd with human blood*" (IV.i.102).

Lee's final play, *Constantine the Great* (1683), contains (in the words of Bonamy Dobrée) only "vague reminiscences of Webster . . . which are merely floating references."[91] These consist mostly of images or phrases that had undoubtedly once been associated in Lee's mind with Webster's tragedies but had by now become all but automatic. A traitor is described as "the foul Spring of all these poison'd Waters, / That late had like to overflow the Empire" (I.i.176–177), a fairly prevalent image but one that could have been suggested to Lee by Antonio's comparison of "a prince's court" to a "common fountain" that "Some curs'd example" may "poison" at the source and so spread "*Death, and diseases through the whole land*" (*The Duchess of Malfi*, I.i.11–15). Lycinius, a pagan, defies the power of the Christian emperor with the exclamation, "why let him take my Head" (I.ii.26), which sounds like a borrowing of Lodovico's self-assured "Why took they not my head then?" when Gasparo reminds the count of "certain murders" (*The White Devil*, I.i.31–33).

The fear-wracked villain Arius seems to allude to Ferdinand's fate in *The Duchess of Malfi* when he cries out,

> Oh I could play the Mad-man!
> Men of our Make so poorly hide a Murder,
> That Dogs can Rake it up. Spies, Spies by Hell!
> (II.i.2–4)

Webster's duke distractedly imagines that the body of his sister will be discovered:

> The wolf shall find her grave, and scrape it up:
> Not to devour the corpse, but to discover
> The horrid murder.
> (IV.ii.309–311)

And indeed Cornelia's dirge in *The White Devil* also alludes to the same superstition:

> *But keep the wolf far thence, that's foe to men,*
> *For with his nails he'll dig them up agen.*
> (V.iv.103–104)

Arius also complains that Constantine's brother has brought him to disaster, "to my eternal Ruine" (II.i.17), an apparent echo of Bracciano's charge to Vittoria that she had led him "To my eternal ruin" (IV.ii.91). Serena takes leave of Crispus, saying "I shall never, never see thee more" (IV.i.246), a probable recollection of Ferdinand's farewell to the Duchess of Malfi, "I will never see you more" (III.ii.136).

Finally, the wicked Arius dies in a poisoned bath when his own stratagem to have the empress executed ironically goes amiss. In a desperate attempt to evade his fate, he pretends at the last moment that the bath was after all harmless. As Lee's editors have pointed out, Arius's panicky behavior here is somewhat like that of the Cardinal in *The*

Duchess when his deadly trickery recoils upon and destroys him.[92] Considering his sensationalism and love of the macabre, his themes of seduction, jealousy, revenge, and sexually motivated crime, and his virtually constant imitation of Webster's imagery and phraseology, it would not be unjust to call Nathaniel Lee the Restoration neo-Websterian extraordinary.

After Lee and indeed during the decade of his dramatic productivity, imitation of Webster by Restoration tragedians became virtually a reflex action. As a consequence, it is sometimes difficult to separate specific debts to the Jacobean dramatist from the more generalized influence of what had now become merely traditional. Thomas Otway's early rhymed tragedy *Don Carlos, Prince of Spain* (1676) illustrates the problem. This play is replete with themes and situations assimilated from Elizabethan drama (particularly *Othello*, *The Duchess of Malfi*, and Ford's *Broken Heart*) or from drama that imitated aspects of these, but the indebtedness to Webster is nonverbal and consists chiefly of broad parallels of characterization and atmosphere that may or may not have been inspired by direct contact with the originals. Philip II, who is aroused to criminal jealousy by the queen's fondness for the prince, tortures his wife in a manner that strongly suggests Ferdinand's behavior in Webster's play. He administers a slow-working poison to prolong her sufferings, confines her in a darkened room, appears to her in her death agonies disguised as her lover, and goes mad after her death in a spasm of guilty despair. In his sadism the king employs a spy and tool, Rui-Gomez, who is mainly a recrudescence of Iago but who also recalls Bosola and Flamineo in a few places. The sexual jealousy and the incest motif are superficially Webster-like, but, since the death of Don Carlos (by slow bleeding on stage) seems to be copied from the execution of Orgilus in *The Broken Heart*, it is probable that Otway had a composite Jacobean and Caroline model that merely included the tragedies of Webster.

Webster's influence upon Otway's masterpiece, *Venice Preserved, or a Plot Discovered* (1682), is somewhat easier to document. A reliable editor of the play informs us truly that "The macabre theatrical climax of love, murder, suicide, and madness . . . was inspired" by the Jacobean tragedian.[93] But one can be more specific than this. Jaffeir's conspiratorial friend Pierre is a cynical malcontent whose idealism, poisoned by oppression and vice in high places, reminds us from time to time of Bosola's similarly troubled spirit. Jaffeir, too, takes on some of Bosola's bitterness when Pierre persuades him to join the plot against Venice; the reluctant proselyte's "Tell me which way I must be damned for this" (II.ii.38) sounds as though it had been inspired by Ferdinand's henchman anticipating some new deed of darkness: "Whose throat must I cut?" (*The Duchess of Malfi*, I.i.249). Otway also employs a naked dagger with a symbolism reminiscent of Webster's tragedy. For a pledge of loyalty to his fellow conspirators Jaffeir presents them with his weapon as he turns his beloved Belvidera over to their keeping. The surface meaning is that they should "strike it to her heart" if he should "prove unworthy" of their trust (II.iii.198–199), but the dagger is mentioned later as a love token (V.ii.206) and the threat is not without overtones that express Jaffeir's erotic passion for the lady. Otway uses the dagger to suggest the conflict in his hero between love and politics rather as Webster symbolizes the conflict between sexual desire and hatred in Ferdinand when the duke menaces his sister with his poniard (*The Duchess of Malfi*, III.ii.71).

Later when Belvidera persuades Jaffier to betray his friends, he voices his pain in an image of animal sacrifice that has been elaborated from *The White Devil*:

> Come, lead me forward now like a tame lamb
> To sacrifice. Thus in his fatal garlands,
> Decked fine and pleased, the wanton skips and plays,
> Trots by the enticing flattering priestess' side,
> And much transported with his little pride,
> Forgets his dear companions of the plain,
> Till by her, bound, he's on the altar lain;
> Yet then too hardly bleats, such pleasure's in the pain.
>
> (IV.i.87–94)

This passage represents an extraordinary prettification of Bracciano's anguished cry to Vittoria:

> Thou hast led me, like an heathen sacrifice,
> With music, and with fatal yokes of flowers
> To my eternal ruin.
>
> (*The White Devil*, IV.ii.89–91)

And it will be remembered that Dryden also imitated these lines in *All for Love*.[94]

When the conspirators confront Jaffeir upon discovering him to be the cause of their downfall, one of them echoes another of Webster's famous speeches: "Death's the best thing we ask or you can give" (IV.ii.161). This of course is based on the Duchess of Malfi's definition of death (in reference to her brothers) as "Best gift . . . they can give, or I can take" (IV.ii.225).[95] Ironically, as if half to fulfill Pierre's urging at the start of the play that his friend "Curse [his] dull stars" (I.i.252), Jaffeir in his agony heaps execration upon the entire earth:

> Final destruction seize on all the world!
> Bend down, ye Heavens, and shutting round this earth,
> Crush the vile globe into its first confusion. . . .
>
> (V.ii.93–95)

Both Pierre's and Jaffeir's words seem to be recollections of the passionate hyperbole by Webster's Duchess—as noted elsewhere, much admired in the Restoration: "I could curse the stars . . . nay the world / To its first chaos" (*The Duchess of Malfi*, IV.i.97–99).[96] Otway seems to copy a final touch from Webster's tragedy when Jaffeir parts from Belvidera for the last time before mounting the scaffold:

> We have a child, as yet a tender infant,
> Be a kind mother to him when I am gone,
> Breed him in virtue and the paths of honor. . . .
>
> (V.ii.209–211)

This is obviously more sentimental and less specific than Webster, but one recalls the Duchess of Malfi's similar domesticity before her own execution:

> I pray thee, look thou giv'st my little boy
> Some syrup for his cold, and let the girl
> Say her prayers, ere she sleep.
>
> (IV.ii.203–205)

And there may be a further echo of Antonio's parting words to the Duchess: "Be a good mother to your little ones . . ." (III.v.85). At least in the case of his best-known play, we have convincing evidence that Otway, like Lee, was an admirer and user of Webster.

The most significant and original tragic dramatist of the Restoration after Dryden, Lee, and Otway was probably John Banks. Since he was drawn to historical or quasi-historical subjects and especially given to dramas in which heroines outshine their male counterparts, it is hardly surprising to learn that he too knew and imitated Webster. *Virtue Betrayed, or Anna Bullen* (1682), for instance, pays *The White Devil* the homage of linguistic borrowing. The young queen of the title, who has been forced to break off her engagement to Percy in order to marry Henry VIII, cries out against the dangers and hypocrisies of life at court:

> Ha, *Piercy*! I'm betray'd. Advise me Heav'n!
> What shall I do!—Be gone, this place is Hell. . . .
>   (III.i)[97]

Banks appropriates the final phrase from the scene of Bracciano's strangling to which Vittoria's response is "O me! this place is hell" (V.iii.179). It is easy to see why, for both contexts involve the separation and frustration of lovers. Like Anna, Percy is forced into a marriage of politics rather than of love, and he anticipates his unhappy union with Lady Diana Talbot in rhetoric that also derives, though more vaguely, from the same play:

> Then turn us loose, like two Condemn'd, lone Wretches;
> Banisht from Earth, no Creature but our selves,
> In an old Bark on wide and Desart Seas,
> In Storms by Night and Day, unseen by all,
> Unpity'd tost, not one dear Morsel with us
> To ease our Hunger, nor one drop of Drink
> To quench our raging Thirst, and which is worse,
> Without one jot of Rigging, Sail, or Steer to guide us.
>   (III.i)[98]

Here Banks seems to have incorporated Lodovico's explosive opening speech, "Banish'd?" (I.i.1) with Vittoria's famous death: "My soul, like to a ship in a black storm, / Is driven I know not whither" (V.vi.248–249). Characteristically, the Restoration tragedian softens and extends the imagery of isolation at sea in such a way as to substitute mere self-indulgent pathos for Webster's dignified metaphysical pessimism.

At the tragic conclusion, just before King Henry orders Anna and Lords Norris and Rochford beheaded, the monarch stumbles momentarily upon an unaccustomed sensation of fellow feeling for his victims:

> Dispatch my Orders straight, and fetch the Traytors—
> What's this that gives my Soul a sudden Twitch?
> And bids me not proceed. Ha! is't Compassion!
> Shall Pity ever fond the Breast of *Harry*!
> 'Tis but a slip of Nature, and I'le on.
>   (V.i)[99]

Again Banks, like Shadwell and Lee before him, appears to have remembered Flamineo's sudden attack of pity before the young cynic consents to involve himself in the horrors of the final act:

> I have a strange thing in me, to th' which
> I cannot give a name, without it be
> Compassion. . . .
> . . . .
> This is beyond melancholy.
> I do dare my fate
> To do its worst. Now to my sister's lodging,
> And sum up all these horrors. . . .
>
> (V.iv.113–146)

Banks had already treated another aspect of Tudor history in *The Unhappy Favourite, or, The Earl of Essex* (1681). This play makes much of the popular legend (alluded to in *The Devil's Law-Case*) that Queen Elizabeth's ring would have saved Essex's life had it not fallen into enemy hands. One of the condemned hero's lines, "Abhor all Courts if thou art brave and wise . . ." (III.i),[100] recalls Antonio's dying sentiment, "let my son fly the courts of princes" (*The Duchess of Malfi*, V.iv.72), but, otherwise, the tragedy is bare of Websterian echoes.

Banks's *The Island Queens, or the Death of Mary, Queen of Scotland* (originally composed in 1684 but forbidden the stage, then altered and retitled *The Albion Queens* in 1704) does seem to take a few stylistic hints from Webster. Bosola's description of the Duchess of Malfi's behavior in her imprisonment,

> so noble
> As gives a majesty to adversity;
> You may discern the shape of loveliness
> More perfect in her tears, than in her smiles. . . .
>
> (IV.i.5–8),

may have suggested to Banks Douglas's similar praise of Queen Mary as she is being temporarily released from confinement:

> You are so good, so perfect and so fair.
> Beauty and sorrow never were so nigh
> A Kin in any but in you. . . .
>
> (II.i)[101]

Also in the next act, when Gifford stares pointedly at Davison, the latter reacts in language suggestive of Webster:

> What art thou that has haunted me so long?
> Thou look'st as if thou mean'st to draw my Picture. . . .
>
> (III.i)[102]

Bosola greets the Cardinal with "I do haunt you still" (*The Duchess of Malfi*, I.i.29), and Francisco in *The White Devil* says of Isabella's ghost,

> methinks she stands afore me;
> And by the quick idea of my mind,
> Were my skill pregnant, I could draw her picture.
> (IV.i.104–106)[103]

We might expect that for *The Innocent Usurper, or the Death of Lady Jane Gray* (published in 1694 but written a decade earlier), Banks would pillage *Sir Thomas Wyatt*, Webster and Dekker's all but forgotten play on the same subject. There is, however, no evidence, verbal or otherwise, that he knew the Jacobean text, and it is curiously in his exotic *Cyrus the Great, or the Tragedy of Love* (1695) that Banks's use of Webster is most striking.

This drama is a tissue of frustrated passions (especially those of the lovers Panthea and Abradatas) furnished with enough "carv'd Limbs and mangled Bodies" (V.i)[104] to make of the stage a virtual abattoir. Of course the fascination with *disjecta membra* in the theatre derives ultimately from Seneca's long speeches of horrific description, and indeed Rothstein traces one of Banks's most sensational scenes to the Roman poet's *Hippolytus*.[105] Plays such as *Cambyses* and *Titus Andronicus*, with their accumulation of sanguinary outrages, also contributed to the tradition. But it is clear that Webster's staged horrors influenced Banks importantly as well. There is a curious obsession with severed hands in *Cyrus the Great* that almost certainly owes much to the famous scene of *The Duchess of Malfi* in which Ferdinand cruelly surprises his sister in the dark by giving her a dead man's hand to kiss (IV.i.42–45). When King Cyrus condemns Abradatas to death, Panthea runs to seize her lover's hand, refusing to be separated from him:

> Come bear him to his Fate—By Constancy,
> I vow this Hand shall go along with him,
> Nor all your Torments, Pincers, nor Devices
> Shall wrench these Knots asunder; no, unless
> You cut this off, so you may part our Bodies,
> But then my Spirits shall retire that moment,
> Flying to th' part that's nearest to my Love,
> And my lost Hand shall hold him still thus fast,
> And Perish with him as the Body wou'd.
> (IV.i)[106]

Later, when Abradatas together with many others has been ripped to pieces by scythed chariots, we see a suicidal Panthea grieving over his corpse, which she has lovingly reassembled from the carnage, the "*Limbs . . . seemingly fix'd to his Body*" (V.i)[107] as the stage directions specify. Just as Panthea stabs herself, Cyrus enters and remorsefully kisses the hand of Abradatas, only to experience the same ghastly surprise as Webster's Duchess:

> *Cyrus.*   O forgive me, blest *Panthea*;
> ·
> And tell him how I took his hand in mine,
> Wash'd with thy Tears, and bath'd in my Repentance,
> And put it to my eager Lips, and ask'd
> His pardon thus——Ha! Horror! Worse than Horror.

> [Cyrus *taking* Abradatas' *hand, offering to put it to his*
> *mouth, it comes from the Body*; Panthea *places it again.*]
> *Panthea.* What have you done? Why touch you him so rudely?
> Give me this Hand back to my Lips again—
> These marvellous Limbs with industry I sought
> Admidst an hundred heaps of mangl'd Bodies,
> And pick'd and cull'd em, as is sifted Gold
> Parted from loads of common Dross;
> And plac'd each torn-off Member in its proper state,
> Just as you see—Forbear again to touch him. . . .
>
> (V.i.)[108]

Not content with this excess, Banks adds yet a further nightmarish detail, the description of an ominous vision in which a deity writes with "A Bloody Hand" whose "Finger . . . distill'd warm Gore" (V.i).[109] Nothing so much as this fixation on mutilated hands better illustrates the tendency of Banks and his age to combine horror with sentimentality and utterly to dissipate Webster's concentrated effects of psychic shock and ironic symbolism by extending and coarsening them. Moreover, we can hardly be astonished by any enormity in a play whose opening curtain discloses a battlefield *"cover'd with dead Bodies"* and in which *"A dead Carkass of one of the slain rises"* (I.i) and speaks.[110]

A number of phrasal and imagistic similarities to Webster confirm him as one of Banks's important sources. King Croesus, threatened with execution, for instance, echoes the popular "I am Duchess of Malfi still" (IV.ii.142): "Yet in / Despite of all thou canst, I'm *Croesus* still" (II.i).[111] Cyrus, addressing the ghost of a lady he has driven mad by refusing her love, cries

> Ha! Thou art fled, and hid
> As in a mist, thou dazelest every Sense,
> And mak'st thy *Cyrus* giddy to behold thee.
> (V.i)[112]

Here Banks appears to amalgamate Webster's distinctive death-mist imagery with Ferdinand's often quoted "Cover her face: mine eyes dazzle: she died young" (*The Duchess of Malfi*, IV.ii.264). And a little later he probably levies on the same speech when Queen Thomyris gives orders for the final disposition of Panthea's and Abradatas's corpses:

> cover the Bodies from their Eyes,
> Then in a Mourning Chariot place the Bridegroom,
> And his pale Bride so leaning on his Cheek—
> (V.i)[113]

Panthea's indignant "What, can't I be obey'd in Death?" (V.i)[114] recalls Vittoria's even more assertive "I will be waited on in death . . ." (*The White Devil*, V.vi.217), and the text contains at least two instances of whirlwind imagery, a favorite with Webster.

Banks's idea of exploiting Webster's detail of the severed hand for pathetic effect had already been anticipated a year earlier by Thomas Southerne in *The Fatal Marriage, or The Innocent Adultery* (1694). Indeed, the passage from *Cyrus* (quoted above) in which Panthea protests her unwillingness to part from her lover may really be Banks's imitation of a speech in Southerne's drama. Isabella, torn between the claims of two husbands (the first having supposedly died and then reappeared), agonizes hyperbolically,

> They rack, they tear; let 'em carve out my limbs,
> Divide my body to their equal claims. . . .
>
> (V.i)[115]

Then later in the same scene, after the earlier spouse has been killed in a street brawl, Isabella must be forcibly separated from the corpse:

> O, they tear me! Cut off my Hands,
> Let me leave something with him,
> They'll clasp him fast—. . . .
>
> (V.i)[116]

Some time ago, Allardyce Nicoll noted that such passionate exclamations "remind us of Ford and Webster at their best."[117] Whether or not we can agree with the qualifying phrase, "at their best," Nicoll's main assertion rings true. As if to corroborate this hint of Websterian inspiration in *The Fatal Marriage*, we find a few additional Websterian features at the conclusion. Isabella madly raves and hallucinates like Webster's Ferdinand, and, like him too, she does so partly for reasons of sexual guilt. Then, like the Duchess of Malfi, she shows motherly concern for her child when she approaches death.

Mary de la Rivière Manley, obviously impressed by the sensationalism of Banks's *Cyrus*, copied with only slight variations the idea of a bereaved lady collecting the scattered remains of her lover. In Mrs. Manley's *The Royal Mischief* (1696), the villain Osman suffers execution by being stuffed into the mouth of a cannon and blown up, whereupon his wife Selima, in her grief and madness, is described as she "ranges the fatal Plain, / Gathering the smoaking Relicks of her Lord," heaping the fragments into a pile, and "bestowing burning Kisses / And Embraces on every fatal piece" (V.i).[118] Mrs. Manley, although undoubtedly prompted by Banks, was clearly drawing on the Webster tradition. Her play is a heady mixture of the Websterian themes of adultery, lust, incest, murder, and revenge. More importantly, she focuses at the end (like Webster) on the ironic juxtaposition of love and death and on the idea of psychic dislocation. But her effect is typically un-Websterian because she literalizes and sentimentalizes so nauseatingly. Webster's Duchess under terrible duress can imagine herself "fly[ing] in pieces" "like to a rusty o'ercharg'd cannon" (III.v.105–106), an ironic anticipation, as it were, of her horrible surprise with the severed hand. But Mrs. Manley's brand of horror—making love to a pile of human fragments—belongs to a different and altogether more decadent sensibility. The dilettante lady all but confesses her dependence on contemporary and earlier playwrights in her self-effacing epistle of dedication: "I have unenvied, read and admir'd, the Eminent Poets of our Age; I durst not once presume to hope, my Pen shou'd ever equal the least of them; but when thus employ'd, methinks the Eloquence of both ancient and modern, are too faint representatives; I cou'd (by a noble Ambition) wish them all united in me. . ." (sig. A2ᵛ).

Although *The Conspiracy, or the Change of Government* (1680) by William Whitaker contains no verbal borrowings from Webster, the play is nevertheless a pastiche of Websterian effects and atmosphere that reminds us of Killigrew's *Imperial Tragedy* and Aphra Behn's *Forc'd Marriage*. A skeleton appears on stage to personify death, and a

"Heavenly Shape" descends "in the Clouds" (III.i)[119] to sing a Webster-like dirge for a murdered man in octasyllabic couplets. Whitaker includes an elaborate stage direction at the end that seems to draw many of its details in compressed form from the climactic fourth act of *The Duchess of Malfi*:

a Room hung all with black; . . . several of the Royal Party are plac'd in Order, with Coffins before them, on which stand a dim Taper, and Mutes standing ready as to strangle them; then Enter eight or ten Blackmoors, drest like Fiends, and dance an Antic; having done, they go out, and after fearful groans and horrid Shriekings; some of them return with burnt Wine, which they fill out in Sculls to the King's Friends, who, as fast as they drink, dy: at which the Queen and all the rest seem pleas'd.

(V.i)[120]

John Bancroft and Edward Ravenscroft are chiefly notable for their obsessive imitation of Shakespeare. But Webster—or at least the popular Webster conventions—are also discernible in their drama. Neo-chronicle plays on medieval English kings were Bancroft's specialty. Both of his works in this genre attest to his familiarity with the non-Shakespearean drama of the Renaissance. His *King Edward the Third, with the Fall of Mortimer Earl of March* (1690) contains (not surprisingly) a few reminiscences of Marlowe; his *Henry the Second, King of England, with the Death of Rosamond* (1692) echoes Webster. In the latter work, Henry's mistress yields to his persuasions in words that recall Bracciano's infatuation with Vittoria;

> Oh I am lost!
> My thirsty Soul drinks up his Words,
> And, pleas'd with the rich Philtre, craves for more.
> (II.ii)[121]

Later, confronted by the jealous queen, Rosamond repeats the phrase in its grimmer but equally Websterian sense:

> *Rosamond.* Oh, I am lost!
> *Queen.*　　　Thou art indeed:
> But my Revenge is starv'd. . . .
> (III.i)[122]

Bancroft also introduces the familiar mist imagery when Rosamond dies: "A sudden mist intrudes upon my sight, / My Limbs grow numb . . ." (V.iii).[123]

Ravenscroft's *Titus Andronicus, or the Rape of Lavinia* (1679?), a reworking of Shakespeare's play in a manner more sensationally bloody than the original, includes a grotesque tableau that seems to owe something to the spectacular staging of the Duchess of Malfi's confrontation with the apparently executed bodies of her husband and children: "*A Curtain drawn discovers the heads and hands of* Dem[etrius] *and* Chir[on] *hanging up against the wall. Their bodys in Chairs in bloody Linnen*" (V.i).[124] But *The Italian Husband* (1697) is Ravenscroft's attempt, as his "Praelude" informs us, to write "in the stile of the *Italian* Tragedies."[125] Consequently, the play teems with vague reminiscences of Jacobean and Caroline tragedy. Apart from the obvious and predictable parallels to *Othello*, Ravenscroft shows us a duchess whose secret amours with her lover are rudely interrupted by her husband and whose cruel punishment for adultery is foreshadowed first by her dressing "*in black*" and "*leaning on a Deaths head*" (II.i)[126] and later by her discovery of the lover's corpse in a bed to which the duke, pretending both forgiveness and erotic excitement, has lured her. (Alphonso, the lover, has been trapped in a mechanical chair during a banquet, presented emblematically with a "brace of Deaths heads" [III.ii],[127] and then poisoned.) After strangling his unfaithful duchess, the duke completes the symmetry of his savage justice by placing the two cadavers in bed together, after which he retires unscathed to a monastery to do penance for his monstrous retribution. Like Flamineo in *The White Devil*, the Italian husband experiences a moment of human tenderness before harsher values get the better of him, and, like Ferdinand in *The Duchess of Malfi*, he is moved by the beauty of the woman he has murdered:

> Behold how Beauty still revels in her Cheeks,
> And gets the Victory o're Death and my Revenge.
> Soft Compassion creeps into my Soul,
> And I cou'd now forget my Injuries.
> But let the noble sense of Honour drive it out:
> Hence then all tender thoughts, and foolish pity.
>
> (III.ii)[128]

Ravenscroft's play reads almost like a parody of the most morbid and sensational elements in Webster's two Italian tragedies—especially, of course, *The Duchess of Malfi*—stirred together in a potpourri of similar details or episodes from such dramas as *The Revenger's Tragedy*, *The Second Maiden's Tragedy*, Ford's *Broken Heart*, Massinger's *Duke of Milan*, and Shirley's *Traitor*. But in a late play like *The Italian Husband*, it has become virtually impossible to disentangle genuine Websterian influence from a generalized taste for extravagant neo-Jacobean admixtures of sex and horror.

Our long list of tragedies that show the impact of Webster comes to an end with William Congreve's *The Mourning Bride* (1697), in its own day the author's most popular play. Apart from its general and obvious indebtedness to Jacobean drama, the tragedy's most celebrated passage, singled out by Dr. Johnson as perhaps "the most poetical paragraph" in "the whole mass of English poetry," imitates Webster significantly.[129] The romantic heroine, Almeria, accompanied by her friend Leonora, visits a tomb to mourn her supposedly dead husband, just as Antonio, attended by Delio, visits what is apparently the grave of his wife, the Duchess of Malfi. Although the verbal debt (if any) is slight and probably unconscious, and perhaps indeed *because* of this distance (the two scenes share only a few of the same words—"reverend," "ancient," "echo," "bones," "face"), Congreve's passage evokes a sepulchral atmosphere of gloom, mystery, and terror that is strikingly close to Webster's effect:

> *Almeria.* No, all is hush'd, and still as Death—'Tis dreadful!
> How rev'rend is the Face of this tall Pile,
> Whose antient Pillars rear their Marble Heads,
> To bear aloft its arch'd and pond'rous Roof,
> By its own Weight, made stedfast, and immoveable,
> Looking Tranquility. It strikes an Awe
> And Terror on my aking Sight; the Tombs
> And Monumental Caves of Death, look Cold,

And shoot a Chilness to my trembling Heart.
Give me thy Hand, and speak to me, nay, speak,
And let me hear thy Voice;
My own affrights me with its Echo's.
Leonora. Let us return; the Horrour of this Place
And Silence, will encrease your Melancholy.
Almeria. It may my Fears, but cannot add to that.
No, I will on: shew me *Anselmo*'s Tomb,
Lead me o'er Bones and Skulls, and mouldring Earth
Of Humane Bodies; for I'll mix with them,
Or wind me in the Shroud of some pale Coarse
Yet green in Earth. . . .

(II.i.58–77)[130]

The corresponding scene in *The Duchess of Malfi* is too long to quote entire, but its opening speeches with their description of the echo and their philosophical reflections on man-made architecture (although Webster stresses its transience rather than its permanence) exemplify the similarity of mood:

Delio. Yon's the cardinal's window:—this fortification
Grew from the ruins of an ancient abbey;
And to yon side o'th' river, lies a wall,
Piece of a cloister, which in my opinion
Gives the best echo that you ever heard,
So hollow, and so dismal, and withal
So plain in the distinction of our words,
That many have suppos'd it is a spirit
That answers.
Antonio.   I do love these ancient ruins:
We never tread upon them but we set
Our foot upon some reverend history.
And questionless, here in this open court,
Which now lies naked to the injuries
Of stormy weather, some men lie interr'd
Lov'd the church so well, and gave so largely to't,
They thought it should have canopy'd their bones
Till doomsday; but all things have their end:
Churches and cities, which have diseases like to men,
Must have like death that we have.
Echo.   *Like death that we have.*
Delio. Now the echo hath caught you:
Antonio.   It groan'd methought, and gave
A very deadly accent.
Echo.   *Deadly accent.*

(V.iii.1–21)

That Congreve did have Webster's play somewhere at the back of his mind is confirmed by the appearance some forty lines later of a characteristically Websterian phrase: Alphonso, Almeria's beloved, is referred to as "that wretched thing" (II.ii.35). In *The Duchess of Malfi* Bosola calls Antonio "that wretched thing" (V.ii.144), and in fact Webster applies variants of this locution to people no fewer than four additional times in close proximity to the echo scene.[131] A few incidental details from *The Mourning Bride* are also suggestive. Congreve may have tapped Webster, although again probably unconsciously, for such lines as Osmyn's "Then, bear me in a Whirl-wind to my Fate . . ." (II.ii.140) and Almeria's "Oh I am lost—" (IV.i.299). Nor can an attentive reader miss the Webster-like horrors, by now of course a staple of the genre—Almeria's distracted vision, for instance, of "a grizled, pale / And ghastly Head . . . all smear'd with Blood . . . and after it . . . a damp, dead Hand . . ." (IV.i.387–390). Additional effects include the ominous presence of mute stranglers and the display onstage of a headless corpse that Queen Zara mistakes for the body of the man she loves.

It seems bizarre to associate the polished craftsman of *The Way of the World* with the grotesqueries of Webster and the traditions of love tragedy that Webster did so much to promote. But *The Mourning Bride* is simply a final illustration of how influential a play like *The Duchess of Malfi* remained even at the end of the seventeenth century. Oscar Wilde's epigram that "imitation is the compliment mediocrity pays to genius" has its obvious limitations, for playwrights of stature—among them Fletcher, Middleton, Ford, Shirley, Wycherley, Dryden, Lee, Otway, and Congreve—did in fact follow where Webster had led. Nevertheless, they could hardly have done so had they not perceived in Webster a "genius" for effective language and action in the theatre. Like Shakespeare, Webster turned out to be one of those burdens of the past whom many dramatists were not free to ignore. And, if the critical test of cultural authority, as Morton Bloomfield has implied,[132] is the *Nachleben* that a poet continues to live as embodied, whether consciously or not, in the language of posterity—a language he himself has uniquely enriched and helped to shape—Webster may well have ranked, at least for seventeenth-century tragedians, next below Shakespeare.

NOTES

PART I

1. See Mary Edmond, "In Search of John Webster," *Times Literary Supplement* (24 December 1976), pp. 1621–1622. Mark Eccles, prompted by Edmond's article, contributed some additional data in a letter to the *TLS* (21 January 1977), p. 71, and Edmond followed up with still more information in two further letters: *TLS* (11 March 1977), p. 272; (24 October 1980), p. 1201. M. C. Bradbrook in *John Webster, Citizen and Dramatist* (London: Weidenfeld and Nicolson, 1980) has reconstructed a lively but highly speculative picture of Webster's education as well as of the local influences upon his career.

2. Edmond, "In Search of John Webster," p. 1621.

3. Jean Robertson and D. J. Gordon, eds., *A Calendar of Dramatic Records in the Books of the Livery Companies of London, 1485–1640; Collections*, III (Oxford: The Malone Society, 1954), 60.

4. This suggestion was originally Leslie Hotson's; see Edmond, "In Search of John Webster," p. 1621 (n. 32).

5. Ibid., p. 1622 (n. 42).

6. Ibid., p. 1621 (n. 14).

7. *Historical Manuscripts Commission: Report on the Manuscripts of . . . Reginald Rawdon Hastings, Esq.* (London: His Majesty's Stationery Office, 1928), I, 373.

8. Mark Eccles, "John Webster," *TLS* (21 January 1977), p. 71; Mary Edmond, "John Webster," *TLS* (11 March 1977), p. 272.

9. R. G. Howarth, "Two Notes on John Webster," *Modern Language Review*, 63 (1968), 786.

10. Edmond, "In Search of John Webster," p. 1622 (n. 42).

11. See Hans Hartleb, *Deutschlands Erster Theaterbau* (Berlin and Leipzig: Walter de Gruyter & Co., 1936), pp. 27–28; also E. K. Chambers, *The Elizabethan Stage* (Oxford: Clarendon Press, 1923), II, 277–279.

12. Thomas Hall, *Histrio-Mastix, A Whip for Webster . . .* , in Hall's *Vindiciae Literarum* (London, 1654), sigs. O, O3ᵛ.

13. J. P. Collier, ed., *The Alleyn Papers* (London: The Shakespeare Society, 1843), pp. 14–15; G. F. Warner verifies the document in his *Catalogue of the Manuscripts and Muniments of Alleyn's College of God's Gift at Dulwich* (London, Longmans, Green, and Co., 1881), p. 127.

14. See R. A. Foakes and R. T. Rickert, eds., *Henslowe's Diary* (Cambridge: Cambridge University Press, 1961), Appendix I, p. 273.

15. Ibid., p. 6. Joan Woodward, Henslowe's stepdaughter, married Edward Alleyn 22 October 1592.

16. Warner, *Catalogue of the Manuscripts . . . of Alleyn's College*, p. 51.

17. See C. M. Clode, *Memorials of the Guild of Merchant Taylors* (London: Harrison and Sons, 1875), p. 596. Clode, however, misidentifies John Webster senior with the dramatist.

18. R. T. D. Sayle, *Lord Mayors' Pageants of the Merchant Taylors' Company in the 15th, 16th, and 17th Centuries* (London: Eastern Press, 1931), p. 82; Robertson and Gordon, eds., *A Calendar of Dramatic Records*, p. 69.

19. Clode, *Memorials of the Guild of Merchant Taylors*, pp. 149, 172.

20. Edmond, "In Search of John Webster," p. 1621 (n. 32); also see n. 4 above.

21. F. L. Lucas, ed., *Works*, III, 260.

22. John Russell Brown, ed., *The White Devil*, p. 187.

23. Lucas, ed., *Works*, IV, 42–43.

24. See Edmond, "Webster's Wife," *TLS* (24 October 1980), p. 1201; also Edmond, "John Webster," *TLS* (11 March 1977), p. 272.

25. Eccles, "John Webster," *TLS* (21 January 1977), p. 71.

26. Edmond, "John Webster," p. 272.

27. Edmond, "Webster's Wife," p. 1201.

28. Edmond, "John Webster," p. 272.

29. Margery Pate died in 1617; see Edmond, "In Search of John Webster," p. 1622 (n. 60); also Eccles, "John Webster," p. 71; also Henry F. Waters, *Genealogical Gleanings in England* (Boston: New England Historic Genealogical Society, 1901), line 327.

30. Lucas, ed., *Works*, III, 313, 315, 320–321.

31. Howarth, "Two Notes on John Webster," p. 786; also see Edmond, "In Search of John Webster," p. 1622 (n. 43).

32. It is interesting that John Gore was himself "born free" of the Merchant Taylors. He took out his freedom in the company by patrimony on 22 June 1590 and was elected sheriff, one of the usual stepping stones to the Lord Mayorship, in 1615, the same year the dramatist became free.

33. Sayle, *Lord Mayors' Pageants of the Merchant Taylors' Company*, pp. 110–111; Robertson and Gordon, eds., *A Calender of Dramatic Records*, p. 107.

34. Sayle, *Lord Mayors' Pageants of the Merchant Taylors' Company*, p. 117.

35. Edmond, "In Search of John Webster," p. 1621 (n. 8).

36. Ibid., p. 1622 (n. 50).

37. Ibid., p. 1622.

38. Ibid., p. 1622 (n. 45).

39. Ibid., p. 1622 (n. 47).

40. Ibid., p. 1622 (n. 49). Also see E. K. Chambers, *William Shakespeare: A Study of Facts and Problems* (Oxford: Clarendon Press, 1930), II, 154–159.

41. C. M. Clode, *The Early History of the Guild of Merchant Taylors* (London: Harrison and Sons, 1888), I, 66.

42. See the manuscript *Merchant Taylors' Accounts*, XIII, folio 6, at Merchant Taylors' Hall; Howarth, "Two Notes on John Webster," p. 786; Sayle, *Lord Mayors' Pageants of the Merchant Taylors' Company*, p. 118.

43. Edmond, "In Search of John Webster," p. 1622 (n. 18).

44. Ibid., p. 1622.

45. Ibid., p. 1622 (n. 54).

46. Robert Latham and William Matthews, eds., *The Diary of Samuel Pepys* (Berkeley and Los Angeles: University of California Press, 1970–83), IX, 352.

47. Edmond, "In Search of John Webster," p. 1622.

48. See Mary Edmond, "New Light on Jacobean Painters," *Burlington Magazine*, 118 (February 1976), 79; also Edmond, "In Search of John Webster," p. 1622 (n. 46).

49. L. W. C., *A Very Perfect Discourse and Order How to Know the Age of a Horse, and the Diseases That Breed in Him with the Remedies to Cure the Same . . .* (1601); *A Strange Report of Six Most Notorious Witches, Who by Their Diuelish Practices Murdred Aboue the Number of Foure Hundred Small Children: Besides the Great Hurtes They Committed Vpon Diuers Other People . . .* (1601).

50. R. B. McKerrow, gen. ed., *A Dictionary of Printers and Booksellers in England, Scotland and Ireland, and of Foreign Printers of English Books, 1557–1640* (London: Blades, East & Blades, 1910), p. 288.

51. Edmond, "In Search of John Webster," p. 1622 (n. 54).

52. Ibid., p. 1622 (n. 51).

53. Ibid., p. 1622 (n. 40).

54. For Okes's collaboration with George Eld and William White, see Peter W. M. Blayney, *The Texts of "King Lear" and their Origins: Volume I, Nicholas Okes and the First Quarto* (Cambridge: Cambridge University Press, 1982), p. 295. Blayney quotes Heywood's praise of Okes (from *An Apology for Actors*, sigs. G4-G4^v), p. 294.

55. Edmond, "In Search of John Webster," p. 1622.

56. Ibid., p. 1622 (n. 59).

57. Edmond, "John Webster," p. 272.

58. John Stow, *A Survey of London*, ed. C. L. Kingsford (Oxford: Clarendon Press, 1908), II, 33.

59. C. H. Cooper and T. Cooper, *Athenae Cantabrigienses* (Cambridge: Deighton, Bell, and Co., 1861), II, 546. Also see Henry B. Wheatley, *London, Past and Present: Its History, Associations, and Traditions* (London: John Murray, 1891), III, 230. Wheatley cites two contemporary letters bearing on the event.

60. C. H. Herford and Percy and Evelyn Simpson, eds., *Ben Jonson* (Oxford: Clarendon Press, 1925–52), VIII, 88–89.

61. Edmond, "In Search of John Webster," p. 1621. Edmond also cites an "exceptionally detailed subsidy roll" for the parish, listing in 1641 "some fourteen-hundred families (well over four-thousand names, in general not including children)" (p. 1622, n. 57).

62. *The Devil Is an Ass*, in C. H. Herford and Percy and Evelyn Simpson, eds., *Ben Jonson*, VI, 268; *Bartholomew Fair*, ed. E. A. Horsman (London: Methuen, 1960), p. 13.

63. The quoted words are from Mary Edmond's characterization of a document to which Mark Eccles originally drew attention. See Eccles, "John Webster," p. 71, and Edmond, "John Webster," p. 272.

64. The references to Pie Corner and Ruffians' Hall are both quoted by C. H. Herford and Percy and Evelyn Simpson in *Ben Jonson*, X, 55, and IX, 648.

65. Fredson Bowers, ed., *The Dramatic Works of Thomas Dekker* (Cambridge: Cambridge University Press, 1953–68), I, 324.

66. C. H. Herford and Percy and Evelyn Simpson, eds., *Ben Jonson*, X, 185–186.

67. E. A. Horsman, ed., *Bartholomew Fair*, p. 18.

68. Howarth, "Two Notes on John Webster," p. 786 (n. 6).

69. Edmond, "In Search of John Webster," p. 1622 (n. 43).

70. William Kent, ed., *An Encyclopaedia of London* (London: J. M. Dent, 1970), p. 108.

71. Ibid., p. 256. Also see the enlarged edition of Stow's *Survey of London* (London, 1633), pp. 419–420.

72. Hugh Peters, *A Dying Father's Last Legacy to an Onely Child* (London, 1660), p. 100.

73. Quoted from a Rawlinson manuscript (B158.166) at the Bodleian Library, Oxford, in G. H. Salter, *A Watcher at the City Gate for Thirty-Eight Reigns* (London: Hodder and Stoughton, 1956), p. 116. Salter's book is a useful history of the fabric and traditions of St. Sepulchre's Church.

74. A. H. Bullen, ed., *The Works of Thomas Middleton* (London: John C. Nimmo, 1885–86), VIII, 25.

75. Edmond, "New Light on Jacobean Painters," p. 79.

76. Ibid., p. 78 (n. 34).

77. Ibid., pp. 74 (nn. 14 and 15), 79.

78. Ibid., p. 74.

79. Francis Meres, *Palladis Tamia; Wit's Treasury* (London, 1598), sig. Oo7.

80. Edmond, "New Light on Jacobean Painters," pp. 74, 80.

81. Edmond, "In Search of John Webster," pp. 1621, 1622 (n. 31).

82. Ibid., p. 1622 (n. 62). Also see C. J. Sisson, *Lost Plays of Shakespeare's Age* (Cambridge: Cambridge University Press, 1936), p. 92.

83. Another signature of John Webster senior survives on the will of the printer Ninian Newton, whose house was in Elliot's (or Ellis) Court (marked g 68 on the Ogilby-Morgan map), running westward off Little Old Bailey in the southern region of St. Sepulchre's parish, and who died early in 1590/91. Newton printed an edition of Caesar's *Commentaries* (1585), Rembert Dodoens's *A New Herball* (1586), and other classical and religious books. According to Edmond, Webster senior served as "overseer and signed as a witness," while his wife Elizabeth (the playwright's mother) also "made her mark" as a witness. See Edmond, "In Search of John Webster," pp. 1621, 1622 (n. 34).

84. Edmond prints a photograph of these signatures in her "New Light on Jacobean Painters," p. 81. For the quotations from the Salisbury petition and additional information about the signatories, see Edmond, "In Search of John Webster," p. 1621. "Raphe Smyth" was admitted to the privilege of wearing Merchant Taylor livery in connection with a fund drive for Sir Robert Lee's mayoral celebration in 1602. In 1603 the Merchant Taylors assessed him for expenses "towardes the chardgs of the pageants, entended against the Kings Coronation." See Clode, *Memorials of the Guild of Merchant Taylors*, pp. 589–591, 598.

85. C. M. Clode, *The Early History of the Guild of Merchant Taylors*, I, 159–160.

86. Ibid., I, 388–389.

87. Ibid., I, 160.

88. Ibid., I, 389.

89. Anon., *A True Report of the Araignment, tryall, conuiction, and condemnation, of a Popish Priest, named Robert Drewrie . . . Also the tryall and death of Humphrey Lloyd . . .* (London, 1607), sigs. B4-B4ᵛ.

90. Wheatley, *London, Past and Present*, III, 229.

91. Clode, *The Early History of the Guild of Merchant Taylors*, I, 160.

92. Salter reproduces a photograph of the handbell in *A Watcher at the City Gate for Thirty-Eight Reigns*, p. 42. A portrait of Dowe by an unknown artist is reproduced in Frederick M. Fry, *A Historical Catalogue of the Pictures, Herse-Cloths, and Tapestry at Merchant Taylors' Hall . . .* (London: Chapman and Hall, 1907), p. 97.

93. Thomas Fuller records that "Robert Smith, citizen and merchant tailor of London, was born at Market Harborough" in Leicestershire, was "one of four attorneys in the mayor's court" in London "betwixt the years 1609 and 1617," gave funds to maintain a lectureship in his hometown as well as "for several other pious uses," and "died . . . about 1618." See Fuller, *The History of the Worthies of England*, ed. P. Austin Nuttall (London: Thomas Tegg, 1840), II, 242.

94. Edmond, "In Search of John Webster," p. 1622 (n. 40).

95. *Notes from Black-Fryers* is a section of Henry Fitzgeffrey's *Satyres and Satyricall Epigrams* (London, 1617). G. E. Bentley reprints the relevant passage (sigs. F6ᵛ-F7) in *The Jacobean and Caroline Stage* (Oxford: Clarendon Press, 1941–68), V, 1242.

96. *Satirical Essayes, Characters, and Others* was printed by Nicholas Okes. The second edition (also 1615 but issued by a different printer) was retitled *Essayes and Characters, Ironicall, and Instrvctive*.

97. G. C. Moore Smith, ed., *William Hemminge's Elegy on Randolph's Finger* (Oxford: B. Blackwell, 1923), p. 12. Bentley reprints the quoted lines in *The Jacobean and Caroline Stage*, V, 1243.

98. Thomas P. Roche, Jr., ed., *Edmund Spenser: "The Faerie Queene"* (New Haven: Yale University Press, 1978), p. 442.

99. See J. G. Nichols, ed., *The Diary of Henry Machyn* (London: Camden Society, 1848), pp. 187–188. Machyn, a Merchant Taylor and furnisher of funeral trappings, wrote when John Webster senior was a boy.

100. E. Hockliffe, ed., *The Diary of the Rev. Ralph Josselin, 1616–1683* (London: Camden Society, 1908), p. 128.

101. E. S. de Beer, ed., *The Diary of John Evelyn* (Oxford: Clarendon Press, 1955), III, 76, 185, 490, 545.

102. See Lucas, ed., *Works*, II, 179–180; also David M. Bergeron, "The Wax Figures in *The Duchess of Malfi*," *Studies in English Literature, 1500–1900*, 18 (1978), 331–339. A contemporary picture of the Prince's hearse was printed with George Chapman's *An Epicede or Funerall Song* (London, 1612), to which a detailed description of the ceremonies was subjoined. Official mourners accompanying the funeral chariot numbered about two thousand.

103. Edmond, "In Search of John Webster," p. 1621 (n. 23). Rippon, according to John Stow, had made the first coach in England in 1555 for the Earl of Rutland; see Stow, *A Survey of London*, ed. Kingsford, II, 282, where Kingsford quotes from the 1604 edition of Stow's *Summary Abridged*. Rippon also made coaches for both Queen Mary and Queen Elizabeth.

104. Clode, *Memorials of the Guild of Merchant Taylors*, p. 545.

105. Myra Lee Rifkin gives an account of mourning customs and their costliness to the merchant and upper classes in her "Burial, Funeral, and Mourning Customs in England, 1558–1662," Diss. Bryn Mawr 1977, pp. 70–140.

106. F. P. Wilson, *The Plague in Shakespeare's London* (London: Oxford University Press, 1927). For the statistics of deaths in St. Sepulchre's parish, see p. 185; for the quotations from Wither (from canto 4 of *Britain's Remembrancer* [London, 1628], sig. gg[v] [p. 117a]), p. 44; for the "dead-carts" and the exodus from London illustrated, pp. 149, 158; for the quotation about "mercenary coaches" (from *London Topographical Record*, VIII [1912–13], 123), p. 134.

107. Godfrey Goodman, *The Court of King James the First* (London: R. Bentley, 1839), II, 146–147.

108. Stow, *A Survey of London*, ed. Kingsford, I, 83–84.

109. As noted earlier, the coachmaking trade in England centered on Smithfield and Cow Lane. Sometimes coaches made abroad were altered after import to suit English style. A "strong cowche with all maner of furniture therto belonging . . . and viii wheles" was ordered from Pomerania at a cost of forty-two pounds for Sir Henry Sidney in 1576. The "same cowche was att Smithfield in London uncovered and made higher" (to accommodate the tall conical hats with plumes then in vogue) for eight pounds, ten shillings. See J. Crofts, *Packhorse, Waggon and Post: Land Carriage and Communications under the Tudors and Stuarts* (London: Routledge and Kegan Paul, 1967), p. 137.

110. Stow, *A Survey of London*, ed. Kingsford, II, 282. Stow, a freeman of the Merchant Taylors, had presented his *Annals* to the company in 1592 and toward the end of his life received a pension from his philanthropic brother of the guild, Robert Dowe—the same man who endowed the St. Sepulchre's ministry to Newgate prisoners. Stow, who died in 1605, may well have known the elder John Webster personally and perhaps the dramatist as well. He was on friendly terms with Ben Jonson (see Kingsford's "Life of Stow" in his introduction to the *Survey*, I, viii, xxiv–xxvi).

111. See "The Traffic Problems in London During the Seventeenth Century" in Norman G. Brett-James, *The Growth of Stuart London* (London: Allen & Unwin, 1935), pp. 420–443; also Edmond, "In Search of John Webster," p. 1621.

112. The quotations from Taylor are all from *The World Runnes on Wheeles*, reprinted in *Works of John Taylor, the Water-Poet* ([Manchester]: The Spenser Society, 1869), III, 233, 237, 238.

113. Hugh Macdonald, ed., *"Coach and Sedan," Reprinted from the Edition of 1636* (London: Westminster Press, 1925), sig. B2.

114. Taylor, *The World Runnes on Wheeles*, in *Works of John Taylor, the Water-Poet*, III, 239.

115. Alexander B. Grosart, ed., *The Non-Dramatic Works of Thomas Dekker* (London: Hazel, Watson, and Viney, 1885), II, 50.

116. R. A. Foakes, ed., *The Revenger's Tragedy* (Cambridge, Mass.: Harvard University Press, 1966), p. 41.

117. C. H. Herford and Percy and Evelyn Simpson, eds., *Ben Jonson*, IV, 264.

118. R. W. Van Fossen, ed., *Eastward Ho* (Manchester: Manchester University Press, 1979), p. 111.

119. Ibid., p. 122.

120. Ibid., pp. 123–124.

121. A. H. Bullen, ed., *The Works of Thomas Middleton*, I, 153.

122. Ibid., IV, 59.

123. *The World Runnes on Wheeles* in *Works of John Taylor, the Water-Poet*, III, 241.

124. Fredson Bowers, ed., *The Dramatic Works of Thomas Dekker*, III, 295; R. B. Parker, ed., *A Chaste Maid in Cheapside* (London: Methuen, 1969), p. 74.

125. *Satyre III: "Redde, age, quae decinceps risisti"* (ll. 121–124), *The Scourge of Villanie*, in Arnold Davenport, ed., *The Poems of John Marston* (Liverpool: Liverpool University Press, 1961), p. 115.

126. Lucas, ed., *Works*, I, 49–50 (n. *h*). The original entry is in Latin: "Primo die Augusti anno 1598, Magister Johannes Webster nuper de Novo Hospicio generosus filius et heres apparens Johannis Webster de London generosi admissus est in Societatem Medii Templi." Also see Charles H. Hopwood, ed., *Middle Temple Records* (London: Butterworth & Co., 1904–05), I, 388.

127. *The Annales, or Generall Chronicle of England, Begun first by Maister Iohn Stow, and . . . continued and augmented . . . by Edmond Howes . . .* (London, 1615), p. 811.

128. John Venn and J. A. Venn, *Alumni Cantabrigienses, Part I* (Cambridge: Cambridge University Press, 1922–27), IV, 356.

129. Lucas, ed., *Works*, III, 315, 317, 327.

130. Frances A. Shirley, ed., *The Devil's Law-Case*, pp. 3–4.

131. John Russell Brown, ed., *The White Devil*, pp. 2–3.

132. See R. G. Howarth, "John Webster's Classical Nescience" in *Diary, Drama and Poetry: Presentations and Recoveries* (Cape Town: Privately printed, University of Cape Town, 1971), pp. 38–69; Howarth published a briefer version of this essay in the *Sidney University Union Recorder*, 33 (14 October 1954), 224–226; also see R. W. Dent, *John Webster's Borrowing* (Berkeley and Los Angeles: University of California Press, 1960).

133. Howarth, "John Webster's Classical Nescience," p. 68.

134. Webster was probably following Lodowick Lloyd, who in *Linceus Spectacles* (1607) mistranslates Valerius Maximus's "Alcestidi" (Alcestis in the dative) as "Alcestides"; see Brown, ed., *The White Devil*, p. 3.

135. Ibid., p. 4.

136. Howarth, "John Webster's Classical Nescience," p. 69.

137. John Russell Brown, ed., *The Duchess of Malfi*, p. 73.

138. Howarth, "John Webster's Classical Nescience," p. 43; F. S. Boas, ed., *The Works of Thomas Kyd*, rev. ed. (Oxford: Clarendon Press, 1955), pp. 273, 455.

139. Kellett, "John Webster" in *The Encyclopaedia Britannica*, 14th ed. (London: Encyclopaedia Britannica Co., 1929), XXIII, 472; Dent, *John Webster's Borrowing*, p. 317.

140. Peter Haworth, "Prelude to the Study of Webster's Plays" in *English Hymns and Ballads and Other Studies in Popular Literature* (Oxford: Basil Blackwell, 1927), p. 79; W. A. Edwards, "John Webster," *Scrutiny*, 2 (1934), 13–14.

141. Lagarde, *John Webster* (Toulouse: Association des Publications de la Faculté des Lettres et Sciences Humaines, 1968), I, 25–29; Bradbrook, *John Webster, Citizen and Dramatist*, pp. 19–20.

142. F. W. M. Draper, *Four Centuries of Merchant Taylors' School, 1561–1961* (London: Oxford University Press, 1962), p. 9. The Manor of the Rose, in the parish of St. Lawrence, Poultney, had once belonged to the tragic Duke of Buckingham whose fall Shakespeare dramatizes in *Henry*

VIII. The play contains an allusion to "The Duke being at the Rose, within the parish / Saint Lawrence Poultney" (I.ii.152–153).

143. Draper, *Four Centuries of Merchant Taylors' School*, Appendix I, pp. 241–251.

144. Robertson and Gordon, eds., *A Calendar of Dramatic Records*, pp. 59–60.

145. John Bruce, ed., *Liber Famelicus of Sir James Whitelocke*, Camden Society Publications, no. 70 (London: Camden Society, 1858), p. 12.

146. M. F. J. McDonnell, *A History of St. Paul's School* (London: Chapman and Hall, 1909), p. 151.

147. E. T. Campagnac, ed., *Mulcaster's "Elementarie"* (Oxford: Clarendon Press, 1925), p. 269.

148. Stow, *A Survey of London*, ed. Kingsford, II, 38.

149. "I was once of Clement's Inn, where I think they will talk of mad Shallow yet." Shallow dwells upon the "swinge-bucklers" or roisterers of the Inns and their recourse to "bona-robas" or harlots (*2 Henry IV*, III.ii.13–24).

150. J. C. Smith and E. de Selincourt, eds., *The Poetical Works of Edmund Spenser* (London: Oxford University Press, 1912), p. 602.

151. Wilfrid R. Prest, *The Inns of Court under Elizabeth I and the Early Stuarts, 1590–1640* (Totowa, N.J.: Rowman and Littlefield, 1972), p. 7.

152. Hunold Nibbe, ed., *"The Fleire" by Edward Sharpham*, in W. Bang, gen. ed., *Materialien zur Kunde des älteren Englischen Dramas*, no. 36 (Louvain: A. Uystpruyst, 1912), p. [9].

153. Sir Thomas Smith, *De Republica Anglorum* (London, 1583), p. 27. Smith had been educated at the Middle Temple.

154. See Buc's Appendix (entitled "The Third University of England") to John Stow's *Annals* (London, 1615), p. 968.

155. Stow, *A Survey of London*, ed. Kingsford, I, 76–77.

156. C. H. Herford and Percy and Evelyn Simpson, eds., *Ben Jonson*, III, 421.

157. My account of life at the Middle Temple and of the Inns of Court generally is heavily indebted to Philip J. Finkelpearl's *John Marston of the Middle Temple: An Elizabethan Dramatist in His Social Setting* (Cambridge, Mass.: Harvard University Press, 1969). I have also profited greatly from J. Bruce Williamson's *The History of the Temple, London, From the Institution of the Order of the Knights of the Temple to the Close of the Stuart Period* (New York: E. P. Dutton and Co., 1924).

158. Robert Krueger, ed., *The Poems of Sir John Davies* (Oxford: Clarendon Press, 1975), pp. 148–149.

159. J. Bruce and T. T. Perowne, eds., *Correspondence of Matthew Parker*, The Parker Society (Cambridge: Cambridge University Press, 1853), p. 384.

160. Quoted from a contemporary manuscript, by Prest, *The Inns of Court under Elizabeth I and the Early Stuarts*, p. 179.

161. See John Hutchinson, *A Catalogue of Notable Middle Templars* (London: Butterworth and Co., 1902), p. 125.

162. Fuller, *The History of the Worthies of England*, ed. Nuttall, I, 423.

163. Thomas Fuller, *The Church History of Britain from the Birth of Jesus Christ until the Year 1648*, ed. James Nichols (London: Thomas Tegg, 1842), III, 129.

164. Izaak Walton, *The Lives of John Donne, Sir Henry Wotton, Richard Hooker, George Herbert, and Robert Sanderson*, ed. George Saintsbury (London: Oxford University Press, 1927), p. 209.

165. See Dent, *John Webster's Borrowing*, p. 312.

166. Albert Peel, ed., *Tracts Ascribed to Richard Bancroft* (Cambridge: Cambridge University Press, 1953), p. 57.

167. *Epigrammes* in C. H. Herford and Percy and Evelyn Simpson, eds., *Ben Jonson*, VIII, 27.

168. Hopwood, ed., *Middle Temple Records*, I, 318.

169. Louise Brown Osborn, *The Life, Letters, and Writings of John Hoskyns, 1566–1638* (New Haven: Yale University Press, 1937), p. 203.

170. Adolphus W. Ward, *Sir Henry Wotton: A Biographical Sketch* (London: Archibald Constable and Co., 1898), p. 46.

171. Elizabeth Jenkins, *Elizabeth the Great* (New York: Coward-McCann, Inc., 1959), p. 315.

172. Robert P. Sorlien, ed., *The Diary of John Manningham of the Middle Temple, 1602–1603* (Hanover, N.H.: University Press of New England, 1976), p. 235.

173. J. B. Leishman, ed., *The Three Parnassus Plays* (London: Ivor Nicholson & Watson, 1949), p. 241.

174. Hopwood, ed., *Middle Temple Records*, I, 386.

175. Finkelpearl's entire volume, *John Marston of the Middle Temple*, is relevant; Bradbrook's "The Middle Temple: A Literary Centre," chapter 2 of her *John Webster, Citizen and Dramatist*, is also suggestive. See, also, A. Wigfall Green's more general study, *The Inns of Court and Early English Drama* (New Haven: Yale University Press, 1931).

176. "W. I." [John Weever], *The Whipping of the Satyre* (London, 1601), sig. E4ᵛ.

177. Prynne, "To the Right Christian Generovs Yovng Gentlemen-Students . . . ," *Histrio-Mastix: The Player's Scovrge* (London, 1633), sig. **3ᵛ; Finkelpearl, *John Marston of the Middle Temple*, p. 27. Also see "In Rufum, 3" in Krueger, ed., *The Poems of Sir John Davies*, p. 130.

178. Finkelpearl, *John Marston of the Middle Temple*, pp. 50–51.

179. Judith M. Kennedy, ed., *A Critical Edition of Yong's Translation of George of Montemayor's "Diana" and Gil Polo's "Enamoured Diana"* (Oxford: Clarendon Press, 1968), p. 3.

180. 1 January 1662; de Beer, ed., *The Diary of John Evelyn*, III, 307. Twenty years earlier (15 December 1641) Evelyn had been "elected one of the Comptrollers of the Middle-Temple-Revellers, as the fashion of the Young Students & Gentlemen was" (Ibid., II, 77).

181. Krueger, ed., *The Poems of Sir John Davies*, p. 303.

182. H. Harvey Wood, ed., *The Plays of John Marston* (Edinburgh: Oliver and Boyd, 1934–39), II, 257.

183. G. K. Hunter, ed., *The Malcontent* (London: Methuen, 1975), p. 126.

184. W. Reavley Gair, ed., *Antonio's Revenge* (Manchester: Manchester University Press, 1978), p. 136.

185. See Hutchinson, *A Catalogue of Notable Middle Templars*.

186. See Hopwood, ed., *Middle Temple Records*, Index, IV, 57, 60.

187. Heywood, *The Hierarchie of the Blessed Angells* (London, 1635), sig. Sᵛ (p. 206); also quoted partially in Lucas, ed., *Works*, I, 52.

188. See C. J. Sisson, *Lost Plays of Shakespeare's Age* (Cambridge: Cambridge University Press, 1936), p. 102 (n. 1). Lucas, Webster's editor, believed that Dekker was still alive in 1634 (*Works*, I, 52), but see Mark Eccles, "Thomas Dekker: Burial-Place," *Notes & Queries*, 177 (1939), 157; also Bentley, *The Jacobean and Caroline Stage*, III, 243.

189. See R. G. Howarth, "John Webster's Burial," *Notes & Queries*, NS 1 (1954), 114–115; also Sisson, *Lost Plays of Shakespeare's Age*, p. 102 (n. 1).

190. Quoted by Bentley in *The Jacobean and Caroline Stage*, V, 1242, from *Satyres and Satyricall Epigrams* (London, 1617), sigs. F6ᵛ-F7; the passage reappears in a reissue of Fitzgeffrey's book, entitled *Certain Elegies, Done By Svndrie Excellent Wits* (London, 1618).

191. Lucas, ed., *Works*, I, 55 (n. 2).

192. Ibid., I, 56.

193. Fitzgeffrey, Epigram 36, in *Satyres and Satyricall Epigrams*, sig. D4.

194. Ibid., sigs. E3ᵛ-E4.

PART II

Chapter 1

1. R. A. Foakes and R. T. Rickert, eds., *Henslowe's Diary* (Cambridge: Cambridge University Press, 1961), p. 201. In this and subsequent quotations, for the sake of clarity, I have modernized Henslowe's eccentric spelling.

2. Ibid., p. 202.

3. Ibid., pp. 218–219.

4. See F. L. Lucas, ed., *The Complete Works of John Webster* (London: Chatto & Windus, 1927), IV, 239.

5. See M. F. Martin's unpublished "Critical Edition of *The Famous History of Sir Thomas Wyat*" (University of London thesis, 1930), pp. 57–94; Philip Shaw, "*Sir Thomas Wyat* and the Scenario of *Lady Jane*," *Modern Language Quarterly*, 13 (1952), 227–238; and especially Cyrus Hoy, *Introduction, Notes, and Commentaries to Texts in "The Dramatic Works of Thomas Dekker" Edited by Fredson Bowers*, 4 vols. (Cambridge: Cambridge University Press, 1980), I, 312–314.

6. Hoy, *Commentaries to Texts in "The Dramatic Works of Thomas Dekker,"* I, 318.

7. Like Richard II, the Northumberland of *Sir Thomas Wyatt* laments the sudden desertion of his followers: "I left liuing . . . at least fiue hundred friendes, / And now I haue not one, simply not one . . ." (II.ii.75–76); a scene later the sheriff who arrests Suffolk compares the duke's betrayer to Judas: "So Iudas kist his Maister" (II.iii.38). Taken together, the two passages could be an imitation of Richard's

> Yet I well remember
> The favors of these men. Were they not mine?
> Did they not sometime cry, "All hail!" to me?
> So Judas did to Christ. But he, in twelve,
> Found truth in all but one; I, in twelve thousand, none.
>   (IV.i.168–172)

An exchange between the young lovers may also be indebted to Shakespeare's tragedy, although the irony of the word "must" as applied to kings was not uncommon:

> *Jane.* My learned carefull King, what must we goe?
> *Guilford.* We must.
> *Jane.* Then it must be so.
> *Northumberland.* Set forward then.
>   (I.ii.55–58)

Compare Richard's arrest:

> *King Richard.* Set on towards London, cousin, is it so?
> *Bolingbroke.* Yea, my good lord.
> *King Richard.*   Then I must not say no.
>   (III.iii.208–209)

Guilford's comment on the death of his father is a more direct appropriation from Prince Hal's words over the body of Hotspur (*1 Henry IV*, V.iv.100–101):

> Peace rest his soule,
> His sinnes be buried in his graue,
> And not remembered in his Epitaph. . . .
>   (III.ii.40–42)

8. Gervase Markham and Lewis Machin present an interestingly visual form of this paradox in *The Dumb Knight*, played by the Children of the King's Revels at Whitefriars (1607–1608). Mariana in that play ascends a portable scaffold to be executed as though it were a chair of estate: "This first step lower / Mounts to this next; this thus and thus hath brought / My body's frame unto its highest throne . . ." (III.i; W. Carew Hazlitt, ed., *Dodsley's Old English Plays* [London: Reeves and Turner, 1875], X, 155).

9. Fernand Lagarde, *John Webster* (Toulouse: Association des Publications de la Faculté des Lettres et Sciences Humaines, 1968), I, 71.

10. Bradbrook, *The Growth and Structure of Elizabethan Comedy* (London: Chatto & Windus, 1955), p. 130.

11. Morris Palmer Tilley, *A Dictionary of the Proverbs in England in the Sixteenth and Seventeenth Centuries* (Ann Arbor: University of Michigan Press, 1950), L116.

12. Hoy, *Commentaries to Texts in "The Dramatic Works of Thomas Dekker,"* I, 314–315. Although Webster and Dekker change the order of the two executions for dramatic effect, they follow Foxe in making Dudley, who shed tears on the scaffold, the less mature and composed of the youthful sufferers; Hoy, pp. 349–350.

13. For several insights in the treatment of *Sir Thomas Wyatt* I am indebted to my student, Joseph Candido. See his "Renaissance Biographical Practice and the Tudor Biographical Play," Diss. Indiana University, 1977, pp. 140–153.

14. Foakes and Rickert, eds., *Henslowe's Diary*, p. 219.

15. The late Professor Howarth communicated this speculation to me in a private letter.

16. Henry Chettle, *England's Mourning Garment* (London: V. S[ims], [1603]), sig. D3.

17. See C. M. Ingleby, *Shakespere Allusion-Books, Part I*, The New Shakespere Society (London: N. Trübner & Co., 1874), p. xiv; and Brinsley Nicholson, "On Shakespeare's Pastoral Name," *Notes & Queries*, 5th series, 1 (1874), 110.

18. See George K. Hunter, ed., *The Malcontent* (London: Methuen, 1975), pp. xli–xlvi. All citations of the play are to this edition.

19. Ibid., p. xliv.

20. It has also been suggested that the King's Men in playing *The Malcontent* may have been retaliating for the children's theft of *The First Part of Jeronimo*, a King's Men play; see E. K. Chambers, *The Elizabethan Stage* (Oxford: Clarendon Press, 1923), IV, 23.

21. Hunter, ed., *The Malcontent*, pp. xlvi–liii. Hunter (p. xlix) thinks the character of Passarello was conceived with Armin in mind. But William A. Ringler, Jr., pointing out the dangers of assuming that Elizabethan actors were regularly type-cast, argues that Armin was a "quick-change artist" and probably played Edgar rather than the Fool in *King Lear*; see Wendell M. Aycock, ed., *Shakespeare's Art from a Comparative Perspective* (Lubbock, Texas: Texas Tech Press, 1981), pp. 183–194.

22. Hunter finds this division of labor an attractive, if admittedly hypothetical, solution to the problem of collaboration; *The Malcontent*, p. li.

23. Lake, "Webster's Additions to *The Malcontent*: Linguistic Evidence," *Notes & Queries*, NS 28 (April 1981), 158.

24. See R. W. Dent, *John Webster's Borrowing* (Berkeley and Los Angeles: University of California Press, 1960), p. 122.

25. See Anthony Caputi, *John Marston, Satirist* (Ithaca: Cornell University Press, 1961), p. 140.

26. Kirsch, *Jacobean Dramatic Perspectives* (Charlottesville: University Press of Virginia, 1972), p. 32.

27. See Harris, ed., *The Malcontent* (London: Ernest Benn, 1967), p. xv.

28. C. H. Herford and Percy and Evelyn Simpson, eds., *Ben Jonson* (Oxford: Clarendon Press, 1925–52), IV, 39. For a more extended discussion of Jonson's inductions and Webster's in-

debtedness, see Thelma N. Greenfield, *The Induction in Elizabethan Drama* (Eugene: University of Oregon Books, 1969), pp. 75–87.

29. Andrew Gurr, following George Steevens, has made the interesting suggestion that, by flourishing his hat, Sly parodies "his own playing" of the part of Osric in *Hamlet*; see Gurr, *The Shakespearean Stage, 1574–1642*, 2nd ed. (Cambridge: Cambridge University Press, 1980), p. 164. Sly echoes Osric's words, "for mine ease" (cf. *Hamlet*, V.ii.105) at line 34. See Hunter's note on Webster's line; *The Malcontent*, p. 10. Blackfriars was the center of the plume and feather industry in London.

30. See E. E. Stoll, *John Webster: The Periods of His Work as Determined by His Relations to the Drama of His Day* (Boston: Alfred Mudge, 1905), pp. 61, 79; and Rupert Brooke, *John Webster & the Elizabethan Drama* (London: Sidgwick & Jackson, 1916), p. 82.

31. Berry, *The Art of John Webster* (Oxford: Clarendon Press, 1972).

32. R. W. Van Fossen, ed., *Eastward Ho* (Manchester: Manchester University Press, 1979).

33. The tricking of "respectable" characters into marriage with prostitutes derives from the Italian tradition of *commedia dell' arte* and quickly became a staple of Middletonian city comedy; versions of the device occur in *A Mad World, My Masters* (Follywit), *Michaelmas Term* (Lethe), *A Trick to Catch the Old One* (Hoard), *Your Five Gallants* (the gallants), and *A Chaste Maid in Cheapside* (Tim Yellowhammer). The prodigal son theme was, of course, even more conventional, having been established on the English secular stage at least as early as 1547–1553 with plays such as *Lusty Juventus* and *Nice Wanton*. See Ervin Beck, Jr., "Prodigal Son Comedy: The Continuity of a Paradigm in English Drama, 1500–1642," Diss. Indiana University, 1972.

34. C. G. Petter in his edition of *Eastward Ho* argues, not without force, however, that Jonson was responsible for the plotting and overall design of the play; Petter, ed., *Eastward Ho* (London: Ernest Benn, 1973), pp. xiii–xxi.

35. Nicoll, "The Dramatic Portrait of George Chapman," *Philological Quarterly*, 41 (1962), 215–228.

36. Hunold Nibbe, ed., *The Fleire*, in W. Bang's *Materialien zur Kunde des älteren Englischen Dramas*, 36 (Louvain: A. Uystpruyst, 1912), [29].

37. Murray, "The Collaboration of Dekker and Webster in *Northward Ho* and *Westward Ho*," *Papers of the Bibliographical Society of America*, 56 (1962), 485. Noting that the two plays were printed in different shops and that the same patterns of usage prevail in both, Murray is able to show that the variations in question must be authorial rather than compositorial. He concludes that Webster wrote I, III, and IV.i of *Westward Ho*; I.i, II.ii, III, and V.i to a point between lines 263 and 359 of *Northward Ho*. Cyrus Hoy in general endorses Murray's apportionment of both plays; see *Commentaries to Texts in "The Dramatic Works of Thomas Dekker"*, II, 163, 247. For additional evidence, see D. J. Lake, *The Canon of Thomas Middleton's Plays* (Cambridge: Cambridge University Press, 1975), p. 45, and "Webster's Additions to *The Malcontent*: Linguistic Evidence," *Notes & Queries*, NS 28 (1981), 154, n. 6.

38. Price, *Thomas Dekker* (New York: Twayne Publishers, 1969), p. 28; and Gibbons, *Jacobean City Comedy: A Study of Satiric Plays by Jonson, Marston, and Middleton* (Cambridge, Mass.: Harvard University Press, 1968), p. 140.

39. Leggatt, *Citizen Comedy in the Age of Shakespeare* (Toronto: University of Toronto Press, 1973), p. 134.

40. Knights, *Drama and Society in the Age of Jonson* (London: Chatto & Windus, 1937), pp. 228–234. If we accept Murray's objective evidence for the apportionment of shares (see n. 37 above), the passages that Knights quotes "to show how unlike Dekker . . . the satire is" (p. 234, n. 3) were written not by Webster but by his collaborator. Knights of course wrote before Murray, but his assumption shows the danger of relying merely on impressions.

41. Brooke, *John Webster & the Elizabethan Drama*, p. 84.

42. Hoy, *Commentaries to Texts in "The Dramatic Works of Thomas Dekker,"* II, 163.

43. Lagarde, *John Webster*, I, 73–128.

44. Stoll, *John Webster: The Periods of His Work*, p. 69.

45. Petter, ed., *Eastward Ho*, p. xxviii. The borrowed phrase is from Louis B. Wright, *Middle-Class Culture in Elizabethan England* (Chapel Hill: University of North Carolina Press, 1935), p. 630.

46. Although "westward for smelts" was a proverbial expression, it seems likely that *Westward Ho* twice alludes (II.iii.80–81, IV.ii.199–200) to the popular collection of fabliaux told by five fishwives on a boat journey from Queenhithe to Kingston.

47. Price, "The Function of Imagery in Webster," *PMLA*, 70 (1955), 717–739. If Murray is correct, the reference to "Dun-is-in-the-mire" is Dekker's, not Webster's, but the imagery of both plays has a consistency that argues for the two dramatists working with an impressive harmony of conception.

48. K. H. Ansari comments on the pattern of bird imagery in *The Duchess of Malfi* and its relation to themes of victimization, imprisonment, and execution; Ansari, *John Webster: Image Patterns & Canon* (New Delhi: Jalaluddin Rumi Publications, 1969), pp. 127–128.

49. The text reads, "I hold my life the blacke-beard her husband whissels for her [Mistress Tenterhook]"; the pun on "blackbird" is probably intentional in view of the many other bird images.

50. Suggestions for Justiniano may also have come from the duke in Shakespeare's *Measure for Measure* and the prince in Middleton's *The Phoenix*.

51. Stoll points out the possible debt of this episode to two scenes in Marston's *Sophonisba* (printed 1606); *John Webster: The Periods of His Work*, p. 63. But the tragedy is probably too late for this; if there is influence, it may flow in the opposite direction.

52. Possibly the name Fabian was suggested by another character of *Twelfth Night*, one of Olivia's servants. Arthur H. King points out the linguistic influence of Jonson's Tucca on Sir Gosling; see *The Language of Satirized Characters in "Poetaster"* (Lund: C. W. K. Gleerup, 1941), pp. 162–163.

53. Juliet calls her nurse "Ancient damnation" at III.v.236. The nurse also complains to Juliet about being sent "To catch my death with jauncing up and down" (II.v.52) and later cries out, "Give me some aqua vitae" (III.ii.88).

54. Nicoll, "The Dramatic Portrait of George Chapman," p. 219.

55. Chapman's play could not have been onstage before 1608, but his predilection for French subjects was well known; conceivably, the authors of *Northward Ho* had notice that Chapman was writing or intended to write on Byron.

56. *Absolom and Achitophel*, l. 163; and *A Midsummer Night's Dream*, V.i.7–8. Compare also Nashe's *Summer's Last Will and Testament*: "There is no excellent knowledge without mixture of madness" (R. B. McKerrow, ed., *The Works of Thomas Nashe* [Oxford: Basil Blackwell, 1958], III, 265). The idea was, of course, proverbial; see Tilley, *A Dictionary of the Proverbs in England*, W579.

57. Alexander Dyce, ed., *The Works of John Webster* (London: Pickering, 1830), I, vi.

58. Middleton also liked to exploit the money-sex relationship. For instance, in *The Phoenix* (acted by Paul's Boys in 1603–1604, almost contemporaneously with the *Ho* plays), a jeweler's wife conducts an adulterous affair with a knight in which their nicknames for each other are "Revenue" and "Pleasure."

59. Dekker's *Satiromastix* (1601) had been performed by both the Lord Chamberlain's Men and the Children of Paul's; Webster, as already noted, had just finished helping adapt *The Malcontent*, originally written for the Children of the Queen's Revels, for performance at the Globe.

60. Hoy, *Commentaries to Texts in "The Dramatic Works of Thomas Dekker,"* II, 163–164.

61. Webster repeated the cannon image in *The Duchess of Malfi* (III.v.105–106), reinforced no doubt (as Lucas has pointed out) by lines 181–182 of Donne's *Second Anniversary* (1612); see Lucas, ed., *Works*, II, 177.

62. See John Russell Brown's note on this passage in his edition of *The Duchess of Malfi*, p. 14.

63. Dekker does credit Middleton but omits mention of Jonson. The several contemporary accounts of the events differ in certain details.

PART II

Chapter 2

1. See R. W. Dent, *John Webster's Borrowing* (Berkeley and Los Angeles: University of California Press, 1960), pp. 57–58.

2. Fredson Bowers, ed., *The Dramatic Works of Thomas Dekker* (Cambridge: Cambridge University Press, 1953–68), III, 136, 163.

3. Ibid., p. 119.

4. Ibid., p. 120. For the identification of Dekker's "*Worthy Friend*" with Webster, see John Russell Brown, ed., *The White Devil*, pp. xx–xxi.

5. Andrew Gurr points out that most dramatists, including Nashe, Heywood, Marston, Chapman, Beaumont, Fletcher, Dekker, and Jonson, were at one time or another unflattering to their audiences; Gurr, *The Shakespearean Stage, 1574–1642*, 2nd ed. (Cambridge: Cambridge University Press, 1980), p. 206. Webster would no doubt have agreed with Jonson in his court prologue to *The Staple of News* that good plays are best appreciated by "Schollers, *that can iudge, and faire report / The sense they heare, aboue the vulgar sort / Of Nut-crackers, that onely come for sight*"; C. H. Herford and Percy and Evelyn Simpson, eds., *Ben Jonson* (Oxford: Clarendon Press, 1925–52), VI, 283. Indeed, Webster deliberately copies the critical terminology from Jonson's "To the Readers" in *Sejanus* (1605).

6. Vittoria Corambona was not Venetian, although at one point she and her lover fled to Venice. The city was notorious for its glamorous prostitutes, however, and Webster no doubt wished to associate his character with this tradition.

7. See John Russell Brown, "The Printing of Webster's Plays (I)," *Studies in Bibliography*, 6 (1954), 117–140.

8. See Samuel Schoenbaum, "*The Revenger's Tragedy*: A Neglected Source," *Notes & Queries*, 195 (1950), 338. William Rowley also uses the term "white devil" (c. 1619–1620) in *All's Lost By Lust* (II.vi.66); Charles W. Stork, ed., *"All's Lost By Lust" and "A Shoemaker a Gentleman"*, Publications of the University of Pennsylvania, series in Philology and Literature (Philadelphia, 1910), p. 109.

9. F. L. Lucas, ed., *Works*, III, 260–261.

10. See E. K. Chambers, *The Elizabethan Stage* (Oxford: Clarendon Press, 1923), II, 186–190.

11. *A Monumental Column* was also issued independently with the same date (1613) on its title page. The entry in the Stationers' Register is dated 25 December 1612.

12. Webster specifically refers to Chapman, who had dedicated his translation of Homer's *Iliad* to Prince Henry, as "my frend" (l. 268).

13. C. H. Herford and Percy and Evelyn Simpson, eds., *Ben Jonson*, VII, 324. Like Webster, Jonson invokes the familiar comparison of Prince Henry to his namesake Henry V (*Prince Henry's Barriers*, ll. 285–298).

14. In *The White Devil* Bracciano refers to Vittoria as "the devil in crystal" (IV.ii.88); Lodovico, with gallows humor, speaks of the noose with which he throttles Bracciano as a wedding present "Sent from the Duke of Florence" (V.iii.175).

15. F. L. Lucas, ed., *Works*, III, 287.

16. *The Countess of Pembroke's Arcadia*, ed. Maurice Evans (Harmondsworth: Penguin Books, 1977), p. 469.

17. See the edition by G. R. Proudfoot (Lincoln: University of Nebraska Press, 1970), p. xxiv.

18. Compare *The Duchess of Malfi* (I.i.209). Webster borrowed the image from Sir William Alexander's *Alexandrean Tragedy* (III.ii; ll. 1318–1319).

19. Brown, ed., *The Duchess of Malfi*, pp. xxii–xxiv.

20. Quoted from the translation of Busino in G. H. and S. K. Hunter, eds., *John Webster: A Critical Anthology* (Harmondsworth: Penguin Books, 1969), p. 32. Busino appears to have confused the poisoning of Julia with the murder of the Duchess.

21. See Gerald Eades Bentley, *The Jacobean and Caroline Stage* (Oxford: Clarendon Press, 1941–68), I, 27–28.

22. Baldwin, *The Organization and Personnel of the Shakespearean Company* (Princeton: Princeton University Press, 1927); see Baldwin's charts of actors and roles, pp. 198 ff.

23. Ibid.

24. Bandello assumes the name "Delio" in his sonnets. See also F. L. Lucas, ed., *Works*, II, 11.

25. See Gunnar Boklund, *"The Duchess of Malfi": Sources, Themes, Characters* (Cambridge, Mass.: Harvard University Press, 1962), p. 19.

26. See Charles R. Forker, "A Possible Source for the Ceremony of the Cardinal's Arming in *The Duchess of Malfi*," *Anglia*, 87 (1969), 398–403.

27. Lope's play was not printed until 1618, but Webster could theoretically have seen a performance or a manuscript copy before 1613.

28. See Inga-Stina Ekeblad, "The 'Impure Art' of John Webster," *Review of English Studies*, 9 (1958), 253–267.

29. Brown, ed., *The Duchess of Malfi*, p. xxx.

30. John Russell Brown, "The Printing of John Webster's Plays (II)," *Studies in Bibliography*, 8 (1956), 117, 122.

31. In dedicating *The Devil's Law-Case*, Webster actually refers to his other plays as "works." Jonson and Dekker in their respective prefaces to *Sejanus* (1603) and *The Whore of Babylon* (1607) had both used the term "poem" for these dramas, and Webster had already followed suit by calling *The White Devil* a "dramatic poem."

32. "Gentry is but a relique of Time-paste"; see *A Wife* in *The Overburian Characters*, ed. W. J. Paylor, Percy Reprints, XIII (Oxford: B. Blackwell, 1936), p. 103; compare *The Devil's Law-Case* (I.i.39) and *The Duchess of Malfi* (Dedication, l. 14).

33. In 1615, John Stephens, a lawyer of Lincoln's Inn, published *Satirical Essays, Characters, and Others*, which included a strongly derogatory portrait of *A Common Player*. That Webster took offense and was specifically answering Stephens in *An Excellent Actor* we know from a heated digression in the dramatist's piece (see Lucas, ed., *Works*, IV, 8–10). This retort is really not germane to the rest of the character and was dropped from all subsequent reprintings. Nevertheless, it hit its mark, for Stephens (apparently alluding obliquely to his assailant's identity by glancing at the Webster family's association with horses) almost instantly flung back at Webster with a second edition of his own. This book made a point of addressing some very rude remarks *"To the namelesse Rayler* [i.e., Webster]: *who hath lengthened his* Excellent Actor, *a most needy Caracter . . . with a peece of dog-skin witt; dressed ouer with oyle of sweaty Post-horse."* Not content with reproving the author of *An Excellent Actor* personally, Stephens enlisted two of his young lawyer friends, John Cocke and George Greene, both of whom felt animus against actors and contributed to the book their own separate abuse of the *"namelesse Detractor before mentioned"* (see Paylor, ed., pp. xx–xxiv). Cocke, too, may have been adverting to Webster's connection with the coach-hiring business in his reference to the "hackney similitudes" of the "botcher" of his own work.

M. C. Bradbrook, not finding a John Cocke in the published records of Lincoln's Inn, concludes that the name is pseudonymous (see Bradbrook, *John Webster, Citizen and Dramatist* [London: Weidenfeld and Nicolson, 1980], p. 168). This is certainly possible, for Cocke's attack on Webster is especially insulting and the writer might well have wished to protect himself by veiling his identity. In addition, Bradbrook ascribes *A Common Player* to Cocke rather than to Stephens, but the preliminaries to the latter's "second impression" would seem to prove her mistaken.

In his address "To the Reader" Stephens mentions "*my poore detractor*," thus appearing to credit himself with the character to which Webster had taken exception; then, directly addressing Webster ("*the namelesse Rayler*"), he says, "*You haue . . . beene bolde with me . . .*" before going on specifically to answer the charge of imitation (in *An Excellent Actor* Webster had referred to the writer of *A Common Player* as "the imitating Characterist" [Lucas, ed., *Works*, IV, 43]). Further confirmation of Stephens's authorship appears in one of the epigrams that Greene addressed to his fellow at Lincoln's Inn: "Forbeare my freind to write against that man [i.e., Webster] . . . who hath wrong'd thy *name*. . . ."

34. See Paylor, ed., pp. xxv–xxxi.

35. Ibid., p. 144.

36. Webster liked to introduce pieces of set description into his dramas, as, for instance, Monticelso's "perfect character" of a whore in *The White Devil* (III.ii.78–101) and the sinister portraits of the Aragonian brothers that Bosola and Antonio offer in the opening scene of *The Duchess of Malfi* (I.i.49–54, 156–186).

37. Paylor, ed., pp. xvii–xxiv.

38. Ibid., p. 2.

39. Compare *The Duchess of Malfi*: "for know whether I am doom'd to live, or die, / I can do both like a prince" (III.ii.70–71); and see Dent, *John Webster's Borrowing*, pp. 282–283.

40. Compare Bracciano's characterization of Vittoria as "the devil in crystal" in *The White Devil* (IV.ii.88); and see Dent, *John Webster's Borrowing*, p. 283.

41. Webster borrows this image from Pierre Matthieu's *Henry the Fourth*; see Dent, *John Webster's Borrowing*, p. 280.

42. E. K. Chambers was the first to suggest this identification; *The Elizabethan Stage*, IV, 257. See also Lucas, ed., *Works*, IV, 57.

43. G. K. Hunter, "English Folly and Italian Vice: The Moral Landscape of John Marston," in *Jacobean Theatre*, ed. John Russell Brown and Bernard Harris, Stratford-upon-Avon Studies, 1 (New York: St. Martin's Press, 1960), pp. 85–111.

44. Compare Numbers, 13:27, and Golding's translation of Ovid's *Metamorphoses*, I.i.27, ed. W. H. D. Rouse (New York: Norton, 1966), p. 23.

45. The circle, with its obvious relevance to the Renaissance cosmology of concentric spheres and its connections with the Neoplatonic and hermetic traditions, was a commonplace symbol of mystical order. George Puttenham wrote that its "ample capacitie doth resemble the world or vniuers" and that its "indefiniteness hauing no speciall place of beginning nor end, beareth a similitude with God and eternitie"; *The Arte of English Poesie* (1589), ed. G. D. Willcock and A. Walker (Cambridge: Cambridge University Press, 1936), p. 98. Compare, for instance, Henry Vaughan's use of the symbol in "The World."

46. *Christian Morals*, in *Works of Sir Thomas Browne*, ed. Geoffrey Keynes (London: Faber & Gwyer, 1928–31), I, 112. All quotations from Browne are from Keynes's edition.

47. Ibid., p. 113.

48. See Dent, *John Webster's Borrowing*, p. 284.

49. Browne, *Musaeum Clausum, or Bibliotheca Abscondita*, in *Works*, V, 138.

50. See Dent, *John Webster's Borrowing*, pp. 283–284.

51. Browne, *Christian Morals*, p. 144.

52. Ibid.

53. See the discussion of *Westward Ho* and *Northward Ho* in Pt. II, chap. 1, above.

54. Browne, *Christian Morals*, p. 140.

55. R. G. Howarth, "Webster's *Guise*," *Notes & Queries*, 13 (1966), 294–296.

56. Edward Grimestone, trans., *A General Inventorie of the History of France* by John de Serres and Pierre Matthieu (London, 1607), pp. 708, 724. This section of the history was, however, written by de Serres, not Matthieu. Webster's friend Chapman used the book as his principal source for the *Byron* plays.

57. In *The Revenge of Bussy D'Ambois* Epernon refers to "the guises / That vulgar great ones make their pride and zeal" (I.i.155–156) in a context where the Duc de Guise is present and being discussed. See T. M. Parrott, ed., *The Plays and Poems of George Chapman: The Tragedies* (London: Routledge, 1910), p. 85.

58. H. J. Oliver, ed., *"Dido Queen of Carthage" and "The Massacre at Paris"* (London: Methuen, 1968). Other quotations of *The Massacre* are taken from this edition.

59. Weil, *Christopher Marlowe, Merlin's Prophet* (Cambridge: Cambridge University Press, 1977), p. 102.

60. Wilson, *Marlowe and the Early Shakespeare* (Oxford: Clarendon Press, 1953), pp. 88–89.

61. Quoted in Hyder E. Rollins, "Samuel Sheppard and His Praise of Poets," *Studies in Philology*, 24 (1927), 554.

62. See Lucas, ed., *Works*, II, 217–218, 339. As Shirley points out in her edition, Webster's reference to "Betray[ing] a town to th' Turk" looks like "a specific allusion" (p. 59) to the Marlowe drama. Moreover, Barabas, reveling (like Romelio) in his villainies, brags of his Italian nurture in crime: "Being young, I studied physic, and began / To practise first upon the Italian" (II.iii.183–184); see N. W. Bawcutt, ed., *The Jew of Malta* (Manchester: Manchester University Press, 1978), p. 115.

63. Bentley, *The Jacobean and Caroline Stage*, V, 1251.

64. Bentley, reasoning from the insistence on dates in the scene (IV.ii) where Romelio's age is at issue, urges 1610 as the date of composition, but he dismisses the evidence of later sources much too lightly; *The Jacobean and Caroline Stage*, V, 1250–1251. See John Russell Brown, "The Date of John Webster's *The Devil's Law-Case*," *Notes & Queries*, 5 (1958), 100–101; and Dent, *John Webster's Borrowing*, pp. 58–59.

65. M. C. Bradbrook speculates that Webster dedicated the play to Sir Thomas Finch because he lived in Drury Lane, the vicinity of the Cockpit Theatre, and would presumably take a special interest in plays produced there. See *John Webster: Citizen and Dramatist*, pp. 171–172.

66. See Baldini, *John Webster e il linguaggio della tragedia* (Rome: Edizioni dell' Ateneo, 1953), pp. 208–209; and Berry, *The Art of John Webster* (Oxford: Clarendon Press, 1972), p. 167.

67. See Lucas, ed., *Works*, II, 215–216; and Dent, *John Webster's Borrowing*, pp. 308–309.

68. See Forker, "A Possible Source for the Ceremony of the Cardinal's Arming in *The Duchess of Malfi*," pp. 399–401.

69. Gunnar Boklund, "*The Devil's Law-Case*—An End or a Beginning?" in *John Webster*, ed. Brian Morris (London: Ernest Benn, 1970), pp. 113–130.

70. Ibid., p. 117. Boklund errs, however, in deriving the name of Leonora from Rowley's play. The queen's name in that drama is Leodice (not Leonora) and her lover is Crispinus (not Crispianus, who is a brother). The mistake presumably arose from the speech prefixes in the 1638 quarto, which read respectively "*Leo.*" and "*Cris.*"

71. Compare *Sejanus* (I.568–570); and see Dent, *John Webster's Borrowing*, p. 295.

72. The phrase is Berry's. See *The Art of John Webster*, p. 164.

73. See n. 29 above.

74. It is possible that Webster had already alluded to this legend in *The Duchess of Malfi*. When Ferdinand leaves a ring with his imprisoned sister as "a love-token," he adds, "when you need a friend / Send it to him that ow'd it" (IV.i.47–50). Of course, the ring in this case is on the severed hand of a dead man whom the Duchess later takes to be her husband. The grotesquerie of the allusion in so macabre a context would, of course, be typically Websterian. Chapman in *The Tragedy of Charles Duke of Byron* (a play that Webster seems to have admired) had also alluded to Essex's imprisonment and the queen's wish to spare her favorite at the last moment, but in Chapman the earl's execution resulted not from the miscarriage of a ring but from Essex's refusal to "ask . . . her mercy" (V.iii.141). Chapman based his account directly on Grimestone's *General Inventorie of the History of France* (1607), p. 984, a work that Webster also knew; see Parrott, ed., *The Plays and Poems of George Chapman: The Tragedies*, pp. 262, 620. The Restoration play-

wright John Banks, several of whose tragedies show the influence of Webster (see Appendix, p. 524) dramatized the legend of the queen's ring in *The Unhappy Favourite, or, The Earl of Essex* (1681).

75. Lucas, ed., *Works*, II, 215.

PART II

Chapter 3

1. See Sykes, "A Webster-Middleton Play: *Anything for a Quiet Life*," *Notes & Queries*, 9 (1921), 181–183, 202–204, 225–226, 300; reprinted in *Sidelights on Elizabethan Drama* (London: Humphrey Milford, Oxford University Press, 1924), pp. 159–172. Fernand Lagarde sums up the controversy and much of the evidence for Webster's hand with admirable objectivity and thoroughness; see his *John Webster* (Toulouse: Association des Publications de la Faculté des Lettres et Sciences Humaines, 1968), I, 179–187. Lagarde probably goes too far, however, in claiming that "Dans toutes les scènes, sauf celles qui sont consacrées exclusivement à Sweetball le barbier-chirurgien et aux ruses de George Cressingham et du jeune Franklin, la main de Webster apparaît aussi distinctement que le permet le sujet middletonien"; pp. 183–184. See also R. W. Dent, *John Webster's Borrowing* (Berkeley and Los Angeles: University of California Press, 1960), pp. 60–61. The chief minority voice has been that of G. E. Bentley, who dismisses the internal evidence as mere impressionism; *The Jacobean and Caroline Stage* (Oxford: Clarendon Press, 1941–68), IV, 859–861. David M. Holmes and M. C. Bradbrook, disdaining to re-examine the question, simply echo Bentley; Holmes, *The Art of Thomas Middleton* (Oxford: Clarendon Press, 1970), p. 160; and Bradbrook, *John Webster, Citizen and Dramatist* (London: Weidenfeld and Nicolson, 1980), p. 199. Peter B. Murray also doubts Webster's hand, but the orthographic evidence he takes seriously is incomplete; Murray, *A Study of John Webster* (The Hague: Mouton, 1969), pp. 261–263.

2. See Elmer Edgar Stoll, *John Webster: The Periods of His Work as Determined by His Relations to the Drama of His Day* (Boston: A. Mudge & Son, 1905), pp. 34–37.

3. Power, "Double, Double," *Notes & Queries*, 6 (1959), 4–8.

4. See A. W. Ward, *A History of English Dramatic Literature to the Death of Queen Anne* (London: Macmillan, 1899), II, 523; and Holmes, *The Art of Thomas Middleton*, p. 153.

5. See Dent, *John Webster's Borrowing*, pp. 295, 221.

6. See, for instance, *The Changeling*, III.iv.167 and V.ii.54–55, ed. N. W. Bawcutt (London: Methuen, 1961), pp. 65, 99. See also the Appendix, pp. 496–497.

7. See especially F. L. Lucas, ed., *The Complete Works of John Webster* (London: Chatto & Windus, 1927), IV, 250–256. See also R. H. Barker, *Thomas Middleton* (New York: Columbia University Press, 1958), pp. 191–192.

8. Lake, *The Canon of Thomas Middleton's Plays* (Cambridge: Cambridge University Press, 1975), pp. 175–184. Lake adduces "Pew wew" in *The White Devil* (Lucas ed., I.ii.72) and "Pew" in *The Devil's Law-Case* (Lucas ed., V.iv.97); he also points out that Webster is unique among Renaissance dramatists in his regular use of *of't*, which appears in all his unaided plays—*The White Devil* (four times), *The Duchess of Malfi* (three times), and *The Devil's Law-Case* (six times).

9. See Shand's review of Lake's *Canon of Thomas Middleton's Plays* in *Shakespeare Studies*, 11 (1978), 311–314.

10. Jackson, *Studies in Attribution: Middleton and Shakespeare* (Salzburg: Institut für Anglistik und Amerikanistik, Universität Salzburg, 1979), p. 144. See also Jackson's review of Lake's *Canon of Thomas Middleton's Plays* in the *Journal of English and Germanic Philology*, 75 (1976), 414–417.

11. See Margery Fisher, "Notes on the Sources of Some Incidents in Middleton's London Plays," *Review of English Studies*, 15 (1939), 283–293; Fisher cites parallels to the episode of Water-Chamlet's gulling.

12. Lucas, ed., *Works*, IV, 76.

13. Lagarde, *John Webster*, I, 192.

14. A. C. Swinburne, *The Age of Shakespeare* (London: Chatto & Windus, 1908), p. 160; reprinted in Edmund Gosse and T. J. Wise, eds., *The Complete Works of Algernon Charles Swinburne* (London: William Heinemann, 1925–27), XI, 391.

15. Lagarde, *John Webster*, I, 177, 193; and Holmes, *The Art of Thomas Middleton*, p. 153.

16. Lucas, ed., *Works*, IV, 69–70.

17. Parker, "Middleton's Experiments with Comedy and Judgement," in *Jacobean Theatre*, ed. John Russell Brown and Bernard Harris, Stratford-upon-Avon Studies, 1 (New York: St. Martin's Press, 1960), p. 183.

18. Ibid., p. 183.

19. Margot Heinemann observes that the surprise ending "is of course a weakness, and makes the neglect of the play in later times less surprising"; Heinemann, *Puritanism and Theatre: Thomas Middleton and Opposition Drama under the Early Stuarts* (Cambridge: Cambridge University Press, 1980), p. 119.

20. Heinemann, who argues that Middleton is generally more sympathetic with citizen values than has often been allowed, stresses Old Franklin's "severe" condemnation of the prank against the mercer; *Puritanism and Theatre*, p. 118. But, as I have already suggested, the play undermines the moralist's own ethical authority.

21. Thomas Heywood gives "wrack" (= destroy, ruin) as "rac," a spelling cited by the *OED*. See *The Iron Age* (printed 1632), ed. Arlene W. Weiner (New York: Garland Press, 1979): "*Troy* was twice rac't and *Troy* deseru'd that wracke . . ." (I.i.32).

22. See *The Duchess of Malfi*, IV.ii.113.

23. I have discussed these elements more thoroughly in "Shakespearean Imitation in Act V of *Anything for a Quiet Life*," *Papers on Language and Literature*, 7 (1971), 75–80.

24. De Witt T. Starnes and Gertrude E. Noyes, *The English Dictionary from Cawdrey to Johnson, 1604–1755* (Chapel Hill: University of North Carolina Press, 1946), p. 27. Starnes and Noyes devote a chapter to Cockeram's compilation; pp. 26–37.

25. Lucas, ed., *Works*, III, 261.

26. See C. J. Sisson, *Lost Plays of Shakespeare's Age* (Cambridge: Cambridge University Press, 1936), p. 84.

27. Ibid., p. 102n.

28. See Mary Edmond, "In Search of John Webster," *Times Literary Supplement* (24 December 1976), pp. 1621–1622.

29. Sir Henry Herbert's license cannot be dated precisely, but it was granted between 3 and 15 September 1624, the dates that immediately precede and follow the entry for *A Late Murder*; see J. Q. Adams, *The Dramatic Records of Sir Henry Herbert* (New Haven: Yale University Press, 1917), p. 29.

30. Sisson, *Lost Plays of Shakespeare's Age*, pp. 80–124.

31. See Bentley, *The Jacobean and Caroline Stage*, III, 253.

32. Sisson, *Lost Plays of Shakespeare's Age*, p. 96 and plate ii facing.

33. Ibid., p. 103.

34. Ibid., p. 106.

35. Ibid., p. 111.

36. For additional examples and Fletcher's possible influence on the lost play to which Webster contributed, see Charles R. Forker, "*Wit Without Money*: A Fletcherian Antecedent to *Keep the Widow Waking*," *Comparative Drama*, 8 (1974), 172–183.

37. R. T. D. Sayle, *Lord Mayors' Pageants of the Merchant Taylors' Company in the 15th, 16th, & 17th Centuries* (London: Eastern Press, 1931), p. 108.

38. Ibid., p. 2. Sayle quotes from William Smythe, whose *A Breffe Description of the Royall Citie of London* (1575) gives the classical account of the annual ceremonies.

39. Sayle, *Lord Mayors' Pageants*, pp. 110–111.

40. Lucas, ed., *Works*, III, 320.

41. Ibid., p. 327.

42. David M. Bergeron, *English Civic Pageantry, 1558–1642* (Columbia: University of South Carolina Press, 1971), p. 212.

43. Ibid., pp. 207–208.

44. See Bernard M. Wagner, "New Verses by John Webster," *Modern Language Notes*, 46 (1931), 403–405.

45. William Gifford and Alexander Dyce, eds., *The Dramatic Works and Poems of James Shirley* (London: John Murray, 1833), VI, 396–397.

46. British Museum 1849–3–15–15. On the dating, see Wagner, "New Verses by John Webster."

47. See Fernand Lagarde, "Les Emprunts de John Webster,"*Études Anglaises*, 16 (1963), 248–250; also see Lagarde's *John Webster*, I, 365–367, 398, n. 33.

PART II

Chapter 4

1. The most important discussions of the authorship of *A Cure for a Cuckold* are to be found in Lucas's edition of the *Works*, III, 10–18; in Fernand Lagarde's *John Webster* (Toulouse: Publications de la Faculté des Lettres et Sciences Humaines, 1968), I, 245–250, 332–344 (especially nn. 142–143); and in Peter B. Murray's *A Study of John Webster* (The Hague: Mouton, 1969), pp. 215–216, 265–268. Each summarizes earlier investigations of the problem.

2. See F. P. Wilson, *The Plague in Shakespeare's London* (Oxford: Clarendon Press, 1927), pp. 170–171.

3. Edmund Gosse emphasized the educational theme in 1883 by suggesting to S. E. Spring-Rice that the main action of the play be detached from its subplot and printed as *Love's Graduate* (see Gosse's *Seventeenth-Century Studies* [London: Kegan Paul, 1883], p. 67, and Spring-Rice's edition of *Love's Graduate* [Oxford: H. Daniel, 1885]). Peter B. Murray develops the point *in extenso* in *A Study of John Webster*, pp. 215–236.

4. Daniel's *Queen's Arcadia* (1605) is the source for two passages in *A Cure for a Cuckold*; see Lucas, ed., *Works*, III, 110–111.

5. When Clare reveals her "violent affection" to Bonvile, he responds (in the quarto):

> Violent indeed; for it seems it was your purpose
> To have ended it in violence on your friend:
> The unfortunate *Lessingham* unwittingly
> Should have been the Executioner.
>
> (IV.ii.163–167)

Lucas, following Rupert Brooke, alters Q's "violence on your friend" to "violence: and your friend," arguing that Bonvile's statement and Clare's assent to it contradict what Clare has earlier said about Lessingham's misreading of her letter and her plan that he should give her poison (see *Works*, III, 117). Murray contends that Bonvile's "seems" saves the text from inconsistency but fails to explain how Lessingham could have killed Bonvile in a duel "unwittingly" (*A Study of John Webster*, p. 229). There may well be some textual corruption at this point or some unresolved conflict resulting from imperfect collaboration, but surely it is not impossible that Webster simply wished to cloud the whole question of Clare's intention.

6. Joseph Harris's *The City Bride, or the Merry Cuckold* (1696) is a stage adaptation of the Compass story detached from the main plot; see also n. 3 above.

7. Murray, *A Study of John Webster*, pp. 219, 230. Jacqueline Pearson also notes "the repetition of significant words" in her discussion of the play; see *Tragedy and Tragicomedy in the Plays of John Webster* (Totowa, N.J.: Barnes & Noble, 1980), pp. 119–121.

8. Lucas, ed., *Works*, III, 29.

9. See *The Plays and Poems of Philip Massinger*, ed. Philip Edwards and Colin Gibson (Oxford: Clarendon Press, 1976), II, 102–104.

10. In Painter, the tale of the Countess of Celant comes directly after Webster's source for *The Duchess of Malfi*.

11. See Lucas, ed., *Works*, IV, 147; and G. E. Bentley, *The Jacobean and Caroline Stage* (Oxford: Clarendon Press, 1941–68), III, 336–339. One scene contains an allusion to the Puritan tailor Ball, who had wagered money on his prediction that James I would become pope; since Ball is referred to as having lost his bet (V.ii.77–80), it seems likely that the king was already dead by the time these lines were written.

12. Cyrus Hoy, "The Shares of Fletcher and His Collaborators in the Beaumont and Fletcher Canon (V)," *Studies in Bibliography*, 13 (1960), 100–108.

13. Murray, *A Study of John Webster*, p. 263.

14. Lake, *The Canon of Thomas Middleton's Plays* (Cambridge: Cambridge University Press, 1975). MacD. P. Jackson, working independently, generally corroborates Lake's data, although neither scholar is principally concerned with Webster and neither discusses *The Fair Maid of the Inn*. See Jackson, *Studies in Attribution: Middleton and Shakespeare* (Salzburg: Institut für Anglistik und Amerikanistik, Universität Salzburg, 1979), pp. ii–iii (Preface) and p. 188 (Table II).

15. See Hoy's table of forms in "The Shares of Fletcher and His Collaborators . . . (V)," p. 108.

16. Sykes, "A Webster-Massinger Play," *Notes & Queries*, 12 (1915), 134–137, 155–156, reprinted in *Sidelights on Elizabethan Drama* (London: Humphrey Milford, Oxford University Press, 1924), pp. 140–172; Lucas, ed., *Works*, IV, 148–152. Lagarde (*John Webster*, I, 216–217) conveniently summarizes the various ascriptions of authorship that have been made in the past.

17. Although mentioned in the text of *The Duchess* and apparently acted by N. Towley in the original performance, Forobosco has no speaking part in the 1623 quarto. See John Russell Brown's edition (London: Methuen, 1964), p. lxvii.

18. See R. W. Dent, *John Webster's Borrowing* (Berkeley and Los Angeles: University of California Press, 1960), p. 306.

19. Gabriele Baldini, *John Webster e il linguaggio della tragedia* (Rome: Edizioni dell' Ateneo, 1953), pp. 220–221.

20. This is not, of course, to rule out a certain amount of overlapping between collaborators within a scene, perhaps as the result of revision. Hoy has pointed to one passage of *The Fair Maid* (II.i.127–131) where Ford may be overwriting Webster ("The Shares of Fletcher and His Collaborators . . . [V]," pp. 102–103). It is equally possible that Webster may have had something to do with the "Ford scene" in which the Host commends his wife's remark during a discussion of Bianca's wooers with the sexual joke, "Well put in wife!" (III.i.113). This recalls Flamineo's bawdy double-entendre at the exchange of jewels between Bracciano and Vittoria in *The White Devil*: "well put in duke" (I.ii.225).

21. M. C. Bradbrook's surprising statement that "there is no support for Webster's part in *The Fair Maid of the Inn*" obviously oversimplifies this issue; see *John Webster, Citizen and Dramatist* (London: Weidenfeld and Nicolson, 1980), p. 199. More prudently, Jacqueline Pearson allows the possibility of Webster's part authorship; see *Tragedy and Tragicomedy in the Plays of John Webster*, p. 55.

22. Baldwin Maxwell in "The Source of the Principal Plot of *The Fair Maid of the Inn*," *Modern Language Notes*, 59 (1944), 122–127, suggested Robert Dallington's account of the Florentine episode in his *A Survey of the Great Dukes State of Tuscany* (London, 1605). Bertha Hensman, however, has established beyond reasonable doubt that the play is directly indebted to Beding-

field's English version of Machiavelli's *History of Florence*; see *The Shares of Fletcher, Field, and Massinger in Twelve Plays of the Beaumont and Fletcher Canon* (Salzburg: Institut für Englishche Sprache und Literatur, Universität Salzburg, 1974), II, 361–362.

23. The tale of the mother who denies her parenthood of a son and is then commanded to marry him may derive from the *Sainte Cour* of Nicholas Caussin (Paris, 1624) or from some earlier rendering of a familiar plot motif; see Lucas, ed., *Works*, II, 219–221, and IV, 147.

24. See Albert E. Sloman, "The Spanish Source of *The Fair Maid of the Inn*," in *Hispanic Studies in Honour of I. González Llubera*, ed. Frank Pierce (Oxford: Dolphin, 1959), pp. 331–341. Fletcher and Massinger seem to have known Spanish. Sloman suggests that a lost version of Lope's play may have been available in England.

25. T. W. Baldwin assigns seven of the roles in *The Fair Maid* to actors who had earlier performed in *The Duchess of Malfi*: Alberto to John Lowin (Bosola), Cesario to Joseph Taylor (Ferdinand), Prospero to Richard Robinson (the Cardinal), the Duke of Florence to Robert Benfield (Antonio), Mentivole to Richard Sharpe (the Duchess), Mariana to John Thompson (Julia), and Clarissa to Robert Pallant (Cariola). See Baldwin's chart of actors and roles in *The Organization and Personnel of the Shakespearean Company* (Princeton: Princeton University Press, 1927), pp. 198 ff.

26. See W. W. Greg, *Pastoral Poetry and Pastoral Drama* (London: A. H. Bullen, 1906), p. 70.

27. Hoy, "The Shares of Fletcher and His Collaborators . . . (V)," pp. 100–101.

28. Lucas, ed., *Works*, IV, 153.

29. Lagarde, *John Webster*, I, 324 (n. 65).

30. The name Forobosco may derive ultimately from the character in *Antonio and Mellida*, from which play Webster may have picked it up for *The Duchess of Malfi*; see n. 17 above.

31. Lucas gives the Forobosco sections entirely to Webster (see *Works*, IV, 154), and Lagarde concurs. Hoy assigns the "surprise scene" (IV.ii) to him.

32. See *The Fair Maid of the Inn* (IV.ii.27–31) and *The Duchess of Malfi* (IV.ii.104–106).

33. Bertha Hensman in *The Shares of Fletcher, Field, and Massinger in Twelve Plays*, II, 347–354, argues that the inconsistencies and anomalies are "serious crudities" (p. 348) and "signs of far-reaching revision" (p. 347) that "disrupt the flow of the play as drama and make it difficult to believe that the extant play could ever have been staged at all" (p. 349). In my opinion, she greatly exaggerates the problem.

34. Lucas summarizes the arguments (*Works*, III, 122–123).

35. Dent, *John Webster's Borrowing*, p. 62.

36. See Marcia Lee Anderson, "Webster's Debt to Guazzo," *Studies in Philology*, 36 (1939), 192–205.

37. See Steppat, "John Webster's *Appius and Virginia*," *American Notes and Queries*, 20 (March–April 1982), 101.

38. See Lucas, ed., *Works*, III, 125–126.

39. See Lagarde, *John Webster*, I, 279–281; also see Leech, *John Webster: A Critical Study* (London: Hogarth Press, 1951), p. 94.

40. Heywood's *Hierarchie of the Blessed Angels* was licensed 7 November 1634. See Lucas, ed., *Works*, I, 52 (n. 3); and Bentley, *The Jacobean and Caroline Stage*, V, 1244.

41. M. C. Bradbrook, connecting the starvation of Virginius's troops with Sir Horace Vere's campaign in the Netherlands, suggests that Webster composed the play in 1622 for boy actors (*John Webster, Citizen and Dramatist*, pp. 178–179).

42. See Rupert Brooke, *John Webster and the Elizabethan Drama* (London: Sidgwick & Jackson, 1916), pp. 161–205; and A. M. Clark, "The Authorship of *Appius and Virginia*," *Modern Language Review*, 16 (1921), 1–17.

43. Gray, "*Appius and Virginia*: By Webster and Heywood," *Studies in Philology*, 24 (1927), 275–289; and Lucas, ed., *Works*, III, 134–135.

44. Lagarde, *John Webster*, I, 297–300, 342–343 (n. 215); and Murray, *A Study of John Webster*, pp. 237–238, 269–270. Murray shows that, whereas Webster often uses *i'th'*, *'tis*, *in't*, *in's*, *see't*, and analogous forms, Heywood tends to avoid these. Lagarde studies a greater variety of usages but gets substantially the same results. In the main both corroborate Lucas.

45. See David M. Bevington, *From "Mankind" to Marlowe* (Cambridge, Mass: Harvard University Press, 1962), p. 32.

46. I quote Ernest Cary's translation of Dionysius's *Roman Antiquities* in the Loeb Classical Library (Cambridge, Mass.: Harvard University Press, 1950), XI, 7.

47. Lucas (*Works*, III, 226–227) believes that Webster did consult Sylburg's Greek text, arguing that the 1654 quarto reads "*Agidon*" (I.i.135), a form that is closer to a mistake in the Greek manuscript uncorrected by the German editor than to the Latin *Algidus*. The evidence seems rather slender to me.

48. Appius's equivocal argument that accepting the Roman magistracy means banishment "from all my kindred and my friends" (I.i.91) seems to derive from an anecdote in *The Lord Coke his Speech and Charge* (1607); see Dent, *John Webster's Borrowing*, pp. 62–63.

49. Cary, ed., *Roman Antiquities*, VII, 43–45.

50. Ibid., p. 155.

51. Lucas first pointed out most of these resemblances (*Works*, III, 132); see also Philemon Holland, trans., *The Romane Historie Written by T. Livius of Padua* (London, 1600), pp. 122, 121, 126, and 128 respectively.

52. Holland, trans., *The Romane Historie*, p. 117.

53. Ibid., p. 126.

54. Ibid., pp. 126–127.

55. Ibid., p. 109.

56. Ibid., p. 118; see Lucas, ed., *Works*, III, 239–240.

57. The 1654 quarto spells the name variously as "Calpharina," "Colpharnia," and "Calphurina"; compare the Shakespeare First Folio's "Calphurnia."

58. E. E. Stoll, *John Webster: The Periods of His Work as Determined by His Relations to the Drama of His Day* (Boston: Alfred Mudge, 1905), pp. 194–195.

59. Compare "a pearl . . . Richer than all his tribe" (*Othello*, V.ii.356–357).

60. See I.i.66–67 and III.ii.383–384; also see Lucas's commentary (*Works*, III, 226 and 240). Virginius's concern lest the Roman mob with "violent hands" should "drag hence / This impious Judg, piece-meal to tear his limbs" (V.ii.43–45) may also have been suggested by the fate of Jonson's villain; see *Sejanus* (V.vi.808–826) in C. H. Herford and Percy and Evelyn Simpson, eds., *Ben Jonson* (Oxford: Clarendon Press, 1925–52), IV, 467–468.

61. George Saintsbury, *A History of Elizabethan Literature* (New York: Macmillan, 1887), p. 274.

62. "The Physician's Tale" (ll. 155–156) in F. N. Robinson, ed., *The Works of Geoffrey Chaucer* (Boston: Houghton Mifflin, 1957), p. 146.

63. See *Sejanus* in C. H. Herford and Percy and Evelyn Simpson, eds., *Ben Jonson*, IV, 350.

64. Both Livy and Dionysius suggest the analogy with Lucrece, and the tradition continued into the Middle Ages; the stories of both martyrs are juxtaposed, for instance, in Book VII of Gower's *Confessio Amantis*.

65. Cary, ed., *Roman Antiquities*, VII, 117.

66. Ibid., p. 95.

67. A stage direction in *The Devil's Law-Case* designates Contilupo "*a spruce lawyer*" (IV.i.77).

68. Conceivably, Webster took the name from Nero's famous general whom the emperor suspected of conspiracy and therefore ordered to commit suicide. At one point, the comic implies that he is destined for execution (III.iv.4). Fletcher had alluded to the historical Corbulo in *Valentinian*

(IV.i.135–141); see Fredson Bowers, gen. ed., *The Dramatic Works in the Beaumont and Fletcher Canon* (Cambridge: Cambridge University Press, 1966–), IV, 339.

69. See Stoll, *John Webster: The Periods of His Work*, pp. 197–200; and Brooke, *John Webster and the Elizabethan Drama*, pp. 189–191.

70. See *Appius and Virginia* (III.ii.47–58); and Lucas's note (*Works*, III, 236); compare *An ordinarie Widdow* (*Works*, IV, 39).

71. Archer, "Webster, Lamb, and Swinburne," *New Review*, 8 (1893), 105.

72. William Hazlitt, *Lectures on the Dramatic Literature of the Age of Elizabeth* (London: John Warren, 1821), p. 114; reprinted in P. P. Howe, ed., *The Complete Works of William Hazlitt* (London: J. M. Dent, 1930–34), VI, 234.

73. Stoll, *John Webster: The Periods of His Work*, p. 40; Brooke, *John Webster and the Elizabethan Drama*, p. 169; and Lucas, ed., *Works*, III, 147.

74. Haworth, "Prelude to the Study of Webster's Plays," in *English Hymns and Ballads and Other Studies in Popular Literature* (Oxford: Basil Blackwell, 1927), pp. 137–148.

75. Seiden, "Two Notes on Webster's *Appius and Virginia*," *Philological Quarterly*, 35 (1956), 416; and Murray, *A Study of John Webster*, p. 252.

76. Eliot, "Thomas Heywood," in *Selected Essays* (London: Faber and Faber, 1951), p. 172.

77. M. C. Bradbrook, *Themes and Conventions of Elizabethan Tragedy* (Cambridge: Cambridge University Press, 1935), p. 186.

78. T. S. Eliot, "John Marston," in *Selected Essays*, p. 230.

79. Ibid., p. 232.

80. *The Rape of Lucrece*, l. 687.

81. See Steppat, "John Webster's *Appius and Virginia*," p. 101; and p. 201 above.

82. Lucas, ed., *Works*, III, 146.

83. Icilius tells Numitorius, apart from "A thousand things which I have now forgot," that he confronted Appius with evidence of the judge's pursuit of Virginia, "known circumstance, / That he might well excuse, but not deny," and that Appius "swore to me quite to abjure her love" (III.i.102–110). But, in fact, we have observed Appius imply that the incriminating letters are forgeries and, far from abjuring Virginia, disclaim any interest in her: "wee are far / Even in least thought from her; and for those Letters, / Tokens and Presents, wee acknowledg none" (II.iii.145–147).

84. Leech, *John Webster: A Critical Study*, p. 94.

85. See also I.i.123–126 and V.ii.124–125.

86. Ekeblad, "Storm Imagery in *Appius and Virginia*," *Notes & Queries*, 3 (1956), 5–7.

87. Compare *The Duchess of Malfi* (I.i.466–467); see also Dent, *John Webster's Borrowing*, p. 191.

88. See Lucas, ed., *Works*, III, 239.

89. See Bentley, *The Jacobean and Caroline Stage*, V, 1248.

90. See Robert Latham and William Matthews, eds., *The Diary of Samuel Pepys* (Berkeley and Los Angeles: University of California Press, 1970–83), IX, 552–553.

PART III

Chapter 5

1. In Provençal the word for love was spelled *l'amor* and to the ear was indistinguishable from *la mort*. A play on the two words also appears in medieval French—in the prose *Tristan* where Brengain says after the lovers have drunk the love potion, "dans la coupe maudite, vous avez bu l'amour et la mort" (see Joseph Bedier, *Le Roman de Tristan et Iseut* [Paris: H. Piazza, 1962], p. 50).

2. Novel 50 in Arthur Machen's translation of the *Heptameron* ([London?]: Privately printed, 1886), p. 298. The first complete translation in English was Robert Codrington's in 1654, but the work was apparently well known. A number of Marguerite's tales are included in the first volume of William Painter's *Palace of Pleasure* (1566).

3. Frederick S. Boas, ed., *The Tragedie of Soliman and Perseda*, in *The Works of Thomas Kyd*, 2nd ed. (Oxford: Clarendon Press, 1955).

4. Christopher Marlowe, *"Dido Queen of Carthage" and "The Massacre at Paris,"* ed. H. J. Oliver (London: Methuen, 1968); compare Shakespeare's *Antony and Cleopatra*: "Eternity was in our lips and eyes, / Bliss in our brows' bent . . ." (I.iii.35–36).

5. A. H. Bullen, ed., *The Works of Thomas Middleton* (London: John C. Nimmo, 1885; rept. New York: AMS Press, 1964), VI, 395.

6. Lord Guilford Dudley and Lady Jane Grey are the youthful lovers of Dekker and Webster's *Sir Thomas Wyatt* (1607), tragically victimized by the political ambition of their fathers; see pt. II, chap. 1, pp. 66–68, 72. The Pyramus and Thisbe story, an analogue to *Romeo and Juliet*, is best known to students of the drama through Shakespeare's parody in *A Midsummer Night's Dream*, but an English company is known to have performed a play of this title at Nordlingen in 1604; see A. Harbage, *Annals of English Drama*, rev. S. Schoenbaum (London: Methuen, 1964), p. 206.

7. C. H. Herford and Percy and Evelyn Simpson, eds., *Ben Jonson* (Oxford: Clarendon Press, 1925–52), VII, 19–20. Later citations are to this edition.

8. Denis de Rougemont, *Love in the Western World*, trans. Montgomery Belgion, 2nd ed. (Garden City, N.Y.: Doubleday, 1957).

9. M. L. Wine, ed., *The Tragedy of Master Arden of Faversham* (London: Methuen, 1973).

10. Robert Burton, *The Anatomy of Melancholy*, ed. Holbrook Jackson (London: Dent, 1964), III, 49.

11. William Gifford and Alexander Dyce, eds., *The Works of John Ford* (London: Lawrence and Bullen, 1895; rept. New York: Russell & Russell, 1965), I, 69.

12. The word "courage" in Renaissance English was often used to denote "sexual vigour and inclination, lust" (see *OED*).

13. Thomas Middleton, *Women Beware Women*, ed. J. R. Mulryne (London: Methuen, 1975). Later citations are to this edition.

14. John Ford, *'Tis Pity She's a Whore*, ed. Derek Roper (London: Methuen, 1975).

15. *"Nihil usitatius apud monachos, cardinales, sacrificulos, etiam furor hic ad mortem, ad insanum"* (*The Anatomy of Melancholy*, III, 51).

16. *Christopher Marlowe's "Edward II": Text and Major Criticism*, ed. Irving Ribner (New York: Odyssey Press, 1970).

17. Thomas Kyd, *The Spanish Tragedy*, ed. Philip Edwards (London: Methuen, 1959).

18. James Shirley, *The Cardinal*, ed. Charles R. Forker (Bloomington: Indiana University Press, 1964).

19. See the Cleveland Museum of Art's catalogue, *European Paintings Before 1500, Part I* (Cleveland: The Museum, 1974), pp. 35–36.

20. See Elizabeth Jenkins, *Elizabeth the Great* (New York: Coward-McCann, 1959), pp. 17, 28. Like Webster's Duke Ferdinand, Seymour "had possessed himself of a master key" to his relation's bedchamber, and on one occasion so frightened the princess by his intrusion that "she ran out of her bed to her maidens and then went behind the curtains of the bed" while he "tarried a long time in hopes she would come out" (p. 27).

21. Even a very early play such as the Inner Temple *Gismond of Salerne* (1566), rev. by Robert Wilmot as *Tancred and Gismund* (1581), provides a classic example. That the couple in this drama have to meet in a secret cave located beneath Gismund's bedchamber serves to emphasize the tyrannical suppression of emotional and sexual fulfillment that is a *donnée* of the action. The moment the lovers emerge above ground, they court their destruction in the form of a hostile father

and can realize their commitment to each other only through dying. Looked at symbolically, the entire action could be read as a conflict between libido and guilt—irreconcilable in life but capable of being sublimated (and therefore resolved) in death.

22. Bloemaert's allegorical *Death and the Lovers* (sometimes entitled *Vanity*) is drawing no. 3744 in the Witt Collection at the Courtauld Institute of Art, London; it was reproduced in *Life*, 71 (13 August 1971), 43, in an article on historical attitudes toward women.

23. Thomas Clayton, ed., *The Works of Sir John Suckling: The Non-Dramatic Works* (Oxford: Clarendon Press, 1971), pp. 66–68.

24. Sir Herbert Grierson, ed., *The Poems of John Donne* (London: Oxford University Press, 1933).

25. Anon., *The Second Maiden's Tragedy* (I.ii.247–248), ed. Anne Lancashire (Manchester: Manchester University Press, 1978).

26. *The Examination, Confession, and Condemnation of Henry Robson* (London, 1598), sig. A4. See the unique copy in the Bodleian Library, Oxford.

27. Charles S. Mish, ed., *Short Fiction of the Seventeenth Century* (New York: New York University Press, 1963), pp. 38–39.

28. John Marston, *Antonio's Revenge*, ed. G. K. Hunter (Lincoln: University of Nebraska Press, 1965).

29. John Ford, *The Broken Heart*, ed. T. J. B. Spencer (Manchester: Manchester University Press, 1980).

30. John Marston, *The Fawn*, ed. Gerald A. Smith (Lincoln: University of Nebraska Press, 1968). The punishment of binding live bodies to dead ones derives from Virgil's *Aeneid*, VIII, 485–488 (the passage to which Marston alludes in *The Fawn*), but it became a familiar emblem of unhappy marriage (see R. W. Dent, *John Webster's Borrowing* [Berkeley and Los Angeles: University of California Press, 1960], p. 231). Not surprisingly, Milton refers to it in *The Doctrine and Discipline of Divorce* (Frank A. Patterson, ed., *The Works of John Milton* [New York: Columbia University Press, 1931–40], III, 478). Burton in a passage listing sexual enormities mentions certain Egyptians "who lie with beautiful cadavers" ("*qui cum formosarum cadaveribus concumbunt*"; *The Anatomy of Melancholy*, III, 51).

31. *The Wonder of Women, or The Tragedy of Sophonisba*, in A. H. Bullen, ed., *The Works of John Marston* (London: John C. Nimmo, 1887), II, 289.

32. Ben Jonson, *Volpone*, ed. Alvin B. Kernan (New Haven: Yale University Press, 1962); *The Sad Shepherd*, in C. H. Herford and Percy and Evelyn Simpson, eds., *Ben Jonson*, VII, 14.

33. Fredson Bowers, gen. ed., *The Dramatic Works in the Beaumont and Fletcher Canon* (Cambridge: Cambridge University Press, 1966–), II, 108.

34. Ibid., I, 439–440.

35. John Donne, "A Valediction: Forbidding Mourning" (ll. 22–23), and "The Canonization" (ll. 26–27).

36. Andrew Marvell, "The Definition of Love" (ll. 3–4), and "To His Coy Mistress" (ll. 31–32).

37. Both lovers expire on lines that utilize the same familiar pun: compare Romeo's "Thus with a kiss I die" (V.iii.120) and Juliet's "O happy dagger! / This is thy sheath; there rust, and let me die" (V.iii.169–170). The concept of love here dramatized is well expressed by the eighteenth-century German mystic Novalis, who wrote, "A union formed even unto death is a marriage bestowing on each a companion for Night. It is in death that love is sweetest. Death appears to one still alive as a nuptial night, the heart of sweet mysteries" (trans. M. C. D'Arcy in his *The Mind and Heart of Love* [New York: Meridian, 1956], p. 45).

38. John Lawlor, "*Romeo and Juliet*," in *Early Shakespeare*, ed. John Russell Brown and Bernard Harris, Stratford-upon-Avon Studies, 3 (London: Edward Arnold, 1961), p. 139.

39. Othello uses this phrase insultingly in one of his most brutal attacks upon his wife, but it nevertheless seems to embody his earlier conception of her purity—the conception that Iago has now so fatally shattered. The precise meaning is admittedly problematic, since the syntax of the

entire passage in which the quoted words appear is a much debated textual crux. Interpretation depends upon several factors, chiefly upon a choice of various ways of punctuating the passage as well as upon a choice between quarto and Folio readings (see M. R. Ridley's New Arden edition [London: Methuen, 1958], pp. 153–154, for a full discussion of the particulars). I follow Ridley in supposing that "cherubin" is a sarcastic epithet for Desdemona and "not an address to a personified virtue" (Patience).

40. Roman drama and Elizabethan history coincide astonishingly at this point. In 1601 the beheading of Sir Charles Danvers for complicity in the Essex rebellion provoked an eye witness to describe the sufferer as "put[ting] off his Gowne and Doublet in most cheerefull manner, rather like a Bridegrome, then a prisoner appointed for death; . . . kneeling . . . upon the sudden, as if hee had flowne, [he] threw his necke upon the blocke, and whilest he there held it seemed to smile . . ." (John Stow, *Annales; or, A Generall Chronicle of England* [London, 1631], sig. XXXI). The equation of violent death with marriage has religious precedent. A famous incident in the life of St. Catherine of Siena (1347–1380), frequently represented in painting and sculpture, concerns the saint's ministrations to one Niccolo di Toldo, an adolescent noble unjustly condemned to decapitation. Catherine held the boy's head as the axe descended, exhorting him to regard his death as his "nuptials" (see Michael de la Bedoyere, *Catherine, Saint of Siena* [London: Hollis & Carter, 1947], p. 57).

41. See Paul Robert, *Dictionnaire alphabétique et analogique et de la Langue Francaise* (Paris: Société du nouveau Littré, 1953–1964), II, 1485; also John Bayley, *The Characters of Love* (New York: Basic Books, 1960), p. 4. Ellis, to whom Bayley attributes the second epigram, was probably echoing Coleridge, who reported that "A person [apparently Wordsworth] once said to me, that he could make nothing of love, except that it was friendship accidentally combined with desire" (*Table Talk* [1835], 27 September 1830); see T. Ashe, ed., *The "Table Talk" and "Omniana" of Samuel Taylor Coleridge* (London: George Bell, 1884), p. 112. Coleridge had already expressed the same idea in "The Improvisatore" (1828): "But is not Love the union of both [i.e., of 'Friendship' and 'passion']?" See *The Poetical Works of Samuel Taylor Coleridge*, ed. E. H. Coleridge (London: Oxford University Press, 1912), p. 464.

PART III

Chapter 6

1. Eliot, "Whispers of Immortality," ll. 1–2, in *The Complete Poems and Plays* (New York: Harcourt, Brace, 1952), p. 32.

2. See the title page of the first edition (1612) also p. 545, n. 6, above.

3. Hoy, "Shakespeare and the Drama of His Time," in G. B. Evans, ed., *Shakespeare: Aspects of Influence* (Cambridge, Mass.: Harvard University Press, 1976), p. 37.

4. Francisco would have Bracciano, if possible, "Led . . . to Florence," there to be "crown'd . . . with a wreath of stinking garlic" (V.i.82–83); Octavius intends, apparently, to "lead" Cleopatra "in triumph," to "hoist [her] up . . . to the shouting varletry / Of censuring Rome" (V.ii.54–56, 108).

5. Hoy suggests that Shakespeare's episode (III.xiii–xiv) provided Webster with a hint for the parallel scene in *The White Devil*. See "Shakespeare and the Drama of His Time," p. 36.

6. The historical Bracciano suffered intensely from an ulcer on his leg. As J. W. Lever has suggested, Webster may be echoing a detail from his source that he suppressed in the dramatic characterization of the duke. See Lever, *The Tragedy of State* (London: Methuen, 1971), p. 79. Clearly Webster's figure is romantically attractive, virile, and energetic.

7. Thomas Kyd, *The Spanish Tragedy*, ed. Philip Edwards (London: Methuen, 1959).

8. Webster's proliferation of revengers to include the subordinates Gasparo, Pedro, and Carlo in addition to the major figures (Francisco, Monticelso, and Lodovico) emphasizes the terri-

fying pressures that menace any search for emotional satisfaction beyond the boundaries of self. If Christopher Lasch had written his popular book, *The Culture of Narcissism* (New York: Norton, 1978), about Jacobean England rather than about the America of the 1970s, he might have said that Webster was giving dramatic expression to such a culture "in an age of diminishing expectations."

9. George Holland, in "The Minor Characters in *The White Devil*," *Philological Quarterly*, 52 (1973), 43–54, argues that Francisco "is initially a good man who later changes to evil ways" (p. 45). His case rests chiefly upon taking the duke's moralistic remarks to Monticelso in IV.i as sincere. It seems plain to me that, like Malcolm testing Macduff, Francisco merely feels out Monticelso in this scene, dissembling here as cleverly as elsewhere. His eagerness to make use of the cardinal's "black book" and his resolve not to trust the churchman, uttered the moment he is out of earshot, establish the duke's deviousness beyond reasonable doubt.

10. The Commendatio Animae or commendation of the departing soul to God was a ceremony of the Roman church that called for a candle to be lit, a crucifix to be presented for contemplation, and a litany to be prayed antiphonally by the priest and bystanders for salvation of the soul. At the moment of death, aspirations to Christ were whispered into the dying person's ears. As has been pointed out, Lodovico and Gasparo cruelly invert this ritual, and Bracciano's final cry to Vittoria rather than to his Savior suggests his damnation. See Susan H. McLeod, "The *Commendatio Animae* and Bracciano's Death Scene in Webster's *The White Devil*," *American Notes and Queries*, 14 (December 1975), 50–52.

11. It may be more than a coincidence that Middleton's cardinal in *Women Beware Women*, ed. J. R. Mulryne (London: Methuen, 1975), warns his brother against damnable sin (IV.i.189–229) in terms reminiscent of Monticelso's preaching to Lodovico. Cardinal Ferdinando de Medici, the brother of the Duke Francisco who figures as a major villain in both tragedies, was associated historically with the vengeance taken against Bracciano and is mentioned in sources that Webster probably knew (see Gunnar Boklund, *The Sources of "The White Devil"* [Cambridge, Mass.: Harvard University Press, 1957], pp. 90–92, 149). But Margot Heinemann is mistaken in asserting that Webster's Monticelso-Paul IV (Montalto-Sixtus V of the sources) is "Historically . . . the same Cardinal as Middleton's" (*Puritanism and Theatre* [Cambridge: Cambridge University Press, 1980], p. 197). Cardinal Ferdinando succeeded his brother as Grand Duke of Tuscany in 1587, later resigned his red hat, and never became pope.

12. Like Lodovico, Carlo and Pedro also take vows "seal'd with the sacrament" (V.i.64) to second Francisco in revenge.

13. Jokes about vaulting and vaulting horses were common. The Host in Jonson's *The New Inn*, for instance, speaks of the decline of chivalrous values in terms of the tendency "To mount the Chambermaid; and for a leape / O' the vaulting horse, to ply the vaulting house . . ." (I.iii.73–74). See also Middleton's *A Mad World, My Masters* in which Follywit, referring to sexual intercourse, uses the expression "to vault into his master's saddle" (IV.i.35). I quote from *Ben Jonson*, ed. C. H. Herford and Percy and Evelyn Simpson, eds., (Oxford: Clarendon Press, 1925–52), VI, 412, and from *A Mad World, My Masters*, ed. Standish Henning (Lincoln: University of Nebraska Press, 1965), p. 70.

14. R. W. Dent doubts the sexual quibble in Flamineo's words, pointing out that the character appropriates a familiar proverb: " 'tis an easier Matter to raise the Devil, than 'tis to lay him"; see Dent, *John Webster's Borrowing* (Berkeley and Los Angeles: University of California Press, 1960), p. 137. But since, as Dent admits, similar erotic meanings are clear in *Romeo and Juliet* (II.i.24–27) and Middleton's *Women Beware Women* (I.i.80–83), I see little reason to exclude such a significance from Webster. Lucas (*Works*, I, 249) and Brown (*The White Devil*, p. 129) agree. Additional evidence for Webster's bawdry in this passage can be found in a famous story from Boccaccio's *Decameron* (III, 10) in which the monk Rustico introduces the naive Alibech to sexual intercourse by teaching her how to put his "devil" "back into [her] Hell." Boccaccio makes it plain that the sexual joke on *devil* had become commonplace: Alibech's townsfolk "coined a proverbial

saying . . . to the effect that the most agreeable way of serving God was to put the devil back in Hell. The dictum later crossed the sea to Italy, where it survives to this day." See G. F. McWilliam, trans., *The Decameron* (Harmondsworth: Penguin Books, 1972), pp. 316–319.

15. Cornelia's anxiety over the dead Marcello, particularly her mention of looking glass and feathers as a means of determining whether breath is still in his body (V.ii.38–40), obviously imitates Lear's words over the corpse of Cordelia.

16. Holland points out that Webster's choice of the name Cornelia "recalls the famous mother of the Gracchi," a woman much admired for strength of character ("The Minor Characters in *The White Devil*," p. 48). It might be added that the Roman matron's two sons, Tiberius and Gaius, like Marcello and Flamineo in Webster's play, both died violently.

17. "On the Life of Man" in Agnes M. C. Latham, ed., *The Poems of Sir Walter Ralegh* (London: Routledge and Kegan Paul, 1951), pp. 51–52.

18. Boklund points out that Webster's sources support this disturbing interpretation: "The Grand Duke of Tuscany certainly does not die in the Fugger version of Vittoria's life or in any other narrative that Webster is likely to have used, nor is he punished for his participation in the murders at Padua" (*The Sources of "The White Devil"*, p. 172). Webster suggests that Francisco has already escaped retribution by having Lodovico urge him to depart from Padua in the preceding scene:

> My lord upon my soul you shall no further:
> You have most ridiculously engag'd yourself
> Too far already.
>
> . . . .
>   My lord leave the city,
> Or I'll forswear the murder.
>
>   (V.v.1–8)

19. Kroll, "The Democritean Universe in Webster's *The White Devil*," *Comparative Drama*, 7 (1973), 3.

20. Ibid., p. 9.

21. T. M. Parrott, ed., *The Plays and Poems of George Chapman: The Tragedies* (London: Routledge, 1910), p. 266.

22. Dent, *John Webster's Borrowing*.

23. A possible fourth occurrence may be *The Fair Maid of the Inn* (V.i.118); see pt. II, chap. 4, p. 199.

24. F. L. Lucas, ed., *Works*, III, 326–327.

25. Chauncey Brewster Tinker, ed., *The English Dictionarie of 1623 by Henry Cockeram* (New York: Huntington Press, 1930), p. 103; Randle Cotgrave, *A Dictionaire of the French and English Tongues* (London: Adam Islip, 1611; facsim. rept. Menston: Scolar Press, 1968).

26. The quotations are from *Bussy D'Ambois* (III.ii.91) and *The Conspiracy of Byron* (II.ii.72–73); Nicholas Brooke, ed., *Bussy D'Ambois* (London: Methuen, 1964), p. 66, and Parrott, ed., *The Plays and Poems of George Chapman: The Tragedies*, p. 173.

27. Eugene M. Waith, *The Herculean Hero in Marlowe, Chapman, Shakespeare, and Dryden* (New York: Columbia University Press, 1962), p. 16.

28. Allardyce Nicoll, ed., *Chapman's Homer*, Bollingen Series, 41 (Princeton: Princeton University Press, 1967), II, 4.

29. Parrott, ed., *The Plays and Poems of George Chapman: The Tragedies*, p. 323.

30. MacLure, *George Chapman: A Critical Study* (Toronto: University of Toronto Press, 1966), p. 110.

31. Parrott, ed., *The Plays and Poems of George Chapman: The Tragedies*, p. 263.

32. Both passages may reflect the words of St. Jerome as quoted by Montaigne and translated by Florio: "*The divels master-point lies in our loines . . .*" (*Essays*, III.v, ed. L. C. Harmer [London: Dent, 1965], III, 86). Marston had also quoted the passage in Latin ("*Diaboli virtus in lumbris*

est") in *The Dutch Courtesan* (1605), II.i.89; see the edition by M. L. Wine (Lincoln: University of Nebraska Press, 1965), p. 26. See also n. 14 above.

33. This allusion to the common practice of barber-surgeons begging corpses from the hangman for purposes of anatomical investigation recalls *Northward Ho* (IV.i.140) and anticipates *Anything for a Quiet Life* (III.ii.24–29).

34. As John Russell Brown points out in his edition of *The White Devil* (p. 167), Venus carries lilies in Jonson's *Masque of Beauty* (1608), the flowers being designated as "speciall *Hieroglyphicks* of loueliness."

35. Brown, ed., *The Duchess of Malfi* (London: Methuen, 1964), p. xlvii.

36. The line counts are taken from John Russell Brown's Revels edition of the play. Of course, Webster's use of prose in some scenes makes the figures only approximate.

37. Eliot, "Four Elizabethan Dramatists," in *Selected Essays* (London: Faber and Faber, 1951), p. 117.

38. Later in the play Flamineo, with equal self-approval, echoes his sister: "This is my resolve— / I would not live at any man's entreaty / Nor die at any's bidding" (V.vi.47–49).

39. Charles Lamb, *Specimens of English Dramatic Poets Who Lived About the Time of Shakespeare*, in E. V. Lucas, ed., *The Works of Charles and Mary Lamb* (London: Methuen, 1903–05), IV, 190.

40. Eleanor Prosser analyzes "the convention of immortal vengeance" in Elizabethan drama between 1585 and 1642; Prosser, *Hamlet and Revenge* (Stanford: Stanford University Press, 1967), pp. 186–191, 261–275. See also Harold Jenkins, ed., *Hamlet* (London: Methuen, 1982), pp. 513–515.

41. Snyder, *The Comic Matrix of Shakespeare's Tragedies* (Princeton: Princeton University Press, 1979), pp. 173–179. Webster himself was aware of the association. In *The Duchess of Malfi*, Antonio confronts his wife at their parting: "Do not weep: / Heaven fashion'd us of nothing; and we strive / To bring ourselves to nothing . . ." (III.v.81–83). I must finally disagree with Howard Felperin, who in a provocative discussion of the theatricality of Jacobean tragedy regards the self-dramatizing quality of Webster's heroes as blocking their growth toward genuine selfhood even at death. For Felperin, Flamineo's dying words reflect a character who is still "imprisoned within a condition of theatricality from which death is indeed the only release," a character, like Vittoria, who remains "the victim of an ontological flippancy at the heart of things." Felperin argues that the quest for identity in Webster ends ultimately in "*dis*establishment," "*un*definition," and "depersonalization" (see *Shakespearean Representation: Mimesis and Modernity in Elizabethan Tragedy* [Princeton: Princeton University Press, 1977], pp. 188–191). That Felperin has acutely observed an important tendency in Websterian characterization I have no wish to deny, but the difficult problem of whether construction or deconstruction of authentic selfhood is more fundamental to Webster's universe depends finally on subjective responses to specific moments of high emotion in the plays. Felperin seems to me to overlook the sense of moral victory or self-respect that Webster often invites us to share with his doomed figures, a self-respect that transcends impotent gestures and that mysteriously reconciles the encompassing void with the conviction of human value and uniqueness "eterne in mutabilitie."

42. Brooke, *John Webster and the Elizabethan Drama* (London: Sidgwick and Jackson, 1916), p. 158.

PART III

Chapter 7

1. Alfonso Piccolomini, the Duchess's son by her first marriage, succeeded to the title and ruled as the Second Duke of Amalfi until his death. Painter, of course, follows history in this regard.

2. John Russell Brown, ed., *The Duchess of Malfi* (Cambridge, Mass.: Harvard University Press, 1964), pp. 184, 192–193. Brown reprints the Painter source in Appendix I.

3. Clifford Leech in *John Webster* (London: Hogarth Press, 1951) was the first to popularize the argument that the Duchess is culpable in marrying Antonio (pp. 68–77), and he amplified his original discussion in *Webster: The Duchess of Malfi* (Great Neck, N.Y.: Barron's Educational Series, 1963), pp. 51–57. Meanwhile, Inga-Stina Ekeblad reinforced Leech's position in her influential essay, "The 'Impure Art' of John Webster," *Review of English Studies*, 9 (1958), 253–267. James L. Calderwood also censured the Duchess's infraction of degree and "disrespect for external realities" in "*The Duchess of Malfi*: Styles of Ceremony," *Essays in Criticism*, 12 (1962), 113–147. With Robert F. Whitman's assertion in "The Moral Paradox of Webster's Tragedy," *PMLA*, 90 (1975), 894–903, that the Duchess "puts her own wishes before the welfare of others" and "openly defies her traditional duties" as a ruler (p. 897), such opinions came close to achieving the status of orthodoxy. Peterson, who quotes Whitman with approval, devotes her entire volume to moral criticism of the Duchess.

4. See Frank W. Wadsworth, "Webster's *Duchess of Malfi* in the Light of Some Contemporary Ideas on Marriage and Remarriage," *Philological Quarterly*, 35 (1956), 394–407.

5. I have suggested elsewhere that the authors of *Keep the Widow Waking* may have been influenced by Fletcher's comedy. See "*Wit Without Money*: A Fletcherian Antecedent to *Keep the Widow Waking*," *Comparative Drama*, 8 (1974), 172–183.

6. Gunnar Boklund, "*The Duchess of Malfi*": *Sources, Themes, Characters* (Cambridge, Mass.: Harvard University Press, 1962), p. 17; Brown, ed., *The Duchess of Malfi*, p. 203.

7. R. C. Bald, *John Donne: A Life* (Oxford: Clarendon Press, 1970), pp. 138–140.

8. "Critical Edition of Thomas Drue's *Dutchess of Suffolke*," ed. Allan John Martin, Diss. Case Western Reserve, 1969; subsequent quotations are from this work.

9. *The Shoemaker's Holiday*, ed. R. L. Smallwood and Stanley Wells (Manchester: Manchester University Press, 1979).

10. See M. P. Tilley, *A Dictionary of the Proverbs in England in the Sixteenth and Seventeenth Centuries* (Ann Arbor: University of Michigan Press, 1950), L499, L505, L531.

11. I quote from Arthur Machen's translation of *The Heptameron* ([London?]: Privately printed, 1886), pp. 246–253.

12. J. R. Mulryne, "*The White Devil* and *The Duchess of Malfi*," in *Jacobean Theatre*, ed. John Russell Brown and Bernard Harris, Stratford-upon-Avon Studies, 1 (London: Edward Arnold, 1960), p. 222.

13. Various critics have pointed out that Ferdinand could scarcely hope to profit materially from his sister's murder inasmuch as her son by her first husband would logically inherit the duchy. John Russell Brown in his note on this passage suggests (rightly, it seems to me) that the duke's words represent "an instinctive attempt to 'cover up' . . . deep feeling" (*The Duchess of Malfi*, p. 132).

14. The Bawd in Shakespeare's *Pericles*, for instance, employs the term in its sexual meaning: "she'd do the deeds of darkness . . ." (IV.vi.28). See also *King Lear*: "A servingman . . . serv'd the lust of my mistress' heart, and did the act of darkness with her . . ." (III.iv.84–87). Jonson uses the phrase in *The Devil Is an Ass* (V.vi.50). Emilia puns on the expression in answer to Desdemona's question, "Woulds't thou do such a deed for all the world?": "I might do 't as well i' th' dark" (*Othello*, IV.iii.66–69).

15. Vernon, *The Garden and the Map: Schizophrenia in Twentieth-Century Literature and Culture* (Urbana: University of Illinois Press, 1973), pp. 23–24.

16. Brennan, "The Relationship between Brother and Sister in the Plays of John Webster," *Modern Language Review*, 58 (1963), 493–494.

17. Otto Rank, *The Double: A Psychoanalytic Study*, trans. and ed. Harry Tucker, Jr. (Chapel Hill: University of North Carolina Press, 1971), p. 33.

18. See R. E. R. Madelaine, "*The Duchess of Malfi* and Two Emblems in Whitney and Peacham," *Notes & Queries*, 29 (1982), 146–147.

19. F. L. Lucas, although he notices the hint of incest in *The Fair Maid of the Inn*, regards this element in *The Duchess* as "merely a suggestion, and an inessential one" (*Works*, II, 24). To Gunnar Boklund the motive of incest "seems . . . improbable" because "the tenor of the decisive passages" is so like that of Painter (*"The Duchess of Malfi": Sources, Themes, Characters*, p. 99). Muriel Bradbrook, while granting that "the modern reading of [Ferdinand's] impulses as incestuous allows a valid presentation," believes that "in Webster's day the same effect upon the audience would have been reached by different means" (Bradbrook, *John Webster, Citizen and Dramatist* [London: Weidenfeld and Nicolson, 1980], p. 159).

20. In the first scene, Webster establishes Ferdinand's disturbing habit of abruptly changing the subject of discourse.

21. See Gabriele Baldini, *John Webster e il linguaggio della tragedia* (Rome: Edizioni dell' Ateneo, 1953), p. 169.

22. Conceivably Webster also remembered Shakespeare's haughty Cardinal Beaufort, Bishop of Winchester, whom the Earl of Salisbury describes in *2 Henry VI* as being "More like a soldier than a man o' th' church . . ." (I.i.184).

23. Fromm, *The Anatomy of Human Destructiveness* (Greenwich, Conn.: Fawcett Publications, 1975), p. 369.

24. Ibid., p. 450.

25. Ibid., p. 377.

26. The first edition of *The Duchess* (1623), unlike that of *The White Devil* (1612), specifies divisions by act. Since Webster carefully supervised the publication of his own tragedy, these divisions would appear to be authorial or at least to possess authorial sanction.

27. The apricock episode does not appear in Painter. R. W. Dent cites a passage, based on an incident in Livy, from Guevara's *Diall of Princes* (a book from which the dramatist drew other matter) as a conceivable source; Dent, *John Webster's Borrowing* (Berkeley and Los Angeles: University of California Press, 1960), p. 193. Webster may also have taken a hint from Marlowe's *Doctor Faustus* (ed. John D. Jump [Cambridge, Mass.: Harvard University Press, 1962]) in which the title figure, with the aid of Mephistopheles, produces grapes out of season for the pregnant Duchess of Vanholt. Webster's "dainties" could be an echo of Marlowe's "rare and dainty" morsels (xvii.12–13). Also Bosola's role as betrayer of the Duchess has its Mephistophelean aspect, for Webster identifies the cynic closely with devil imagery: Antonio says, for instance, that Bosola "would look up to heaven" but "The devil . . . stands in [his] light" (II.i.94–95). And Bosola earlier refers to himself as a "familiar" and "a very quaint invisible devil, in flesh" (I.i.259–260).

28. The Duchess's reference to "molten brass" derives, at least indirectly, from the threatened punishment of God as referred to in Deuteronomy 28:23. The comparison of her sufferings to those of a "galley-slave" is appropriated from a passage in Grimestone's *General Inventorie of the History of France* (p. 817) in which the author quotes Jacqueline d'Entremont (widow of the Protestant martyr Admiral Coligny), who was also persecuted for her religion and, like the Duchess of Malfi, imprisoned and tortured in Italy. Dent documents both sources (*John Webster's Borrowing*, pp. 234–235). But Webster's phrase, "acquainted with sad misery," is curiously reminiscent, whether fortuitously or not, of the King James rendering of Isaiah's prophecy of Christ's Passion: "He is despised and rejected of men; a man of sorrows, and acquainted with grief" (Isaiah 53:3).

29. Raleigh, *The History of the World* (1614), Book V; see the abridged edition by C. A. Patrides (Philadelphia: Temple University Press, 1971), p. 396.

30. Eugene M. Waith suggests that for the Duchess's most famous line Webster may be indebted to Seneca's Medea, who asserts "Medea superest" (*Medea*, l. 166) at a point when all help has deserted her; Waith, *Ideas of Greatness: Heroic Drama in England* (London: Routledge & Kegan Paul, 1971), p. 145. John Studley, the sixteenth-century translator of *Medea*, renders the state-

ment "Medea yet is left"; see Thomas Newton, ed., *Seneca His Tenne Tragedies*, 1581 (London: Constable and Co., 1927; rept., 2 vols. in 1, Bloomington: Indiana University Press, 1964), II, 62.

31. The execution scene may contain one further reminiscence of *Richard II*, although the echo (if it is one) is rather faint. The Duchess's exasperated phrase directed to Bosola and her other persecutors, "any way, for heaven-sake, / So I were out of your whispering" (IV.ii.222–223), sounds suspiciously similar to Richard's impatience with Bolingbroke at the end of the deposition scene: "Whither you will, so I were from your sights" (IV.i.316).

32. Adrian Noble's 1981 Manchester Royal Exchange Theatre production of *The Duchess of Malfi* at the Round House, London, in which Peter Postlethwaite played Antonio, apparently emphasized this change; see the review by Ian Stewart in *Country Life* (23 April 1981), p. 1111.

33. Irving Ribner, ed., *Christopher Marlowe's "Edward II": Text and Major Criticism* (New York: Odyssey Press, 1970), p. 23; also see Mark H. Curtis, "The Alienated Intellectuals of Stuart England," *Past & Present*, no. 23 (1962), 24–43.

34. Donne, *Of the Progress of the Soul*, ll. 165–166; see Dent, *John Webster's Borrowing*, p. 237.

35. See Ewbank, "Webster's Realism, or, 'A Cunning Piece Wrought Perspective,'" in *John Webster*, ed. Brian Morris, Mermaid Critical Commentaries (London: Ernest Benn, 1970), pp. 159–178.

36. Ibid., p. 161.

37. See Colie's *Paradoxia Epidemica* (Princeton: Princeton University Press, 1966) and Grudin's *Mighty Opposites: Shakespeare and Renaissance Contrariety* (Berkeley and Los Angeles: University of California Press, 1979).

38. In *Romeo and Juliet* Shakespeare uses the same paronomasia: "These times of woe afford no times to woo" (III.iv.8).

39. Henry King employs the same pun to splendid effect in his famous "Exequy" (c. 1624): "So close the ground, and 'bout her shade / Black curtains draw, my bride is laid" (ll. 79–80).

40. For an illuminating essay on Webster's use of the *ars moriendi* tradition, see Bettie Anne Doebler, "Continuity in the Art of Dying: *The Duchess of Malfi*," *Comparative Drama*, 14 (1980), 203–215.

41. Bosola (I.i.289), Ferdinand (I.i.308), the Duchess (I.i.351), and Antonio (I.i.460–461) all speak of the matter. Later Bosola predicts "fame" (III.ii.297) for Antonio, and the "ditty" intoned at the shrine of Our Lady of Loretto prays that "*Fame*" will sing loud the military "*pow'rs*" (III.iv.22) of the Cardinal. Webster associates all five major figures with the idea. The prominence of the theme, although common in Renaissance literature, seems to derive directly from Painter, who dwells much on Antonio's reputation as well as on the Duchess's concern for preserving hers.

42. See Berry, *The Art of John Webster* (Oxford: Clarendon Press, 1972). Berry identifies the astrologian with Bosola, who understands horoscopes, the licentious priest with the Cardinal, the lunatic doctor with the quack who believes he can cure Ferdinand, and the crazy lawyer with the duke, who is represented as a perverted judge (pp. 43–44).

43. See Brown's edition of the play, pp. xxii–xxiv.

44. Boklund, *"The Duchess of Malfi": Sources, Themes, Characters*, pp. 130–132.

45. Murray, *A Study of John Webster* (The Hague: Mouton, 1969), p. 259.

46. Gunby, *"The Duchess of Malfi: A Theological Approach*," in *John Webster*, ed. Brian Morris (London: Ernest Benn, 1970), p. 181.

47. Ornstein, *The Moral Vision of Jacobean Tragedy* (Madison: University of Wisconsin Press, 1960), p. 134.

48. Boklund, *"The Duchess of Malfi": Sources, Themes, Characters*, p. 129.

49. Paul Oskar Kristeller, *Eight Philosophers of the Italian Renaissance* (Stanford: Stanford University Press, 1964), p. 78.

50. Grudin, *Mighty Opposites: Shakespeare and Renaissance Contrariety*, p. 28.

51. Rabkin, "Rabbits, Ducks, and *Henry V*," *Shakespeare Quarterly*, 28 (1977): 279–296.

52. See Colie, *Paradoxia Epidemica*.

PART III

Chapter 8

1. [Baker], *The Companion to the Play-House* (London, 1764), I, sig. F3. Later expansions of this work (1782, 1812) repeat Baker's statement; see D. E. Baker, I. Reed, and S. Jones, eds., *Biographia Dramatica* (London: Longman, 1812), II, 160–161.

2. Cotgrave, *The English Treasury of Wit and Language* (London, 1655); see also Gerald Eades Bentley, "John Cotgrave's *English Treasury of Wit and Language* and the Elizabethan Drama," *Studies in Philology*, 40 (1943), 198.

3. See Phillips, *Theatrum Poetarum, or a Compleat Collection of the Poets* . . . (London, 1675), sigs. Ee10ᵛ–Ee11 (pp. 116–117); Winstanley, *The Lives of the Most Famous English Poets* . . . (London, 1687), sig. K6ᵛ (p. 140); Langbaine, *Momus Triumphans: or the Plagiaries of the English Stage* . . . (London, 1687), sig. E (p. 25); Langbaine, *An Account of the English Dramatick Poets* (Oxford, 1691), sigs. Ii6ᵛ–Ii7ᵛ (pp. 508–510); [Gildon] ed., *The Lives and Characters of the English Dramatick Poets* (London, [1699]), sigs. Lᵛ–L2 (pp. 146–147).

4. Arthur C. Kirsch, "A Caroline Commentary on the Drama," *Modern Philology*, 66 (1968–69), 257. Kirsch prints texts of all Wright's manuscript observations on plays.

5. Thomas Hall, *Histrio-Mastix: A Whip for Webster (as 'tis conceived) the Quondam Player* . . . , in Hall's *Vindiciae Literarum* (London, 1654), sig. P5 (p. 217). *Histrio-Mastix* has its own title page also dated 1654; the anonymous appendix containing the quoted words is entitled "An Examination of Mr Webster's Illogical Logick, and Reasoning even against Reason."

6. Beaumont, "Gamble Pays Off with Lucid, Witty Revival," *Yorkshire Evening Press* (5 June 1980), p. 3.

7. Cushman, "Travelling Nowhere," *Observer* (15 June 1980), p. 31.

8. de Jongh, "The Lust Tycoon," *Guardian* (7 June 1980), p. 10.

9. Chaillet, "*The Devil's Law-Case*," (London) *Times* (9 June 1980), p. 7.

10. Fredson Bowers, gen. ed., *The Dramatic Works in the Beaumont and Fletcher Canon* (Cambridge: Cambridge University Press, 1966–), III, 497.

11. Giambattista Guarini, *The Compendium of Tragicomic Poetry* (1599), in Allan H. Gilbert, ed., *Literary Criticism: Plato to Dryden* (New York: American Book Co., 1940), p. 507.

12. Ibid., p. 512.

13. G. Blakemore Evans, ed., *The Plays and Poems of William Cartwright* (Madison: University of Wisconsin Press, 1951), pp. 518–519.

14. *An Essay of Dramatic Poesy* in W. P. Ker, ed., *Essays of John Dryden* (Oxford: Clarendon Press, 1900), I, 73.

15. Brennan, ed., *The Devil's Law-Case* (London: Ernest Benn, 1975), p. xxiii.

16. Ibid., p. 116. Brennan (unlike Dyce, Lucas, and Shirley) restores the word order of Q: "How could you know / Of your first child: when you quickened?" This reading seems to make the best sense, and I am heavily indebted to her gloss on the passage.

17. See M. P. Tilley, *A Dictionary of the Proverbs in England in the Sixteenth and Seventeenth Centuries* (Ann Arbor: University of Michigan Press, 1950), W416.

18. Tertullian's so-called rule of faith, *Certum est qui impossibile est* (*De Carne Christi*, V), was much cited or paraphrased in Webster's age; see Robert Burton, *The Anatomy of Melancholy*, ed. Holbrook Jackson (London: Dent, 1964), III, 351, and Sir Thomas Browne, *Religio Medici*, section 9, in Geoffrey Keynes, ed., *Works of Sir Thomas Browne* (London: Faber & Gwyer, 1928–31), I, 13. Francis Bacon also uses the idea: "And, therefore, the more absurd and incredible any di-

vine mystery is, the greater honour we do to God in believing it . . ." (*De Augmentis Scientiarum,* IX, in Joseph Devey, ed., *The Physical and Metaphysical Works of Lord Bacon* [London: George Bell, 1904], p. 369).

19. *Essays*, I, 31; see L. C. Harmer, ed., *Montaigne's Essays . . . Translated by John Florio* (London: Dent, 1965), I, 230.

20. Sidney, *The Defence of Poesie* in T. W. Craik, ed., *Sir Philip Sidney: Selected Poetry and Prose* (London: Methuen, 1965), p. 26.

21. Browne, *Religio Medici*, section 9, in Keynes ed., *Works of Sir Thomas Browne*, I, 13. The Capuchin's "look upwards" echoes his earlier "Look up, sir," spoken to Ercole after his preservation "beyond natural reason" (II.iv.1). R. W. Dent cites other uses of the expression, "Look up," in secular contexts; see *Proverbial Language in English Drama Exclusive of Shakespeare, 1495–1616: An Index* (Berkeley and Los Angeles, 1984): University of California Press, L431.1 (p. 482).

22. As Ralph Berry has pointed out, Webster at this point seems to draw upon Jonson's *Masque of Blackness* (1605)—an entertainment in which James I's queen appeared as "an Aethiope," her face and arms painted black to represent one of the twelve daughters of the Niger. Jonson's conceit, like Webster's, depends on the notion of beauty in a foreign and paradoxical disguise, and his opening song parallels Webster's imagery:

> Fayre NIGER, sonne to great OCEANVS,
> Now honord, thus,
> With all his beautious race:
> Who, though but blacke in face,
> Yet, are they bright,
> And full of life, and light.
> To proue that beauty best,
> Which not the colour, but the feature
> Assures vnto the creature.
>
> (ll. 100–108)

See Berry, "Masques and Dumb Shows in Webster's Plays," in G. R. Hibbard, ed., *The Elizabethan Theatre VII* (Hamden, Conn.: Archon Books, 1980), pp. 142–144; also C. H. Herford and Percy and Evelyn Simpson, eds., *Ben Jonson* (Oxford: Clarendon Press, 1925–52), VII, 170–172.

23. "So goes it every where: *Rarenesse and difficulty giveth esteeme unto things*" (*Essays*, II, 15); see Harmer, ed., *Montaigne's Essays*, II, 335.

24. Jacqueline Pearson, *Tragedy and Tragicomedy in the Plays of John Webster* (Totowa, N.J.: Barnes & Noble, 1980), p. 96.

25. T. S. Eliot, "Four Elizabethan Dramatists," in *Selected Essays* (London: Faber and Faber, 1951), p. 116.

26. For a detailed study of demonology in relation to *The White Devil* and *The Duchess of Malfi*, see Muriel West, *The Devil and John Webster* (Salzburg: Institut für Englische Sprache und Literatur, Universität Salzburg, 1974).

27. Burton, *The Anatomy of Melancholy*, III, 325–326.

28. Pearson, *Tragedy and Tragicomedy in the Plays of John Webster*, p. 97.

29. Stone, *The Family, Sex and Marriage in England, 1500–1800* (London: Weidenfeld and Nicolson, 1977), pp. 105–119. Lee Bliss in a provocative chapter on *The Devil's Law-Case* emphasizes the theme of familial and social crack-up; see Bliss, *The World's Perspective: John Webster and the Jacobean Drama* (New Brunswick, N.J.: Rutgers University Press, 1983), p. 178.

30. Shakespeare's Richard II, for instance, says that "music" has "holp madmen to their wits" (*Richard II*, V.v.61–62). Also see Burton, *The Anatomy of Melancholy*, II, 115–119.

31. Cyril Tourneur, *The Revenger's Tragedy*, ed. R. A. Foakes (London: Methuen, 1966), p. 72.

32. Stevens, *The Necessary Angel: Essays on Reality and the Imagination* (New York: Alfred A. Knopf, 1951), p. 72.

33. Francis Bacon, *The Advancement of Learning*, II, 14, in Arthur Johnston, ed., *"The Advancement of Learning" and "New Atlantis"* (Oxford: Clarendon Press, 1974), p. 126.

34. *Timber, or Discoveries*, in C. H. Herford and Percy and Evelyn Simpson, eds., *Ben Jonson*, VIII, 593, 620–621, 624–625.

35. From *A True and Perfect Relation of the proceedings at the several Arraignments of the Late Most Barbarous Traitors* (London: Robert Barker, 1606), pp. T1–T2, quoted in Henry N. Paul, *The Royal Play of "Macbeth"* (New York: Octagon Books, 1971), p. 241.

36. George Puttenham, *The Arte of English Poesie* (1589), ed. G. D. Willcock and A. Walker (Cambridge: Cambridge University Press, 1936), p. 154.

37. Samuel Johnson, "Preface to Shakespeare," in Arthur Sherbo, ed., *Johnson on Shakespeare* (New Haven: Yale University Press, 1968), I, 74.

38. Quintilian, *Institutio Oratoria* (VI.iii.89), ed. and trans., H. E. Butler (Cambridge, Mass.: Harvard University Press, 1921), II, 487.

39. Jane Donawerth, *Shakespeare and the Sixteenth-Century Study of Language* (Urbana: University of Illinois Press, 1984), p. 119.

40. Essays, I, 19; see Harmer, ed., *Montaigne's Essays*, I, 80.

41. "Of Love," in Michael J. Hawkins, ed., *Francis Bacon: Essays* (London: J. M. Dent, 1972), p. 29.

42. See George R. Price, ed., *A Fair Quarrel* (Lincoln: University of Nebraska Press, 1976), pp. xvii–xxvi; also Fredson Bowers, "Middleton's *Fair Quarrel* and the Duelling Code," *Journal of English and Germanic Philology*, 36 (1937), 40–65. G. P. V. Akrigg gives a lively account of Jacobean quarrels and James I's attempts to curb them in his *Jacobean Pageant* (London: Hamish Hamilton, 1962), pp. 248–258.

43. G. K. Hunter quotes the archaic definition of "security" as well as R. Willis's contemporary description of *The Cradle of Security* in his edition of *Macbeth* (Harmondsworth: Penguin Books, 1967), pp. 21–23.

44. See Ralph Berry, *The Art of John Webster* (Oxford: Clarendon Press, 1972), pp. 162–166. My discussion of the legal theme is heavily indebted to Berry.

45. *Timber, or Discoveries*, in C. H. Herford and Percy and Evelyn Simpson, eds., *Ben Jonson*, VIII, 597.

46. See Bliss, *The World's Perspective: John Webster and the Jacobean Drama*, p. 171; Berry, *The Art of John Webster*, p. 151; Robert Ornstein, *The Moral Vision of Jacobean Tragedy* (Madison: University of Wisconsin Press, 1965), pp. 149–150; and Madeleine Doran, *Endeavors of Art: A Study of Form in Elizabethan Drama* (Madison: University of Wisconsin Press, 1954), p. 354.

47. Peter Haworth, "Prelude to the Study of Webster's Plays" in *English Hymns and Ballads and Other Studies in Popular Literature* (Oxford: Basil Blackwell, 1927), p. 136.

48. Baldini, *John Webster e il linguaggio della tragedia* (Rome: Edizioni dell' Ateneo, 1953), pp. 175–210; Glier, *Struktur und Gestaltungsprinzipien in den Dramen John Websters* (Munich: Memmingen-Allgäu, 1957), pp. 46–54.

49. D. C. Gunby, "*The Devil's Law-Case*: An Interpretation," *Modern Language Review*, 63 (1968), 546, 558; also see the introduction to Gunby's edition, *John Webster: Three Plays* (Harmondsworth: Penguin Books, 1972), pp. 27–28.

50. Peter B. Murray, *A Study of John Webster* (The Hague: Mouton, 1969), pp. 185, 214.

51. Berry, *The Art of John Webster*, p. 167.

52. Pearson, *Tragedy and Tragicomedy in the Plays of John Webster*, pp. 108, 110.

53. Beaumont, "Gamble Pays Off with Lucid, Witty Revival," p. 3.

54. Bliss, *The World's Perspective: John Webster and the Jacobean Drama*, pp. 175, 179, 185 (italics added).

55. Helen Gardner and Timothy Healy, eds., *John Donne: Selected Prose Chosen by Evelyn Simpson* (Oxford: Clarendon Press, 1967), p. 377.

56. William R. Elton, *"King Lear" and the Gods* (San Marino, Calif.: Huntington Library, 1966), p. 335.

57. *Essays*, II, 12; see Harmer, ed., *Montaigne's Essays*, II, 323.

58. Gunnar Boklund, "The Devil's Law-Case—An End or a Beginning?" in *John Webster*, ed. Brian Morris (London: Ernest Benn, 1970), p. 130.

59. See Rosalie L. Colie, *The Resources of Kind: Genre-Theory in the Renaissance* (Berkeley and Los Angeles: University of California Press, 1973).

60. John F. Danby, *Elizabethan and Jacobean Poets: Studies in Sidney, Shakespeare, Beaumont and Fletcher* (London: Faber and Faber, 1964), pp. 164–165, 170.

61. Johnston, ed., *The Advancement of Learning*, II, 10 (p. 113); II, 4 (p. 80).

62. E. P. Coleridge, trans., Euripides' *Andromache* (ll. 1284–1288), in Whitney J. Oates and Eugene O'Neill, Jr., eds., *The Complete Greek Drama* (New York: Random House, 1938), I, 878. Webster alludes to Euripides in his preface to *The White Devil* (ll. 27–33), and Samuel Sheppard in his epigram on the same play compares Webster to the Greek tragedian; see G. K. and S. K. Hunter, eds., *John Webster: A Critical Anthology* (Harmondsworth: Penguin Books, 1969), p. 36.

63. Sherbo, ed., *Johnson on Shakespeare*, I, 404.

64. Robert Grams Hunter, *Shakespeare and the Comedy of Forgiveness* (New York: Columbia University Press, 1965).

65. Frank Kermode, *The Sense of an Ending: Studies in the Theory of Fiction* (Oxford: Oxford University Press, 1967), p. 39.

66. Ibid., p. 18.

67. T. S. Eliot, *Four Quartets*, in *The Complete Poems and Plays* (New York: Harcourt, Brace, 1952), p. 125.

68. Stevens, *The Collected Poems of Wallace Stevens* (New York: Alfred A. Knopf, 1954), p. 332.

PART IV

1. R. G. Collingwood, *Speculum Mentis, or the Map of Knowledge* (Oxford: Clarendon Press, 1924), pp. 81–82.

2. Webster did, of course, imitate Shakespeare in more direct ways. The most obvious instance is probably Cornelia's mad scene in *The White Devil* (V.iv), which echoes both *Hamlet* and *King Lear* (see David L. Frost, *The School of Shakespeare: The Influence of Shakespeare on English Drama, 1600–42* [Cambridge: Cambridge University Press, 1968], pp. 145–154).

3. N. W. Bawcutt, ed., *The Jew of Malta* (Manchester: Manchester University Press, 1978), p. 91.

4. Garber, " 'Infinite Riches in a Little Room': Closure and Enclosure in Marlowe," in Alvin Kernan, ed., *Two Renaissance Mythmakers: Christopher Marlowe and Ben Jonson*, Selected Papers from the English Institute, 1975–76 (Baltimore: Johns Hopkins University Press, 1977), pp. 3–21.

5. Irving Ribner, ed., *"Edward II": Text and Major Criticism* (New York: Odyssey Press, 1970), p. 50.

6. H. S. Bennett, ed., *"The Jew of Malta" and "The Massacre at Paris"* (London: Methuen, 1931), p. 19.

7. Harbage, *Shakespeare and the Rival Traditions* (New York: Macmillan, 1952), pp. 176–177.

8. Gerald Eades Bentley analyzes the frequencies in "John Cotgrave's *English Treasury of Wit and Language* and the Elizabethan Drama," *Studies in Philology*, 40 (1943), 186–203.

9. See Gabriele Baldini, *John Webster e il linguaggio della tragedia* (Rome: Edizioni dell' Ateneo, 1953), pp. 234–237.

10. Wright's manuscript notes on Renaissance plays have been published by Arthur C. Kirsch in "A Caroline Commentary on the Drama," *Modern Philology*, 66 (1968–69), 256–261; I quote from Kirsch's article. Also see James G. McManaway, "Excerpta Quaedam per A. W. Adolescentem" in Thomas P. Harrison et al., eds., *Studies in Honor of De Witt T. Starnes* (Austin: University of Texas Press, 1967), pp. 117–129.

11. Quoted by Lucas (*Works*, I, 101), who repunctuates a confusing passage; for the original, see Sheppard, *Epigrams theological, philosophical, and romantic* (London, 1651), sigs. L–L^v.

12. Sheppard's *Fairy King* has never been printed in its entirety. I quote from Hyder E. Rollins's extract of the manuscript (Bodleian MS. Rawlinson Poet. 28, stanza 70) in his "Samuel Sheppard and his Praise of Poets," *Studies in Philology*, 24 (1927), 554.

13. *The Annales, or Generall Chronicle of England, Begun first by Maister Iohn Stow, and . . . continued and augmented . . . by Edmond Howes . . .* (London, 1615), p. 811.

14. Richards, *The Celestiall Pvblican, A Sacred Poem* (London, 1630): "Then like a mastlesse Barke in stormy weather, / The soule driues vp & downe, it knowes not whether . . ." (sig. C); the soul "like a spent Taper burnes / Onely for a flash, ready to goe out . . ." (sig. C2). Also see the Appendix, p. 502 (and Appendix nn. 32–33).

15. Anon., *A Citie-Dog in a Saints Doublet* (London, 1648), sig. A3^v.

16. Mercurius Pragmaticus [pseud.], *The Second Part of Crafty Crvmwell, or Oliver in his Glory as King* (London, 1648), sig. A2 (p. 3); Samuel Holland, *Wit and Fancy in a Maze, or the Incomparable Champion of Love and Beautie* (London, 1656), sig. H3^v (p. 109).

17. J[ohn] P[hillips], ed., *Wit and Drollery, Jovial Poems Never Before Printed* (London, 1656), sig. A3^v.

18. James Wright, *Country Conversations*, ed. Charles Whibley (London: Peter Davies, 1927), pp. 55–56.

19. See Charles R. Forker, "Robert Baron's Use of Webster, Shakespeare, and Other Elizabethans," *Anglia*, 83 (1965), 176–198.

20. See Joseph Angus, ed., *The Works of Thomas Adams* (Edinburgh: James Nichol, 1861–62), I, 493. R. W. Dent documents Webster's debts to Adams in *John Webster's Borrowing* (Berkeley and Los Angeles: University of California Press, 1960), also pointing out the reverse indebtedness (see Dent's index and pp. 111–112). Webster borrowed from Adams's *The Gallant's Burden* (1612) for Bosola's lines, "Security some men call the suburbs of hell, / Only a dead wall between" (*The Duchess of Malfi*, V.ii.337–338); then Adams appears to have reborrowed from the play in his *Meditations upon the Creed* (1629) by adding to his original ("Security is the very suburbs of hell") an imitation of Webster's phrase: "there is nothing but a dead wall between." See Angus, ed., *The Works of Thomas Adams*, I, 299, and III, 191. It is possible, of course, that a common source might explain this seeming two-way street between Adams and Webster, but none has yet been discovered.

21. In Phillips's edition of Buchler's *Thesaurus*, a separate title page introduces the *Compendiosa Enumeratio: Tractatulus de Carmine Dramatico Poetarum Veterum . . .* (London, 1670); the allusion to Webster occurs on sig. R8^v (p. 400). For an English version of the section of Phillips's book in which the Elizabethan dramatists are mentioned, see Daniel G. Calder and Charles R. Forker, *Edward Phillips's History of the Literature of England and Scotland: A Translation from the "Compendiosa Enumeratio Poetarum" with an Introduction and Commentary* (Salzburg: Institut für Englische Sprache und Literatur, Universität Salzburg, 1973), pp. 52–53. For the treatment of Webster in Phillips's later book, see the *Theatrum Poetarum, or A Compleat Collection of the Poets* (London, 1675), II, 116–117.

22. Winstanley, *The Lives of the Most Famous English Poets, or the Honour of Parnassus* (London, 1687), p. 140; Langbaine, *Momus Triumphans, or the Plagiaries of the English Stage* (London, 1687), sig. E (p. 25) and title page.

23. Langbaine, *An Account of the English Dramatick Poets* (London, 1691), pp. 508–510; Gildon, reviser, *The Lives and Characters of the English Dramatick Poets . . . First Begun by Mr. Langbain . . .* (London, 1699), pp. 146–147.

24. Wright, *Historia Histrionica: An Historical Account of the English Stage* . . . (London, 1699), sigs. B2–B2ᵛ (pp. 3–4).

25. Downes, *Roscius Anglicanus, or an Historical Review of the Stage* (London, 1708), pp. 9, 25.

26. Robert Latham and William Matthews, eds., *The Diary of Samuel Pepys* (Berkeley and Los Angeles: University of California Press, 1970–83), III, 209; VII, 352, 358; IX, 375.

27. Ibid., II, 190–191.

28. Ibid., IX, 552–553; Downes, *Roscius Anglicanus*, p. 30.

29. Anon., *A Defence of Drammatick Poetry: Being A Review of Mr. Collier's View* . . . (London, 1698), pp. 34–35; quoted from John Munro, ed., *The Shakespere Allusion-Book* (London: Humphrey Milford, 1932), II, 413.

30. Tate, *Injur'd Love, or the Cruel Husband, a Tragedy* (London, 1707), Prologue, sig. A2.

31. Ibid., Epilogue, sig. K2.

32. Ibid., sig. Bᵛ (p. 6).

33. See Hazelton Spencer, "Tate and *The White Devil*," *ELH, A Journal of English Literary History*, 1 (1934), 235–249. Spencer gives a careful synopsis of Tate's plot, analyzing the deviations from Webster and noting the burlesque treatment by Fielding (p. 235, n. 2). L. J. Morrissey points out the numerous borrowings from *Injur'd Love* in the commentary notes of his edition of *The Tragedy of Tragedies* (Edinburgh: Oliver and Boyd, 1970). Clifford Leech also discusses *Injur'd Love* in his *John Webster, A Critical Study* (London: Hogarth Press, 1951), pp. 15–19.

34. B. L. Joseph quotes from the letter to Warburton in "Lewis Theobald and Webster," *Comparative Literature Studies* (Cardiff), 17–18 (1945), 29–31, italicizing five passages in the two soliloquies that derive from Webster.

35. Lewis Theobald, *The Fatal Secret, A Tragedy* (London, 1735), Prologue, sig. A6.

36. *Gentlemen's Magazine* (April 1733), p. 194.

37. Theobald, *The Fatal Secret*, Preface, sig. A4ᵛ.

38. Ibid., Preface, sigs. A4ᵛ–A5.

39. Ibid., Preface, sigs. A5–A5ᵛ.

40. Ibid., sig. C9ᵛ. Not surprisingly, Theobald's prosaic rewriting of Ferdinand's speech is more akin to prose lines in the anonymous domestic tragedy, *A Warning for Fair Women* (1599), possibly Webster's source, than to the verse in *The Duchess of Malfi* that the adapter thought he was improving:

> *Old John.* Marie amen, for I tel thee my heart is heavie, God send me good luck: my
> eies dazel, and I could weepe. . . .
>
> *Jone.* O master, master . . . I shall swound, cut my lace, and cover my face, I die
> else. . . .
>
> (viii, ll. 1446–1452; sig. F2)

See Charles Dale Cannon, ed., *A Warning for Fair Women: A Critical Edition* (The Hague: Mouton, 1975), p. 139; also R. G. Howarth, "Dramatic Alchemy," in *A Pot of Gillyflowers: Studies and Notes* (Cape Town: Privately printed, 1964), p. 10.

41. Theobald, *The Fatal Secret*, Epilogue, sig. D6.

42. Leech, *John Webster*, pp. 22–23.

43. The New York Public Library possesses a copy of Daniel's text that once belonged to the actor Sidney Wilkins and has been marked up in preparation for an elaborate professional production. Frank W. Wadsworth discusses this prompt book; see n. 69 below.

44. See D. E. Baker, I. Reed, and S. Jones, eds., *Biographia Dramatica* (London: Longman, 1812), I, 465. Don D. Moore in *John Webster and His Critics, 1617–1964* (Baton Rouge: Louisiana State University Press, 1966) reports mistakenly that Malone's "Historical Account of the English Stage" (in vol. I, pt. 2, of Malone's *The Plays and Poems of William Shakespeare* [London: J. Rivington, 1790]) contains "a page of Webster-Shakespeare parallels" (p. 23).

45. The quotations from Lamb are all taken from E. V. Lucas, ed., *The Works of Charles and Mary Lamb* (London: Methuen, 1903–05), IV, 190, 192, 179.

46. William Hazlitt, *Lectures on the Dramatic Literature of the Age of Elizabeth*, in P. P. Howe, ed., *The Complete Works of William Hazlitt* (London: J. M. Dent and Sons, 1930–34), VI, 175.

47. Ibid., VI, 240–241.

48. Ibid., VI, 246.

49. Hazlitt, "On Reason and Imagination" in *The Plain Speaker* (1826); see Howe, ed., *The Complete Works of William Hazlitt*, XII, 53–54.

50. Ibid., VI, 245.

51. Alexander Dyce, ed., *The Works of John Webster: Now First Collected with Some Account of the Author, and Notes* (London: W. Pickering, 1830), I, xi–xii.

52. Quoted from the *Annual Review and History of Literature*, 7 (1809), 568, by Don D. Moore in *Webster: The Critical Heritage* (London: Routledge & Kegan Paul, 1981), p. 53.

53. "H. M.," "Analytical Essays on the Early English Dramatists, Nos. IV and V," *Blackwood's Edinburgh Magazine*, II (March 1818), 657–658, and III (August 1818), 562.

54. Anon., "English Dramatists," *European Magazine*, 78 (1820), 420, 424.

55. Anon., "Webster's Plays," *Retrospective Review*, 7 (1823), 88.

56. ["Barry Cornwall," i.e., Bryan Procter], Review of James Sheridan Knowles's *Virginius* and Thomas L. Beddoes's *The Bride's Tragedy*, *Edinburgh Review*, 38 (February 1823), 197–198. Cornwall reprinted this piece in his *Essays and Tales in Prose* (Boston: Ticknor, Reed, and Fields, 1853), II, 82–124.

57. "J. M.," "The Early English Drama, Nos. III and IV," *Gentleman's Magazine*, 103 (May 1833) 416–417, and (June 1833), 490.

58. Drake, *Shakespeare and His Times* (London: T. Cadell and W. Davies, 1817), II, 564–565; Campbell, *Specimens of the British Poets* (London: John Murray, 1819), III, 216.

59. Hallam, *Introduction to the Literature of Europe* (London: J. Murray, 1837–39), III, 619–621. I quote from both editions of Shaw's work; see Thomas B. Shaw, *Outlines of English Literature* (London: John Murray, 1849), pp. 150–151, and the revised *A Complete Manual of English Literature* (New York: Sheldon & Co., 1867), p. 163.

60. Read, "In Defence of Shelley," in *The True Voice of Feeling: Studies in English Romantic Poetry* (London: Faber and Faber, 1953), p. 234.

61. Medwin, *The Life of Percy Bysshe Shelley* (London: Oxford University Press, 1913), p. 256.

62. Rowland E. Prothero, ed., *The Works of Lord Byron: Letters and Journals* (London: John Murray, 1898–1901), V, 218; Ernest J. Lovell, Jr., ed., *Medwin's Conversations of Lord Byron* (Princeton: Princeton University Press, 1966), p. 139.

63. Claude Colleer Abbott, ed., *The Life and Letters of George Darley* (Oxford: Clarendon Press, 1928), pp. 97–98.

64. Horne, Preface to his edition of *The Duchess of Malfi, Reconstructed for Stage Representation* (London: John Tallis, 1850), quoted in G. K. and S. K. Hunter, eds., *John Webster: A Critical Anthology* (Harmondsworth: Penguin Books, 1969), pp. 58–60.

65. (London) *Times* (21 November 1850), p. 8.

66. *Athenaeum* (23 November 1850), pp. 1225–1226.

67. *Spectator* (23 November 1850), p. 1113.

68. G. H. Lewes, "*The Duchess of Malfi*," *The Leader* (30 November 1850), p. 859; reprinted in William Archer and Robert Lowe, eds., *Dramatic Essays: John Forster, George Henry Lewes* (London: Walter Scott, 1896), pp. 118–122.

69. Quoted from Horne's 1950 text (opposite p. 137, in the scene of the Duchess's execution) by Frank W. Wadsworth, " 'Shorn and Abated'—British Performances of *The Duchess of Malfi*," *Theatre Survey*, 10 (1969), 94. Wadsworth also documents the nineteenth-century theatre history

of Webster's *Duchess* in two additional articles; see his "Some Nineteenth-Century Revivals of *The Duchess of Malfi*," *Theatre Survey*, 8 (1967), 67–83, and "Webster, Horne, and Mrs. Stowe: American Performances of *The Duchess of Malfi*," *Theatre Survey*, 11 (1970), 151–166.

70. See "D.- G." [George Daniel], ed., *The Duchess of Malfi: A Tragedy in Five Acts Adapted from John Webster*, Cumberland's British Theatre Series, No. 379 (London: Davidson, [1853?]), pp. 6–7.

71. Horne, *The Duchess of Malfi*, Tallis's Acting Drama (London: John Tallis and Co., [1851]); this edition of Horne's adaptation lacks the author's preface but contains a "Memoir of Miss Glyn" by J. A. H[eraud].

72. Eliot, "Four Elizabethan Dramatists," in *Selected Essays* (London: Faber and Faber, 1951), p. 117.

73. Kingsley, *Plays and Puritans and Other Historical Essays* (London: Macmillan and Co., 1885), p. 18.

74. Ibid., pp. 48–49.

75. Watson, "Some Literary Idolatries," in *Excursions in Criticism* (London: Elkin Mathews & John Lane, 1893), pp. 15–18.

76. Archer, "Webster, Lamb, and Swinburne," *New Review*, 8 (1893), 96–106; Archer, "*The Duchess of Malfi*," *Nineteenth Century*, 87 (1920), 126–132. In revised form the latter essay appeared in Archer's *The Old Drama and the New* (Boston: Small, Maynard and Co., 1923), pp. 52–63.

77. Shaw, "Our Theatres in the Nineties," in *The Collected Works of Bernard Shaw* (New York: Wm. H. Wise & Co., 1930–32), XXV, 334.

78. Edmund Gosse and T. J. Wise, eds., *The Complete Works of Algernon Charles Swinburne* (London: William Heinemann, 1925–27), V, 177.

79. Swinburne, "John Webster," *Nineteenth Century*, 19 (1886), 861–881; republished in revised form in Swinburne's *The Age of Shakespeare* (London: Chatto & Windus, 1908), pp. 15–59.

80. Symonds, "Vittoria Accoramboni," in *Italian Byways* (New York: Henry Holt, 1883), pp. 142–175. Symonds had already praised Webster in a more general essay on Elizabethan drama; see "The English Drama During the Reigns of Elizabeth and James," *Cornhill Magazine*, 11 (1865), 604–618, 706–716.

81. Symonds, Introduction to *Webster and Tourneur* (London: Vizetelly & Co., 1888), pp. xii–xxii.

82. Review in the (London) *Times* (22 October 1892), p. 6.

83. Gosse and Wise, eds., *The Complete Works of Algernon Charles Swinburne*, XVIII, 445–446.

84. Ibid., VI, 316–317.

85. Poel, "A New Criticism of Webster's *Duchess of Malfi*," *Library Review*, 2 (1893), 21–24.

86. Whipple's lectures were printed in the *Atlantic Monthly* during 1867–1868 and published together in *The Literature of the Age of Elizabeth* (Boston: Fields, Osgood & Co., 1869). I quote from the ninth edition (Boston: Houghton, Mifflin, 1884), p. 145.

87. Minto, *Characteristics of English Poets*, 2nd ed. (Edinburgh: William Blackwood and Sons, 1885), pp. 354–357; Ward, *A History of English Dramatic Literature to the Death of Queen Anne* (London: Macmillan, 1875), II, 256, 259–260.

88. Lowell, *Old English Dramatists* in *The Works of James Russell Lowell* (Boston: Houghton, Mifflin, 1892), XI, 243–245, 260–261.

89. See Gosse, *The Jacobean Poets* (London: John Murray, 1894), pp. 166–173; also Gosse, *Seventeenth Century Studies* (London: William Heinemann, 1914), p. 50. The original version of the latter essay appeared in *Fraser's Magazine*, 9 (1874), 620–634.

90. See Brooke, *John Webster and the Elizabethan Drama* (London: Sidgwick & Jackson, 1916), pp. 129, 147, 155–156, 158.

91. Stacton's *A Dancer in Darkness* was first published in London (Faber and Faber, 1960), then in New York (Pantheon, 1962); the author invents a sister of Bosola (an intellectual, humanis-

tic nun), arranges a sexual affair between Bosola and Cariola, and leaves the Cardinal unpunished at the end. G. K. and S. K. Hunter describe Amis's *A Question of Hell* in *John Webster: A Critical Anthology*, pp. 310–311; Voodo rites replace Webster's Christian supernaturalism. A review of the two operas by Oliver and Burton appeared in *Time*, 112 (4 September 1978), 80; see also a review of Oliver's *Duchess of Malfi* by Kurt Oppens in *Opernwelt*, 19 (October 1978), 39–40. Oliver's libretto reduces the number of the Duchess's children to one and eliminates the character of Julia.

92. Ludwig Tieck, *Vittoria Accorombona: ein Roman in fünf Büchern* (Breslau: Josef Max, 1840); Clifford Bax, *The Life of the White Devil* (London: Cassell and Co., 1940).

93. See Una Ellis-Fermor, *The Jacobean Drama: An Interpretation* (London: Methuen, 1936; rev. ed., 1958), pp. 170–190; Ian Jack, "The Case of John Webster," *Scrutiny*, 16 (1949), 38–43; Clifford Leech, *John Webster: A Critical Study* (London: Hogarth Press, 1951); Gunnar Boklund, *The Sources of "The White Devil"* (Uppsala: A. B. Lundequistska Bokhandeln, 1957); Robert Ornstein, *The Moral Vision of Jacobean Tragedy* (Madison: University of Wisconsin Press, 1960), pp. 128–150.

94. See Irving Ribner, *Jacobean Tragedy: The Quest for Moral Order* (London: Methuen, 1962), pp. 97–122; Peter B. Murray, *A Study of John Webster* (The Hague: Mouton, 1969); D. C. Gunby, "*The Duchess of Malfi*: A Theological Approach," in Brian Morris, ed., *John Webster*, Mermaid Critical Commentaries (London: Ernest Benn, 1970), pp. 181–204; Ralph Berry, *The Art of John Webster* (Oxford: Clarendon Press, 1972).

95. Price, "The Function of Imagery in Webster," *PMLA*, 70 (1955), 717–739.

96. See Inga-Stina Ekeblad, "The 'Impure Art' of John Webster," *Review of English Studies*, 9 (1958), 253–267; James L. Calderwood, "*The Duchess of Malfi*: Styles of Ceremony," *Essays in Criticism*, 12 (1962), 133–147; James R. Hurt, "Inverted Ritual in Webster's *The White Devil*," *Journal of English and Germanic Philology*, 61 (1962), 42–47.

APPENDIX

1. Frost, *The School of Shakespeare: The Influence of Shakespeare on English Drama, 1600–1642* (Cambridge: Cambridge University Press, 1968), pp. 145–156.

2. William Gifford and Alexander Dyce, eds., *The Works of John Ford* (London: Lawrence and Bullen, 1895), I, 7. Since Gifford and Dyce do not number lines, further references to this edition will include volume and page numbers in brackets following act and scene references.

3. T. J. B. Spencer, ed., *The Broken Heart* (Manchester: Manchester University Press, 1980).

4. Derek Roper, ed., *'Tis Pity She's a Whore* (London: Methuen, 1975). All quotations are taken from this edition.

5. Peter Ure, ed., *The Chronicle History of Perkin Warbeck* (London: Methuen, 1968).

6. Some of these imitations have previously been noted by H. J. Oliver in *The Problem of John Ford* (Melbourne: Melbourne University Press, 1955), pp. 65, 80; and by Clifford Leech in *John Ford and the Drama of His Time* (London: Chatto & Windus, 1957), pp. 79, 95.

7. N. W. Bawcutt, ed., *The Changeling* (London: Methuen, 1958).

8. Dorothy M. Farr thinks "many theatre-goers might remember" Webster's earlier use; see *Thomas Middleton and the Drama of Realism* (Edinburgh: Oliver & Boyd, 1973), p. 126.

9. J. R. Mulryne, ed., *Women Beware Women* (London: Methuen, 1975).

10. Farr, *Thomas Middleton and the Drama of Realism*, p. 126.

11. J. W. Harper, ed., *A Game at Chess* (London: Ernest Benn, 1966). Dorothy Farr has noted the echoes from Webster in *A Game at Chess*; see *Thomas Middleton and the Drama of Realism*, p. 127.

12. See Charles R. Forker, "*Wit Without Money*: A Fletcherian Antecedent to *Keep the Widow Waking*," *Comparative Drama*, 8 (1974), 172–183.

13. Fredson Bowers, gen. ed., *The Dramatic Works in the Beaumont and Fletcher Canon* (Cambridge: Cambridge University Press, 1966–), IV, 599.

14. See R. W. Dent, *John Webster's Borrowing* (Berkeley and Los Angeles: University of California Press, 1960), p. 201; and John Russell Brown's note in his edition of *The Duchess of Malfi*, p. 63. Elizabeth M. Brennan notes but does not specify Fletcher's "echoes of *The Duchess of Malfi*"; see " 'An Understanding Auditory': An Audience for John Webster," in Brian Morris, ed., *John Webster*, Mermaid Critical Commentaries (London: Ernest Benn, 1970), p. 11.

15. Philip Edwards and Colin Gibson, eds., *The Plays and Poems of Philip Massinger* (Oxford: Clarendon Press, 1976), II, 102–104.

16. Bradbrook, *Themes and Conventions of Elizabethan Tragedy* (Cambridge: Cambridge University Press, 1935), p. 135.

17. Edwards and Gibson, eds., *The Plays and Poems of Philip Massinger*, I, 372.

18. See T. A. Dunn, *Philip Massinger: The Man and the Playwright* (Edinburgh: Thomas Nelson, 1957), pp. 204–210; and Frost, *The School of Shakespeare*, pp. 103, 112–115.

19. Edwards and Gibson, eds., *The Plays and Poems of Philip Massinger*, I, 296.

20. Ibid., p. 203.

21. Ibid., p. 79.

22. Eliot, "Philip Massinger" in *Selected Essays* (London: Faber and Faber, 1951), pp. 208–209; Edwards and Gibson, eds., *The Plays and Poems of Philip Massinger*, III, 67, and V, 189.

23. Eliot, "Philip Massinger," p. 208. Also see Edwards and Gibson, eds., *The Plays and Poems of Philip Massinger*, III, 66. Gibson points out (V, 189) that in this passage Massinger may be imitating Jonson's *Sejanus* (II.406).

24. William Gifford and Alexander Dyce, eds., *The Dramatic Works and Poems of James Shirley* (London: John Murray, 1833), I, xxxix. See also "The Character and Writing of James Shirley," *London Magazine* (attributed to John Payne Collier by T. R. Hughes), July 1820, II, 36–41.

25. For a more extended treatment of Shirley's debt to Webster in his final tragedy, see my edition of *The Cardinal* (Bloomington: Indiana University Press, 1964), pp. xlviii–liii. Citations of the play are from this edition.

26. J. S. Cunningham, ed., *Tamburlaine the Great* (Manchester: Manchester University Press, 1981).

27. J. S. Carter, ed., *The Traitor* (Lincoln: University of Nebraska Press, 1965).

28. Compare "I am in a tempest, / And I know not how to steer" (*The Young Admiral*, III.i; Gifford and Dyce, eds., *The Dramatic Works and Poems of James Shirley*, III, 136). All further citations of Shirley are taken from the Gifford-Dyce edition and are noted in the text, following the act and scene references, by volume and page in brackets.

29. Shirley's imitations of Webster in *The Brothers* and *The Gentleman of Venice* were noted by F. L. Lucas in *The Complete Works of John Webster*, I, 265, 268, 269; II, 138.

30. Allardyce Nicoll, ed., *The Tragedy of Osmond the Great Turk* (Waltham Saint Lawrence, Berkshire: Golden Cockerel Press, 1926), p. 46; J. C. Maxwell pointed out the borrowing in "Ludowick Carlell: An Echo of Webster," *Notes & Queries*, 16 (1969), 288.

31. James Maidment and W. H. Logan, eds., *The Dramatic Works of Sir William D'Avenant* (Edinburgh: William Patterson, 1872), I, 86; compare Flamineo's "I have caught / An everlasting cold. I have lost my voice / Most irrecoverably . . ." (*The White Devil*, V.vi.270–272).

32. A. R. Skemp, ed., *Nathanel Richards' "Tragedy of Messalina"*, Materialien zur Kunde des älteren Englischen Dramas, vol. 30 (Louvain: A. Uystpruyst, 1910), p. 88.

33. Ibid., p. 154.

34. [Cavendish], *The Country Captaine, and the Varietie, Two Comedies . . . Written by a Person of Honor* (London, 1649), sigs. C6ᵛ–C7 (pp. 60–61).

35. See M. P. Tilley, *A Dictionary of the Proverbs in England in the Sixteenth and Seventeenth Centuries* (Ann Arbor: University of Michigan Press, 1950), D310; and Adams, *The Works of Thomas Adams* (London, 1629), pp. 32–60, rept. in Joseph Angus, ed., *The Works of Thomas Adams* (Edinburgh: James Nichol, 1861–62), II, 221–253.

36. L. A. Beaurline, ed., *The Works of Sir John Suckling* (Oxford: Clarendon Press, 1971), II, 114. Further citations of Suckling are to this edition. Suckling's play exists in two versions. It was originally written as a tragedy, then revised in the final act to end happily. Both versions betray the influence of Webster.

37. Compare "I could curse . . . the world / To its first chaos" (*The Duchess of Malfi*, IV.i.96–99).

38. See A. Hamilton Thompson, ed., *The Works of Sir John Suckling* (London: Routledge & Kegan Paul, 1910), p. 399.

39. Hemminge, *The Fatal Contract, A French Tragedy* (London, 1653), sigs. C3ᵛ–C4. There is no pagination in this edition.

40. Ibid., sig. G2ᵛ.

41. See pt. I, pp. 24–25, above.

42. Harding, *Sicily and Naples, or The Fatal Union* (Oxford, 1640), sig. A4. The commendatory verses are by "S. Hall" of Exeter College.

43. The quotations are taken from A. J. Martin, ed., "Critical Edition of Thomas Drue's *Dutchess of Suffolke*," Diss. Case Western Reserve, 1969. See also Joseph Candido, "Websterian Imitation in Thomas Drue's *Duchess of Suffolk*," *American Notes and Queries*, 22, nos. 5–6 (January–February 1983), 67–69.

44. Porter, *The Villain* (London, 1663), sig. N3ᵛ (p. 94).

45. Ibid., sig. K3 (p. 69).

46. Tilley, *A Dictionary of the Proverbs in England*, H356, W427. Heywood applies the idea to cursing in *A Challenge for Beauty* (1634–1635?): "all my attempts / Like curses shall against the winde flie back / In mine owne face and soile it" (IV.i); see R. H. Shepherd, ed., *The Dramatic Works of Thomas Heywood* (London: John Pearson, 1874), V, 57.

47. Cary, *The Marriage Night* (London, 1664), sig. H2 (p. 51).

48. See Alfred Harbage, "Elizabethan-Restoration Palimpsest," *Modern Language Review*, 35 (1940), 297–304.

49. Howard, *The Great Favourite, or the Duke of Lerma* (London, 1668), sig. D (p. 17).

50. Ibid., sig. D4ᵛ (p. 24).

51. Ibid., sig. K2 (p. 67).

52. R. W. Dent cites only a single instance of the glowworm's heatless light before Webster's—in a sermon by George Benson (1609); Dent, *Shakespeare's Proverbial Language: An Index* (Berkeley and Los Angeles: University of California Press, 1981), G142.1 (pp.119–120).

53. [Killigrew], *The Imperial Tragedy: Written by a Gentleman For his own Diversion* (London, 1669), sig. B (p. 1).

54. Ibid., sig. O (p. 49).

55. Ibid.

56. Ibid., sig. L2ᵛ (p. 40).

57. Montague Summers, ed., *The Works of Aphra Behn* (London: William Heinemann, 1915), III, 373.

58. Ibid., II, 39; compare *The Duchess of Malfi*, IV.i.96.

59. See H. T. Swedenberg, Jr., gen. ed., *The Works of John Dryden*, X (Berkeley and Los Angeles: University of California Press, 1970), 384.

60. Ibid., p. 150. Marlowe also uses these words in *The Jew of Malta* (II.i.37); see the edition by N. W. Bawcutt (Manchester: Manchester University Press, 1978), p. 100. R. W. Dent cites several additional pre-Websterian examples in his *Proverbial Language in English Drama Exclusive of Shakespeare, 1495–1616: An Index* (Berkeley and Los Angeles: University of California Press, 1984), D585.11 (p. 303).

61. David M. Vieth, ed., *All for Love* (Lincoln: University of Nebraska Press, 1972). Citations are from this edition.

62. Lucas notes this particular imitation in *The Complete Works of John Webster*, I, 241.

63. Thomas B. Stroup and Arthur L. Cooke, eds., *The Works of Nathaniel Lee* (New Brunswick, N.J.: Scarecrow Press, 1954), I, 442–443. Stroup and Cooke note the parallel; see ibid., I, 483.

64. See Dent, *John Webster's Borrowing*, p. 239.

65. Stroup and Cooke, eds., *The Works of Nathaniel Lee*, II, 459.

66. L. A. Beaurline and Fredson Bowers, eds., *Don Sebastian* in *John Dryden: Four Tragedies* (Chicago: University of Chicago Press, 1967), p. 394.

67. Fernand Lagarde, "Wycherley et Webster," *Caliban*, NS I (1965), 33–45.

68. Ibid., p. 34.

69. Gerald Weales, ed., *The Complete Plays of William Wycherley* (New York: New York University Press, 1966), p. 17.

70. See Dent, *John Webster's Borrowing*, p. 140.

71. Weales, ed., *The Complete Plays of William Wycherley*, p. 168.

72. Ibid., p. 198.

73. Ibid., p. 408.

74. Ibid., p. 491.

75. Ibid., p. 479.

76. See pt. II, chap. 2, pp. 140–141, above.

77. H. N. Payne, *The Fatal Jealousie, A Tragedy* (London, 1673), sig. E (p. 25).

78. Settle, *The Empress of Morocco, a Tragedy* (London, 1673), sig. I (p. 57); see Maximillian E. Novak's facsimile edition of the original quarto in *"The Empress of Morocco" and Its Critics*, Augustan Reprint Society (Los Angeles: William Andrews Clark Memorial Library, University of California, 1968), p. 57.

79. Ibid., sig. K3 (p. 69).

80. Ibid., sig. K3ᵛ (p. 70).

81. Montague Summers, ed., *The Complete Works of Thomas Shadwell* (London: Fortune Press, 1927), III, 68.

82. All quotations of Lee's dramas are taken from Stroup and Cooke, eds., *The Works of Nathaniel Lee*, cited above.

83. R. W. Dent cites other instances of the phrase "devil in crystal"; see *John Webster's Borrowing*, p. 125.

84. For Ferdinand's cruel fantasy, Webster probably imitated Painter's account of Otho, Earl of Monferratto; see Dent, *John Webster's Borrowing*, p. 203.

85. Bonamy Dobrée sees "no earthly reason" for the detail other than a gratuitous imitation of *The White Devil*; see *Restoration Tragedy, 1660–1720* (Oxford: Clarendon Press, 1929), pp. 123–124.

86. Stroup and Cooke, eds., *The Works of Nathaniel Lee*, I, 292.

87. Van Lennep, "The Life and Works of Nathaniel Lee: A Study of the Sources," Diss. Harvard, 1933, I, 225.

88. Ibid., II, 381.

89. Webster's Julia dies when she kisses a poisoned Bible (*The Duchess of Malfi*, V.ii.276 ff.); the detail of the poisoned gloves may derive from Marlowe's *The Massacre at Paris* (iii.1–20) in which the Queen Mother of Navarre is so dispatched.

90. Dent (*John Webster's Borrowing*, p. 172) cites parallels in Sidney and Sharpham.

91. Dobrée, *Restoration Tragedy*, p. 123.

92. Stroup and Cook, eds., *The Works of Nathaniel Lee*, II, 609.

93. Malcolm Kelsall, ed., *Venice Preserved* (Lincoln: University of Nebraska Press, 1969), p. xvi. Quotations are taken from this edition.

94. R. W. Dent has suggested privately to me that Webster, Dryden, and Otway may all share some common source for the comparison to animal sacrifice, but until one is discovered, we may credit Webster with the idea.

95. Webster in turn took the idea from Sir William Alexander's *Alexandrean Tragedy* (IV.ii); see Dent, *John Webster's Borrowing*, p. 239.

96. Thomas B. Stroup calls attention to part of this imitation in "Otway's Bitter Pessimism," *Studies in Philology*, extra series, no. 4 (1967), 68.

97. Banks, *Vertue Betray'd: or, Anna Bullen* (London, 1682), sig. F4ᵛ (p. 40); see Diane Dreher's facsimile edition of the original quarto, Augustan Reprint Society, 205–206 (Los Angeles: William Andrews Clark Memorial Library, University of California, 1981).

98. Ibid., sigs. G2–G2ᵛ (pp. 43–44).

99. Ibid., sig. K2ᵛ (p. 68).

100. Banks, *The Unhappy Favourite, or, The Earl of Essex* (London, 1682), sig. Gᵛ (p. 42); see Thomas Marshall Howe Blair's facsimile edition of the original quarto (New York: Columbia University Press, 1939).

101. Banks, *The Island Queens . . . Publish'd only in Defence of the Author . . .* (London, 1684), sig. D3ᵛ (p. 22).

102. Ibid., sig. E3 (p. 29).

103. But compare Ophelia's description of Hamlet: "He falls to such perusal of my face / As 'a would draw it" (*Hamlet*, II.i.87–88). Webster may have been imitating Shakespeare.

104. Banks, *Cyrus the Great: or, The Tragedy of Love* (London, 1696), sig. G3ᵛ (p. 46).

105. Eric Rothstein, *Restoration Tragedy: Form and the Process of Change* (Madison: University of Wisconsin Press, 1967), p. 155.

106. Banks, *Cyrus the Great*, sig. F4ᵛ (p. 40).

107. Ibid., sig. H3 (p. 53).

108. Ibid., sig. H3ᵛ (p. 54).

109. Ibid., sig. G4ᵛ (p. 48).

110. Ibid., sigs. B–B3 (pp. 1–5).

111. Ibid., sig. C2ᵛ (p. 12).

112. Ibid., sig. H2 (p. 51).

113. Ibid., sig. H4ᵛ (p. 56).

114. Ibid., sig. H3 (p. 53).

115. Southerne, *The Fatal Marriage: or, The Innocent Adultery* (London, 1694), sig. K3ᵛ (p. 70).

116. Ibid., sig. K4ᵛ (p. 72).

117. Nicoll, *A History of English Drama, 1600–1900* (Cambridge: Cambridge University Press, 1952–61), I, 154.

118. Manley, *The Royal Mischief, A Tragedy* (London, 1696), sig. G3ᵛ (p. 46).

119. Whitaker, *The Conspiracy, or the Change of Government, A Tragedy* (London, 1680), sig. E3ᵛ (p. 30).

120. Ibid., sig. H2 (p. 51).

121. Bancroft, *Henry the Second, King of England; with the Death of Rosamond, A Tragedy* (London, 1693), sig. D2 (p. 19).

122. Ibid., sig. Eᵛ (p. 26).

123. Ibid., sig. Hᵛ (p. 50).

124. Ravenscroft, *Titus Andronicus, or the Rape of Lavinia; a Tragedy* (London, 1687), sig. H3ᵛ (p. 54).

125. Ravenscroft, *The Italian Husband, A Tragedy* (London, 1698), sig. A3ᵛ.

126. Ibid., sig. C4 (p. 15).

127. Ibid., sig. E4 (p. 31).

128. Ibid., sig. G (p. 41). Ravenscroft also imitates *Romeo and Juliet* here: "Thou art not conquer'd; beauty's ensign yet / Is crimson in thy lips and in thy cheeks, / And death's pale flag is not advanced there" (V.iii.94–96).

129. Arthur Waugh, ed., *"Lives of the English Poets" by Samuel Johnson* (London: Oxford University Press, 1952), II, 30–31. D. Crane Taylor in *William Congreve* (London: Oxford University Press, 1931) notes that in the play's "devices for securing an atmosphere of gloom and cold horror, in its cavernous darkness, we can detect the influence of Ford and Webster" (p. 96).

130. Herbert Davis, ed., *The Complete Plays of William Congreve* (Chicago: University of Chicago Press, 1967), p. 339. All other quotations of *The Mourning Bride* are taken from this edition. Almeria's phrase, "some pale Coarse / Yet green in Earth," is a borrowing from Shakespeare's *Romeo and Juliet*: "bloody Tybalt, yet but green in earth" (IV.iii.42).

131. Compare "a thing so wretch'd" (IV.i.89); "A most wretched thing" (V.iv.48); "Thou wretched thing of blood" (V.v.92); and "These wretched eminent things" (V.v.113). See pt. III, chap. 7, p. 330, above.

132. Morton W. Bloomfield, "Quoting and Alluding: Shakespeare in the English Language," in G. B. Evans, ed., *Shakespeare: Aspects of Influence* (Cambridge, Mass.: Harvard University Press, 1976), pp. 1–20.

INDEX

Works mentioned or discussed in this volume (as distinguished from those merely cited in the notes for purposes of documentation) are listed by both author and title with cross references. Anonymous works appear under their titles only. Collaborative writings in which Webster is thought to have taken a share will generally be found under Webster, even in cases when he was not the principal or dominant partner.

Charles R. Forker is Professor of English at Indiana University, where he has taught since 1959. He has also taught at the Universities of Wisconsin and Michigan and at Dartmouth College. He has produced scholarly editions of Shirley's *Cardinal* and Shakespeare's *Henry V*, has compiled (with Joseph Candido) an extensive annotated bibliography of *Henry V*, and has contributed many essays and reviews on Shakespeare and Renaissance drama to scholarly journals. Currently, he serves on the editorial boards of *Hamlet Studies* and of *Medieval and Renaissance Drama in England*.